solutions@syngress.com

With more than 1,500,000 copies of our MCSE, MCSD, CompTIA, and Cisco study guides in print, we continue to look for ways we can better serve the information needs of our readers. One way we do that is by listening.

Readers like yourself have been telling us they want an Internet-based service that would extend and enhance the value of our books. Based on reader feedback and our own strategic plan, we have created a Web site that we hope will exceed your expectations.

Solutions@syngress.com is an interactive treasure trove of useful information focusing on our book topics and related technologies. The site offers the following features:

- One-year warranty against content obsolescence due to vendor product upgrades. You can access online updates for any affected chapters.
- "Ask the Author" customer query forms that enable you to post questions to our authors and editors.
- Exclusive monthly mailings in which our experts provide answers to reader queries and clear explanations of complex material.
- Regularly updated links to sites specially selected by our editors for readers desiring additional reliable information on key topics.

Best of all, the book you're now holding is your key to this amazing site. Just go to **www.syngress.com/solutions**, and keep this book handy when you register to verify your purchase.

Thank you for giving us the opportunity to serve your needs. And be sure to let us know if there's anything else we can do to help you get the maximum value from your investment. We're listening.

www.syngress.com/solutions

SYNGRESS®

SYNGRESS®

1 YEAR UPGRADE
BUYER PROTECTION PLAN

ASP.NET
Web Developer's Guide

Mesbah Ahmed
Chris Garrett
Jeremy Faircloth
Chris Payne
DotThatCom.com
Wei Meng Lee Series Editor
Jonothon Ortiz Technical Editor

Syngress Publishing, Inc., the author(s), and any person or firm involved in the writing, editing, or production (collectively "Makers") of this book ("the Work") do not guarantee or warrant the results to be obtained from the Work.

There is no guarantee of any kind, expressed or implied, regarding the Work or its contents. The Work is sold AS IS and WITHOUT WARRANTY. You may have other legal rights, which vary from state to state.

In no event will Makers be liable to you for damages, including any loss of profits, lost savings, or other incidental or consequential damages arising out from the Work or its contents. Because some states do not allow the exclusion or limitation of liability for consequential or incidental damages, the above limitation may not apply to you.

You should always use reasonable care, including backup and other appropriate precautions, when working with computers, networks, data, and files.

Syngress Media®, Syngress®, "Career Advancement Through Skill Enhancement®," and "Ask the Author UPDATE®," are registered trademarks of Syngress Publishing, Inc. "Mission Critical™," "Hack Proofing™," and "The Only Way to Stop a Hacker is to Think Like One™" are trademarks of Syngress Publishing, Inc. Brands and product names mentioned in this book are trademarks or service marks of their respective companies.

KEY	SERIAL NUMBER
001	ANVE48952P
002	WNBN9433ET
003	7BANL4P2WR
004	QNV984UTAP
005	KVAW939RE4
006	6JSE4FHU9W
007	4MAS8TYGF2
008	DAUTGFLRGT
009	2983K74SLF
010	VFR4MHY7Q2

PUBLISHED BY
Syngress Publishing, Inc.
800 Hingham Street
Rockland, MA 02370

ASP.NET WEB DEVELOPER'S GUIDE

Copyright © 2002 by Syngress Publishing, Inc. All rights reserved. Printed in the United States of America. Except as permitted under the Copyright Act of 1976, no part of this publication may be reproduced or distributed in any form or by any means, or stored in a database or retrieval system, without the prior written permission of the publisher, with the exception that the program listings may be entered, stored, and executed in a computer system, but they may not be reproduced for publication.

Printed in the United States of America

1 2 3 4 5 6 7 8 9 0

ISBN: 1-928994-51-2

Technical Editor: Jonothan Ortiz
Series Editor: Wei Meng Lee
Co-Publisher: Richard Kristof
Acquisitions Editor: Catherine B. Nolan
Developmental Editor: Kate Glennon
CD Production: Michael Donovan

Freelance Editorial Manager: Maribeth Corona-Evans
Cover Designer: Michael Kavish
Page Layout and Art by: Shannon Tozier
Copy Editors: Janet Zunkel and Michael McGee
Indexer: Robert Saigh

Distributed by Publishers Group West in the United States and Jaguar Book Group in Canada.

Acknowledgments

We would like to acknowledge the following people for their kindness and support in making this book possible.

Richard Kristof and Duncan Anderson of Global Knowledge, for their generous access to the IT industry's best courses, instructors, and training facilities.

Ralph Troupe, Rhonda St. John, and the team at Callisma for their invaluable insight into the challenges of designing, deploying, and supporting world-class enterprise networks.

Karen Cross, Lance Tilford, Meaghan Cunningham, Kim Wylie, Harry Kirchner, Kevin Votel, Kent Anderson, and Frida Yara of Publishers Group West for sharing their incredible marketing experience and expertise.

Mary Ging, Caroline Hird, Simon Beale, Caroline Wheeler, Victoria Fuller, Jonathan Bunkell, and Klaus Beran of Harcourt International for making certain that our vision remains worldwide in scope.

Annabel Dent of Harcourt Australia for all their help.

David Buckland, Wendi Wong, Daniel Loh, Marie Chieng, Lucy Chong, Leslie Lim, Audrey Gan, and Joseph Chan of Transquest Publishers for the enthusiasm with which they receive our books.

Kwon Sung June at Acorn Publishing for his support.

Ethan Atkin at Cranbury International for his help in expanding the Syngress program.

Contributors

Todd Carrico (MCDBA, MCSE) is a Senior Database Engineer for Match.com. Match.com is a singles portal for the digital age. In addition to its primary Web site, Match.com provides back-end services to AOL, MSN, and many other Web sites in its affiliate program. Todd specializes in design and development of high-performance, high-availability data architectures primarily on the Microsoft technology. His background includes designing, developing, consulting, and project management for companies such as Fujitsu, Accenture, International Paper, and GroceryWorks.com. Todd resides in Sachse, TX, with his wife and two children.

Jeremy Faircloth (CCNA, MCSE, MCP+I, A+) is a Systems Analyst for Gateway, Inc. In this position, he develops and maintains enterprise-wide client/server and Web-based technologies. He also acts as a technical resource for other IT professionals, using his expertise to help others expand their knowledge. As a Systems Analyst with over 10 years of real-world IT experience, he has become an expert in many areas of IT including Web development, database administration, enterprise security, network design, and project management. Jeremy currently resides in North Sioux City, SD and wishes to thank Christina Williams for her support in his various technical endeavors.

Mesbah Ahmed (PhD and MS, Industrial Engineering) is a Professor of Information Systems at the University of Toledo. In addition to teaching and research, he provides technical consulting and training for IT and manufacturing industries in Ohio and Michigan. His consulting experience includes systems design and implementation projects with Ford Motors, Dana Corporation, Riverside Hospital, Sears, and others. Currently, he provides IT training in the areas of Java Server, XML, and .NET technologies. He teaches graduate level courses in Database Systems, Manufacturing Systems, and Application Development in Distributed and Web Environment. Recently, he received the University of Toledo Outstanding Teaching award, and the College of Business Graduate Teaching Excellence award. His current research interests are in the areas of data warehousing and data mining. He has published many research articles in academic journals such as *Decision Sciences, Information & Management, Naval Research Logistic Quarterly, Journal of Operations Management, IIE Transaction*, and *International Journal of Production Research*. He has also presented numerous papers and seminars in many national and international conferences.

Patrick Coelho (MCP) is an Instructor at The University of Washington Extension, North Seattle Community College, Puget Sound Center, and Seattle Vocational Institute, where he teaches courses in Web Development (DHTML, ASP, XML, XSLT, C#, and ASP.NET). Patrick is a Co-Founder of DotThatCom.com, a company that provides consulting, online development resources, and internships for students. He is currently working on a .NET solution with contributing author David Jorgensen and nLogix. Patrick holds a bachelor's of Science degree from the University of Washington, Bothell. Patrick lives in Puyallup, WA with his wife Angela.

David Jorgensen (MCP) is an Instructor at North Seattle Community College, University of Washington Extension campus, and Puget Sound Centers. He is also developing courses for Seattle Vocational Institute, which teach .NET and Web development to the underprivileged in the Seattle area. David also provides internship opportunities through his company DotThatCom.com, which does online sample classes and chapters of books. David holds a bachelor's degree in Computer Science from St. Martin's College and resides in Puyallup, WA with his wife Lisa and their two sons Scott and Jacob.

Adam Sills is an Internet Programmer at GreatLand Insurance, a small insurance company parented by Kemper Insurance. He works in a small IT department that focuses on creating applications to expedite business processes and manage data from a multitude of locations. Previously, he had a small stint in consulting and also worked at a leading B2B eCommerce company designing and building user interfaces to interact with a large-scale enterprise eCommerce application. Adam's current duties include building and maintaining Web applications, as well as helping to architect, build, and deploy new Microsoft .NET technologies into production use. Adam has contributed to the writing of a number of books for Syngress and is an active member of a handful of ASP and ASP.NET mailing lists, providing support and insight whenever he can.

Chris Garrett is the Technical Manager for a large European Web agency. He has been working with Internet technologies since 1994 and has provided technical and new media expertise for some of the world's biggest brands. Chris lives in Yorkshire, England, with his wife Clare and his daughter Amy.

Chris Payne, author of *Teach Yourself ASP.NET in 21 Days*, is the Co-Founder and CIO of Enfused Media, Inc., which designs and develops applications to automate and facilitate business processes. Chris has taught ASP and solution techniques through articles and tutorials and has a background in writing both technical and nontechnical material. Chris holds a bachelor's degree in Engineering from Boston University and is currently lives with his wife, Eva, in Orlando, FL.

Technical Editor and Contributor

Jonothon Ortiz is Vice President of Xnext, Inc. in Winter Haven, FL. Xnext, Inc. is a small, privately owned company that develops Web sites and applications for prestigious companies such as the New York Times. Jonothon is the head of the programming department and works together with the CEO on all company projects to ensure the best possible solution. Jonothon lives with his wife Carla in Lakeland, FL.

Series Editor and Contributor

Wei Meng Lee is Series Editor for Syngress Publishing's .NET Developer Series. He is currently lecturing at The Center for Computer Studies, Ngee Ann Polytechnic, Singapore. Wei Meng is actively involved in Web development work and conducts training for Web developers and Visual Basic programmers. He has co-authored two books on WAP. He holds a bachelor's degree in Information Systems and Computer Science from the National University of Singapore. The first book in the .NET series, *VB.NET Developer's Guide* (ISBN: 1-928994-48-2), is currently available from Syngress Publishing.

About the CD

This CD-ROM contains the code files that are used in each chapter of this book. The code files for each chapter are located in a "chXX" directory. For example, the files for Chapter 8 are in ch08. Any further directory structure depends on the projects that are presented within the chapter.

Chapters 4, 6, and 9 contain code that apply to the situations described in their sections. This code will be extremely useful for understanding and enhancing the way you use ASP.NET. Specifically, Chapter 4 has various examples on dealing with the internal configuration of ASP.NET while Chapter 6 deals with how to optimize the various caching methods available through ASP.NET and Chapter 9 contains code on how to work with the debugging system of .NET with ASP.NET.

Chapters 3 and 8 contain code that deal with improved technologies in ASP.NET. Chapter 3 discusses examples on how to work with ASP Server Controls while Chapter 8 deals with a concise introduction to what XML is and how XML affects .NET.

Chapters 7, 11, 12, and 13 contain low-to-heavy duty applications, exactly in that order. Chapter 7 will introduce you to a sample application that deals with an address book, from start to finish. This example code will also introduce you to how code looks and operates in ASP.NET. Chapter 11, our XML.NET Guestbook, will show you how XML in .NET can easily be worked with by using the standard classes within ADO.NET, bridging the gap between XML and ADO. Chapters 12 and 13 take XML and ADO to the next level by introducing a Shopping Cart (Chapter 11) and a Message Board (Chapter 13). Both applications in Chapters 12 and 13 require an SQL Server backend, but either of these databases can be easily converted to an Access database.

Look for this CD icon to obtain files used in the book demonstrations.

Contents

Foreword   xxv

Chapter 1 Introducing ASP.NET   1

Introduction   2
Learning from the History of ASP   2
   The Origins of ASP   2
      Why ASP Was Needed   3
      Why ASP Was Not Originally Embraced   4
   Developing ASP 1.x   5
   Developing ASP 2.x   6
      Major Changes with ASP 2   6
      Weaknesses in the ASP 2 Model   7
   Developing ASP 3.0   7
      Final Changes to Original ASP Model   8
      Weaknesses in the ASP 3 Model   8
      The Need for a New ASP Model   9
   The ASP Timeline   10
Reviewing the Basics of the ASP.NET Platform   11
   Utilizing the Flexibility of ASP.NET   12
      Converting Code into Multiple Languages   13
   Comparing Improvements in ASP.NET to
      Previous ASP Models   14
How Web Servers Execute ASP Files   15
   Client-Server Interaction   16
   Server-Side Processing   17
      Compiling and Delivering ASP.NET Pages   18
   Running ASP.NET Web Pages   19
      Obtaining and Installing .NET   19
      Creating Your First ASP.NET Application   20

Debugging ASP.NET Applications

Debugging under classic ASP was a hit-and-miss affair, usually forcing the developer to add *Response.Write* statements through the code until he or she found the failure point. ASP.NET introduces much better debugging, thanks to the .NET Framework and Common Language Runtime (CLR).

Upgrading from Classic ASP	26
Taking Security Precautions	28
Summary	29
Solutions Fast Track	29
Frequently Asked Questions	32
Chapter 2 ASP.NET Namespaces	**35**
Introduction	36
Reviewing the Function of Namespaces	36
Using Namespaces	37
Using the Microsoft.VisualBasic Namespace	38
Understanding the Root Namespace: System	38
Supplied Functionality	38
Integral Numbers	39
Floating-Point Numbers	39
Dates	40
Strings	40
Booleans	40
Objects	40
Grouping Objects and Data Types with the System.Collections Namespace	43
Supplied Functionality	43
Enabling Client/Browser Communication with the System.Web Namespace	45
Supplied Functionality	45
System.Web.UI Namespace Set	46
System.Web.Services Namespace Set	51
Working with Data Sources Using the System.Data Namespace	52
Supplied Functionality	52
Processing XML Files Using the System.XML Namespace	53
Supplied Functionality	53
Summary	55
Solutions Fast Track	56
Frequently Asked Questions	58

Reviewing the Function of Namespaces

To use a namespace in an ASP.NET page, you must use the *Import* directive. Unlike in classic ASP, ASP.NET pages are compiled before they are run. You build ASP.NET pages using a compiled language, such as VB.NET or C#.

Chapter 3 ASP Server Controls — 61

Introduction — 62
Major Features of ASP.NET Server Controls — 62
    Collecting Data Using HTML Forms — 63
Server-Side Processing in ASP.NET — 65
    A Simple Application Using Conventional HTML Controls — 66
    A Simple Application Using ASP Server Controls — 68
    Mapping Server Controls and Preserving Their States — 69
    Including Scripts in an .aspx File — 69
        Loading a List Box via Script — 70
    Using the *IsPostBack* Property of a Page — 72
    AutoPostBack Attributes of Server Controls — 73
        Structure of an ASP.NET Web Form — 75
        Page Directives — 76
        The Order of Event Execution — 77
Code-Behind versus In-Page Coding — 77
    Using Code-Behind without Compilation — 79
    Using Code Behind with Compilation — 81
    Using VS.Net for Developing a Web Application — 84
Using HTML Server Controls — 87
    Using the *HtmlAnchor* Control — 88
    Using the *HtmlTable* Control — 88
    Using *HtmlInputText* and *HtmlTextArea* Controls — 90
    Using *HtmlButton* and *HtmlImage* Controls — 91
    Using the *HtmlInputFileControl* — 93
    Using the *HtmlSelect* Control with Data Binding to a *SortedList* Structure — 95
        Creating and Loading the *SortedList* — 97
    Using *HtmlCheckBox* and *HtmlInputRadioButton* Controls — 98
Using ASP.NET Web Controls — 100

Developing ASP.NET Web Forms

When you develop an ASP.NET Web form, you can use the following type of controls:

- HTML Server Controls
- Web Server Controls (also known as Web Controls or ASP.NET Web Form Controls)
- Validation Controls
- Custom Controls

Basic Web Controls	101
Using *Labels*, *TextBoxes*, *RadioButtons*, *CheckBoxes*, and *DropDownLists*	103
Using the *ListControl* Abstract Class	106
Using *HyperLink* Controls	110
Binding a *ListControl* to an *ArrayList*	111
Validation Controls	113
The *RequiredFieldValidator* Control	114
The *RegularExpressionValidator* Control	115
The *CompareValidator* Control	117
The *RangeValidator* Control	118
The *CustomValidator* Control	118
CustomValidator with Explicit Client-Side Validation Function	120
Displaying the Error Message with Style	122
The *ValidationSummary* Control	123
Validating Patterned Strings, Passwords, and Dates	126
</form></body></html> The *Databound ListControls* Family	130
Using the *Repeater* Server Control	132
Using the *DataList* Control	139
Using the *DataGrid* Control	144
Providing Paging in *DataGrid*	152
Navigating to a Selected Page	154
Providing Data Editing Capability in a *DataGrid* Control	157
Creating Custom ASP Server User Controls	161
Creating a Simple Web User Control	161
Exposing Properties of a User Control	163
Developing the Payroll User Control	164
Consuming the Payroll User Control	166
Summary	168
Solutions Fast Track	168
Frequently Asked Questions	171

Chapter 4 Configuring ASP.NET 173

Introduction 174
Overview of ASP.NET Configuration 174
Uses for a Configuration File 177
    Application Configuration 179
        Setting Static Variables Using the <appSettings> Tag 179
        Providing Global Support Using the <globalization> Tag 180
        Configuring Application Identity Using the <identity> Tag 181
        Setting Page-Specific Attributes Using the <pages> Tag 181
        Configuring the Tracing Service Using the <trace> Tag 183
    System Configuration 184
        Determining Client Capabilities Using the <browserCaps> Tag 184
        Setting Compilation Options Using the <compilation> Tag 187
        Controlling Connections Using the <connectionManagement> Tag 190
        Defining Custom Errors Using the <customErrors> Tag 191
        Mapping Requests Using the <httpHandlers> Tag 192
        Configuring HTTP Modules Using the <httpModules> Tag 193
        Setting Runtime Options Using the <httpRuntime> Tag 194
        Setting Process Model Options Using the <processModel> Tag 195
        Configuring the Session State Using the <sessionState> Tag 200
        Configuring Request Modules Using the <webRequestModule> Tag 202

SECURITY ALERT!

With the standard ASP.NET *machine.config* file, all configuration files are secured and cannot be downloaded by a client system. This allows for some protection of critical information such as user IDs and passwords for DSN sources, but keep in mind that any system can be hacked with enough time and effort. Always keep security in mind when planning your Web application.

Contents

Configuring Web Services Using the <webServices> Tag	203
Security	204
Authenticating Users Using the <authentication> Tag	205
Configuring Security Modules Using the <authenticationModules> Tag	207
Controlling Access Using the <authorization> Tag	208
Configuring Encryption Keys Using the <machineKey> Tag	209
Mapping Security Policies Using the <securityPolicy> Tag	210
Applying Trust Levels Using the <trust> Tag	211
Anatomy of a Configuration File	211
Creating a Configuration File	215
Retrieving Settings	220
Summary	223
Solutions Fast Track	223
Frequently Asked Questions	224

Chapter 5 An ASP.NET Application — 227

Introduction	228
Understanding ASP.NET Applications	228
Managing State	229
Analzying Global.asax	231
Understanding Application State	232
Using Application State	232
Application Cache Object	233
Static Variables	234
State Example	234
Using Application Events	236
Supported Application Events	236
More Events	237
Working with Application Events	238
Threading Use	239

Working with Application Events

To use application events in your project, you must do the following:

- Create a Web application folder using the MMC.
- Create a file called Global.asax in the directory you marked as an application.
- Within the Global.asax, enter script tags with the language you are using (e.g., VB).
- Insert subroutines using the name of the event you wish to use. Any code you add to this subroutine will run when the event fires.

Understanding Session State		240
Configuring Sessions		241
Using Session Events		243
Working with Session Events		245
Comparing Application and Session States		246
Static Values		249
Caching Data		252
Expiring the Cache		258
Summary		259
Solutions Fast Track		259
Frequently Asked Questions		262

Chapter 6 Optimizing Caching Methods — 265

Introduction	266
Caching Overview	266
Output Caching	269
Using the @ *OutputCache* Directive	269
Using the *HttpCachePolicy* Class	275
Advantages of Using Output Caching	276
Fragment Caching	277
Advantages of Using Fragment Caching	281
Data Caching	281
Using the Cache Method	282
Using the *cache.add* and *cache.insert* Methods	285
Using the Dependency Option	285
Using the Expiration Policy Option	287
Using the Priority Options	288
Using the *CacheItemRemovedCallback* Delegate	289
</HTML>Using the *Cache.Remove* Method	292
Advantages of Using Data Caching	292
Best Uses for Caching	293
Output Caching	294
Fragment Caching	294
Data Caching	294

Answers to Your Frequently Asked Questions

Q: I have been asked to migrate an application from ASP to ASP.NET. In the ASP application, several third-party utilities have been used to provide for caching. Should I use these or use ASP.NET's internal caching?

A: Use ASP.NET's caching when possible. With automatic scavenging features and integrated memory management, ASP.NET provides a more tightly integrated caching system than existing third-party utilities.

The tblAddress Layout

	Summary	295
	Solutions Fast Track	296
	Frequently Asked Questions	297

Chapter 7 Introduction to ADO.NET: A Simple Address Book — 299

	Introduction	300
	Understanding the Changes in ADO.NET	300
	Supported Connectivity	305
	The *System.Data* Namespace	305
	The *System.Data.Common* Namespace	307
	The *System.Data.OleDb* Namespace	307
	The *System.Data.SqlClient* Namespace	308
	The *System.Data.SqlTypes* Namespace	308
	Creating Connection Strings	310
	Where to Put the Connection String	312
	Creating an Address Book Application	314
	Connecting to a Database: Exercise	319
	Browsing a Database: Exercise	323
	Adding to a Database: Exercise	330
	Updating Data in a Database: Exercise	335
	Deleting from a Database: Exercise	339
	Summary	342
	Solutions Fast Track	343
	Frequently Asked Questions	345
	Frequently Asked Questions	345

Chapter 8 Using XML in the .NET Framework — 347

	Introduction	348
	An Overview of XML	348
	What Does an XML Document Look Like?	349
	Creating an XML Document	350
	Creating an XML Document in VS.NET XML Designer	351
	Components of an XML Document	352
	Well-Formed XML Documents	355

Schema and Valid XML Documents		356
Structure of an XML Document		360
Processing XML Documents Using .NET		361
Reading and Writing XML Documents		362
Storing and Processing XML Documents		363
Reading and Parsing Using the XmlTextReader Class		364
Parsing an XML Document:		365
Navigating through an XML Document to Retrieve Data		367
Writing an XML Document Using the XmlTextWriter Class		370
Generating an XML Document Using *XmlTextWriter*		370
Exploring the XML Document Object Model		373
Navigating through an *XmlDocument* Object		374
Parsing an XML Document Using the *XmlDocument* Object		376
Using the *XmlDataDocument* Class		378
Loading an *XmlDocument* and Retrieving the Values of Certain Nodes		379
Using the Relational View of an *XmlDataDocument* Object		381
Viewing Multiple Tables of a *XmlDataDocument* Object		383
Querying XML Data Using XPathDocument and XPathNavigator		388
Using *XPathDocument* and *XPathNavigator* Objects		390
Using *XPathDocument* and *XPathNavigator* Objects for Document Navigation		392
Transforming an XML Document Using XSLT		396
Transforming an XML Document to an HTML Document		397

Exploring the Components of an XML Document

An XML document contains a variety of constructs. Some of the frequently used ones are as follows:

- **Declaration**
- **Comment**
- **Schema or Document Type Definition (DTD)**
- **Elements**
- **Root Element**
- **Attributes**

	Transforming an XML Document	
	into Another XML Document	400
	Working with XML and Databases	405
	Creating an XML Document	
	from a Database Query	406
	Reading an XML Document into a DataSet	408
	Summary	410
	Solutions Fast Track	410
	Frequently Asked Questions	414

Chapter 9 Debugging ASP.NET   417

	Introduction	418
	Handling Errors	418
	Syntax Errors	419
	Compilation Errors	419
	Runtime Errors	420
	Unstructured Error Handling	421
	Structured Error Handling	423
	Logic Errors	426
	Page Tracing	426
	Using the *Trace* Class	427
	Sorting the *Trace* Information	430
	Writing the *Trace* Information to the	
	Application Log	432
	Application Tracing	432
	Using Visual Studio .NET Debugging Tools	434
	Setting Breakpoints	434
	Enabling and Disabling Debug Mode	435
	Viewing Definitions Using the Object	
	Browser	436
	Using the Class Viewer	436
	Summary	438
	Solutions Fast Track	438
	Frequently Asked Questions	439

Properties in the Trace Class

Property	Description
IsEnabled	Indicates whether tracing is enabled for the current request.
TraceMode	Sets the trace mode: sortByCategory or sortByTime.

Chapter 10 Web Services — 441

Introduction	442
Understanding Web Services	443
Communication between Servers	448
.asmx Files	450
WSDL	455
Using XML in Web Services	460
An Overview of the System.Web.Services Namespace	461
The *System.Web.Services.Description* Namespace	461
The *System.Web.Services.Discovery* Namespace	461
The *System.Web.Services.Protocols* Namespace	462
Type Marshalling	464
Using DataSets	466
Summary	469
Solutions Fast Track	469
Frequently Asked Questions	471

Understanding Web Services

Web Services are objects and methods that can be invoked from any client over HTTP. Web Services are built on the Simple Object Access Protocol (SOAP) which enables messaging over HTTP on port 80 (for most Web servers) and uses a standard means of describing data.

Chapter 11 Creating an XML.NET Guestbook — 473

Introduction	474
Functional Design Requirements of the XML Guestbook	475
Constructing the XML	476
Adding Records to the Guestbook	478
Understanding the *pnlAdd* Panel	482
Adding a Thank-You Panel with *PnlThank*	484
Exploring the Submit Button Handler Code	484
Viewing the Guestbook	488
Displaying Messages	488
Advanced Options for the Guestbook Interface	490
Manipulating Colors and Images	491
Modifying the Page Output	495

Summary	498
Solutions Fast Track	498
Frequently Asked Questions	500

Chapter 12 Creating an ADO.NET Shopping Cart — 501

Introduction	502
Setting Up the Database	502
Setting Up the Table "Books"	505
Setting Up the Table "Categories"	505
Setting Up the Table "Customer"	505
Setting Up the Table "Orders"	505
Setting Up the Table "BookOrders"	506
Creating an Access Database	506
SQL Server Database	510
Creating the Stored Procedures	512
Creating the Web Services	518
Overview of the Book Shop Web Services	518
Creating the Data Connection	520
Creating a Web Service	521
Testing a Web Service	527
Using WSDL Web References	531
Building the Site	533
Site Administration	533
Creating the Administration Login (adminLogin.aspx)	535
Creating the Administrator Page (adminPage.aspx)	537
Retrieving the Data: Creating the *getBooks.AllBooks* Web Method	537
Displaying the Data: Binding a *DataGrid* to the *DataSet*	540
Adding New Books to the Database: Creating the *allBooks.addItem* Web Method	541
Deleting Books: Deleting from the *DataGrid* and the Database	541

Using WSDL Web References

- Disco, or vsdisco, written in WSDL, enables access to all Web Services and methods for that site. This provides a one-stop shop, if you will, into the server's cupboards.

- Proxy classes can easily be generated using WSDL, which enables code to access remote services as if they were local classes.

Updating Book Details: Updating the *DataGrid* and the Database	542
Creating the *addBook* Page (addBook.aspx)	543
Customer Administration	543
Creating the Customer Admin Section	543
Creating the *loginCustomer* Page	544
Creating the *updateCustomerInfo* Page	545
Creating an ADOCatalog	547
Creating the BookCatalog Class	548
Creating the *CreateSummaryTable* Method	549
Creating the *InitCatalog* Method	550
Creating the *Catalog* Method	550
Creating the *catalogItemDetails*, *catalogRange*, and *catalogByCategory* Methods	550
Creating the *catalogRangeByCategory* Method	551
Building an XMLCart	553
Creating the User Interface	556
Creating the start.aspx Page	556
Rendering the Catalog	558
Rendering the Cart	559
Creating the Code	559
Summary	562
Solutions Fast Track	562
Frequently Asked Questions	566

Chapter 13 Creating a Message Board with ADO and XML — 567

Introduction	568
Setting Up the Database	568
MSAccess Database	569
SQL Server Database	572
Designing Your Application	576
Designing Your Objects	579
Creating Your Data Access Object	579

Designing the *User* Class	581
Designing the *Board* Class	591
Designing the *ThreadList* Class	599
Designing the *Thread* class	603
Designing the *PostList* Class	606
Designing the *Post* Class	608
Designing the *MessageBoard* Class	611
Designing the User Interface	612
Setting Up General Functions	614
Building the Log-In Interface	621
Designing the Browsing Interface	628
Board Browsing	628
Thread Browsing	631
Message Browsing	635
Creating the User Functions	638
Editing the Member Profile	638
Creating Threads and Posts	641
Building the Administrative Interface	645
Summary	658
Solutions Fast Track	658
Frequently Asked Questions	661

Index   **663**

Setting Up the Database

Setting up the database is one of the most important parts of any application. How do you represent your ideas in a structured, well-formed way? The first and most important step is to break down what you know you want your application to do, analyze those tasks, and then extract the important parts.

Foreword

Since 1996, ASP programmers have faced one upgrade after another, often with no extremely visible advantages until version 3.*x*—it's been quite a wild ride. Now we have the first significant improvement in ASP programming within our grasp—ASP.NET. Our reliance on a watered-down version of Visual Basic has been alleviated now that ASP.NET pages may be programmed in both Microsoft's new and more powerful version of Visual Basic or the latest version of C++: C#, which is more Web friendly. ASP.NET allows programmers and developers to work with both VB.NET and C# within the same ASP.NET page. .NET itself is a milestone for Microsoft; it marks Microsoft's entry into the "run once, run everywhere" compiler market alongside Java and Ruby. .NET is also notable for its extreme flexibility; unlike the other choices available, .NET allows the programmer to use any number of .NET-compliant languages to create its code (however, as of this writing, only VB.NET and C# are allowed for ASP.NET) and have it run anywhere through the robust .NET Framework. Visual Basic and C++ have undergone changes as well; Visual Basic was already somewhat Web-oriented through its sibling, Visual Basic Script (VBS).

Since VBS was not visually orientated, like Visual Basic, this meant that a lot of the prewritten code employed by Visual Basic did not create performance issues. This did mean, however, that VBS was not graced with an IDE to debug or troubleshoot with, making the server logs and the browser error messages a programmer's only hope of figuring out what went wrong and where. The lack of an IDE led to several complications and eventually programmers had to create their own error-handling system, usually consisting of a log file and e-mail notification.

VBS had another obstacle to overcome in attempting to offer programmers more than what originally was basically a scaled-down version of Visual Basic. VBS lacked many of Visual Basic's strong features due to the way that the IIS was limited at the time, especially with object creation and cleanup. Programmers experienced code or objects locking up before destruction, rampant memory leaks, and even buffer overflows that were caused by IIS, not by the code itself.

With .NET in general, Visual Basic and VBS are now one and the same. All of the Web-oriented abilities of VBS have been given to Visual Basic and it has received a significant retooling of the language and syntax. Many previous problems, such as poor memory management and object control, have been resolved by the .NET Common Language Runtime (CLR) and internal programming additions, such as the inclusion of the Try/Catch error-handling system and more low-level abilities than before. All in all, Visual Basic can now be called a true programming language.

C++ retained all the aspects that made it a powerful programming language, such as its excellent object control and error-handling techniques, in its new version, C#. It has now gained a very good IDE as well as being more Web-based, a trait that can be attributed to the .NET Framework and ASP.NET. It is expected that many programmers will still use C# for object control while combining it with Visual Basic's ease of use for GUI and presentation.

This book is meant to show all ASP programmers, new and old, just how powerful ASP.NET now is. Unlike ASP 1.*x* through 3.*x*, which worked in Windows 95 through the Personal Web Server tool, you will need at least Windows 2000, all the latest service packs, Internet Explorer 6, IIS 5.*x* (up to date), and the .NET SDK installed. As of this writing, the latest version of .NET is Beta 2, which covers the framework, ASP, and its programming languages. Remember, this book is meant to be an introduction to ASP.NET, not VB.NET or C#. If you need a good book on VB.NET or C#, I recommend looking to two other books published by Syngress Publishing: *The VB.NET Developer's Guide* (ISBN 1-928994-48-2) and *The C#.NET Web Developer's Guide* (ISBN 1-928994-50-4).

Chapter 1 of this book will give you a brief overview of the history of ASP and offer insights into why and how it has evolved in its particular fashion. We'll take a look at its inception from Microsoft, the ups and downs of previous ASP versions, and how ASP.NET will change the way we look at ASP from this point forward. From there, we'll start getting into the foundations of ASP.NET by looking at how client-side and server-side viewing takes place. However, since this is still a beta release, we will mention any possible security precautions that should be taken with

ASP.NET. Chapter 2 will add to our .NET foundation by introducing us to namespaces (special attention will be given to the most commonly used namespaces):

- System
- System.Collections
- System.Web
- System.Data
- System.XML

ASP.NET makes heavy use of these namespaces; therefore, it is vital we understand their purpose!

With this foundation well in place, we can start looking at the innovations ASP.NET brings with it. In Chapter 3, we will concentrate on ASP Server Controls. Server Controls are used by ASP instead of the standard HTML form objects, such as text boxes and select items. This allows for greater flexibility in your code design by allowing for the creation of "forms," which can be considered the ASP.NET method of coding <DIV> layers. ASP Server Controls also allow you to call specific functions as a response to particular actions within the form displayed, allowing for greater programming control and flexibility.

Another innovation to ASP.NET is the usage of configuration files. Chapter 4 will describe how ASP.NET uses configuration files, how to edit them, and how configuration files add to the flexibility of the way ASP.NET deals with data and options. Chapter 5 continues this by introducing us to the layout of a standard ASP.NET application. In many ways, the manner in which we look at an ASP application hasn't changed structurally, even though its inner workings have changed greatly. We will also cover how Application State and Server State have changed in .NET and the differences between the two. Managing the two states in ASP.NET is a vital part of application creation and can literally make or break your program. Chapter 6 introduces us to one of the more commonly misunderstood concepts of ASP.NET: caching. Caching in ASP.NET retains ASP's caching method (output caching), but also adds fragment caching and data caching, as well as the capability to pick and choose between the two within the application at any time.

Chapter 7 provides you with an in-depth look at one of the more common namespaces, *System.Data*. *System.Data* is the .NET equivalent of ADO and contains all the necessary functions for database control and creation as well as basic XML control. We'll first see how the *System.Data* namespace is structured, and then, by working with a basic address book, our first general-use ASP.NET application, we will take a look at how *System.Data* allows us to do the following:

- Connect to a database
- Browse a database
- Add to a database
- Delete from a database

We will start coding this little application after we have had an opportunity to fully understand the *System.Data* namespace. Basic XML support is provided through *System.Data*. We will take a look at the basics of XML in Chapter 8. In general, XML is structured similarly to HTML but it's free from any type of tag rule—the tags are totally arbitrary. However, we have to provide the tag names, content, and so on. This means that we also have to sometimes do more work with XML than what *System.Data* allows. XML provides us with various other tools, such as XSL and XPath, to properly query and work with XML. While *System.XML* provides the tools to work with XSL and XPath, they cannot help us much if we don't understand what the tools are for, so this is what Chapter 8 focuses on.

The .NET Framework provides ASP.NET with a powerful new debugging tool through the Visual Studio .NET IDE. Chapter 9 shows us how to debug in ASP.NET, also covering error handling, tracing, and how to work with the SDK debugger. Many ASP programmers will tell you that these abilities were missing in ASP and sorely needed! ASP threw error messages that were sometimes even more arcane than Visual Basic and required checking of both IIS and the ASP error messages in order to track down the problem.

ASP.NET can also use .NET's Web Services. Web Services allow ASP greater flexibility over the Internet by allowing it to work with other applications through the Internet as if it was a standard LAN network. It uses XML to transmit the data to and from different sources. Web Services can also be considered as a connectivity tool—objects, data sets, and even cached objects can be passed to and from other servers.

We will finally walk through the development of three different sample applications so we can use what we've learned in the book. Chapter 11 will show us a guestbook with a couple of nice touches; it is easy to implement, design, and upgrade, using a combination of *System.Data* and *System.XML*. Chapter 12 will move our programming up a notch by walking us through a simple ASP.NET shopping cart, using most of ADO.NET's capabilities. Lastly, Chapter 13 will round things out by showing the development of a threaded ASP.NET message board that relies on both ADO.NET and System.XML.

So, what we are looking at here is a huge new version of ASP within .NET. We'll be able to go through the basics, understand more of the innovations, and even have a good grounding in what .NET is all about when it comes to the Web and ASP. Let's get started with Chapter 1.

—Jonothon Ortiz, Technical Editor

Chapter 1

Introducing ASP.NET

Solutions in this chapter:

- Learning from the History of ASP
- Reviewing the Basics of the ASP.NET Platform
- How Web Servers Execute ASP Files
- Taking Security Precautions

☑ Summary
☑ Solutions Fast Track
☑ Frequently Asked Questions

Introduction

With the advent of ASP.NET we see a shift from traditional scripting to the beginning of full-fledged programming online. VBScript isn't the only option anymore, as programmers can now employ the full power that lies behind both Visual Basic (VB) and C within their ASP.NET assemblies.

There is no denying the widespread acceptance that .NET received from the developer community. It's proven itself to be a well-developed framework with solid ideas on how the programming world should continue to change. The introduction of a software solution that enables anyone to code in any language that is compatible with the framework is groundbreaking to say the least.

In this chapter we will take a look at how Active Server Pages (ASP) itself began just a couple of years ago and how it has captivated programmers ever since. It has had some problems, of course, but the .NET architecture seems to have found solutions to many preexisting programming problems. There have also been changes with how ASP works with the server and client, to provide the user with the information that you want to provide.

Even though this is a stable beta, and many people are assuming already that what we are seeing within Beta 2 is basically the "freeze" for many features, it still has a couple of caveats, due to its beta nature. Learning from these problems within the framework can allow for preparation against it.

Learning from the History of ASP

You can trace the history of ASP right back to 1995 and the momentous occasion when Microsoft realized they were falling behind in a fundamental shift in the industry by not embracing the Internet. Up until that point Microsoft had been developing their proprietary technologies, tools, and network protocols for the Microsoft Network; all of a sudden they needed an Internet strategy and fast.

Microsoft has gone from a position of playing catch-up to one close to dominance, with the Internet Explorer Web browser having a strangle-hold on the Web browsing market, and Internet Information Server (IIS) installed at the majority of Fortune 1000 companies.

The Origins of ASP

Back in the mid '90s, when the commercial Web world was still young, there was not a great deal of choice of tools for the Web developer who wanted to make his or her Web site a truly useful place to do business. The choices were limited in both available server-side programming platforms and also desktop development tools to produce the solutions. In the end, the programmer was stuck with clumsy Common Gateway Interface (CGI) programs using compiled languages such as C, Delphi, and Visual Basic, or interpreted scripting languages like Perl or Rexx, and operating system shell scripts on systems such as UNIX.

In early 1996 Microsoft had a first stab at improving the situation by including the Internet Server Application Programming Interface (ISAPI) technology as part of Internet Information Server. ISAPI is an extension to the Windows Win32 API. It was developed as a way to create Web server software that interacts with the inner workings of Internet Information Server, bringing what was claimed to be a five-fold increase in performance. As you can well imagine from this description, as well as the immediate performance increase, it also had a side effect of increasing the complexity of the development for the programmer. It wasn't for the faint hearted, and it takes some serious hardcore programming knowledge to do ISAPI applications right. As well as ISAPI, Microsoft encouraged developers to embrace their Internet Database Connector (IDC) technology. This was a new way to connect Web sites to back-end databases through Open Database Connectivity (ODBC).

The ISAPI and IDC technologies lifted Microsoft's youthful and as yet unproven Web server from being a glorified file server to being a basic interactive application server platform for the first time.

Other vendors had tools out there, and several were very popular, such as Netscape Livewire. Livewire was a technology that ran under Netscape's Web server and used a version of JavaScript for page logic, and also used Java components. Unfortunately, Livewire had similar limitations to ISAPI in that it was a compiled technology and the server needed stopping and starting to make changes visible.

Why ASP Was Needed

Not all Web developers have the programming skills needed to write ISAPI applications, and because ISAPI requires the compilation of programs, there are extra steps in producing an ISAPI-based site that slow development down. Novice and intermediate programmers found the need to learn an industrial-strength language, such as C++, and compile even the simplest of their page logic into .dll files a real barrier.

Visual Basic programs, although easier to develop, when used for CGI, performed poorly and the overhead hogged resources. Other languages such as Perl require the Web server to launch a separate command-line program to interpret and execute the requested scripts, increasing page-load time and reducing server performance. CGI itself hogs resources because every page request forces the Web servers to launch and kill new processes and communicate across these processes. This is time consuming and also uses up precious RAM.

Another problem facing development teams in the mid '90s was the fact that a Web site is a mixture of Hypertext Markup Language (HTML) and logic. They needed a way to mix the programmer's code with the designer's page-layout HTML and designs without one messing up the other. There were many solutions to this problem, ranging from custom template systems to Sever Side Include (SSI) statements that told the server to execute code based on special HTML comment tags.

Database-driven interactivity was another challenge. The demand for complex Web sites had just kicked off, and developers needed to supply that demand in a manageable fashion, but the tools available did not make this an easy task. Those who could achieve it demanded rewards that matched the difficulty of what they were being asked to do.

What was needed was a solution for the rest of us. It needed to be a simple scripted text-based technology like Perl, so developers could tweak and alter their pages without compilation and with simple text-editing tools such as Notepad. It needed to have low resource requirements while keeping high performance; therefore it needed to be executed within the server environment just like ISAPI, but without the complexity. Designers and cross-discipline teams demanded that it should include SSI and template features to make integrating page layouts simpler to manage. To be truly popular, it should run off a language that would be easy to pick up and was familiar to a large community of developers. Enter Active Server Pages!

Why ASP Was Not Originally Embraced

Active Server Pages was not an overnight success, though understandably it did capture the imagination of a large sector of the development community, particularly those already well versed in Visual Basic programming or Visual Basic for applications scripting.

Others who did not have an investment in Visual Basic knowledge found the limitations of Visual Basic, and by extension Visual Basic Scripting, reasons to avoid the technology. Faults included poor memory management, the lack of strong string management abilities, such as Regular Expressions, found in other established languages. When compared to CGI with Perl, ASP was found lacking.

At that time, Internet Information Server was in its infancy, and take-up was low, despite Microsoft's public relations juggernaut going into full flow after the company's much-reported dramatic turnaround. In comparison to current versions of the software it seems very poor, but it was still competitive on performance.

Until 1997, back-end Web programming was pretty much owned by CGI and Perl. High-performance Web sites usually had a mix of C-compiled programs for the real business engine, and Perl for the more lightweight form processing.

There was a fair amount of doubt and suspicion around Microsoft's Internet efforts, including IIS and Internet Explorer, and ISAPI had not done all that much to bring across a huge sector of the development community. Despite this uncertain atmosphere, Microsoft saw many Windows NT 4 licenses being bought specifically for Web hosting and development increasing. Third-party support for anything other than small components was initially slow, but, as with all Microsoft products, after the first couple of releases they usually get things right, and ASP was no exception.

Whereas Perl had a huge community of developers led by the heroic figure of Larry Wall, the ASP developer was not yet well supported. A Perl programmer was encouraged from the top to share and make his or her code open, so the community thrived, with every conceivable solution or library just a few clicks away at the Comprehensive Perl Archive Network (CPAN) site, or at one of the many other Web sites and news groups. Contrast this with the ingrained competitive and financially led philosophies of the third-party component vendors in the Windows Distributed Internet Applications (DNA) world. Of course, it did not take the ASP community long to grow to be the loving, sharing success it is now.

Developing ASP 1.x

ASP 1 was an upgrade to Internet Information Server 2, bringing it up to version 3, and was installed as an optional downloaded component. The public beta was first made available in October 1996 and the final release was a factor in IIS quickly overtaking Netscape in the server market.

Around the same period, Microsoft had purchased and further developed a Web site authoring tool called FrontPage that brought with it a new organizational and hosting concept of the FrontPage Web, enabling the developer to deploy Web applications in drag and drop style without using the File Transfer Protocol (FTP). This concept would be carried through into Microsoft Visual Interdev, Microsoft's new HTML and ASP editing environment.

ASP 1 was surprisingly feature-rich for a version 1 product. It included much of the revolutionary functionality ASP that today's programmers take for granted, such as ActiveX Data Objects that shield the programmer from differences in database implementations, with record sets to easily access and navigate database query results, and the ability to mix and match logic and presentation code in the same page. Programmers found the limitations of some areas frustrating, for example, options for reading and writing to the file system; but overall, ASP 1 was a breath of fresh air, and many developers quickly and eagerly adopted it.

Developing ASP 2.x

Once ASP 1 had settled and become established, Microsoft released a new version of Internet Information Server and an upgrade to ASP, with a combined download called the Windows NT 4 Option Pack. This time, ASP was built in to the Web server setup and was not seen as an extra. The Web server was a big improvement, with better support and functionality all round and the addition of a Simple Mail Transfer Protocol (SMTP) Mail service.

With ASP 2, the technology matured to the point where developers could really implement powerful, large-scale solutions. Big-name companies adopted the Microsoft platform for their high traffic transactional sites and the technology proved itself time and again against the demands of serving up millions of page views.

From launch, ASP 2 showed improvements across the board, such as increased file system functionality, added components, and language improvements. Third-party developers released components into the market place that filled in every conceivable gap in functionality, and developers were producing their own bespoke components through ASP's Component Object Model (COM)-based architecture.

Developer tools also had upgrades, with Visual Interdev becoming much improved and better integrated into the Visual Studio suite, with access to Visual Source Safe for source control. Third-party tool vendors had also developed their own solutions, with many wizard-style developers' toolkits and integrated environments coming to market, such as the popular Macromedia Ultradev.

More recently, Microsoft extended the language code with incremental releases of the language runtime Scripting Engines, allowing for improvements in the languages, such as support for Regular Expressions, without the need for full new versions of Active Server Pages.

Major Changes with ASP 2

Moving to Active Server Pages 2 brought the developer into a more stable and feature-rich environment. All aspects of the technology were tuned and tweaked, and programmers really felt that things had settled into a stable technology. This newfound confidence was in part due to the evidence of successful transactional sites actually showing that the platform could deliver, but also the fact that the technology had been boosted under the hood with tighter integration with Microsoft Transaction Server (MTS). In fact, IIS 4 was rebuilt to be a MTS application, and so ASP and MTS components were actually running in the same processes. Another improvement was the work with Microsoft Message Queue. This allowed ASP and components to communicate across networks, ideal for large-scale applications with complex backend requirements, for example, e-commerce systems integrating with existing legacy enterprise resource planning (ERP) infrastructures.

Weaknesses in the ASP 2 Model

Failings in the ASP 2 model were most noticeable when the platform was contrasted against newcomers and developments in other technologies, such as Java Server Pages (JSP), Perl 5, PHP, and ColdFusion.

The main contender for ASP mind-share in Microsoft's most-needed marketplace, large-scale blue chip projects, was Java Server Pages. Microsoft could dismiss the others as low-rent small to medium business and hobbyist technologies, and had an army of certified solutions companies and consultants to take care of those. On the other hand, products from Microsoft's biggest competitors, such as IBM, Oracle, and Sun, supported Java, and these companies had massive opinion-forming clout in the world's largest corporations. As well as products such as IBM Net.Commerce (now Websphere), other vendors such as ATG and Broadvision were releasing application servers based around Java. To make matters worse, Microsoft could not claim to have the better technology.

JSP was outperforming and out-scaling ASP, plus the application servers and host operating systems proved time and again to be more robust and stable, and had lower cost of ownership and higher uptime!

The Java Server Pages and Servlets technologies allowed performance gains against ASP 2 partly because the code is compiled before execution. The Java language also had better error handling, object orientation, housekeeping, and variable typing. ASP, on the other hand, was based around interpreted scripting and languages that were compromised shadows of their already flawed parents.

Developing ASP 3.0

With the release of Windows 2000, Active Server Pages 3 was available. Performance was increased considerably by the addition of a step in the execution of the pages that checked for a previously cached version of the compiled page, and the compiler checking for script elements rather than always processing the page line by line.

The Windows 2000 operating system and features in IIS5 that included the option to selectively separate out Web applications and processes addressed stability issues.

Functionally, it did not have many revolutionary additions (perhaps they were waiting for .NET, which was already on the drawing board at Microsoft), but developers did get several features they had been asking for, such as server-side redirects to replace the Hypertext Transfer Protocol (HTTP)-header client-side implementation, better error handling, and dynamic includes.

Final Changes to Original ASP Model

With version 3, Microsoft introduced the concept of server scriptlets. These were COM objects that were developed as Extensible Markup Language (XML)-based text files. This enabled programmers to rapidly prototype multi-tiered application business logic without the "change, recompile, upload, stop the server, register, test, change" cycle of component development.

ASP and ActiveX Data Objects (ADO) were given a boost in capability with the addition of XML-processing abilities. XML was, at this point, a massive deal in the developer community, and Microsoft wanted to appear to be fully embracing it, and so the whole of Microsoft's product line seemed to be receiving an XML makeover.

As well as the new script execution changes mentioned earlier, it included many other performance improvements, such as the ability of the Web server to self-tune, checking adding threads when needed, and having response buffering on by default.

Weaknesses in the ASP 3 Model

Despite the great achievements of Active Server Pages, particularly in the areas of speed and stability, the platform was still based on incomplete scripting languages of VBScript and JScript, and third-party languages such as Perl.

Scripting languages required the developer to compromise coding standards and bolster the application with components written in a second language, usually C++ or VB. The languages were not properly object oriented, although they were object-aware, and could never perform very well whenever they required an interpreter to execute.

The reliance on the systems administrator for Web server configurations was also a problem; the administrator must register components, settings, and permissions on the server, and so deployment was not as simple as just uploading your files. Programmers were bound to ask, after several years of Java programmer colleagues evangelizing Java Server Pages, "What is Microsoft going to do?"

The Need for a New ASP Model

It was evident that Microsoft would require a fundamental change to bring ASP up to the standard of industrial-strength programming. Active Server Pages was a technology based on the foundations of COM. ActiveX and COM technology provided much of its strength, but also many of its limitations. Microsoft would need to have a long hard look at COM to see how it could improve, and these changes would be bound to affect ASP. At the same time, Microsoft realized that the developers' playing field was changing, with new standards arriving all the time, particularly in information-sharing and distributed applications using XML, such as Simple Object Access Protocol (SOAP) and XML-RPC. Web services were becoming all the rage; Java was everywhere, and XML was taking the developer community by storm. A new version of ASP was not going to be enough to meet these demands; the changes must be more far-reaching if they were not just going to catch up but also take the lead against such tough challenges.

ASP and Windows DNA, being based on early 1990's COM and Win32 API technologies, did not provide a very coherent technical architecture roadmap for modern distributed applications, whereas with Java 2 Enterprise Edition (J2EE), Sun had a suite of technologies that developers could follow, starting small with Standard Edition projects and scaling up to full Enterprise JavaBeans.

In today's world, we do not have to contend just with different Web browsers but also with different distribution channels and modes of operation, with mobile phones and computers, interactive digital TV, intelligent appliances, digitally networked homes, and possibly moving from Web pages to disposable applications and Web services.

No doubt, as Microsoft was looking at their own technologies they must have analyzed the competition. As they announced the .NET framework, they also introduced a new language for the twenty-first century, C#. C# and .NET would address all of the criticisms, provide for a whole new way of looking at applications and the Web, and replace everything that had gone before, including Microsoft's flagships Visual C++, Visual Basic, and Active Server Pages.

The ASP Timeline

Before looking at ASP.NET, let's briefly take a look at the short but eventful history of Active Server Pages to see how we got to where we are today:

- **December 1995** Microsoft makes a dramatic U-turn and announces that their whole product lineup will be refocused to embrace the Internet. Up until this point they had largely ignored the Internet market and had fallen dangerously behind the competition.

- **February 1996** Microsoft releases Internet Information Server to the public for free download. Microsoft spokespeople claim that the server offers a four-fold increase in performance over Netscape Netsite server. IIS includes ISAPI and IDC technologies.
  - With the release of Windows NT 4, IIS version 2 is bundled, while IIS 1 is available for Windows NT 3.51.

- **October 1996** Microsoft releases the public beta for IIS 3 as an optional upgrade to IIS 2. The major change with this version is the inclusion of a new development environment called Active Server Pages, formerly known under its project name of "Denali." As part of their public relations campaign, Microsoft claims they are beating Netscape 2-1 in the server market. IIS no longer supports MIPS and NT 3.51.

- **August 1997** Microsoft releases ASP 2 with IIS 4. IIS now includes the Microsoft Management Console (MMC) to make administering the server more straightforward, and the SMTP server is now bundled, having previously been a part of the Commercial package. IIS and ASP are now tightly integrated with Microsoft Transaction Server, and this is seen as a real step forward in making the platform a credible choice for large-scale deployment.

- **1998–2000** Microsoft started releasing incremental versions of the language Scripting Engines, adding language features and functionality without the need for full ASP version updates, such as the addition of Regular Expressions for VBScript programmers.
  - With the release of Windows 2000 with IIS 5, Active Server Pages 3 became available. ASP 3 allowed for server-side redirects, better error support, ADO 2.5 with support for XML, and caching of compiled code. IIS 5 enabled the administrator to finely separate processes to prevent crashing of the server.

- **July 2000** .NET makes their first public announcement, revealing their new C# language, promising to deliver better functionality and flexibility than ever before, and promising support for a wide variety of Internet standards.

Reviewing the Basics of the ASP.NET Platform

Microsoft has done a great job of bringing ASP and their older languages into the twenty-first century with .NET. ASP.NET, using VB.NET, is now a full-fledged object-oriented Web application development platform, and has seen many improvements; but the past legacy languages should not hold back a new initiative as massive as .NET, so Microsoft developed a new headline-grabbing language for the .NET Framework, called C#.

C# was built from scratch as *the* .NET language. While it has features familiar to C programmers, and it has some of the great RAD features so beloved by Visual Basic programmers, it is completely new. Some have said that C# is Microsoft's "me too" language to compete with Sun's Java.

If Microsoft does one thing well, that is building developer tools, (remember, the product that first put Microsoft on the map was their version of Basic), and C# with Visual Studio.NET certainly lives up to expectations. C# is a truly modern language with all the features you could wish for, such as full object-orientation (unlike the C++ bolted-on approach), automatic memory management, and housekeeping.

The following are some key points about ASP.NET:

- ASP.NET is a key part of the wider Microsoft .NET initiative, Microsoft's new application development platform.

- .NET is both an application architecture to replace the Windows DNA model and a set of tools, services, applications and servers based around the .NET Framework and common language runtime (CLR).

- Rather than just being ASP 4 or an incremental upgrade, ASP.NET is a complete rewrite from the ground up, using all the advanced features .NET makes available.

- ASP.NET can take advantage of all that .NET has to offer, including support for around 20 or more .NET languages from C# to Perl.NET, and the full set of .NET Framework software libraries.

- Web applications written in ASP.NET are fast, efficient, manageable, scalable, and flexible, but, above all, easy to understand and to code!

- Components and Web applications are all compiled .NET objects written in the same languages, and they offer the same functionality, so no need to leave the ASP environment for purely functional reasons.

- You'll have less need for third-party components. With a few lines of code, ASP.NET can talk to XML, serve as or consume a Web service, upload files, "screen scrape" a remote site, or generate an image.

Utilizing the Flexibility of ASP.NET

With the .NET Framework and ASP.NET, Microsoft has not just shown itself to be a contender in Web development technologies, but many commentators also believe Microsoft has taken the lead. ASP.NET is well equipped for any task you want to put to it, from building intranets to e-business or e-commerce megasites. Microsoft has been very careful to include the functionality and flexibility developers will require, while maintaining the easy-to-use nature of ASP.

- With ASP.NET you now have a true choice of languages. All the .NET languages have access to the same foundation class libraries, the same type of systems, equal object orientation and inheritance abilities, and full interoperability with existing COM components.

- You can use the same knowledge and code investment for everything from Web development to component development or enterprise systems, and developers do not have to be concerned about differences in APIs or variable type conversions, or even deployment.

- ASP.NET incorporates all the important standards of our time, such as XML and SOAP, plus with ADO.NET and the foundation class libraries, they are arguably easier to implement than in any other technology, including Java.

- An ASP.NET programmer still only needs a computer with Notepad and the ability to FTP to write ASP code, but now with the .NET Framework command-line tools and the platform's XML-based configuration, this is truer than before!

- Microsoft has included in the .NET Framework an incredibly rich feature set of library classes, from network-handling functions for dealing with Transmission Control Protocol/Internet Protocol (TCP/IP) and

Domain Name System (DNS), through to XML data and Web Services, to graphic drawing.

- In the past, the limitations of ASP scripting meant components were required for functionality reasons, not just for architectural reasons. ASP.NET has access to the same functionality and uses the same languages in which you would create components, so now components are an architectural choice only.
- A .NET developer is shielded from changes in the underlying operating system and API, as the .NET technologies deal with how your code is implemented; and with the Common Type System, you don't have to worry whether the component you are building uses a different implementation of a string or integer to the language it will be used in.

Developing & Deploying…

Deploying ASP.NET Applications

In previous ASP versions, deploying your application required careful planning, particularly if the system was large and complex. This was because of various factors, including the requirement to upload, install, and register components, necessitating stopping and starting the Web server and ensuring that you had the correct version. You had to configure Web servers through Microsoft Management Console, ADSI, or command-line tools, also often requiring you to stop and restart services.

With ASP.NET, this has all been simplified. ASP files, components, and configuration options are all files that you upload together. You do not need to register components, and you can specify nearly all configuration changes using XML format text files. ASP.NET has even simplified software version dependencies by enabling you to host several versions of a component on the same system.

Converting Code into Multiple Languages

As supplied by Microsoft, ASP.NET and the .NET Framework consist of three main languages: JScript.NET, VB.NET, and C#. Other vendors have available or have announced many more, such as Perl.NET, COBOL.NET, and a version of Python.

JScript has been updated to be a full-fledged language and to take account of the object-oriented nature of .NET. Experienced JScript developers should feel very at home and be pleasantly surprised at the new additions.

VB.NET replaces VBScript support, but is similar enough in operation that it isn't too steep a learning curve for VBScript programmers, and as with JScript above, it provides you with full access to all that .NET has to offer, including, for the first time, full object orientation.

C# has been (perhaps unfairly) described as J++ mark 2. There is more to it than that. C# is effectively C++ built from scratch. The problems with C++ are well documented, so there is no need to go into them here, but suffice it to say that in C++, object orientation was an optional bolted-on afterthought, whereas in C#, it was built in from the ground up.

All the functionality and support of the .NET Framework is available to any of the .NET languages, and in addition, objects written under one language can be used, inherited, and extended under any of the others. This is a very powerful concept and introduces the idea of language independence. This is achieved through the Common Language Runtime technology.

The CLR takes your .NET language code and converts it into an intermediate language (Microsoft Intermediate Language [MSIL]), and this intermediate language is then compiled to target machine-specific binary code. The Intermediate Language specification is one of the many .NET technologies that have been submitted to standards bodies, and several projects are under way to transport the software over to non-windows platforms, such as Mono and Portable.NET in the open source community, and to developments from Corel and Borland.

Comparing Improvements in ASP.NET to Previous ASP Models

The first difference an experienced ASP developer will notice is that VBScript support has been dropped in favor of VB.NET. This is not as much of a hurdle as it sounds like, as the syntax is quite similar, and VB.NET is a full-fledged language and so provides a lot richer environment than VBScript ever could.

As described above, all ASP.NET languages are object oriented, event driven, and server compiled. This brings many benefits, especially where improvements were needed most, namely performance, stability, scalability, and manageability.

With Classic ASP, you pretty much had to code your whole application from scratch. ASP.NET has several labor-saving additions to make life easier. Web forms introduce a new Visual Basic Rapid Development-style way of looking at forms in Web pages. With Web Forms, the developer uses new form components that you can add in the traditional way or through code, and they enable the programmer to call on server-side event-driven programming and true separation of layout and logic. You can separate the layout code and functions by using *code behind* pages that use inheritance to add methods to the form. .NET form controls maintain the session state so the users input remains when the page is submitted, and the controls' property values are available to the ASP code without resorting to querying the request object.

The framework foundation class libraries contain exciting new features, previously only available from third parties such as the System.Drawing tools, which enable you to build dynamic images on the fly, built-in browser-based file upload and system network services for working with TCP/IP and DNS.

With Web Services and built-in support for SOAP you can distribute code and applications. Your ASP.NET scripts can consume services across the Web, and publish and expose routines as services just as easily.

Deployment, including server configuration, is mostly just a matter of transferring files with configuration that was previously only available from the MMC now implemented with XML files. Now you do not need to register and unregister components, and the server can handle multiple versions of the same component without conflicts.

Mission critical services has increased support with load balancing and several state-management options, including the ability to store state information in an SQL Server database and pass the session ID on the URL to avoid requiring the user to have cookies.

How Web Servers Execute ASP Files

When a site visitor requests a Web page address, the browser contacts the Web server specified in the address URL and makes a request for the page by formulating a HTTP request, which is sent to the Web server. The Web server on receiving the request determines the file type requested and passes processing to the appropriate handler. ASP.NET files are compiled, if necessary, into .NET Page classes and then executed, with the results sent to the client's browser.

Compilation means that on first load ASP.NET applications take longer to display than previous versions of ASP, but once compiled they are noticeably faster.

Client-Server Interaction

ASP.NET applications are a mixture of client side markup and code, and server side processing. When an ASP.NET Web form page is downloaded to the visitor's Web browser, additional code is included to previous ASP versions. This extra code enables richer form functionality, including server and client side events, validation, and the ability to maintain form value state. The server determines the visitor's browser type and sends markup to match the browser's abilities.

Some client interactions will be dealt with within the visitor's browser, while others will require information to be posted to the server for processing and the altered page returned.

As form responses are received, the form values are maintained in a new facility of ASP.NET "State Bags" and are compressed into a hidden form element containing the page "Viewstate." This allows the form elements that the visitor has interacted with to maintain the same values as when the page was submitted.

As illustrated in Figure 1.1, the browser can request information from and send information to the server using two HTTP methods, *GET* and *POST*.

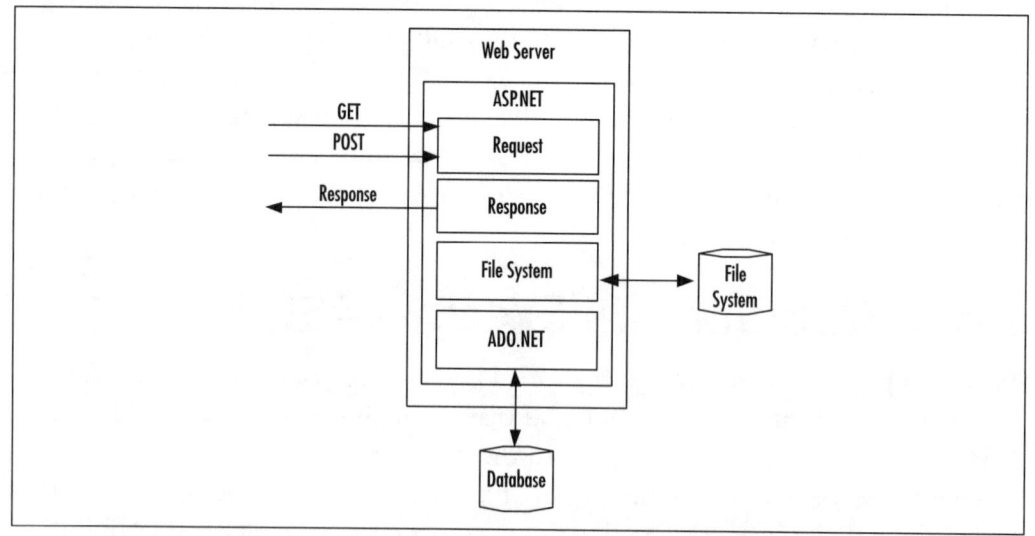

Figure 1.1 How the Client and Server Communicate

GET is simply the method in which the browser compiles a URL. A typical URL in this context will consist of a protocol, for example, HTTP for hypertext or FTP for file transfer, a fully qualified domain name, such as "www.aspalliance.com," followed by a path, such as "/chrisg/", and then the page to *GET*, such as "default.asp" or "index.html." You can add information as parameters, called a *querystring*. This is separated from the rest of the URL with a question mark, and the parameters take the form of keywords and values such as "keyword=value," for example, "article=5." Multiple parameters are separated with ampersands, so if we have two parameters, *foo* and *bar*, they would be presented like **foo=a&bar=z**. So, a full GET request including querystring could be **http://www.abcxyz123.com/site/index.asp?page=5**.

When a browser sends information using the *POST* method, the parameters are compiled in the same way but sent separately in the HTTP header, and so are not seen in the URL portion of the browser like *GET* requests are. Forms often use *POST* for this very reason.

Other information goes into the HTTP request header, such as what browser the user is using and so on. As you will see later, your ASP can pick up this header information and the querystring parameter values.

Server-Side Processing

When the server receives this request, it will find the page that was requested using the path information specified, and the relevant system will process the page. In the case of Classic ASP, there was not much to this process, although a certain amount of caching happened. As you will see in Figure 1.2, with ASP.NET the process is a fair amount more involved but provides for much faster processing and delivery.

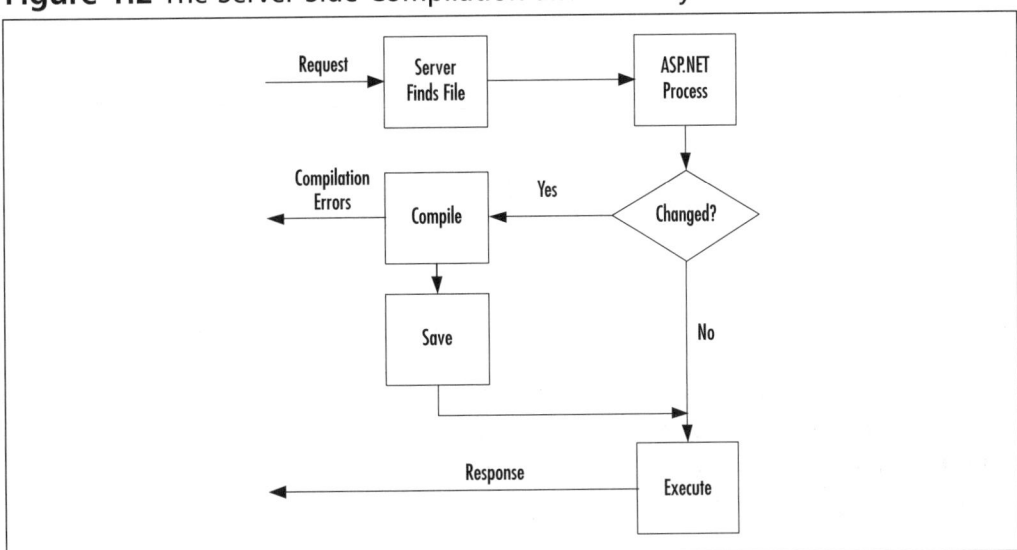

Figure 1.2 The Server-Side Compilation and Delivery Process

The server will process the ASP.NET page using a special .dll especially for ASP.NET. As with previous versions of ASP, ASP.NET has a large collection of objects that deal with processing certain functions such as the HTTP request, databases, the file system, and forming the response.

When the response is complete, it is flushed back out to the user's browser, usually as HTML but not necessarily, and the browser renders this page as it arrives as the page on screen.

Compiling and Delivering ASP.NET Pages

The process of compiling and delivering ASP.NET pages goes through the following stages:

1. IIS matches the URL in the request against a file on the physical file system (hard disk) by translating the virtual path (for example, /site/index.aspx) into a path relative to the site's Web root (for example, d:\domains\thisSite\wwwroot\site\index.aspx).

2. Once the file is found, the file extension (.aspx) is matched against a list of known file types for either sending on to the visitor or for processing.

3. If this is first visit to the page since the file was last changed, the ASP code is compiled into an assembly using the Common Language Runtime compiler, into MSIL, and then into machine-specific binary code for execution.

4. The binary code is a .NET class .dll and is stored in a temporary location.

5. Next time the page is requested the server will check to see if the code has changed. If the code is the same, then the compilation step is skipped and the previously compiled class code is executed; otherwise, the class is deleted and recompiled from the new source.

6. The compiled code is executed and the request values are interpreted, such as form input fields or URL parameters.

7. If the developer has used Web forms, then the server can detect what software the visitor is using and render pages that are tailored to the visitors requirements, for example, returning Netscape specific code, or Wireless Markup Language (WML) code for mobiles.

8. Any results are delivered back to the visitor's Web browser.

9. Form elements are converted into client side markup and script, HTML and JavaScript for Web browsers, and WML and WMLScript for mobiles, for example.

Running ASP.NET Web Pages

In order to run and host ASP.NET Web pages, you will need to have installed the .NET Framework onto a machine already running Windows 2000 professional or server and Internet Information Server 5. Microsoft recommends that you develop under Windows 2000, although it is possible to use Windows XP. Unfortunately, Windows 98 and Windows NT 4 are *not* supported at the time of this writing, although you can use Visual Studio.

There are two versions of the software development kit (SDK): the standard .NET Framework download and the premium version. The main difference between the two is that the premium edition provides support for multiple processors, Web farms, and sandbox security.

Obtaining and Installing .NET

You can get the .NET Framework Software Development Kit on CD-ROM from Microsoft by request or via their developer's network subscription service. If you do not have access to an installation CD-ROM, be prepared for a hefty download (almost 20 MB).

- The SDK is available for download from www.asp.net and www.gotdotnet.com as well as from Microsoft's corporate site, but look out for other mirrors appearing closer to home to improve download time.

- Installation is really simple and it is advisable that you install all components including the ADO update (version 2.7) and the samples, if you are installing on your own development machine. The documentation is excellent, so it would be a shame to leave it out, although it is available to view on the Web.

- You can install sample applications, a set of databases in a desktop version of Microsoft SQL Server, called the Microsoft Data Engine (or Microsoft SQL Server Desktop Edition according to the installation program), as part of the full installation by selecting the option once all SDK files are set up.

- Several Internet Service Providers (ISPs) are already supporting ASP.NET with beta 2, such as www.Orcsweb.com, and even providing free hosting, for example, www.brinkster.com.

Creating Your First ASP.NET Application

For your first sample ASP.NET projects, let's take a look at some very simple examples, first using VB.NET, and then, for comparison, the same project built with C#. As you will see, ASP.NET is very easy, and you will be up and running in no time at all.

1. Start a new document in either Visual Studio.NET or the text editor of your choice.
2. Enter the code from Figure 1.3 into the document, and then go to **File | Save As** and name it **HelloWorld.ASPX** in your Web root folder.

Figure 1.3 Hello World Example

```
<html>

<head>
<title>Example 1: Hello World</title>
</head>

<body bgcolor=white>

<h1>
<% response.write("Hello World") %>
</h1>

</body>

</html>
```

3. Launch your Web browser and enter the location of the new file (e.g., localhost/helloworld.aspx). You should see something like the screenshot in Figure 1.4.

This HTML markup should all be familiar; it is just a basic Web page. The main difference you will notice is the addition of code within <% and %> tags. This is our ASP.NET code. By default, ASP.NET uses VB.NET language (we will look at C# later).

```
<% response.write("Hello World") %>
```

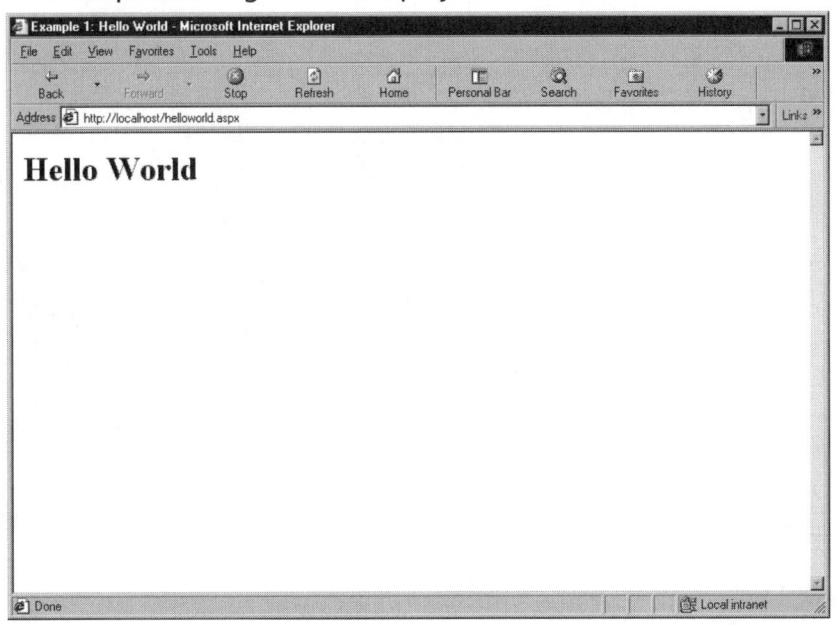

Figure 1.4 Script from Figure 1.3 Displayed in a Browser

This code tells the server to output the text "Hello World" to the user's browser. Alternative shorthand for outputting values is to use the following form, where *value* is the variable or literal you wish to output.

`<%=value%>`

Since that is not much of an example, and nothing you couldn't do as well in classic ASP, or HTML for that matter, let's expand the example a bit. With the code in Figure 1.5, we will use the ASP.NET browser capability function of the *Request* object.

Figure 1.5 Hello World with Browser Capabilities Example

```
<html>

<head>
<title>Example 1: Hello World</title>
</head>

<body bgcolor=white>
```

Continued

Figure 1.5 Continued

```
<%
dim strUsersBrowser as string
strUsersBrowser&=request.browser.browser
strUsersBrowser&=cstr(request.browser.majorversion)
strUsersBrowser&="."
strUsersBrowser&=cstr(request.browser.minorversion)
response.write("<h1>Your web browser is " & strUsersBrowser & "</h1>")
%>

</body>

</html>
```

Within this code, you can see that we first declare we want to use a new string variable, which we will use to store and display the user's browser type:

`dim strUsersBrowser as string`

Next, we add the result of the **Request.Browser.Browser** object property to our string. This method returns the name of the visitor's browser:

`strUsersBrowser+=request.browser.browser`

Then, we use the **.majorversion** and **.minorversion** properties converted to strings using **CStr,** which will return the version numbers of the browser:

`strUsersBrowser+=cstr(request.browser.majorversion)`

Finally, we output the result to the user with **Response.Write**.

In Classic ASP we would have had to create a reference to a browser capabilities component and ensured that our browsecap.ini configuration file was up to date. With the new in-built browser capabilities feature, we simply have to request the values, and in theory at least the browser name and version should always be up to date as the browser version is detected by using regular expressions. Figures 1.6 and 1.7 show the script display in IE6 and Netscape 6.

As explained earlier, Microsoft has introduced a new language especially for .NET, called C#. As this is now Microsoft's flagship language, and the most likely language to be supported by Open Source projects, it is probably useful to show you now how our previous example looks when coded in C#.

Figure 1.6 Browser Detect with IE6

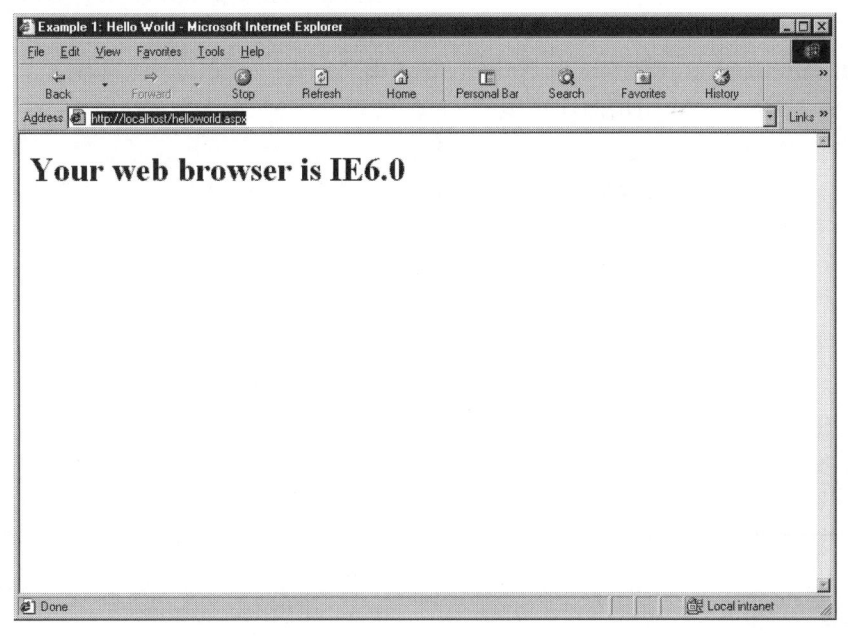

Figure 1.7 Browser Detect with Netscape 6.0

Figure 1.8 takes the browser detection example and simply recodes it into the C# syntax. The very first line shows the first distinction between this and the VB.NET version. VB.NET is the default language of ASP.NET, and, therefore, to use that language you just start coding. On the other hand, if you want to use C#, you must declare this with the language declaration.

Another major difference is that C# is case sensitive. If you had entered **request** rather than **Request**, the compiler will return with "The type or namespace name 'request' could not be found." This is a common source of errors for VBScript programmers learning C#; as in VBScript, case is largely a matter of personal programming style.

The third difference is how lines of code are terminated. In C#, lines end with a semicolon, while in VBScript and VB.NET the lines end with a carriage return.

Comments in C# take the form of two forward slashes ("//"). In VB.NET and VBScript it was an apostrophe. This form of comment must not flow over more than one line. If you require multi-line comments, then either enter double slashes at the beginning of each line or use the alternative form of "/*" at the beginning of the comment and "*/" at the end.

Remaining differences are the variable declaration where we use "string variablename" rather than "dim variablename" and we use ".ToString()" instead of "CStr," and strings are concatenated with a plus symbol instead of the ampersand in VB.

Migrating...

Running in Parallel

You are not forced into changing to ASP.NET just by installing the .NET Framework. ASP.NET pages and applications will run quite happily alongside classic ASP scripts. ASP.NET and Global files use new file extensions and run under new runtime environments. You can continue to use your old COM components in your ASP.NET applications; plus, any new .NET components you create you may use as COM components within your Classic ASP projects. Interestingly, Microsoft states that you will be able to run any future versions of .NET in parallel with previous versions, too.

C# will of course be familiar to C programmers, but also should be quite familiar to anyone who has programmed in Java, JavaScript, and so on. It is a nice, fresh, clean language, with all of the best bits of C++ and Visual Basic without the clumsy baggage. Even though VB.NET will be many programmers' bread and butter language, C# is well worth the effort to learn.

Figure 1.8 Example C# Code

```
<%@ page language="c#" %>

<html>

<head>
<title>Chapter 1</title>
</head>

<body bgcolor=white>

<%

/*
comments are either entered with slashes like below
or multi-line comments can be entered like this
*/

// # we declare string variables with string rather than dim
string strUsersBrowser = "";

// # make sure you use the correct case!
strUsersBrowser+=Request.Browser.Browser;
strUsersBrowser+=Request.Browser.MajorVersion.ToString();
strUsersBrowser+=".";
strUsersBrowser+=Request.Browser.MinorVersion.ToString();

// # strings are concatenated with + in C#
Response.Write("<h1>Your web browser is " + strUsersBrowser + "</h1>");
%>
```

Continued

Figure 1.8 Continued

```
</body>

</html>
```

Upgrading from Classic ASP

Many ASP developers will have years and years' worth of historical code, and thousands of live Web sites are running happily. As mentioned previously, the installation of the .NET Framework will not stop anything from working, so just by installing the software you are not forcing a decision to upgrade. What do you do, though, if you want to upgrade?

You may not need to actually upgrade, but instead add new .NET-based modules piecemeal. This is probably preferable from a simplicity point of view. This approach has a couple of problems. First problem is that your new ASP.NET programs will not be able to share built-in application or session state information. You will need to find some sort of bespoken workaround or compromise solution. The second problem is the possible performance penalty, but depending on the project, this may or may not be so noticeable.

If you do want to upgrade your Classic ASP projects and applications to run under .NET, then you will need to make quite a few changes to your code. The first change you must make is to rename all .asp files to the new .aspx extension and "Global.asa" to "Global.asax."

The upgrade will be less painful for JScript programmers as very little has changed (although much has been improved) in the language. VB.NET is broadly similar to VBScript as they share common ancestry, but several important points need to be taken into account:

- ASP.NET pages support only a single language per page, whereas ASP enabled you to mix and match, provided each language was in its own script blocks.

- Page functions must be declared in script blocks; they cannot be declared in scriptlet sections.

- HTML displaying functions are not supported; that is, you cannot have a subroutine that displays HTML using %> <% script style. HTML must be sent to the browser using Response unless outside a function definition.

- Set and Let assignments are no longer supported. In VB.NET, object assignments are done directly.
- Nonindexed default properties are not supported in VB.NET; you must address an object's property values directly.
- Parentheses are required for calling all methods in VB.NET, whether they are functions or not.
- *If* statements must always start a new line after *then,* whereas with ASP you could just continue straight into the command to execute.
- ASP.NET pages can use COM and COM+ components. .NET objects can interact with classic ASP scripts as if they are using COM. In order for all projects to see a component, the component must be registered in the Global Assembly Cache, as by default they are only visible to the application they were deployed to. Visual Studio.NET has a wizard for upgrading COM component projects to .NET components that should simplify migrating business logic, and there is an ASP Page Compatibility directive to allow for better compatibility with components that use ASP intrinsic objects.
- The ASPError object has been removed.
- By default, *Option Explicit* is set to true, so you must either declare all variables or set it to false in your script, or within Web.config, to prevent compilation errors.

Debugging...

Debugging ASP.NET Applications

Debugging under classic ASP was a hit-and-miss affair, usually forcing the developer to add *Response.Write* statements through the code until he or she found the failure point. ASP.NET introduces much better debugging, thanks to the .NET Framework and Common Language Runtime (CLR). Visual Studio.NET and the command-line tools provide much more debugging functionality, almost comparable to the tools available when developing desktop applications. The server has a debug mode enabling the developer to switch on a trace that will output all the server's variables when the page is requested.

Taking Security Precautions

As with all new technologies or software systems, ASP.NET will require a bedding-in period before we can fully call it a stable technology. While Beta 2 is widely considered to be the full final release, it may still have bugs and security holes waiting to be discovered. The buzz surrounding the .NET technologies will attract the unethical as well as, or maybe more than, the ethical, and some are sure to try to exploit everything they can to their own ends.

It is well worth developing your applications with .NET; there are already ISPs who will host and support .NET-based sites, and Microsoft has a program in which you can already launch your site under the Beta 2.

Having said this, you would be well advised to be cautious. As with all Beta software, Microsoft programmers will be constantly developing and bug-fixing right up until launch. This makes the .NET Framework a bit of a moving target from a security point of view.

If you do intend to host a .NET site on a live environment, make sure you have not inadvertently included any of the example sites or codes in your upload. As well as being an unnecessary additional upload, the code may have vulnerabilities that could be exploited, and the code will have been well researched by now. Secondly, as part of the .NET Framework installation, a slimmed-down developer's version of Microsoft SQL Server is included, called Microsoft Data Engine (MSDE), which is a desktop edition of SQL Server scaled down to five concurrent users. This acts as a working SQL Server installation, including support for stored procedures. Unfortunately, an administration user named "SA" is installed by default *without a password*. This means that a remote user can log into a .NET-equipped host using the SQL Query Analyzer as SA and, using built-in stored procedures, gain access to your systems command line—nasty!

Another area the developer should be aware of is the debug tracing that the server can now perform. In the past, programmers would add parameters into the application memory to conveniently store things like database connection strings, usernames, and passwords. Unfortunately, now this is not practical, as a page fault or a developer manually switching on tracing would cause these values to be output to the screen. An alternative method is available by adding these parameters into the applications configuration files instead, and they are just as easily accessible.

In order to be forewarned and to avoid these security problems, and keep up to date in general, it would be a good idea to subscribe to one or more of the many e-mail discussion lists and newsletters out there that are covering ASP.NET.

Summary

ASP has come a long way in a very short time. It is not difficult to see why it is so popular, when the languages are so easy to learn and novice developers do not need any special software or platform knowledge, just notepad and their current desktop operating system. Contrast this against, say, Java Server Pages, where the language can be tricky for new programmers, and the application server installation can seem daunting.

Over the few years since version 1, consecutive versions have improved the technology into a platform large businesses can trust to host their Web applications and perform reliably around the clock. Now with ASP.NET, those applications can be even more reliable, scalable, robust, and manageable, with better functionality, while adhering to the popular standards of our time.

The playing field has been leveled; now developers have freedom to choose the languages that suit them, and each .NET language has equal access to the full .NET functionality and abilities.

It is an exciting time to be a Web developer, and it will be interesting to see where .NET will take us next. Several Open Source projects are under way to bring .NET to non-Windows platforms, and you can be guaranteed that Microsoft already has work under way on .NET version 2.

Solutions Fast Track

Learning from the History of ASP

- ☑ Before Active Server Pages (ASP), developers had to use Common Gateway Interface (CGI) programs and scripts to achieve server-side interactivity and database-driven content.

- ☑ ASP offered Web site developers the tools that could quickly and efficiently provide them with effective Web solutions.

- ☑ Internet Information Server (IIS) releases upgraded ASP from version 1 to version 3.

- ☑ Each release from Microsoft improved on the last without any dramatic changes to the underlying structure until finally being completely rebuilt with ASP.NET.

Reviewing the Basics of the ASP.NET Platform

- ☑ ASP.NET is part of the wider Microsoft .NET initiative.
- ☑ .NET is a set of tools, services, applications, and servers based around the .NET Framework and common language runtime (CLR).
- ☑ VBScript support has been dropped in favor of VB.NET. The CLR enables you to use a choice of full-fledged object-oriented and event-driven server-compiled languages for the first time.
- ☑ .NET languages are compiled using an intermediate language and then into machine-specific code, so language differences are now more a matter of style and personal preference rather than functionality and performance. Objects can interact and inherit from components written in any language.
- ☑ ASP.NET pages are built with (and are) .NET components, providing all the benefits of an object-oriented approach.
- ☑ Web forms introduce a new Visual Basic forms-style way of looking at Web pages, allowing for server-side event-driven coding and true separation of layout and logic with code behind. .NET form controls maintain session state, and the controls properties are available to the ASP code without resorting to querying the request object.
- ☑ The functionality available has been increased to encompass such exciting features as building dynamic images on the fly, browser-based file upload, and network services without the need for third-party components.
- ☑ You can now distribute code and applications easily and effectively with .NET Web services and standards-based protocols.
- ☑ Deployment, including server configuration, is mostly just a matter of transferring files with configuration implemented with Extensible Markup Language (XML) files. Now you do not need to register and unregister components.
- ☑ Mission critical services now have increased support, with load balancing and several state management options, including the ability to store state information in an SQL Server database.

How Web Servers Execute ASP.NET Files

- ☑ The site visitor requests a page URL from the Web server.
- ☑ IIS matches the URL against a file on the physical file system (hard disk).
- ☑ If this is the first visit to the page since the file was last changed, the code is compiled.
- ☑ The compiled code is executed, and the parameters, events, and form submissions are processed.
- ☑ Results are delivered to the visitor's browser as HTML, WML, and so on.

Taking Security Precautions

- ☑ Do not install the example code on a live-hosted environment.
- ☑ Configure your development environment to not allow requests from outside the network with user or IP security.
- ☑ Keep sensitive information such as usernames and passwords out of application variables and files in the Web root.
- ☑ Ensure the file system and Web server security is locked down; too strict is better than not strict enough.
- ☑ Keep sensitive or vulnerable computers (such as databases storing personal data) inaccessible from the public Internet, for example, behind a firewall.
- ☑ Change the SA password on any MSDE installations.

Frequently Asked Questions

The following Frequently Asked Questions, answered by the authors of this book, are designed to both measure your understanding of the concepts presented in this chapter and to assist you with real-life implementation of these concepts. To have your questions about this chapter answered by the author, browse to **www.syngress.com/solutions** and click on the **"Ask the Author"** form.

Q: What do I need to get my scripts up and running?

A: You will need a Windows 2000 server or Windows XP development machine, IIS configured, and the .NET Framework SDK downloaded and installed from www.asp.net.

Q: Will I have to recode my old ASP Scripts?

A: Classic ASP pages will happily run alongside ASP.NET scripts.

Q: Can I rename my ASP files to ASPX files?

A: If you want to upgrade your scripts to run under .NET, you will first need to make some syntactical changes to your code.

Q: Will my existing investment in third-party components be wasted?

A: Not necessarily, ASP.NET pages can use COM components to give you a transition period, but many of the functions you previously looked to bought-in components to perform, you can now achieve within the .NET framework for free.

Q: Will I be able to deploy on non-Windows platforms?

A: Currently ASP.NET requires IIS. Having said that, several Open Source projects are under way to port .NET to non-windows platforms, but as yet, none are complete enough to be certain what functionality will be brought across and how successful they are. One intriguing project aims to deliver .NET functionality by running the CLR within the Java Virtual Machine, meaning that you will be able to deploy .NET on any platform where a Java Virtual Machine is available. Most of these development efforts are concentrating on core .NET services, such as a C# compiler and so on, though at the time of this writing, none have announced support for ASP yet.

Q: Are there any ASP.NET hosting companies?

A: More companies are coming out to support ASP.NET all the time. Two are Orcsweb (www.orcsweb.com), who host several ASP community Web sites such as www.aspalliance.com, and Brinkster (www.brinkster.com), who even provide free hosting!

Chapter 2

ASP.NET Namespaces

Solutions in this chapter:

- **Reviewing the Function of Namespaces**
- **Using the Microsoft.VisualBasic Namespace**
- **Understanding the Root Namespace: System**
- **Grouping Objects and Data Types with the System.Collections Namespace**
- **Enabling Client/Browser Communication with the System.Web Namespace**
- **Working with Data Sources Using the System.Data Namespace**
- **Processing XML Files Using the System.XML Namespace**
- ☑ Summary
- ☑ Solutions Fast Track
- ☑ Frequently Asked Questions

Introduction

Microsoft defines namespaces as "a logical naming scheme for grouping related types." What that means to us is that all objects used in ASP.NET are grouped by type, making them easy to find and to use. Imagine the .NET namespaces as a file cabinet. You use file cabinets to group related things to make finding them easier, and to preserve your sanity. For example, you may place the deed to your house and your mortgage coupons in one folder, while college loan papers and stubs go in another. Namespaces represent exactly the same concept. Like objects are grouped together: an *HTMLInputTextBox* object is grouped in the same namespace as the *HTMLAnchor* object, because they both represent HTML-user interface controls displayed to the user. In subsequent sections we'll be looking at all the major namespaces that ASP.NET will take advantage of.

System is the root of the namespaces. Within each namespace we can find anywhere from one to several other subnamespaces that provide programmers with the functionality needed to create and provide Web-based applications.

System.Web is a great example. Within its namespace it contains over 10 different sub-namespaces that fulfill many of the basic Web functions and then some. *System.Data* contains various database connectivity methods, such as communication with SQL databases and some limited Extensible Markup Language (XML) connectivity. For specialized XML connectivity we can use *System.XML*, which can provide everything from parsing to translating XML schemas.

Reviewing the Function of Namespaces

As mentioned in the introduction, namespaces are logical collections of objects. You'll reference many namespaces and their objects throughout your ASP.NET development, so it's helpful to dig a bit deeper into the technology.

You should already have a grasp on the conceptual ideas behind namespaces—that they are containers for objects. However, how is this represented physically on your computer? A namespace is usually contained in a file called an *assembly*. These files look outwardly just like dynamically linked libraries (DLLs), and they even end in the .dll extension. If you are familiar with DLLs, then you'll know that prior to .NET, they were used to supply additional functionality and objects for your applications. In .NET, they do exactly the same thing, except that everything within the DLL file belongs to a specified namespace.

The main difference between .NET and non-.NET DLLs is that .NET DLLs are not compiled into machine language. Rather, they are compiled into the

www.syngress.com

Microsoft Intermediate Language (MSIL), which is understood by the Common Language Runtime (CLR). Therefore, the two types of DLLs are not interchangeable (although you can build wrappers around non-.NET DLLs to make them compatible—see the .NET Framework Documentation under the *tlbimp.exe* tool).

Note that you can also create your own namespaces, or add to existing ones. See "Programming with Assemblies" in the .NET Framework Documentation for more information.

Using Namespaces

To use a namespace in an ASP.NET page, you must use the *Import* directive. For example, the following statement placed at the top of your ASP.NET page enables you to use the objects in the *System.Data* namespace:

```
<%@ Import Namespace="System.Data" %>
'more code
```

That's all you need to do. Behind the scenes, this instruction tells the CLR to reference this namespace when it compiles your ASP.NET application. The objects in the namespace then are dynamically loaded when they are called in your pages.

Namespaces are a very powerful tool for developers. Because everything is grouped logically, you'll be able to find and infer an object's functionality much more easily than before. Often, just by knowing what namespace an object belongs to, you'll be able to use it without having to refer to documentation. Now let's take a look at the major namespaces available to ASP.NET.

> **Migrating...**
>
> **Compiling ASP.NET Pages**
>
> If you're familiar with classic ASP, the beginning of this section may have confused you. Classic ASP pages were not compiled—they were built with scripting languages (such as VBScript) and interpreted by the ASP.NET engine when they were called.
>
> ASP.NET pages, however, are compiled before they are run. You build ASP.NET pages using a compiled language, such as VB.NET or C#. This serves to increase performance and strength tremendously over classic ASP.

Using the Microsoft .VisualBasic Namespace

The *Microsoft.VisualBasic* namespace, which is exclusive to Microsoft's Visual Basic, contains just one class, *VBCodeProvider*, and provides access to the Visual Basic.NET runtime, enabling you to interact with the compiler directly.

You won't be using this namespace often in your dealings with ASP.NET, unless you need to change the way ASP.NET pages are compiled (which is a very rare occurrence), so we'll move on. However, if you are interested in working more with VB.NET outside of ASP.NET, you should definitely explore this namespace further.

Understanding the Root Namespace: System

The *System* namespace is the root namespace for the entire .NET Framework; thus, it contains all the basic and generic classes you'll use in ASP.NET. These include the primitives (integers, strings, and so on), as well as all of the other namespaces in .NET. Since it is the root namespace, it is necessary to explore some of the major objects in this collection because they'll be used throughout all your future applications.

Supplied Functionality

Most of the functionality you'll be accessing from the *System* namespace involves the primitive data types, which the following sections will cover specifically. These include integral numbers, floating point numbers, date and time structures, string values, and Booleans, and additionally, the *Object* data type, which is generic. Table 2.1 describes the data types available.

Table 2.1 .NET Primitives

Primitive	Category	Description
Byte	Integers	1-byte integral number (*System.Int*)
Short	Integers	2-byte integral number (*System.Int16*)
Integer	Integers	4-byte integral number (*System.Int32*)
Long	Integers	8-byte integral number (*System.Int64*)

Continued

Table 2.1 Continued

Primitive	Category	Description
Single	Floating-points	4-byte number with decimal point (*System.Single*)
Double	Floating-points	8-byte number with decimal point (*System.Double*)
Decimal	Floating-points	12-byte number with decimal point (*System.Decimal*)
Char	Strings	A single Unicode character (*System.Char*)
Date	Dates	Date and/or time value (*System.DateTime*)
Boolean	Booleans	True or false value (*System.Boolean*)

Integral Numbers

Integral numbers are whole numbers that do not have decimal values. For instance: 1, 12353, and −10. If you are familiar with computer programming, you'll probably recognize the *Byte*, *Short*, *Integer*, and *Long* data types. These are 8, 16, 32, and 64 bit integers respectively, and each requires different amounts of memory. In other words, they can hold different ranges of values. For example, the *Integer* data type can hold values from −2,147,483,648 to 2,147,483,647.

You can reference these data types by the names in the preceding paragraph, or by the .NET names: *System.Int*, *System.Int16*, *System.Int32*, and *System.Int64*. Either name will work—the choice is up to you.

Floating-Point Numbers

Floating-point numbers are numbers with fractions or decimal points, such as 3.141592654 or −0.45. The specific data types are: *Single* (*System.Single*, 4 byte), *Double* (*System.Double*, 8 byte), and *Decimal* (*System.Decimal*, 12 byte). Let's take a look at a simple example. The following code illustrates the difference between integers and floating-point numbers:

```
1:   dim intA, intB as Integer
2:   dim fltA, fltB as Single
3:
4:     intA = 4
5:     fltA = 5.6
6:     intB = intA * fltA
```

Line 6 should return the value 22.4, but since we've assigned it to *intB*, an Integer, the returned value is 22—ASP.NET has dropped the decimal point. The following line, however, will return the correct answer:

```
7:   fldB = intA * fltA
```

Be sure to use the proper data type for your applications!

Dates

A *DateTime* data type can be in many formats: "5/6/01," "Wednesday, July 4th, 2001," or "8:30:34 PM," for example. This provides you with great flexibility in representing your date values, and enables you to perform simple arithmetic (such as adding or subtracting days or hours) on your values. As you move through this book, you'll encounter many of these operations.

There is another date data type that you won't use as often, but is helpful to know: the *TimeSpan* data type, which represents a time interval such as "8 hours" or "13 days." Note that it cannot be used to hold specific times, such as "8 PM." Use the *DateTime* type for these values instead.

Strings

The *String* data type that most programmers are familiar with is actually a class in VB.NET, rather than a primitive. This enables you to create new instances, override, and inherit from a *String*, which gives the programmer a lot of power when designing applications. This is probably one of the most common classes you'll be using in your ASP.NET applications.

There is also the *Char* data type, which represents a single Unicode character. Because it is Unicode, it can represent a lot more than just the alphanumeric characters, in case you ever need to use them. You'll see methods that will enable you to convert from *Chars* to *Strings*.

Booleans

Booleans are simply true-or-false values, such as 1/0, yes/no, and so on. Although the *Boolean* data type in VB.NET strictly uses true/false to represent data, you can easily convert it to the other pairs of values.

Objects

Finally, the *Object* data type is a generic type that's used for a variable if no other type is specified. For example, if you use the VB.NET statement, then you'll be creating an *Object* data type:

```
Dim strMyVariable
```

> **NOTE**
>
> It is generally a good practice to always explicitly declare your variable types. This saves you the trouble of having to convert later, as well as providing you with more functionality that can be used with your variables.

Your ASP.NET pages automatically import the *System* namespace, so you needn't import it explicitly. For example, the ASP.NET page shown in Figure 2.1 is equivalent to Figure 2.2—the latter is probably easier for the developer, and doesn't hurt performance at all.

Figure 2.1 Importing the *System* Namespace Explicitly

```
1:    <%@ Page Language="VB" %>
2:    <%@ Import Namespace="System" %>
3:    <script runat="server">
4:    dim MyInt as System.Integer
5:    </script>
```

Figure 2.2 Allowing ASP.NET to Implicitly Import the *System* Namespace

```
1:    <%@ Page Language="VB" %>
2:    <script runat="server">
3:    dim MyInt as Integer
4:    </script>
```

The *System* namespace also includes one more object that is very useful for ASP.NET developers: the *Array*. Even though this class belongs to the *System* namespace, we'll discuss it in the next section, under *System.Collections*.

Table 2.2 lists all of the namespaces directly under the *System* namespace—it's quite a long list, and each of these namespaces often have even more subnamespaces. We'll cover a few of the more important ones (when dealing with ASP.NET) in the subsequent sections.

Table 2.2 The Namespace Collection

Namespaces	Description
CodeDom	Contains objects that represent the elements of a source code document.
Collections	Contains collection objects, such as lists, queues, and hash tables.
ComponentModel	Contains the classes that enable you to control the run and design-time behavior of components and controls.
Configuration	Provides methods and objects that enable you to access .NET configuration settings.
Data	Contains classes that enable you to interact with data sources; constitutes ADO.NET.
Diagnostics	Contains classes that enable you to debug and follow the execution of your applications.
DirectoryServices	Provides access to Active Directory services.
Drawing	Contains classes that enable you to use basic, graphical display interface (GDI) capabilities.
EnterpriseServices	Contains objects that enable you to control how components behave on a server.
Globalization	Contains classes that define culture-related information.
IO	Contains classes that enable you to read and write to data streams and files.
Management	Provides classes used to interface with WMI events and objects.
Messaging	Contains classes to interact with messages over a network.
Net	Provides classes to work with network protocols.
Reflection	Contains classes that enable you to view information about other types in the .NET Framework.
Resources	Contains classes that enable you to manage culture-specific resources.
Security	Provides access to the .NET security framework.
ServiceProcess	Enables you to interact with services.
Text	Contains classes that represent ASCII, Unicode, UTF-7, and UTF-8 character encodings.
Threading	Contains classes that enable multi-threaded programming.
Timers	Contains classes to raise events on specified time intervals.

Continued

Table 2.2 Continued

Namespaces	Description
Web	Provides client/browser communications; represent the bulk of objects that will be used with ASP.NET.
Xml	Contains classes that process XML data.

Grouping Objects and Data Types with the System.Collections Namespace

The *System.Collections* namespace contains much of the functionality you'll need for grouping objects and data types into collections. These include lists, arrays, hash tables, and dictionaries, as well as some collections that you won't see as often in ASP.NET: stacks, comparers, and queues.

Supplied Functionality

The classes in the *System.Collections* namespace are often very useful, but unfortunately are often not in the spotlight in ASP.NET. They each have specific uses that just may come in handy for your applications. They are listed in Table 2.3.

Table 2.3 The *System.Collections* Classes

Name	Description
ArrayList	Creates an array whose size is dynamically increased as necessary.
BitArray	Provides an array of bits (Boolean values).
CaseInsensitiveComparer	Provides case-insensitive comparison of two objects.
CaseInsensitiveHashCodeProvider	Creates hash codes for objects, ignoring cases for strings.
CollectionBase	The base class for a strongly typed collection. This class must be inherited from—it cannot be directly instantiated.
Comparer	A case-sensitive object comparison class.
DictionaryBase	The base class for a strongly typed collection of key/value pairs. This class must also be inherited from.

Continued

Table 2.3 Continued

Name	Description
Hashtable	A collection of key/value pairs organized by the hash value of the key.
Queue	A first-in, first-out collection of objects.
ReadOnlyCollectionBase	Just like the *CollectionBase* class, but the values are read-only.
SortedList	A collection of key/value pairs sorted by the key value.
Stack	A last-in, first-out collection of objects.

In addition to the classes outlined in Table 2.3, there is the *System.Array* class, which holds collections of values. Let's take a look at an example. The following code creates an array of integers, initialized to the numbers 1 to 5:

```
Dim arrIntegers() As Integer = {1, 2, 3, 4, 5}
```

The size of this array is 5, and the index values are 0 to 4. For example, to access the number 3 in this array, you would use this:

```
arrIntegers(2)
```

Note that you cannot declare a size for an array and assign values at the same time. The following code would produce an error:

```
Dim arrIntegers(5) As Integer = {1, 2, 3, 4, 5}
```

Instead, separate the declaration and assignment into two steps:

```
Dim arrIntegers(5)
arrIntegers(0) = 1
arrIntegers(1) = 2
'and so on
```

The *Array* class has quite a few useful methods and properties as well, such as the *Copy* and *Sort* methods, and the *Length* and *Rank* properties. You'll examine these more as you progress through the book.

Enabling Client/Browser Communication with the System.Web Namespace

Perhaps one of the most important namespace for ASP.NET, the *System.Web* namespace contains most of the functionality for building ASP.NET pages. You'll be covering the classes and functionality of this namespace extensively in later chapters (you'll have to, in order to learn ASP.NET!), so we'll only touch on its members here.

Supplied Functionality

Specifically, the *System.Web* interface provides the functionality that enables client/browser communication, which is key for ASP.NET pages. The *System.Web.HttpResponse* class encapsulates Hypertext Transfer Protocol (HTTP) response information. Likewise, the *System.Web.HttpRequest* object encapsulates HTTP values sent from a client.

In addition, you now have the *HttpServerUtility* object, which provides helper methods that parse HTTP information and return server variables.

> **Migrating…**
>
> **Response and Request Objects**
>
> If you are familiar with classic ASP, the *Response* and *Request* objects should sound familiar to you. The *Request* and *Response* objects in ASP 3.0 are used for exactly the same functionality, and have most of the same methods as the new ASP.NET objects, such as the all-too-familiar *Response.Write* method.
>
> In fact, ASP.NET makes it easy for you by enabling you to use the same names for these objects as previous versions of ASP. When an ASP.NET page is created, the Common Language Runtime (CLR) creates *HttpResponse* and *HttpRequest* object variables named *Response* and *Request* respectively. Thus, you can use *Response.Write* just as you did in classic ASP.
>
> The *HttpServerUtility* is also instantiated as an object variable named *Server*. It contains all the familiar methods as well, such as *Server.MapPath* and *Server.HTMLEncode*.
>
> *Continued*

> These objects in ASP.NET are much more powerful, however, than their older counterparts. They are fully object-oriented, which means you can inherit or extend them, and they also provide a multitude of new methods and properties that will be useful for ASP.NET developers.
>
> Note, however, that the *Request* and *Response* objects hearken back to the days of the Request/Response model of Internet communication. One of the main benefits of ASP.NET is that it abstracts this older model with an event-driven model, which allows for more intuitive application programming. In general, you'll want to use an event-driven method to interact with data rather than using *Request* or *Response*. For example, rather than using the following code snippet to display text to the user:
>
> ```
> Response.Write("Hello World!")
> ```
>
> You should use something like this:
>
> ```
> lblText.Text = "Hello World!"
> ```
>
> Where *lblText* is a label object in the UI.

This namespace also has classes for dealing with many common HTTP related functions: the *HttpCookie* object lets you create and read cookies; the *HttpApplication* class provides control over the ASP.NET application itself; *HttpCachePolicy* is used to set HTTP headers that specify how you can cache ASP.NET pages; and the *HttpFileCollection* class provides access to files uploaded by clients. There are quite a few other useful classes in this namespace as well—see the .NET Framework SDK Documentation for more information.

System.Web.UI Namespace Set

In the *System.Web* namespace, the *System.Web.UI* subnamespace is probably the most used collection of objects in ASP.NET. It provides all the functionality you'll need to create, render, and display user interface (UI) elements to the end user.

The *System.Web.UI.Control* object is the base class for almost all of the UI objects you'll be using in ASP.NET. It provides methods and properties that are common to all ASP.NET server controls, thus making it easy to learn how each control works. Figure 2.3 shows the hierarchy of objects based on this class.

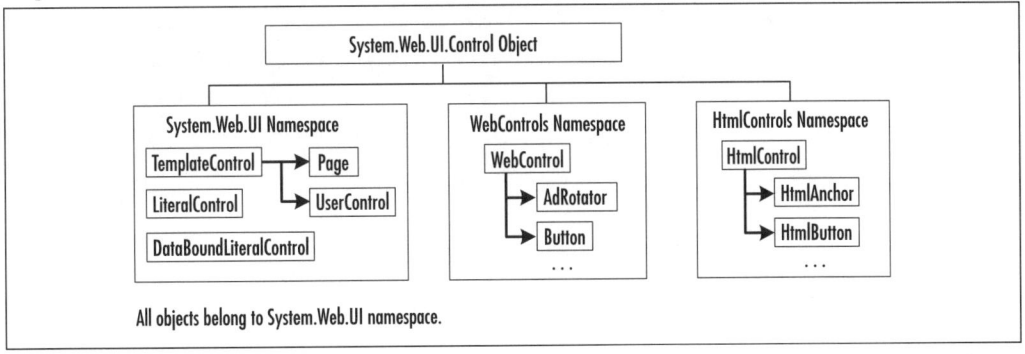

Figure 2.3 The Hierarchy of UI Objects

```
                    System.Web.UI.Control Object
          ┌──────────────────┼──────────────────┐
  System.Web.UI Namespace   WebControls Namespace   HtmlControls Namespace
   TemplateControl → Page      WebControl              HtmlControl
   LiteralControl  → UserControl  ↓ AdRotator           ↓ HtmlAnchor
   DataBoundLiteralControl       ↓ Button               ↓ HtmlButton
                                   ...                    ...

        All objects belong to System.Web.UI namespace.
```

The *System.Web.UI.HtmlControls* and *System.Web.UI.WebControls* subnamespaces provide the classes that render actual UI elements such as HTML input text boxes and forms. You'll learn more about these in Chapter 3. For example, Figure 2.3 shows the *HTMLAnchor* object in the *System.Web.UI.HtmlControls* namespace. The minimum amount of ASP.NET code that would utilize this object is shown in Figure 2.4.

Figure 2.4 Using Objects in the *System.Web.UI* Namespace

```
1:   <%@ Page Language="VB" %>
2:
3:   <html><body>
4:   <a href="blah.aspx" runat="server">Click me!</a>
5:   </body></html>
```

This listing simply displays an anchor in the Web page, as shown in Figure 2.5. Notice that it looks just like a regular HTML page with the exception of the *@Page* and *runat="server"* attributes. The *runat="server"* tells ASP.NET that this control isn't just a normal HTML anchor, but rather an instance of the server object *HTMLAnchor*, which contains properties and methods. You can easily turn most HTML controls into their ASP.NET object counterparts simply by adding the *runat="server"* attribute.

Using objects from the *WebControls* namespace is a bit different, but no more difficult. Figure 2.6 shows an example.

Figure 2.5 A Simple *HTMLAnchor* Control

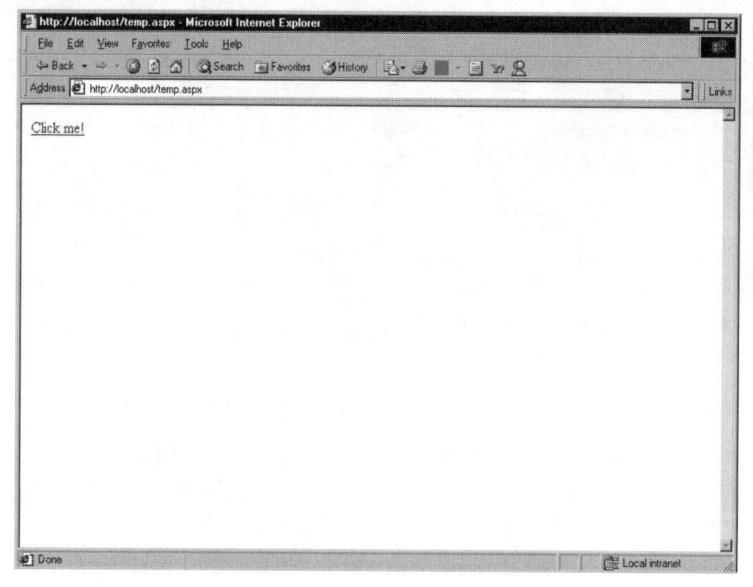

Figure 2.6 A *TextBox* Web Control

```
1:   <%@ Page Language="VB" %>
2:
3:   <html><body>
4:   <asp:TextBox value="Welcome to ASP.NET!" runat="server"/>
5:   </body></html>
```

This syntax is a bit different than normal HTML, but is one that you'll be seeing very often in ASP.NET pages, as well as later in this book. Again notice the *runat="server"* on line 4—this attribute is vital for ASP.NET controls to function correctly. Without it, ASP.NET believes that you are just trying to create a customized tag that it doesn't recognize, and so it will just send it as is to the browser, which won't produce the right results. Figure 2.6 produces the result shown in Figure 2.7.

It is necessary to mention a subset of ASP.NET controls that deal with data, as they are very important in ASP.NET: the *Repeater*, *DataList*, and *DataGrid* controls. These controls have no specific counterparts in HTML, but rather present a complex UI consisting of HTML tables and lists. Any time you have a data source, you can simply bind it to these objects (you can actually bind data to any type of ASP.NET controls, but more on that in later chapters) and the object will provide the UI for you, no matter how complex it may be. Figure 2.8 shows an example of the *DataGrid* in action.

Figure 2.7 An ASP.NET *TextBox* Control

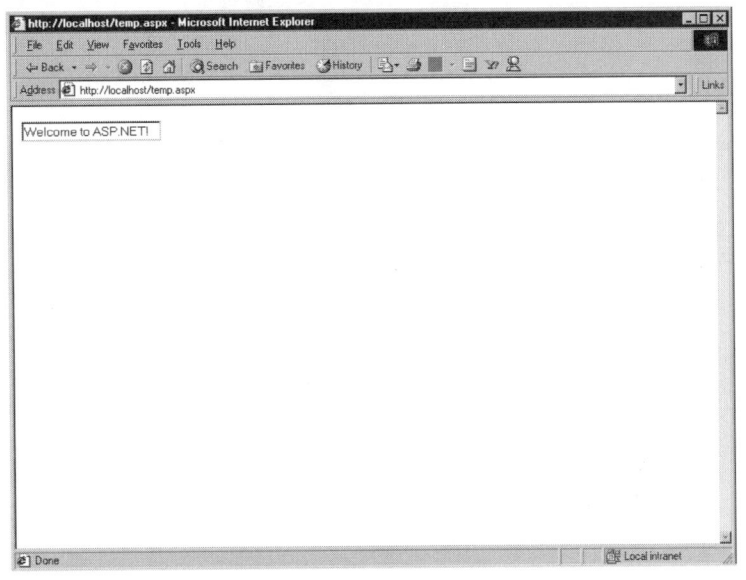

Figure 2.8 The *DataGrid* Web Control

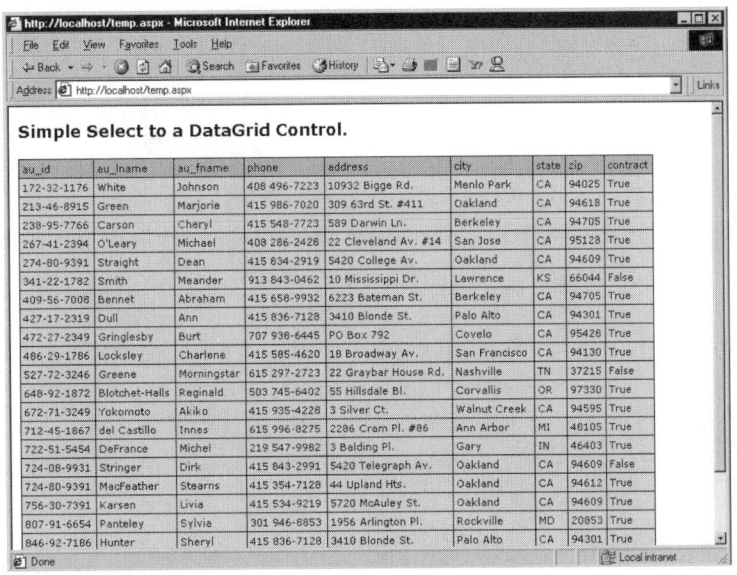

The code to generate Figure 2.8 is shown in Figure 2.9.

Figure 2.9 Using a *DataGrid* Control in ASP.NET

```
1:   <%@ Page Language="VB" %>
2:   <%@ Import Namespace="System.Data" %>
3:   <%@ Import Namespace="System.Data.SqlClient" %>
4:
5:   <script runat="server">
6:      Sub Page_Load(Src As Object, e As EventArgs)
7:         Dim myConnection As SqlConnection
8:         Dim myCommand As SqlDataAdapter
9:
10:           myConnection = new _
11:    SqlConnection("server=localhost;uid=sa;pwd=;" _
12:            & "database=pubs")
13:         myCommand = new SqlDataAdapter("SELECT * FROM Authors", _
14:            myConnection)
15:
16:         Dim ds As DataSet = new DataSet()
17:         myCommand.Fill(ds)
18:
19:         MyDataGrid.DataSource = ds
20:         MyDataGrid.DataBind()
21:      End Sub
22:   </script>
23:
24:   <html><body>
25:      <h3><font face="Verdana">
26:         Simple Select to a DataGrid Control.
27:      </font></h3>
28:      <ASP:DataGrid id="MyDataGrid" runat="server"
29:         Width="700"
30:         BackColor="#ccccff"
31:         BorderColor="black"
32:         ShowFooter="false"
33:         CellPadding=3
```

Continued

Figure 2.9 Continued

```
34:          CellSpacing="0"
35:          Font-Name="Verdana"
36:          Font-Size="8pt"
37:          HeaderStyle-BackColor="#aaaadd"
38:          MaintainState="false"
39:      />
40: </body></html>
```

You can see that there is no code to loop through any data. Simply assign the *DataGrid* a data source, as shown on line 19, call the *DataBind* method, and you're set to go!

System.Web.Services Namespace Set

Web services are a new feature to ASP.NET. They enable anyone to access your application over the Internet, just as if it were on their local machine. For example, Microsoft could maintain one copy of Microsoft Office on their servers, and when you need to run Word, you could just connect to their servers and run it like normal. Web services promise a lot of benefits for both clients and developers.

Web services enable you to do this because they are based on existing, non-proprietary standards such as XML and Simple Object Access Protocol (SOAP). Using these protocols, a Web service client communicates with the Web service over the Internet, sending commands and data back and forth as plain XML. This means that such applications can work even across firewalls. Figure 2.10 illustrates this process; note that both Web service and client can be ASP.NET pages, as well as traditional applications.

When the Web service on the server receives a command, it processes it just as if it were a local application. The server can access databases, local files, user lists, or even other Web services. Any data that needs to be returned is then sent back to the client as XML.

You may be wondering how this is different than regular ASP.NET pages. First, ASP.NET pages usually require a UI—a Web service does not. It simply provides functionality that another application can take advantage of. The second difference is that any application can use a Web service, from an ASP.NET page to a desktop-based calculator. ASP.NET pages have to be served up through a Web server. Don't think, however, that Web services are a replacement for ASP.NET pages—each technology simply provides different functionality for different situations.

Figure 2.10 How a Web Service Works

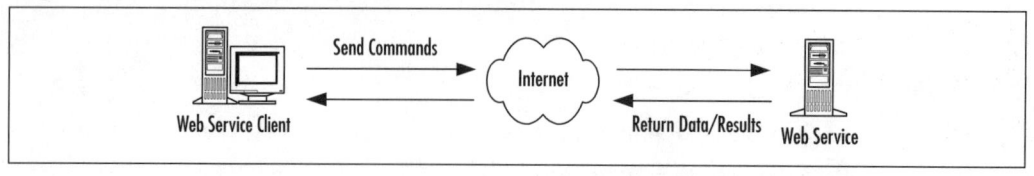

Working with Data Sources Using the System.Data Namespace

The *System.Data* namespace contains most of the objects associated with ADO.NET, such as *DataReaders* and *DataSets*. These objects enable you to interface with all sorts of data sources, from text files to Microsoft SQL Server, to Oracle, or even with custom data sources you create yourself. You'll be spending a large amount of time dealing with ADO.NET in Chapter 7 and in subsequent chapters.

Supplied Functionality

Any time you need to deal with an outside data source, you'll likely use objects in the *System.Data* namespace. One of the most important classes in this namespace is the *DataSet*. It provides a complete, disconnected representation of any data source, whether a traditional database, an XML file, or even a file system. As you start building data-enabled ASP.NET pages, you'll see just how powerful both this object and ADO.NET are.

The *System.Data* namespace also provides objects to interact with connected data sources, such as streams. These objects are usually more efficient than the disconnected data objects such as the *DataSet,* because they don't have to represent a complete database with keys, constraints, and other objects. However, due to that limited representation, they are also limited in functionality.

There are a few Web controls that are often associated with ADO.NET: the *Repeater*, *DataList*, and *DataGrid* controls. Though these controls are not part of the *System.Data* namespace, they are often associated with ADO.NET because of the way they interact with data sources. See the "System.Web.UI Namespace Set" section earlier in the chapter for more information.

Finally, the *System.Data* object also provides limited functionality to interact with XML data sources. You can load XML data and write it to a database, and vice versa. However, if you want to examine XML data in more depth, you should use the objects in the *System.Xml* namespace, which we'll discuss next.

> **Migrating...**
>
> ### ADO.NET from ADO
>
> Though much of ADO.NET is similar to ADO, a few things have changed. Most notably, the move from *Recordset* to *Dataset* objects, and the inclusion of XML data representation.
>
> There are a lot of similarities between the *Recordset* and *DataSet* objects, but there are several things to be aware of. First, a *Recordset* was a simple representation of a table—it did not contain information on relationships, constraints, keys, and so on. A *DataSet*, however, does contain this information, as well as being able to contain more than one table of data at a time. This makes it much more functional than the *Recordset*.
>
> Secondly, a *DataSet* is a completely separate entity from the database. You can even fill it manually without using a data source. This disconnected data provides a large performance boost over the connected data in a *Recordset* by not requiring extensive locks and active connections on data.
>
> Finally, a *DataSet* represents its data internally with XML. Thus, you can easily retrieve data from a database with a *DataSet*, and then write it directly to an XML file. Or, conversely, you can load an XML file into a *DataSet*, and then insert it into a database. The *Recordset* object had no such capability.

Processing XML Files Using the System.XML Namespace

The *System.Xml* namespace provides all of the methods to process XML files—creating, parsing, transforming, searching, and so on. XML is a large part of ASP.NET (and ADO.NET, as discussed in the previous section), so you'll spend quite a bit of time with it later in the book.

Supplied Functionality

XML files are essentially pure text databases. Using a system of tags (like HTML), you can declare any type of data you'd like. For example, the following code shows a simple book database:

```
<?xml version=1.0?>
<library>
    <book>
        <title>To Kill A Mockingbird</title>
        <author>Harper Lee</author>
    </book>
</library>
```

You could easily insert this data into a database such as Microsoft SQL Server, but then you'd lose the readability and portability of the data. Thus, XML is designed to make any type of data universally available.

The *XmlTextReader* and *XmlTextWriter* objects are two of the most used objects in *System.Xml* because they provide lightweight and easy access to the data in XML files. You can navigate through an XML file with these objects just as you would a *DataSet* in ADO.NET. There are also objects that represent each part of an XML file, such as an *XmlNode* and *XmlElement*.

Also of interest are the *System.Xml.Schema*, *System.Xml.Serialization*, *System.Xml.XPath*, and *System.Xml.Xsl* sub-namespaces. These groups of objects provide additional functionality that will be very useful when dealing with XML data.

Summary

Microsoft.VisualBasic is a Microsoft specific namespace that provides access to the VB.NET compiler and code generator. You probably won't spend much time in this namespace unless you're interested in the inner workings of VB.NET.

The *System* namespace provides all of the foundations for the other namespaces, including the various data types and the *Array*. You'll be using the objects in this namespace quite a bit, and often without even realizing it.

System.Collections provides the base classes for the other collection objects in the .NET Framework, as well as a few useful regular classes, such as the *HashTable* and *BitArray*. You cannot use all of the base classes directly—they must be inherited from a custom class, or you can use one of the many existing classes that already inherit from them.

System.Web is a very important namespace for ASP.NET. It contains all of the functionality required to communicate between client and server; in essence, it is the heart of ASP.NET. The *HttpRequest* and *HttpResponse* objects enable you to examine data returned from a client (such as data from a form) and send information back to the client (for example, by using *Response.Write*). You can access the *HttpServerUtility* object through the *Server* object variable, and it provides additional functionality that helps when dealing with Internet communications.

Under the *System.Web* namespace are two very important subnamespaces: *System.Web.UI.HtmlControls* and *System.Web.UI.WebControls*. These two namespaces provide all of the objects you'll use to display user interfaces to the client browser. Without these, you could not interact properly with users, if at all.

System.Data is essentially ADO.NET. In this namespace you'll find all of the tools you'll need to communicate with any type of data that ADO.NET can access. These classes can even interact with XML.

Finally, *System.Xml* enables you to handle and manipulate XML data. Note that *System.Xml* and *System.Data* are highly intertwined; you can use each namespace's classes to read and write each type of data, so the choice of which to use is often up to you.

You will be working with these namespaces throughout this book. For deeper information about these namespaces, the .NET Framework Documentation is an excellent resource.

Solutions Fast Track

Reviewing the Function of Namespaces

- ☑ Namespaces are logical collections of objects. A namespace is usually contained in a file called an *assembly*. These files outwardly look just like dynamically linked libraries (DLLs), and even end in the .dll extension.

- ☑ The main difference between .NET and non-.NET DLLs is that .NET DLLs are not compiled into machine language. Rather, they are compiled into the Microsoft Intermediate Language (MSIL), which is understood by the Common Language Runtime (CLR).

- ☑ To use a namespace in an ASP.NET page, you must use the *Import* directive. Unlike in classic ASP, ASP.NET pages are compiled before they are run. You build ASP.NET pages using a compiled language, such as VB.NET or C#.

Using the *Microsoft.VisualBasic* Namespace

- ☑ The *Microsoft.VisualBasic* namespace provides access to the VB.NET runtime.

- ☑ It enables you to access the compiler and code generator.

Understanding the Root Namespace: *System*

- ☑ The *System* namespace contains the foundation for the .NET Framework.

- ☑ It contains classes and structures representing the primitive data types (*Integers*, *Strings*, and so on).

- ☑ It also contains the very useful *Array* class.

Grouping Objects and Data Types with the *System.Collections* Namespace

- ☑ The *System.Collections* namespace provides the base classes for all other collection objects in the .NET Framework.

- ☑ It contains the *HashTable* object, which you may notice quite often in ASP.NET.

Enabling Client/Browser Communication with the *System.Web* Namespace

- ☑ The *System.Web* namespace is the foundation for all ASP.NET pages.
- ☑ It contains the *System.Web.UI.WebControls* and *System.Web.UI.HtmlControls* subnamespaces, which provide the objects used to build UIs.
- ☑ It also contains the *System.Web.Services* namespace, which encapsulates the functionality needed to create and consume Web services.

Working with Data Sources Using the *System.Data* Namespace

- ☑ The classes in *System.Data* make up ADO.NET.
- ☑ It uses XML to represent data internally, enabling you to use XML files just as if they were a traditional data source.

Processing XML Files Using the *System.XML* Namespace

- ☑ The *System.XML* namespace provides access to XML files just as ADO.NET does with databases.
- ☑ *XmlTextReader* and *XmlTextWriter* objects allow for easy, lightweight manipulation of XML data.
- ☑ It provides tight integration with the objects in *System.Data* (ADO.NET).

Frequently Asked Questions

The following Frequently Asked Questions, answered by the authors of this book, are designed to both measure your understanding of the concepts presented in this chapter and to assist you with real-life implementation of these concepts. To have your questions about this chapter answered by the author, browse to **www.syngress.com/solutions** and click on the **"Ask the Author"** form.

Q: Where are the namespaces located? How do I find them?

A: All of the .NET namespaces are located in assemblies (previously known as dynamically linked libraries, or DLLs). For example, *System* is located in the file System.dll. Note, however, that namespace names do not always represent the DLL files they are located in. For example, *System.Web.UI* is located in System.Web.dll, not in System.Web.UI.dll.

Q: What namespaces are automatically imported into ASP.NET pages?

A: *System, System.Collections, System.IO, System.Web, System.Web.UI, System.Web.UI.HtmlControls,* and *System.Web.UI.WebControls* all are imported implicitly by ASP.NET; you do not need to make explicit references to these.

Q: Do I have to import namespaces not included in the previous list?

A: No, there is no requirement to import additional namespaces. If you like, you can just reference an object not imported by default by its full namespace name. For example, if you don't import the *System.Drawing* namespace, you could use the following line in your code:

```
Dim objColor as System.Drawing.ColorConverter
```

Had you imported the *System.Drawing* namespace, you could simply use the following:

```
Dim objColor as ColorConverter
```

Q: Does importing namespaces add overhead to my applications?

A: Simply importing namespaces does not add overhead. The objects within the namespace are loaded only if they are needed, so you could import every namespace in the .NET Framework and notice no performance hit.

www.syngress.com

Q: Is there a way to view an assembly's methods and objects without programming or using the *System.Reflection* objects?

A: Absolutely! The Intermediate Language Disassembler enables you to view the technical details of any .NET assembly. You can run it from the command prompt with the command *ildasm.exe*. You can also use the object browser in Visual Studio .NET, which provides a more user-friendly listing of the objects and their methods/properties. Both of these methods are excellent tools for examining namespaces that you are curious about.

Q: How can I deploy custom namespaces?

A: Thanks to the .NET Framework, deploying namespaces and applications is very easy: all that is required is to copy the files to the target computer. There is no need to install or register assemblies or applications because the Common Language Runtime handles everything for you. There is one requirement, however, if you want the CLR to make custom assemblies automatically available to your applications: Place them in a *\bin* directory in your application folder. Assemblies in this folder are automatically loaded by the .NET runtime, though you can manually load assemblies that are not in this directory. See the .NET Framework Documentation for more details.

Chapter 3

ASP Server Controls

Solutions in this chapter:

- **Major Features of ASP.NET Server Controls**
- **Server-Side Processing in ASP.NET**
- **Code-Behind versus In-Page Coding**
- **Using HTML Server Controls**
- **Using ASP.NET Web Controls**
- **Creating Custom ASP Server User Controls**

☑ **Summary**

☑ **Solutions Fast Track**

☑ **Frequently Asked Questions**

Introduction

ASP.NET supplies ASP.NET programmers with a much-needed solution to an age-old problem—HTML form controls. Up until .NET, ASP programmers had to move back and forth between HTML and ASP in order to provide interactivity between Web pages. This also meant that an ASP page was not as dynamic as it could be if it were done through Java or through some extensive JavaScript/Cascading Style Sheet (CSS) coding.

In short, ASP had the short end of the stick as far as Web interactivity went. With the advent of ASP server controls, all that will change. Imagine being able to do real-time value verification and having the Web page instantly spit out an error when someone tries to skip a required field. Imagine being able to dynamically replace data on a Web page without having to force the user to access another page or restart completely. With ASP.NET, all this and more is possible! The exercises illustrated in this chapter will demonstrate to you the power of ASP.NET.

Major Features of ASP.NET Server Controls

When you develop an ASP.NET Web Form, you can use the following type of controls:

- **HTML Server Controls** You can manipulate these controls at the server-side. Before dispatching a form to the client, the ASP Engine converts them to the equivalent HTML elements. These controls are included in the *System.Web.UI.HtmlControls* namespace.

- **Web Server Controls (also known as Web Controls or ASP.NET Web Form Controls)** These are the new generation's controls developed by Microsoft. They have many useful built-in features, and a standard set of properties. In the HTML or .aspx file, these are typically referenced with an asp: prefix such as asp:Label, asp:Button, or asp:TextBox. Besides the form-type server controls such as labels, button, and dropdown, there are a number of special-purpose controls like the *Calendar* and *AdRotator* controls. The ASP Engine also maps these controls to standard HTML equivalent controls before dispatching the page to the client. These Web server controls are available in the *System.Web.UI.WebControls* namespace.

- **Validation Controls** This set of controls provides Rapid Application Development (RAD) features for automatically checking the specified validity of user inputs. These controls are available in the *System.Web.UI.WebControls* namespace.

- **Custom Controls** You can develop your own server controls by extending an existing control or group of controls to provide additional functionalities. There are two versions of custom controls: Web User Controls and Web Custom Controls. The Web User Controls are easy to develop, and are typically stored as .ascx files. The Web Custom Controls require in-depth knowledge of Object Oriented Programming and the Common Language Runtime (CLR). These are stored in compiled form as assemblies.

In this chapter we will provide an overview of these controls. Before we introduce you to the ASP.NET server controls, we need to focus your attention on a number of procedural issues involved in developing a Web form. These issues are the following: *Collecting Data using HTML Forms, State-less ASP controls* versus *State-full ASP Net controls*, the role of *PostBack*, and *In-Page Code* versus *Code-Behind*.

> **NOTE**
>
> In an IIS environment, the ASP and ASP.NET can run side by side. If you install ASP.NET, your existing ASP applications will continue running. The IIS uses the ASP Engine to process the .asp files, whereas it uses the ASP.NET Engine to process the .aspx files. Session states and application states are not shared between ASP and ASP.NET pages.

Collecting Data Using HTML Forms

HTML uses the Hypertext Transfer Protocol (HTTP) to transmit Web pages. When you enter a URL of a page in your browser, it sends an HTTP message to the server, requesting the desired page. This message is typically known as the *Request* message. If the desired page has a *.html or *.htm extension, the Web server simply retrieves the page from the server's disk and sends it back to your computer (client) via a new HTTP message, known as the *Response* message. It is your browser that interprets the mark-up codes in the Response object and presents the page on your monitor.

In an HTML document, you can use an HTML *form* element to collect data from the user. Typically, other HTML elements like buttons, checkboxes, or textboxes are imbedded in an HTML form. It also provides an HTML **Submit** button in the form. With one click of the **Submit** button, the browser packages the user's given data in a Request message and then sends it to the server. An HTTP message has two parts: the HTTP *Header* and the HTTP *Body*. Thus, the browser can package the user-given data in the Request object in one of two ways. It may augment the URL with the name-value pairs of submitted data. Alternatively, it can package the submitted data inside the *body* part of the Request message. Which of the alternative methods will it use? The answer depends on the specifications in the HTML form element. A typical form tag is shown in Figure 3.1. The *Method* parameter is used to specify the mode of data transmission. If it is "Get", the browser sends the data in the *header* section of the HTTP message. If it is "Post", the data are sent in the *body* section. The *Action* parameter can be used to request a specified html or other documents like .asp or .aspx files.

Figure 3.1 Major Parameters (Attributes) of an HTML Form Element

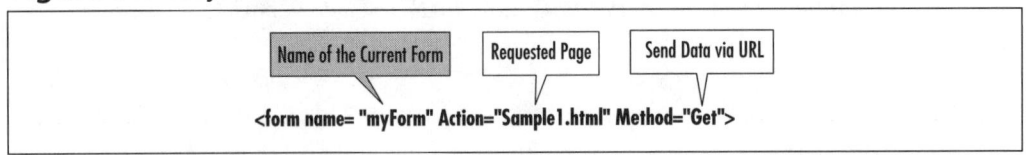

```
           Name of the Current Form    Requested Page     Send Data via URL

           <form name= "myForm" Action="Sample1.html" Method="Get">
```

To demonstrate the data-passing mechanism using the *Get* method, we will present a simple example. Consider the *Sample1.html* document as shown in Figure 3.2, which is included on the CD that accompanies this book. In this code, we have included a HTML form named *myForm*. It has a **Submit** button, and a **textbox**. The user will enter a hobby and click the **Submit** button. On click of the **Submit** button, the browser will request the html document named *Sample1.html* and pass the submitted data to the server in the augmented URL. In this particular example, the browser will actually request the same html document (named *Sample1.html*). Figure 3.3 shows the URL of the requested form as submitted by the browser to the Web server. You will see that the browser has augmented the URL, and the new URL is http://ahmed2/Chapter3/sample1.html?txtHobby=Fishing. That means the data are submitted as a *name=value* pair in the URL itself. The first such pair is prefixed with a question mark.

Figure 3.2 A Simple Data Collection HTML Form (Sample1.html)

```
<!-- Chapter3\Sample1.html -->
<html><head></head><body>
<form name="myForm" Action="Sample1.html" Method="Get">
Your Hobby? <input type="text" name="txtHobby" size=10>
<input  type="submit" Value="Submit">
</form></body></html>
```

Figure 3.3 Submitting Data in the Augmented URL: *Get* Method

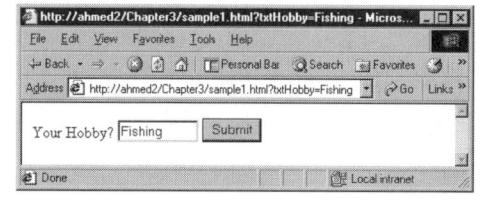

If we specify *Method="Post"* in the *form* tag, the data are packaged as *name-value* pairs in the *body* section of the HTTP message. Unfortunately, we cannot have a peak inside the *body* section, and thus it cannot be shown. Once the data are submitted, what do we do with it? Well, that is where the server-side scripting comes into the scenario. We will briefly discuss the ASP.NET server-side processing in the next section.

Server-Side Processing in ASP.NET

An ASP.NET file has an *.aspx extension. Typically, it contains HTML elements, server-side codes and client-side codes. As shown in Figure 3.4, when a user requests an ASPX page, the server retrieves it from the disk and then sends it to the ASPX Engine for further processing. The ASPX Engine compiles the server side codes and generates the page class file. It then instantiates the class file and executes the instructions to develop the response object. During the execution stage, the system follows the programmatic instructions (in the server-side code) to process the data submitted by the user. Finally, the server transmits the response object to the client. In short, the major steps in processing a request for an ASPX page are as follows:

1. The server receives a request for a desired ASPX page.
2. The server locates the page in the disk.

3. The server gives the page to the ASP.NET Engine.

4. The ASP.NET Engine compiles the page and generates the page class. If the class had already been loaded, it simply provides a thread to the running class instead of regenerating the class. During compilation, it may require other code classes, such as code-behind classes and component classes. These are assembled during this step.

5. The ASP.NET instantiates the class, performs necessary processing, and it generates the *Response* object.

6. The Web server then sends the *Response* object to the client.

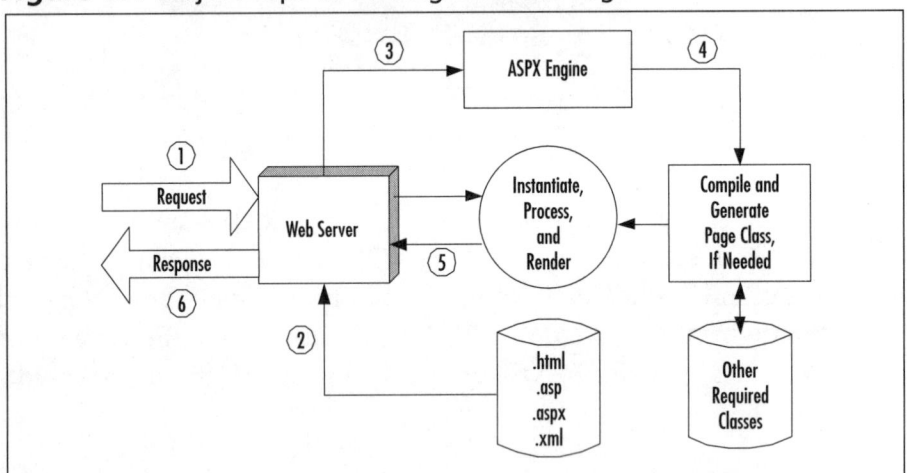

Figure 3.4 Major Steps in Serving an ASPX Page

Now that we know about the HTML Forms and Web server environment, we will start discussing the server controls. To demonstrate the basic principles of server controls, we will kick off this section by presenting a simple application using conventional HTML controls. Then we will develop the same application using the ASP.NET Web controls and highlight the major differences.

A Simple Application Using Conventional HTML Controls

As shown in Figure 3.5, we will display some flower names using conventional HTML controls. On click of a command button we will request the same form from the server. The code for this form is shown in Figure 3.6 and can be found on the CD that accompanies this book.

Figure 3.5 Conventional HTML Form and Controls

Figure 3.6 A Simple .aspx File Using Conventional HTML Controls (Conventiona1.aspx)

```
<!-- Chapter3\Conventional1.aspx -->
<html><head></head>
<form action="htmlListbox.aspx" method="post">
<body>Select a flower and then either click on the
submit button or refresh the page.
You will see that your selection has been lost
in successive requests of the page. <br/><br/>
<select name="lstFlowers"  size="3">
    <option value="Tulip">Tulip</option>
    <option value="Poppy">Poppy</option>
    <option value="Iris">Iris</option>
</select> <br/><br/>
<input type="submit" value="Submit"/>
</body></form></html>
```

Once the form is displayed, we will select a flower from the list box, and either click on the **Submit** button or refresh the page. In both cases, the system will return the same form, but we will see that our selection has been lost. This is due to the *state-less* nature of HTTP protocol. On each request, the server serves the requested page, however, it does not remember the values of the controls assigned in its prior invocation. In ASP days, we had to include a good amount of codes to preserve the states of the controls. Well, ASP.NET has made life easier! It preserves the states of controls automatically.

A Simple Application Using ASP Server Controls

In this example, we will develop the same application using ASP.NET Server Controls. At this stage, we have two choices. We may either use HTML Server controls or Web Server controls. Just for the sake of experimentations, we will use the *<asp:listbox>* Web Server Control, and the *<input type="button">* HTML Server Control. Irrespective of which type of controls we use, we will need to add a new attribute in the tags for these controls. When we create an instance of these controls, we will specify its *runat* attribute to be "server" such as *<asp:listbox id= "lstFlowers" runat="server" />*. The output is shown in Figure 3.7. Its revised code is shown in Figure 3.8 and can be found on the CD that accompanies this book.

Once a flower is selected and the command button is clicked, the client will receive a new instance of the form from the server, however, the selected value of the list box will persist. This phenomenon is known as *state-full*. This is because the ASP.NET controls maintain their states in spite of the state-less nature of the HTTP protocol.

Figure 3.7 The Flower Selection Application Using ASP.NET Server Controls

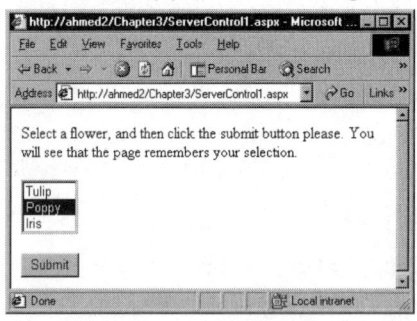

Figure 3.8 The Code for ServerControl1.aspx (ServerControl1.aspx)

```
<!-- Chapter3\ServerControl1.aspx -->
<html><head></head><body>
<form runat="server" action ="ServerControl1.aspx">
Select a flower, and then click the submit button please. You
will see that the page remembers your selection.<br/><br/>
<asp:ListBox runat="server" rows="3">
     <asp:ListItem>Tulip</asp:ListItem>
     <asp:ListItem>Poppy</asp:ListItem>
     <asp:ListItem>Iris</asp:ListItem>
```

Continued

Figure 3.8 Continued

```
</asp:ListBox><br/><br/>
<input type="submit" value="Submit" runat="server"/>
</body></form></html>
```

Mapping Server Controls and Preserving Their States

In our previous example, we have preserved the state of the list box. Of course, the ASP.NET framework has assisted us in doing so. Now, how does the system map the server controls, and how does it preserve the states of the controls? Answers to both of these questions are actually available in the source document received by the client. Once we run the application, we may view the source code received by our browser using the **View | Source** menu of Internet Explorer. The contents of the source code are shown in Figure 3.9. In this figure, please note that the system has mapped our *asp:listbox* control to a conventional HTML <select name="ctrl1" size="3"> tag. The system has also added an <input type="hidden"> tag with many attributes.

Figure 3.9 The Source Code of the Document Received by the Browser

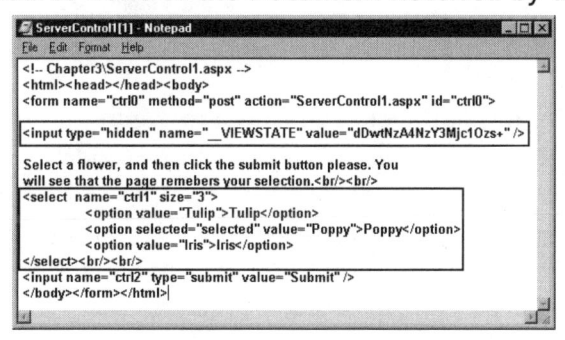

```
<!-- Chapter3\ServerControl1.aspx -->
<html><head></head><body>
<form name="ctrl0" method="post" action="ServerControl1.aspx" id="ctrl0">

<input type="hidden" name="__VIEWSTATE" value="dDwtNzA4NzY3Mjc1Ozs+" />

Select a flower, and then click the submit button please. You
will see that the page remebers your selection.<br/><br/>
<select name="ctrl1" size="3">
        <option value="Tulip">Tulip</option>
        <option selected="selected" value="Poppy">Poppy</option>
        <option value="Iris">Iris</option>
</select><br/><br/>
<input name="ctrl2" type="submit" value="Submit" />
</body></form></html>
```

It is via this hidden field that the system transfers the user-given values to the server. In summary, the server controls are mapped to standard HTML controls, and the ASP.NET employs hidden fields to maintain the states of the controls.

Including Scripts in an .aspx File

So far our examples have been very simple, and we have not yet included any script in the examples. In the previous exercise (Figure 3.8), we have hard-coded the values of the list box in its definition. Suppose that we need to load the list box via code. We will need to do that when the values to be loaded are unknown during the design time, and would come from an external source like a text file, an XML document, or from a database query. Although we will not venture into the XML or database topics right now, it is still beneficial to know how to load the list box programmatically. This is what we will do in our next example.

Loading a List Box via Script

In this example we will accomplish two objectives. First, we will load the list box via code. Secondly, we will provide a command button. The user will select a flower and then click the button. On the **click()** event of the button we will display his or her selection. The output of the example is shown in Figure 3.10.

Figure 3.10 The Output Generated by Figure 3.11

The complete listing of the code is shown in Figure 3.11, which can also be found on the CD that accompanies this book. In the code, the following statements are of major interests:

- We have added a *Page Declaration:*

    ```
    <%@ page language="VB" debug="true" %>
    ```

- At the initial stage, the debug="true" helps us a lot by providing detailed explanations of our errors during the run-time. The debug="true" specification drains the system's resources, and hence, we should delete it from our finished work.

- We have defined an *asp:button* and *"wired up"* its click event with a sub-procedure named *showSelection()* as the following:

    ```
    <asp:button id="btnSubmit" runat="server" text="Submit"
                onclick="showSelection" />
    ```

- The list box is loaded in the *Page_Load* event as follows:

  ```
  Sub Page_Load(source As Object, e As EventArgs)
          lstFlowers.Items.Add(New ListItem("Tulip"))
          lstFlowers.Items.Add(New ListItem("Poppy"))
          lstFlowers.Items.Add(New ListItem("Iris"))
          lstFlowers.SelectedIndex=0   'Selection by default
  End Sub
  ```

  As you can see from the previous code, we are setting "Tulip" as the default selection in the list box.

- Finally, we are displaying the selection in the *showSelection* procedure:

  ```
  Sub showSelection(sender As Object, e As EventArgs)
      lblMessage.Text ="You have selected " + _
          lstFlowers.SelectedItem.Text
  End Sub
  ```

Figure 3.11 ServerControl2.aspx (ServerControl2.aspx)

```
<!-- Chapter3\ServerControl2.aspx -->
<%@ page language="VB" debug="true" %>
<html><head></head><body><form runat="server">
Select a flower, and then click the submit button please:<br/><br/>
<asp:listbox id="lstFlowers" runat="server" rows="3" /><br/><br/>
<asp:button id="btnSubmit" runat="server" text="Submit" onclick
    ="showSelection" />
<br/><br/>
<asp:label id=lblMessage runat="server"></asp:Label>
</body></form></html>
<script language="VB" runat="server">
  Sub Page_Load(source As Object, e As EventArgs)
          lstFlowers.Items.Add(New ListItem("Tulip"))
          lstFlowers.Items.Add(New ListItem("Poppy"))
          lstFlowers.Items.Add(New ListItem("Iris"))
          lstFlowers.SelectedIndex=0  'Selection by default
  End Sub
```

Continued

Figure 3.11 Continued

```
Sub showSelection(sender As Object, e As EventArgs)
        lblMessage.Text ="You have selected " +
   lstFlowers.SelectedItem.Text
   End Sub
</script>
```

The code appears to be very simple. However, the code still has some intentional bugs. When we run this application, we will observe that the page behaves very erratically. First, irrespective of the selection we make, it will always display "You have selected Tulip". Secondly, on repeated clicks of the command button, the list box will continue growing with duplicate entries. Now, that is a surprise, isn't it? Let us try to figure out this strange behavior of the application in our next section!

Using the *IsPostBack* Property of a Page

An ASPX page is loaded upon each request. In our previous example, when we click the command button, it submits the form back to the server and requests the same page. This phenomenon is known as *PostBack*. The system will load the page again, and hence, the *Page_Load* event will take place on every request. That is why, if we run the code shown in Figure 3.11, our list box will keep on growing in size. This is also why the *SelectedItem* property of the list box will keep on being reset to "Tulip" on each *post back*.

In this case, we should rather load the list box only once during the first invocation of the page. Wait a minute! If we do not load the list box again, how would it get populated when the page is reloaded? Well, therein lies the beauty of ASP.NET. The server controls automatically retain their values (state-full and not state-less), thus we do not need to load the list box repetitively on successive requests of the page. How do we achieve that? In the *Page_Load* event, we may use the *Page.IsPostBack* property as shown in Figure 3.12. You can also find this code for Figure 3.12 (SeverControl3.aspx) on the accompanying CD.

Figure 3.12 Loading a List Box Correctly (ServerControl3.aspx)

```
<script language="VB" runat="server">
   Sub Page_Load(source As Object, e As EventArgs)
        If Not Page.IsPostBack Then
```

Continued

Figure 3.12 Continued

```
            lstFlowers.Items.Add(New ListItem("Tulip"))
            lstFlowers.Items.Add(New ListItem("Poppy"))
            lstFlowers.Items.Add(New ListItem("Iris"))
            lstFlowers.SelectedIndex=0 'Selection by default
        End If
    End Sub
    Sub showSelection(sender As Object, e As EventArgs)
         lblMessage.Text ="You have selected "+ _
             lstFlowers.SelectedItem.Text
    End Sub
</script>
```

Now, go ahead and replace the script in Figure 3.11 with the previous script shown in Figure 3.12. The application will work fine! The complete code for this application is available in ServerControl3.aspx in the CD.

AutoPostBack Attributes of Server Controls

In this section, we will illustrate an important behavior of certain server-side controls. Some server-side controls can generate automatic *postbacks* on selected events. That means, to submit a form, we may not have to wait until the user clicks the submit button. For example, the *SelectedIndexChange* event of an *asp:ListBox* is an event that is capable of triggering a *postback*. If we want this mechanism to work, we will have to set the *AutoPostBack* property of the List box to "True."

To illustrate the *AutoPostBack* attribute of an asp control, we will revise our flower selection example. We will remove the **Submit** button (although we could have kept it, too, without any loss of functionality). We will set the *AutoPostBack* attribute of the list box to be True, and we will attach the *showSelection* VB function on its *onSelectedIndexChanged* attribute. When you run this form, every time you select a new flower, the system will display your selection in the label. We do not need the **Submit** button because the *onSelectedIndexChanged* event will generate a *postback*. The output of this application is shown in Figure 3.13, and its code is shown in Figure 3.14 (which is also available on the CD that accompanies this book).

Figure 3.13 A List Box with Its *AutoPostBack* Property Set to True

Figure 3.14 Complete Code (ServerControl4.aspx)

```
<!-- Chapter3\ServerControl3.aspx -->
<%@ Page Language="VB" Debug="true" %>
<html><head></head><body><form runat="server">
Select a flower, and then click the submit button please:<br/><br/>
<asp:listbox id="lstFlowers" runat="server" rows="3"
   AutoPostBack="true" onSelectedIndexChanged="showSelection"/>
    <br><br>
<asp:Label id=lblMessage runat="server" />  <br/><br/>
</body></form></html>
<script language=vb runat="server">
  Sub Page_Load(source As Object, e As EventArgs)
    If Not Page.IsPostBack Then
       lstFlowers.Items.Add(New ListItem("Tulip"))
       lstFlowers.Items.Add(New ListItem("Poppy"))
       lstFlowers.Items.Add(New ListItem("Iris"))
       lstFlowers.SelectedIndex=0
    End If
  End Sub
  Sub showSelection(source As Object, e As EventArgs)
        lblMessage.Text="You have selected " + _
                 lstFlowers.SelectedItem.Text
  End Sub
</script>
```

> **NOTE**
>
> While using the *AutoPostBack* attribute, we need to be careful. An *AutoPostBack* submits the form to the server; thus, the system will eventually slow down significantly if we use too many of these *AutoPostBacks*.

Structure of an ASP.NET Web Form

A *Web Form* is an ASP.NET technology that we use to create a programmable Web page. It can present information, using any markup language, to the user in any browser, and can use code on the server to implement application logic. In .NET documentation, Microsoft has outlined the following characteristics of a Web form:

- A Web form of your design can run on a specific browser of your choice, or it can run on any browser and automatically render the browser-compliant HTML.
- It is built on the Common Language Runtime, thereby providing a managed execution environment, type safety, inheritance, and dynamic compilation. It can be programmed in any CLR-supported language.
- It supports WYSIWYG editing tools and development tools such as VS.NET.
- It supports a rich set of controls that enables you to encapsulate page logic into reusable components and declaratively handle page events.
- It allows for separation between code and content on a page.
- It provides a set of state management features that preserves the view state of a page between requests.

As shown in Figure 3.15, a Web form may contain directives, server-side scripts, client-side scripts, static texts, Web controls, HTML controls, and many others. In the remainder of this section, we will provide an overview of ASP.NET Page directives.

Figure 3.15 Typical Contents of a Web Form

```
<% Page Language="VB" %>          ← Page Directives

<html><body><form runat="server">
  Enter you hobby:                ← Static Text
  <asp:TextBix id="txtHobby" runat="server"/
>
  <input type="submit">           ← Web Control Tag
</form></body>
<script runat="server">
  Sub Page_Load(…, …)             ← Html Control
  … …
  End Sub
</script>                         ← Server-Side Code
<script lanuguage="javascript">
function --- ----
{ ---                             ← Client-Side Code
}
</script></html>
```

Page Directives

Page directives are used to set various attributes about a page. The ASP Engine and the compiler follow these directives to prepare a page. There are many kinds of directives. The most frequently ones are the following: @ Page, @ Import, @ Implements, @ Register, @ OutputCache and @ Assembly directives. These directives can be placed anywhere in a page, however, these are typically placed at the top. Table 3.1 briefly describes the major use of these directives.

Table 3.1 Page Directives and Their Functions

Page Directive	Description and Example
@ Page	We may use this directive to declare many page-related attributes about a particular page. For example, we use this directive to declare the language to be used in a page, such as <%@ Page Language="VB" Debug="true" %> page. There are numerous attributes of this directive. Some of the frequently used ones are these: *AutoEventWireup, Buffer, ClientTarget, EnableSessionState, ErrorPage, Debug, Trace, TraceMode*, and so on.
@ Import	We use this directive to import a namespace in the page class file. For example, in the following directive, we are importing the *System.Data.OleDb* namespace in our page: <%@ *Import Namespace="System.Data.OleDb" %>.*

Continued

Table 3.1 Continued

Page Directive	Description and Example
@ OutputCache	We can use this directive to specify how to cache the page. In the following example, we are setting the duration that a page or user control is output cached: <%@ OutputCache Duration="10" /%>.
@ Register	This directive is used to register a custom control in a page. In the following example, we are registering one of our user custom controls in page: <%@ Register tagprefix ="utoledo" tagname="Time" Src="TimeUserControl.ascx"%>.
@ Assembly	We use this directive to link to an assembly to the current page or user control. The following example shows how to link to an assembly-named payroll: <%@ Assembly Name="Payroll" %>.
@ Implements	This directive enables us to implement an interface in our page. In the following example, we are implementing the *IpostBackEventHandler* interface in one of our user controls: <%@ Implements Interface="System.Web.UI .IPostBackEventHandler" %>.

The Order of Event Execution

One of the novel offerings of ASP.NET is that it enables us to write server-side code to handle events that are triggered at the client. When a *postback* occurs, the page is reloaded, and the events are handled by the system. However, it is worthwhile to know the sequence of these activities. As shown in Figure 3.16, the order of execution is *Page_Init, Page_Load, Change events, Action events*, and finally the *Page_Unload* event. *The Page_Init* does not completely load all of the controls. In the *Page_Load* event, the states of the controls are set. Then the system takes care of the change and action events that occurred at the client's site. These are executed only in case of a *postback*.

Code-Behind versus In-Page Coding

In our previous example, we have placed a certain amount of VB code inside the .aspx file. We will refer to this practice as In-Page coding (also referred to as *inline coding* by some programmers). In ASP days, all ASP applications had to be developed using in-page coding because that was the only way to develop an ASP page. (In those days, the ASP developers envied the VB developers, because the VB developers had a nice way to split their codes and visual presentation.)

Figure 3.16 Event Execution Sequence

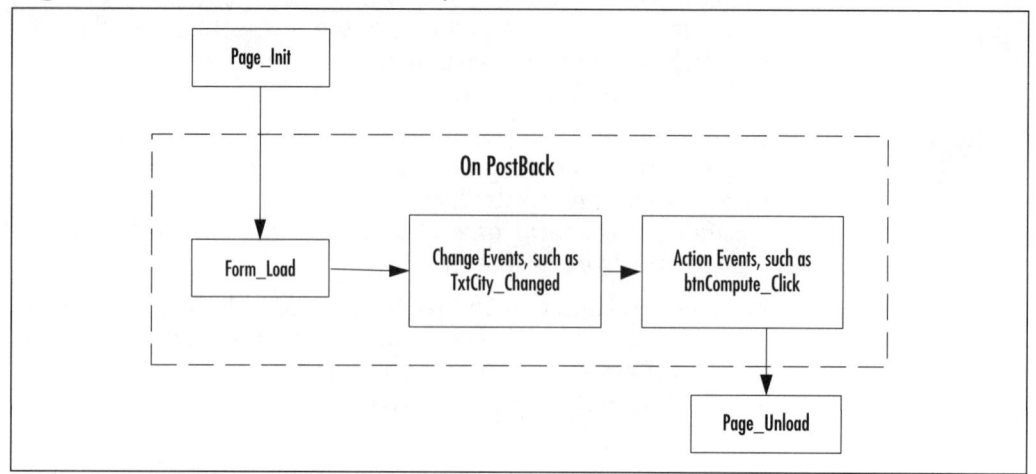

Often, the intermixed HTML and scripting codes in a large page become cryptic and difficult to read and maintain. Fortunately, ASP.NET provides a way out of this problem. We may develop the html code in a file with an .aspx extension, and then we may write the necessary code in a separate C# or VB code file. This practice is known as *Code-Behind*. Basically, the *Code-Behind* follows the Visual Basic model of developing an application. Here, we develop an .aspx file where we define the layout of the controls in a page, and then we include the code in a separate VB or C# class file. As shown in Figure 3.17, this mechanism separates the page layout design activities from the code development activities. When we develop an ASP.NET application using VS.NET, we are automatically forced to use *Code-Behind*.

Obviously, the .aspx file has to be somehow linked to the class file. We may link the .aspx file with the code file in one of two ways:

- Develop the class file and save it without compilation in the same directory of the .aspx file, or
- Compile the class file and save the .dll file in the *bin* subdirectory of our virtual directory.

It is intuitively assumed that the former will execute more slowly than the latter. Here, we will provide two examples. In both of these cases, we will develop our flower selection page using alternative *Code-Behind* techniques. First, we will demonstrate an example using VB.NET without compilation and then we will present a code behind example using C# with compilation.

Figure 3.17 In-Page Code versus Code Behind

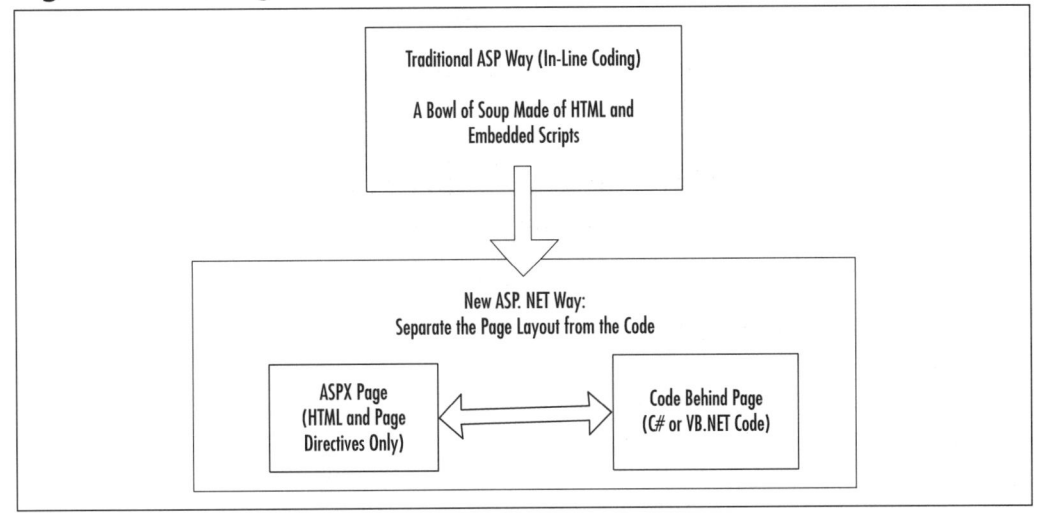

Using Code-Behind without Compilation

The output of this application is shown in Figure 3.18.

Figure 3.18 Run-Time Display of the VB Code-Behind Application

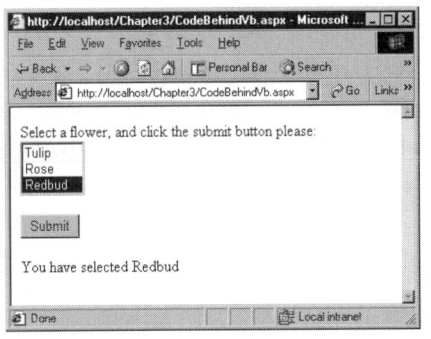

In this method, you do not need to compile the VB or C# source file. Just save the source file and the .aspx file in the same virtual directory. You will need to enter the following *Page Declarative* statement at the top of your .aspx file. Here, the *Src* attribute specifies the name of the source file, and the *Inherits* attribute specifies the name of the class to inherit. In the following illustration, we assume that the VB source file named *vbCb.vb* has a class named *VbCb* in a namespace *myVbCodeBehind*. The complete listing for Figure 3.19 is also available in the CodeBehind.aspx file in the accompanying CD.

```
<%@ page language="VB" src="vbCb.vb" inherits="myVbCodeBehind.vbCb" %>
```

1. Develop the page layout in an .aspx file (shown in Figure 3.19). Be sure to include the page directive.

Figure 3.19 The .aspx File for the Code-Behind Example (CodeBehindVB.aspx)

```
<!- Chapter3\CodeBehindVb.aspx ->
<%@ page language="VB" debug="true" src="vbCb.vb"
        inherits="myVbCodeBehind.vbCb" %>
<html><head></head><body>
<form runat="server">
Select a flower, and click the submit button please: <br>
<asp:ListBox id="lstFlowers" runat="server" rows="3">
</asp:ListBox><br><br>
<asp:Button id="btnSubmit" runat="server"
     text="Submit" onclick="showSelection" /><br><br>
<asp:Label id=lblMessage runat="server" />
</body></form></html>
```

2. Develop the VB class file (shown in Figure 3.20) and save it in the same directory. In this particular application, we need to import the *System* and the *System.WebUI.WebControls* namespaces. Depending on the nature of your applications, you may need to import other namespaces, too. The code for Figure 3.20 is also available in the accompanying CD.

Figure 3.20 The VB Class File for the Code-Behind Example (vbCb.vb)

```
' Chapter3\vbCb.vb
Option Strict Off
Imports System
Imports System.Web.UI.WebControls
Namespace myVbCodeBehind
Public Class vbCb : Inherits System.Web.UI.Page
   Public lstFlowers As System.Web.UI.WebControls.ListBox
```

Continued

Figure 3.20 Continued

```
   Public lblMessage As System.Web.UI.WebControls.Label
   Public btnSubmit As System.Web.UI.WebControls.Button
   Protected Sub Page_Load(ByVal sender As Object, ByVal e As EventArgs)
      If Not IsPostBack Then
         lblMessage.Text="No Selection Yet"
         lstFlowers.Items.Add(new ListItem("Tulip"))
         lstFlowers.Items.Add(new ListItem("Rose"))
         lstFlowers.Items.Add(new ListItem("Redbud"))
         lstFlowers.SelectedIndex=0
      End If
   End Sub
   Protected Sub showSelection(ByVal obj As Object, ByVal e As
EventArgs)
      lblMessage.Text="You have selected " + _
               lstFlowers.SelectedItem.Text
   End Sub
End Class
End Namespace
```

3. Test the ASPX application. It should work fine.

Using Code Behind with Compilation

In this method, you will need to compile your VB or C# source file to a .dll file first. Then copy the .dll file and save it in the *bin* subdirectory of your virtual directory. Rather than manually copying the .dll file to the *bin* directory, you may also use the */out* parameter of the *compilation* command to save the .dll file directly to your *bin* directory, as follows:

```
G:\MyAspNets\CodeBehind>vbc /out:..\bin\vbCb.dll /t:library vbCb.vb
```

In the *compilation* command, we assume that the name of the VB file is vbCb.vb. This command will create the *vbCb.dll* file in the bin directory directly upon compilation. Now we need to enter a page declarative at the top of our ASPX page as follows. Here, the name of the source file (*cs* or *vb*) should be specified in the *Code-Behind* attribute. The *Inherits* attribute should include the *namespace.className* of the class file:

```
<%@ page language="VB" codebehind="vbCb.vb"
        inherits="myCodeBehind.vbCb" %>
```

Although we are staging this example using C#, you may change the VB code shown in the previous example very easily to implement this application in VB. The output of this example would appear exactly similar to the one shown in Figure 3.18.

1. Develop the .aspx file (Figure 3.21). Here, we assume that you will develop the C# class in a file named *CsharpCodeBehind.cs*. We further assume that the name of the class will be *cSharpCb* in a namespace *myCsCodeBehind*. Thus, be sure to include the *Code-Behind* attribute to link the page to the code behind class file as follows. The code shown in Figure 3.21 is also available in the accompanying CD in a file named *CodeBehindCS.aspx*.

```
<%@ page language="cs" debug="true" codebehind="CSharpCodeBehind.cs"
        inherits="myCsCodeBehind.cSharpCb" %>
```

Figure 3.21 Complete Listing (CodeBehindCS.aspx)

```
<!-- Chapter3\CodeBehindCS.aspx -->
<%@ page language="cs" Debug="true" codebehind="CSharpCodeBehind.cs"
        inherits="myCsCodeBehind.cSharpCb" %>
<html><head></head><body>
<form runat="server">
Select a flower, and click the submit button please: <br>
<asp:ListBox id="lstFlowers" runat="server" rows="3">
</asp:ListBox><br><br>
<asp:Button id="btnSubmit" runat="server"
    text="Submit" onclick="showSelection" /><br><br>
<asp:Label id=lblMessage runat="server" />
</body></form></html>
```

2. Develop the Code-Behind class file as shown in Figure 3.22. The code shown in Figure 3.22 is also available in the accompanying CD in a file named CsharpCodeBehindCS.cs.

Figure 3.22 Complete Listing for CSharpCodeBehind.cs

```csharp
// Chapter\CSharpCodeBehind.cs
namespace myCsCodeBehind
{ using System;
  using System.Web.UI.WebControls;
   public class cSharpCb : System.Web.UI.Page
   {  public System.Web.UI.WebControls.ListBox lstFlowers;
      public System.Web.UI.WebControls.Label lblMessage;
      public System.Web.UI.WebControls.Button btnSubmit;
      protected void Page_Load(object sender, EventArgs e)
      { if   (!IsPostBack)
         {    lblMessage.Text="No Selection Yet";
              lstFlowers.Items.Add(new ListItem("Tulip"));
              lstFlowers.Items.Add(new ListItem("Redbud"));
              lstFlowers.Items.Add(new ListItem("Poppy"));
         }
      }
      protected void showSelection(object obj, EventArgs e)
         {         lblMessage.Text="You have selected " +
lstFlowers.SelectedItem.Text;
         }
    }
  }
```

3. Compile the class file as follows. Note: If you are using the VB version, just replace the **csc** keyword with **vbc**, and change the name of the source file.

`csc /t:library /r:System.dll /r:System.Web.dll CSharprpCodeBehind.cs`

4. Copy the .dll file in the *bin* directory of your virtual directory. You are done.

When we develop Web applications using VS.Net, it forces us to implement the *code-behind* methodology. In the next section we will walk you through the steps for developing a simple application using VS.Net.

Using VS.Net for Developing a Web Application

In this section we will provide a step-by-step procedure to develop a simple Web page using VS.Net. Our finished page will be displayed in the browser as shown in Figure 3.23.

Figure 3.23 The Flower Selection Page Developed Using VS.Net

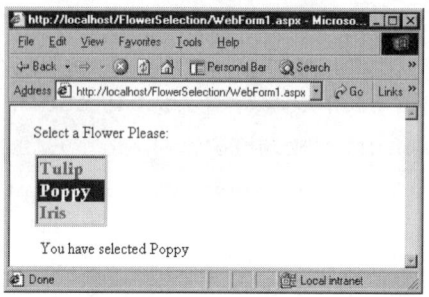

1. Start a new Visual Basic ASP.NET project as shown in Figure 3.24. Be sure to provide a name for your project.

    Figure 3.24 Starting a New VB ASP.NET Web Application

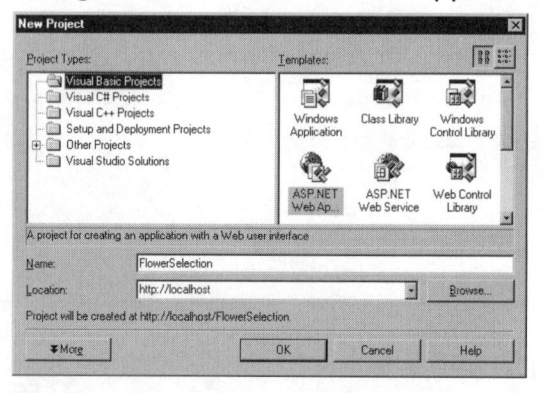

2. After you click **OK**, the system will display the VS.Net IDE screen. Do not get intimidated by the complex appearance of the screen. With some practice, you will start loving the environment. You will see an empty Web page with two tabs at the bottom: *Design* and *HTML*. If the toolbox is not visible, use the **View | ToolBox** of the system menu to

display the toolbox. Click on the **Web Forms** tab of the toolbox. You will see all of the server controls in the toolbox. Draw a Label. If the **Property Window** is not visible, use F4 (or **View | Property Window** menu) to display the property window of the label. Change its *Text* property to **Select a Flower Please** as shown in Figure 3.25. Please note that the system is building the *WebForm1.aspx* file automatically for you.

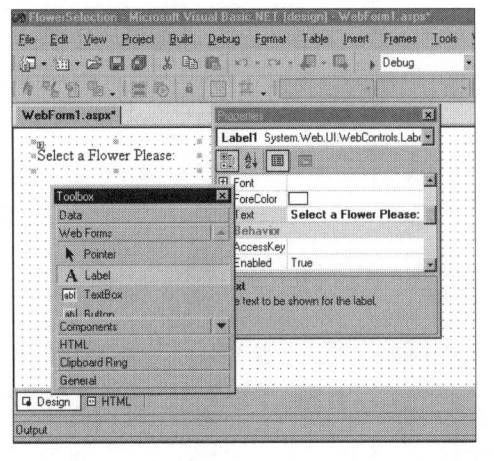

Figure 3.25 The VS.Net IDE Screen

3. Draw a *ListBox* control. Change its *ID* property and Rows property *lstFlower* and 3, respectively. You may also change its background *Color* and *Font* to your taste. Be sure to set its *AutoPostBack* property to *True*. Now double-click on any empty place of the form. The system will bring the code screen as shown in Figure 3.26. Please note that the system has already generated the VB *Code-Behind*. It has named it *WebForm1.aspx.vb*. In the *Page_Load* event, enter the necessary code for loading the list box.

4. You are almost done. Go back to the design view of the *WebForm1.aspx*. Draw a label at the bottom of the list box, and change its *ID* property to *lblMessage*. Now double-click the list box. The system will bring the code screen with the template for the *lstFlower_SelectedIndexChanged* event procedure. Enter the following code in this event:

```
lblMessage.Text="You have selected " + _
     lstFlowers.SelectedItem.Text
```

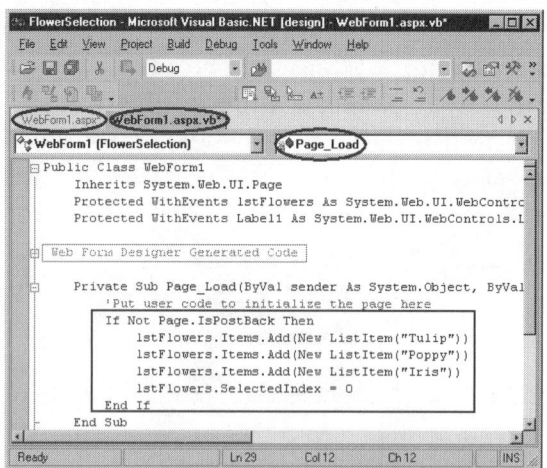

Figure 3.26 Code-Behind Screen in VS.Net

Migrating...

ASP Skills Are Not Obsolete

If you are an experienced ASP developer, your skills are not lost. The new ASP.NET programming model will seem very familiar to you. However, most of your existing ASP pages will have to be modified if you want to run them under ASP.NET. The modifications would be quite simple. Some of the VB Script codes would have to be changed to VB.NET code, and the new ADO.NET would replace your ADO-related codes. In most cases, though, the necessary changes will involve only a few lines of code. You may choose to rewrite existing ASP applications to gain the performance, readability, and maintainability improvements of the new development environment. However, because a Web application can contain both ASP and ASP.NET pages, the conversion does not necessarily have to be carried out all at once.

You are done. Go ahead and test it. Before you test it, you may use the **Build** menu to build your project (compile the code), and then use the **Start** icon or **Debug | Start** of the main menu to run the application. Knowingly or unknowingly, you have developed an ASP.NET Web application. The VS.Net has created a virtual directory in your IIS. If you display the *Solution Explorer* window, you will see that the VS.Net has done a lot of work for you. By the way, if you look at the HTML code in the *WebForm1*.aspx file, you will see that VS.Net has styled the list box as follows (only selected attributes are shown):

```
<asp:ListBox id="lstFlowers" runat="server"  Rows="3"
   BackColor="#FFE0C0" Font-Bold="True" AutoPostBack="True"
   Font-Names="Book Antiqua" Font-Size="Medium"  ForeColor="#C04000">
</asp:ListBox>
```

That means when we develop our .aspx files manually, we can also use these attributes to style our controls.

Using HTML Server Controls

Conventional HTML elements are not programmable at the server side. Their values do not persist in postbacks. These are essentially treated as opaque texts that are passed to the browser. In ASP.NET, we may convert an HTML element to an HTML server control by adding an attribute *runat="server."* This notifies the ASP Engine to create an instance of the control during parsing. We will, of course, need to specify an *ID* of the element so that we can manipulate it programmatically at the server side. These controls are particularly useful for migrating ASP applications to ASP.NET applications.

HTML server controls have been derived directly or indirectly from the base class *System.Web.UI.HtmlControls.HtmlControl* and map directly to HTML elements. The hierarchy of HTML server control classes is shown in Figure 3.27. Basically, the hierarchy divides the classes into three major categories: the classes that mimic the HTML <input> tag, the classes that may act as container classes, and finally the *HtmlImage* class. Several classes in the second category also employ the HTML <input> tag. HTML server controls must reside within a containing <form> control with the *runat="server"* attribute.

In this section, we will present a number of examples of HTML server controls. If you are relatively new to ASP, be sure to go through these examples. Most of these examples can also be enhanced using the Web controls. Most importantly, the concepts learned in this section will enable you to develop better applications using Web controls.

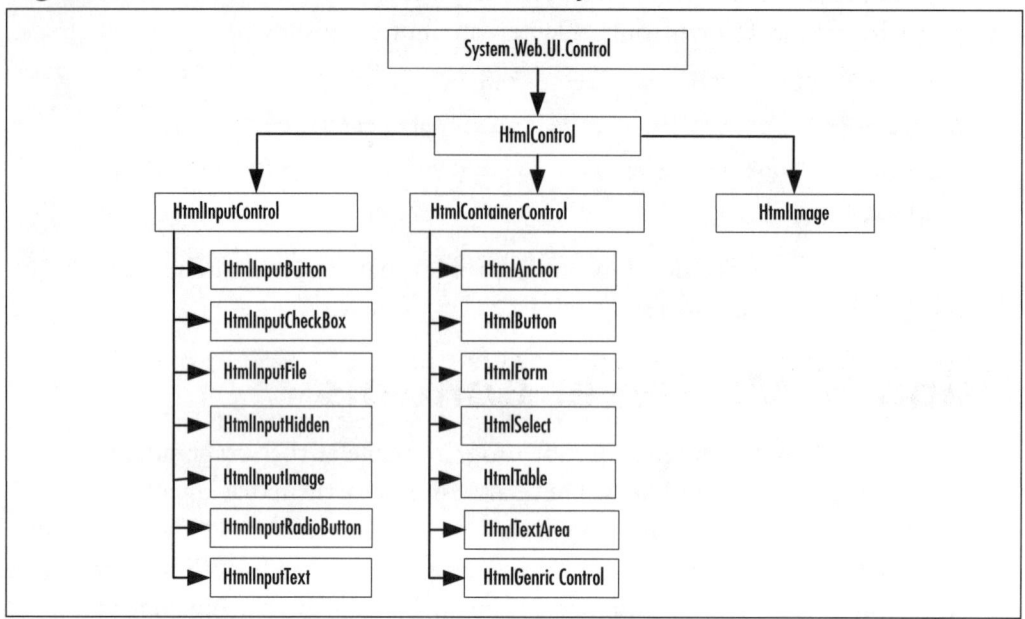

Figure 3.27 HTML Server Controls Hierarchy

```
                         System.Web.UI.Control
                                  │
                                  ▼
                              HtmlControl
                                  │
        ┌─────────────────────────┼─────────────────────────┐
        ▼                         ▼                         ▼
  HtmlInputControl         HtmlContainerControl         HtmlImage
        │                         │
        ├─► HtmlInputButton       ├─► HtmlAnchor
        ├─► HtmlInputCheckBox     ├─► HtmlButton
        ├─► HtmlInputFile         ├─► HtmlForm
        ├─► HtmlInputHidden       ├─► HtmlSelect
        ├─► HtmlInputImage        ├─► HtmlTable
        ├─► HtmlInputRadioButton  ├─► HtmlTextArea
        └─► HtmlInputText         └─► HtmlGenric Control
```

Using the *HtmlAnchor* Control

You can use the *HtmlAchor* control (<a>) to navigate from a page to another page. This basically works almost like the Html anchor tag; the only difference is that it works on the server. It has the following attributes:

```
<a runat="server" id="programmaticID" href= "linkurl"
   name="bookmarkname" OnServerClick="onserverclickhandler"
   target="linkedcontentframeorwindow" title="titledisplayedbybrowser">
```

If necessary, we can use this control to dynamically modify the attributes and properties of the <a> element and display hyperlinks from a data source. The *href* attribute contains the URL of the page to be linked to. We have shown an example of anchor controls in Figure 3.28.

Using the *HtmlTable* Control

The *HtmlTable* control mimics the Html <table> tag. We may define rows using <tr> tags. Table cells are defined using <td> tags. This control is a container control, and so we can embed other controls in its cells. It has the following attributes:

```
<table runat="server" id="programmaticID" align=left | center | right
    bgcolor="bgcolor"  border="borderwidthinpixels"
    bordercolor="bordercolor" cellpadding="spacingwithincellsinpixels"
    cellspacing="spacingbetweencellsinpixels" height="tableheight"
    rows="collectionofrows" width="tablewidth" >
</table>
```

In the following example, as you can see in Figure 3.28, we will build an *HtmlTable* with two rows and two columns. Each cell of the table will contain an *HtmlAnchor* control.

Figure 3.28 Embedded *HTMLAnchor* Controls in an *HtmlButton* Control

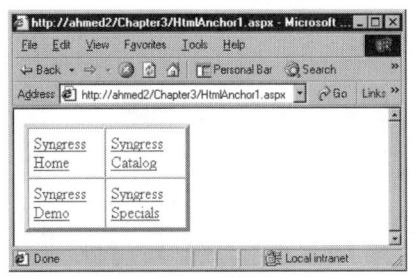

The code for this application, as shown in Figure 3.29, is self-explanatory. Each pair of **<tr>** and **</tr>** entries enable us to define a row, and within each row, we nest a pair of **<td> </td>** to define the table's data (cell). In this example, we have embedded an *HtmlAnchor* control in each cell. The code shown in Figure 3.29 is available in the accompanying CD in a file named HtmlAnchor1.aspx.

Figure 3.29 HtmlAnchor1.aspx

```
<!- Chapter3\HtmlAnchor1.aspx ->
<html><head></head><form runat="server">
  <table style= width: 170px; height: 50px" cellSpacing="0"
      cellPadding="5" width="170" border="4">
    <tr><td><a id="anchor1" runat="server"
          href="http://www.syngress.com">Syngress Home</a>
      </td>
        <td><a id="acnhor2" runat="server"
          href="http://www.syngress.com/book_catalog/index.htm">
```

Continued

Figure 3.29 Continued

```
                Syngress Catalog</a>
        </td>
    </tr>
    <tr><td><a id="anchor3" runat="server"
            href="http://www.syngress.com/demo/index.htm">
            Syngress Demo </a>
        </td>
        <td><a id="anchor4" runat="server"
            href="http://www.syngress.com/specials/index.htm">
            Syngress Specials</a>
        </td>
    </tr>
</table></form></html>
```

Using *HtmlInputText* and *HtmlTextArea* Controls

You can use both of these controls to collect text data from the user. You can use the *HtmlInputText* control to implement server-side code against the HTML *<input type=text>* and *<input type=password>* tags. Its major attributes are these: *type* (text or password), *runat, id, maxlength, size* , and *value*. The *HtmlTextArea* control enables the user to enter multi-line text. Thus, it is the server-side equivalent to the HTML *<textarea>* element. Its *rows* and *cols* properties can be used to define its size. You can use its *onserverchange* attribute to run an event handling function.

We will illustrate the usage of these controls with an example. In this application, the user will enter a short story in a text area, and then he or she will enter the name in a textbox, and the password in a password-type textbox. On the click event of a button, we will check the password and display the appropriate message in an html <span> element. The run-time view of the application is shown in Figure 3.30. The code (shown in Figure 3.31) for this application is pretty straightforward and more or less self-explanatory. The code shown in Figure 3.31 is also available in the accompanying CD in a file named HtmlText1.aspx.

Figure 3.30 Using *HtmlInputText* and *HtmlTextArea* Controls

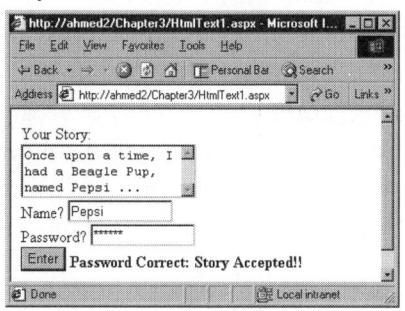

Figure 3.31 HtmlText1.aspx

```
<!-- Chapter3/HtmlText1.aspx -->
<html><form method="post" runat="server">
Your Story:<br>
<TextArea id="txtAreaStory" runat="server" cols="20" rows="3"/><br>
Name?<input type="text" id="txtName" size="12" runat="server"/><br>
Password? <input type="password" id="txtPwd" runat="server" size="12"/>
<br><input type="Button" runat="server"  value="Enter"
      OnServerClick="CheckPassword"/>
<span id="spnMessage" runat="server"> </span></h2>
</form></html>
<script language="VB" runat="server">
Sub checkPassword(source As Object, e As EventArgs)
   If txtName.Value="Pepsi" And txtPwd.Value="Beagle" Then
      spnMessage.InnerHtml="<b>Password Correct: Story Accepted!!</b>"
   Else
      spnMessage.InnerHtml="<b>Bad Password: Story Rejected!!</b>"
   End If
End Sub
</script>
```

Using *HtmlButton* and *HtmlImage* Controls

You will find two of these controls: *HtmlInputButton* and *HtmlButton*. The *HtmlInputButton* supports the HTML **Reset** and **Submit** button types. On the

92 Chapter 3 • ASP Server Controls

other hand, the *HtmlButton* control can be used to develop server-side code against the HTML *<button>* element. We can provide custom code for the *OnServerClick* event. You can customize its appearance and imbed other controls in it. We have used *HtmlButton* controls in many of our previous examples. In our next example, we will embed an HTML *<img>* element inside a button. We have used the *OnMouseOver* and *OnMouseOut* attributes of a button control to provide rollover effects. We have also shown how to use an in-line style attribute that you can use to format many of the controls. The run-time view of the application and its code listing are shown in Figure 3.32 and Figure 3.33, respectively. The relevant code is also available on the accompanying CD in a file named HtmlButton1.aspx.

Figure 3.32 Using the *HtmlImage* Control in an *HtmlButton* Control

> **NOTE**
>
> To run this code, you will need to copy the *SmallSpinReel1.jpg* in the *Images* folder of your virtual directory.

Figure 3.33 HtmlButton1.aspx

```
<html><form runat="server">
<h4><font face="Verdana">
HtmlButton Sample With  Embedded &lt;img&gt; Tag And Rollover
    </font></h4>
<font face="Verdana" size="-1"><p>
<Button id="btnReel"
```

Continued

Figure 3.33 Continued

```
    OnServerClick="btnReel_OnClick"
    OnMouseOver="this.style.backgroundColor='yellow'"
    OnMouseOut="this.style.backgroundColor='white'"
    style="font: 8pt verdana; background-color:lightgreen;
           border-color:blue; height:100;  width:170"
    runat="server">
    <img src="images/SmallSpinReel1.jpg"/><b> Bass Master!</b>
</Button><p>
<Span id=span1 runat="server" />
</font></form></body></html>
<script language="VB" runat="server">
    Sub btnReel_OnClick(Source As Object, e As EventArgs)
        span1.InnerHtml="You clicked Bass Master"
    End Sub
</script>
```

Using the *HtmlInputFile* Control

The *HtmlInputFile* control has been designed to program against the HTML *<input type=file>* element. We can use this control to enable users to upload binary or text files from a browser to a directory that we specify in our Web server. Its major attributes are as follows:

```
<input    type=file    runat="server"   id="programmaticID"
   accept="MIMEencodings"   maxlength="maxfilepathlength"
   size="widthoffilepathtextbox"    postedfile="uploadedfile"
>
```

When this control is rendered, it automatically displays a Browse button for directory browsing. Figure 3.34 illustrates the usage of an *HtmlInputFile* control. The user may upload a file from his or her machine to our *c:\temp* directory of the Web server. The code for this application is shown in Figure 3.35 and is available on the CD in a file named HtmlFile1.aspx. As you will observe from this code, we have used the *fileControl.PostedFile.SaveAs(("c:\temp\" + targetName.Value))* statement to accomplish the objective.

Figure 3.34 Using the *HtmlFile* Control for Uploading Files to the Server

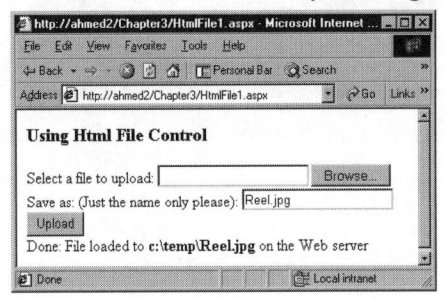

Figure 3.35 HtmlFile1.aspx

```
<!-- HtmlFile1.aspx --><html><head></head>
<h3>Using Html File Control</h3>
<form enctype="multipart/form-data" runat="server">
Select a file to upload:
<input type="file" id="fileControl"  runat="server"><br>
Save as: (Just the name only please):
<input id="txtTargetName" type="text" runat="server"><br>
<input type=button  id="btnLoad" value="Upload"
       OnServerClick="btnLoad_Click" runat="server"><br>
<span id=span1 runat="server" /><br>
</form></html>

<script language="VB" runat="server">
Sub btnLoad_Click(s As Object, e As EventArgs)
   If txtTargetName.Value="" Then
      span1.InnerHtml="Error: you must enter a file name"
      Return
   End If
   If Not (fileControl.PostedFile Is Nothing) Then
     Try
        fileControl.PostedFile.SaveAs(("c:\temp\" + targetName.Value))
        span1.InnerHtml="Done: File loaded to <b>c:\temp\" + _
        txtTargetName.Value & "</b> on the Web server"
     Catch err As Exception
```

Continued

Figure 3.35 Continued

```
        span1.InnerHtml="Error saving file <b>c:\temp\" + _
            txtTargetName.Value & "</b><br>" & err.ToString()
    End Try
  End If
End Sub
</script>
```

Using the *HtmlSelect* Control with Data Binding to a *SortedList* Structure

The *HtmlSelect* control has been offered to program against the HTML *<select>* element. Basically, it enables us to develop a combo box (dropdown list) or a list box. If the *size* attribute is set to 1, then it behaves like a dropdown list. We may allow the selection of multiple items by using its *Multiple* property. If we allow multiple selections, we will need to use its *Items(i).Selected* property to test if its element *i* has been selected. An *HtmlSelect* control can be bound to an external data source. Figure 3.36 shows an example of a bound *HtmlSelect* control.

Figure 3.36 Binding an *HtmlSelect* Control to a *SortedList* Object

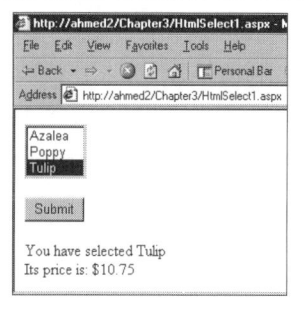

At first sight, the example will appear to be very simple. However, we have employed a number of common ASP.NET techniques here. Please review the example carefully as it will become very handy when you deal with more challenging applications using Web server controls. Our objective is to bind an *HtmlSelect* control with a field of a commonly used structure named *SortedList*. The *SortedList* structure, like the *ArrayList* and *HashTable,* is an offering in the Net SDK Collection Class. We may use a *SortedList* to store a collection of objects in alphabetic order of a key field. Subsequently, we may retrieve a desired value either by using array-like addressing or by its key. The complete code for this application is shown in Figure 3.37 (and can also be found in the accompanying CD in a file named HtmlSelect1.aspx).

Figure 3.37 HtmlSelect1.aspx

```
<!— Chapter3\HtmlSelect1.aspx —>
<%@ page language="VB" debug="true" %>
<html><head></head><form runat="server">
<select id= "lstFlowers"  size="3" runat="server" /><br/><br/>
<input id="btnSubmit" type="button" runat="server" value="Submit"
       onServerClick="showSelection"><br/><br/>
<span id=spnMessage runat="server"/><br>
<span id=spnPrice runat="server"/><br>
</form></html>
<script language="VB" runat="server">
Sub Page_Load(source As Object, e As EventArgs)
   If Not IsPostBack Then
      Dim sortedList1 As New SortedList()
      ' Load the SortedList object
      sortedList1.Add("Tulip", 10.75)
      sortedList1.Add("Poppy",20.22)
      sortedList1.Add("Azalea",30.33)
      Dim i As Integer
      ' Bind the HtmlSelect control (list box) with the key values
      ' of the SortedList object
      lstFlowers.DataSource=sortedList1.Keys
      lstFlowers.DataBind()
      Session.Timeout=10 'Set the session timeout to 10 minutes
      ' Save the populated SortedList in the session
      Session("savedList")=sortedList1
   End If
End Sub
Sub showSelection(sender As Object, e As EventArgs)
   Dim sortedList1 As New SortedList()
      ' Load the Session's savedList into an instance of a SortedList
```

Continued

Figure 3.37 Continued

```
    sortedList1=Session("savedList")
    Dim i As Integer
    Dim msg As String
    Dim dblPrice as Double
    dblPrice=sortedList1.GetValueList(lstFlowers.SelectedIndex)
    spnMessage.InnerHtml="You have selected " + lstFlowers.Value
    spnPrice.InnerHtml="Its price is: " + FormatCurrency(dblPrice)
End Sub
</script>
```

Creating and Loading the *SortedList*

In the *Page_Load* event, we have loaded the *SortedList* as follows:

```
Dim sortedList1 As New SortedList()
sortedList1.Add("Tulip", 10.75)
sortedList1.Add("Poppy",20.22)
sortedList1.Add("Azalea",30.33)
```

By default, the name of a flower (the first parameter) will be loaded in the sorted list as the key-field. The price of the flower (the second parameter) will be stored as its *value*. After the sorted list object is loaded, we have bound the *HtmlSelect* control to the key-field of the sorted list as follows:

```
lstFlowers.DataSource=sortedList1.Keys
lstFlowers.DataBind()
```

On the click event of the button, our intention is to display the price of the selected flower. Where will we get the price? Obviously, we want to retrieve it from the sorted list object. However, there is a minor problem. Whereas the values of the controls in an ASP.NET page are state-full, the values of the variables are state-less. Hence, on postback, the sorted list would not be available. We may solve this problem in many ways. The easiest way is to load the sorted list again. Placing the relevant code outside the *If Not IsPostBack* block can do that. But that will cause repetitive loading of the sorted list object on each postback. Therefore, we have instead saved the sorted list in a *Session* object. Subsequently, we have retrieved the sorted list object from the session variable in the *showSelection* procedure. The value of the sorted list has been retrieved using its *GetValueList* method.

Using *HtmlCheckBox* and *HtmlInputRadioButton* Controls

We can use the *HtmlInputCheckBox* control to develop server-side code against the HTML *<input type=checkbox>* element. This is done using the *Checked* property of this control. The *HtmlInputRadioButton* control can be used to provide server-side programmability to an HTML *<input type=radio>* element. We can group these controls together by specifying a *name* property common to all *<input type=radio>* elements within the group. Only one radio button in a group can be checked at a time. Figure 3.38 shows a simple example of these controls. The complete code is shown in Figure 3.39. The code, shown in Figure 3.39, is self-explanatory and can be found in a file named HtmlInputCheck1.aspx in the accompanying CD.

Figure 3.38 Using *HtmlCheckBox* and *HtmlInputRadioButton* Controls

Figure 3.39 HtmlInputCheck1.aspx

```
<!-- Chapter3\HtmlInputCheck1.aspx -->
<%@ page language="VB" debug="true" %>
<html><head></head><form runat="server">
Select a room type<br>
<input type="radio" id="radOceanFront" name="rgrView"
    runat="server"/>Ocean Front: $600.00<br>
<input type="radio" id="radOceanView" name="rgrView"
    runat="server"/>Ocean View: $400.00<br><br>
Select one or more special facilities: <br>
<input type="checkbox"  id= "chkFishing"
runat="server"/> Deep Sea Fishing: $450.00<br>
```

Continued

Figure 3.39 Continued

```
<input type="checkbox"   id= "chkGolf"
  runat="server" />Golf at Diamond's Head: $150.00<br>
<input id="btnSubmit" type="button" runat="server" value="Submit"
        onServerClick="showPrice"><br><br>
<span id=spnPrice runat="server"/><br>
</form></html>


<script language="VB" runat="server">
Sub showPrice(sender As Object, e As EventArgs)
    Dim totalPrice As Double=0
    If radOceanFront.Checked Then
       totalPrice += 600.00
    End If
    If radOceanView.Checked Then
       totalPrice += 400.00
    End If
    If chkFishing.Checked Then
        totalPrice += 450.00
    End If
    If chkGolf.Checked Then
        totalPrice += 150.00
    End If
    spnPrice.InnerHtml="Total Price is: " + FormatCurrency(totalPrice)
End Sub
</script>
```

> **Developing & Deploying…**
>
> ### HTML Server Controls versus Web Controls
>
> At first sight, the parallel existence of these two sets of controls may appear questionable. However, these two types of controls have their advantages and disadvantages. HTML server controls make it easy to convert an existing HTML or ASP page to a Web Form. By converting individual HTML elements to HTML server controls, we can quickly add Web Forms functionality to the page without affecting the rest of the page. Furthermore, if we plan to use a heavy amount of client-side scripts, the HTML server control is the way to go! However, all values in HTML server controls are essentially of *string* type, and thus there is no type safety.
>
> On the other hand, the Web server controls have a richer and more consistent object model. They automatically generate correct HTML for *down-level* (HTML 3.2) and *up-level* (HTML 4.0) browsers. You will need them when you prefer a VB-like programming model, and when you are creating applications with nested controls. However, with server controls we have less direct control over how a server control is rendered in a Response object. We can mix these controls in the same page.

Using ASP.NET Web Controls

The ASP.NET Web controls are also known as Web form controls. Microsoft has included a plethora of Web controls in the *System.Web.UI.WebControls* namespace. For discussion purposes, we will divide these controls into three major categories:

- **Basic Web Controls** These Web controls are similar to HTML server controls but have additional features. These controls have a richer and more consistent object model.

- **Validation Controls** These controls have been developed exclusively for input validation (to be discussed later in this chapter).

- **Databound ListControls** These belong to the new generation of controls that provide additional power and development speed. These are also typically referred to as *Templated Web Controls*.

All Web controls are derived from the generic class named *WebControl*. Thus, the Web controls inherit a common set of class members. Some of the frequently used members include *BackColor, BorderColor, BorderStyle BorderWidth, DataBind, Enabled, Font, ForeColor, Height, Page, Parent, Site, TabIndex, ToolTip, Visible, Init, Load, Unload, Dispose, ToString, OnInit, OnLoad,* and *OnDataBinding.*

Basic Web Controls

Table 3.2 briefly describes several server controls that we have classified as basic Web controls. Some of these controls behave similarly. For example, the usages and characteristics of a *CheckBoxList* control are almost identical to those of a *RadioButtonList* control. This is why we have grouped these controls under single captions in Table 3.2.

Table 3.2 Basic Server Controls

Server Control	Characteristics
Label	A *Label* is used to display text. If we want to display static text, we do not need a *Label* server control; we should instead use HTML. We should use a *Label* server control only if we need to change its properties via server code.
TextBox	A *TextBox* control enables the user to enter text. By default, the *TextMode* property is *SingleLine*, but it can also be set to *Multiline* or *Password.* In case of *Multiline* text box, the *Rows* property determines the height. If its *AutoPostBack* property is set to *True*, it generates a *PostBack* on its *Text_Changed()* event.
Buttons: ■ Button ■ LinkButton ■ ImageButton	All three types of buttons cause *PostBacks* when the user clicks them. *Button* controls can be placed inside other container controls, such as *DataList, DataGrid* and *Repeater.* The *LinkButton* renders a hyperlink in the page. The *ImageButton* displays an image that responds to mouse clicks. We can also use it as an image map. Thus, we may pinpoint where in the graphic the user has clicked.
CheckBox	It enables the user to input *Boolean* data: true or false, yes or no. Its *Checked* property can also be bound to a data field of a data source. Its *CheckedChanged* event can be used for *AutoPostBack.*
ListControls: ■ CheckBoxList ■ DropDownList ■ ListBox ■ RadioButtonList	These controls are derived from the ListControl abstract class. Note: these controls will be discussed in detail in a later section of this chapter.

Continued

Table 3.2 Continued

Server Control	Characteristics
HyperLink	It displays a link to another page. It is typically displayed as text specified in its *Text* property. It can also be displayed as an image specified in the *ImageUrl* property. If both the *Text* and *ImageUrl* properties are set, the *ImageUrl* property is displayed. If the image does not exist, then the text in the *Text* property is shown. Internet Explorer uses the *Text* property to display ToolTip.
Image	We may use the *Image* control to display an image on the Web page. The *ImageUrl* property specifies the path to the displayed image. When the image does not exist, we can specify the text to display in place of the image by setting the *AlternateText* property. The *Image* control only displays an image. If we need to capture mouse clicks on the image, we should instead use the *ImageButton* control.
Panel	This can be used as a container of other controls. This control is rendered as an *HTML <div>* element.
RadioButton	It creates an individual radio button on the page. We can group them to present mutually exclusive choices.
Table	It enables us an HTML table. A table can be built at design time with static content, but the *Table* control is often built programmatically with dynamic contents. Programmatic additions or modifications to a table row or cell do not persist on *PostBack*. Changes to table rows or cells must be reconstructed after each post to the server. In these cases, better alternatives are *DataList* or *DataGrid* controls.
Xml	This control can be used to transform XML documents.

Many of the basic server controls work very similarly to their HTML server control counterparts. All of the Web controls are prefixed with *asp:* in their tags. For example, the tag for a label Web control is *<asp:Label>*. Their uses are also mostly intuitive. All of the examples illustrated in the HTML server control section can also be effectively developed using Web controls. In this section we will present a number of additional examples to demonstrate the uses of Web controls.

Using *Labels*, *TextBoxes*, *RadioButtons*, *CheckBoxes*, and *DropDownLists*

In this example, we will develop a simple payroll estimation application to demonstrate *Labels, TextBoxes, RadioButtons, CheckBoxes* and a *DropDownList*. We will use a button control to submit a user's given data to the server. We will collect data on hours worked, and hourly rate using two textboxes. Insurance-related data will be collected using two radio buttons: "No Insurance ($0.00)," and "Family Coverage ($40.00)." We will group these two radio buttons in a group named *rgrInsurance*. The objective of grouping buttons is to enable the user to select at most one button from the group.

We will provide two check boxes to collect data on company facility use. We will assume that there are two facilities: Parking ($15.00) and Swimming Pool ($10.00). The user should be able to check both items. Finally, we will provide a **DropDownList** box to collect data on employee status. There will be two types of employees: White-Collar and Workhorse. A white-collar worker will receive a bonus of $100, whereas the bonus for a workhorse is assumed to be $65.88. The run-time view of the application is shown in Figure 3.40. The code for the application is pretty much straightforward. We have shown the code in Figure 3.41. The code is also available in a file named BasicServerControls1.aspx in the accompanying CD.

Figure 3.40 Using *Label*, *TextBox*, *RadioButton*, *CheckBox*, and *DropDownList* Web Controls

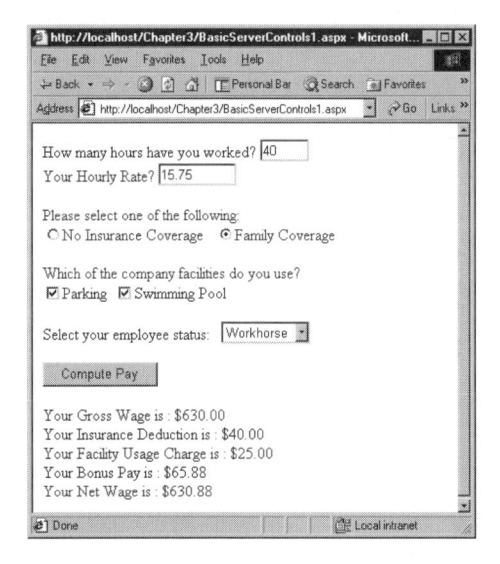

Figure 3.41 Complete Code for BasicServerControls1.aspx

```aspx
<!-- Chapter3\BasicServerControls1.aspx -->
<html><head></head><body><form runat="server">
How many hours have you worked?
<asp:TextBox id="txtH" rows="1" width="50" runat="server"/><br>
Your Hourly Rate?
<asp:TextBox id="txtR" rows="1" width="80" runat="server" /><br>
<br>Please select one of the following:<br>
<asp:RadioButton id="rbtnNoCov" groupName="rgrInsurance"
 text="No Insurance Coverage" checked="true" runat="server"/> 
<asp:RadioButton id="rbtnFamCov" groupName="rgrInsurance"
 text="Family Coverage" runat="server"/><br><br>
Which of the company facilities do you use?<br>
<asp:CheckBox id="chkPark" text="Parking" runat="server"/> 
<asp:CheckBox id="chkPool" text="Swimming Pool" runat="server"/>
<br><br>Select your employee status:  
<asp:DropDownList id="ddLStatus" runat="server">
 <asp:ListItem> White Collar</asp:ListItem>
 <asp:ListItem> Workhorse</asp:ListItem>
</asp:DropDownList><p>
<asp:Button id="btnCompute" runat="server"
 text="Compute Pay" onclick="computePay"/><br><br>
<asp:Label id="lblPayMsg" runat="server"/>
<asp:Label id="lblPay" runat="server"/><br>
<asp:Label id="lblInsMsg" runat="server"/>
<asp:Label id="lblInsCharge" runat="server"/><br>
<asp:Label id="lblFacilityMsg" runat="server"/>
<asp:Label id="lblFacilityCharge" runat="server"/><br>
<asp:Label id="lblBonusMsg" runat="server"/>
<asp:Label id="lblBonusPay" runat="server"/><br>
<asp:Label id="lblNetWageMsg" runat="server"/>
<asp:Label id="lblNetWage" runat="server"/>
</form></body></html>
<script language=vb runat="server">
```

Continued

Figure 3.41 Continued

```
Sub computePay (Sender As Object, E As EventArgs)
   Dim h, r, g, netWage, insCharge As Single
   Dim facilityCharge, bonus As Single
   h=CSng(txtH.Text)
   r=CSng(txtR.Text)
   lblPayMsg.Text="Your Gross Wage is : "
   g=h * r      ' Compute gross wage
   ' Compute Insurance Deduction
   If rbtnNoCov.Checked Then
       insCharge=0 ' No Insurance Charge
   Else
       insCharge=40.00
   End If
   ' Compute Facility Usage Charge
   facilityCharge=0
    If chkPark.Checked Then
       facilityCharge += 15    ' Parking
    End If
    If chKPool.Checked Then
       facilityCharge += 10    ' Swimming Pool
    End If
    ' Compute Bonus
    Select Case ddlStatus.SelectedIndex
       Case 0
          bonus=100.00 ' White Collar
       Case 1
          bonus= 65.88 ' Workhorse
    End Select
    netWage=g + bonus - insCharge - facilityCharge
    ' Display Results
    lblPay.Text=FormatCurrency(g)
    lblInsMsg.Text="Your Insurance Deduction is :"
    lblInsCharge.Text=FormatCurrency(insCharge)
```

Continued

Figure 3.41 Continued

```
    lblFacilityMsg.Text= "Your Facility Usage Charge is :"
    lblFacilityCharge.Text=FormatCurrency(facilityCharge)
    lblBonusMsg.Text="Your Bonus Pay is : "
    lblBonusPay.Text=FormatCurrency(bonus)
    lblNetWagemsg.Text="Your Net Wage is :"
    lblNetWage.Text=FormatCurrency(netWage)
  End Sub
</script>
```

Using the *ListControl* Abstract Class

A number of basic Web controls have been derived from the *ListControl* abstract class. These are *CheckBoxList, DropDownList, ListBox,* and *RadioButtonList*. Their usages and characteristics follow a common pattern. If warranted, each of these can be used as a container control. For example, a *CheckBoxList* control can contain a collection of *CheckBoxes*. We can set their *AutoPostBack* properties to *true* to trigger postbacks on their *SelectedIndexChanged* events. Each of them has a property named *Item.Count* that contains the number of items in the collection. The *Items(i).Selected* property can be used to check if the user has selected an item in the list. Finally, the *Items(i).Text* property enables us to extract the text of the selected item.

To demonstrate the identical behavior of the controls in the *ListControl* family, we will develop a simple example. We will load a *ListBox* control with certain flower names, a *RadioButtonList* control with some state names, and a *CheckBoxList* control with some facility names. Just for demonstration purposes, we will set the *AutoPostBack* properties of all of these controls to *true*. On click of each of these controls, we will display the user's selections. We will enable the user to select multiple entries from our list box. Of course, by default, the *CheckBoxList* control will enable the user to select more than one entry. The complete application, when displayed in IE, will appear as shown in Figure 3.42.

We have developed this application using VS.Net. The design time view of the form is shown in Figure 3.43. As you can observe from this figure, we have applied a certain amount of styling in the controls.

The VS.Net created a virtual directory and generated a Web application for this work. It has also generated two major files: *WebForm1.aspx* and *WebFrom1.aspx.vb* (the code-behind). It has compiled the *WebForm1.aspx.vb* to a .dll file and has saved it in the *bin* directory automatically. The entire application is available in the

Chapter3\TestingWebControls directory of the accompanying CD. To test the application, you will need to copy the *TestingWebControls* directory to your *Inetpub\wwwroot* directory. Then use the following URL to display the page in your browser: http://localhost/TestingWebControls/WebForm1.aspx.

Figure 3.42 Displaying and Manipulating Various *List* Controls

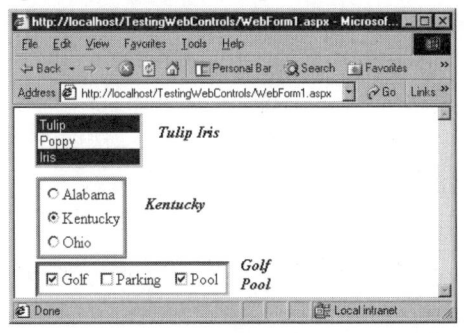

Figure 3.43 Design Time View of the *ListControl* Demonstration in VS.Net

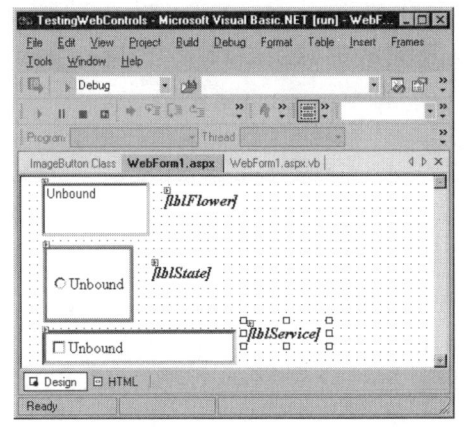

We will not reproduce the entire code here. In short, we have created three list controls. The *RepeatDirection* attribute of the *CheckBoxList* control has been set to "Horizontal" to align the check boxes horizontally. A truncated version of the *WebForm1.aspx* file as generated by VS.Net is shown in Figure 3.44.

Figure 3.44 Truncated Code Listing for WebForm1.aspx File: VS.NET (TestWebControls directory)

```
<%@ Page Language="vb" AutoEventWireup="false"
    Codebehind="WebForm1.aspx.vb"
```

Continued

Figure 3.44 Continued

```
     Inherits="TestingWebControls.WebForm1"%>
<body MS_POSITIONING="GridLayout">
<form id="Form1" method="post" runat="server">
<asp:RadioButtonList id="rblStates" style="Z-INDEX: 103; LEFT: 22px;
     POSITION: absolute; TOP: 69px" runat="server" AutoPostBack="True"
     Width="93px" Height="77px" BorderStyle="Ridge"
     BorderColor="#E0E0E0"></asp:RadioButtonList>
<asp:CheckBoxList id="cblServices" style="Z-INDEX: 104; LEFT: 21px;
     POSITION: absolute; TOP: 154px" runat="server" AutoPostBack="True"
     Width="200px" Height="35px" BorderStyle="Inset" RepeatDirection
     ="Horizontal" BorderColor="#E0E0E0"></asp:CheckBoxList>
--- --- Similar Code for the asp:ListBox id="lstFlowers" --- ---
<asp:Label id="lblState" style="Z-INDEX: 105; LEFT: 134px; POSITION:
     absolute; TOP: 87px" runat="server" Width="66px" Height="19px"
Font-
     Bold="True" Font-Italic="True"></asp:Label>
--- --- Similar Codes for other Labels --- ---
</form></body>
```

In the *WebForm1.aspx.vb* code-behind file, we have loaded all of the *ListControls* in the *Page_Load* event. In the appropriate events of these controls, we included the instructions to display the selections in respective labels. The user may select more than one entry in the *CheckBoxList*. Hence, we used a loop to iterate through each of the items. If the item was selected, we included its *text* in the output. Identical procedures were used to display the selected values in the list box. A truncated version of the relevant code for *WebForm1.aspx.vb* file is shown in Figure 3.45.

Figure 3.45 Partial Listing of WebForm1.aspx.vb

```
Private Sub Page_Load(ByVal sender As System.Object, ByVal e As _
                    System.EventArgs) Handles MyBase.Load
  'Put user code to initialize the page here
  If Not Page.IsPostBack Then
    ' Load the CheckBoxList
```

Continued

Figure 3.45 Continued

```
        cblServices.Items.Add(New ListItem("Golf"))
        cblServices.Items.Add(New ListItem("Parking"))
        cblServices.Items.Add(New ListItem("Pool"))
        ' Load the RadioButtonList
        rblStates.Items.Add(New ListItem("Alabama"))
        rblStates.Items.Add(New ListItem("Kentucky"))
        rblStates.Items.Add(New ListItem("Ohio"))
        ' Load ListBox
        lstFlowers.Items.Add(New ListItem("Tulip"))
        lstFlowers.Items.Add(New ListItem("Poppy"))
        lstFlowers.Items.Add(New ListItem("Iris"))
    End If
End Sub
Private Sub rblStates_SelectedIndexChanged(ByVal sender As _
        System.Object, ByVal e As System.EventArgs) Handles _
        rblStates.SelectedIndexChanged
    lblState.Text=rblStates.SelectedItem.Text
End Sub
Private Sub cblServices_SelectedIndexChanged(ByVal sender As _
        System.Object, ByVal e As System.EventArgs) Handles _
        cblServices.SelectedIndexChanged
    Dim i As Integer
    lblService.Text=" "
    For i=0 To cblServices.Items.Count - 1
        If cblServices.Items(i).Selected Then
            lblService.Text += cblServices.Items(i).Text + " "
        End If
    Next
End Sub
' Similarly, develop the SelectedIndexChanged event procedure for the
' other controls.
```

Using *HyperLink* Controls

The *HyperLink* server control enables us to link to a different page. Its *Text* property is displayed on the screen as a hyperlink. On click of the hyperlink, it links to a page specified in its *NavigateUrl* property. The displayed text can be replaced by an image by specifying the *ImageUrl* property. In our next example, we will develop a page with two *HyperLink* controls. One of them will display text, and the other will display an image. We will specify the *"http://ahmed2/Chapter3/ServerControl4.aspx"* in both of their *NavigateUrl* properties. The completed application will be displayed in IE as shown in Figure 3.46. When the user clicks any of the controls, the system will display the specified page. The complete code for the application is shown in Figure 3.47 and is also available in a file named HyperLink1.aspx in the accompanying CD.

Figure 3.46 Illustration of the *HyperLink* Server Control

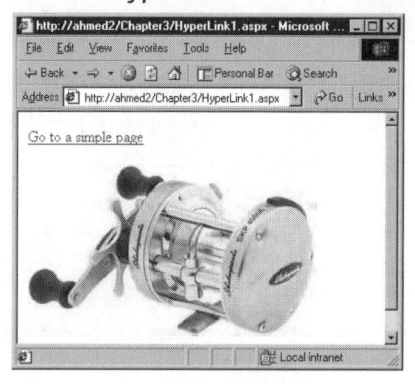

Figure 3.47 Complete Listing for HyperLink1.aspx

```
<!-- Chapter3\HyperLink1.aspx -->
<%@ Page Language="VB" Debug="true" %>
<html><head></head><body>
<form runat="server">
<asp:HyperLink id="HyperLink1" runat="server"
     NavigateUrl="http://ahmed2/Chapter3/ServerControl4.aspx"
     Text="Go to a simple page"/><br><br>
<asp:HyperLink id="HyperLink2" runat="server"
     NavigateUrl="http://ahmed2/Chapter3/ServerControl4.aspx"
     ImageUrl="http://ahmed2/Chapter3/BaitcastReel1.jpg"
```

Continued

Figure 3.47 Continued

```
      Text="World's Best Fishing Reel"/><br><br>
</body></form></html>
```

Binding a *ListControl* to an *ArrayList*

In most of our previous examples, we loaded a list box via code in the *Page_Load* event. In this section, we will introduce an important concept of a typical ASP.NET development practice. Rather than populating a specific control via code, we may bind a control to a data source (something that contains data). In this case, the control will automatically assume the value or values contained in the data source. At this stage, you may not see the benefit of this approach, but it will shine like a jewel when we learn how to display and manipulate data from databases. In the example shown in Figure 3.36 and Figure 3.37, we have shown a similar example of binding an *HtmlSelect* control to a *SortedList*). Since the *ArrayList* object is also very common in ASP.NET framework, we will bind our *ListControl* to an *ArrayList* in our next example.

Often we create and load a collection of objects into certain structures. These structures are known as *collection* objects. For example, an *ArrayList* is a *collection* object. It is actually very similar to a dynamic array of objects. Suppose that one of these *ArrayList* objects contains the names of some flowers. If needed, we may bind one or more controls to this *ArrayList*. That way, the controls will be automatically loaded with the values in the *ArrayList*. Don't worry! We will not deprive you of binding controls to databases. Those examples will appear later in this chapter.

Binding a control to a data source is very simple. Rather than developing a data loading procedure, we just set the *DataSource* property of a control to a data source. Then we employ the *DataBind()* method of the control to accomplish the binding task. In our example, we will first create an *ArrayList* of flowers, and then we will bind a list box *(lstFlower)* with the *ArrayList*. Figure 3.48 shows the runtime view of the application. The complete listing of the code is shown in Figure 3.49 (also available in the accompanying CD in a file named DataBind1.aspx).

Figure 3.48 Binding a *ListControl* to an *ArrayList*

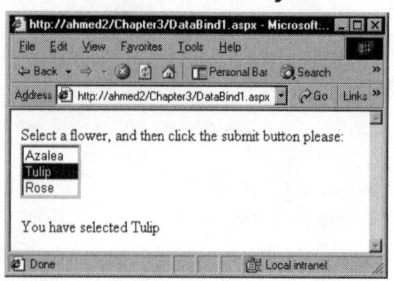

Figure 3.49 Complete Listing of DataBind1.aspx

```
<!— Chapter3\DataBind1.aspx —>
<%@ Page Language="VB" Debug="true" %>
<html><head></head><title></title><body>
<form runat="server">
Select a flower, and then click the submit button please:<br>
<asp:ListBox id="lstFlowers" runat="server" rows="3"
AutoPostBack="True" onSelectedIndexChanged="showSelection"/>
</asp:ListBox><br><br>
<asp:Label id=lblMessage runat="server"></asp:Label></p>
</body></form></html>
<script language=vb runat="server">
Sub Page_Load(source As Object, e As EventArgs)
  If Not Page.IsPostBack Then
     Dim myArrayList As New ArrayList
    ' Populate the ArrayList: This will be a data source
     myArrayList.Add("Azalea")
     myArrayList.Add("Tulip")
     myArrayList.Add("Rose")
     ' Step 1: Specify the Datasource property of the list control
     lstFlowers.DataSource= myArrayList
     ' Step 2: Employ the DataBind() method to load the
     ' list control from its DataSource automatically
     lstFlowers.DataBind()
     lstFlowers.SelectedIndex=0
```

Continued

Figure 3.49 Continued

```
  End If
End Sub
Sub showSelection(sender As Object, e As EventArgs)
  lblMessage.Text="You have selected "+lstFlowers.SelectedItem.Text
End Sub
</script>
```

Validation Controls

A validation control enables us to validate an input and display an error message if necessary. It is very much like other server-side controls with certain additional methods and properties. First, the server treats it as an invisible control. After the user has entered erroneous data, it becomes visible. It is a powerful, rapid application development feature; however, a developer needs to understand its behavior and the methods thoroughly before he or she can appreciate it. There are certain rough edges in the Beta 2 version, which hopefully will be polished in the final product. The best strategy to learn the family of controls is to learn them one at a time, and finally to apply the summary validation.

Various types of validation controls are as follows:

- **RequiredFieldValidator** Checks if the input control has any value.
- **RegularExpressionValidator** Checks the value against a regular expression (pattern).
- **CompareValidator** Checks if the value is acceptable compared to a given value or compared to the content of another control.
- **RangeValidator** Checks if the input control's value is within a specified range.
- **CustomValidator** Allows you to develop custom validation.
- **ValidationSummary** Reports a summary of all errors.

By default, each of the validation controls performs the validation task at the client-side as well as at the server-side. Except for the *RequiredFieldValidator*, all other validation controls treat an empty field as a valid field. Therefore, we will need to apply a *RequiredFieldValidator* to every input field that we want to validate. You can attach more than one validation control to an input. For example, we may use a *RequiredFieldValidator* and a *RangeValidator* to ensure that an input is not empty and falls within a specified range.

There are a number of common properties in these controls. The major ones are:

- **ErrorMessage** In case of an error, the system displays this message at the location of the control, and in the summary report, if any.

- **Display** A validation control is kept invisible until a bad input is entered. In case of a bad input, the system has to display the error message. The display mechanism can be handled in one of three ways.

    - **Display= "static"** Initially, enough room in the page is reserved for the expected error message.

    - **Display= "dynamic"** No room is initially reserved. In case of an error, the message is displayed by displacing existing contents of the page.

    - **Display="none"** The message won't be displayed at the location of the control; however, it will be reported in the summary report, if any.

The *RequiredFieldValidator* Control

In the following example, the user is expected to enter two values. If he or she skips any one of the values and clicks the **Submit** button, the system will report the error. Please notice that we do not require any extra code for performing this validation. When the **Submit** button is clicked, the form will be sent to the server, and the server will do the automatic validation. The run-time view of this application is shown in Figure 3.50. The code for this application, as shown in Figure 3.51, is self-explanatory and is also available in the accompanying CD in a file named Validator1.aspx.

Figure 3.50 Using the *RequiredFieldValidator* Control

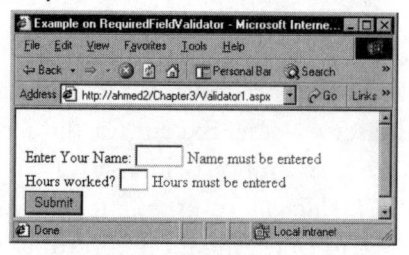

Figure 3.51 Validator1.aspx

```
<!-- Chapter3\Validator1.aspx -->
<!- Required Field Validator -->
<html><head></head>
<title>Example on Required Field validator</title><body>
<form runat="server"><br> Enter Your Name:
<asp:TextBox id="txtName" rows="1 " width="50" runat="server"/>
<asp:RequiredFieldValidator id="validTxtName"
    runat="server"   controlToValidate="txtName"
    errorMessage="Name must be entered"  display="static">
</asp:RequiredFieldValidator></br>
Hours worked?
<asp:TextBox id="txtH" width ="30" runat="server" />
<asp:RequiredFieldValidator id="validTxtH"  runat="server"
    controlToValidate="txtH" errorMessage="Hours must be entered"
    display="static">
</asp:RequiredFieldValidator></br>
<asp:Button id="btnSubmit" runat="server" text="Submit"   />
</form></body></html>
```

The *RegularExpressionValidator* Control

The *RegularExpressionValidator* control is typically used to match an input pattern. As an example, let us assume that the value of hours-worked field must have one to three digits. In this case, we will add a *RegularExpressionValidator* to the *txtH* control. In the *RegularExpression* property of the *RegularExpressionValidator*, we will specify a pattern */d{1,3}*. This will force the system to raise an error if the user input is not one-to-three digits long. The output of this application is shown in Figure 3.52. The code for this example is shown in Figure 3.53 and is also available on the accompanying CD in a file named Validator2.aspx.

Figure 3.52 Using *RegularExpressionValidator* Controls

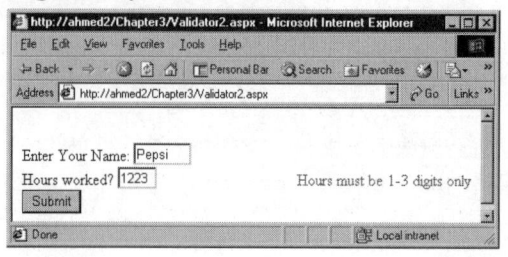

Figure 3.53 Validator2.aspx

```
<!-- Chapter3\Validator2.aspx -->
<%@ Page Language="VB" Debug="true" %>
<html><head></head><body>
<form runat="server"><br>
Enter Your Name:
<asp:TextBox id="txtName" rows="1 " width="60"  runat="server"/>
<asp:RequiredFieldValidator id="validTxtName"    runat="server"
   controlToValidate="txtName" errorMessage="Name must be entered"
   display="static">
</asp:RequiredFieldValidator></br>
Hours worked?
<asp:TextBox id="txtH" width ="40" runat="server" />
<asp:RequiredFieldValidator id="validTxtH"   runat="server"
   controlToValidate="txtH"  errorMessage="Hours must be entered"
   display="static">
</asp:RequiredFieldValidator>
<asp:RegularExpressionValidator id="regvH"
   runat="server"   display="static"   controlToValidate="txtH"
   errorMessage="Hours must be 1-3 digits only"
   validationExpression="\d{1,3}">
</asp:RegularExpressionValidator></br>
<asp:Button id="btnSubmit" runat="server" text="Submit"    />
</form></body></html>
```

NOTE

The details of regular expressions can be found in any Perl book. You may also review http://msdn.microsoft.com/scripting/default.htm?/scripting/JScript/doc/jsobjregexpression.htm.

We have found the following source to be adequate: www.microsoft.com/mind/defaulttop.asp?page=/mind/1098/jscript/jscript.htm&nav=/mind/1098/inthisissuecolumns1098.htm.

The *CompareValidator* Control

The *CompareValidator* control compares an input to a specified value or to the value of another control. You can also use it to check if the input is of any particular data type. In our next example, we will add a textbox named *txtR*. In this textbox, the user will enter the hourly rate. Suppose that we want the data-type of this field to be *Double*. We will apply a *CompareValidator* control to test the data-type of the *txtR*. Note that if the data entered is convertible to the desired data-type, the validation will succeed. The run-time view of the application is shown in Figure 3.54.

Figure 3.54 Using the *CompareValidator* Control

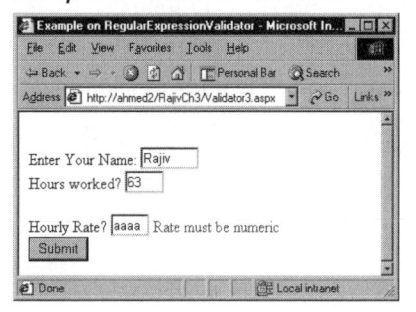

We have added the code following code to accomplish this objective (you may review the complete code in the file named Validator3.aspx on the CD). Please notice that we have set the *type* property to *"Double,"* and the *operator* property to *"DataTypeCheck."*

```
<asp:CompareValidator id="comvR" runat="server" display="static"
    controlToValidate="txtR" errorMessage="Rate must be numeric"
    type="Double" operator="DataTypeCheck">
</asp:CompareValidator></br>
```

In the *type* property of the *CompareValidator*, we may specify: *String*, *Integer*, *Double*, *DateTime*, and *Currency*. In the *operator* property, we may specify: *Equal*, *NotEqual*, *GreaterThan*, *LessThan*, *GreaterThanEqual*, *LessThanEqual*, and *DataTypeCheck*.

The *RangeValidator* Control

You can use this control to check if an input is within an acceptable range. Suppose that we want to provide a textbox for collecting data on "number of dependents." We want to enforce a constraint that this field should be from 0 to 10. Figure 3.55 illustrates the use of a *RangeValidator* in this particular situation.

Figure 3.55 Using the *RangeValidator* Control

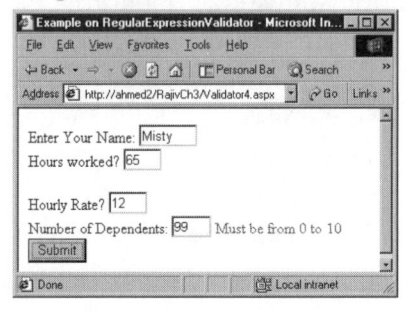

In our code, we have used the *type*, *minimumValue*, and *maximumValue* properties of a *RangeValidator* to apply the constraint. We have applied the *RangeValidator* as follows: (The complete code is available in *Validator4.aspx*.)

```
<asp:RangeValidator id="ranvDependents" runat="server"
    display="static" controlToValidate="txtDependents"
    errorMessage="Must be from 0 to 10"
    type="Integer" minimumValue=0  maximumValue=10>
</asp:RangeValidator></br>
```

The *CustomValidator* Control

In many situations, we may not be able to use the existing validators to validate a complex rule. In that case, we may apply a *CustomValidator*. When applying a *CustomValidator*, we may provide our own functions that will return true or false. We may develop the code for server-side validation only, or we may develop the code for server-side as well as the client-side validation. Suppose that the user will enter the data about his or her department number. Also suppose that the department number must be evenly divisible by 10. We will develop a simple custom validator to enforce this rule at the server-side. The run-time display of this application is shown in Figure 3.56.

Figure 3.56 Using the *CustomValidator* Control

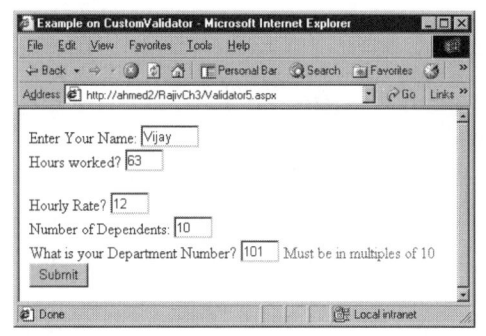

We have developed a VB function named *validateDeptNum* to perform the check. We have also specified its name in the *onServerValidate* property of the *CustomValidator* control. An excerpt from the complete code for this application is shown in Figure 3.57. The complete code is available on the CD in the file named Validator5.aspx.

Figure 3.57 The Code for *CustomValidator* (Validator5.aspx)

```
What is your Department Number?
<asp:TextBox id="txtDeptNum" width ="40" runat="server" />
<asp:CustomValidator id="cusvDeptNum" runat="server"
     display="static" controlToValidate="txtDeptNum"
     onServerValidate="validateDeptNum"
     errorMessage="Must be in multiples of 10" >
</asp:CustomValidator></br>
<asp:Button id="btnSubmit" runat="server" text="Submit"  />
</form></body></html>

<script language="VB" runat="server">
Sub validateDeptNum(source As Object, s as ServerValidateEventArgs)
  If (CInt(s.Value) Mod 10)=0 Then
     s.IsValid= True
  Else
```

Continued

Figure 3.57 Continued

```
    s.IsValid=False
  End If
End Sub
</script>
```

Although this example illustrates the server-side validation, ASP.NET automatically writes client-side code to perform the validation. There are various options available to prevent this from occurring and also not to display the code that shows the client-side JavaScript validation. We will not be going into these in detail. In the server-side custom validation, the validation function is included in the server-side script tag *<script language="VB" runat="server">*. We need to specify the name of the validation function in the *OnServerValidate* property of the *CustomValidator* control. The *validator* control calls this function with two parameters: the first parameter is the control itself, whereas the second parameter is an instance of the *ServerValidateEventArgs* class. This object encapsulates the methods and properties that enable us to access the value of the control being validated and to return whether the control has been validated or not.

> **NOTE**
>
> If the client-side validation is active (which is the default), the browser does not submit the form back to the server until all corrections have been made on the client-side. If you have a "server-side-only" custom validator along with some other fields that employ client-side validation, then on click of the submit button, the form may not appear to work properly. That is expected because the browser will not submit the form until all client-side validated fields are correct.

CustomValidator with Explicit Client-Side Validation Function

In the *CustomValidator*, we may specify a twin client-side validation function. To employ the client-side validation, we will have to specify the name of the client-side validation function in the *ClientValidationFunction* property of the *CustomValidator* control. The client-side function needs to be coded in JavaScript, and it should also return true or false. Obviously, the client-side validation should perform the same checks that are done by the server-side validation function.

We will revise our previous example to include a client-side validation function. We have already developed the server-side validation function for the department number textbox. Now we will implement the client-side validation. The run-time display of the application is shown in Figure 3.58.

Figure 3.58 Using *CustomValidator* with Explicit Client-Side Validation

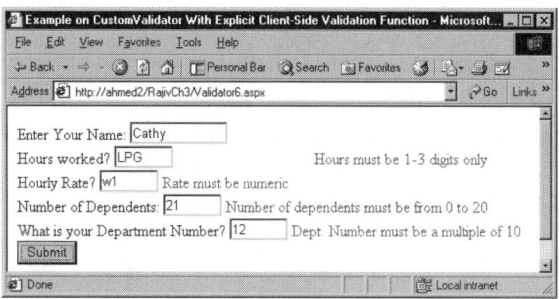

The part of the code that is pertinent to our example is shown in Figure 3.59. In this code, you will notice that we have specified the name of the JavaScript validation function in the *ClientValidationFunction* property of the control to be validated. The complete code is available in Validator6.aspx in the CD.

Figure 3.59 Partial Listing of Validator6.aspx

```
<asp:CustomValidator id="cusvDeptNum" runat="server"
    display="dynamic" controlToValidate="txtDeptNum"
    onServerValidate="validateDeptNum"
    ClientValidationFunction="checkModTen"
    errorMessage="Dept. Number must be a multiple of 10" >
</asp:CustomValidator></br>
<script language="javascript" >
function checkModTen(source, s)
{ var y=parseInt(s.Value);
  if ((y % 10) == 0 && !(isNaN(y)))
    s.IsValid=true;
  else
    s.IsValid=false;
```

Continued

Figure 3.59 Continued

```
}
</script>
```

Displaying the Error Message with Style

In this example, we will set various properties of the validation controls to display its message with style. The output of the application is shown in Figure 3.60. We have set a number of properties, such as *forecolor*, *bordercolor*, *tooltip*, and so on, to our number of dependent validators.

Figure 3.60 Displaying Error Message with Style

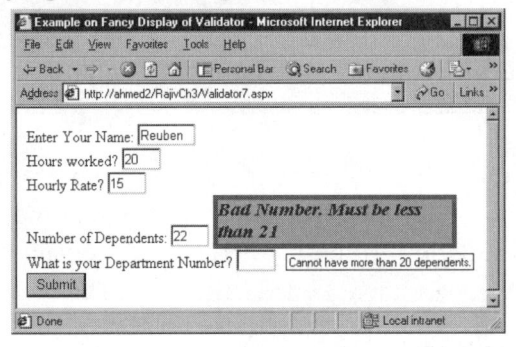

The part of the code that is relevant to format the validator is shown in Figure 3.61. The complete code is available in the file named Validator7.aspx on the CD.

Figure 3.61 Validator7.aspx

```
<asp:RangeValidator id="ranvDependents" runat="server"
    backcolor="salmon" forecolor="blue" bordercolor="green"
    borderstyle=Solid  borderwidth=5 font-bold=True font-italic=True
    font-size="14"     height="20"
    tooltip="Cannot have more than 20 dependents."
    text="Bad Number. Must be less than 21"
    width="250" display="dynamic" controlToValidate="txtDependents"
    errorMessage="Number of dependents must be from 0 to 20"
    type="Integer" minimumValue=0 maximumValue=10>
</asp:RangeValidator></br>
```

The *ValidationSummary* Control

The *ValidationSummary* control enables us to display all errors in a given location. It displays the *"errorMessage"* properties of respective controls in the summary report. Since the error messages are displayed in the summary, often we suppress the detailed error message in the individual *ValidatorControls* by placing an asterisk (*) or a short message right after the validator control's start-tag. Major properties of the *ValidationSummary* control are the following:

- **headerText** This is simply a header.
- **displayMode** Displays the errors in one of the following ways:
  - List
  - BulletList (default)
  - Singleparagraph
- **ShowSummary: (True or False)** This property can be used to display or hide the summary report programmatically.

Figure 3.62 illustrates the use of a *ValidationSummary* control. In our example, we have defined the *ValidationSummary* control as follows.

```
<asp:ValidationSummary id="valSummary" runat="server"
headerText="Please correct the following errors"
display="static" showSummary= "True" />
```

Figure 3.62 Using the *ValidationSummary* Control

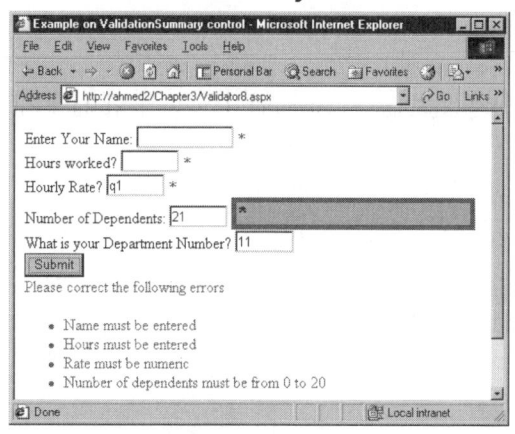

The complete code for the application is shown in Figure 3.63 and is available in the file named Validator8.aspx on the CD.

Figure 3.63 The Complete Code for the Application (Validator8.aspx)

```
<!-- Chapter3\Validator8.aspx -->
<%@ Page Language="VB" Debug="true" %>
<html><head></head>
<title>Example on ValidationSummary control </title>
<body><form runat="server">
Enter Your Name:
<asp:TextBox id="txtName" rows="1" width="100" runat="server"/>
<asp:RequiredFieldValidator id="validTxtName" runat="server"
    controlToValidate="txtName" errorMessage="Name must be entered"
    display="static">*
</asp:RequiredFieldValidator></br>
Hours worked?
<asp:TextBox id="txtH" width ="60" runat="server" />
<asp:RequiredFieldValidator id="validTxtH" runat="server"
    controlToValidate="txtH" errorMessage="Hours must be entered"
    display="static">*
</asp:RequiredFieldValidator>
<asp:RegularExpressionValidator id="regvH" runat="server"
    display="static" controlToValidate="txtH"
    errorMessage="Hours must be 1-3 digits only"
    validationExpression="\d{1,3}">*
</asp:RegularExpressionValidator></br>
Hourly Rate?
<asp:TextBox id="txtR" width ="60" runat="server" />
<asp:CompareValidator id="comvR" runat="server" display="static"
    controlToValidate="txtR" errorMessage="Rate must be numeric"
    type="Double" operator="DataTypeCheck">*
</asp:CompareValidator></br>
Number of Dependents:
<asp:TextBox id="txtDependents" width ="60" runat="server" />
<asp:RangeValidator id="ranvDependents" runat="server"
```

Continued

Figure 3.63 Continued

```
      backcolor="salmon" forecolor="blue" bordercolor="green"
      borderstyle="Solid" borderwidth="5" font-bold="True"
      font-italic="True" font-size="14" height="20"
      tooltip="Cannot have more than 20 dependents."
      text="Bad Number. Must be less than 21" width="250"
      display="dynamic" controlToValidate="txtDependents"
      errorMessage= "Number of dependents must be from 0 to 20"
      type="Integer" minimumValue="0" maximumValue="10">*
</asp:RangeValidator><br>
What is your Department Number?
<asp:TextBox id="txtDeptNum" width ="60" runat="server" />
<asp:CustomValidator id="cusvDeptNum" runat="server"
      display="dynamic" controlToValidate="txtDeptNum"
      onServerValidate="validateDeptNum"
      ClientValidationFunction="checkModTen"
      errorMessage= "Dept. Number must be a multiple of 10" >*
</asp:CustomValidator><br>
<asp:Button id="btnSubmit" runat="server" text="Submit"/><br><br>
 <asp:ValidationSummary id="valSummary" runat="server"
      headerText="Please correct the following errors" display="static"
      showSummary= "True" /><br>
 </form></body></html>
<script language="VB" runat="server">
Sub validateDeptNum(source As Object, s as ServerValidateEventArgs)
   If (CInt(s.Value) Mod 10)=0 Then
      s.IsValid= True
   Else
      s.IsValid =False
   End If
End Sub
</script>
<script language="javascript">
function checkModTen(source, s)
```

Continued

Figure 3.63 Continued

```
{   var y=parseInt(s.Value);
    if (isNaN(y) && !((y % 10) == 0))
        s.IsValid=false;
    else
        s.IsValid=true;
}
</script>
```

Validating Patterned Strings, Passwords, and Dates

Suppose that we want the user to enter the phone number, date of birth, hire-date, password, and confirmation of password. Also suppose that the business environment dictates that we enforce the following constraints:

- The phone number must follow a pattern like (ddd)ddd-dddd for employees in the USA. It should match dd.dd.dd.dd for employees in France.
- The date of birth must be between 1/1/1940 and 1/12/1985.
- Hire date must be after the date of birth and before 6/15/2001.
- The user should enter the password twice, and both entries must be identical.

We have developed an application to enforce these business rules. The output of the application is shown in Figure 3.64.

Figure 3.64 Validating Patterned Strings and Passwords

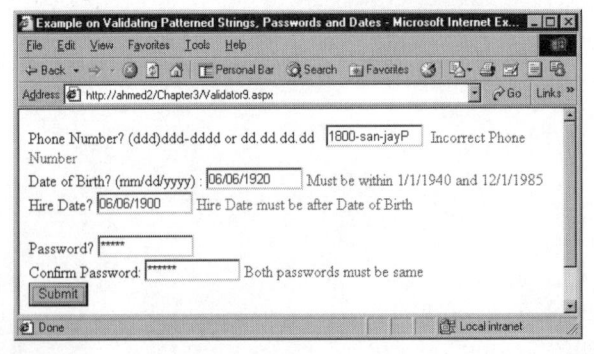

The complete code for this application is shown in Figure 3.65 and is available on the CD in the file named Validator9.aspx. We have enforced the underlying constraints as follows:

Constraint 1. We will use a regular expression to implement this constraint. The following regular expressions are identical. Both of these expressions will test the pattern (ddd)ddd-ddd:

```
ValidationExpression="\(\d\d\d\)\d\d\d\-\d\d\d\d">
ValidationExpression="\(\d{3}\)\d{3}\-\d{4}"
```

However, for French employees we must also test a pattern like dd.dd.dd.dd. The regular expression for this pattern would be this:

```
ValidationExpression="\d{2}\.\d{2}\.\d{2}\.\d{2}"
```

We may parenthesize these two expressions and connect them with a pipe (|) symbol to specify that any one of the expressions needs to be satisfied, as follows:

```
ValidationExpression="(\(\d{3}\)\d{3}\\d{4})|
   (\d{2}\.\d{2}\.\d{2}\.\d{2})"
```

Constraint 2. We have used a *RangeValidator* to enforce this rule.

Constraint 3. We have used a combination of the *CompareValidator* and the *RangeValidator*. The *CompareValidator* checks whether the date in *txtDateHired* is greater than that in *txtDateOfBirth*. The code for that is as follows:

```
Hire Date?
<asp:TextBox id="txtDateHired" rows="1" width="100" runat="server"/>
<asp:CompareValidator id="compDateHired" runat="server"
   display="dynamic"
   controlToValidate="txtDateHired"
   controlToCompare="txtDateOfBirth"
   errorMessage="Hire Date must be after Date of Birth"
   type="String" operator="GreaterThan">
</asp:CompareValidator><br/>
```

The RangeValidator checks whether the date in *txtDateHired* is less than "6/15/2001." The *minimumValue* is set to "1/1/1900" because the

RangeValidator will not work unless both the *minimumValue* and *maximumValue* are both present. The code snippet follows:

```
<asp:RangeValidator id="ranvDateHired" runat="server" type="Date"
    display="dynamic" controlToValidate="txtDateHired"
    errorMessage="Hire date must be before 6/1/2001"
    minimumValue="1/1/1900" maximumValue="6/15/2001" >
</asp:RangeValidator><br/>
```

Constraint 4. Two *asp:TextBox* controls have been used. The *TextMode* properties have been set to *"Password"*. *CompareValidator* has been attached to the *txtConfirmPassword*. Its *ControlToCompare* property has been set to *"txtPassword."*:

```
controlToValidate="txtConfirmPassword" controlToCompare="txtPassword"
    type="String" operator="Equal"
```

Figure 3.65 Validator9.aspx

```
<!-- Chapter3\Validator9.aspx -->
<html><head></head><body><form runat="server">
Phone Number? (ddd)ddd-dddd or dd.dd.dd.dd  
<asp:TextBox id="txtPhone" rows="1 " width="100" runat="server"/>
<asp:RequiredFieldValidator id="validTxtName" runat="server"
    controlToValidate="txtPhone" errorMessage="Name must be entered"
    display="dynamic">
</asp:RequiredFieldValidator>
<asp:RegularExpressionValidator id="regvPhone" runat="server"
  display="dynamic" controlToValidate="txtPhone"
  errorMessage="Incorrect Phone Number"
  validationExpression=
      "(\(\d{3}\)\d{3}\-\d{4})|(\d{2}\.\d{2}\.\d{2}\.\d{2})">
</asp:RegularExpressionValidator><br>
Date of Birth? (mm/dd/yyyy) :
<asp:TextBox id="txtDateOfBirth" rows="1" width="100" runat="server"/>
<asp:RangeValidator id="ranvDob" runat="server" type="Date"
    display="dynamic" controlToValidate="txtDateOfBirth"
```

Continued

Figure 3.65 Continued

```
         errorMessage= "Must be within 1/1/1940 and 12/1/1985"
         minimumValue="1/1/1940" maximumValue="12/1/1985">
</asp:RangeValidator></br>
Hire Date?
<asp:TextBox id="txtDateHired" rows="1 " width="100" runat="server"/>
<asp:CompareValidator id="compDateHired" runat="server"
    display="dynamic" controlToValidate="txtDateHired"
    controlToCompare="txtDateOfBirth"
    errorMessage="Hire Date must be after Date of Birth" type="String"
    operator="GreaterThan">
</asp:CompareValidator><br/>
<asp:RangeValidator id="ranvDateHired" runat="server" type="Date"
       display="dynamic" controlToValidate="txtDateHired"
       errorMessage="Hire date must be before 6/1/2001"
       minimumValue="1/1/1900" maximumValue="6/15/2001" >
</asp:RangeValidator><br/>
Password?
<asp:TextBox id="txtPassword" textmode="password" width="100"
    runat="server"/><br/>
Confirm Password:
<asp:TextBox id="txtConfirmPassword" textMode="password" width="100"
    runat="server" />
<asp:CompareValidator id="comvConfirmPassword" runat="server"
    display="static" controlToValidate="txtConfirmPassword"
    controlToCompare="txtPassword"
    errorMessage="Both passwords must be same" type="String"
    operator="Equal">
</asp:CompareValidator><br/>
<asp:Button id="btnSubmit" runat="server" text="Submit"/> <br><br><br>
```

</form></body></html> The *Databound ListControls* Family

In this section, we will discuss the *Databound ListControls*. This family of controls is new to ASP developers. These controls provide rapid application development to display and manipulate data from any data source. The following controls shown in Table 3.3 belong to this family.

Table 3.3 The *Databound ListControls* Family

CheckBoxList	DataGrid	DataList	DropDownList
HtmlSelect	ListBox	RadioButtonList	Repeater

In earlier sections of this chapter, we illustrated data binding examples on *HtmlSelectControl* (Figure 3.36), and *asp:ListBox* control (Figure 3.48). We may use similar techniques to bind data to a *CheckBoxList, DropDownList*, or a *RadioButtonList* control. In this section, we will instead introduce three of the most prominent members of this family: *Repeater, DataList*, and *DataGrid*.

In our demonstrations, we will use a sample database named Products.mdb, which you can find on the CD accompanying this book. It is a Microsoft Access 2000 database. It contains only one table, named *Products*. Figure 3.66 shows some sample records in this table. Basically, the table has four columns: *ProductId* (AutoNumbered Long Integer), *ProductName* (Text 50), *ImagePath* (Text 150) and *Price* (Currency). The *ImagePath* column contains the name and location of an image relative to a virtual directory.

Figure 3.66 Sample Records in the Products Table

ProductID	ProductName	ImagePath	Price
1	Shimano Calcutta	Images/BaitcastReel1.jpg	$45.89
2	Bantam Lexica	Images/BaitcastReel2.jpg	$33.22
3	Ambassadeur Original	Images/BaitcastReel3.jpg	$21.11
4	Quantum Micro	Images/SpinReel1.jpg	$79.12
5	SpiderCase 2000	Images/SpinReel2.jpg	$55.55
6	Minnow by Daiwa	Images/SpinReel3.jpg	$11.35

Record: 6 of 21

You will learn database connectivity issues in Chapter 7. When we connect to a database, we typically run a query and populate a data table of a data set with the results of the query. In this chapter, we will not discuss the mechanics of how to connect to a database. To understand the remainder of this chapter, it will be sufficient to know that we can bind a *ListControl* to a data table of a data set. In most of the examples, we will use a subprocedure to populate a *DataSet* named *myDataSet*. The listing of a similar subprocedure is shown in Figure 3.67. Temporarily, we will treat this code as a black box (until you have read Chapter 7). This code will populate a data set and subsequently bind a specific *ListControl* to the data set.

Figure 3.67 Populating *myDataSet* and Binding a *ListControl*

```
1.  Sub bindListControl()
2.    Dim myConn As OleDbConnection
3.    Dim myOleDbAdapter As OleDbDataAdapter
4.    Dim connStr, sqlStr As String
5.    Dim myDataSet As New Dataset
6.    connStr="Provider=Microsoft.Jet.OLEDB.4.0;" _
7.        + "Data Source=D:\Products.mdb"
8.    sqlStr="SELECT ProductId, ProductName, Price, ImagePath " _
9.        + "FROM Products WHERE Price>45.00 ORDER BY Price"
10.   myConn= New OleDbConnection(connStr)
11.   myConn.Open()
12.   myOleDbAdapter =New OleDbDataAdapter(sqlStr,myConn)
13.   myOleDbAdapter.Fill(myDataSet,"dtProducts")
14.   repeater1.DataSource=myDataSet.Tables("dtProducts")
15.   repeater1.DataBind()
16.  End Sub
```

> **NOTE**
>
> To try the examples in the remainder of this chapter, you will need to do the following:
>
> 1. Copy the *Products.mdb* in your hard drive. In each sample program, locate the *bindListControl* subprocedure (shown in Figure 3.67), and adjust its line number 7 to specify your drive. For example, if you have loaded *Products.mdb* in your C drive, then change line number 7 of the *bindListControl* procedure to Data Source=C:\Products.mdb.
>
> 2. Copy the image files from *Chapter3/Images* directory of the CD and paste them in the *Images* subdirectory of your virtual directory.

Actually, the preceding code is not difficult to understand. First we have defined the necessary object variables to connect to a database. In lines 6 and 7, we have provided the information about the driver to be used, and the location of the database. A SQL statement is constructed in lines 8 and 9. We have instantiated the connection object in line 10, and opened the connection in line 11. An *OleDbDataAdapter* object was instantiated using the *SQL* string and *connection* string. The *dtProducts* data table of the *myDataSet* data set is populated in line 14. Then we set the *DataSource* property of a repeater control to the *dtProducts*. Finally, in line 15, we have bound the repeater to its data source. We will be using similar logic in each of our *ListControl* examples with minor variations in the SQL statement.

Using the *Repeater* Server Control

The *Repeater* is essentially a template-driven data-bound list. The *Repeater* control allows fragments of html tags inside the templates. For example, we may start a <table> in the *Header* template and end the table (</table>) in the *Footer* template, if necessary. The control binds its *Item* collection to the its *DataSource*. We may use the *Item Command* event to process events that are raised from the templates of the control.

We may specify the following templates for a *Repeater* control:

- **Item Template** Specifies the *DataItem* fields to be displayed, and the layout (required).
- **AlternatingItemTemplate** Defines the layout of the zero-based odd indexed items (optional).
- **SeparatorTemplate** In this template, we can specify the separator such as <hr> or <br> between repeating items (optional).
- **HeaderTemplate** Specifies the header of the list (optional).
- **FooterTemplate** Specifies the footer of the list (optional).

We will provide two examples to illustrate the behavior of a repeater control. In the first example, we will display our product information using a repeater control. In the second example, we will illustrate how to capture an event from a control residing inside a repeater control (known as *Event Bubbling*).

Displaying Data in a Repeater Control

Suppose that we want to display our products data for the products that cost more than $45.00. The expected display for this application is shown in Figure 3.68. The code for this application is shown in Figure 3.69 and is also available in the accompanying CD in a file named Repeater1.aspx.

Figure 3.68 Displaying Data in a *Repeater* Control

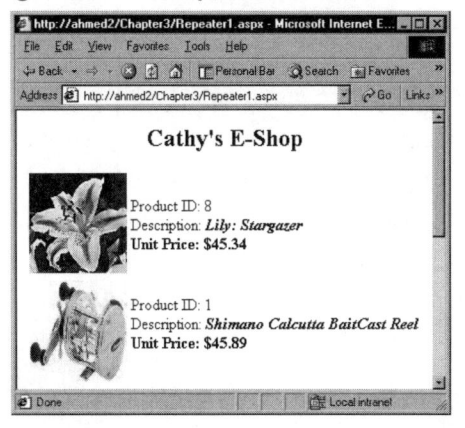

In this application we have defined three templates for our repeater. The *Header* template starts an HTML table with a <table> tag. The *Footer* template completes the table with a </table> tag. The *ItemTemplate* contains the table cells to house the data values. We will extract data from the *Products* table from the *Products.mdb* database. First we will populate a data set object, and then we will bind the repeater to this data set. Detailed code for populating the data set and binding the repeater is shown in Figure 3.69.

Figure 3.69 Repeater1.aspx

```
<!-- Chapter3/Repeater1.aspx -->
<%@ Import Namespace="System.Data" %>
<%@ Import Namespace="System.Data.OleDb" %>
<html><head></head>
<script language="VB" Debug="true" runat="server">
Sub Page_Load(src As Object, e As EventArgs)
   If Not IsPostBack
      bindListControl
   End If
End Sub
Sub bindListControl()
   Dim myConn As OleDbConnection
```

Continued

Figure 3.69 Continued

```
    Dim myOleDbAdapter As OleDbDataAdapter
    Dim connStr, sqlStr As String
    Dim myDataSet As New Dataset
    connStr="Provider=Microsoft.Jet.OLEDB.4.0;" _
        + "Data Source=D:\Products.mdb"
    sqlStr="SELECT ProductId, ProductName, Price, ImagePath " _
        + "FROM Products WHERE Price>45.00 ORDER BY Price"
    myConn= New OleDbConnection(connStr)
    myConn.Open()
    myOleDbAdapter =New OleDbDataAdapter(sqlStr,myConn)
    myOleDbAdapter.Fill(myDataSet,"dtProducts")
    repeater1.DataSource=myDataSet.Tables("dtProducts")
    repeater1.DataBind()
End Sub
</script>
<body><h2><center>Cathy's E-Shop</h2>
<asp:Repeater id="repeater1" runat="server" >
    <HeaderTemplate><table></HeaderTemplate>
    <ItemTemplate><tr>
      <td><asp:Image height=100 width=100
          Img src='<%# Container.DataItem("ImagePath")%>'
          runat="server"/>
      </td>
      <td>Product ID:
         <%# Container.DataItem("ProductId")%><br>
            Description: <b><i>
         <%# Container.DataItem("ProductName")%></b><i><br>
            <b>Unit Price:
         <%# FormatCurrency(Container.DataItem("Price"))%></b><br>
      </td></tr>
    </ItemTemplate>
    <FooterTemplate>
      </table>
```

Continued

Figure 3.69 Continued

```
    </FooterTemplate>
</asp:Repeater>
</center></body></html>
```

Once a data table has been populated, only two statements are required to bind a repeater. We need to set its *DataSource* property to the appropriate data table, and then we can apply its *DataBind()* method to accomplish the job. These two statements are as follows:

```
repeater1.DataSource=myDataSet.Tables("dtProducts").DefaultView
repeater1.DataBind()
```

We know that the *dtProducts* table of our data set will contain columns like *ProductId, ProductName*, etc. Our objective is to develop an ItemTemplate where we want to specify which column should be shown in what format. For each row of the table in the data set, the repeater will employ this template to display the data. A typical way to display a desired field is to use the *<%# Container .DataItem("columnName")%>* syntax. For example, the following *ItemTemplate* will display the *ProductId* in a cell of a table (assuming that the <table> tag has been specified in the HeaderTemplate):

```
<ItemTemplate>
    <tr><td><%# Container.DataItem("ProductId") %>
    </td></tr>
</ItemTemplate>
```

Similarly, as shown in the following statement, an *Img* control can also be specified to render an image:

```
Img src='<%# Container.DataItem("ImagePath") %>'
```

Using Event Bubbling and Capturing Events in a Repeater Control

You can use the *Repeater* control to accomplish much more than just displaying data. In its templates, we may insert other controls. In this example, we will place an *asp:Button* control in the *ItemTemplate* of our repeater. As shown in Figure 3.70, the repeater will display a button for every record in its data source. We may capture the click event of this button and perform appropriate processing. In this

136 Chapter 3 • ASP Server Controls

example, we will just display the selected *ProductId*. Would it not be an excellent way to enable the users to select items in a shopping cart application? On each selection, we could have written the selected data in a database.

Figure 3.70 Event Bubbling in a *Repeater* Control

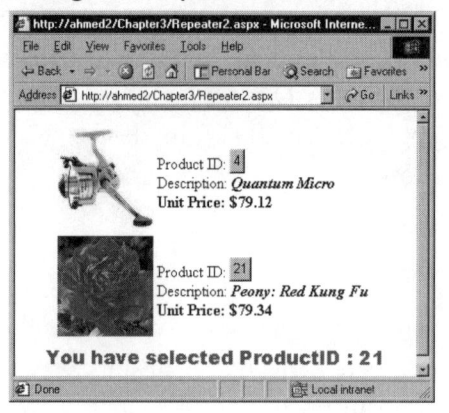

The complete code for this application is shown in Figure 3.71 (and is also available in a file named Repeater2.aspx, in the accompanying CD). A repeater is essentially a container control. When we defined the repeater, we set its *OnItemSelection* attribute to a function named *"showSelection"* as follows:

`<asp:Repeater id=repeater1 OnItemCommand="showSelection" runat="server">`

Whenever a child control in a repeater raises an event, it will report it to its parent, the repeater. The repeater will fire the *showSelection* function. This phenomenon of a child reporting an event to its parent is known as *Event Bubbling*. A *Repeater* (or any such parent) may receive events from many embedded child controls; hence, it may not clearly identify which of the children raised the event. Therefore, the child needs to pass certain information about itself when reporting an event. This is accomplished by the second parameter of the event procedure. The second parameter is defined as *e As RepeaterCommandEventArgs*. Naturally, the parameter *e* will be of a *RepeaterCommandEventArgs* object type (data type), and its *CommandSource* will identify the child raising the event. Similar event bubbling is employed in many cases where a parent control contains child controls. That is how, as shown in the following code excerpt, we are displaying the value of the *ProductId* in our message:

```
Sub showSelection(s As Object, e As RepeaterCommandEventArgs)
    lblMessage.Text="You have selected ProductID : " _
```

```
                    + e.CommandSource.Text
End Sub
```

But, wait a minute! How did we get the *ProductId* value displayed on a button anyway? Well, that is actually very easy. As shown in the following code excerpt, the button was placed inside the *ItemTemplate*, and we set its text property to the "<%# Container.DataItem("ProductId")%>".

```
<ItemTemplate><tr>
  <td>Product ID:
  <asp:Button text=<%# Container.DataItem("ProductId")%>
              runat="server"/>
 </ItmpTemplate>
```

The remainder of the code is self-explanatory.

Figure 3.71 Repeater2.aspx

```
<!-- Chapter3/Repeater2.aspx -->
<%@ Import Namespace="System.Data"%>
<%@ Import Namespace="System.Data.OleDb"%>
<html><head></head>
<script language="VB" Debug="true" runat="server">
Sub Page_Load(src As Object, e As EventArgs)
   If Not IsPostBack Then
      bindListControl
   End If
End Sub
Sub bindListControl()
Dim myConn As OleDbConnection
   Dim myOleDbAdapter As OleDbDataAdapter
   Dim connStr, sqlStr As String
   Dim myDataSet As New Dataset
   connStr="Provider=Microsoft.Jet.OLEDB.4.0; " _
        + "Data Source=D:\Products.mdb"
   sqlStr="SELECT ProductId, ProductName, Price, ImagePath " _
        + "FROM Products WHERE Price>79.00 ORDER BY Price"
   myConn= New OleDbConnection(connStr)
```

Continued

Figure 3.71 Continued

```
   myConn.Open()
   myOleDbAdapter =New OleDbDataAdapter(sqlStr,myConn)
   myOleDbAdapter.Fill(myDataSet,"dtProducts")
   repeater1.DataSource=myDataSet.Tables("dtProducts")
   repeater1.DataBind()
End Sub
Sub showSelection(s As Object, e As RepeaterCommandEventArgs)
   lblMessage.Text="You have selected ProductID : "   _
                    + e.CommandSource.Text
   ' Some references convert the CommandSource object to a button object
   ' first as shown below. It is not necessary though.
   ' CType(e.CommandSource, Button).Text
End Sub
</script>
<body><form runat= "server"><center>
<asp:Repeater id=repeater1 OnItemCommand="showSelection" runat="server">
<HeaderTemplate><table></HeaderTemplate>
<ItemTemplate><tr>
   <td><asp:Image height=100 width=100
   Img src='<%# Container.DataItem("ImagePath") %>' runat="server"/>
   </td><td> Product ID:
   <asp:Button text=<%# Container.DataItem("ProductId")%>
         runat="server"/> <br>Description: <b><i>
   <%# Container.DataItem("ProductName")%></b></i><br>
       <b>Unit Price:
   <%# FormatCurrency(Container.DataItem("Price"))%></b><br>
   <td></tr>
</ItemTemplate>
<FooterTemplate></table></FooterTemplate>
</asp:Repeater>
<asp:Label id=lblMessage runat="server" ForeColor="Brown"
   Font-Size="14pt" Font-Weight="700" Font-Name="Arial Black,Arial">
</asp:Label></center>
</form></body></html>
```

Using the *DataList* Control

The *DataList* control is similar to the *Repeater* control. However, it has some additional properties and templates that you can use to display its data in a diverse fashion. The *Repeater* control does not have any built-in layout or style. We are forced to specify all formatting-related HTML elements and style tags. On the other hand, a *DataList* control provides more flexibility to display data in a desired layout. It also provides data selection and editing capabilities. How does it do it? Well, in addition to the five templates that a repeater has, the *DataList* control has two more templates: *SelectedItemTemplate*, and *EditItemTemplate*. These templates are useful for allowing data selection and data editing functionalities. Furthermore, the *RepeatDirection* and *RepeatColumns* properties of a *DataList* control can be exploited to lay out the data in horizontal or vertical fashions.

In this section, we will present two examples. The first example will illustrate the use of the *RepeatDirection* and *RepeatColumns* properties. The second example will demonstrate how to enable the user to select a particular data being displayed using a *DataList*.

Using RepeatDirection *and* RepeatColumn *Properties of a* DataList

In this example, our objective is to display the product's data in a fashion as shown in Figure 3.72. A data table in a data set is essentially a relational database-like table in the computer's cache. It has rows (records) and columns (fields) of data extracted from the database. When we bind a *ListControl* to a data table, each record of the data table becomes an *Item* in the *ItemList* collection of the *ListControl*. In this particular example, we want to display three of these *Items* in each row of our display (horizontally). This is why we have defined the *DataControl* as follows:

```
<asp:DataList id="dataList1" border=0
    RepeatDirection="Horizontal" RepeatColumns="3" runat="server">
```

The remainder of the code for this application, as shown in Figure 3.73, is straightforward. The code is also available in a file named DataList1.aspx in the accompanying CD.

Figure 3.72 Displaying Data Using *RepeatDirection* and *RepeatColumn* Properties

Figure 3.73 Listing of DataList1.aspx

```
<!-- Chapter3\DataList1.aspx -->
<%@ Import Namespace="System.Data" %>
<%@ Import Namespace="System.Data.OleDb" %>
<html><head></head>
<script language="VB" Debug="true" runat="server">
Sub Page_Load(src As Object, e As EventArgs)
   If Not IsPostBack Then
      bindListControl
   End If
End Sub
Sub bindListControl()
   Dim myConn As OleDbConnection
   Dim myOleDbAdapter As OleDbDataAdapter
   Dim connStr, sqlStr As String
   Dim myDataSet As New Dataset
   connStr="Provider=Microsoft.Jet.OLEDB.4.0;Data Source=D:\Products.mdb"
   sqlStr="SELECT ProductId, ProductName, Price, ImagePath " _
         + "FROM Products ORDER BY Price"
```

Continued

Figure 3.73 Continued

```
    myConn= New OleDbConnection(connStr)
    myConn.Open()
    myOleDbAdapter =New OleDbDataAdapter(sqlStr,myConn)
    myOleDbAdapter.Fill(myDataSet,"dtProducts")
    dataList1.DataSource=myDataSet.Tables("dtProducts")
    dataList1.DataBind()
End Sub
</script>
<body bgcolor="white">
<asp:DataList id="dataList1" border=0
    RepeatDirection="Horizontal" RepeatColumns="3" runat="server">
    <ItemTemplate><table><tr>
      <td> <asp:Image   height=80 width=80
         ImageURL='<%# Container.DataItem("ImagePath") %>'
         runat="server" />
      </td></tr><tr>
      <td> Product ID:
         <%# Container.DataItem("ProductId")%><br>
         Description:<b><i><%# Container.DataItem("ProductName")%>
         </b></i><br><b>Unit Price: $
          <%# Container.DataItem("Price")%></b><br>
      </td></tr></table>
    </ItemTemplate>
</asp:DataList></body></html>
```

Capturing Selected Items in a DataList Control

In this example, we will use a *DataList* control to display the product names in a tabular fashion. Within the *DataList* control, the product names are displayed using *link buttons*. The output of this application is shown in Figure 3.74. Once the user selects a particular product name, our objective is to display the name of the selected product. We will also display the index number of the selected item. What index number? Well, you already know that when a *ListControl* is bound to a data table, all rows of the table are included as *Items* in the *ItemList* collection of the *ListControl*. The first such *Item* will have an index value of 0, the second item will have an index value of 1, and so on…! It is the value of that index which we will display.

Figure 3.74 Capturing Selected Items in a *DataList* Control

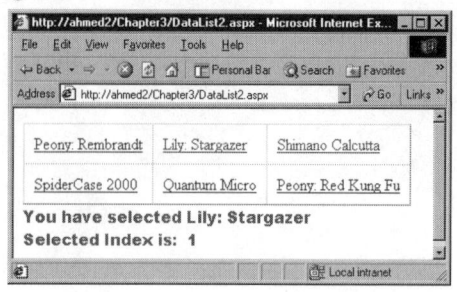

The definition of the *DataList* is itself very simple. We have included the *OnItemCommand* attribute of the *DataList* to the *showSelection* procedure, as follows:

```
<asp:DataList id="dataList1" gridlines="both" cellpadding="10"
    RepeatColumns="3" RepeatDirection="Horizontal"
    onItemCommand="showSelection"
    runat="server">
```

Subsequently, we have embedded a *LinkButton* control in the *ItemTemplate* of the *DataList*. On the click event of this *LinkButton,* it will send the *ProductName* as the *CommandArgument* to the *showSelection* function. These are accomplished as follows:

```
<ItemTemplate>:
    <asp:LinkButton id="myLinkBtns"
    text='<%# Container.DataItem( "ProductName" )%>'
    CommandArgument='<%# Container.DataItem( "ProductName" )%>'
    runat ="server"/>
</ItemTemplate>
```

In the *showSelection* procedure, we are simply displaying the desired information as shown in the following code excerpt:

```
Sub showSelection(s As Object, e As DataListCommandEventArgs)
        lblSelectedIndex.Text ="Selected Index is: " + " " + _
        e.Item.ItemIndex.toString()
lblSelectedProductName.Text="You have selected " + e.CommandArgument
```

The complete code for this application is shown in Figure 3.75 (and is also available in a file named DataList2.aspx in the accompanying CD).

Figure 3.75 DataList2.aspx

```
<!-- Chapter3\DataList2.aspx -->
<%@ Import Namespace="System.Data" %>
<%@ Import Namespace="System.Data.OleDb" %>
<html><head></head>
<script language="VB" Debug="true" runat="server">
Sub Page_Load(src As Object, e As EventArgs)
  If Not IsPostBack Then
     bindListControl
  End If
End Sub
Sub bindListControl()
  Dim myConn As OleDbConnection
  Dim myOleDbAdapter As OleDbDataAdapter
  Dim connStr, sqlStr As String
  Dim myDataSet As New DataSet
  connStr="Provider=Microsoft.Jet.OLEDB.4.0;Data Source=D:\Products.mdb"
  sqlStr="SELECT  ProductId, ProductName, Price " _
        + " FROM Products WHERE Price > 40 ORDER BY Price"
  myConn= New OleDbConnection(connStr)
  myConn.Open()
  myOleDbAdapter=New OleDbDataAdapter(sqlStr,myConn)
  myOleDbAdapter.Fill(myDataSet,"dtProducts")
  dataList1.DataSource=myDataSet.Tables("dtProducts")
  dataList1.DataBind()
  myConn.Close()
 End Sub
Sub showSelection(s As Object, e As DataListCommandEventArgs)
  lblSelectedIndex.Text ="Selected Index is: " + " " + _
         e.Item.ItemIndex.toString()
  lblSelectedProductName.Text="You have selected " + e.CommandArgument
End Sub
```

Continued

Figure 3.75 Continued

```
</script>
<form runat="server">
<asp:DataList id="dataList1" gridlines="both" cellpadding="10"
    RepeatColumns="3" RepeatDirection="Horizontal"
    onItemCommand="showSelection"
    runat="server">
<ItemTemplate><asp:LinkButton id="myLinkBtns"
    text='<%# Container.DataItem( "ProductName" )%>'
    CommandArgument='<%# Container.DataItem( "ProductName" )%>'
    runat ="server"/>
 </ItemTemplate>
</asp:DataList>
<asp:Label id="lblSelectedProductName" runat="server" ForeColor="Brown"
    Font-Size="12pt" Font-Weight="500" Font-Name="Arial Black,Arial"/>
<br>
<asp:Label id="lblSelectedIndex" runat="server" ForeColor="Brown"
    Font-Size="12pt" Font-Weight="500" Font-Name="Arial Black,Arial"/>
</form></html>
```

Using the *DataGrid* Control

The *DataGrid* Control happens to be the most versatile and powerful member of the data-bound control family. In addition to the functionalities offered by a *DataList,* the *DataGrid* control offers sorting and paging capabilities. We can employ its *<AllowSorting>* property to dynamically sort and re-display data on selection of a column header. In case of very large data source, we can use its *<Allow Paging>* property to display a selected page of data.

Essentially, a *DataGrid* control can be used to display bound data in tabular format. Each record in the data source is displayed as a row in the grid. By default, the data grid maps each field of the data source as a column in the grid. Obviously, we may override the default value of its *AutoGenerateColumn* property to display selected columns in a particular order. In this section, we will present five examples to demonstrate various features of a *DataGrid*.

Displaying Data in a DataGrid Control Using Default Column Mapping

In this example, we will use the default layout of a data grid to display the bound data. The expected output of this example is shown in Figure 3.76. Exactly like a *Repeater*, or a *DataList* control, the *DataGrid* control also requires binding to an appropriate data source. Besides the binding chore, the specification of the data grid, particularly in this example, is extremely simple as follows:

```
<asp:DataGrid id="dataGrid1" runat="server" />
```

Figure 3.76 Displaying Data in a *DataGrid* Control

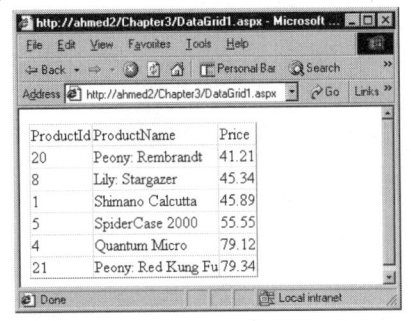

The complete listing of the application is shown in Figure 3.77. The code is also available in the accompanying CD in the file named DataGrid1.aspx.

Figure 3.77 DataGrid1.aspx

```
<!-- Chapter3/DataGrid1.aspx -->
<%@ Import Namespace="System.Data" %>
<%@ Import Namespace="System.Data.OleDb" %>
<html><head></head>
<script language="VB" Debug="true" runat="server">
Sub Page_Load(Source As Object, E As EventArgs)
    If Not IsPostBack Then
        bindListControl
    End If
End Sub
Sub bindListControl()
    Dim myConn As OleDbConnection
```

Continued

Figure 3.77 Continued

```
    Dim myOleDbAdapter As OleDbDataAdapter
    Dim connStr, sqlStr As String
    Dim myDataSet As New Dataset
    connStr="Provider=Microsoft.Jet.OLEDB.4.0;Data Source=D:\Products.mdb"
    sqlStr="SELECT  ProductId, ProductName, Price " _
         + "FROM Products WHERE Price > 40 ORDER BY Price"
    myConn= New OleDbConnection(connStr)
    myConn.Open()
    myOleDbAdapter =New OleDbDataAdapter(sqlStr,myConn)
    myOleDbAdapter.Fill(myDataSet,"dtProducts")
    DataGrid1.DataSource=myDataSet.Tables("dtProducts")
    DataGrid1.DataBind()
    myConn.Close()
  End Sub
</script>

<body bgcolor="white">
<asp:DataGrid id="dataGrid1" runat="server" />
</center></body></html>
```

Displaying Formatted Data with Styles

In this example, we will illustrate how to format and style the contents of a *DataGrid*. We will also demonstrate how to lay out the columns in a different order other than the original order of the columns in the data source. The runtime view of the application is shown in Figure 3.78. The complete code is shown in Figure 3.79. Please notice that our SQL statement for the data extraction procedure is "SELECT *ProductID, ProductName, Price* FROM *Products* WHERE *Price* > 40 ORDER BY *Price*". That means the data table *"dtProducts"* will contain three columns exactly in that order. However, the sequence of the columns displayed in the data grid is *ProductId, Price* and *ProductName*. Furthermore, we have formatted the *Price* field. We have also changed the captions in the column headings.

Figure 3.78 Displaying Formatted Data with Styles

Product ID	Description	Unit Price
20	Peony: Rembrandt	$41.21
8	Lily: Stargazer	$45.34
1	Shimano Calcutta	$45.89
5	SpiderCase 2000	$55.55
4	Quantum Micro	$79.12
21	Peony: Red Kung Fu	$79.34

First, we have to set the **AutoGenerateColumn** property to **False** to suppress the automatic generation of the columns in the **DataGrid**. The **DataGrid** has a **<Column>** collection property. Inside the **<Column>** tag, we can include the column names of the desired columns using the **<BoundColumn>** property. We do not have to necessarily include all of the columns, and we can list the columns in the desired order. The necessary formatting instructions for a column can be specified inside the **<BoundColumn>** tag. We can also include the **<ItemStyle>** property of a **<BoundColumn>** object to specify the alignment of the text. For example, we have formatted the **Price** column as follows:

```
<asp:BoundColumn HeaderText="Unit Price" DataField="price"
        DataFormatString="{0:c}">
    <ItemStyle HorizontalAlign="Right"/>
</asp:BoundColumn>
```

We have used the *<HeaderStyle>* property to define the look of the header. Finally, the *<AlternatingItemStyle>* property has been used to display the rows in alternating background colors. The complete code for this application is shown in Figure 3.79 and can be found on the CD that accompanies this book in the file named DataGrid2.aspx.

Figure 3.79 DataGrid2.aspx

```
<!-- Chapter3/DataGrid2.aspx -->
<%@ Import Namespace="System.Data" %>
<%@ Import Namespace="System.Data.OleDb" %>
<html><head></head>
<script language="VB" Debug="true" runat="server">
```

Continued

Figure 3.79 Continued

```
Sub Page_Load(Source As Object, E As EventArgs)
  If Not IsPostBack Then
    bindListControl
  End If
End Sub
Sub bindListControl()
  Dim myConn As OleDbConnection
  Dim myOleDbAdapter As OleDbDataAdapter
  Dim myDataSet As New DataSet
  Dim connStr, sqlStr As String
  connStr="Provider=Microsoft.Jet.OLEDB.4.0;Data Source=D:\Products.mdb"
  sqlStr="SELECT  ProductId, ProductName, Price " _
       + " FROM Products WHERE Price > 40 ORDER BY Price"
  myConn= New OleDbConnection(connStr)
  myConn.Open()
  myOleDbAdapter =New OleDbDataAdapter(sqlStr,myConn)
  myOleDbAdapter.Fill(myDataSet,"dtProducts")
  DataGrid1.DataSource=myDataSet.Tables("dtProducts")
  DataGrid1.DataBind()
  myConn.Close()
End Sub
</script>
<asp:DataGrid runat="server" id="DataGrid1" AutoGenerateColumns="false"
    Width="75%" BackColor="White" BorderWidth="1px" BorderStyle="Solid"
    CellPadding="2" CellSpacing="0" BorderColor="Salmon"
    Font-Name="Verdana" Font-Size="8pt">
    <HeaderStyle Font-Size="8" Font-Names="Arial" Font-Bold="True"
      BackColor="Yellow" HorizontalAlign="center">
    </HeaderStyle>
    <Columns>
      <asp:BoundColumn HeaderText="Product ID" DataField="ProductId" >
        <ItemStyle HorizontalAlign="Right"/>
      </asp:BoundColumn>
```

Continued

Figure 3.79 Continued

```
        <asp:BoundColumn HeaderText="Unit Price" DataField="price"
           DataFormatString="{0:c}">
           <ItemStyle HorizontalAlign="Right"/>
        </asp:BoundColumn>
        <asp:BoundColumn HeaderText="Description" DataField="ProductName">
           <ItemStyle Width="130"/>
        </asp:BoundColumn>
    </Columns>
    <AlternatingItemStyle BackColor="Beige"/>
</asp:DataGrid>
</center></body></html>
```

Sorting DataGrid

Yes, on click of any of the column headers, we can dynamically sort the records of a data grid. However, please bear in mind that the *DataGrid* itself does not provide the sorting algorithm. It rather provides a mechanism to enable us to call a sorting routine. Fortunately, in our example (as shown in Figure 3.80), we do not need to implement a sorting algorithm ourselves. We have used the SQL ORDER BY clause to automatically sort the retrieved data.

Figure 3.80 Sorting Data in a *DataGrid* Control

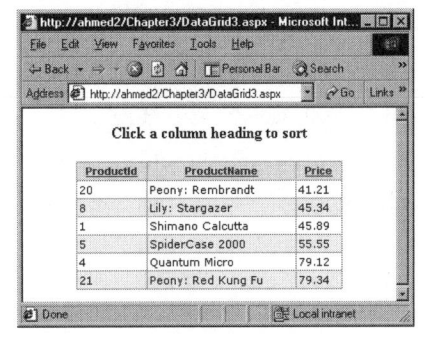

The code for this application is shown in Figure 3.81. The code is also available on the CD that accompanies this book in the file named DataGrid3.aspx. On the click event of a column header, our intention is to exploit the SQL's ORDER BY clause to perform the sorting. This forces us to recreate the data set and subsequently to rebind the data grid. Please observe that we have designed the *bindDataGrid* routine slightly differently from the similar procedures in our previous examples. We included an optional parameter to this procedure so that we can pass a column name when we call this routine. This subprocedure will then extract the data from the database in the ascending order of the passed column. In the *DataGrid* tag, we have specified its *AllowSorting* property to be *true*. We have also set its *OnSortCommand* to a subprocedure named *sortGrid*. On the click event of any of the column header, the *sortGrid* subprocedure will be called.

Figure 3.81 DataGrid3.aspx

```
<!-- Chapter3/DataGrid3.aspx -->
<%@ Page Language="VB" Debug="true" %>
<%@ Import Namespace="System.Data" %>
<%@ Import Namespace="System.Data.OleDb" %>
<script language="VB" Debug="true" runat="server">
Sub Page_Load(Source As Object, E As EventArgs)
    If Not IsPostBack Then
        bindDataGrid
    End If
End Sub
Sub bindDataGrid(Optional sortField As String="ProductId")
    Dim myConn As OleDbConnection
    Dim myOleDbAdapter As OleDbDataAdapter
    Dim connStr, sqlStr As String
    Dim myDataSet As New Dataset
    connStr="Provider=Microsoft.Jet.OLEDB.4.0;Data Source=D:\Products.mdb"
        sqlStr="SELECT  ProductId, ProductName, Price " _
            +   " FROM Products WHERE Price > 40 ORDER BY " +
sortField
    myConn= New OleDbConnection(connStr)
    myConn.Open()
    myOleDbAdapter =New OleDbDataAdapter(sqlStr,myConn)
    myOleDbAdapter.Fill(myDataSet,"dtProducts")
    dataGrid1.DataSource=myDataSet.Tables("dtProducts")
    dataGrid1.DataBind()
```

Continued

Figure 3.81 Continued

```
  myConn.Close()
End Sub
Sub sortGrid(s As Object, e As DataGridSortCommandEventArgs)
    bindDataGrid(e.sortExpression)
End Sub
</script>
<html><head></head><body><form runat="server"><center>
<h4>Click a column heading to sort</h4>
<asp:DataGrid runat="server" id="dataGrid1"
    AutoGenerateColumns="true"
    AllowSorting="true"
    OnSortCommand="sortGrid"
    Width="75%"
    BackColor="White"
    BorderWidth="1px" BorderStyle="Solid"
    CellPadding="2" CellSpacing="0"
    BorderColor="Salmon"
    Font-Name="Verdana" Font-Size="8pt">
    <HeaderStyle Font-Size="8" Font-Names="Arial"
          Font-Bold="True" BackColor="Yellow"
          HorizontalAlign="center">
    </HeaderStyle>
    <AlternatingItemStyle BackColor="Beige"/>
</asp:DataGrid>
</center></form></body></html>
```

> **NOTE**
>
> If needed, we may also use the *Sort* method of a *DataView* object to sort the columns of the underlying data table. In this case we may use the following types of code:
>
> ```
> Dim myDataView As DataView
>     myDataView=myDataSet.Tables("dtProducts").DefaultView
> ```

```
myDataView.Sort=sortField
dataGrid1.DataSource=myDataView
dataGrid1.DataBind()
```

Providing Paging in *DataGrid*

In case of a large data table, we may want to provide paging capability to the user. We may implement the paging functionality in many different ways. In this context, we will present two examples. First, we will illustrate how to provide a pair of VCR style icons to enable the user to navigate to the previous or the next page of the data displayed in a data grid. Later, we will present an example that will show how to enable the user to navigate to a particular desired page.

Using Previous Page and Next Page Icons

The run-time view of this application is shown Figure 3.82. To accomplish the paging, we have set the following properties of the data grid:

- AllowPaging="true"
- PageSize="5"
- PagerStyle-HorizontalAlign="Center"
- OnPageIndexChanged="*doPaging*"

Figure 3.82 Using VCR Style Icons for Page Navigation

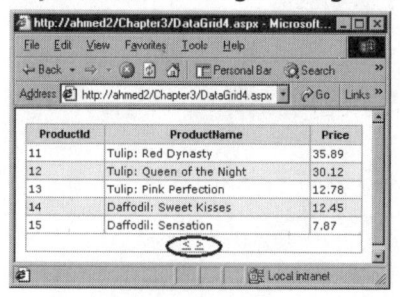

The data grid automatically generates the previous page and next page icons. When any one of these icons is clicked, the *doPaging* subprocedure is triggered. The click event passes a *DataGridPageChangedEventArgs* parameter to the subprocedure. In the *doPaging* procedure we have set the *currentPageIndex* property of the data grid to the *newPageIndex* property of this parameter. Then we issued a call to the *bindDataGrid* procedure as shown in the following code excerpt. The complete code for this application is shown in Figure 3.83 and can be found on the CD that accompanies this book in the file named DataGrid4.aspx.

```
Sub doPaging(s As Object, e As DataGridPageChangedEventArgs)
    dataGrid1.CurrentPageIndex=e.NewPageIndex
    bindDataGrid
End Sub
```

Figure 3.83 DataGrid4.aspx

```
<!-- Chapter3/DataGrid4.aspx -->
<%@ Page Language="VB" Debug="true" %>
<%@ Import Namespace="System.Data" %>
<%@ Import Namespace="System.Data.OleDb" %>
<script language="VB" Debug="true" runat="server">
Sub Page_Load(Source As Object, E As EventArgs)
  If Not IsPostBack Then
        bindDataGrid
  End If
End Sub
Sub bindDataGrid
    Dim myConn As OleDbConnection
    Dim myOleDbAdapter As OleDbDataAdapter
    Dim connStr, sqlStr As String
    Dim myDataSet As New Dataset
    connStr="Provider=Microsoft.Jet.OLEDB.4.0; " _
            + "Data Source=D:\Products.mdb"
    sqlStr="SELECT  ProductId, ProductName, Price " _
            + "FROM Products ORDER BY ProductId"
    myConn= New OleDbConnection(connStr)
    myConn.Open()
    myOleDbAdapter=New OleDbDataAdapter(sqlStr,myConn)
    myOleDbAdapter.Fill(myDataSet,"dtProducts")
    dataGrid1.DataSource=myDataSet.Tables("dtProducts")
    dataGrid1.DataBind()
    myConn.Close()
```

Continued

Figure 3.83 Continued

```
End Sub
Sub doPaging(s As Object, e As DataGridPageChangedEventArgs)
    dataGrid1.CurrentPageIndex=e.NewPageIndex
    bindDataGrid
End Sub
</script>
<html><head></head><form runat="server">
<asp:DataGrid runat="server" id="dataGrid1" AutoGenerateColumns="true"
   AllowPaging="true" PageSize="5" PagerStyle-HorizontalAlign="Center"
   OnPageIndexChanged="doPaging" BackColor="White" BorderWidth="1px"
   BorderStyle="Solid" Width="100%" BorderColor="Salmon"
   CellPadding="2" CellSpacing="0" Font-Name="Verdana" Font-Size="8pt">
   <HeaderStyle Font-Size="8" Font-Names="Arial" Font-Bold="True"
        BackColor="Yellow" HorizontalAlign="center">
   </HeaderStyle>
   <AlternatingItemStyle BackColor="Beige"/>
</asp:DataGrid>
</center></form></html>
```

> **NOTE**
>
> Every time we navigate to a different page, the entire data table is populated again, even we if are viewing only five records. Thus, for a very large data table, the speed of execution will slow down significantly. In that case, an alternative technique would involve keeping track of the page numbers programmatically. That can be accomplished by operating on the underlying data table's rows in the cache. We may also employ a *Parameterized Stored Procedure* to alleviate this problem.

Navigating to a Selected Page

In our previous example, we could only move to the previous or next page. We can sure do better than that! We can display a list of page numbers, and the user can click any one of these page numbers to move to the desired page. In this example we will illustrate how to accomplish this objective. The run-time view of the application is shown in Figure 3.84. The code for the application is shown in Figure 3.85 and can be found on the CD that accompanies this book in the file named DataGrid5.aspx. There is actually nothing much new in the code, except that we have set several paging related properties as follows:

```
AllowPaging="true" PageSize="5" PagerStyle-Mode="NumericPages"
    PagerStyle-HorizontalAlign="Center" OnPageIndexChanged="doPaging"
```

Figure 3.84 Paging in a *DataGrid* Control

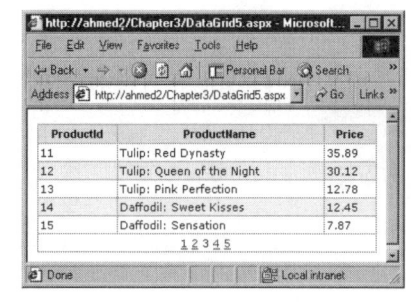

Figure 3.85 DataGrid5.aspx

```
<!-- Chapter3/DataGrid5.aspx -->
<%@ Page Language="VB" Debug="true" %>
<%@ Import Namespace="System.Data" %>
<%@ Import Namespace="System.Data.OleDb" %>
<script language="VB" Debug="true" runat="server">
Sub Page_Load(Source As Object, E As EventArgs)
 If Not IsPostBack Then
        bindDataGrid
 End If
End Sub
Sub bindDataGrid
 Dim myConn As OleDbConnection
 Dim myOleDbAdapter As OleDbDataAdapter
 Dim connStr, sqlStr As String
 Dim myDataSet As New Dataset
 connStr="Provider=Microsoft.Jet.OLEDB.4.0; " _
```

Continued

Figure 3.85 Continued

```
        + "Data Source=D:\Products.mdb"
 sqlStr="SELECT  ProductId, ProductName, Price " _
        + "FROM Products ORDER BY ProductId"
 myConn= New OleDbConnection(connStr)
 myConn.Open()
 myOleDbAdapter =New OleDbDataAdapter(sqlStr,myConn)
 myOleDbAdapter.Fill(myDataSet,"dtProducts")
 dataGrid1.DataSource=myDataSet.Tables("dtProducts")
 dataGrid1.DataBind()
 myConn.Close()
End Sub
Sub doPaging(s As Object, e As DataGridPageChangedEventArgs)
   dataGrid1.CurrentPageIndex=e.NewPageIndex
   bindDataGrid
End Sub
</script>
<html><head></head><form runat="server">
<asp:DataGrid runat="server" id="dataGrid1" AutoGenerateColumns="true"
    AllowPaging="true" PageSize="5" PagerStyle-Mode="NumericPages"
    PagerStyle-HorizontalAlign="Center" OnPageIndexChanged="doPaging"
     BackColor="White" BorderWidth="1px" BorderStyle="Solid"
     Width="100%" BorderColor="Salmon" CellPadding="2" CellSpacing="0"
     Font-Name="Verdana" Font-Size="8pt">
   <HeaderStyle Font-Size="8" Font-Names="Arial" Font-Bold="True"
     BackColor="Yellow" HorizontalAlign="center">
   </HeaderStyle>
   <AlternatingItemStyle BackColor="Beige"/>
</asp:DataGrid>
</center></form></html>
```

Providing Data Editing Capability in a *DataGrid* Control

We can enable the user to edit data in a *DataGrid* or *DataList* control. Typically, we accomplish this by employing the *OnEditCommand, OnCancelCommand,* and *OnUpdateCommand* properties. If needed, we can also use the *OnDeleteCommand* property of a *DataGrid* control to allow deletion of a selected record. The *OnDeleteCommand* property is not available in a *DataList*. In this example, we will illustrate how to allow data editing capability to the user. The run-time view of the application is shown in Figure 3.86.

Figure 3.86 Editing Data in a *DataGrid* Control

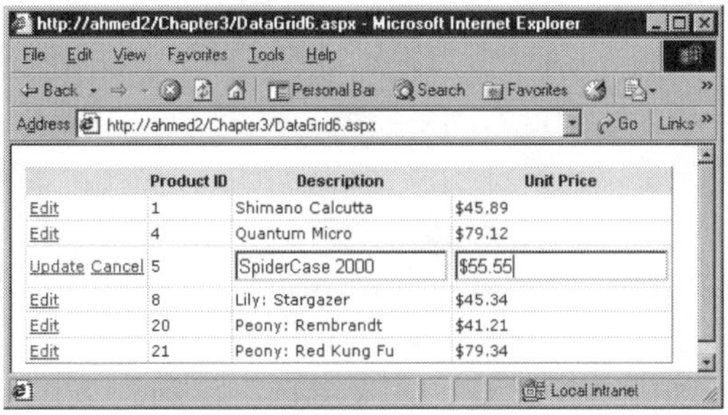

The code for this application is shown in Figure 3.87. The code is also available in the CD that accompanies this book in the file named DataGrid6.aspx. We have a number of major issues to cover here. First, we have used four additional properties of the *DataGrid* as shown in the following code excerpt:

```
DataKeyField="ProductId"  OnEditCommand="setEditMode"
OnCancelCommand="cancelEdit"  OnUpdateCommand="updateDataBase"
```

As you can see from the previous code, we have set the *OnEditCommand* property to a subprocedure named *setEditMode*. When we specify such a property, the data grid automatically places a *ButtonList* control captioned as "Edit" in the first column of the displayed table. On the click of this **ButtonList**, the control triggers the *OnEditCommandEvent* and passes a *DataGridCommandEventArgs* parameter to the wired-up event procedure (in this case, to the *setEditMode* procedure). In our *setEditMode* subprocedure, we have simply placed the clicked row in the edit mode as follows:

```
Sub setEditMode(s As Object, e As DataGridCommandEventArgs)
    dataGrid1.EditItemIndex= e.Item.ItemIndex
```

158   Chapter 3 • ASP Server Controls

```
bindDataGrid
End Sub
```

When the **Edit** button is clicked, the data grid also displays the **Update** and **Cancel** buttons automatically. Furthermore, the editable columns in the clicked row (item) are replaced with textboxes. The user can enter appropriate data in these textboxes and subsequently click the **Update** or **Cancel** button.

Second, on the click event of the **Update** button, we need to update the database. But how would we know which record in the database to update? This is why we have used the *DataKeyField* property (in the *DataGrid* tag) to identify the *ProductId* field as the key field. Our primary objective is to prepare an appropriate SQL Update statement like UPDATE *Products* SET *ProductName='givenName'*, Price='*givenPrice'* WHERE ProductID='*selectedProductId'*. When the *Update* procedure is triggered, it is passed with a *DataGridCommandEnentArgs*-type parameter. We can retrieve the key value of the clicked row as *dataGrid1.EditItemIndex= e.Item.ItemIndex*.

Getting the value of the key field is not enough. We will also have to know the new values of the other edited columns. The desired values can be retrieved using the *DataGridCommandEventArgs,* too. For example, the *ProductName* field happens to be the second cell of the selected row. The *Controls(0)* of a given *Cell* of an *Item* object contains the value. But the parameter was passed to the routine as an object. Thus, we need to cast the *Controls(0)* to a textbox type, so that we can extract its *Text* data. The following statement will capture the new data in the ProductName column and will place it in a string varianble. Once we have done all these things, it is just a matter of building the necessary SQL string for the appropriate UPDATE query.

```
strPName=(CType(e.Item.Cells(2).Controls(0), Textbox)).Text
```

An UPDATE query is typically executed by using the *ExecuteNonQuery* method of a *Command* object (to be learned in the database chapter). This is what we did here. Finally, we need to set the edit-mode off. We have done this with the *dataGrid1.EditItemIndex=−1* statement. Obviously, we do not want the user to edit the primary key. Therefore, we have set the *ReadOnly* property of the *ProductID* column to *True*.

Figure 3.87 Editing in *DataGrid* (DataGrid6.aspx)

```
<!— Chapter3/DataGrid6.aspx —>
<%@ Import Namespace="System.Data" %>
```

Continued

Figure 3.87 Continued

```
<%@ Import Namespace="System.Data.OleDb" %>
<script language="VB" Debug="true" runat="server">
Sub Page_Load(Source As Object, E As EventArgs)
  If Not IsPostBack Then
       bindDataGrid
  End If
End Sub
Sub bindDataGrid
  Dim myConn As OleDbConnection
  Dim myOleDbAdapter As OleDbDataAdapter
  Dim connStr, sqlStr As String
  Dim myDataSet As New Dataset
  connStr="Provider=Microsoft.Jet.OLEDB.4.0; Data Source=D:\Products.mdb"
  sqlStr="SELECT  ProductId, ProductName, Price " _
       + " FROM Products WHERE Price > 40 ORDER BY ProductId"
  myConn= New OleDbConnection(connStr)
  myConn.Open()
  myOleDbAdapter =New OleDbDataAdapter(sqlStr,myConn)
  myOleDbAdapter.Fill(myDataSet,"dtProducts")
  dataGrid1.DataSource=myDataSet.Tables("dtProducts")
  dataGrid1.DataBind()
  myConn.Close()
End Sub
Sub setEditMode(s As Object, e As DataGridCommandEventArgs)
   dataGrid1.EditItemIndex= e.Item.ItemIndex
   bindDataGrid
End Sub
Sub cancelEdit(s As Object, e As DataGridCommandEventArgs)
   dataGrid1.EditItemIndex=-1
   bindDataGrid
End Sub
Sub updateDatabase(s as Object, e As DataGridCommandEventArgs)
   Dim myConn As OleDbConnection
```

Continued

Figure 3.87 Continued

```
    Dim connStr, sqlStr, strPName  As String
    Dim myUpdateCommand As OleDbCommand
    Dim intPid As Integer
    Dim dblPrice As Double
    ' Get the key-value of the clicked row
    intPid=dataGrid1.DataKeys.Item(e.Item.ItemIndex)
    ' Get the new value of ProductName
    strPName=(CType(e.Item.Cells(2).Controls(0), Textbox)).Text
    ' Get the new value of Price
    dblPrice=cDbl((CType(e.Item.Cells(3).Controls(0), Textbox)).Text)
    ' Build the SQL
    sqlStr="UPDATE Products SET ProductName=' " + strPName _
         + " ', Price="  + dblPrice.ToString _
         + " WHERE ProductID=" + intPid.ToString
    connStr="Provider=Microsoft.Jet.OLEDB.4.0;Data Source=D:\Products.mdb"
    myConn= New OleDbConnection(connStr)
    myConn.Open()
    myUpdateCommand=New OleDbCommand(sqlStr, myConn)
    ' Execute the Update SQL statement
    myUpdateCommand.ExecuteNonQuery
    myConn.Close()
    dataGrid1.EditItemIndex=-1
    BindDataGrid
End Sub
</script>
<html><head></head><form runat="server">
<asp:DataGrid id="dataGrid1" AutoGenerateColumns="False"
  DataKeyField="ProductId" OnEditCommand="setEditMode"
  OnCancelCommand="cancelEdit" OnUpdateCommand="updateDataBase"
  CellPadding="2" Font-Name="Verdana" Font-Size="8pt" runat="server">
  <HeaderStyle Font-Size="8" Font-Names="Arial" Font-Bold="True"
     BackColor="Yellow" HorizontalAlign="center"></HeaderStyle>
  <Columns>
```

Continued

Figure 3.87 Continued

```
    <asp:EditCommandColumn EditText="Edit"
        UpdateText="Update" CancelText="Cancel">
    </asp:EditCommandColumn>
    <asp:BoundColumn HeaderText="Product ID" DataField="ProductId"
        ReadOnly="True" />
    <asp:BoundColumn HeaderText="Description" DataField="ProductName"/>
    <asp:BoundColumn HeaderText="Unit Price" DataField="price"
        DataFormatString="{0:c}" />
  </Columns>
</asp:DataGrid></form></html>
```

Creating Custom ASP Server User Controls

We may develop our own server controls by extending an existing control or a group of controls to provide additional functionalities. As stated earlier, there are two versions of custom controls: *Web User Controls* and *Web Custom Controls*. The Web User Controls are easy to develop and these are typically stored as *ascx* files. The Web Custom Controls require in-depth knowledge of Object Oriented Programming and CLR. These are stored in compiled form as assemblies.

A user control, if developed correctly, functions like any other controls. It can be placed inside any other host ASP page (often called the "*Consumer*" of a control). In this section we will provide two examples on how to develop and use a *Web User Control*. In the first example, we will develop a very simple user control. In the second example, we will develop a user control that will expose some of its properties to its host page class.

Creating a Simple Web User Control

Suppose that we want to build the control as shown in Figure 3.88. If a host page embeds this control, it will automatically display the current time in the server's time zone. Once we build this control, we can use it in any subsequent page. We will provide a step-by-step procedure to build this control.

Chapter 3 • ASP Server Controls

Figure 3.88 A Sample User Control

> The time in server land is 03:30:40

1. Develop the necessary code for the control. The code for this example is shown in Figure 3.89 and can be found on the CD that accompanies this book in the file named TimeUserControl.ascx. The code is essentially very simple. We are using use a *<table>* tag with an embedded *<asp:Label>* control. In the *Page_Load* event, we will display the current time in the label.

Figure 3.89 The Code for the User Control (TimeUserControl.ascx)

```
<!— Chapter3/TimeUserControl.ascx —>
<table border ="5" cellpadding="5" rules="none"
    bgcolor="lightyellow"  bordercolor="orange">
 <tr valign="middle"><td><h3>The time in server land is</h3></td>
    <td><h3><asp:Label id="lblDateTime"  runat="server"/></h3></td>
 </tr>
</table>
<script Language="vb" runat ="server">
Sub Page_Load(s As Object, e As EventArgs)
   If Not Page.IsPostBack Then
        ' lblDateTime.Text=System.DateTime.Now.ToLongTimeString()
        lblDateTime.Text=Format(Now,"hh:mm:ss")
   End If
End Sub
</script>
```

2. Save the code with an extension of *.ascx in your virtual directory.
3. Test the User Control: A control cannot be tested unless it is hosted in an ASPX page. Thus, start a new page, and enter the code shown in Figure 3.90. The code can be found on the CD that accompanies this book in the file named TestTimeUserCntrol1.aspx. First, a host page needs to register a user control using the *Register* directive. The *Register* directive has three major attributes. We provide a prefix in the *tagprefix*

attribute (it can be any prefix of your choice). Then we need to provide a name of the registered control in the *tagname* attribute. Finally, we must also specify the name of the source code (of the .ascx file) using the *Src* attribute. Can you believe that you are done? Go ahead and open the page in your browser. You will see a page very similar to the one shown in Figure 3.91.

Figure 3.90 Testing the User Control (TestTimeUserCntrol1.aspx)

```
<!- Chapter3/TestTimeUserControl1.aspx ->
<%@ Register tagprefix ="utoledo" tagname="Time"
     Src="TimeUserControl.ascx" %>
<html><head></head><form><body>
<b>I am a host page. Suppose that I don't know how to show the time.
Hence, I will use the TimeUserControl. I am using an instance of the
    TimeUserControl below:<p>
<utoledo:Time runat="server" /><br/>
Now I can do my other work... <b/>
</body></form></html>
```

Figure 3.91 Using a User Control

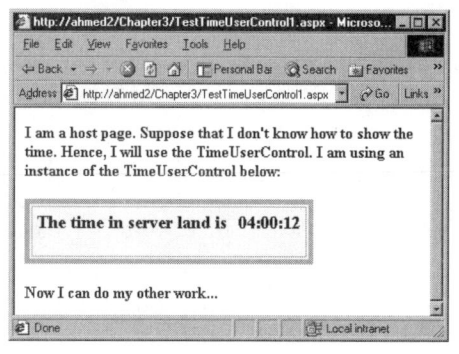

Exposing Properties of a User Control

Obviously, the control developed in our previous example does not do much more than display the current time. If judiciously designed, a user control can actually play an extremely crucial role in systems development practice. We can develop user controls to encapsulate standard business processes. A user control is

164   Chapter 3 • ASP Server Controls

essentially a visual component (almost like ActiveX controls and visual JavaBeans), except that it is much easier to develop. Once we develop the component, it can be plugged in many applications, thereby making it easy for the front-end application developers. More importantly, it provides the mechanism to implement standard business processes and maintain their integrity.

We will illustrate this concept with an example. In this example, we will encapsulate a simple business rule for computing gross wage. The interesting feature of this control is that it will pass the result of its computation to the host page for further processing. It will also accept a title from the host page and display it within itself. That means we will provide two-way communication between the control and the host page. The run-time view of the control when hosted in a page is shown in Figure 3.92.

Figure 3.92 Exposing Properties of a User Control

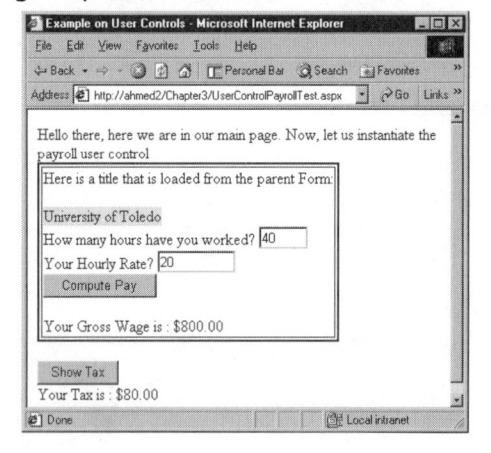

Developing the Payroll User Control

The code for this user control is shown in Figure 3.93 and can be found on the CD that accompanies this book in the file named UserControlPayroll.ascx. As can be observed in the listing, we have provided number of labels, two textboxes, and a button in this user control. These are named *lblTitle, txtH, txtR,* and *cmdCompute*. In the script, we have provided two properties: *Title* and *grossWage*. The *grossWage* property is defined as *ReadOnly,* so the host page will not be able to change its value. The *Title* property simply returns the content of the *lblTitle*. However, the host page will be able to set its value during the run-time.

Figure 3.93 UserControlPayroll.ascx

```
<!-- AspNet/UserControls/UserControlPayroll.ascx -->
<table border='2' bordercolor="blue"><tr><td>
Here is a title that is loaded from the parent Form: <br/>
<asp:Label id="lblTitle" backcolor="yellow" Height=15 runat="server"/>
    <br>How many hours have you worked?
<asp:TextBox id="txtH" rows="1 " width="50"  runat="server"/></br>
Your Hourly Rate? <asp:TextBox id="txtR" rows="1" width="80"
    runat="server"/><br>
<asp:Button id="btnCompute" runat="server" text="Compute Pay"
    onclick="computePay"/>
<p/><asp:Label id="lblPayMsg" runat="server"/>
<asp:Label id="lblPay" runat="server"/><br></tr></td></table>
<script language=vb runat="server">
Public Property  Title() As String
  Set
    lblTitle.Text=value
  End Set
  Get
    return lblTitle.Text
  End Get
End Property
Private grWage As Single
Public ReadOnly Property grossWage() As Single
  Get
    return cSng(lblPay.Text)
  End Get
End Property
Protected Sub computePay (Sender As Object, E As EventArgs)
  Dim h, r, g As Single
  h=CSng(txtH.Text)
  r=CSng(txtR.Text)
  lblPayMsg.Text="Your Gross Wage is : "
  g=h * r
```

Continued

Figure 3.93 Continued

```
    lblPay.Text=FormatCurrency(g)
    grWage=g
End Sub
</script>
```

Consuming the Payroll User Control

We have tested the previous user custom control in a page named *UserControlPayrollTest.aspx*. The code for this page is shown in Figure 3.94, and can be found on the CD that accompanies this book in the file named UserControlPayrollTest.aspx. First, we have registered the user control with a *tagprefix* of *userCtrlPayroll* and a *tagname* of *payroll*. We inserted one of these controls in our page using the *runat="server"* attribute. This will ensure that the controls in the user control persist during *postbacks*. We have set the *Title* property of the control to "The University of Toledo" as follows:

```
<usrCtrlPayroll:payroll id="usrPayCtrl" runat="server"
    Title="University of Toledo"/><br>
```

After the user enters the data in the user control, he or she will click the **Compute Pay** button inside the user control. The user control will apply its own business logic (*comptePay* procedure) to compute the gross wage. As a consumer of the user control, we do not need to know the details of how the gross wage is being computed. However, we need its value to compute appropriate tax in our own application (page). Fortunately, the user control has exposed the value of the gross wage as a property. Thus, we have developed the following code to compute the value of tax:

```
Sub computeTax (s As Object, e As EventArgs)
    Dim t, gWage As Single
    gWage=usrPayCtrl.grossWage()
    t=gWage * 0.10
    --- ---
End Sub
```

In this example, we have demonstrated how to develop a user control and expose its properties. We have maintained the states of the properties of the user control. This was accomplished by exploiting the controls embedded in the custom control and by using the *runat="server"* attribute. In an advanced custom control, we may avoid this trait by maintaining the states of the variables using objects similar to the old ActiveX Controls *"PropertyBags"*. However, that topic is not within the bounds of this chapter.

Figure 3.94 Consuming the Payroll User Control (UserControlPayrollTest.aspx)

```
<!-- Chapter3\UserControlPayrollTest.aspx -->
<!-- Uses the UserControlPayroll.ascx -->
<%@ Register tagprefix="usrCtrlPayroll" Tagname="payroll"
    src="UserControlPayroll.ascx" %>
<html><head</head><title>Example on User Controls</title>
<body><form runat="server">
Hello there, here we are in our main page.
Now, let us instantaite the payroll user control <br>
<usrCtrlPayroll:payroll id="usrPayCtrl" runat="server"
                Title="University of Toledo"/><br>
<asp:Button id="btnShowTax" runat="server" text="Show Tax"
    onclick="computeTax" />
<br><asp:Label id="lblTaxMsg" runat="server"/>
<asp:Label id="lblTax" runat="server"/><br>
</form></body></html>

<script language=vb runat="server">
  Sub computeTax (s As Object, e As EventArgs)
    Dim t, gWage As Single
    gWage=usrPayCtrl.grossWage()
    t=gWage * 0.10
    lblTaxMsg.Text="Your Tax  is : "
    lblTax.Text=FormatCurrency(t)
  End Sub
</script>
```

Summary

This chapter has been about ASP.NET Web Controls. The ASP.NET controls are placed in Web pages. Thus, we cannot isolate them and discuss them without knowing how the ASP.NET Engine works, and how it maintains the states of the server controls. Hence, we presented brief overviews of various concepts like HTML Forms, server-side processing, and in-page coding vs. code-behind. We have also given a step-wise procedure to develop a simple ASP.NET project using VS.NET.

We have essentially covered almost all of the HTML server and Web server controls in this chapter. We have also introduced you to a very promising technology named *Custom User Control*. We have not presented two special purpose controls, namely the *Calendar* and the *AdRotator* controls in this chapter. Detail examples of these controls are available in plenty of sources (including the SDK documentations). After you practice the examples presented in this chapter, you will not have much difficulties in tackling these two controls.

The ASP.NET server controls are here to stay. They provide exceptional functionalities and abilities to develop server-side codes just like the VB 6 codes we used to develop in the old days. The bound controls make it easy for us to develop powerful data-oriented applications on the Web very fast. We have illustrated many of these controls with simple examples. However, each of these controls has many properties and events beyond the materials presented in this chapter. A complete book can be written on data-bound list controls, and still the richness of these controls would not be covered in full. The details of the beauties and the beasts behind these controls are anxiously waiting for you in the SDK documentation. After you complete this chapter, be sure to go and grab them from the SDK documentation! Pretty soon, you will be one of the most successful ASP.NET developers.

Solutions Fast Track

Major Features of ASP.NET Server Controls

- ☑ There are four types of ASP.NET server controls: *HTML Server Controls, Web Server Controls, Validation Controls,* and *Custom Controls*. HTML server controls can be used to run server-side code against conventional HTML controls. The Web server controls follow standard object-oriented programming model and provide rich functionalities. Custom controls enable users to develop their own controls. The Validation controls allow data validation.

- HTML uses HTTP protocol. HTTP is state-less.
- The client can submit data to the server using the *GET* or *POST* method. The *GET* method transmits the data by augmenting the data in the URL. The *POST* method packages the data inside the BODY of a HTTP massage.

Server-Side Processing in ASP.NET

- When a server receives a request for a page, it retrieves the page from the disk and gives it to the ASP Engine. The ASP Engine compiles the page and creates a page class. Subsequently, the class is instantiated and executed, thereby providing a *Response* object. The server sends this *Response* object back to the client.
- ASP.NET server controls are state-full. The system maintains the states of the controls automatically. All server controls are typically defined with a *runat="server"* attribute.
- When a user enters data and submits a form back to the server, it is known as *PostBack*. On a *PostBack,* the server reloads the form, and the events generated at the client-side are handled at the server. In conventional HTML, typically a **Submit** button is used to submit data from the client to the server. However, many Web server controls can also trigger *PostBacks*.
- When a page is loaded and executed, the sequence of events are: *Page_Init, Page_Load, Change* events, *Action* events, and finally the *Page_Unload*.

Code-Behind versus In-Page Coding

- In an ASP page, scripts and HTML tags are usually intermixed. This is known as In-Page Coding. ASP.NET pages can be developed using this procedure. However, ASP.NET provides an alternative methodology to develop a page. It enables separation of HTML tags (presentation) from the processing logic (code). This is known as *Code-Behind*. It is essentially very similar to the VB development model.

- ☑ VS.NET follows *Code-Behind* methodology for ASP.NET development.

Using HTML Server Controls

- ☑ HTML controls are not programmable at the server-side. Their values do not persist. The HTML server controls have been developed both of these problems. The ASP Engine maps the HTML server controls to HTML controls before a page is sent to the client.

- ☑ Certain HTML server controls can be bound to a data source. For example, if a list box is bound to a data source, it is automatically loaded with the data in the data source. This is known as data binding.

- ☑ If necessary, we can mix HTML server controls and Web server controls in the same page.

Using ASP.NET Web Controls

- ☑ These controls are similar to the HTML server controls; however, these controls have a richer and more consistent object model.

- ☑ Some of the new and powerful Web controls are: *Repeater, DataList,* and *DataGrid.* These are also known as *Data-Bound Templated* control. These controls allow displaying data from a data source almost automatically. The *DataGrid* and *DataList* controls allow data selection and data editing.

- ☑ A validation control enables us to validate an input and display an error message if necessary.

- ☑ There are six Validation Controls: *RequiredFieldValidator, RangeValidator, CompareValidator, RegularExpressionValidator, CustomValidator,* and *ValidationSummary.*

- ☑ The Validation controls automatically generates client-side and server-side validation code. If necessary, you can also develop custom validation functions.

Creating Custom ASP Server User Controls

- ☑ Custom controls are similar to ActiveX controls, except that these are much easier to develop.

- ☑ There are two types of custom controls: *Web User Controls* and *Web Custom Controls*.
- ☑ A custom control can be used exactly like any other Web server controls.

Frequently Asked Questions

The following Frequently Asked Questions, answered by the authors of this book, are designed to both measure your understanding of the concepts presented in this chapter and to assist you with real-life implementation of these concepts. To have your questions about this chapter answered by the author, browse to **www.syngress.com/solutions** and click on the **"Ask the Author"** form.

Q: How much will ASP syntax change during the transition from Beta 2 to the final version?

A: Microsoft has "predicted" that there will be no syntactical changes. This should be good news to developers who were faced with some confusion when certain classes were dropped, added, and modified during the last transition from Beta 1 to Beta 2.

Q: What happens to the existing ASP applications when the .Net Beta 2 SDK is installed and .aspx files enter the picture?

A: Nothing! The good news is that files extensions used by ASP (.asp, .asa, etc.) are completely separate from the ones used by ASP.NET (.aspx, .asax, .ascx, etc.) and do not override each other even in the same directory. The bad news is that settings made in the global.asa file are not accessible to those made in the *global.asax* file, and therefore you have to redo some setting to get some consistency.

Q: Are paths such as HREFs in user controls relative to the user control or to the host page that they are in?

A: The paths are relative to the user control and not to the host page. This makes it much easier for the user control to find things irrespective of what directory the calling .aspx file is. Another interesting feature in paths is that you can use the "~" to represent the application root to shortcut the use of the Request Application path. This really makes the building of large Web sites more manageable.

Chapter 4

Configuring ASP.NET

Solutions in this chapter:

- **Overview of ASP.NET Configuration**
- **Uses for a Configuration File**
- **Anatomy of a Configuration File**

☑ Summary

☑ Solutions Fast Track

☑ Frequently Asked Questions

Introduction

As applications became more complex and started offering more configurable features, a natural progression was to use configuration files to store these values. It has since become a required feature of any application to support the use of configuration files to control various aspects of itself and to avoid hard-coding of variable data. Most Windows applications support this with the use of *.ini* files or entries in the Windows registry. ASP.NET includes this support by the use of machine.config and web.config files. These files are standard text files written using XML formatting and can be edited with any text editor such as Notepad or an XML parser. With the use of these files, ASP.NET provides the ability to modify many standard settings used within Web applications as well as allowing the creation of custom settings.

The configuration of a given Web application is computed in a hierarchical manner when the application is first accessed and then cached to speed up future references to the configuration. ASP.NET then monitors the configuration files for any changes, and if a change is detected, the cached configuration is flushed and recomputed.

In this chapter, we will go over the way ASP.NET uses its configuration files and how we can best take advantage of this feature. We will also discuss the application, system, and security aspects of the configuration files and work through the creation of a web.config file.

Overview of ASP.NET Configuration

The configuration files used by ASP.NET are processed in a hierarchical manner. This means that the files located at a higher level of the hierarchy can override the options set within each file. An exception to this rule is provided to allow for locking down some settings. This exception uses the *allowOverride* attribute and the <location> tag to lock down the settings. The use of this option is explained in the "Anatomy of a Configuration File" section later in this chapter.

The machine.config file is used on a per-server basis and controls the base configuration of ASP.NET on the system. The machine.config is located in the *C:\winnt\Microsoft.NET\Framework\version\CONFIG* directory and is the highest-level configuration file. The web.config file can be located in your root application directory as well as in any subdirectories below it in order to set Web application specific configuration. If a value is not explicitly defined in a lower level configuration file and is defined in a higher-level file, the value will be inherited from the higher level configuration file. This process is outlined in Figure 4.1.

Figure 4.1 Configuration Inheritance

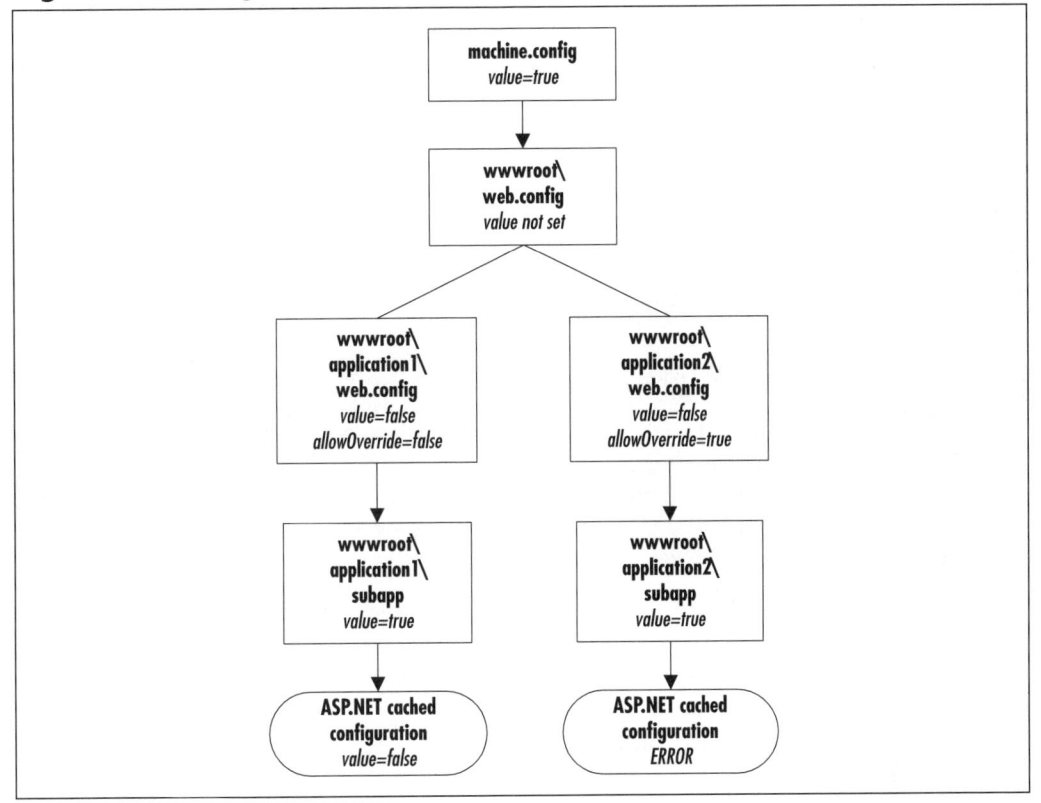

```
                    machine.config
                     value=true
                          │
                          ▼
                      wwwroot\
                      web.config
                     value not set
                     ╱          ╲
                    ╱            ╲
         wwwroot\                  wwwroot\
        application1\            application2\
          web.config               web.config
          value=false              value=false
       allowOverride=false      allowOverride=true
              │                        │
              ▼                        ▼
          wwwroot\                 wwwroot\
        application1\            application2\
           subapp                   subapp
         value=true               value=true
              │                        │
              ▼                        ▼
       ( ASP.NET cached )       ( ASP.NET cached )
       ( configuration  )       ( configuration  )
       (  value=false   )       (     ERROR      )
```

Figure 4.1 illustrates several important points regarding ASP.NET's use of configuration files. Let's walk through what this illustration shows.

First, the order in which the configuration files are processed is shown. The machine.config file is processed first. Any values specified within the machine .config file are inherited throughout every ASP.NET application on your Web server. The web.config file in each consecutive subdirectory is then processed with each lower-level file overriding the configuration files above it unless otherwise instructed.

Secondly, if a value is not explicitly defined in a lower-level configuration file, the value is inherited from the higher-level file. This is a very important feature to keep in mind as values set in a higher-level file may cause problems with an application stored at lower level.

Security Alert!

With the standard ASP.NET machine.config file, all configuration files are secured and cannot be downloaded by a client system. This allows for some protection of critical information such as user IDs and passwords for DSN sources, but keep in mind that any system can be hacked with enough time and effort. Always keep security in mind when planning your Web application.

Debugging...

Configuration Hierarchy

An important note to keep in mind when planning your usage of configuration files is the hierarchical manner in which ASP.NET computes the effective configuration of your application. When ASP.NET reads in the web.config in each consecutive directory, it goes from each physical subdirectory to the next.

Virtual directories cause this processing to occur somewhat differently. Let us assume as an example that you have a web.config file physically located in *E:\wwwroot\mainapp* and have the virtual directory *app* assigned to this directory.

Later you add another application in *E:\wwwroot\mainapp\subapp* and assign the virtual directory *subapp* to this directory. If you access your sub-application by using *http://localhost/app/subapp/myapp.aspx*, the settings in the machine.config as well as the web.config stored in the *mainapp* are applied. However, if your sub-application is accessed via *http://localhost/subapp/myapp.aspx*, only the settings configured in the machine.config are applied.

This caveat of configuration inheritance is very important to keep in mind when designing your virtual directory structure. If structured incorrectly, your applications could experience errors, or could fail.

Finally, we can see how the use of the *allowOverride* attribute affects an application's configuration. The default value for the *allowOverride* attribute is *true*, which allows any lower level configuration file to override the configuration specified in a higher-level file. You can change this behavior by setting the *allowOverride* attribute to *false,* which prevents lower-level configuration files from overriding configuration options set at a higher level. If a lower-level configuration file attempts to override this setting, an error will occur. We will go into more detail on the *allowOverride* attribute for the <location> tag later in the chapter.

Uses for a Configuration File

When examining the uses for ASP.NET's configuration files, we must look at the machine.config file as well as the web.config file. The main difference between these two files is that the machine.config file is applied system-wide while the web.config is applied to each application based on the inheritance rules. Each configuration option set within the machine.config file is applied to every application and by using the *allowOverride* attribute in conjunction with the <location> tag; you can prevent individual web.config files from overriding these settings.

When ASP.NET is initially installed, a default machine.config file is set up for your system with the standard configuration section handlers used within ASP.NET as well as many other configuration items. You can edit this default file to tailor your ASP.NET configuration to your requirements. You can also configure the same options in the lower-level web.config files in order to give you more granular control over individual applications.

You can configure almost all functional items of ASP.NET through the configuration files. The options available to you using the default ASP.NET machine.config file include everything from browser compatibility options to secure authentication options. Table 4.1 details the standard tags available through the ASP.NET configuration files; however, you can define additional tags by defining new configuration section handlers.

Table 4.1 Standard Configuration Tags

Configuration Tag	Description	Group
<appSettings>	Allows the configuration of custom settings for your applications.	Application
<authentication>	Allows configuration of ASP.NET's authentication support.	Security
<authenticationModules>	Allows the definition of modules necessary for ASP.NET's authentication support.	Security

Continued

Table 4.1 Continued

Configuration Tag	Description	Group
<authorization>	Allows configuration of ASP.NET's authorization support.	Security
<browserCaps>	Allows configuration of settings for the browser capabilities component.	System
<compilation>	Allows configuration of all ASP.NET compilation settings.	System
<connectionManagement>	Allows configuration of client connection options.	System
<customErrors>	Allows the definition of custom error messages for your application.	System
<defaultProxy>	Allows the configuration of proxy server usage by ASP.NET.	System
<globalization>	Allows the configuration of globalization settings for your applications.	Application
<httpHandlers>	Allows mapping of incoming URL requests to appropriate IHttpHandler classes or IhttpHandlerFactory classes.	System
<httpModules>	Allows the configuration of HTTP modules used within an application.	System
<httpRuntime>	Allows the configuration of HTTP runtime settings.	System
<identity>	Controls the identity used by your application.	Application
<machineKey>	Allows configuration of keys for encryption and decryption of form's authentication cookie data.	Security
<pages>	Allows configuration of page-specific settings.	Application
<processModel>	Allows configuration of ASP.NET process model settings.	System
<securityPolicy>	Allows the mapping of defined security levels to policy files.	Security

Continued

Table 4.1 Continued

Configuration Tag	Description	Group
<sessionState>	Allows configuration of the session state HTTP module.	System
<trace>	Allows configuration of the ASP.NET trace service.	Application
<trust>	Allows configuration of the code access security permission set used to run your application.	Security
<webRequestModules>	Allows configuration of ASP.NET's use of modules for request processing based on the prefix.	System
<webServices>	Allows configuration of ASP.NET Web Services settings.	System

You can break up these standard configuration tags into three main configuration groups:

- ASP.NET Application Configuration
- ASP.NET System Configuration
- ASP.NET Security Configuration

Each standard tag in Table 4.1 has been categorized as belonging to one of these three configuration groups, and we will review each option and its function in the following sections. Many of these tags do overlap between the configuration groups, but this breakdown serves as a general guideline for defining your configuration.

Application Configuration

The application configuration tags are generally used to control application-specific settings. You can set all of these tags either within the machine.config file or a web.config file at any level.

Setting Static Variables Using the <appSettings> Tag

The <appSettings> tag supports only two attributes, a *key* and a *value*. This setting enables you to set static variables for your application. One excellent use for this configuration setting is to set all of your application specific variables in a single location. This gives you the ability to completely control your application through a single configuration file. In previous ASP versions, these options were set through the use of application variables, but ASP.NET's utilization of this feature is much more efficient. The following code shows the use of this tag in setting a data source name for your application.

```
<configuration>
    <appSettings>
        <add key="dsn" value="localhost;uid=readonly;pwd=user"/>
    </appSettings>
</configuration>
```

Providing Global Support Using the <globalization> Tag

The <globalization> tag enables you to configure your application to accept requests or respond to requests using different encoding options. Using this configuration setting will allow your site to respond in the specific encoding used by any country accessing your site. The default for *requestEncoding* and *responseEncoding* within the machine.config file is *utf-8* for English-language systems, and if this setting is removed, ASP.NET defaults to your system's locale setting. This tag supports five attributes as shown in Table 4.2.

Table 4.2 <globalization> Tag Attributes

Attribute	Description
requestEncoding	Specifies the assumed encoding for incoming requests.
responseEncoding	Specifies the encoding for Web application responses.
fileEncoding	Specifies the default encoding for .aspx, .asmx, and .asax file parsing.
culture	Specifies the default culture for processing incoming requests.
uiCulture	Specifies the default culture for processing locale-dependent resource searches.

The following code is an example of how to use this tag to set the globalization options to a different encoding format such as Japanese:

```
<configuration>
    <system.web>
```

```
        <globalization
            requestEncoding="Shift-JIS"
            responseEncoding="Shift-JIS"
        />
    </system.web>
</configuration>
```

Configuring Application Identity Using the <identity> Tag

The <identity> tag enables you to configure the application identity for your Web application. You can then use this identity throughout your application for access to resources without explicitly including the user id and password elsewhere. This can be very useful when accessing a remote database or databases. You also have the option of setting the application identity to impersonate the client. The default within the machine.config is to set the *impersonate* attribute to *false*. The <identity> tag supports only three attributes. The *impersonate* attribute can be set to either *true* or *false*. If the *impersonate* attribute is *false*, you can set the *userName* and *password* attributes to a specific user id and password for your application to use. This is shown in the following code example:

```
<configuration>
    <system.web>
        <identity impersonate="false" userName="mainapp" password="mainpass" />
    </system.web>
</configuration>
```

Setting Page-Specific Attributes Using the <pages> Tag

The <pages> tag presents several page-specific attributes that you can configure. These are used to set *response buffering* options, *session,* and *view* states, *code-behind* classes, and *page events* options. By changing these options, you can control the way pages act within your site. As an example, if you wish to disable page events, you can set the *autoEventWireup* tag to *false*. These attributes and their options are detailed in Table 4.3.

Table 4.3 `<pages>` Tag Attributes

Attribute	Options	Description
buffer	On/Off/ReadOnly	Specifies whether the page uses response buffering. You can turn response buffering on or off. The ReadOnly option allows an application to read, but not modify session state variables.
enableSessionState	true/false	This specifies whether session state is enabled or disabled.
enableViewState	true/false	This specifies whether view state is enabled or disabled.
pageBaseType		This option allows you to specify a code-behind class that .aspx pages inherit.
userControlBaseType		This option allows you to specify a code-behind class that user controls inherit.
autoEventWireup	true/false	This specifies whether page events are automatically enabled or disabled.

The following code is an example usage of the `<pages>` tag:

```
<configuration>
    <system.web>
        <pages
            buffer="true"
            enableSessionState="true"
            enableViewState="true"
            autoEventWireup="true"
        />
    </system.web>
</configuration>
```

Configuring the Tracing Service Using the <trace> Tag

The <trace> tag enables you to configure the ASP.NET tracing service. By enabling this service, you are able to obtain extensive debugging information about your application. This is extremely useful when you are developing an application and want to view all of the information related to the compile or other trace information. This tag supports five attributes as detailed in Table 4.4.

Table 4.4 <trace> Tag Attributes

Attribute	Options	Description
enabled	true/false	Specifies whether the tracing service is enabled or disabled. The default setting in your *machine.config* is *false*.
localOnly	true/false	Specifies whether you can view trace results only from local host or remotely. The default is *true*.
pageOutput	true/false	Specifies whether trace results are appended to the end of a page or available only through the trace utility. The default is *false*.
requestLimit		This is a numeric value that places a limit on the number of trace requests to store on the server. The default is 10.
traceMode	SortByTime/ SortByCategory	Specifies whether to sort trace results by time or by category. The default is *SortByTime*.

The description field in Table 4.4 shows the default settings for the <trace> tag in ASP.NET's machine.config. The code below is an example of how to enable tracing and append it to the page output.

```
<configuration>
    <system.web>
        <trace
            enabled="true"
            localOnly="true"
            pageOutput="true"
            requestLimit="15"
            traceMode="SortByTime"
```

```
            />
    </system.web>
</configuration>
```

System Configuration

The system configuration options are generally best applied when set in the machine.config and applied system-wide. Most of these options control the way ASP.NET itself functions, and enables you to add additional system-level capabilities to your application. In some cases, these configuration options are restricted as to what level they can be applied at. As we examine each option, the levels at which the option is applicable will be defined.

Determining Client Capabilities Using the <browserCaps> Tag

The <browserCaps> tag enables you to configure the browser capabilities component. This tag enables you to determine the type and version of browser and operating system that the remote client is using and define the capabilities that the client has based on this information. Using this enables you to tailor your dynamic page to only include features that the browser is capable of using. For example, if you're using tables within your document and the browser doesn't support tables, the document could end up formatted differently than what you intended. By using this, you would never have sent a table to the browser. The actual data used to obtain this information is pulled by using the *HTTP_USER_AGENT* variable. You can specify this by using the <use> subtag with the <browserCaps> tag. The <result>, <filter>, and <case> subtags are supported in order to populate the <browserCaps> attributes. The settings for most major browsers currently on the market are defined in the default ASP.NET machine.config file. These attributes are detailed in Table 4.5 along with the input data types that they support.

Table 4.5 <browserCaps> Tag Attributes

Attribute	Data Type
browser	string
version	numeric
majorversion	numeric
minorversion	numeric

Continued

Table 4.5 Continued

Attribute	Data Type
frames	boolean
tables	boolean
cookies	boolean
backgroundsounds	boolean
vbscript	boolean
javascript	boolean
javaapplets	boolean
activexcontrols	boolean
win16	boolean
win32	boolean
beta	boolean
ak	boolean
sk	boolean
aol	boolean
crawler	boolean
cdf	boolean
gold	boolean
authenticodeupdate	boolean
tagwriter	object
ecmascriptversion	numeric
msdomversion	numeric
w3cdomversion	numeric
platform	string
clrVersion	numeric
css1	boolean
css2	boolean
xml	boolean

The following code shows an example of the <browserCaps> tag as it would be used to specify some default browser capabilities:

```
<configuration>
    <system.web>
```

```xml
<browserCaps>
    <result type="System.Web.HttpBrowserCapabilities" />
    <use var="HTTP_USER_AGENT" />

    browser="Unknown"
    version=0.0
    minorversion=0
    majorversion=0
    frames=false
    tables=false
    win16=false
    win32=false

    <filter>
        <case match="Windows 95|Win95">
            platform=Win95
        </case>
        <case match="Windows 98|Win98">
            platform=Win98
        </case>
    </filter>

    <filter>
        <case match="16bit|Windows 3.1|Win16">
            win16=true
        </case>
        <case match="Windows 95|Win95|Windows 98|Win98|Windows
            NT|WinNT|Win32">
            win32=true
        </case>
    </filter>
</browserCaps>
</system.web>
</configuration>
```

Setting Compilation Options Using the <compilation> Tag

You set all of ASP.NET's compilation options by using the <compilation> tag. This allows for a very detailed level of control over the compilation of your application. The default settings in the machine.config are usually sufficient for most applications. The only time when these options would need to be changed would be to modify the compilation of your ASP.NET application. The <compilation> tag supports seven attributes and three subtags. The attributes are explained in Table 4.6.

Table 4.6 <compilation> Tag Attributes

Attribute	Options	Description
debug	true/false	Specifies whether to compile retail or debug binaries. By setting this to *true*, debug binaries are compiled. The default option is *false*.
defaultLanguage		Specifies a list of language names to be used in dynamic compilation files. Multiple names are separated by semicolons. The default for this is *vb*.
explicit	true/false	Specifies the setting of the Visual Basic *explicit* compile option. The default is *true*.
batch	true/false	Specifies whether batching is supported as a compile option. This is not defined in the default *machine.config*.
batchTimeout		Specifies a timeout period for batch compilation. If the batch compile is unable to complete before this timeout period expires, ASP.NET reverts to single compilation mode. This is not defined in the default *machine.config*.

Continued

Table 4.6 Continued

Attribute	Options	Description
numRecompilesBeforeApprestart		Specifies the number of recompiles that can occur before ASP.NET restarts the application. NOTE: This attribute is not supported at the directory level. This is not defined in the default *machine.config*.
strict	true/false	Specifies the setting of the Visual Basic *strict* compile option. This is not defined in the default *machine.config*.

The <compilation> tag also supports three subtags: <compilers>, <assemblies>, and <namespaces>. Each of these supports its own subtags in order to give a more granular level of control over the compilation options.

The <compilers> subtag exists only to encapsulate one or more <compiler> subtags. This subtag is used to define a new compiler option. The <compiler> subtag supports five attributes, which are illustrated in Table 4.7.

Table 4.7 <compiler> Subtag Attributes

Attribute	Description
language	Specifies a list of language to be used within dynamic compilation files. You can specify multiple languages by separating them with semicolons.
extension	Specifies file extensions used for dynamic code-behind files. You can specify multiple extensions by separating them with semicolons.
type	Specifies a class/assembly combination that indicates the .NET Framework class used to compile all resources using the specified language(s) or extension(s). You can specify multiple classes by separating them with semicolons.
warningLevel	Specifies compiler warning levels for the specified type.
compilerOptions	Any additional compiler-specific options that need to be passed to the .NET Framework class are specified with this attribute.

The <assemblies> subtag enables you to specify ASP.NET processing directives. It supports three subtags that act as the processing directives: <add>, <remove>, and <clear>. The use of these three subtags is detailed in table 4.8.

Table 4.8 <assemblies> Subtags

Subtag	Description
<add>	Enables you to add an assembly reference for use when a dynamic resource is compiled. This assembly is automatically linked to the resource by ASP.NET when each code module is compiled. The <add> subtag uses the same attributes and syntax as the *AssemblyName* class.
<remove>	Enables you to remove an assembly reference previously specified by using the <add> tag. The assembly name used in the <remove> tag must match the name used in the <add> tag, and wildcards are not supported.
<clear>	Removes *all* assembly references whether they were explicitly defined or inherited.

The <namespaces> subtag enables you to specify additional ASP.NET processing directives. The subtags supported by the <namespaces> subtag are identical to the <assemblies> subtag and perform the same function, using namespaces instead of assemblies.

These <compilation> subtags and attributes are illustrated in the following code sample.

```
<configuration>
    <system.web>
        <compilation
            defaultLanguage="VB"
            debug="true"
            numRecompilesBeforeAppRestart="15">
            <compilers>
                <compiler
                    language="VB;VBScript"
                    extension=".cls"
                    type="Microsoft.VB. VBCodeProvider,System" />
                <compiler
                    language="C#;Csharp"
```

```xml
                    extension=".cs"
                    type="Microsoft.CSharp. CSharpCodeProvider,System" />
                <compiler
                    language="js;jscript;javascript"
                    extension=".js"
                    type="Microsoft.JScript.JScriptCodeProvider,
                        Microsoft.JScript" />
            </compilers>
            <assemblies>
                <add assembly="ADODB" />
                <add assembly="mscorlib" />
            </assemblies>
            <namespaces>
                <add namespace="System.Web" />
                <add namespace="System.Web.UI" />
                <add namespace="System.Web.UI.WebControls" />
                <add namespace="System.Web.UI.HtmlControls" />
            </namespaces>
        </compilation>
    </system.web>
</configuration>
```

Controlling Connections Using the <connectionManagement> Tag

The <connectionManagement> tag enables you to control the number of simultaneous connections allowed per address on your system. By using this tag, you can control the optimization of your pages. As an example, if you want to speed up access to a smaller number of users, then increase the number of simultaneous connections. This tag supports the <add>, <remove>, and <clear> subtags. The <add> subtag specifies the address(es) to set connection limits on. It has two attributes, address and maxconnection. Proper usage of the <add> subtag is illustrated in the following code sample. The <remove> subtag only accepts the address attribute and is used to remove addresses previously specified with the <add> subtag. Wildcards are also supported with the <remove> tag. The <clear> subtag removes all addresses from the configuration whether explicitly defined or inherited.

```
<configuration>
    <system.net>
        <connectionManagement>
            <add
                address="*"
                maxconnection="2"
            />
        </connectionManagement>
    </system.net>
</configuration>
```

Defining Custom Errors Using the <customErrors> Tag

By using the <customErrors> tag, you have the ability to define custom error messages for your application. This is generally used to point users to a friendlier message than the default error messages. This tag supports only two attributes and one subtag. The two attributes supported are *defaultRedirect* and *mode*. The *defaultRedirect* attribute accepts a string value representing the default URL to redirect the browser to when an error occurs. The *mode* attribute has three options: *On*, *Off*, and *RemoteOnly*. These options allow you to enable or disable custom error support or enable custom error support only for remote clients.

The <error> subtag supported by the <customErrors> tag enables you to set pages to redirect specific errors to. The <customErrors> tag supports the use of multiple <error> subtags, enabling you to redirect many different errors to the appropriate URL. The usage of these tags are outlined in the following code example:

```
<configuration>
    <system.web>
        <customErrors
            defaultRedirect="error/unspecifiederror.aspx"
            mode="RemoteOnly">
            <error
                statusCode="500"
                redirect="error/internalerror.aspx"
            />
```

```
                <error
                    statusCode="404"
                    redirect="error/notfound.aspx"
                />
            </customErrors>
        </system.web>
</configuration>
```

Mapping Requests Using the <httpHandlers> Tag

The <httpHandlers> tag is used to map incoming requests to the appropriate *IHttpHandler* or *IhttpHandlerFactory* class. This is done based on the URL requested and the verb used to request it. Some example verbs used by this are *GET*, *POST*, and *PUT*. You would use this if you had a custom handler that you wanted to implement when files with a certain extension are requested. As an example, you could use this if you had a custom virus scanner needed to be run against all files sent with a *PUT* request that have the *.ZIP* extension. You could develop a custom handler to do this and assign the handler to the *.ZIP* extension in combination with the *PUT* verb. This can also be used to restrict certain files from being viewed, by pointing them to the *System.Web.HttpForbiddenHandler* handler. The <httpHandlers> tag supports three subtags to control this configuration option: <add>, <remove>, and <clear>.

The <add> subtag is used to add new entries to the list and supports three attributes. The first is the *verb* attribute, which specifies specific verbs to apply this *IHttpHandler* or *IhttpHandlerFactory* to. This attribute does accept wildcards. The second attribute is *path*, which specifies either a specific URL path or a wildcard string. The final attribute is *type*, which specifies the class/assembly combination. ASP.NET has a specific search order for finding the appropriate DLL. It first checks in the application's *"bin"* directory, and then in the system assembly cache.

The <remove> subtag accepts only the *path* and *type* attributes and is used to remove a previously specified mapping from the list. The <clear> subtag removes all mappings from the list whether they are explicitly defined or inherited.

The following code sample illustrates the use of the <httpHandlers> tag by adding a mapping for all .tmp files to be forbidden:

```
<configuration>
    <system.web>
        <httpHandlers>
```

```
            <add verb="*" path="*.tmp" type="System.Web
                    .HttpForbiddenHandler, System.Web, Version=1.0.2411.0,
                    Culture=neutral />
        </httpHandlers>
    </system.web>
</configuration>
```

Configuring HTTP Modules Using the <httpModules> Tag

The <httpModules> tag enables you to configure the HTTP modules used within your application. This tag supports the <add>, <remove>, and <clear> subtags. The <add> subtag specifies the HTTP module class to add to your application. It has two attributes, type and name. Proper usage of the <add> subtag is illustrated in the following code sample. The <remove> subtag accepts the same attributes of type and name and is used to remove HTTP modules previously specified with the <add> subtag. Wildcards are also not supported with the <remove> tag. The <clear> subtag removes all addresses from the configuration whether explicitly defined or inherited.

```
<configuration>
    <system.web>
        <httpModules>
            <add
                name="OutputCache"
                type="System.Web.Caching.OutputCacheModule"
            />
            <add
                name="Session"
                type="System.Web.SessionState.SessionStateModule"
            />
            <add
                name="WindowsAuthentication"
                type="System.Web.Security.WindowsAuthenticationModule"
            />
        </httpModules>
```

```
        </system.web>
</configuration>
```

Setting Runtime Options Using the <httpRuntime> Tag

The <httpRuntime> tag enables you to set various runtime options for ASP.NET's HTTP processing. These options are represented by the three available attributes for the <httpRuntime> tag. By changing these attributes, you can control the way ASP.NET functions when performing operations requested by the user.

The first attribute is *useFullyQualifiedRedirectUrl*. This attribute supports a boolean value of *true* or *false*, and configures whether ASP.NET uses fully qualified client-side redirects or relative redirects. The default is *false*, which specifies relative redirects. Fully qualified redirects are only used for some mobile controls or very early-stage Web browsers.

The second available attribute is *executionTimeout*, which specifies the maximum amount of time that a request is allowed to process before being terminated by ASP.NET. This is used both to terminate hung applications as well as to prevent badly coded applications from using up all your system resources. This attribute accepts a numeric value specified in seconds.

The final attribute for the <httpRuntime> tag is *maxRequestLength*. This attribute specifies a maximum file size that ASP.NET will accept as an upload. This is primarily used to prevent users from performing a denial of service attack by uploading large files to your server. In addition, it can help manage your disk capacity by limiting the size of the files your server accepts. This attribute accepts a numeric value in megabytes. These attributes are illustrated in the following code:

```
<configuration>
    <system.web>
        <httpRuntime
            executionTimeout="90"
            maxRequestLength="4096"
            useFullyQualifiedRedirectUrl="false"
        />
    </system.web>
</configuration>
```

Setting Process Model Options Using the <processModel> Tag

The <processModel> tag is used to set various options for the ASP.NET process model. These options are represented by the 15 attributes supported by the <processModel> tag and are described in Table 4.9. The <processModel> tag can only be used within the machine.config file.

Table 4.9 <processModel> Tag Attributes

Attribute	Options	Description	Default
enable	true/false	Allows you to enable or disable the process model.	true
timeout	Infinite/hh:mm:ss	Allows you to specify a timeout period at the end of which ASP.NET will launch a new worker process. This value is expressed as hh:mm:ss or a special value of *Infinite*.	Infinite
idleTimeout	Infinite/hh:mm:ss	Enables you to specify a timeout period based on inactivity at the end of which ASP.NET will automatically shut down the worker process. This value is expressed as hh:mm:ss or a special value of *Infinite*.	Infinite
shutdownTimeout	Infinite/hh:mm:ss	Enables you to specify a length of time for the worker process to shut itself down. When this time period runs	00:00:05

Continued

Table 4.9 Continued

Attribute	Options	Description	Default
		out, the worker process will be terminated by ASP.NET. This value is expressed as hh:mm:ss or a s pecial value of *Infinite*.	
requestLimit	Infinite/numeric	Enables you to specify the maximum number of requests to process before ASP.NET restarts the worker process.	Infinite
requestQueueLimit	Infinite/numeric	Enables you to specify the number of requests to store in the queue before ASP.NET starts responding with an error message.	5000
memoryLimit	Infinite/numeric	Enables you to specify the maximum amount of memory that a worker process can consume before ASP.NET starts a new worker process and begins reassigning requests. This value is a numeric value representing the percentage of the total system memory.	60
cpuMask	decimal bitmask	Enables you to assign specific processors in a multi-processor system to	0xffffffff

Continued

Table 4.9 Continued

Attribute	Options	Description	Default
		run ASP.NET processes. This enables you to dedicate processors completely to just process ASP.NET threads. The value for this attribute is the decimal conversion of the binary representation of processors that you wish to specify. For example, in a four-processor system, let's assume that you wish to dedicate processors 0 and 1 to ASP.NET. The binary mask for this would be 0011. Translated to decimal, the value is 3. Processors 2 and 3 exclusively would be masked as 1100, which is 12 in decimal. This attribute is only valid on multi-processor systems that have the *webGarden* attribute set to *false*.	
webGarden	true/false	Enables you to specify whether to control processor utilization on multi-processor systems by using the operating system or specific processor masks	false

Continued

Table 4.9 Continued

Attribute	Options	Description	Default
		defined in the *cpuMask* attribute. A value of *false* signifies to use the *cpuMask* attribute, and a value of *true* signifies usage of the operating system.	
userName	string	Enables you to specify a specific user id to start the worker process under. This attribute accepts the value of a valid user account or two special names, *System* and *Machine.* The *System* name runs the worker process under the system account. The *Machine* name, when used with a password of *Autogenerate,* runs the worker process under an unprivileged system account.	System
password	AutoGenerate/ string	Enables you to specify a password to use with the user id specified in the *userName* attribute. This attribute accepts either a valid password or a value of *AutoGenerate* for use with the *Machine* user id.	AutoGenerate

Continued

Table 4.9 Continued

Attribute	Options	Description	Default
logLevel	All/None/Errors	Enables you to specify the ASP.NET logging level for debugging information. This value specifies the events to log to the system event log. Supported values are *All*, *None*, or *Errors*.	Errors
clientConnectedCheck	hh:mm:ss	Enables you to specify a default length of time for a request to be queued before ASP.NET checks to make sure that the client is still connected. This value is formatted as hh:mm:ss.	0:00:05
comAuthenticationLevel	Default/None/ Connect/ Call/Pkt/ PktIntegrity/ PktPrivacy	Enables you to specify the authentication level for DCOM security. The available values listed in the *Options* column enables you to control what level of authentication you wish to use.	Connect
comImpersonationLevel	Default/ Anonymous/ Identify/ Impersonate/ Delegate	Enables you to specify the authentication level for COM security. The available options are shown in the *Options* column.	Impersonate

The following code shows the use of these options as they could be configured for a multiprocessor system:

```
<configuration>
    <system.web>
        <processModel
            enable="true"
            timeout="Infinite"
            idleTimeout="Infinite"
            shutdownTimeout="0:00:10"
            requestLimit="Infinite"
            requestQueueLimit="8000"
            restartQueueLimit="10"
            memoryLimit="70"
            webGarden="true"
            cpuMask="13"
            userName="SYSTEM"
            password="AutoGenerate"
            logLevel="All"
            clientConnectedCheck="0:00:10"
            comAuthenticationLevel="Connect"
            comImpersonationLevel="Impersonate"
        />
    </system.web>
</configuration>
```

Configuring the Session State Using the <sessionState> Tag

The <sessionState> tag enables you to configure the session state HTTP module. This tag supports five attributes, which are detailed in Table 4.10. For further information on session state, please refer to Chapter 5.

Table 4.10 <sessionState> Tag Attributes

Attribute	Options	Description	Default
mode	Off/InProc/ StateServer/ SqlServer	Enables you to specify where to store the session state. The *Off* value disables session state, the *InProc* value stores the session state locally, the *StateServer* stores the session state on a remote server, and the *SqlServer* value stores the session state on a SQL server.	InProc
cookieless	true/false	Enables you to specify whether sessions without cookies should be used to identify client sessions with a value of *true*, indicating that sessions without cookies should be used.	false
timeout		Enables you to specify the amount of time in minutes before an idle session is abandoned.	20
stateConnectionString		Enables you to specify the server name and port to use when the session state is stored remotely, as specified with the *StateServer* value under the *mode* attribute.	tcpip= 127.0.0.1:42424
sqlConnectionString		Enables you to specify a SQL connection string to use when the session state is stored on a SQL server, as specified with the *SqlServer* value under the *mode* attribute.	data source= 127.0.0.1; user id= sa;password=

www.syngress.com

An example use of this tag is illustrated in the following code sample:

```
<configuration>
    <system.web>
        <sessionState>
            mode="SqlServer"
            sqlConnectionString="data source=10.10.10.1;user
                id=sa;password=mypass"
            cookieless="false"
            timeout="25"
        </sessionState>
    </system.web>
</configuration>
```

Configuring Request Modules Using the <webRequestModule> Tag

The <webRequestModules> tag enables you to configure the request modules used within your application. These modules control the way that ASP.NET will respond to different requests. As an example, one of the default modules is the *System.Net.FileWebRequestCreator* module. Whenever a request prefaced with "file://" is sent to the server, the *System.Net.FileWebRequestCreator* module is called to handle the request.

This tag supports the <add>, <remove>, and <clear> subtags. The <add> subtag specifies the request module class to add to your application. It has two attributes, prefix and type. Proper usage of the <add> subtag is illustrated in the following code sample. The <remove> subtag accepts the same attributes of *prefix* and *type* and is used to remove request modules previously specified with the <add> subtag. Wildcards are not supported with the <remove> tag. The <clear> subtag removes all request modules from the configuration whether explicitly defined or inherited.

```
<configuration>
    <system.net>
        <webRequestModules>
            <add
                prefix="http"
                type="System.Net.HttpRequestCreator"
```

```
                />
                <add
                    prefix="https"
                    type="System.Net.HttpRequestCreator"
                />
                <add
                    prefix="file"
                    type="System.Net.FileWebRequestCreator"
                />
            </webRequestModules>
        </system.net>
</configuration>
```

Configuring Web Services Using the <webServices> Tag

The <webServices> tag enables you to configure aspects of ASP.NET's web services and how they function. Web services are explained in detail in Chapter 10. By using various subtags, you can add protocol types, writer and reader types, as well as configure many other options. All of the subtags supported by the <webServices> tag support the three attributes of *add*, *remove*, and *clear*. There are two different styles of subtags supported, standard subtags, and type subtags. When using a standard subtag, the *add* and *remove* attributes use the *name* value. When using a type subtag, these attributes use the *type* value.

There are many subtags supported by the *<webServices>* attribute. Table 4.11 contains a partial list of these subtags and describes the style of each subtag.

Table 4.11 <webServices> Tag Subtags

Subtag	Style
protocolTypes	type
protocols	standard
returnWriterTypes	type
returnWriters	standard
parameterReaderTypes	type
parameterReaders	standard

Continued

Table 4.11 Continued

Subtag	Style
protocolReflectorTypes	type
protocolReflectors	standard
mimeReflectorTypes	type
mimeReflectors	standard
protocolImporterTypes	type
protocolImporters	standard
mimeImporterTypes	type
mimeImporters	standard
protocolInfoTypes	type
protocolInfo	standard
mimeInfoTypes	type
mimeInfo	standard
referenceResolverTypes	type
referenceResolvers	standard
discoverySearchPatternTypes	type
discoverySearchPatterns	standard
soapExtensionTypes	type
soapExtensions	standard
soapExtensionReflectorTypes	type
soapExtensionReflectors	standard
soapExtensionImporterTypes	type
soapExtensionImporters	standard

Security

Security is a very important area of configuration for ASP.NET. The tags provided in this section enable you to configure several aspects of ASP.NET security including encryption and authentication. When planning any application, you should always keep security in mind and make sure that all aspects of your application are as secure as possible. These tags, when configured properly, can assist in reaching the goal of a secure application.

Authenticating Users Using the <authentication> Tag

Authentication refers to the portion of ASP.NET, which verifies that the users accessing your application are indeed who they say they are. This should be used to verify the identity of your users for security reasons as well as personalization of the application. The *mode* attribute specifies the type of authentication to use. Table 4.12 shows the available options for this attribute and what they mean. When Windows authentication is referred to, this includes all forms of authentication supported by IIS such as basic, digest, NTLM/kerberos, or certificates.

Table 4.12 *mode* Attribute Options

Option	Description
Windows	Specifies Windows/IIS authentication mode.
Forms	Specifies an ASP.NET forms-based authentication mode.
Passport	Specifies the use of Microsoft Passport authentication mode.
None	No authentication specified. This should only be used for anonymous access-based applications or applications designed with their own authentication scheme.

The <authentication> tag also supports two subtags, <forms> and <passport>. The <forms> tag is used to specify configuration information for using ASP.NET's forms-based authentication mode. This subtag supports five attributes and one subtag. These attributes are shown in Table 4.13.

Table 4.13 <forms> Subtag Attributes

Attribute	Options	Description
name		Enables you to specify a cookie name to use for authentication. ASP.NET defaults to .ASPXAUTH.
loginUrl		If the specified cookie is not found, the user will be redirected to the URL specified in this attribute to log in. ASP.NET defaults to default.aspx.
protection	All/None/Encryption/Validation	The *All* option specifies that the application uses both validation and encryption to protect the authentication cookie. This is the default value. The *None* option specifies that neither validation nor encryption

Continued

Table 4.13 <forms> Subtag Attributes

Attribute	Options	Description
		is used, and therefore the cookie is not secure. This should only be used when there are no security requirements and the authentication features are only being used for personalization.
timeout		Enables you to specify a maximum length of time for the authentication cookie to remain valid. This value is in seconds and the default is 30.
path		Enables you to specify a specific path for storing cookies used by your application. The default is /.

The <forms> subtag supports the <credentials> subtag. This subtag enables you to specify user id and password credentials within the configuration file. This is done by using the *passwordFormat* attribute and the <user> subtag. The *passwordFormat* attribute accepts three values, which specifies the password encryption. These values are as follows:

- **Clear** No encryption
- **MD5** Encrypted with the MD5 hash algorithm
- **SHA1** Encrypted with the SHA1 hash algorithm

The <user> subtag supports the use of the *name* and *password* attributes. These values are simply text values containing the user's id and password.

The second subtag supported by the <authentication> tag is <passport>. This subtag has a single attribute of *redirectUrl*, and enables you to specify a default URL to redirect the user to if the passport mode is used and the user has not signed on with passport. The following code sample shows the use of these options:

```
<configuration>
    <system.web>
        <authentication
            mode="Forms">
            <forms
                name=".ASPXAUTH"
                loginUrl="authenticate.aspx"
```

```
                protection="All"
                timeout="45"
                path="/">
                <credentials
                    passwordFormat="SHA1">
                        <user
                            name="myuser"
                            password="mypass"
                        />
                </credentials>
            </forms>
        </authentication>
    </system.web>
</configuration>
```

Configuring Security Modules Using the <authenticationModules> Tag

The <authenticationModules> tag enables you to add or remove the security modules used within ASP.NET for authentication. This will only be used if you wish to add some other form of authentication to ASP.NET. This may evolve in the future with the use of smart cards and biometric authentication. This tag supports the <add>, <remove>, and <clear> subtags. The <add> subtag specifies the authentication module class to add to your application. It uses the type attribute to specify the class. Proper usage of the <add> subtag is illustrated in the following code sample. The <remove> subtag accepts the same attribute of type and is used to remove authentication modules previously specified with the <add> subtag. Wildcards are not supported with the <remove> tag. The <clear> subtag removes all authentication modules from the configuration whether explicitly defined or inherited.

```
<configuration>
    <system.net>
        <authenticationModules>
            <add type="System.Net.DigestClient" />
            <add type="System.Net.NegotiateClient" />
            <add type="System.Net.KerberosClient" />
```

```
                <add type="System.Net.NtlmClient" />
                <add type="System.Net.BasicClient" />
            </authenticationModules>
        </system.net>
</configuration>
```

Controlling Access Using the <authorization> Tag

The <authorization> tag is used to control access to specific resources based on permissions granted to the user or role. For any application, you want only authorized users to access your application in certain ways. Historically this has been controlled by the use of user databases, but for small applications this works well. In addition, if a method of access is needed, should the backend database fail, this provides a good failsafe.

This is done by using the two subtags, <allow> and <deny>. The <allow> subtag controls which users or roles are granted access, and the <deny> subtag controls which users or roles to which access is denied. Both subtags support the same three attributes. These are described in Table 4.14. All permissions specified through this configuration are read and applied by ASP.NET from the top down; therefore the order in which you specify your permissions is very important.

Table 4.14 <allow> and <deny> Subtag Attributes

Attribute	Description
users	Enables you to designate a list of users to either be allowed or denied access. User names should be separated with a comma. The ? and * symbols are used to specify anonymous or all users, respectively.
roles	Enables you to designate a list of roles to either be allowed or denied access. You should separate roles with a comma.
verbs	Enables you to specify a list of verbs to either allow or deny access to. These include GET, HEAD, POST, and DEBUG. You should separate verbs with a comma.

The following code sample illustrates the use of these tags:

```
<configuration>
    <system.web>
        <authorization>
            <allow
```

```
                users="austin,bobby,chris,dave"
                roles="Admins"
            />
            <deny
                users="*"
            />
        </authorization>
    </system.web>
</configuration>
```

Configuring Encryption Keys Using the <machineKey> Tag

The <machineKey> tag enables you to configure encryption keys for use with encryption and decryption of forms authentication cookie data. This is very important to use when high security is necessary for your application. When this is in place, cookies used for forms authentication are encrypted. Forms authentication is explained in the earlier section of this chapter on the <authentication> tag. The <machineKey> tag supports three attributes as shown in Table 4.15. You can specify this tag on any level with exception of the subdirectory level.

Table 4.15 <machineKey> Tag Attributes

Attribute	Options	Description
validationKey	AutoGenerate/value	Specifies the key used for validation.
decryptionKey	AutoGenerate/value	Specifies the key used for decryption.
validation	SHA1/MD5/3DES	Specifies the type of encryption being used for validation.

As shown in Table 4.15, the *validationKey* and *decryptionKey* attributes can either be set to *AutoGenerate* a key or have a specific value set. This value must be at least 40 characters long and have a maximum limit of 128 characters. The recommended length is 128 hexadecimal characters, for maximum security. If you are using multiple Web servers with your application in a Web farm environment, these keys must match between all Web servers. If you use *AutoGenerate* with a Web farm, your keys will not match, and your application will not work correctly. The following sample code illustrates the usage of this tag.

```
<configuration>
    <system.web>
        <machineKey validationKey="AutoGenerate"
decryptionKey="AutoGenerate"
    validation="SHA1"/>
    </system.web>
</configuration>
```

Mapping Security Policies Using the <securityPolicy> Tag

The <securityPolicy> tag enables you to map policy files to specific security level names. By doing so, you can then easily implement your own custom security configuration throughout your application. This tag accepts the subtag of <trustLevel>. Multiple <trustLevel> subtags can be placed within a <securityPolicy> tag. The <trustLevel> subtag accepts two attributes, *name* and *policyFile*. The *name* attribute is used to specify a logical name to designate the policy, and the *policyFile* attribute specifies the policy file. The default names set up with ASP.NET are *Full*, *High*, *Low*, and *None*. The following code shows these names as well as one custom name and their associated policy files:

```
<securityPolicy>
    <trustLevel
        name="Full"
        policyFile="internal"
    />
    <trustLevel
        name="High"
        policyFile="web_hightrust.config"
    />
    <trustLevel
        name="Low"
        policyFile="web_lowtrust.config"
    />
    <trustLevel
        name="None"
        policyFile="web_notrust.config"
```

```
        />
        <trustLevel
            name="MyLevel"
            policyFile="web_mypolicy.config"
        />
</securityPolicy>
```

Applying Trust Levels Using the <trust> Tag

The <trust> tag enables you to apply specific trust levels to your application. By using this tag, you are able to use security policy files with your Web applications. This tag accepts only two attributes, *level* and *originUrl*. The *level* attribute is used to reference a trust level previously specified with the <trustLevel> tag. The *originUrl* tag specifies an application's origin URL. This is used for certain permissions that allow connectivity back to the origin host, such as *Socket* and *WebRequest*. If the permissions that you are applying require a host to function correctly, then you must specify this attribute. The use of this tag is illustrated in the following code:

```
<configuration>
    <system.web>
        <trust
            level="High"
            originUrl="http://localhost/myapp/default.aspx"
        />
    </system.web>
</configuration>
```

Anatomy of a Configuration File

The machine.config and web.config files are written using standard XML formatting. These files consist of a hierarchy of tags and subtags. Each tag or subtag contains attributes that contain the actual configuration values. All of the tags, subtags, and attributes in the configuration files are case-sensitive, and your application will generate errors if a tag or attribute is formatted incorrectly.

Fortunately, there are specific rules that XML uses to help in getting the case correct. All tags, subtags, and attributes are camel-cased, which means that the first "word" of the name is lower case and any additional "words" in the name are capitalized. For example, take the tag <webRequestModules>. This tag consists of the three words: web, request, and modules. The first word is all lower case, and the remaining two are capitalized.

XML, much like HTML, requires that each tag have a beginning and an end. This can be accomplished within a single statement by opening the tag and closing with a "/>" at the end. The example code for the <machineKey> tag uses this method:

```
<machineKey validationKey="AutoGenerate" decryptionKey="AutoGenerate"
    validation="SHA1"/>
```

When a tag contains subtags, you cannot begin and end a tag within the same statement. You must use a separate beginning and ending tag in this situation. A good example for this is the <configuration> tag itself:

```
<configuration>
    <system.web>
        <machineKey validationKey="AutoGenerate" decryptionKey="AutoGenerate"
    validation="SHA1"/>
    </system.web>
</configuration>
```

The first part of the machine.config file is the definition of *configuration section handlers*. These are the classes used by the tags within the rest of the configuration file to apply configuration settings. The default configuration section handlers are detailed in the previous section, so we are now going to look at how to create additional handlers. These are generally created in the machine.config file for use between all applications, but can also be created within web.config files for application-specific configuration section handlers.

You can create your own .NET Framework class for this by creating a class that supports the *IconfigurationSectionHandler* interface. For our example, we will be using the *System.Configuration.NameValueFileSectionHandler* class, which is the same class used by the <appSettings> tag.

All configuration section handlers are specified within the <configSections> tag. They are then defined by using the <section> tag. This tag accepts the *name* and *type* attributes. The *name* attribute specifies the tag that you will later be using to reference this class, and the *type* attribute contains the actual class/assembly combination.

> **NOTE**
>
> You cannot define any new configuration section handlers beginning with the keyword "config."

In addition, you can group configuration section handlers into sections by using the <sectionGroup> tag. This tag accepts the *name* attribute, which specifies the tag you will later use to reference this section. So, we can put this all together as shown in the following sample code:

```
<configuration>
    <configSections>
        <sectionGroup name="myAppSettings.group">
            <section
                name="myAppSettings"
                type="System.Configuration.NameValueFileSectionHandler,
                    System"
            />
        </sectionGroup>
    </configSections>

<myAppSettings.group>
    <myAppSettings>
        <add
            key="tableBackgroundColor"
            value="lightyellow"
        />
        <add
            key="tableForegroundColor"
            value="brown"
        />
    </myAppSettings>
</myAppSettings.group>

</configuration>
```

We have one more tag to go over before we go through the creation of a configuration file. This tag is the <location> tag and is used to designate certain configuration options to apply only to specific files or directories. This tag can also be used to lock down configuration options so that they cannot be changed at a lower level. The <location> tag accepts the *path* and *allowOverride* attributes. The *path* attribute enables you to specify a location to apply a set of configuration options to. If you are using the <location> tag within a machine.config file, the *path* attribute can specify either virtual directories or applications. If you are using it within a web.config file, the *path* attribute enables you to specify a directory, subdirectory, application, or file. The *allowOverride* attribute accepts a value of either *true* or *false* and enables you to lock down the configuration options. This tag is illustrated in the following code sample:

```
<configuration>
    <location path="myapp.aspx">
        <appSettings>
            <add
                key="mykey"
                value="myvalue"
            />
        </appSettings>
    </location>
    <location path="secureapp.aspx" allowOverride="false">
        <system.web>
            <identity
                impersonate="false"
                userName="dbaccess"
                password="seCur1e"
            />
        </system.web>
        <appSettings>
            <add
                key="secured"
                value="true"
            />
        </appSettings>
```

```
        </location>
</configuration>
```

Creating a Configuration File

At this point, we've covered the default tags provided with ASP.NET, learned how to create our own configuration section handlers, and have gone over how to assign configuration options to specific locations. Now, let's create a configuration file for an application. We'll call our application "TestConfig" and store it within its own virtual directory to avoid inheriting any configuration other than the machine.config.

We'll start off our web.config file by opening the <configuration> tag and defining a new configuration section handler. We'll place this handler within a new section group, just in case we need to add more handlers to the application at some point in the future.

```
<configuration>
    <configSections>
        <sectionGroup name="testConfig.group">
            <section
                name="mainAppSettings"
                type="System.Configuration.NameValueFileSectionHandler,
                    System"
            />
        </sectionGroup>
    </configSections>
```

Next, we'll go ahead and define some custom settings for this section group:

```
<testConfig.group>
    <mainAppSettings>
        <add
            key="tableBackgroundColor"
            value="lightyellow"
        />
        <add
            key="tableForegroundColor"
            value="brown"
```

```
            />
        </mainAppSettings>
</testConfig.group>
```

Now let's assume that we have another page within our application located in a subdirectory that should use different settings for its tables. We also want to lock this setting down so that it can't be changed by a web.config file that another developer may place in the subdirectory. We'll accomplish this by using the <location> tag:

```
<location path="execreports" allowOverride="false">
    <configTest.group>
        <mainAppSettings>
            <add
                key="tableBackgroundColor"
                value="lightyellow"
            />
            <add
                key="tableForegroundColor"
                value="red"
            />
        </mainAppSettings>
    </configTest.group>
```

We want to make sure that this page uses resource buffering as well as the session and view states. We also want to enable page events automatically. These should be all the special configuration options that we need to specify for this application, so we'll also go ahead and close our <location> tag as well.

```
    <system.web>
        <pages
            buffer="true"
            enableSessionState="true"
            enableViewState="true"
            autoEventWireup="true"
        />
    </system.web>
</location>
```

Let's also set our application to require Windows authentication, and allow access only to a couple of individuals for testing purposes. Just to be sure, we'll also explicitly deny access to everyone else.

```
<system.web>
    <authentication mode="Windows" />
    <authorization>
        <allow
            users="faircjer,devtest,devtest2"
        />
        <deny
            users="*"
        />
    </authorization>
```

As this is our test application, we're also going to enable tracing so we can see what's happening as we go along:

```
    <trace
        enabled="true"
        localOnly="true"
        pageOutput="true"
        requestLimit="15"
        traceMode="SortByTime"
    />
```

That should do it for configuration on this application, so let's close off our tags:

```
    </system.web>
</configuration>
```

So, what's our end result? The web.config file we created is shown in Figure 4.2 and can be found on the included CD as web.config.

Figure 4.2 Sample File (web.config)

```
<configuration>
    <configSections>
        <sectionGroup name="testConfig.group">
```

Continued

Figure 4.2 Continued

```xml
            <section
                name="mainAppSettings"
                type="System.Configuration.NameValueFileSectionHandler,
                    System"
            />
        </sectionGroup>
        <sectionGroup name="sectiontest.group">
            <section
                name="mainAppSettings"
                type="System.Configuration.NameValueFileSectionHandler,
                    System"
            />
        </sectionGroup>
    </configSections>
    <testConfig.group>
        <mainAppSettings>
            <add
                key="tableBackgroundColor"
                value="lightyellow"
            />
            <add
                key="tableForegroundColor"
                value="brown"
            />
        </mainAppSettings>
    </testConfig.group>

    <location path="execreports" allowOverride="false">
        <testConfig.group>
            <mainAppSettings>
                <add
                    key="tableBackgroundColor"
                    value="lightyellow"
                />
```

Continued

Figure 4.2 Continued

```xml
                    <add
                        key="tableForegroundColor"
                        value="red"
                    />
                </mainAppSettings>
        </testConfig.group>
        <system.web>
            <pages
                buffer="true"
                enableSessionState="true"
                enableViewState="true"
                autoEventWireup="true"
            />
        </system.web>
    </location>

    <system.web>
        <authentication mode="Windows" />
        <authorization>
            <allow
                users="faircjer,devtest,devtest2"
            />
        </authorization>
        <trace
            enabled="true"
            localOnly="true"
            pageOutput="true"
            requestLimit="15"
            traceMode="SortByTime"
        />
    </system.web>
</configuration>
```

Retrieving Settings

Many of the settings used within the web.config and machine.config files simply modify the way that ASP.NET works. Others enable us to dynamically customize our applications based on many factors. In order to customize our applications, we have to be able to retrieve settings from the configuration.

When we retrieve data, we are not retrieving it from any specific configuration file, but from the cached configuration. This cached configuration includes all inherited configuration and any location specific configuration information. For the examples used in this section, we will be using the "TestConfig" application that we designed the preceding web.config file for.

ASP.NET exposes intrinsic static methods for some configuration options. An example of this is the *Session* method. When you have set session state configuration by using the <sessionState> tag, you can read this in by using the *Session* method. This process is shown in the following code sample:

```
Dim nocookies As Boolean = Session.Cookieless
```

The second method of retrieving settings is only applicable to settings configured using the <appSettings> tag. To retrieve these settings, you simply use the *ConfigurationSettings.AppSettings* method and supply the key. This method will return the value stored under that keyname. This method is shown in the following code sample:

```
Dim myvalue As String = ConfigurationSettings.AppSettings("mykey")
```

You can use the final retrieval method to obtain any value within the configuration. This is the *ConfigurationSettings.GetConfig* method. In order to use this, you must know the exact path to the configuration setting that you wish to retrieve. The syntax for this method is shown in Figure 4.3. This code is available on the included CD as testconfig.aspx.

Figure 4.3 Application (TestConfig.aspx)

```
<html>

<script language="VB" runat="server">

Public tblBack As String = ""
Public tblFore As String = ""
```

Continued

Figure 4.3 Continued

```
    Sub Page_Load(source As Object, E As EventArgs)
        dim config As NameValueCollection=
            ConfigurationSettings.GetConfig
            ("testConfig.group/mainAppSettings")

        dim strTblBack as string = config("tableBackgroundColor")
        dim strTblFore as string = config("tableForegroundColor")

        if strTblBack <> nothing then
           tblBack=strTblBack
        else
           tblBack="lightgreen"
        end if

        if strTblFore <> nothing then
           tblFore=strTblFore
        else
           tblFore="purple"
        end if

    End Sub

</script>

<head>
<title>Test Configuration</title>
</head>
<body>
<table border=1 bgcolor=<%=tblBack%> bordercolor=<%=tblFore%>>
    <tr>
        <td>Some</td>
        <td>Important</td>
        <td>Data</td>
```

Continued

Figure 4.3 Continued

```
        </tr>
        <tr>
            <td>Some</td>
            <td>More</td>
            <td>Data</td>
        </tr>
</table>
</body>
</html>
```

This code uses configuration sections that we defined within our web.config file in the previous section. The full possibilities of this configuration can be realized by first running the code in its own virtual directory, and then running the same code within an "execreports" subdirectory. This will show you how the configuration options change based on the <location> tag.

Summary

The configuration capabilities provided by ASP.NET enable you to configure almost every aspect of ASP.NET and the way that your applications are processed. It provides this ability through the use of the machine.config file and web.config files. These files are processed in a hierarchical manner with each higher-level file overriding previous settings. All settings are cached, and when a change is detected in the configuration files, the configuration is then recached.

When using the configuration files to configure ASP.NET, various tags, sub-tags, attributes, and options are used. Each of these enables you to control built-in configuration options or create new configuration options as you see fit. By using the available options, you can control everything from application variables down to compilation options.

The configuration files used by ASP.NET are formatted in XML and are case-sensitive. Using the correct formatting for these files is critical if you want your configuration to work correctly. All values within your configuration are accessible by using one of the three methods listed in the "Retrieving Settings" section.

Solutions Fast Track

Overview of an ASP.NET Configuration

- ☑ ASP.NET configuration settings are stored in the machine.config and the web.config files.
- ☑ ASP.NET processes the configuration settings in a hierarchical manner. It does this by processing the machine.config first, and then processing all web.config files.
- ☑ You can override the hierarchal method of configuration file processing by the use of the *allowOverride* attribute and the <location> tag.

Uses for a Configuration File

- ☑ By using the machine.config file as well as web.config files, you can configure ASP.NET at a very granular level.
- ☑ You can use configuration files to control most aspects of ASP.NET including application, security, and system-related options.

- ☑ You can configure additional configuration tags by creating new configuration section handlers.

Anatomy of a Configuration File

- ☑ The ASP.NET configuration files are configured using XML formatting.
- ☑ Tags and subtags contain attributes that control the various configuration options available in ASP.NET.
- ☑ You can retrieve all configuration settings within ASP.NET at any time from within your application.

Frequently Asked Questions

The following Frequently Asked Questions, answered by the authors of this book, are designed to both measure your understanding of the concepts presented in this chapter and to assist you with real-life implementation of these concepts. To have your questions about this chapter answered by the author, browse to **www.syngress.com/solutions** and click on the **"Ask the Author"** form.

Q: Should I modify the machine.config file or create a web.config file for my application?

A: That depends on the situation. If you have multiple applications running on a server, and several configuration options need to be shared between them, then place the shared configuration settings in the machine.config and any application specific settings in individual web.config files. If you only have one application on your server, just create a web.config file with all your configuration settings.

Q: Why should I use configuration files at all? Can't I just define everything in my application?

A: Some options available within the configuration files are not available within an application. One good example of this is the use of compilation options. If you aren't working at this level of configuration, then there are still several advantages to using the configuration files: They provide a single reference point for configuration, configuration options are cached and load quickly, and they enable you to distribute changes to static variables within your application easily.

Q: I don't understand what some of the configuration options do. How can I find out more about them?

A: There are two resources that I highly recommend. The first is Microsoft's MSDN site, which contains all of the ASP.NET documentation. The second is hands-on practice. If want to learn everything about a configuration option, try it yourself in as many ways as possible.

Q: Are the configuration files case-sensitive?

A: Yes! Make sure that you follow the case guidelines for working with your configuration files. If your configuration isn't working correctly, a good thing to look at is the case formatting of your configuration files.

Chapter 5

An ASP.NET Application

Solutions in this chapter:

- **Understanding ASP.NET Applications**
- **Managing State**
- **Analyzing Global.asax**
- **Understanding Application State**
- **Using Application Events**
- **Understanding Session State**
- **Configuring Sessions**
- **Using Session Events**
- **Comparing Application and Session States**
- ☑ Summary
- ☑ Solutions Fast Track
- ☑ Frequently Asked Questions

Introduction

ASP.NET applications have not changed a great deal through ASP's development. Granted, the actual inner workings have definitely changed dramatically, but the application concept itself has not; an ASP.NET application is still defined as the developer-created files and directories that can be requested, invoked, and processed through ASP.NET within its local directory structures.

Each application can have within its own local subdirectory a file named Global.asax that defines application parameters to Internet Information Server (IIS), and to the ASP.NET Web application scripts local to it. Global.asax tells IIS what to do when the application is started and how to handle processing, depending on the state of the application.

An application can have both an application state and a session state. They are both very useful and versatile facilities when used knowledgably, reflecting the functionality that .NET has provided them. Each of these states can be further customized to contain the information needed to refine the application to your purposes.

In this chapter we will look at how you can implement application and session functionality, and will work through examples of using state in ASP.NET projects.

Understanding ASP.NET Applications

As previously outlined, ASP.NET applications collect Web site resources into manageable organizational units within the Web server's file system hierarchy. But what exactly does this mean to the programmer?

A user expects a Web site to simply serve up the pages the visitor has asked for. He or she may be pleasantly surprised that the Web site knows who they are and personalizes their experience, but they will not necessarily expect it. If they choose to use a Web application, on the other hand, their expectations will be very different.

Examples of a Web application could be a multi-page bank account sign-up form. The user would expect to be able to navigate to the next and previous pages without reentering information. Another example may be an intranet. Once logged in, the user would expect the intranet to remember who they are and what they have access to without repeatedly entering the same information.

As well as user-centric information, it is also useful to remember that Web applications are multi-user. It can be handy for the application to be aware of its own application settings and values and all of its logged-in users, especially in some sort of multi-user environment, such as a live chat application or multi-user adventure game.

> **Developing & Deploying...**
>
> **Creating Your Application**
>
> Unfortunately, applications are one of the few areas that must still be managed initially by your Web server administrator through the Microsoft Management Console (MMC). By default, the Web root folder is considered the only application (the default application), and all sub-directories of that can access the application variables of their parent. If you require a new application, you must go into the MMC and either create a new virtual directory, or get the properties of the folder in which you wish to make an application by right-clicking and selecting **Properties** and then clicking the **Create** button. Any scripts in this new application will now access application variables for this application only and will not have access to those of its parent.

Managing State

State management has always been a subject of much debate since Web development began. For smaller projects, state is a little easier to manage and you can pretty much do whatever works best for you, but Web architects still disagree on the subject when discussing multi-million-dollar mega-projects. What is *state*, and why is the subject so difficult?

One of the first things that strike an experienced programmer coming to the Web for the first time is the odd fact that from one transaction to the next, the Web server, and therefore application, forgets who you are. On a desktop application, clicking buttons affects only the action you wish to achieve; it is very easy for the programmer to track what you have done before and what you are likely to do next. With a Web application, each request appears to the server as if it came from a new user, as the connection between the client and server is closed once the request has been processed. A desktop application maintains state by default, whereas the Web is stateless.

Actually, statelessness is one of the many advantages of the Web. If you think for a minute about what would happen if the Web was not stateless, you would see what I mean. Imagine all those millions of Hotmail users logging on to their mailbox first thing in the morning and not logging off until last thing in their work or school day. That would be far too much for even the largest Web farm to cope with. The Web was designed around very short conversations between Web browsers, such as, "Hello, can I have this page please" answered by, "Sure, here you go, goodbye"; there was no need for the connection to be maintained, and this allows for one server to provide pages for thousands of requests per second.

It is only when we try to make our Web applications work in a familiar desktop-style way that we run into problems. For example if you go to a cash machine and enter your personal identification number (PIN), you expect to not have to reenter that number any time within your session unless you have entered it incorrectly. With a Web site, without some means of managing session state, it is quite possible you will have to keep reentering your login details on every page you go to.

Many ways of getting around this problem have been used through the Web's short history, and all of them have advantages and disadvantages. All state management solutions center around storing and persisting information about the site user in some way, and many sites use a mix-and-match approach to achieve these objectives.

The most low-tech solution is to resubmit the information you need to keep alive on the site visitor's behalf, kind of like entering the person's username and password for them but still entering it on every page. This is usually done by putting the information into hidden fields on the Web form so that when the user clicks the **Submit** button, the receiving page gets the old values along with the new, freshly entered information. Of course, this means that every page download and submit is carrying extra data, slowing the page load each time; plus it is more difficult for the programmer and page designer, as they need to keep track of all the data that has been entered before and replicate it in the current page.

The next solution is to set a cookie on the user's browser. Netscape invented cookies as a browser-based state solution; they are a way that information can be set in small text files on the visitor's machine. The Web site and Web browser send information backward and forward in the HTTP headers. Cookies are used a lot on the Web, but unfortunately they are not always reliable, as in some circumstances the browser will turn off cookies. Also, you need to be aware of the inherent privacy and security concerns, as the information is visible to anyone else who uses the machine.

If you can uniquely identify a user, then you can store that user's information on the server or in a database; this is the technique that ASP.NET uses. A new user is provided a unique ID, either in a cookie or optionally as part of the URL, and from then on, until the end of the user's visit, the programmer can set and access information about them.

Analyzing Global.asax

The Global.asax is a special file that tells the server certain information about an application, such as what to do when the application is first started, or when the application is ended. The file affects the whole of the application and any subdirectories and files under it that do not come under another application of their own. While the Global.asax is very useful, the presence of a global file does not make a folder an application, and any configuration of the application is done separately on the server or in the separate web.config file.

Migrating...

Comparing ASP and ASP.NET Applications

Most of this chapter may seem familiar to experienced ASP gurus, but watch out, because there are one or two subtle differences. The most obvious change is the filename Global.asax to replace the old Global.asa. This is partly because you may wish to keep your old ASP scripts running for a time. This allows the two to continue in parallel. Next is the new bin folder. This is where your .NET components are stored, rather than registering into the Windows registry; this can sometimes cause confusion, as these components are now only available to the application and to the scripts under it, whereas COM objects were accessible from anywhere. The last big change is that an application can have its own unique configuration by changing an XML file, called web.config. These application settings are done independently of the MMC and only require FTP write access on the part of the developer, easing the burden on the stressed server administrator.

If you have used ASP applications in the past, you will recognize this concept as the old Global.asa. Global.asax does not replace any ASP application you have, and they will run quite happily in parallel. Unfortunately, they will run only in parallel; they cannot directly share application or session information.

Global.asax files contain directives and code, much like .aspx files. Much of the information in a Global.asax is optional, and a default file is created along with the application, if built as a Visual Studio project.

With directives, you can set certain values such as a description of the application, much like the description HTML metatag. Or, more usefully, the Import directive instructs the server to import specific .NET namespaces.

You can enter code into the Global.asx as events or object declarations, or include them with server-side Include statements. When the application is launched, like other pages in ASP.NET, the Global.asax is compiled into a .NET component, so the same rules for other components follow, enabling the Global.asax to inherit from other components, declare methods and events, and hold property values.

Understanding Application State

ASP.NET application state management is far improved over the previous ASP incarnations. In addition to the previous application variables, there are also two new facilities, the *Cache* and *Static* variables.

Application variables are values that are available to any user or page within an application. For the first time, they can be any value you wish to store. In previous versions of ASP, due to threading limitations, *Visual Basic* objects should not have been stored in application variables. VB.NET components do not have this limitation.

In this section we will take a look at the way we can use application state in our ASP.NET projects, with examples using application variables and the new cache functionality.

Using Application State

You use application variables like hashes or dictionaries, as it is a special type of collection, using the following method, where *"strKeyword"* is the name of the key as a string, and value is whatever you want to store in it:

```
' set an application variable
Application("strKeyword")=value


' output the contents of the variable
Response.write(application("strKeyword"))
```

Because application variables are effectively global variables for the whole application, you should carefully consider what the full implications on the system will be:

- The memory taken up by an application state variable is not readily freed up like the variables that you declare in a page or object, so you must free it up in code by deleting it. Carefully determine if what you store will be necessary and if storing it in application memory is prudent. As well as the memory implications, also remember that application state is in the server process memory only. If you want the information to persist, you should store it in a database or file system.

- Application state is not shared outside of the process in which the application is running. Each application process has its own set of values, on the same server in a multi-process environment, or in a Web farm of multiple machines, so use an external data store to persist state if your application relies on the validity of the data.

- The more locking and unlocking of application state that takes place, the more you risk tying up the server with delays in processing.

If you keep in mind these issues, then you can effectively use application state to give you a dramatic improvement in performance, as requests do not require filesystem, database, or network communication.

Application Cache Object

The cache can be thought of much like the application variable facility, in that it is shared storage that is accessible by the whole application, but the cache goes a fair bit further.

Cache values have some very powerful aspects that extend the application state concept much further than previous implementations, such as the ability to detect when a dependant object has changed and to automatically refresh.

Microsoft realized one of the popular uses for application state was to store frequently used information that would be useful for future users, such as option values from database tables to populate drop-down list boxes. Often these values would only be set when the application was started, so if the source information changed, then the application must be reset to refresh from the data source.

With the cache, you can expire information based on dependencies such as a timestamp (for example, set the data to refresh every day), and if the server finds that information is rarely used, then the data is expired automatically to free up resources.

As you can see from the following code excerpt, at their most basic, cache values are set in the same way as application variables. One major exception is that cache values are self-locking, so we do not have to worry about concurrent accesses as much as with the application values.

```
' set a cache value
cache("strKeyword")=value

' output cache value
response.write(cache("strKeyword"))
```

Static Variables

Static variables are values that are also available across the whole application, but have some performance advantages and fewer overheads.

The main difference to static variables and the previous examples is the fact that static variables are a side benefit of ASP.NET being object-oriented and the global being a .NET class, where as the other two methods are simply special collections. Static variables are declared in the Global.asax by first giving the global itself a class name and then declaring the variables.

We will come back to static variables later. For the moment, remember that using application variables and cache to store information does not require you to write your own Global.asax, but if you want to use static variables, then you must write your own Global.asax.

State Example

The following simple example, shown in Figures 5.1 and 5.2, demonstrates using application variables to count page views in an application. One of the major traps a programmer can fall into with application variables is errors and conflicts, where two processes try to write to the same value simultaneously; our example also shows how to use locking to overcome this.

Figure 5.1 Application State

```
<html>

<head>
<title>Chapter 5</title>
</head>
```

Continued

Figure 5.1 Continued

```
<body bgcolor="white">

<%

'# lock the application to prevent clashes
Application.Lock()

'# increment application counter
Application(page.ToString) += 1

'# unlock application
Application.UnLock()

%>

<p>
This page has been visited <b><%=application(page.toString)%></b> times
    since the application started<br>

</body>
</html>
```

Debugging...

Testing and Error-Checking Your Application

Be very careful to not store sensitive information in session and application variables. A new feature of the ASP.NET environment is the ability to dump tracing information to the Web browser. If this is inadvertently triggered through an error or by switching to debug mode, the server will output all the user's current variable information to screen, possibly

Continued

> including your database connection information, usernames, and passwords. Rather than store this information in application or session variables, it would be better to store them elsewhere; you could possibly use the new options found in the Web configuration files.

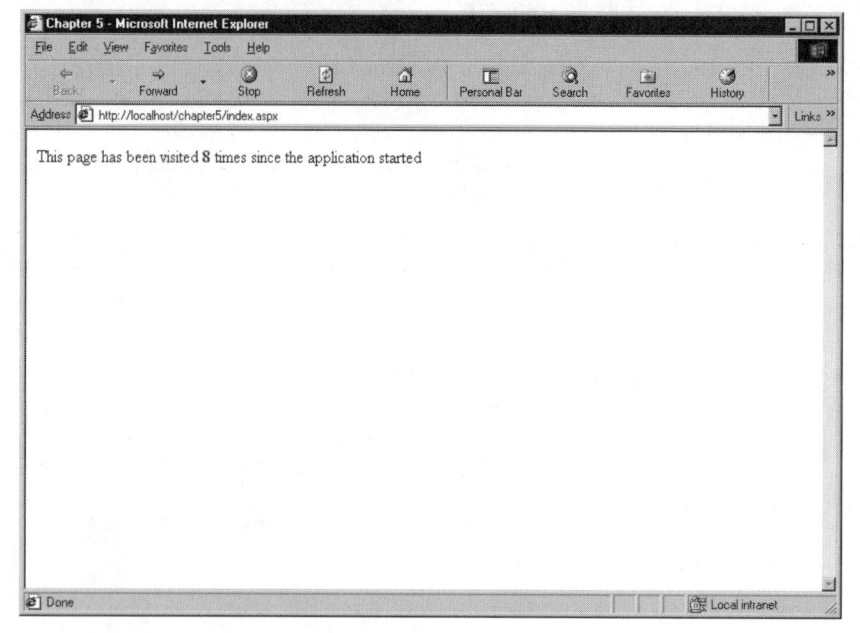

Figure 5.2 Application State at Work

Using Application Events

As stated previously, ASP.NET is object-oriented and event-driven; therefore, you should not be surprised to see that applications are no exception. In total, there are 18 standard events that the programmer can use, plus, if these do not cover what you want, then you can define your own. You do not have to set any event code if you do not want to, though, as you will see, they do bring some interesting and useful functionality to your application.

Supported Application Events

Table 5.1 displays a selection of events you will probably come across. We doubt you will need to use many of these very often, but knowing what they are could come in handy!

Table 5.1 Useful Events Supported by the ASP.NET Application

Event	Description
Application_OnStart	This event is processed when the application or server is started or rebooted. This event is useful for initializing values that will be useful for the whole application, setting up database utility objects and functions, and preloading the cache.
Application_OnEnd	*OnEnd* is complementary to *OnStart*, and is mainly used for cleaning up and freeing up resources by closing down database connections, destroying objects, and clearing the cache.
Application_OnError	If an error is raised but not handled, this event can be called upon. It could be used to alert the administrator or write to a log, for example.
Application_OnBeginRequest	*OnBeginRequest* is executed on and before every page request. This is useful for any processing that needs to take place for every page before any output is generated.

More Events

Table 5.2 shows some examples of the other events you may want to use.

Table 5.2 Less Commonly Used Application Events

Event	Description
Application_OnAcquireRequestState	We can use this event to fill session values using our own state management routines, if we wanted to not use the default ASP.NET state management.
Application_OnAuthenticateRequest	This event enables us to add code to authenticate a request when using IIS/ASP.NET authentication, such as querying a database or XML file.

Continued

Table 5.2 Continued

Event	Description
Application_OnAuthorizeRequest	*AuthorizeRequest* is raised when the above request has been authorized. We could use this for logging purposes or perhaps to allow additional permissions to the user based on a security database.
Application_OnEndRequest	This is the last event before the browser receives the output from our ASP.NET page. We can use this to add tracking code to the page or perhaps a standard copyright message.
Application_OnPostRequestHandlerExecute	*PostRequestHandlerExecute* is raised when the response has all the data to send to the client.
Application_OnPreRequestHandlerExecute	This enables us to perform procedures before the HTTP handler gets the request.
Application_OnReleaseRequestState	After this event is processed, we can no longer gain access to the session state data. This is our last opportunity to persist any required values to permanent storage such as a database or filesystem.
Application_OnResolveRequestCache	This event fires when ASP.NET determines if a page might be provided from the cache.
Application_OnUpdateRequestCache	*UpdateRequestCache* event is raised when the output cache is to be updated.

Working with Application Events

To use application events in your project, you must do the following (Figures 5.5 and 5.9 later in the chapter show examples of Global.asax files that demonstrate how to implement these events in your projects):

- Create a Web application folder using the MMC.
- Create a file called Global.asax in the directory you marked as an application.
- Within the Global.asax, enter script tags with the language you are using (e.g., VB).
- Insert subroutines using the name of the event you wish to use. Any code you add to this subroutine will run when the event fires.

For example, if you only wanted to use the *Application_OnStart* event you could create a Global.asax like the following:

```
<script language="VB" runat="server">
Sub Application_OnStart()


End Sub
</script>
```

Threading Use

As application level values are accessible and writeable by any or all scripts and users within an application, you must be careful when writing values to an application variable, as multiple threads may request the same object. If two processes try to write to the same value simultaneously, you could get unpredictable results and errors.

The application object has methods to get around this. Before writing to the value, you can call the lock method that will stop or delay any other process from changing the value. Once the value is locked, you can go ahead and write to the variable without worrying that another process will attempt to write to it. After you have done writing to the variable you must unlock it so others can write their data.

Application locking must be used carefully as it can introduce delays into your application, but it is far safer than hoping for the best.

Another aspect where threads have an impact is the fact you can now safely use *Visual Basic* objects in your application variables. In the past with ASP, you were not able to do this properly because the Visual Basics threading model would cause unwanted affects. Now with ASP.NET and Visual Basic .NET components, you can happily store your objects in the application state.

Understanding Session State

When a visitor first logs on to your Web application, they are said to have started a new session with your application, and it generates a unique Session ID. This session ID is usually stored in a cookie, but the server can be instructed to use an alternative method of passing the session ID around as part of the URL. ASP sessions enable the developer to store information for that user's session in *Session* variables. *Session* variables are a lot like dictionary values in that they are a keyword and value pair; in an astrology application, a keyword such as "starsign" could have the value "Leo."

You have the option of storing session values in the Web server's memory, specifying one server in a Web farm to maintain the values or specifying the location of a database. Many developers will be glad for the many improvements this brings; the new ASP.NET solutions are broadly how many programmers overcame the limitations of ASP state management in the past.

Despite the solution provided in ASP.NET being greatly improved over the situation we have had in the past, we are still not in a position where everybody is happy. Using server memory has long been criticized, as this hogs a lot of memory resource per user, so does not scale well. Writing to a database moves the load out of memory, but adds a burden to your database management system and relies on connections being made and broken over your network. Think very carefully about what you want to achieve and what effect this will have on your system now and in the future, and, above all, do whatever works for you. If you have a few hundreds of thousands of visitors a month or less, you can probably handle using a few session variables without much concern. Our session state example is shown in Figures 5.3 and 5.4.

Figure 5.3 Session State

```
<html>

<head>
<title>Chapter 5</title>
</head>

<body bgcolor="white">

<%
```

Continued

Figure 5.3 Continued

```
'# lock the application to prevent clashes
Application.Lock()

'# increment application counter
Application(page.ToString) += 1

'# unlock application
Application.UnLock()

'# increment session counter
Session(page.ToString) += 1

%>

<p>

This page has been visited
<b><%=application(page.toString)%></b>
times since the application started<br>

You have visited this page
<b><%=session(page.toString)%></b>
times in this session<br>

</body>
</html>
```

Configuring Sessions

Each user session in ASP.NET is allocated a unique random 120-bit session ID that is communicated across server requests in a cookie or a modified URL, depending on how you choose to work it. If you want the application to not rely on cookies, then you can set the application to put the ID in the URL using the following web.config setting:

```
<sessionstate cookieless="true" />
```

Figure 5.4 Application and Session State

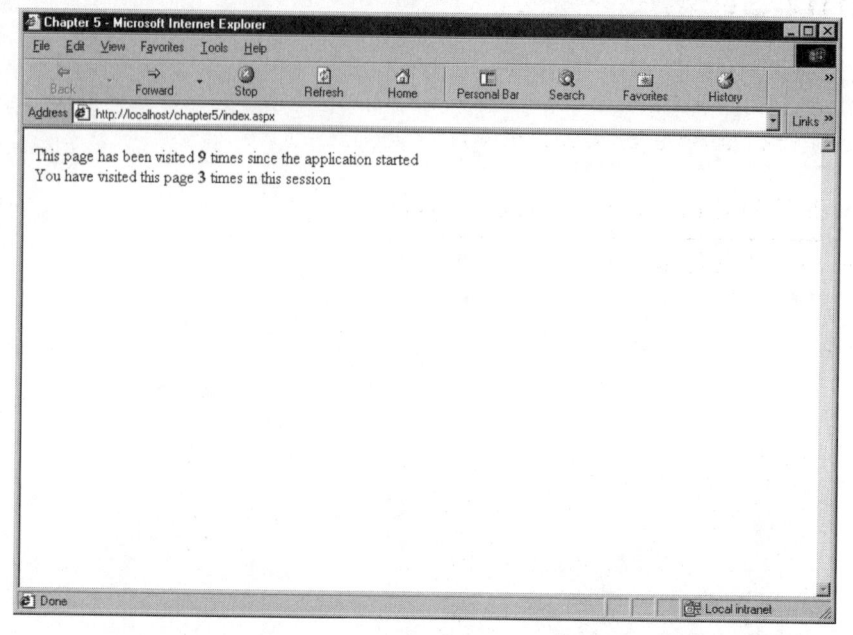

![Figure 5.4: Internet Explorer window showing http://localhost/chapter5/index.aspx with the text "This page has been visited 9 times since the application started" and "You have visited this page 3 times in this session"]

By default, the session will expire due to the user's inactivity after a period of 20 minutes. This is usually a reasonable figure, but there are cases where you would want to change this behavior to another duration, either to a lower amount of time because you require higher security, in case the user walks away from the browser, or change to a longer period. You can set the figure with the following web.config setting:

```
<sessionstate timeout="5" />
```

It is possible to switch off session state management. You may wonder why you would want to do this after reading how useful and easy it can be to use session state management. Session state demands additional processing by your server that may not be necessary, and the default setting sets a cookie on the clients browser that may not be ever used.

You can turn off session state in a single page with the following directive:

```
<%@ Page EnableSessionState="false" %>
```

To turn off session state for the whole application, put the following in the web.config file:

```
<sessionstate mode="off">
```

Using Session Events

Just as applications have events, the session has related events also: *session_OnStart* and *session_OnEnd*. Figures 5.5, 5.6, and 5.7 demonstrate how to implement session and application events within your Global.asax files.

Figure 5.5 Session Events in Global.asax

```
<script runat=server>

    Sub Session_onStart(ByVal sender As Object, ByVal e As EventArgs)

        '# lock the application to prevent clashes
        Application.Lock()

        '# increment application counter
        Application("cntApplication") += 1

        '# unlock application
        Application.UnLock()

    End Sub

</script>
```

Figure 5.6 Using Session Events

```
<html>

<head>
<title>Chapter 5</title>
</head>
```

Continued

www.syngress.com

Figure 5.6 Continued

```
<body bgcolor="white">

<%

'# lock the application to prevent clashes
Application.Lock()

'# increment application counter
Application(page.ToString) += 1

'# unlock application
Application.UnLock()

'# increment session counter
Session(page.ToString) += 1

%>

<p>

The application has been visited
<b><%=application("cntApplication")%></b>
times since the application started<br>

This page has been visited
<b><%=application(page.toString)%></b>
times since the application started<br>

You have visited this page
<b><%=session(page.toString)%></b>
times in this session<br>

</body>
</html>
```

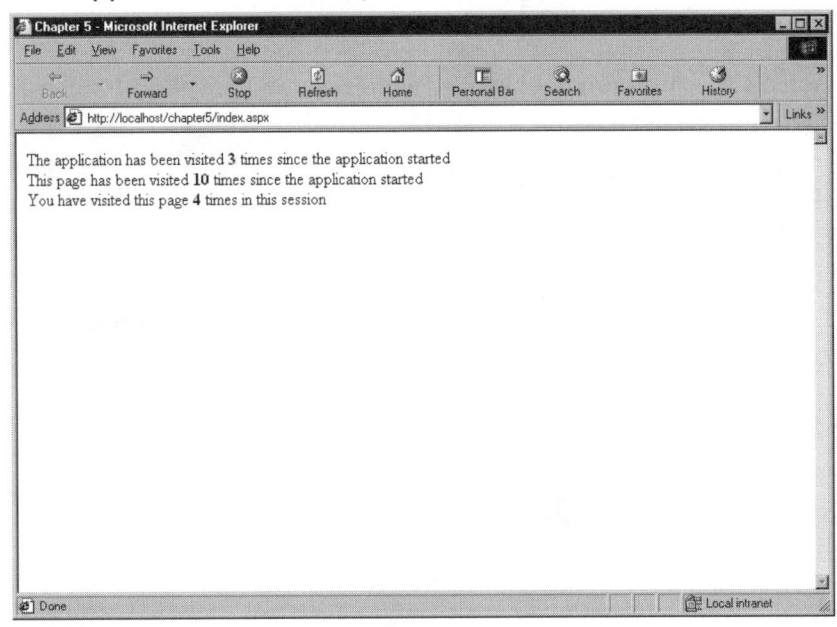

Figure 5.7 Application Variable Updated Using Session Events

[Screenshot: Chapter 5 - Microsoft Internet Explorer showing:
The application has been visited 3 times since the application started
This page has been visited 10 times since the application started
You have visited this page 4 times in this session]

Working with Session Events

As an example of how you might implement *Session* events in your projects, if you wanted to use the *Session_OnStart* event, then you could create a Global.asax like the following:

```
<script language="VB" runat="server">
Sub Session_OnStart()
    session("sessionStart")=DateTime.Now
End Sub


Sub Session_OnEnd()

End Sub
</script>
```

In this example, we have added code for the OnStart, but we do not need to process anything at session end, so we have left that subroutine blank.

Comparing Application and Session States

Application State deals with application-wide issues. Application state impacts every page for every user currently live in the Web application. Session State is only relevant to one user, for the duration of the particular session they are currently taking part in. One user's session does not have any impact on any other, whereas one user can affect values that another user can see and interact with.

As you can see from the code examples and in Figure 5.8, both states complement each other, and you will probably have used many Web applications that demonstrate examples of both.

Figure 5.8 Relationship between Sessions and Applications

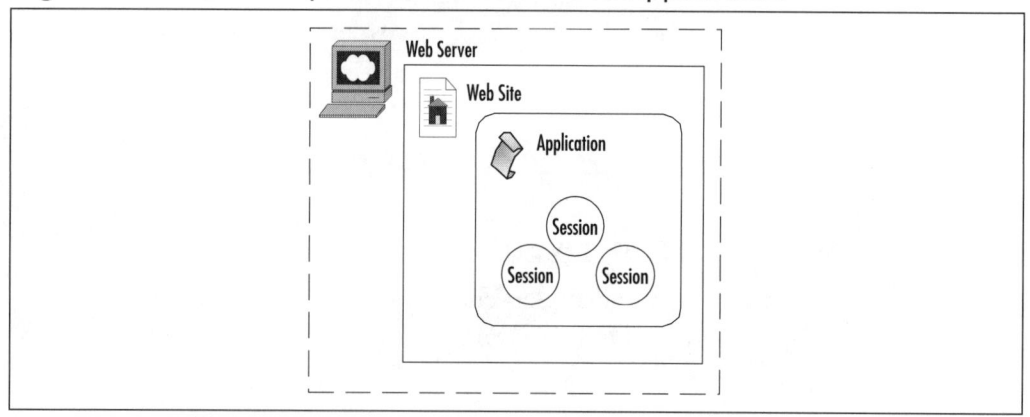

So far in this chapter, all the example code has been in Visual Basic .NET, so in Figures 5.9 and 5.10 we have reworked the existing application example in C# so that you can see the differences in syntax.

Figure 5.9 C# Global.asax

```
<script language="c#" runat=server>

public void Session_onStart()
{
// lock the application to prevent clashes
Application.Lock();
```

Continued

Figure 5.9 Continued

```
// increment application counter
if(Application["cntApplication"] == null)
 {
 Application["cntApplication"] = 0;
 }

Application["cntApplication"]=((int)Application["cntApplication"])+1;

// unlock application
Application.UnLock();


}

</script>
```

Much of the change in code is due to the fact that C# is much more conscious about variable types and conversion of one type to another than in Visual Basic .NET.

In the VB example, we did not have to worry what the application variable contained; we simply incremented whatever was there. Visual Basic would worry about if it was empty, and would simply convert the empty object to be a number.

C# would have an error in this scenario, both because we were trying to increment an object instead of an integer, and also because the object at that point would contain *Null*.

To get around this, we have had to add a check to see what the variable contains. We know if the variable contains Null, then this is the first run through the procedure since the application was started. If this is the case, then we initialize the variable to be a number—zero, to be exact.

We now know that by the time we get to incrementing the counter, there will always be a valid number there. This is where we encounter our next difficulty.

Where in the Visual Basic .NET example we simply incremented whatever was there, using the "+=" facility, in C# it's not that simple. The application variable would not be allowed to simply increment by one; we have to make the variable equal to one plus whatever is currently there, *converted to an integer*. We do this by preceding the application variable with "(int)," which means to the compiler: "Treat the following as an integer."

Other notable differences are that C# syntax, for arrays and collections, uses square brackets rather than the curved brackets used in Visual Basic .NET, and has curly brackets around functions.

Figure 5.10 Example in C#

```
<%@page language="c#" %>

<html>

<head>
<title>Chapter 5</title>
</head>

<body bgcolor="white">

<%

// lock the application to prevent clashes
Application.Lock();

// increment application counter
if(Application[Page.ToString()] == null)
{
 Application[Page.ToString()] = 0;
}

Application[Page.ToString()]=((int)Application[Page.ToString()])+1;

// unlock application
Application.UnLock();

// increment session counter
if(Session[Page.ToString()]==null) Session[Page.ToString()] = 0;
Session[Page.ToString()]=((int)Session[Page.ToString()]) + 1;
```

Continued

Figure 5.10 Continued

```
%>

<p>
The application has been visited
<b><%=Application["cntApplication"]%></b>
times since the application started<br>

This page has been visited
<b><%=Application[Page.ToString()]%></b>
times since the application started<br>

You have visited this page
<b><%=Session[Page.ToString()]%></b>
times in this session<br>

</body>
</html>
```

Static Values

To return to the subject of the alternatives to application, which is caching and static variables, let us look first at an example of how static variables can make our code cleaner and make it perform better (Figure 5.11).

Figure 5.11 A C# Global.asax Class

```
<%@ Application Classname="Chapter5" %>

<script language="c#" runat=server>

public static int cntApplication = 0;

    public void Session_onStart()
      {
```

Continued

Figure 5.11 Continued

```
        // increment application counter
        cntApplication++;

    }

</script>
```

Compare this code to the previous Global.asax. Isn't it much cleaner? The best thing is that it performs faster in many cases, too!

To use our static variable, *"cntApplication,"* we must first name our class. We do this with the very first line. We have called this class *"Chapter5"* in honor of this very chapter you are reading.

Once the class is named, we then declare our static variable. For the variable to be used outside the class, we must make it public. Static means that it retains its value from one access to another, and we have declared this variable as an integer number.

All that remains is to increment the value whenever a new session starts, using the C-like shorthand "++" increment operation. Whereas in the other examples, when we first locked the application before doing our increment and then unlocked the application, here you will see that we do not need to worry about locking at all, as the application class does this for us. Figure 5.12 shows the example C# static variable page.

Figure 5.12 C# Static Variable Page

```
<%@page language="c#" %>

<html>

<head>
<title>Chapter 5</title>
</head>

<body bgcolor="white">

<%
```

Continued

Figure 5.12 Continued

```
// lock the application to prevent clashes
Application.Lock();

// increment application counter
if(Application[Page.ToString()]==null) Application[Page.ToString()]=0;
Application[Page.ToString()]=((int) Application[Page.ToString()])+1;

// unlock application
Application.UnLock();

// increment session counter
if(Session[Page.ToString()] == null) Session[Page.ToString()] = 0;
Session[Page.ToString()] = ((int) Session[Page.ToString()]) + 1;

%>

<p>

The application has been visited
<b><%=Chapter5.cntApplication%></b>
times since the application started<br>

This page has been visited
<b><%=Application[Page.ToString()]%></b>
times since the application started<br>

You have visited this page
<b><%=Session[Page.ToString()]%></b>
times in this session<br>

</body>
</html>
```

For the other counters we still use application variables, as we do not know what the names will be beforehand, or how many there will be, as we could use this script for many pages and the code picks up the name of the page as the application key. To display the value of our static variable counter, we use the name of our class, *"Chapter5"* and the name of the variable, *"cntApplication."* As we are outputting the value using *response.write* (or the shorthand version at least), the variable knows to convert the integer to a string before passing out the value.

Caching Data

Storing frequently used data in memory can give you immediate and large performance gains, and can reduce load on your network and servers immensely. In this example, we will demonstrate how the new ASP.NET caching facility can be implemented in your scripts to improve performance by storing data in a cache object on the first user page request, and then using this cached copy of the data for future requests. The code for this example is shown in Figure 5.13, and the outputs are shown in Figures 5.14, 5.15, and 5.16.

Figure 5.13 Caching Example

```
<%@ Import Namespace="System.Data" %>
<%@ Import Namespace="System.Data.SqlClient" %>
<%@ page debug=true %>
<html>

<head>
<title>
Chapter 5: Caching
</title>
</head>

<body>

<form runat="server">


<p>
<!— a label to display status info —>
<asp:label id="oLabel" runat="server"/>
```

Continued

Figure 5.13 Continued

```
<p>
<!— a button to force a cache refresh —>
<asp:Button
     text="Refresh Cache"
     id="oRefresh"
     OnClick="ReCache"
     runat="server"
/>

<p>
<!— a link to reload the page —>
<a href="cache.aspx">Reload Page</a>

<p>
<!— our data grid to display data —>
<ASP:DataGrid
      id="oDataGrid"
      runat="server"
     BorderColor="silver"
     CellPadding=2
     CellSpacing=2
     Font-Name="Verdana"
     Font-Size="10pt"
     HeaderStyle-BackColor="gray"
/>

</form>
</body>
</html>

<script runat="server">
```

Continued

Figure 5.13 Continued

```
Sub Page_Load(Src As Object, E As EventArgs)

'# show the data grid with data
call ShowGrid()

End Sub

Sub ReCache(Src As Object, E As EventArgs)

'# force the cache to refresh from db
call RefreshCache()
response.redirect("cache.aspx")

end sub

Sub ShowGrid()

'# check to see if we have cache data
If Cache("gridData") Is Nothing

'# cache is empty so read from db
oLabel.Text = "Reading data from Database"
call RefreshCache()

Else

'# ok, we have cached data
oLabel.Text = "Reading data from Cache"

End If

'# set the data grid contents to
'# whatever is in the cache
oDataGrid.DataSource=Cache("gridData")
```

Continued

Figure 5.13 Continued

```
oDataGrid.DataBind()

End Sub

sub RefreshCache()

'# load data from the db into
'# our cache
Dim cn As SqlConnection
Dim da As SqlDataAdapter

'# set up db connection
Dim dsn as String
dsn="server=(local)\NetSDK;"
dsn+="database=pubs;"
dsn+="Trusted_Connection=yes"
cn = New SqlConnection(dsn)

'# load sql query
Dim sql as String
sql="select getDate() as Refreshed,"
sql+=" au_fname + ' ' + au_lname as Name from Authors"
da = New SqlDataAdapter(sql, cn)

'# fill dataset
Dim ds As New DataSet
da.Fill(ds, "Authors")

'# cache the data
Cache("gridData") = New DataView(ds.Tables("Authors"))

end sub

</script>
```

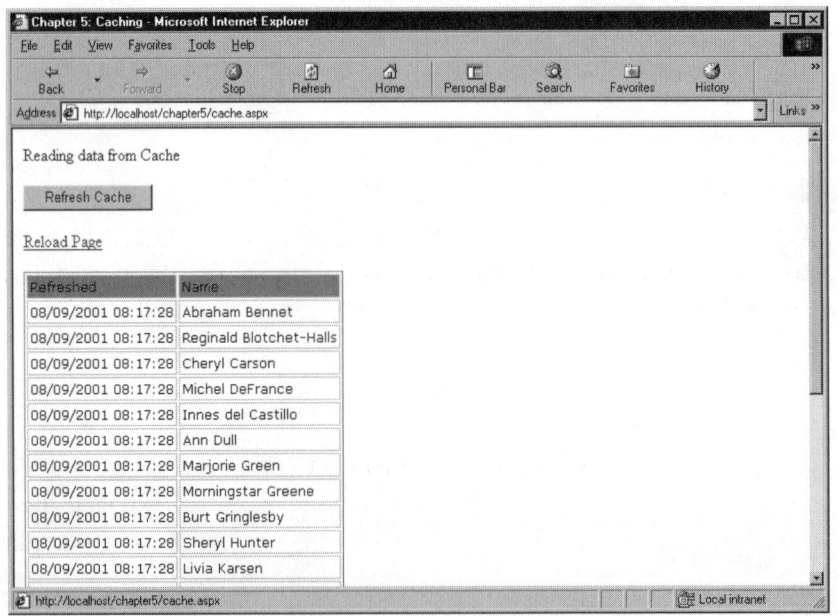

Figure 5.14 Screenshot Showing First Request

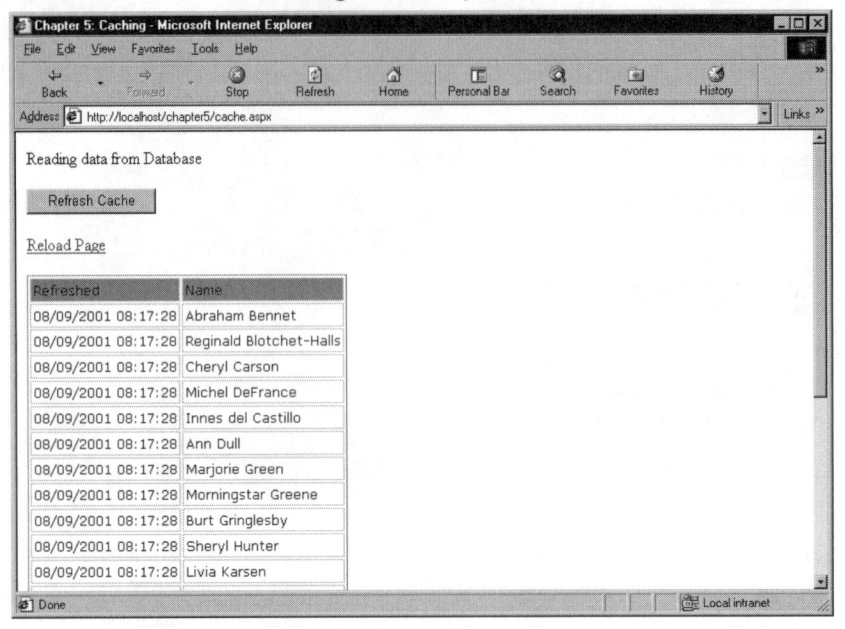

Figure 5.15 Screenshot Showing Subsequent Requests

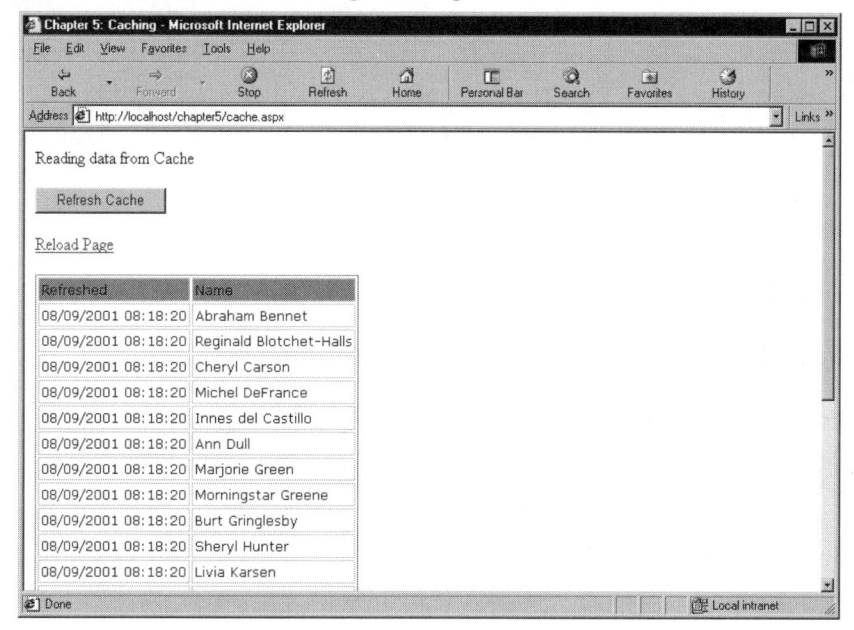

Figure 5.16 Screenshot Showing Forcing Cache Refresh

As you can see, using the cache is really easy to implement; the majority of this page deals with loading data from the database or displaying results.

First the page is set up, and we display the usual HTML head and body information, plus some server-side Web form components. After this, we check to see if a copy of the data has been previously cached. If we are on our first request of the page, then the cache will be empty, so we must extract and store the data in the cache. We fill a datagrid with the data that the cache contains. We know for testing purposes whether the data has been refreshed from the database by setting a label caption. We can force the data to refresh by pushing the button that calls the same routine used when the page is first loaded, to retrieve the database data.

This is fine for circumstances where the data is sure not to change, or, like in our example, we can trust the user to push a button to force a refresh. But what if this is not acceptable?

The cache functionality includes the facility to enable you to expire content based on a time delay, another value, or a dependency on an external file. The next example shows how you can use the timed expiry to make the application refresh the data periodically, and enforce up-to-date values.

Expiring the Cache

The cache has two methods of time expiring a cache value, *absoluteExpiration* and *slidingExpiration*. Absolute expiration is when the cache is deleted at a certain date or time, and sliding expiration is a time after the cache entry was last accessed. Syntax for the *Cache Insert* method is as follows, with the parameters shown in Table 5.3:

```
Cache.insert(key, value, dependencies, absoluteExpiration,
slidingExpiration)
```

Table 5.3 Parameters of the *Cache Insert* Method

Parameter	Description
key	Identifying key for cache item
value	The data to store
dependencies	Check for changes in this value or file to expire content
absoluteExpiration	Remove the cache value at a specific plan
slidingExpiration	Delete so long after the cache value was last accessed

To change our example so that the content is expired at a specific time interval of 10 minutes, we replace the cache-filling statements with the following:

```
'# cache the data
Dim MyData = New DataView(ds.Tables("Authors"))
Cache.insert("gridData", myData, nothing, _
    DateTime.Now.AddMinutes(10),TimeSpan.Zero)
```

Summary

ASP.NET provides an excellent framework for building Web applications. Now even more than in the past, ASP equips the programmer with excellent tools for dealing with application events and maintaining state. State is a very important subject when dealing with Web applications, and Microsoft has clearly looked carefully at how they can help the programmer out in this area.

All through this book you will see references to how Microsoft has built ASP.NET and the .NET framework as a fully object-oriented technology; ASP.NET applications carry this through to great effect, making the application Global.asax a class definition in its own right and allowing its member contents to be accessible to the rest of the application—its static variables especially. As well as application variables and the static variables, there is the new functionality of the cache object, enabling us to avoid lengthy delays over and over again for often-used data, by preloading and caching or caching on first hit. The cache also has the powerful ability to expire at a certain time and detect changes in the source it is dependant upon so that data can be refreshed.

Solutions Fast Track

Understanding ASP.NET Applications

- ☑ ASP.NET applications collect Web site resources into manageable organizational units.
- ☑ An application is made up of the files and directories within its parent folder.
- ☑ Applications can store values that are accessible to the whole application and all the users of that application.
- ☑ Events can be used to run procedures at certain points in the applications lifecycle.

Managing State

- ☑ State management allows the application to "remember" values from one transaction to the next.

- ☑ ASP.NET state management is improved over previous versions by not solely relying on cookies.
- ☑ Data can now be persisted using a database, and it offers more flexibility in load balancing situations.

Analyzing Global.asax

- ☑ Each application has its own Global.asax.
- ☑ Global.asax sets the event code and values for an application using script blocks and directives.
- ☑ When executed, Global.asax is a .NET component with events, values, and inheritance abilities.
- ☑ What is set in the Global.asax affects the whole of the application and scripts contained within it.
- ☑ To use application, session, and cache values, you do not need to write your own Global.asax, but you must if you wish to use static variables.

Understanding Application State

- ☑ The whole of the application code and all application users currently active can access application variables.
- ☑ ASP.NET introduces two new facilities to extend the application functionality, the *Cache* object and static variables.
- ☑ Cache values enable the programmer to preload content and data, with automatic expiry and dependencies.
- ☑ Static variables are the Global.asax application class member variables and are accessible to the whole application; and as they are not object collections, they do not have the overhead of application variables and so they have, in many cases, higher performance.

Using Application Events

- ☑ Application event code is written into the Global.asax as subroutines.
- ☑ Most commonly used events are those that deal with the application starting and ending, errors, or processing a request.

- ☑ Other events deal with authentication and cache issues.

Understanding Session State

- ☑ Session state deals with the information relating to one user for the duration of his or her active session, and any script within the application the user visits has access to all of the user's values.
- ☑ ASP.NET improves on previous versions of ASP session state solutions by allowing centralized state storage and on the ability to allow state management for users without cookies.
- ☑ A server will usually expire a session after 20 minutes of inactivity, but this can be set to a different value by the programmer.

Configuring Sessions

- ☑ Sessions are configured using web.config.
- ☑ Cookies are now no longer a requirement, and sessions can be set to be "cookieless."
- ☑ Using the *timeout* attribute, you can reduce or increase the session timeout value from the default.
- ☑ Pages and applications can turn off session state completely by setting the session-state mode to "off."

Using Session Events

- ☑ *Session* events deal with the processing of one user's session.
- ☑ Using *session_OnStart* and *session_OnEnd,* you can add code to run when the user enters and leaves a site.
- ☑ The session may end when the user closes his or her browser or the session has timed out.

Comparing Application and Session States

- ☑ Application state is the management of information relating to the whole application and all of the currently live users.
- ☑ Session state relates to each user separately.
- ☑ All users and scripts have access to the same application values, whereas one user can only access his or her own session information and can not see another's session variables.

Frequently Asked Questions

The following Frequently Asked Questions, answered by the authors of this book, are designed to both measure your understanding of the concepts presented in this chapter and to assist you with real-life implementation of these concepts. To have your questions about this chapter answered by the author, browse to **www.syngress.com/solutions** and click on the **"Ask the Author"** form.

Q: Must I have a Global.asax?

A: A Global.asax is not required; only use one if you need to. You will not need a Global.asax unless you want to use events or static variables, for example. Application, session, and cache values do not depend on your writing a Global.asax.

Q: Are there any security risks associated with session and application variables?

A: As the state information is stored in storage (server memory or a database) that the user has no direct access to, providing databases are secured, there is no direct security risk. Having said that, ensure that application variables do not contain sensitive information, as they are accessible to the whole application and to all users within it.

Q: Should I use application, cache, or static variables?

A: Use whichever is appropriate for your situation; if in doubt, use application variables. For simple values where the names are known beforehand and do not change, you may find static variables give you cleaner code and faster processing. Cached values are excellent for situations where users will frequently need to read the same data or where the application occasionally needs to refresh this data while the application is running. Application variables are probably best in cases where users might need to both read and write values to the variables often, and the variable names are not necessarily known beforehand.

Q: Can I use application state in a Web farm?

A: Yes, but your application data will only be visible to the process in which it is running. If you want this data to be shared, then you should store it in an external store instead, such as a database. For this reason, application state should not be used in a Web farm or a load-balanced environment when critical values are required.

Q: Can I use session state in a Web farm?

A: Yes, but carefully consider all the implications. Storing session state either puts a load on your servers, or network, or both.

Chapter 6

Optimizing Caching Methods

Solutions in this chapter:

- **Caching Overview**
- **Output Caching**
- **Fragment Caching**
- **Data Caching**
- **Best Uses for Caching**

- ☑ **Summary**
- ☑ **Solutions Fast Track**
- ☑ **Frequently Asked Questions**

Introduction

Data caching was introduced with Internet Information Server (IIS) in order to optimize the transfer of Web pages and speed up the user's access to these pages. ASP 2.*x* did not have any native caching ability and simply made use of the caching provided by IIS. Third-party utilities could also be used to increase the caching abilities of ASP 2.*x* and provide a greater level of control over the IIS cache.

Caching is now available natively within ASP.NET and has three new faces: *output*, *data*, and *fragment* caching. Each of these methods provides new and powerful methods of optimizing the utilization of system resources and increasing application performance.

Output caching is more like the old method of caching provided by IIS; a single page is stored within memory for a small period of time, for any reason that the programmer sees fit. While this model is troublesome in some instances, it can be helpful to the end-user at times. This allows for faster access to pages that contain some dynamic content without having to regenerate the entire page.

Fragment caching is an innovation to output caching; it enables the programmer to determine which parts of a page should be cached for future reference. This is done by breaking the code into separate user controls and then caching the control. This new feature greatly expands on our caching options.

Data caching enables the programmer to have full control over the caching at the object level. You can define which objects and which areas are to be cached and for what length of time, as you see fit. This detailed level of control enables you to save any object to memory that you wish, in order to speed up access to that object.

In this chapter, we are going to go over the three methods of caching that are available in ASP.NET. We will also discuss how and why to use each method and in what situations each method should be used. The options and parameters for each method will be discussed and illustrated. By using this information, you can greatly increase the performance of your application. This objective is key in creating an application that fits well with the needs of your users.

Caching Overview

Caching is a technique used in various aspects of computing to increase performance by decreasing access times for obtaining data. This is accomplished by retaining frequently accessed data within memory. This technique is used by many operating systems to cut down on the number of times that a hard drive must be accessed or a network connection utilized, by storing the needed data in the system's memory. It is also used by some databases to store data retrieved from queries that may be needed again later. As it pertains to a Web application, data is retained from across multiple HTTP requests, and can then be reused without incurring additional access times that would normally be necessary to recreate the data.

ASP.NET makes available three different types of caching, which, when used properly, can greatly increase the overall performance of your application. These types are as follows:

- Output Caching
- Fragment Caching
- Data Caching

We will go into detail in this chapter on each of these caching types, but they all are based off of the basic concept of saving all or a portion of the data generated by your application, with the purpose of presenting the same data again at a later time.

Output caching basically caches the entire content of an output Web page. This can be very useful when the content of your pages changes very little. Programmers familiar with ASP 2.x should be familiar with this concept, as it was the only available caching method for ASP. This method provides the greatest performance increase, but can only be used when nothing on the output page is expected to change within the valid timeframe of the cache.

Fragment caching, which is new in ASP.NET, allows for the caching of portions of your output page. This is an excellent improvement in caching technique, and is best used when your application's output page has content that changes constantly in addition to content that changes very little. While this method does not provide as much of a performance increase as output caching, it does increase performance for applications that would formerly have been unable to use any caching at all due to the strict requirements of output caching.

Data caching, also new in ASP.NET, provides the ability to cache individual objects. Placing objects into the cache in this manner is similar to adding items to a dictionary. By using a simple dictionary-style interface, this method makes for an easy-to-use temporary data storage area while conserving server resources by releasing memory as cached objects expire.

A major consideration in planning your caching strategy is the appropriate utilization of server resources. There is a trade-off when it comes to the use of any kind of caching, in that for every item cached, less memory is available for other uses. While output caching provides the greatest performance increase, it also utilizes more memory than caching a few objects using data caching. On the other hand, due to the overhead required to store multiple objects by using data caching, it may be more logical to cache a portion of the output page by using fragment caching. Suggested uses are listed in Table 6.1; however, the best caching method for your specific application is dependant upon your output.

Table 6.1 Suggested Uses of Caching Types

Situation	Suggested Caching Type
The generated page generally stays the same, but there are several tables shown within the output that change regularly.	Use Fragment Caching in this situation. Cache the portions of the page that remain somewhat static, while dynamically generating the table contents. Also consider using Data Caching for storing some individual objects.
The generated page constantly changes, but there are a few objects that don't change very often.	Use Data Caching for the objects.
The generated page changes every few hours as information is loaded into a database through automated processes.	Use Output Caching and set the duration to match the frequency of the data changes.

Developing & Deploying...

Optimizing Cache versus Optimizing Server Resources

When it comes to optimizing your Web application's performance, there are two factors that you must keep in mind. The first is the caching method(s) that you choose, and the second is server resources. It is not possible to implement a good performance plan without keeping both

Continued

> factors in mind. The choice of caching method will depend on the output of your page more than any other factor. For example, it doesn't matter if you have enough server resources to implement Output Caching, if your output changes constantly.
>
> When data is cached on the server, additional memory resources are used for storage of the cached data. The cached data includes not only the page output or the objects that you cache, but also header information necessary to obtain the correct cached data again later. As you cache more data, less memory is available for other uses. You may need to add more memory to your server to compensate for this in order to provide the highest performance increase. By testing your Web application extensively, you will be able to find the right mix of caching and hardware to provide the best performance at the right price.

Output Caching

Output caching provides the capability to cache response content generated from dynamic pages for the purpose of increasing application performance. This form of caching should be applied when the content of your page is somewhat static. Various options can be set for output caching including the duration.

In order for a page to be cached using output caching, it must have a valid expiration or validation policy. These options can be set either through the *@ OutputCache* directive or through the *HttpCachePolicy* class.

Using the @ *OutputCache* Directive

When the *@ OutputCache* directive is used at the top of the page, ASP.NET basically uses the *Page.InitOutputCache* method to translate the directive parameters into *HttpCachePolicy* class methods. These methods and properties can also be accessed through the *HttpResponse.Cache* property, which will be discussed later in this section. To set the expiration of a page you intend to cache, you can use the following code at the top of the page:

```
<% @ OutputCache Duration="60" VaryByParam="None" %>
```

This sets the cache duration for this page to 60 seconds as well as setting the *VaryByParam* attribute to not provide additional functions. The *VaryByParam* attribute is *required* when using the *@ OutputCache* directive. The *VaryByParam* attribute is one of three attributes used to control caching of multiple pages by the *@ OutputCache* directive. These attributes are as follows:

- VaryByParam
- VaryByHeader
- VaryByCustom

When ASP.NET generates the content of your page, the output can vary based on values that have been passed to the page. By using the *VaryByParam* attribute, you can control the caching of these pages based on a *GET* query string or *POST* parameters. By specifying the *GET* query string parameters or *POST* parameters using this attribute, each request received for that parameter using a different value will be cached. For example, if you specified the "*name*" GET query string parameter, each request received with a different *name* value will be cached separately. The syntax for setting a 60-second cache with the "*name*" parameter is as follows:

```
<% @ OutputCache Duration="60" VaryByParam="name" %>
```

If you use the "*name*" parameter with the *VaryByParam* attribute as shown in the previous code, and the requests shown in Figure 6.1 are received, ASP.NET will cache three pages, each for a duration of 60 seconds.

Figure 6.1 Sample Page Requests

```
http://LocalHost/testing/mypage.aspx?name=bob
http://LocalHost/testing/mypage.aspx?name=bob&cube=C4
http://LocalHost/testing/mypage.aspx?name=charlie
http://LocalHost/testing/mypage.aspx?name=chris&cube=A4
http://LocalHost/testing/mypage.aspx?name=chris&ext=5555
```

If the requests arrived in the order specified in Figure 6.1, the first, third, and fourth pages will be cached. For the duration of their time in the cache, any request with the *name* parameter containing these three names will be satisfied by redisplaying the cached data.

You can specify multiple parameters to the *VaryByParam* attribute by separating them with a semicolon. For example, using the code:

```
<% @ OutputCache Duration="60" VaryByParam="name;cube" %>
```

would result in caching four pages instead of three, if the requests specified in Figure 6.1 were received. In this case, the first, second, third, and fourth pages would be cached. Figure 6.2 shows the source of a small application demonstrating the use of the *VaryByParam* attribute. This code is located on the CD that accompanies this book as *output_cache.aspx*. Figures 6.3, 6.4, and 6.5 display the generated page after clicking on each button. Each page is stored in cache for 60 seconds.

Figure 6.2 Output Cache Example Code (output_cache.aspx0

```
<% @ OutputCache Duration=60 VaryByParam="button" %>

<HTML>
  <SCRIPT language="VB" runat="server">
    Sub Page_Load(Src As Object, E As EventArgs)
        TimeMsg.Text = DateTime.Now.ToString("G")
        PageName.Text = request.querystring("button")
    End Sub
  </SCRIPT>
  <BODY>
    <H3>Output Cache Example</H3>
      <FORM action=output_cache.aspx method=get>
      <P><H4>Click a button</H4>
      <INPUT type="submit" name="button" value="One">
      <INPUT type="submit" name="button" value="Two">
      <INPUT type="submit" name="button" value="Three">
      </FORM>
    <P>Page generated at: <asp:label id="TimeMsg" runat="server"/>
    <P>Page Name: <asp:label id="PageName" runat="server"/>
  </BODY>
</HTML>
```

Figure 6.3 Output Cache Example Page 1

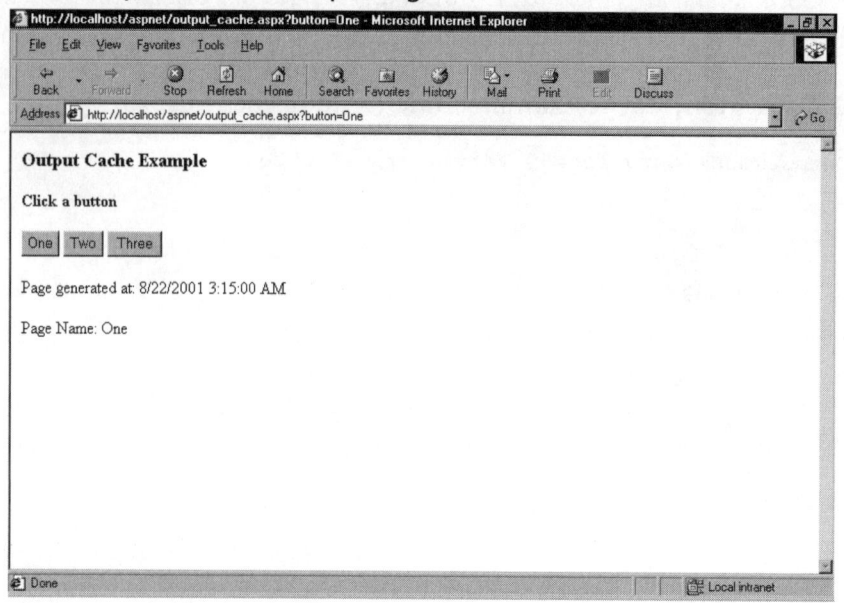

Figure 6.4 Output Cache Example Page 2

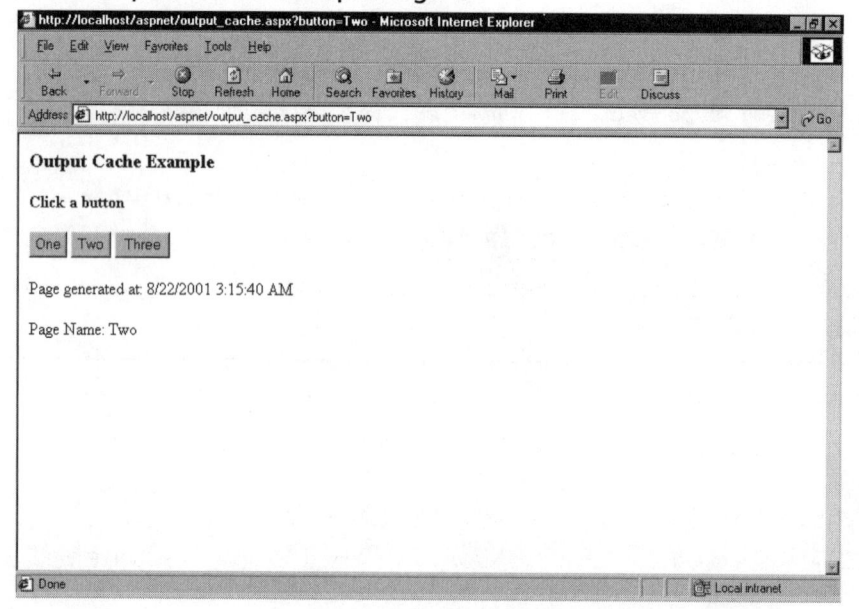

Figure 6.5 Output Cache Example Page 3

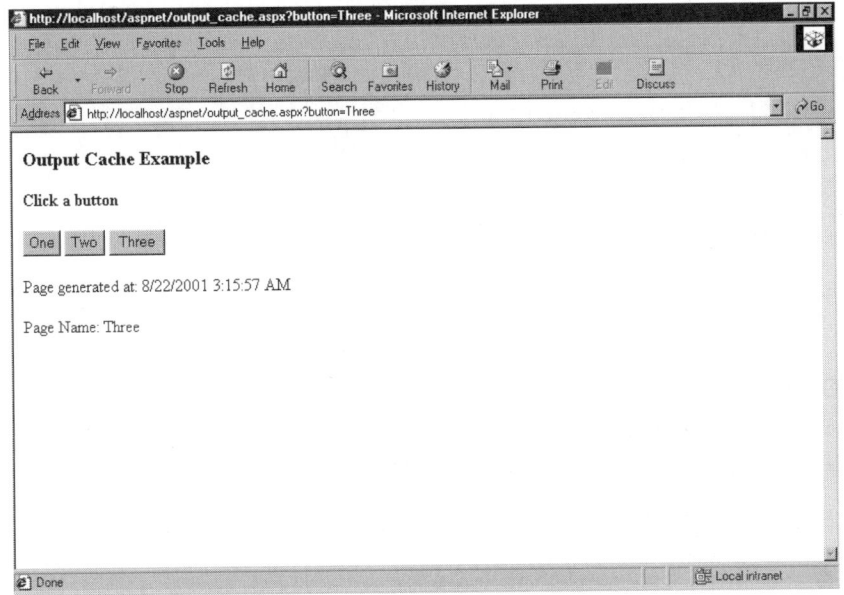

The second available attribute, *VaryByHeader*, enables you to control output caching based on the HTTP header that is passed to the page during a request. This opens up the option of caching multiple versions of pages based on any header variable. A partial list of acceptable HTTP header values available in this context is shown in Table 6.2.

Table 6.2 HTTP Headers

HTTP Headers	Description
ACCEPT	Acceptable media types
ACCEPT-CHARSET	Acceptable character sets
ACCEPT-ENCODING	Acceptable content coding values
ACCEPT-LANGUAGE	Acceptable languages (based off ISO639-2 standards)
ACCEPT-RANGES	Acceptable range requests
AGE	The amount of time since the response was generated
ALLOW	Methods supported by the server
AUTHORIZATIOn	Authorization credentials used for a request

Continued

Table 6.2 Continued

HTTP Headers	Description
CACHE-CONTROL	Cache control directives
CONNECTION	Options that are specified for a particular connection and must not be communicated by proxies over further connections
COOKIE	Cookies associated with the request
DATE	Date and time of request origination
FROM	E-mail address of the requesting user (if provided)
HOST	Address and port of the requested resource
MAX-FORWARDS	Number of proxies or gateways allowed between the requestor and the destination server
MIME-VERSION	The version of MIME used to construct the message
MSTHEMECOMPATABLE	Allow or disallow theme support (Only available in IE6+)
REFERER	URI of the user's last request
REQUEST-METHOD	The verb used for the request
SET-COOKIE	Value of the cookie set for the request
TRANSFER-ENCODING	Message body encoding type
USER-AGENT	Information about the user agent (browser) making the request

As an example, we could cache multiple versions of a page that differs based on the accepted language of the requestor. This would be accomplished by specifying the *Accept-Language* parameter to the *VaryByHeader* attribute as shown in the following code:

```
<% @ OutputCache Duration="60" VaryByParam="none"
    VaryByHeader="Accept-Language" %>
```

If three requests are then received with the *Accept-Language* header values specified in Figure 6.6, two will be cached. Because the third request matches the first, the third request will be fulfilled by the data that was previously cached by the first request.

Figure 6.6 Sample Header Values

en-us

en-uk

en-us

The final available attribute is *VaryByCustom*. This attribute enables you to control caching of the page based on browser version or other custom strings that you define. If you were to want to cache multiple versions of a page based on the browser type of the requestor, you would use the "*browser*" parameter with the *VaryByCustom* attribute.

```
<% @ OutputCache Duration="60" VaryByParam="none"
   VaryByCustom="browser" %>
```

This code has the effect of caching a different version of the page for every request coming from different browser types and versions based on the page's *Request.Browser.Type* property. If a request is made from an Opera browser and an Internet Explorer browser, two versions of the page are made available in the output cache for subsequent requests.

Using the *HttpCachePolicy* Class

Another method of setting the output cache for a page is to use the *HttpCachePolicy* class. This property enables you to control the caching policy at a much more granular level. In the first sample for the @ *OutputCache* directive, we set the cache for a duration of 60 seconds with no other parameters. To perform the same function using the *HttpCachePolicy* class, you could use this code:

```
Response.Cache.SetExpires(DateTime.Now.AddSeconds(60))
Response.Cache.SetCacheability(HttpCacheability.Public)
```

This sets the cache expiration to be 60 seconds from the current system time and gives the page public cache visibility. There are several other properties that can be set for the *HttpCacheability* method. These properties are listed and explained in Table 6.3.

Table 6.3 *HttpCacheability* Method Values

Value	Description
NoCache	This can be specified with or without an optional fieldname. When no field name is specified, the value applies to the entire request, and any shared cache such as a proxy server must requery the Web server instead of sending the cached page. When a field is specified, only the specified field will require a requery, and the rest of the page can be sent from the shared cache.
Private	This is the default value. When this is specified, the page will be cached only on the client end, and will not be cached by a shared cache such as a proxy server.
Public	By setting the *public* value, the page can be cached by a shared cache as well as by the client cache.
Server	This value specifies that the page has only to be cached on the Web server and not the client or a shared cache.

If you would like the cache duration to be extended each time the page is requested, the *SetSlidingExpiration* method can be set to true. This property defaults to false, which sets the page to expire when the time set in the *SetExpires* method lapses.

```
Response.Cache.SetSlidingExpiration(true)
```

It is generally best to use the *@ OutputCache* directive at the beginning of your page and only use the *HttpCachePolicy* class when you need a lower level of control over the caching header. Either of these methods can provide the same functionality, and the only reasons to use one over the other is the level of control that you need and the ease of use.

Advantages of Using Output Caching

The primary advantage of output caching is speed. When a page is cached using output caching, the entire page is stored in memory for the duration specified; therefore, the response to a request for this page is almost instantaneous. Implementing output caching within your application can increase the performance by several hundred percent depending on your content. Consider the access time difference between running a query against a remote database compared to pulling a page directly from memory.

In addition, the usage of output caching cuts down on the number of requests sent to your database server. When a page is dynamically generated for the first time, the data necessary is queried and then presented to the user. If the page is subsequently stored in cache, the database does not need to be queried in order to present the requested information. This can increase performance of your database server by eliminating many unnecessary queries.

Fragment Caching

In order to work with pages that have some dynamic content that needs to be updated regularly, as well as content that remains relatively static, Microsoft has provided the concept of fragment caching. This enables you to break your page into separate sections (fragments) that can be cached individually with their own caching options.

Using fragment caching is very similar to output caching. In fact, you call it in the same way as output caching by using either the *@ OutputCache* directive or the *HttpCachePolicy* class. Fragment caching is implemented by separating user controls out of your main page, and assigning caching parameters to each user control. This gives you a greater level of control over which portions of your page are cached.

An example of a good use for fragment caching is when you have a table within a page that has content generated from a database. In order to cut down on the number of queries being sent to the database, you want to cache the data in the table for a specified time period. However, the page that the table is displayed in has a timestamp that must be updated. The way we would accomplish this is to place the code used for generating the table into a user control and call the control from within the main page. This code is illustrated in Figures 6.7 and 6.8.

Figure 6.7 Fragment Cache Example Code Part 1 (fragment_cache.aspx)

```
<!- First we set up the user control ->

<%@ Register TagPrefix="Tag1" TagName="TestControl"
    Src="fragment_cache.ascx" %>

<HTML>
  <SCRIPT language="VB" runat="server">
      Sub Page_Load(Src As Object, E As EventArgs)

' We'll just load the current date/time into a string
```

Continued

Figure 6.7 Continued

```
            TimeMsg.Text = DateTime.Now.ToString("G")
      End Sub
  </SCRIPT>
  <BODY>
     <H3>Fragment Cache Example</H3>

<!— We'll run the user control first —>

     <Tag1:TestControl runat="server"/>

<!— Then show the time that this page was loaded —>

     <P>Main page generated at: <asp:label id="TimeMsg" runat="server" />
  </BODY>
</HTML>
```

Figure 6.8 Fragment Cache Example Code Part 2 (fragment_cache.ascx)

```
<!— We'll set the cache up for a two minute duration —>

<%@ OutputCache Duration="120" VaryByParam="none" %>

  <SCRIPT language="VB" runat="server">
     Sub Page_Load(Src As Object, E As EventArgs)

' We'll just load the current date/time into a string

         TimeMsg.Text = DateTime.Now.ToString("G")
     End Sub
  </SCRIPT>
  <P>
```

Continued

Figure 6.8 Continued

```
<!- In real use, we'd use data from a database for this.  We'll just make our
    own table for the example. ->

  <TABLE border=1 bordercolor=brown>
     <TR bgcolor=lightyellow>
        <TH>First Name</TH>
        <TH>Last Name</TH>
        <TH>Number</TH>
     </TR>
     <TR>
        <TD>Bob</TD>
        <TD>Marly</TD>
        <TD>555-1234</TD>
     </TR>
     <TR>
        <TD>Lee</TD>
        <TD>Young</TD>
        <TD>555-1235</TD>
     </TR>
  </TABLE>

<!- Show the time that this control was loaded ->

  <P>Table last generated on: <asp:label id="TimeMsg" runat="server" />
```

These code fragments are on the included CD as *fragment_cache.aspx* and *fragment_cache.ascx*. In the second code fragment, I am generating the table data within the code; however, fragment caching in this style is best used when you are pulling data from database tables. When this code is run, you will see two timers as shown in Figure 6.9. The first will list the time that the table was built. This is the time that the user control was called, and based on the *@ OutputCache* directive, this user control will be cached for 120 seconds. The second timer will show the time that the main page was generated. As no caching parameters were set for this page, it will not be cached. If you refresh this page after the initial load, you will see that the first timer will not change if the cache duration has not been passed, and the second timer is changed to the current time.

Figure 6.9 Fragment Caching Example

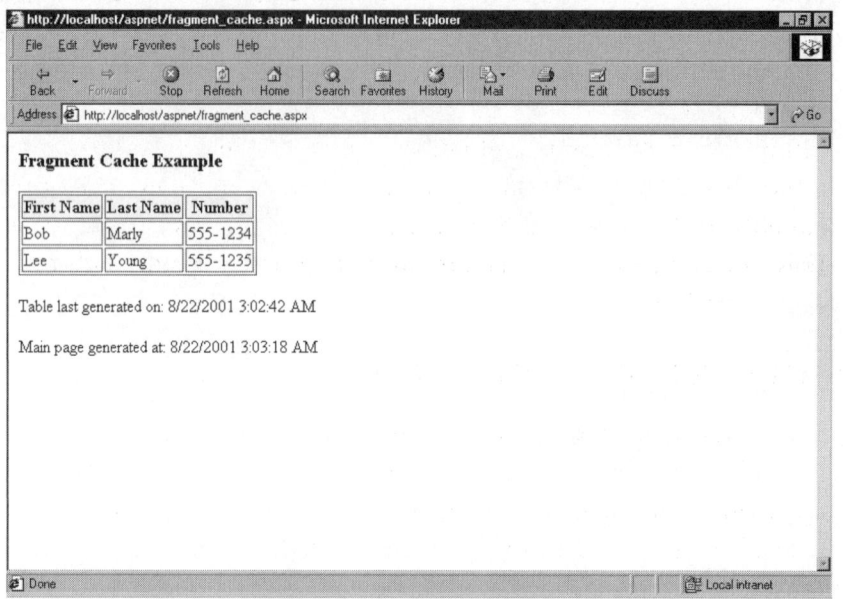

As with output caching, fragment caching can be used either through the *@ OutputCache* directive or programmatically through the *HttpCachePolicy* class. Fragment caching differs in that it only supports the *VaryByParam* attribute as well as a new attribute named *VaryByControl*. The *VaryByParam* attribute is a required attribute in fragment caching as well. Fragment caching does not support the *VaryByHeader* nor the *VaryByCustom* attributes.

The *VaryByParam* attribute works the same way in fragment caching as it does in output caching. Using this attribute, a separate page can be generated and cached for each argument provided to the user control. Just as in output caching, this capability greatly increases the performance of your page.

The additional attribute provided for fragment caching, the *VaryByControl* attribute, enables you to control the cache based on controls within the user control. This attribute can be used with the following syntax:

```
<% @ OutputCache duration="60" VaryByParam="none"
    VaryByControl="name" %>
```

For example, if you have a control in your application that contains a select box control named "name," then ASP.NET would cache a separate version of the page each time the value of the select box control changed.

There is one major aspect of fragment caching that must be kept in mind. If a user control is cached, it can no longer be manipulated. Basically, when the user control is cached, the instance for the control is only created on the first request, and not on subsequent requests when the data is pulled from the cache. Because of this, the logic necessary to create the content of a user control should be stored within the control itself, and not within the calling page. This can be done by using the *Page_Load* event or the *Page_PreRender* event. This enables you to pass arguments to the control and generate new content based on those arguments. This can be further enhanced by using fragment caching with the *VaryByControl* attribute.

Advantages of Using Fragment Caching

The greatest advantage of fragment caching is the ability to cache only portions of a page while generating the remainder of the page dynamically. While this does not provide as much of a performance increase as output caching, it enables you to take advantage of caching in situations when it would previously not be possible to cache the page at all.

A second advantage of fragment caching is the possibility of better use of memory resources. When caching an entire page, all of the data for that page is stored in memory. With fragment caching, only the portions of the page you specify are cached. This advantage is best presented when you have several pages that call a common user control. After the user control is cached on the first request, any subsequent request from any page presents the cached data. This enables you to make the most of your system resources by caching commonly used user controls.

Data Caching

Data caching provides the most granular control of cached data. The data cache is a full-featured cache engine that enables you to store and retrieve data between multiple HTTP requests and multiple sessions within the same application. As with output caching and fragment caching, the cached data and objects are stored in memory, providing fast access to cached information. Another similarity to output caching and fragment caching is that the cache is cleared completely when the application is reset.

Chapter 6 • Optimizing Caching Methods

There are three different methods that you can use to add data or objects to the cache. They all work in a very similar fashion, but offer different levels of control and usage. The *cache* method is used for fast and easy access to the data cache. The *cache.add* and *cache.insert* methods are used to give you a greater amount of control over the data that you cache. Each of these methods has its uses and we will go into detail on each of them in the sections that follow. Table 6.4 outlines the features of the different caching methods.

Table 6.4 Caching Method Features

Method	Stores Data in Cache	Dependency Support	Expiration Policy	Priority Settings	Returns Object
cache	X				
cache.insert	X	X	X	X	
cache.add	X	X	X	X	X

Using the Cache Method

Microsoft has provided a simple dictionary-style interface for using the data cache. Because of this interface, you can store and retrieve data from the cache as easily as you would store and retrieve data from a dictionary. The syntax for storing data in this cache is as follows:

```
cache("keyname")=value
```

Caching data has never been so simple! The retrieval of your data is also a very simple operation. In the following code, we will pull the value from the cache based on the key we specified, and display it.

```
myvalue=cache("keyname")
if value <> null then
    displaydata(myvalue)
end if
```

This method of caching works very well for providing fast access to your objects. In addition to using the simple dictionary-style method of storing and retrieving simple data, you can also use data caching to store arrays or any other object. This technique is illustrated in Figures 6.10, 6.11, and 6.12. You can find the source code in Figure 6.10 on the CD that accompanies this book as data_cache1.aspx.

Figure 6.10 Data Caching Example Code (data_cache1.aspx)

```
<SCRIPT language="VB" runat=server>

Sub Page_Load(source As Object, e As EventArgs)
    dim MyValue as string
    MyValue=cache("MyKey")
    if MyValue <> nothing then
        output.text=MyValue & "<P>This data retrieved from cache"
    else
        Dim stringArray() As string ={"Amy", "Bob", "Chris", "Dave", _
            "Eli", "Franklin", "Gerald"}
        dim MyString as string
        for each MyString in stringArray
            output.Text=output.Text & MyString & "<br>"
        next

        cache("MyKey")=output.Text
    end if
End Sub
</SCRIPT>
<HTML>
<HEAD>
</HEAD>
<BODY>
    <P><asp:label id="output" runat="server"/>
</BODY>
</HTML>
```

Figure 6.11 shows the output of the code sample in Figure 6.10 on the first page request. ASP.NET first checks the cache to see if the key name we specify contains any data. Since at this point it does not, the array is generated and saved to the cache. When the page is viewed a second time, as shown in Figure 6.12, ASP.NET finds the data in cache and displays the cached data as well as the message indicating that the source data is from the cache rather than being generated.

Figure 6.11 Data Caching Example Page 1

Amy
Bob
Chris
Dave
Eli
Franklin
Gerald

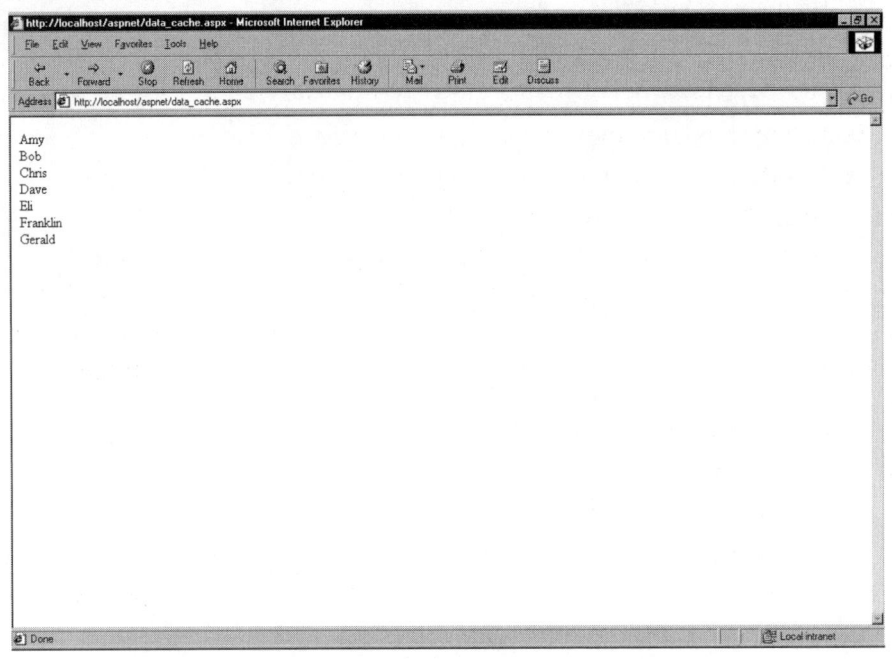

Figure 6.12 Data Caching Example Page 2

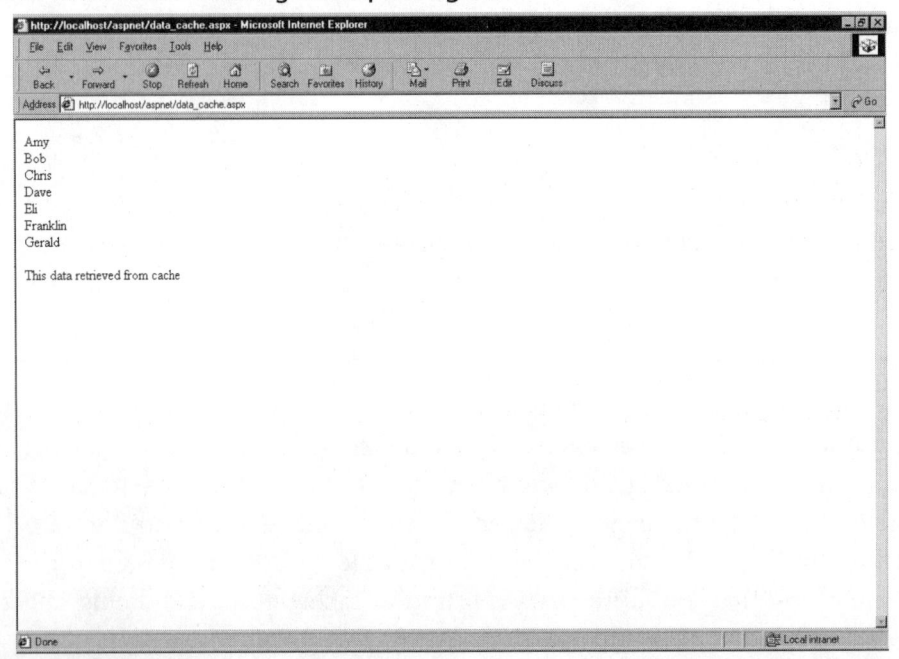

Amy
Bob
Chris
Dave
Eli
Franklin
Gerald

This data retrieved from cache

Using the *cache.add* and *cache.insert* Methods

In the example code in Figure 6.10, we have used the *cache* method in the same manner that we would use a dictionary. Using this method, the data remains in cache for the lifetime of the application or until it is explicitly removed from the cache. For greater control over the data we are storing in the cache, we can use two other methods of storing the data. The first is the *cache.add* method and the second is the *cache.insert* method. These are very similar, but they do differ, in that the *cache.add* method returns an object that represents the cached data, and the *cache.insert* method does not. The code used in the previous section to simply add an object to the cache can be expressed in the following way, using either the *cache.add* or the *cache.insert* method. For this example we will use the *cache.insert* method.

```
cache.insert("keyname", value)
```

Using either the *cache.add* or the *cache.insert* methods, you have three primary options available to us for the manner in which you can control the cached data. The first option is to base the expiration of a cached object on dependency files, directories, or other cached object keys. The second option is comprised of two different methods of controlling the expiration policy of the cached object based on time. The third option is comprised of two methods of controlling the cached object's cache priority, and the final option allows a method of obtaining notification when an object is removed from the cache.

Using the Dependency Option

When you have a dependency object set for a cached object, ASP.NET monitors the dependency object for changes. When a change is detected in the dependent object, the cached item with the dependency option expires. The syntax for using the *cache.add* and *cache.insert* methods with the dependency option is the same, and for this example we will use the *cache.insert* method:

```
cache.insert("keyname", value, New
    CacheDependency(Server.Mappath("data.xml")))
```

There are many ways to put this option to use. For example, if you wish for a cached item to expire when another cached item changes, then set the second cached object to be dependent on the first cached object's key.

It is also possible to make a cached object dependent on multiple other objects. For example, if you have multiple XML files that your page is pulling data from, and wish for a cached item to expire when any of the XML files change, you can list these files in an array and make the array your dependent object. An example of this usage is shown in Figure 6.13, and you can locate this code on the CD that accompanies this book as data_cache2.aspx.

Figure 6.13 Data Caching with Multiple Dependencies Code (data_cache2.aspx)

```
<SCRIPT language="VB" runat=server>

Sub Page_Load(source As Object, e As EventArgs)
    dim MyValue as string
    MyValue=cache("MyKey")
    if MyValue <> nothing then
        output.text=MyValue & "<P>This data retrieved from cache"
    else
        Dim StringArray() As string ={"Amy", "Bob", "Chris", "Dave", _
            "Eli", "Franklin", "Gerald"}
        dim DependentString() as string ={server.mappath _
            ("partofmydata.xml"), server.mappath("theotherpart.xml")}
        dim MyString as string

        for each MyString in StringArray
            output.Text=output.Text & MyString & "<br>"
        next

        cache.insert("MyKey", output.text, new _
            CacheDependency(DependentString))
    end if
End Sub
</SCRIPT>


<HTML>
<HEAD>
</HEAD>
```

Continued

Figure 6.13 Continued

```
<BODY>
    <P><asp:label id="output" runat="server"/>
</BODY>
</HTML>
```

Using the Expiration Policy Option

The second caching option sets the expiration policy of the cached object. There are two ways to set the expiration policy. The first is to use an absolute expiration time that sets the cached object to expire at a specific time. The syntax for this statement is as follows:

```
cache.insert("keyname", value, nothing, _
    datetime.now.addminutes(2), timespan.zero)
```

Even when using just one of the two expiration policy parameters, the other must contain some value. In addition, when using either method, you must set the dependency option to either an object or the *nothing* object. In the case of the previous code, we have set a timespan of 0 for the second parameter, which effectively disables it. This option is useful when you have a cached object that you want to have refreshed on a regular basis regardless of how many times the cached object has been accessed.

The second expiration policy option is to use a sliding expiration. Using this method, the cached object's absolute expiration time is increased by value of the sliding expiration parameter. For example, to force the cached object to expire 10 seconds after the last request for the cached object, you could use the following code:

```
cache.insert("keyname", value, nothing, _
    datetime.maxvalue, timespan.fromseconds(10))
```

Again, as both parameters must contain some value, the absolute expiration parameter has been set to the maxvalue of datetime, which effectively disables the absolute expiration policy.

By using either of these expiration policy options, you can specify the duration of your objects in cache. One caveat to keep in mind is that you must use either an absolute expiration time or a sliding expiration, and ASP.NET does not support the use of both on the same object. Therefore, when setting the expiration policy option, you must use either the *timespan.zero* or the *datetime.maxvalue* option.

Using the Priority Options

All of the options for specifying the duration of an object in cache are secondary to ASP.NET's method of conserving system resources. If your system begins to run low on available memory, the first thing ASP.NET does is begin to clear out the cache until the available system memory reaches a tolerable level. If we had no control over this process, your Web application's performance could be severely degraded by the loss of critical cached items. Fortunately, ASP.NET provides the ability to control the purging of your cached data. This is set through two options for the *cache.add* and *cache.insert* methods.

The first option available is the *CacheItemPriority* setting. This enables you to set different priorities on cached objects based on how critical the cached data is to the performance of your application. The default value is *Normal,* and objects are purged in order of lowest priority to highest, leaving high priority objects in the cache for as long as possible. Table 6.5 outlines the different priority settings available for cached objects.

Table 6.5 *CacheItemPriority* Values

Value	Definition
NotRemoveable	Cached objects with this priority will never be removed from memory when ASP.NET is purging due to a loss of memory resources. Use this option sparingly, as negative results can occur when ASP.NET is prevented from obtaining needed memory resources due to too many unremovable items in the cache.
High	Objects with this priority level are the last to be purged. ASP.NET will clear all lower-priority objects from memory before clearing objects designated as High priority.
AboveNormal	Objects with this priority level are less likely to be purged than items left at the default level.
Normal	This is the default priority level for cached objects. This value is assigned to all cached objects that do not explicitly have a priority level designated.
BelowNormal	Objects with this priority level are considered by ASP.NET to be less critical to your application's performance than normally cached items.
Low	Cached Objects with this priority level are the first to be purged when system memory resources are low.

The second option for setting the priority of cached objects is the *CacheItemPriorityDecay* setting. This option controls the purging of objects from the cache when they are accessed infrequently. This differs from the *CacheItemPriority* setting in that it controls the purging of cached objects based on the frequency of their access, as compared to a loss of system memory resources. As with the *CacheItemPriority* setting, this option has several different values. These values are described in Table 6.6.

Table 6.6 *CacheItemPriorityDecay* Values

Value	Definition
Never	Objects set with a decay of Never will not be removed from the cache if accessed infrequently.
Slow	Objects with a decay of Slow are the last to be purged.
Medium	This is the default setting for any objects without a differing explicit setting.
Fast	Objects with this setting are the first to be purged if they are not frequently accessed.

When you choose to explicitly set the priority of a cached object, both priority options must be set as well as setting a *CacheItemRemovedCallback* delegate, which will be discussed in the next section. To illustrate the use of the priority options, let us assume that we have a dataset to cache. This dataset is very rarely changed and is accessed very often. Although it is large, we have determined that the application would suffer a greater performance loss by not having this data cached than it would by reallocating the memory resources used by the cached dataset. In this scenario, we would want to set the *CacheItemPriority* value to *High* and the *CacheItemPriorityDecay* value to *Slow*. In addition, we will set the *CacheItemRemovedCallback* delegate to *OnRemove*. We do want the data to be refreshed occasionally, so we will also use an absolute expiration of one hour.

```
cache.insert("MyKey", mydataset, nothing, _
    datetime.now.addminutes(60), timespan.zero, _
    CacheItemPriority.High, CacheItemPriorityDecay.Slow, OnRemove)
```

Using the *CacheItemRemovedCallback* Delegate

The *CacheItemRemovedCallback* delegate is a function of the cache that allows the application to be notified when an item is removed from the cache. The

Chapter 6 • Optimizing Caching Methods

CacheItemRemovedCallback delegate returns three parameters that must be accepted by your event handler: the cached item's key, the value of the cached item when it was removed, and the reason for removal. There are four valid reasons for an object to be removed from the cache, and they are outlined in Table 6.7.

Table 6.7 *CacheItemRemovedReason* Values

Reason	Definition
DependencyChanged	When the files, directories, or keys specified in the dependency option are changed, this reason is reported upon the cached object's removal.
Expired	If an expiration policy is set for a cached object, this reason is reported when the absolute expiration time has been met.
Removed	If a cached object is explicitly removed or replaced due to the usage of the same key, this reason is reported.
Underused	If ASP.NET has removed the cached object due to a lack of system resources or because the data is underutilized, the Underused reason is reported.

I have illustrated the use of all the caching options available for the *cache.add* and *cache.insert* methods in the code shown in Figure 6.14. In this code, we first check to see if there is any data stored in the cache under the key "MyKey." If data is there, then note that the data was retrieved from cache, remove the data from the cache, and display the data. If no data is in the cache, then your array is loaded into the cache. When you do remove the cached data, you fire an event that adds the fact that the data was removed from cache as well as the reason code to the array, and then recache the result. When you recache it the second time, you do not add the *CacheItemRemoved* option; otherwise you would end up in a loop. This code is located on the CD that accompanies this book as data_cache3.aspx.

Figure 6.14 Data Caching Full Sample Code (data_cache3.aspx)

```
<SCRIPT language="VB" runat=server>

Private Shared OnRemove as CacheItemRemovedCallback = Nothing

Public Sub RemovedCallback(key as string, value as object, _
```

Continued

Figure 6.14 Continued

```
        reason as CacheItemRemovedReason)
        'At this point, place any code needing to be executed upon
        'an item's removal.  As an example, we will now recache the
        'object after making a change.
        value=value & " *recached due to reason code " & reason & "*<br>"
        cache.insert(key, value, nothing, datetime.maxvalue, _
            timespan.fromseconds(10))
End Sub 'RemovedCallback

Sub Page_Load(source As Object, e As EventArgs)
    onRemove = New CacheItemRemovedCallback(AddressOf _
        Me.RemovedCallback)

    dim MyValue as string
    MyValue=cache("MyKey")
    if MyValue <> nothing then
        output.text=MyValue & "<P>This data retrieved from cache"
        'Now we'll remove the item from cache, just to trigger the
            event'
        Cache.Remove("MyKey")
    else
        Dim StringArray() As string ={"Amy", "Bob", "Chris", "Damien", _
            "Eli", "Franklin", "Gerald"}
        dim DependentString() as string ={server.mappath("test.txt"), _
            server.mappath("test2.txt")}
        dim MyString as string

        for each MyString in StringArray
            output.Text=output.Text & MyString & "<br>"
        next

        cache.insert("MyKey", output.text, nothing, datetime.maxvalue, _
            timespan.fromseconds(10), CacheItemPriority.Low, _
```

Continued

Figure 6.14 Continued

```
                CacheItemPriorityDecay.Fast, onRemove)

    end if
End Sub
</SCRIPT>

<HTML>
<HEAD>
</HEAD>
<BODY>
    <P><asp:label id="output" runat="server"/>
</BODY>
</HTML>
```

Using the *Cache.Remove* Method

Removing data manually from the cache is a useful method of clearing up resources or giving your end user the option of verifying that the data they are viewing is up to date. The way this is done is similar to the simple dictionary cache interface. I have used the *cache.remove* method in Figure 6.14, which illustrates its syntax:

```
cache.remove("MyKey")
```

Advantages of Using Data Caching

We have gone over the plethora of different options available for data caching, and I believe that its many advantages are apparent. With the ability of caching data at the object level, you are given the most granular control over ASP.NET's caching features possible. By using the dictionary interface, you have a simple manner of adding and removing data from the cache. If, however, a greater amount of control is necessary, ASP.NET provides for this with the expiration features and priority levels.

By using all of these features in the best manner possible, you can increase the overall speed of your application without the requirements of using a separate user control or a semi-static page. While data caching does take up more memory per saved object than object or fragment caching, its primary strength is that you can store smaller amounts of data in the cache, thus opening the possibility of saving memory resources overall.

> **Debugging…**
>
> **Implementing Caching**
>
> When building your Web application, it is best to not implement caching on the initial build. There are several reasons for this, the primary being ease of debugging. You will find that it is much easier to get an application completely debugged without having to deal with the question of cached pages and data. When you have the application debugged, begin adding in the caching features of ASP.NET where they are most effective. You will see an immediate performance increase in your application, as well as make your debugging process much faster by following this process.
>
> A second advantage of this method is that you have an opportunity to set a baseline for your application. As memory resources on the server become scarce, cached data is dumped in order to conserve resources. With this baseline performance data, you can provide a worst-case scenario for your application.

Best Uses for Caching

When should you use caching? As often as possible. In order to make your application viable in today's fast-paced world, you have to make your data available as quickly as possible and decrease the wait-time for your end user as much as possible. By using the various types of caching in the best manner possible, you can change your application from slow yet effective to fast and amazing. When users access an application created using ASP.NET's caching features for the first time, the first thing they will notice is the speed increase. In the overall user experience, this is one of the most important impressions that you can make. In the following section, I've listed several of the best uses for the different methods of caching.

Output Caching

Output caching is best used when an entire page needs to be cached. Examples are as follows:

- A semi-static page with data pulled from multiple locations where the data is known not to change too frequently, such as a message board.
- A page that tends to take a long time to load due to its size and complexity.
- A page accessed very frequently even if it contains no dynamic data.

Fragment Caching

You can use fragment caching when only some portions of a page need to be cached and other portions of the same page do not. Examples are as follows:

- Any page that remains mostly static, with the exception of some data pulls, should have those data pulls loaded into a user control and cached.
- A page that must be constantly updated, with the exception of some areas, should have those areas loaded into a user control and cached.
- Any data accessed frequently between multiple pages within an application can be loaded into a user control and cached so that any page can access the cached data.

Data Caching

Data caching is best used for caching data at the object level. Examples are as follows:

- Any page too dynamic for output or fragment caching should have data caching implemented where possible.
- An application with objects that tend to be slow-loading should be cached on first use and used from the cache thereafter.
- Objects frequently accessed from multiple pages within an application should be cached for simple access from any page in the application.

Summary

High performance is one of the most important aspects of any Web application. With the use of ASP.NET's caching features, you can dramatically increase the performance of your application. Any application can benefit from the use of the caching features; by using the correct types of caching in the correct locations, you can optimize these benefits.

Output caching is used to cache entire pages. It is accessed either through the *@ OutputCache* directive or programmatically through the *HttpCachePolicy* cache. By setting the duration option, you can control the length of time that your page is stored in the cache. The additional features provided by the use of the *VaryByParam*, *VaryByHeader*, and *VaryByCustom* parameters enable you to control the various versions of your page that are stored in the cache.

Fragment caching is used to cache portions of pages when an entire page is unable to be cached, or in a situation where caching the entire page is inefficient. Fragment caching is used by breaking out portions of your code into user controls and including the *@ OutputCache* directive at the top of your user control. You can also use the *HttpCachePolicy* to access the features of fragment caching. The parameter of *VaryByControl* is included, in addition to *VaryByParam,* to give you control over the versions of the user control stored in the cache.

Data caching is the lowest level of caching available and enables you to cache data at the object level. Three methods are used to call the data caching functions. The first is the *cache* method, which is used in the same method that you would use a dictionary. There are no additional options available when using data caching with this method. The second and third methods are *cache.add* and *cache.insert*. The syntax and usage of these two methods are identical, and the difference between the two is that *cache.add* returns an object.

Accessing data caching by using the *cache.add* and *cache.insert* methods provides you with several options to control the cached data. The first option is the specification of files, directories, and other cache keys that the cached object is dependent upon. The second option is the use of two methods to specify the length of time that the object is stored in the cache. The third is the setting of priority levels for your cached data. By using priority levels, you control the order in which cached data is removed when ASP.NET purges the cache due to a lack of memory resources or infrequent access. The final option is the ability to specify a callback delegate when the object is removed from cache. The reason the object was removed from the cache as well as the value of the object at the time it was removed are specified to the callback delegate, and you can take any actions necessary based on this information.

Solutions Fast Track

Caching Overview

- ☑ Caching is used to increase performance of your Web application. It does this by storing frequently accessed data in memory.
- ☑ ASP.NET provides three different types of caching: output caching, fragment caching, and data caching.
- ☑ The proper balance of caching and usage of system resources is key to increasing overall application performance.

Output Caching

- ☑ Output caching caches an entire page, and you can cache multiple versions of the page by the use of available parameters.
- ☑ Output caching is accessed through either the *@ OutputCache* directive or the *HttpCachePolicy* class.
- ☑ The options to control data stored with output caching are: *VaryByParam, VaryByHeader,* and *VaryByCustom*.

Fragment Caching

- ☑ Fragment caching caches a portion of a page. This is done by breaking your code out into user controls and caching the control.
- ☑ Fragment caching enables you to take advantage of caching features when you are unable to cache the entire page.
- ☑ The options to control data stored with fragment caching are: *VaryByParam* and *VaryByControl*.

Data Caching

- ☑ Data caching caches individual objects.
- ☑ There are three methods of putting data into the data cache: *cache, cache.add* and *cache.insert*.

www.syngress.com

- ☑ Using the *cache.add* and *cache.insert* methods provide you with options to control cached data based on dependencies, duration, and priority as well as specifying a callback delegate.

Best Uses for Caching

- ☑ Use caching whenever possible to increase the performance of your application.
- ☑ Keep in mind the tradeoff between system memory resources and the caching of data when planning your caching policy.
- ☑ Use the correct type of caching at the correct points in your application for the highest performance increase possible.

Frequently Asked Questions

The following Frequently Asked Questions, answered by the authors of this book, are designed to both measure your understanding of the concepts presented in this chapter and to assist you with real-life implementation of these concepts. To have your questions about this chapter answered by the author, browse to **www.syngress.com/solutions** and click on the **"Ask the Author"** form.

Q: I have been asked to migrate an application from ASP to ASP.NET. In the ASP application, several third-party utilities have been used to provide for caching. Should I use these or use ASP.NET's internal caching?

A: Use ASP.NET's caching when possible. With automatic scavenging features and integrated memory management, ASP.NET provides a more tightly integrated caching system than existing third-party utilities.

Q: Within my application, there is a table populated with data from several different databases. How could I best implement caching in order to share this populated table between multiple pages of my application?

A: Use fragment caching to cache a user control that builds your table. Items stored in the cache are accessible throughout the application.

Q: I am concerned about the use of memory on my server. Prior to implementing caching, the memory utilization of the system was fairly low, but after adding the caching features to every page of my application, the memory utilization has gone up quite a bit. Is it possible to add so many items to the cache that I begin to run into a lack of memory resources?

A: This is possible if all of your items are cached using data caching with the parameters set to never remove the data from cache. However, by caching any data without this parameter opens the cached data up to be removed from the cache if the system becomes low on resources.

Q: Which is the overall best method of caching?

A: There is no "best" method. Each of the different caching options apply under different circumstances, and all of them provide an overall application performance increase when used properly.

Chapter 7

Introduction to ADO.NET: A Simple Address Book

Solutions in this chapter:

- **Understanding the Changes in ADO.NET**
- **Creating Connection Strings**
- **Creating an Address Book Application**

☑ Summary
☑ Solutions Fast Track
☑ Frequently Asked Questions

Introduction

ADO.NET is the latest implementation of Microsoft's universal data access strategy. In the past few years we have gone through many changes to classic ADO as Microsoft made changes, bug-fixes, and enhancements to the venerable libraries. These libraries have made the foundation for many Web sites and applications that are in place today. ADO.NET will be no different in this respect, as Microsoft is positioning ADO.NET to be the primary data access technology for the .NET Framework. This will ensure that the data access architecture is mature and robust, since all the Common Language Runtime (CLR) languages will be using these namespaces for their primary means of communicating with data providers.

Flexible and efficient data access technologies are at the heart of dynamic Web sites and Web applications. Classic ADO serialized data in a proprietary protocol that limited its reach, and it could have been made more efficient. ADO.NET serializes data using XML. This allows ADO.NET to take advantage of a standards-based approach to moving data back and forth in your applications. With rich support for any data source that can create or consume XML, ADO.NET is truly the data access technology for current and future applications. Through ADO.NET, you are able to connect to a myriad of data sources with the speed and flexibility that today's businesses require.

The goal for the developers of the ADO.NET architecture is to continue the tradition of ADO by further removing the complexities of interacting with different data providers, and shielding you from the intricacies that would interfere with the primary mission—packing functionality and usefulness into your applications.

This chapter will delve into the common strategies for viewing, editing, and deleting data in the various ways that ADO.NET allows. The primary data source for the examples will be SQL Server 2000, with Access 2002 as an alternative. The sample application is a straightforward address book. The architecture of our sample is very simple, in order to allow us to concentrate on the task at hand. We will step through the application and discuss some of the best uses of ADO.NET.

Understanding the Changes in ADO.NET

As mentioned above, ADO.NET has a relatively long history. As far as software development goes, if you are going to make dramatic enhancements, it is sometimes necessary to start from scratch, taking what you learned from the last implementation and looking forward with wisdom and clairvoyance. More than likely, it will result in a product that is not backward compatible and that requires significant change to bring older applications up to par.

The same could be said for ADO.NET. It is a vast departure in some ways, but not in others. Suffice to say that you will have to change your existing code to make it work in the ADO.NET world.

To start with, let us talk about the foundation. ADO.NET has taken XML to heart with rich support for XML data, both as a data consumer and as a data provider. Later versions of classic ADO had some support for XML, but the format was difficult to use unless you were exchanging it with another ADO client. The XML documents that ADO.NET creates are consistent with the XML specification and are what is known as "well-defined documents," making them suitable for consumption by any data access technology that understands XML. You can take a plain XML document with just a root node and open it in ADO.NET, add data to it, and save it back out.

The *Recordset* is dead. ADO.NET has a couple of new ways to serve data, which made the *Recordset* obsolete. These new objects are the *DataSet* and the *DataReader*. The *DataSet* has really made the classic ADO *Recordset* object obsolete by providing functionality that goes far beyond what the *Recordset* was able to provide. At the heart of the *Recordset* was the cursor. The classic ADO connection and *Recordset* objects both had a property to set the location of the cursor, either client-side or server-side. This provided a source for confusion, and enabled programmers to open scrolling, updatable cursors directly on the database server. This type of cursor is very expensive for the server to create and maintain. Scrolling, updatable cursors definitely have their uses, and will continue to fill a niche in data access applications.

The *DataSet* is really an in-memory relational database. The block diagram in Figure 7.1 shows the many collections in a *DataSet,* namely the *DataTables* collection, *DataViews* collection, and *DataRelations* collection. A programmer will create one or more *DataTable* objects in a *DataSet* and "fill" them with data. A *DataTable* contains a collection of *DataRows,* each of which contains a collection of *DataColumns*. We can optionally create *DataViews* based on these *DataTables,* and even define relations to enforce data integrity. Again with all this functionality we really don't have the need for a *Recordset* object.

The process of filling a *DataTable* with data is simple, and provides us with a copy of the data from the data source. The *DataSet* does not maintain a connection to the data source. With this copy of our data, the application can enable the user to add, edit, and remove data. The application can then enable the user to save this data back to the original data source. As a matter of fact, this data can be saved to any other data source, persisted to disk, and/or transferred just as if it were any other file. The key to this functionality is the reliance upon XML, and the disconnected nature of ADO.NET.

Figure 7.1 Object Model for the *DataSet*

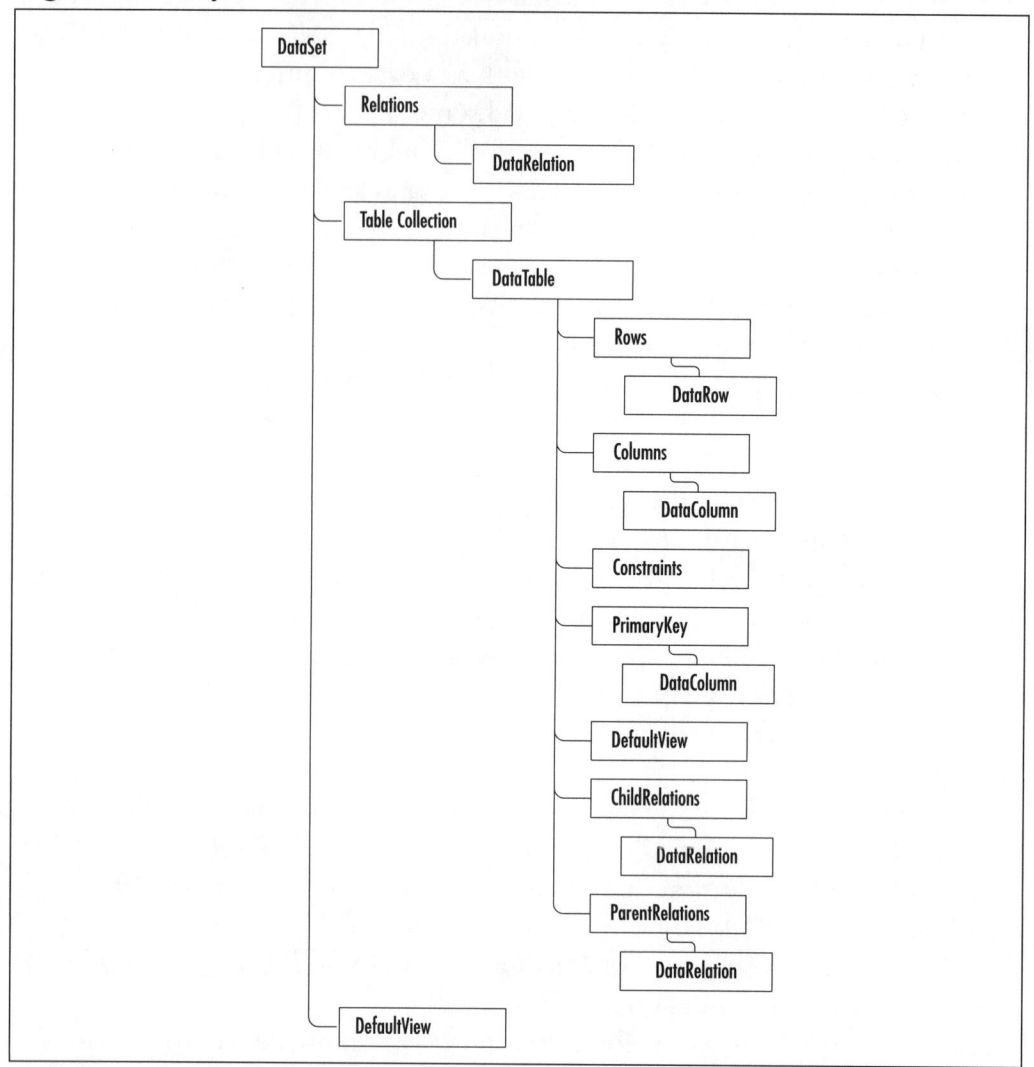

```
DataSet
├── Relations
│   └── DataRelation
├── Table Collection
│   └── DataTable
│       ├── Rows
│       │   └── DataRow
│       ├── Columns
│       │   └── DataColumn
│       ├── Constraints
│       ├── PrimaryKey
│       │   └── DataColumn
│       ├── DefaultView
│       ├── ChildRelations
│       │   └── DataRelation
│       └── ParentRelations
│           └── DataRelation
└── DefaultView
```

The *DataSet* requires a *DataAdapter* to actually interact with a data source. The *DataAdapter* represents the connection to a data source and the commands used to communicate with the data source to "fill" a *DataSet* or update a data source. After we are finished adding or updating data in the *DataSet,* the application would then call the *Update* method of the *DataAdapter* to INSERT, UPDATE, and DELETE records as appropriate at the data source.

Note that you don't have to commit your changes back to the original source; that is, you can transfer data to another data source as long as you have a *DataAdapter* that understands how to communicate between the *DataSet* and the final data source. This really serves to emphasize the total and complete disconnected nature of ADO.NET.

The other thing to keep in mind, especially since we are developing for ASP.NET, is that since a *DataSet* is a disconnected copy of our data, it is most suitable for small amounts of data. For ASP.NET, one would expect to find most of the work of retrieving data to be done using a *DataReader*, with *DataSets* being used for relatively static data that must be retrieved often. A *DataSet* in this scenario could be used at the session level to save some processing at the data source. For example, a Web site might have a drop-down list that contains the 50 states in the United States. If this drop-down list is used more than once on a page, and the number of states is static, we could fill a *DataSet* and bind every instance of the drop-down list to this *DataSet*. This way we hit the database once for all 50 states and for all instances of the drop-down list, thus saving many database hits.

The *DataReader* can be thought of as a firehose *Recordset*. A *firehose Recordset* was a nickname given to a read-only, forward-only *Recordset* in classic ADO. So, a *DataReader* is a forward-only, non-updateable stream of data from the data provider. Consider this as proof of a *DataReader*'s speed; a *DataAdapter* creates a *DataReader* behind the scenes to populate a *DataSet*. Because of this simple fact, the *DataReader* is very useful for ASP.NET work. In a stateless environment such as the Internet, fast access to the data is very important. It may be wasteful to retrieve this data into a *DataSet*, read through it once to render HTML, and then discard it. The point here is to be aware of the overhead that the *DataSet* has and use it when it makes sense.

The next item to discuss is the idea of *Managed Providers*. *Managed Providers* are namespaces that are written specifically to take advantage of the strengths of a particular data source. The ADO.NET Beta 2 release shipped with two *Managed Providers: System.Data.OleDb* and *System.Data.SqlClient*. The idea of *Managed Providers* is somewhat different from classic ADO where the Provider property dictated the data source you were connecting to. For example, if you were connecting to a Microsoft access database, you would use the *Microsoft.Jet.OLEDB.4.0* as the *Provider* attribute in your connection string. For SQL Server, you would use

"SQLOLEDB.1" as the *Provider* attribute. Every thing else about the connection object would be the same.

In the case of the *System.Data.OleDb* namespace, we select the OLEDB provider in much the same way that we selected them in classic ADO. We specify the *Provider* attribute in the connection string. In the case of the *System.Data .SqlClient* namespace, Microsoft has written this namespace to bypass the OLEDB protocol and instead use the Tabular Data Stream (TDS) protocol. The TDS protocol is much more efficient than the OLEDB protocol and allows for much greater speed when working with data. The downside is that the *System.Data .SqlClient* namespace can only be used to interact with SQL Server versions 7.0 and up; therefore, we do not need to specify the *Provider* attribute when using the *System.Data.SqlClient* namespace. These providers are explained in more detail later in the chapter.

For example, a connection to SQL Server in VB6 would look like this:

```
Dim oConn as ADODB.Connection
Dim strConn as String


strConn = "Provider=SQLOLEDB.1;Password=chapter7;User ID=Chapter7;Initial _
    Catalog=Chapter7;Data Source=localhost


SET oConn = New ADODB.Connection
```

It becomes this in VB.NET, using the *OleDb* namespace:

```
Dim oConn as OleDbConnection
Dim strConn as String


strConn = "Provider=SQLOLEDB.1;Password=chapter7;User ID=Chapter7;Initial _
    Catalog=Chapter7;Data Source=localhost


oConn = New OleDbConnection(strConn)
```

And it becomes this in VB.NET, using the *SqlClient* namespace:

```
Dim oConn as SqlConnection
Dim strConn as String
```

```
strConn = "Password=chapter7;User ID=Chapter7;Initial _
    Catalog=Chapter7;Data Source=localhost


oConn = New SqlConnection(strConn)
```

Notice the difference in the connection strings in the previous examples. The major difference in the *OleDb* connection string and the *SqlClient* connection string was the absence of the *Provider* property in the *SqlClient* example. If you leave the *Provider* property in the connection string for an *SqlConnection* object, ADO.NET throws an exception. We discuss connection strings in great detail later in this chapter.

Supported Connectivity

ADO.NET Beta 2 comes with two namespaces. The *System.Data.SqlClient* namespace is used with Microsoft SQL Server version 7.0 and up. The *System.Data.OleDb* namespace is more generic and provides services for MS SQL, MS Access, Oracle, and any other data providers that implement the OLE DB interfaces. Microsoft has tested the *System.Data.OleDb* namespace with SQL Server, MS Access, and Oracle. If your application will be using SQL Server only, then you can comfortably use the *System.Data.SqlClient* namespace and take advantage of the tight integration to the Microsoft SQL Server APIs. If, on the other hand, you are not sure, or you know for sure that your application will use a variety of data sources, then you should use the *System.Data.OleDb* namespace.

With the namespaces explained, we can discuss connectivity. As stated above, ADO.NET is connectionless by nature. That is, we do not open a connection and maintain it. The *DataReader* is sort of a departure from this in the respect that a *DataReader* is connected while it is streaming data, but when the *DataReader* gets to the end of the data, it releases the connection. If you need truly connected scrolling cursors to work with, then you are going to have to go back to classic ADO with the Interop libraries and do things the old-fashioned way. Since we are building a high-performance address book in our example in this chapter, we are not interested in maintaining a connection. We will concentrate on the *DataReader* object, using the *System.Data.SqlClient* and the *System.Data.OleDb* namespaces.

The *System.Data* Namespace

The *System.Data* namespace is the foundation for ADO.NET. This namespace contains the classes that form the ADO.NET architecture. The heart of the architecture is the *DataSet,* which contains a collection of *DataTables.* We will go into detail about these objects later in the chapter. The classes in this namespace are *data source agnostic*; therefore they are independent of the data source and the method used to connect to it.

The *System.Data* namespace is imported in the Code-Behind files in our samples. This keeps us from having to fully qualify the objects in the class definition. For example, Figure 7.2 (A and B) shows the difference between fully qualifying an object name and using the *Imports* keyword for VB.NET, and the *Using* keyword in C#.NET.

Figure 7.2 (A and B) Difference between Fully Qualified Namespace and Using the *Imports* or *Using* Keywords

Figure 7.2A Fully Qualified Namespace in C#.NET

```
// Fully qualified SqlConnection
oConnection = System.Data.SqlClient.SqlConnection(strConn);
// Simplified
using System.Data.SqlClient;
oConnection = SqlConnection(strConn);
```

Figure 7.2B Fully Qualified Namespace in VB.NET

```
'Fully qualified SqlConnection
oConnection = System.Data.SqlClient.SqlConnection(strConn)
'Simplified
Imports System.Data.SqlClient
oConnection = SqlConnection(strConn)
```

Here are some of the common classes in the *System.Data* namespace:

- *DataSet*
- *DataTable*
- *DataView*
- *DataColumn*
- *DataException*

System.Data namespace contains interfaces that are implemented by .NET data providers. You can find more information on these interfaces in the Visual

Studio .NET Documentation, and I urge you to dig into the supplied documentation. Microsoft has put a great deal of effort into the documentation effort.

The *System.Data.Common* Namespace

The classes in the *System.Data.Common* namespace are shared throughout the ADO.NET by the various data providers. These classes form the base classes for common objects in the *SqlClient* and the *OleDb* namespaces. This namespace contains the general classes for connecting to data sources, filling *DataSets,* column mapping, and some simple events. I have included it here for completeness; however, you won't be using it much. The following namespaces play a much bigger role in managing data in ADO.NET.

The *System.Data.OleDb* Namespace

The *System.OleDb* namespace provides objects that enable us to connect to OLE-DB providers. OLE-DB is an open specification for data providers that allow for flexible access to many Microsoft and third-party data sources. This provides us with one data access technology to connect to and manipulate data in several database products, without having to change libraries. The *System.Data.OleDb* namespace has been tested by Microsoft to work with Microsoft Access, Microsoft SQL Server, and Oracle. In theory, any data provider that has an OLE-DB interface can be used in ADO.NET.

ODBC or, Open Database Connectivity, is part of the OLE-DB specification, but Microsoft did not include it with the Beta 2 release. Microsoft has subsequently released the ODBC namespace for download as a separate installation. Microsoft considers OLE-DB to be the replacement for ODBC, and for the most part it has replaced it. Our example here will use *System.Data.OleDb* to connect to an Access 2002 version of the Address Book. More information can be found on OLE-DB at www.microsoft.com/data/oledb/.

Some common classes in the *System.Data.SqlClient* namespace are as follows:

- *OleDbConnection*
- *OleDbCommand*
- *OleDbDataAdapter*
- *OleDbDataReader*

The *System.Data.SqlClient* Namespace

The *System.Data.SqlClient* namespace inherits from the *System.Data.Common* namespace, but uses the TDS protocol that is proprietary to Microsoft SQL Server. Because of the tight integration with SQL Server, developers will only use objects derived from the *System.Data.SqlClient* namespace to connect to and manipulate data in Microsoft SQL Server. This namespace will connect to Microsoft SQL Server versions 7.0 and higher. We will be using SQL Server 2000 for our example, but you could just as easily use SQL 7.0.

The *System.Data.SqlClient* classes have the same properties, methods, and events as the *System.Data.OleDb* class, which makes switching back and forth very easy. Add to this the disconnected nature of the *System.Data* namespace from which most our data objects are derived, and you get the idea of how easy it is to pull and replace one Managed Provider with another.

Some common classes in the *System.Data.SqlClient* namespace are as follows:

- *SqlConnection*
- *SqlCommand*
- *SqlDataAdapter*
- *SqlDataReader*

The *System.Data.SqlTypes* Namespace

The *System.Data.SqlTypes* namespace contains the classes that map .NET data types to native SQL Server data types. This may sound trivial; however, there are many issues with converting data from one type to another that can cause loss of precision. The classes in the *System.Data.SqlTypes* provide a safe and more efficient means of handling these conversion issues. Figure 7.3 (A, B, C, and D) is an example of the different uses for the objects in the *System.Data.SqlTypes* namespace, and the *SqlDbType* enumeration in the *System.Data* namespace.

Figure 7.3 (A, B, C, and D) Difference between *SqlTypes* Namespace and the *SqlDbType* Enumeration

Figure 7.3A Using *SqlTypes* in C#.NET

```
System.Data.SqlTypes.SqlInt32 iAddrsID;
```

Figure 7.3B Using *SqlTypes* in VB.NET

```
Dim iAddrsID As System.Data.SqlTypes.SqlInt32
```

To create a command parameter with a *VarChar* data type:

Figure 7.3C Creating Command Parameters with C#.NET

```
oCmd.Parameters.Add("@FName", SqlDbType.VarChar, 50).Value = FName;
```

Figure 7.3D Creating Command Parameters with VB.NET

```
oCmd.Parameters.Add("@FName", SqlDbType.VarChar, 50).Value = FName
```

Do not confuse the *SqlDbTypes* enumeration in the *System.Data* namespace with the *System.Data.SqlTypes* namespace. The *SqlDbTypes* enumeration is useful for specifying the data type of a parameter that belongs to a *Command* object. The classes in *System.Data.SqlTypes* are used for declaring variables.

The *SqlDbType* and the *System.Data.SQLTypes* may sound the same, but they are very different in nature and in use. Refer to Table 7.1 for the mapping from native SQL Server data types to the types provided in *System.Data.SqlTypes* and to the *SqlDbTypes* enumeration.

Table 7.1 Data Type Mapping

Native SQL Server	System.Data.SqlTypes	SqlDbType from System.Data
Bigint	SqlInt64	BigInt
Binary	SqlBinary	Binary
Bit	SqlBit	Bit
Char	SqlString	Char
Datetime	SqlDateTime	DateTime
Decimal	SqlNumeric	Decimal
Float	SqlDouble	Float
Image	SqlBinary	Image
Int	SqlInt32	Int
Money	SqlMoney	Money
Nchar	SqlString	NChar
Ntext	SqlString	NText

Continued

Table 7.1 Continued

Native SQL Server	System.Data.SqlTypes	SqlDbType from System.Data
Numeric	SqlNumeric	Numeric
Nvarchar	SqlString	NVarChar
Real	SqlSingle	Real
Smalldatetime	SqlDateTime	SmallDateTime
Smallint	SqlInt16	SmallInt
Smallmoney	SqlMoney	SmallMoney
sql_variant	Object	Variant
Sysname	SqlString	VarChar
Text	SqlString	Text
Timestamp	SqlBinary	TimeStamp
Tinyint	SqlByte	TinyInt
Uniqueidentifier	SqlGuid	UniqueId
Varbinary	SqlBinary	VarBinary
Varchar	SqlString	VarChar

Creating Connection Strings

The first step to connecting to a data source, after choosing the Managed Provider, is to create the connection string. The connection string is a list of key/value pairs that the *Connection* object will parse; it will use the information to find the Data Source, authenticate, and establish a connection. Depending on the namespace used, the connection string will vary a little. Basically the connection string for a *SqlConnection* does not have the *Provider* attribute, while the connection string for an *OleDbConnection* does.

Connection to SQL Server is done using the *System.Data.SqlClient* namespace. This namespace contains the classes for the *SqlConnection* object. As described earlier, the connection string is the hardest part of creating a connection. Table 7.2 lists some common keys, and the default values with some simple explanations.

Table 7.2 Connection String Properties

Name	Default	Description
Connect Timeout -or- Connection Timeout	15	Seconds to try and make the connection. When these are up, an exception is thrown.
Data Source -or- Server -or- Address -or- Addr -or- Network Address	<User Defined>	The name or IP address of the SQL Server to make the connection with. For servers with multiple instances of SQL Server, this would be <servername>\<instancename>.
Initial Catalog -or- Database	<User Defined>	The name of the database. If this is not specified you will get a connection to the default database defined for the User ID.
Integrated Security -or- Trusted_Connection	'false'	Whether SQL Server will use the NT user credentials, or expect a SQL Server username and password.
Password -or- Pwd	<User Defined>	The password for the SQL Server account logging on. For integrated security, this is not specified.
Persist Security Info	'false'	When set to 'false,' security-sensitive information, such as the password, is not returned as part of the connection if the connection is open or has ever been in an open state. Resetting the connection string resets all connection string values including the password.
User ID	<User Defined>	The SQL Server login account.

For example, this connection string could be used to connect to a SQL Server that is named "Dataserver" with a user name of "Chapter7" and a password of "Chapter7." The initial catalog, or database, to connect to is "Chapter7":

```
strConn = "Password=chapter7;User ID=Chapter7;Initial _
    Catalog=Chapter7;Data Source=Dataserver"
```

Now you have a connection string that you can use with an *SqlConnection* object. A trick you can use is to create a text file with .udl as the file extension. Executing this file would start the connection wizard and enable you to step through creating the connection string. When finished, open the file in notepad and copy the completed connection string. For an *SqlConnection* you would remove the *Provider* attribute.

Where to Put the Connection String

In the Address Book example, you are putting the connection string in the web.config file. The web.config file has a root node named <configuration>. Under this node is the <system.web> node and you will add another node at this level called <AppSettings>. You then add a new key using the <add> tag. This new item is a key/value pair that you refer to when you need a connection string.

The web.config is an XML document that belongs in the root of your Web application. Figure 7.4 is the abbreviated text from the web.config in the sample Address Book which is included on the CD that accompanies this book. Notice the relationship of the *system.web* node and the *AppSettings* node; they are at the same child level in the document.

Figure 7.4 web.config (cs\web.config)

```
<configuration>
    <system.web>
       ......
    </system.web>
    <appSettings>
       <add key="appStrConnection" value="PWD=pword;UID=webUser;...">
    </AppSettings>
</configuration>
```

To retrieve the value in the data access layer or Code-Behind file, you use the syntax in Figure 7.5 (A and B).

Figure 7.5 (A and B) Retrieving a Connection String from the web.config File

Figure 7.5A C#.NET

```
strConnection = ConfigurationSettings.AppSettings("appStrConnection");
```

Figure 7.5B VB.NET

```
strConnection = ConfigurationSettings.AppSettings("appStrConnection")
```

For ASP 2, and 3, Microsoft Developers Network—the help files for many Microsoft development tools—has many examples of connection strings in the Global.asa. The Global.asa could be compromised using a buffer overrun attack with the end result of giving out the user name and password to your customers' data. The managed code nature of the Common Language Runtime should eliminate the buffer overrun attack as a source of entry for unauthorized access. You should feel secure with leaving the connection string in your web.config file; however, heed the advice in the sidebar titled "Connection Strings and Security."

Developing & Deploying…

Connection Strings and Security

In past versions of ASP, it was common to place the connection string in the Global.asa. This had two problems. First, the file was well known. Its name and location were dictated by the architecture of ASP. Second, this file could be compromised using simple attacks. The attacks were mitigated by patching IIS, but the fact remained that an incorrectly configured server could allow access to this file.

Due the compiled nature of the Common Language Runtime and ASP.NET it is unlikely that these problems will follow you into the future, however, it is still recommended to leave all sensitive data out of the AS(x)X files in ASP.NET. You do have a few options, such as the web.config file in the Address Book example. You can create a component that does nothing but return the connection string to a properly authenticated caller. You could create a text file, and encrypt the connection string in this file. Read it on application start and save it in a variable. This is one area where creativity will pay off.

In addition to putting the connection string in a safe place, the username you use for the application should have minimum access rights to get the job done. In SQL Server this would entail creating a user who has execute permissions to stored procedures but who does not have select permissions to the tables. Then all data access and manipulation is handled using stored procedures. This is a very simple example but is very powerful, at least as far as SQL Server is concerned.

Creating an Address Book Application

The example application is a simple address book. This example will explore the major topics for data access. We will cover inserting, selecting, and updating data using a simple ASP.NET page with a *DataList* and a couple of templates. Figure 7.6 contains the table layout for the application. This table has seven columns of various data types plus a primary key that is of data type Int. The primary key is an auto-incrementing field that will be used to uniquely identify a row.

Figure 7.6 tblAddress Layout

Column Name	Data Type	Length	Allow Nulls
AdrsID	int	4	
FName	varchar	50	✓
LName	varchar	50	✓
Phone	char	15	✓
EMail	varchar	255	✓
WebPage	varchar	255	✓
Age	tinyint	1	✓
Comments	varchar	2000	✓

The Web form consists of a *DataList* that is bound to the address table on page load. A *DataList* is a server-side control that you format using templates. You can bind data to a *DataList* from a *DataReader* or a *DataSet*. Our example uses a *DataReader,* and this is the most common scenario you should expect to find. The *DataSet* is a wonderful tool, with a lot of power. For our example we are going stick to the *DataReader;* the basics of the *DataSet* will be explained at the end of the chapter.

Address.aspx is the primary form for the Address Book. On load you bind the data to the *DataList* and display the records in a read-only grid. Refer to Figure 7.7 for a screen shot of the standard view.

Notice the Edit link in the left-hand column of each row. Click this button to activate the edit template. Several things are going on here. First, when we created our *DataList* in the .aspx file, we specified an *OnEditCommand*. This command receives two parameters from the caller, or in this case, the edit link from our row. Using these parameters in the subprocedure specified by the *OnEditCommand* property of the *DataList*, we can interrogate the row and read its values at runtime. We then set the *editItemIndex* of the *DataList* to the *ItemIndex* of the arguments were passed into the subprocedure. This allows the *DataList* to display the row we selected in our Edit template. The Edit template consists of a table with textboxes and three buttons. These buttons enable us to delete, update, and cancel.

Figure 7.7 Standard View of Our Address Application

Figure 7.8 shows the resulting Edit template. The *DataList* enables us to specify several templates. Table 7.3 is a listing of the templates and a basic description.

Figure 7.8 Editing a Record in Our Address Book

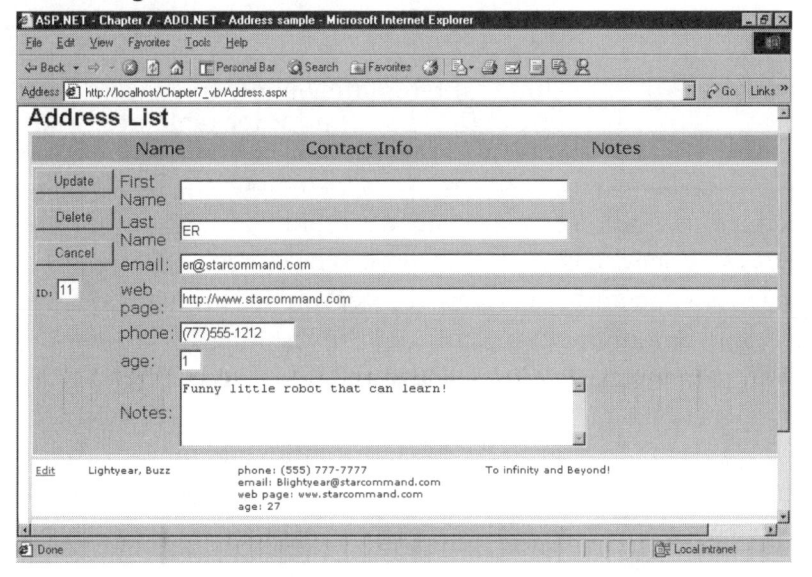

Table 7.3 Templates Supported by the *DataList*

Template Name	Description
HeaderTemplate	Optional template provides for specifying the layout and content of the header. If this template is not defined, a header will not be displayed.
ItemTemplate	This template is the default layout for each row in the *DataList*. This template will be repeated for each row in the Data that is bound to the *DataList*. This template is required.
AlternatingItemTemplate	This template is substituted on a configurable basis for the ItemTemplate. It will default to replacing every other ItemTemplate, but could be configured to replace every 2, 3, 4, etc.
SelectedItemTemplate	Optional template for displaying the selected row in the *DataList*.
EditItemTemplate	Optional template that will specify the format and layout of the row to be edited in the *DataList*.
SeparatorTemplate	Optional template to separate each row. If this template is not specified, no separator will be displayed.
FooterTemplate	Optional template will provide layout for the footer of the *DataList*. If a footer template is not specified, then a footer will not be rendered.

To add records, insert a blank record with some default data and then bind the *DataList* to the new record in edit mode. The stored procedure to add the record returns the Identity of the new record. You use this new identity to call the *getByID* function of the DAL, and bind the resulting *DataReader* to your *DataList*. You then set the *EditItemIndex* to the first record in the *DataReader* and let the Edit Template fill up with your new record. Figure 7.9 shows the *DataList* with your new record in edit mode. After you finish adding your data, click the **Update** button and the data is posted back to the database. The *Page_OnLoad* event populates the *DataList*, and you see your new record.

To get started with the sample application, you can find the sample database on the CD that accompanies this book. Follow the directions for your database as outlined in the following steps.

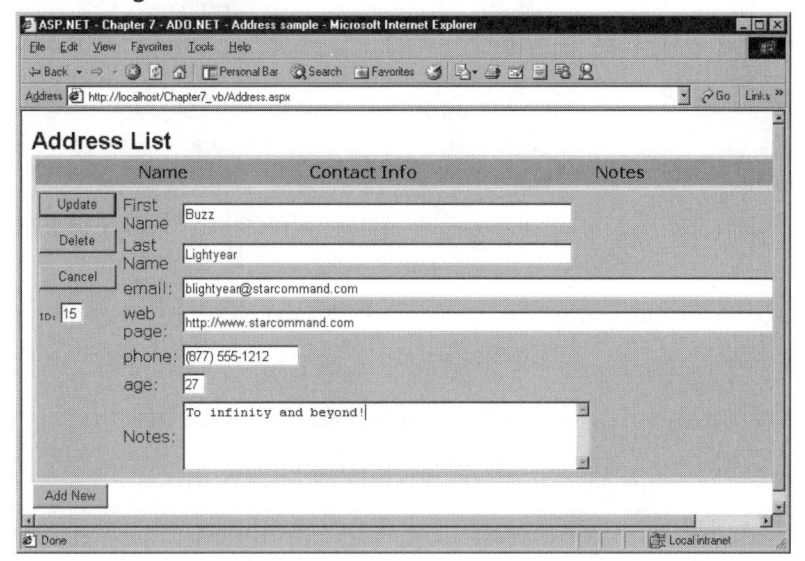

Figure 7.9 Adding a Record to the Address Book

To set up the Database in SQL 2000:

1. You must have SQL Server 2000 installed. You must have 4 MB of space.
2. Copy the following files from this book's CD to your local hard drive.
   - db\Chapter_7.mdf
   - db\Chapter_7.ldf
3. Open the SQL Server Enterprise Manager and right-click on the **Databases** node. Select **All Tasks\Attach Database**, and select the **Chapter_7.mdf** from the files you copied to your hard drive.

To set up the database in SQL 7.0:

1. You must have SQL Server 7.0 installed. You must have 4MB of space.
2. Open the **Query Analyzer**. Choose **File\Open**, and navigate to the **Chapter7\DB Setup** directory. Select the **genDataBase.sql** file and click **OK**.
3. Edit the script by replacing the file path **<your path here>** with the location you would like your database files.
4. Execute the script by pressing the **F5** button. The script should have run without errors.

318　Chapter 7 • Introduction to ADO.NET: A Simple Address Book

To set up the database in Access:

1. Copy the **Chapter7.mdb** file from the db directory on the CD-ROM that accompanies this book to your application directory.

The first step to create the Web application is to open Visual Studio .NET and create a new application. We will call it **Chapter7_cs** (if you are using VB, then name the application **Chapter7_vb**). Then we will copy the front-end code into the project. Finally we will step through adding the DAL into our project and tying it to the front end.

1. Copy the following files from the CD into the root of your application:
   - cs\Address.aspx (or vb\Address.aspx for VB)
   - cs\Address.aspx.cs (or vb\Address.aspx.vb for VB)
   - cs\Address.css (or vb\Address.css for VB)

2. Right-click on the Project name in the Solution Explorer, and select **Add\Class** from the pop-up menu.

3. Name the class **CDalAddress.cs(.vb for VB.NET)** and click **Open**. Visual Studio will create the file and open it in the visual designer window.

4. Right-click on our new file in the solution explorer and select **View Code**.

After you have performed the steps above, the code similar to Figure 7.10 (A and B) should have been generated for you.

Figure 7.10 (A and B) Empty Class Created Using the Visual Studio Class Wizard

Figure 7.10A Empty Class in C#.NET

```
using System;
namespace Chapter7_cs
{
    /// <summary>
    /// Summary description for CDalAddress.
    /// </summary>
    public class CDalAddress
    {
```

Continued

Figure 7.10A Continued

```
        public CDalAddress()
        {
            //
            // TODO: Add constructor logic here
            //
        }
    }
}
```

Figure 7.10B Empty Class in VB.NET

```
Public Class CDalAddress

End Class
```

This will be our workspace. The presentation has already been taken care of so we will only be concerning ourselves with the data access code in our *CDalAddress* class.

Connecting to a Database: Exercise

Making a database connection in ADO.NET is really very simple. The most difficult part of creating the connection is the Connection string. This is a semi-colon delimited string of name—value pairs that we discussed earlier in the chapter. If you have worked with ODBC, or even OLE-DB, then they are basically the same with a twist for the *SqlConnection* object.

It has become common to create what is referred to as the DAL, or Data Access Layer. This implies a multi-tiered approach to application architecture, and ADO.NET lends itself quite well for this purpose. Seeing as how the *System.Data* namespace doesn't really care about the data source or connection, the data container objects such as the *DataSet* and the *DataList* can be populated from any provider that can understand how to connect between them and the data source. So, if our Web form has a page-level *DataList,* it can be populated from an *OleDbDataReader* object, or the *SqlDataReader* object. We can decide on the data source at runtime if we have to, with very little effort. But for now let's focus on the connection part of the DAL in our example.

Chapter 7 • Introduction to ADO.NET: A Simple Address Book

Create a new class file in Visual Studio and add the code in Figure 7.11 (A and B) to the body of the file. Name this file **CDalAddress.vb** for VB.NET and **CDalAddress.cs** for C#.NET.

Figure 7.11 (A and B) Implementing the Connection String Property in the Data Access Layer

Figure 7.11A C#.NET (cs\CDalAddress.cs)

```csharp
using System;
using System.Data;
using System.Data.SqlClient;
using System.Data.SqlTypes;
using System.Data.OleDb;
namespace Chapter7_cs
{
    ///    <summary>
    ///    Summary description for CDalAddress.
    ///    </summary>
    public class CDalAddress
    {
        string strConStr;
        string strError;
        SqlConnection oConn;
        // OleDbConnection oConn;

        public string strConnection
        {
            get
            {
                return strConStr;
            }
            set
            {
                strConStr = value;
                try
                {
```

Continued

Figure 7.11A Continued

```csharp
                        this.oConn = new SqlConnection(value);
                        // oConn = new OleDbConnection(value);
                    }
                    catch (Exception e)
                    {
                        throw e;
                    }
                }
            }
        }
    }
}
```

Figure 7.11B VB.NET (vb\CDalAddress.vb)

```vbnet
Option Explicit On
Imports System
Imports System.Data
Imports System.Data.SqlClient
Imports System.Data.OleDb
Public Class CdalAddress
    '// a conneciton string
    Private strConStr As String
    Private oConn As SqlConnection
    'Private oConn As OleDbConnection
    Public Property strConnection() As String
        Get
            Return strConStr
        End Get
        Set(ByVal Value As String)
            strConStr = Value
            Try
                oConn = New SqlConnection(Value)
                'oConn = New OleDbConnection(Value)
```

Continued

Figure 7.11B Continued

```
            Catch oleE As OleDbException
                Throw oleE
            Catch e As SqlException
                Throw e
            End Try
        End Set
    End Property
End Class
```

We now have a class with one property. On the set operation of the *strConnection* property, set the private variable *strConStr* to the Connection string, and then create the connection with the new operator and the type of connection we are creating. Figure 7.12 (A and B) illustrates instantiating the *Connection* object.

Figure 7.12 (A and B) Instantiating the Connection Object

Figure 7.12A C#.NET

```
// For a SQL Server only connection
oConn = New SqlConnection(Value);
// For an OleDb connection
oConn = New OleDbConnection(Value);
```

Figure 7.12B VB.NET

```
' For a SQL Server only conneciton
oConn = New SqlConnection(Value)
' For an OleDb connection
oConn = New OleDbConnection(Value)
```

The error handling is self-explanatory; basically you just bubble it back to the caller. To recap, you set a reference to the namespace, declare a variable of type *SqlConnection,* and then call the New operator and pass the connection string into the constructor. So, creating the connection comes down to three lines of code.

In our sample, we commented out the lines responsible for creating the *OleDbConnection* object. That and the different connection string are all it takes to switch database connections.

Browsing a Database: Exercise

Now that you are connected to the database, you can retrieve some records. Data retrieval is the most intensive thing that you will do to your database. Online Transaction Processing, or OLTP, applications are designed for inserting and updating data quickly. They are not designed for fast and efficient retrieval of multi-dimensional data. Modern Relational Database technology does a good job of satisfying most needs, but many people often find themselves needing faster access to the data than they are currently getting. Faster is better, right? One of the benefits of ASP.NET are the caching and state management features. They enable you to connect to a database, return some results, and then cache this for a specific period of time. This caching can improve performance dramatically, while reducing the amount of load on the database. It is a true win-win situation.

Our example uses two methods that return data reader objects to the calling procedure. A Data Reader is a read-only, forward-only cursor. You can bind it to a *DataGrid*, a *DataList*, a *DataRepeater*, etc. You can only use it once due to its forward-only nature. This is the workhorse for ADO.NET, and especially for data access in ASP.NET.

Another object for browsing data is the *DataSet*. You can think of the *DataSet* as an in-memory database. You can add *DataTables*, which are synonymous with database tables; you can create *DataViews*, *DataRelations*, and constraints. The *DataSet* is very useful when you are going to access the same data more than twice in a page hit or session. The thing to keep in mind is that it is not connected to the database. Once you fill the *DataTable*, it is disconnected from the data source. The *DataTable* doesn't know anything about the database. As far as ASP.NET goes, *DataTables* are useful for populating drop-downs with data that doesn't change very often, but is used many times in a single session. If you place a *DataSet* in a session, beware that the memory is taken up until the session times out, not just when the user leaves the site. Our example doesn't use the *DataSet*, but a *DataSet* can be bound to the *DataList* in the same manner as the *DataReaders* are.

Our example uses stored procedures extensively for SQL Server, and raw SQL for Access. Not all Relational databases create and consume stored procedures the same way; therefore their implementation is specific to the database. In this example, T-SQL is used to create the stored procedures in SQL Server.

The first stored procedure gets all the records and orders them Last Name, First Name. Refer to Figure 7.13 for the code to create the stored procedure.

Figure 7.13 Selecting Data from the Database T-SQL

```
CREATE PROC usp_tblAddress_sel
AS
SELECT [AdrsID]
, [FName]
, [LName]
, [Phone]
, [EMail]
, [WebPage]
, [Age]
, [Comments]
FROM [dbo].[tblAddress]
ORDER BY [LName], [FName]
```

This stored procedure doesn't take any parameters, so we have a couple of ways to call it. In Access, we would not be able to create the stored procedure, so we will just have to use the SQL Statement in place of the stored procedure name. We are going to use the simpler *Text CommandType* refer to Figure 7.14 (A and B).

Figure 7.14 (A and B) Selecting Data from the Database

Figure 7.14A C#.Net (cs\CDalAddress.cs)

```
public SqlDataReader getAll()
{
    string strSQL = "EXEC usp_tblAddress_sel";
    SqlCommand oCmd = new SqlCommand(strSQL, oConn);
    // OleDbCommand oCmd = new OleDbCommand(strSQL, oConn);
    oCmd.CommandType = CommandType.Text;
    try
    {
        if (oConn.State == ConnectionState.Closed)
        {
            oConn.Open();
```

Continued

Figure 7.14A Continued

```
        }
        return oCmd.ExecuteReader();
    }
    catch (Exception e)
    {
        throw e;
    }
}
```

Figure 7.14B VB.NET (vb\CDalAddress.vb)

```
Public Function getAll() As SqlDataReader
        'Public Function getAll() As OleDbDataReader
        Dim oCmd As SqlCommand
        'Dim oCmd As OleDbCommand
        Dim strSQL As String
        strSQL = "EXEC usp_tblAddress_sel"
        oCmd = New SqlCommand(strSQL, oConn)
        'oCmd = New OleDbCommand(strSQL, oConn)
        oCmd.CommandType = CommandType.Text
        Try
            If oConn.State = ConnectionState.Closed Then
                oConn.Open()
            End If
            Return oCmd.ExecuteReader
        Catch oErr As Exception
            Throw oErr
        End Try
End Function
```

Notice in our *Try Catch* block that we are checking the current state of the connection. If it is closed, then we want to open it. We can check for various states; Table 7.4 lists the available states and gives a brief description of each one. The *ExecuteReader* of our *Command* object returns a *DataReader* that we return to the calling function.

Table 7.4 Connection States

Connection State	Description
Open	Object has located and authenticated the connection, and is ready for commands.
Closed	Not connection to the data source. Default state when a connection object is created.
Connecting	Object is in the process of connecting.
Executing	Object is in the process of executing a command.
Fetching	Object is retrieving, or fetching data.
Broken	Can only happen after a connection is open. To recover from this, a connection must be closed and the reopened.

In our earlier example, we set the SQL statement to *EXEC usp_tblAddress_sel*. EXEC[UTE] is a Transact SQL command to execute a stored procedure and return the result. The text immediately following it, usp_tblAddress_sel is the name of the stored procedure. This is the simplest way to execute a stored procedure. We could have also just specified the Select statement instead. For example, if we were using Access with Jet, it doesn't support stored procedures so we would have to create the select statement and send it to the *OleDbCommand* object. To change the code for Access, refer to Figure 7.15.

Figure 7.15 Switch from a Stored Procedure to Embedded SQL

The line:
```
strSQL = "EXEC usp_tblAddress_sel";
```
Becomes:
```
strSQL = " SELECT [AdrsID]
, [FName]
, [LName]
, [Phone]
, [EMail]
, [WebPage]
, [Age]
, [Comments]
FROM [dbo].[tblAddress]
ORDER BY [LName], [FName]";
```

The results are the same. The reason we use stored procedures in SQL Server is that SQL Server can optimize the query plan and reuse it for subsequent executions. This eliminates the parsing, and compiling that takes place when we send in Embedded SQL. Refer to the sidebar entitled "Embedded SQL Statements" for an explanation of Embedded SQL. It is more flexible than the stored procedure method, but for 95 percent of database operations, dynamic SQL is not the only way to get the job done.

Developing & Deploying...

Embedded SQL Statements

Embedded SQL or Dynamic SQL is a term given to generating SQL statements at runtime and executing it against the database. For Access it is the only method. For SQL Server, Oracle, DB2, and so on, it is optional. For SQL Server the stored procedure is preferred for several reasons. SQL Server can optimize the query plan and cache it for reuse, thus saving the cost of parsing and compiling the statement every time it runs. Also, you can execute a stored procedure against a table that you do not have select access to. SQL Server does this through the ownership chain, where the owner of an object can create a table and a stored procedure. They can give you execute permission on the stored procedure, but not give you select permission on the table. Since they own both objects, SQL Server will grant the user access to the table, but only through the stored procedure that the table owner created.

The next method returns a particular row identified by the Primary key. We use the Primary key to uniquely identify a row, so it is a very reliable way of ensuring that you get exactly the row that you wanted. Figure 7.16 (A and B) contains the Transact SQL for the stored procedure.

Figure 7.16 (A and B) Selecting a Particular Record

Figure 7.16A T-SQL

```
CREATE PROC usp_tblAddress_sel_ByID(@AdrsID INT)
AS
SELECT [AdrsID]
```

Continued

Figure 7.16A Continued

```
, [FName]
, [LName]
, [Phone]
, [EMail]
, [WebPage]
, [Age]
, [Comments]
FROM [dbo].[tblAddress]
WHERE [AdrsID] = @AdrsID
```

Figure 7.16B Access

```
SELECT [AdrsID]
, [FName]
, [LName]
, [Phone]
, [EMail]
, [WebPage]
, [Age]
, [Comments]
FROM [tblAddress]
WHERE [AdrsID] = <replace with your id>
```

Even though we must specify a parameter, we can still use the *Text CommandType* with our *Command* object by concatenating the variable to our command text. Figure 7.17 (A and B) contains the code listing for the getByID function of our DAL.

Figure 7.17 (A and B) GetByID Function—Use Dynamic SQL to Call a Stored Procedure

Figure 7.17A C#.NET (cs\CDalAddress.cs)

```
public SqlDataReader getByID(Int32 AdrsID)
{
    string strSQL = strSQL = "EXEC usp_tblAddress_sel_ByID " +
```

Continued

Figure 7.17A Continued

```csharp
            AdrsID.ToString();
        SqlCommand oCmd = new SqlCommand(strSQL, oConn);
        oCmd.CommandType = CommandType.Text;
        try
        {
            if (oConn.State == ConnectionState.Closed)
            {
                oConn.Open();
            }
            return oCmd.ExecuteReader();
        }
        catch (Exception e)
        {
            throw e;
        }
    }
}
```

Figure 7.17B VB.NET (vb\CDalAddress.vb)

```vbnet
Public Function getByID(ByVal AdrsID As Int32) As SqlDataReader
    Dim oCmd As SqlCommand
    Dim strSQL As String
    strSQL = "EXEC usp_tblAddress_sel_ByID " & AdrsID
    oCmd = New SqlCommand(strSQL, oConn)
    oCmd.CommandType = CommandType.Text
    Try
        If oConn.State = ConnectionState.Closed Then
            oConn.Open()
        End If
        Return oCmd.ExecuteReader
    Catch oErr As Exception
        Throw New Exception(oErr.ToString)
    End Try
End Function
```

Notice how we do not include single quotes? For numerical data we leave our single quotes off and just send the value. This is a very simple way to send parameters into a stored procedure. In the "Adding to a Database" exercise that follows, we explicitly create parameters and return values in them. This is called output parameters, and they are very useful in certain situations.

Adding to a Database: Exercise

Adding data to the database involves many of the same steps that we took to select the data. At the database level, the database engine will open the table, navigate to a new row, and put in your data. This is overly simplistic, but covers the highpoints.

We will use a stored procedure, but this time we will use an output parameter to return the new primary key value of our new record. In SQL Server this is done using the @@IDENTITY function. SQL Server will return the last identity value in your session. This is very important for consistency. We don't want the ID of a record that another user committed right after we committed ours. Figure 7.18 (A and B) contains the text for the stored procedure; note the Output syntax in the parameter declaration:

Figure 7.18 (A and B) Statements for Inserting Records

Figure 7.18A T-SQL

```
CREATE PROC usp_tblAddress_ins(
    @AdrsID    INT = NULL OUTPUT
  , @FName     varchar(50)
  , @LName     varchar(50)
  , @Phone     char(15)
  , @EMail     varchar(255)
  , @WebPage   varchar(255)
  , @Age       tinyint
  , @Comments  varchar(2000)
)
AS
INSERT INTO [dbo].[tblAddress]([FName]
        , [LName]
        , [Phone]
        , [EMail]
```

Continued

Figure 7.18A Continued

```
            , [WebPage]
            , [Age]
            , [Comments])
VALUES(   @FName
            , @LName
            , @Phone
            , @EMail
            , @WebPage
            , @Age
            , @Comments)
SET @AdrsID = @@IDENTITY
```

Figure 7.18B Inserting Records with Access

```
INSERT INTO [tblAddress]([FName]
            , [LName]
            , [Phone]
            , [EMail]
            , [WebPage]
            , [Age]
            , [Comments])
VALUES(   <Replace with @FName>
            , <Replace with @LName>
            , <Replace with @Phone>
            , <Replace with @Email>
            , <Replace with @WebPage>
            , <Replace with @Age>
            , <Replace with @Comments>)
SELECT @@IDENTITY
```

The syntax for inserting records is very simple:

```
INSERT <table name> (<columns>n) VALUES (<values>n)
```

Note

For Access you have to select the @@IDENTITY and return this in a *DataReader*, or use the *ExecuteScalar* method to return a single value.

This results in one record being inserted. Notice how we do not specify the primary key in our field list or values list. Indecently, these two lists must match for count and data type, or else SQL Server will throw an error.

Calling the stored procedure from our DAL, we use the same *Connection* object, but the *Add* method is quite different from our earlier code. Specifically, we are creating parameters and adding them to the parameter collection of our *Command* object. The *SqlCommand* object and the *OleDbCommand* object both have a parameter collection, and the same methods for creating and adding them. Our *Add* function will take a parameter for each column except the primary key, and the method will return a value of type Int32. This is equivalent to the SQL Server data type of INT. They are both capable of holding values between negative 2,147,483,648, and positive 2,147,483,647. Those are plenty of available IDs for our contact list. Figure 7.19 (A and B) contains the code for the *Add* method of our DAL.

Figure 7.19 (A and B) Inserting Records Using a Command Object with Declared Parameters

Figure 7.19A C#.NET (cs\CDalAddress.cs)

```
public Int32 Add(string FName,
     string LName,
     string Phone,
     string EMail,
     string WebPage,
     Int16 Age,
     string Comments)
{
     SqlCommand oCmd;
     SqlParameter oParam;
     string strSQL;
     Int32 AdrsID;
```

Continued

Figure 7.19A Continued

```
    strSQL = "usp_tblAddress_ins";
    oCmd = new SqlCommand(strSQL, oConn);
    oCmd.CommandType = CommandType.StoredProcedure;
    oParam = oCmd.Parameters.Add("@AdrsID", SqlDbType.Int, 4);
    oParam.Direction = ParameterDirection.Output;
    oCmd.Parameters.Add("@FName", SqlDbType.VarChar, 50).Value = FName;
    oCmd.Parameters.Add("@LName", SqlDbType.VarChar, 50).Value = LName;
    oCmd.Parameters.Add("@Phone", SqlDbType.VarChar, 15).Value = Phone;
    oCmd.Parameters.Add("@EMail", SqlDbType.VarChar, 255).Value =
        EMail;
    oCmd.Parameters.Add("@WebPage", SqlDbType.VarChar, 255).Value =
        WebPage;
    oCmd.Parameters.Add("@Age", SqlDbType.TinyInt, 2).Value = Age;
    oCmd.Parameters.Add("@Comments", SqlDbType.VarChar, 2000).Value =
        Comments;
    try
    {
        if (oConn.State == ConnectionState.Closed)
        {
            oConn.Open();
        }
        oCmd.ExecuteNonQuery();
        AdrsID = (Int32)oCmd.Parameters["@AdrsID"].Value;
        return AdrsID;
    }
    catch (Exception oErr)
    {
        throw oErr;
    }
}
```

Figure 7.19B VB.NET (vb\CDalAddress.vb)

```vb
Public Function Add(ByVal FName As String, _
                    ByVal LName As String, _
                    ByVal Phone As String, _
                    ByVal EMail As String, _
                    ByVal WebPage As String, _
                    ByVal Age As String, _
                    ByVal Comments As String) As Int32
    Dim oCmd As SqlCommand
    Dim oParam As SqlParameter
    Dim strSQL As String
    Dim AdrsID As Int32
    strSQL = "usp_tblAddress_ins"
    oCmd = New SqlCommand(strSQL, oConn)
    oCmd.CommandType = CommandType.StoredProcedure
    oParam = oCmd.Parameters.Add("@AdrsID", SqlDbType.Int, 4)
    oParam.Direction = ParameterDirection.Output
    oCmd.Parameters.Add("@FName", SqlDbType.VarChar, 50).Value = FName
    oCmd.Parameters.Add("@LName", SqlDbType.VarChar, 50).Value = LName
    oCmd.Parameters.Add("@Phone", SqlDbType.VarChar, 15).Value = Phone
    oCmd.Parameters.Add("@EMail", SqlDbType.VarChar, 255).Value = EMail
    oCmd.Parameters.Add("@WebPage", SqlDbType.VarChar, 255).Value = _
        WebPage
    oCmd.Parameters.Add("@Age", SqlDbType.TinyInt, 2).Value = Age
    oCmd.Parameters.Add("@Comments", SqlDbType.VarChar, 2000).Value = _
        Comments
    Try
        If oConn.State = ConnectionState.Closed Then
          oConn.Open()
        End If
        oCmd.ExecuteNonQuery()
        AdrsID = oCmd.Parameters("@AdrsID").Value
        Return AdrsID
    Catch oErr As Exception
```

Continued

Figure 7.19B Continued

```
        Throw oErr
    End Try
End Function
```

Notice how the first parameter was explicitly set to a parameter object, and then this object was used to set the direction of the parameter. Valid values are Output, Input (default), Input/Output, and ReturnValue. The return value is useful for integer data, and is generally used to tell the outcome of the procedure; using 0 for success and 1 for failure are common, but any integer is acceptable. Output parameters are much more useful. If you are only returning one row of data, it is more efficient to return a batch of output parameters than a single row of data. We can't bind to it, but is more efficient from the database side of the application.

To get the value out of the parameter, we have to close the connection. By calling the *ExecuteNonQuery* method of the *Command* object, we effectively close the connection after execution, and we can then access our value from the parameter collection. Getting the value is no different than getting it out of any other collection. It is interesting to note that you must name your parameters the same as the Declaration of the stored procedure. It seems that Microsoft decided to use name parameters when they wrote the data access code. This gives us the option of setting them out of order.

Updating Data in a Database: Exercise

In addition to inserting new data, we will want the ability to update the data. Perhaps someone changes his or her phone number or moves. In our sample, we will update all the columns except for the primary key of our table. The syntax for creating the update statement is in Figure 7.20 (A, B, and C). The declaration of our stored procedure is very similar to the *Add* stored procedure, but we are not using an output parameter.

Figure 7.20 (A, B, and C) Updating Data

Figure 7.20A ANSI SQL (ANSI Is the Standard Which All RDBMS Databases Try to Implement)

```
UPDATE <table name>
SET <Column1 name> = <value1>,
```

Continued

Figure 7.20A Continued

```
<Column2 name> = <value2>
WHERE <primary key> = <identifier>
```

Figure 7.20B T-SQL

```
CREATE PROC usp_tblAddress_upd(
    @AdrsID    INT
,   @FName     varchar(50)
,   @LName     varchar(50)
,   @Phone     char(15)
,   @EMail     varchar(255)
,   @WebPage   varchar(255)
,   @Age       tinyint
,   @Comments  varchar(2000)
)
AS
UPDATE [dbo].[tblAddress]
SET [FName]    = @FName
,   [LName]    = @LName
,   [Phone]    = @Phone
,   [EMail]    = @EMail
,   [WebPage]  = @WebPage
,   [Age]      = @Age
,   [Comments] = @Comments
WHERE [AdrsID] = @AdrsID
```

Figure 7.20C Updating Data in Access

```
UPDATE [tblAddress]
SET [FName]    = <Replace with @FName>
,   [LName]    = <Replace with @LName>
,   [Phone]    = <Replace with @Phone>
,   [EMail]    = <Replace with @Email>
,   [WebPage]  = <Replace with @WebPage>
```

Continued

Figure 7.20C Continued

```
, [Age]      = <Replace with @Age>
, [Comments]= <Replace with @Comments>
WHERE [AdrsID] = <Replace with @AdrsID>
```

Again, we will use the *Command* object with parameters. We are using the default direction of Input to send in the new data. Any values that were not changed will just be overwritten with the same data. Refer to Figure 7.21 (A and B) for the *Update* method of our DAL example.

Figure 7.21 (A and B) Updating Data Using a Stored Procedure

Figure 7.21A C#.NET (cs\CDalAddress.cs)

```csharp
public void Update(Int32 AdrsID,
                   string FName,
                   string LName,
                   string Phone,
                   string EMail,
                   string WebPage,
                   Int16 Age,
                   string Comments)
{
  SqlConnection oConn;
  SqlCommand oCmd;
  SqlParameter oParam;
  string strSQL;
strSQL = "usp_tblAddress_upd";
oConn = new SqlConnection(strConStr);
oCmd = new SqlCommand(strSQL, oConn);
oCmd.CommandType = CommandType.StoredProcedure;
oCmd.Parameters.Add("@AdrsID", SqlDbType.Int, 4).Value = AdrsID;
oCmd.Parameters.Add("@FName", SqlDbType.VarChar, 50).Value = FName;
oCmd.Parameters.Add("@LName", SqlDbType.VarChar, 50).Value = LName;
oCmd.Parameters.Add("@Phone", SqlDbType.VarChar, 15).Value = Phone;
oCmd.Parameters.Add("@EMail", SqlDbType.VarChar, 255).Value = EMail;
```

Continued

Figure 7.21A Continued

```
oCmd.Parameters.Add("@WebPage", SqlDbType.VarChar, 255).Value = WebPage;
oCmd.Parameters.Add("@Age", SqlDbType.TinyInt, 2).Value = Age;
oCmd.Parameters.Add("@Comments", SqlDbType.VarChar, 2000).Value =
    Comments;
  try
  {
        if (oConn.State == ConnectionState.Closed)
        {
              oConn.Open();
        }
        oCmd.ExecuteNonQuery();
  }
  catch (Exception oErr)
  {
        throw oErr;
  }
}
```

Figure 7.21B VB.NET (vb\CDalAddress.vb)

```
Public Function Update(ByVal AdrsID As Int32, _
                  ByVal FName As String, _
                  ByVal LName As String, _
                  ByVal Phone As String, _
                  ByVal EMail As String, _
                  ByVal WebPage As String, _
                  ByVal Age As String, _
                  ByVal Comments As String) As Int32
    Dim oConn As SqlConnection
    Dim oCmd As SqlCommand
    Dim oParam As SqlParameter
    Dim strSQL As String
    strSQL = "usp_tblAddress_upd"
    oConn = New SqlConnection(strConStr)
```

Continued

Figure 7.21B Continued

```
        oCmd = New SqlCommand(strSQL, oConn)
        oCmd.CommandType = CommandType.StoredProcedure
        oCmd.Parameters.Add("@AdrsID", SqlDbType.Int, 4).Value = AdrsID
        oCmd.Parameters.Add("@FName", SqlDbType.VarChar, 50).Value = FName
        oCmd.Parameters.Add("@LName", SqlDbType.VarChar, 50).Value = LName
        oCmd.Parameters.Add("@Phone", SqlDbType.VarChar, 15).Value = Phone
        oCmd.Parameters.Add("@EMail", SqlDbType.VarChar, 255).Value = EMail
        oCmd.Parameters.Add("@WebPage", SqlDbType.VarChar, 255).Value =
            WebPage
        oCmd.Parameters.Add("@Age", SqlDbType.TinyInt, 2).Value = Age
        oCmd.Parameters.Add("@Comments", SqlDbType.VarChar, 2000).Value =
            Comments
    Try
        If oConn.State = ConnectionState.Closed Then
            oConn.Open()
        End If
        oCmd.ExecuteNonQuery()
    Catch oErr As Exception
        Throw New Exception(oErr.ToString)
    End Try
End Function
```

Notice the use of the *SqlDbType* enumeration for specifying our data types. The *ExecuteNonQuery* method is more efficient, since we are not returning any data.

Deleting from a Database: Exercise

To delete data from your database, you will use the Delete syntax with your primary key to delete just the row you specify. The syntax for the Delete statement is shown in Figure 7.22 (A, B, and C).

It is important to include the Where clause here, or you will end up deleting all the records in your table. The stored procedure will take one parameter, the primary key of record to delete.

Figure 7.22 (A, B, and C) Delete Syntax

Figure 7.22A T-SQL

```
DELETE
FROM <table name>
WHERE <primary key> = <id>
```

Figure 7.22B Delete Syntax for Access

```
DELETE *
FROM <table name>
WHERE <primary key> = <id>
```

Notice that T-SQL does not use the asterisk between the DELETE and the FROM keywords, and Access does.

Figure 7.22C Deleting a Particular Address in T-SQL

```
CREATE PROC usp_tblAddress_del(@AdrsID INT)
AS
DELETE FROM [dbo].[tblAddress]
WHERE [AdrsID] = @AdrsID
```

The Delete method of our DAL is simple after we have completed the methods earlier in the chapter. The finished code for the Delete Method is in Figure 7.23 (A and B).

Figure 7.23 (A and B) Calling the Delete Stored Procedure

Figure 7.23A C#.NET (cs\CDalAddress.cs)

```csharp
public void Delete(Int32 AdrsID)
{
    string strSQL = "EXEC usp_tblAddress_del " + AdrsID;
    SqlCommand oCmd = new SqlCommand(strSQL, oConn);
    oCmd.CommandType = CommandType.Text;
    try
    {
        if (oConn.State == ConnectionState.Closed)
```

Continued

Figure 7.23A Continued

```
                {
                    oConn.Open();
                }
                oCmd.ExecuteNonQuery();
        }
        catch (Exception oErr)
        {
            throw oErr;
        }
}
```

Figure 7.23B VB.NET (vb\CDalAddress.vb)

```
Public Sub Delete(ByVal AdrsID As String)
    Dim oCmd As SqlCommand
    Dim strSQL As String
    strSQL = "EXEC usp_tblAddress_del " & AdrsID
    oCmd = New SqlCommand(strSQL, oConn)
    oCmd.CommandType = CommandType.Text
    Try
        If oConn.State = ConnectionState.Closed Then
            oConn.Open()
        End If
        oCmd.ExecuteNonQuery()
    Catch oErr As Exception
        Throw New Exception(oErr.ToString)
    End Try
End Sub
```

The code to call the Delete Stored procedure is similar to the first method you used to select the records by their ID. Again, the *ExecuteNonQuery* tells ADO.NET that you are not interested in returning any rows and to close the connection when you are done. This requires less overhead for the data provider.

Summary

Microsoft has put a lot effort into .NET, and it shows in the 2500-plus objects that they have provided you in the .NET Framework. ADO.NET continues the tradition of ADO simplifying data access, while allowing for more flexible and powerful solutions than ever. Microsoft has added much power to ADO.NET, and provided clear ties to classic ADO that enable the veteran ADO programmer to easily move into the new environment.

We have gone over the changes in ADO.NET from classic ADO and talked about the new architecture. We discussed that ADO.NET was based on XML and how this compared to the proprietary protocol that classic ADO was based on. We talked about the rich support for XML and that it is part of the native architecture of ADO.NET. We discussed the fact that the *Recordset* no longer exists, and that it has been replaced with two objects that offer more than the *Recordset* ever could have: specifically, the *DataSet,* which can hold more than one result set for a data provider. We discussed the disconnected nature of the ADO.NET architecture and made great use of the *DataReader* object in our Address Book example.

We went into great detail about the configuration of a connection string, and where to keep this valuable piece of information. Specifically, by adding the <appSettings> node to the web.config file, and using the <add> tag, you can create a *ConfigurationSettings* variable that can be accessed globally in the Web application. We discussed the differences in the connection strings of the two major namespaces for data access. More to the point, we said that OleDB connection strings really haven't changed, but that if you are using the *SqlConnection* object, then you will need to remove the *Provider* attribute, or ADO.NET will raise an exception.

We introduced you to the Data Access Layer concept, and created a sample application the used the DAL to insert data using Embedded SQL statements, and Stored procedures. We used the *System.Data.SqlTypes* and the *SqlDbTypes* enumeration, and discussed that they are related, but have very different uses, such as the *System.Data.SqlTypes* namespace provider objects that are used to create SQL Server-compatible variables in our code, and then use the *SqlDbTypes* enumeration to specify the data type of a *Parameter* object for a command.

We showed you the ease in which operations can be performed using the various namespaces. We created the *strConnection* property of our DAL, and demonstrated the ease in which you can change from *OleDbConnections* to *SqlConnections* by declaring new variables and changing the connection string.

Solutions Fast Track

Understanding the Changes in ADO.NET

- ☑ ADO.NET is not *ActiveX Data* objects for ported to .NET, but an entirely new class of data access technologies.
- ☑ ADO.NET makes extensive use of XML, with rich support for consuming and creating XML documents.
- ☑ The *Recordset* has been removed, and new and more powerful objects have been provided. The *DataSet* is an in-memory relational database with support for multiple result sets from multiple data sources.
- ☑ ADO.NET is connectionless by nature, and does not maintain a connection to the data source.

Creating Connection Strings

- ☑ The first step to connecting to a data source, after choosing the Managed Provider, is to create the connection string.
- ☑ The connection string is a list of key/value pairs that the *Connection* object will parse; it will use the information to find the Data Source, authenticate, and establish a connection. Depending on the namespace used, the connection string will vary a little.

Connecting to a Database: Exercise

- ☑ Introduce the concept of the Data Access Layer, or DAL, as the data tier of a multi-tier application architecture.
- ☑ Create the correct Connection string for your data provider, and place it in a safe place such as the web.config file.
- ☑ The connection string for a *SqlConnection* is different than the connection string for an *OleDbConnection*; specifically, the *SqlConnection* does not allow for a *Provider* attribute.
- ☑ Provide the minimum database permissions to the user.

Browsing a Database: Exercise

- ☑ Use stored procedures as much as possible, for both security and for performance.
- ☑ Use a *DataReader* instead of a *DataSet* to return data from a Method in VB.NET or C#.NET.
- ☑ Bind data of the *DataReader* to a *DataList*, *DataGrid*, or *DataRepeater*.
- ☑ Return only the rows and columns you need.

Adding to a Database: Exercise

- ☑ Use parameterized stored procedure to insert data, and return the identity of the new record in MS SQL.
- ☑ Use Dynamic SQL to add records in Access, and you can still use the @@IDENTITY to return the identity that the database gave the new record.
- ☑ Use the *ExecuteNonQuery()* to improve performance.

Updating a Database: Exercise

- ☑ Use parameterized stored procedures to update data using the primary key to identify the row to update.
- ☑ Use *ExecuteNonQuery()* to improve performance.

Deleting from a Database: Exercise

- ☑ Do not forget the Where clause!
- ☑ Use *ExecuteNonQuery()* to improve performance.

Frequently Asked Questions

The following Frequently Asked Questions, answered by the authors of this book, are designed to both measure your understanding of the concepts presented in this chapter and to assist you with real-life implementation of these concepts. To have your questions about this chapter answered by the author, browse to **www.syngress.com/solutions** and click on the **"Ask the Author"** form.

Frequently Asked Questions

Q: Where is the best place to put the connection string?

A: In this chapter, we put our samples in the web.config file. This provides a central point to administer the connection strings, and allows for a reasonable level of security. You should guard the web.config from prying eyes regardless of where the connection string is. You really have a lot of options for placing the connection string. You can put the connection string in an encrypted in a file, custom object, and so on. The best place really depends on your environment, the applications purpose, and the level of security desired.

Q: Can I reuse a connection?

A: Yes, connections can be reused. Remember to test for state before you do, as ADO.NET may close the connection if it thinks it is not being used. You cannot use a connection twice at the same time. It would not be wise to open a connection at the application level, as you could very easily end up with simultaneous attempts to use the same connection.

Q: In SQL Server, which data type is more suitable for a primary key, INT, BIGINT or a uniqueidentifier?

A: Generally speaking, the INT going to be sufficient. An INT can hold between −2,147,483,648 and 2,147,483,648. That is a lot of records. If you were to seed an identity column with −2,147,483,648 negative number and insert one record a second, it would take 136 years to use all of them up. If you need more than that, then BIGINT is an alternative, but uniqueidentifier would probably be more appropriate. The other good use for the uniqueidentifier is to keep disconnected records from colliding with one another. This is often an issue with replication, and the uniqueidentifier is the method used to prevent it.

Q: How can I add a record to Access and return the ID of the new record in the same call?

A: Yes, you can. Access 2002 with ADO.NET supports the @@IDENTITY function. This function returns the last identity that was written in your session. This ensures that the identity value that you got was not from another user's session.

Q: How can I add a record to Microsoft SQL Server and return the ID of the new record in the same call?

A: The technique for returning the identity in SQL server is much the same as for Access; however, you have a couple of other options. You can return the identity as a return value. You can create an output parameter that is populated after the insert. You can also select the @@IDENTITY and return a record to the caller. The latter is not the most efficient way. The return value and the output parameter are comparable; however, the return value is limited to a data type of integer, while the output value can be any data type that SQL Server supports.

Chapter 8

Using XML in the .NET Framework

Solutions in this chapter:

- **An Overview of XML**
- **Processing XML Documents Using .NET**
- **Reading and Parsing Using the XmlTextReader Class**
- **Writing an XML Document Using the XmlTextWriter Class**
- **Exploring the XML Document Object Model**
- **Querying XML Data Using XPathDocument and XPathNavigator**
- **Transforming an XML Document Using XSLT**
- **Working with XML and Databases**
- ☑ Summary
- ☑ Solutions Fast Track
- ☑ Frequently Asked Questions

Introduction

The Extensible Markup Language (XML) is the latest offering in the world of data access. Microsoft has been actively supporting this language since its conception. XML provides a universal way for exchanging information between organizations. Its structure makes it perfect for online applications and working with data residing on the local or remote data sources.

Like Hypertext Markup Language (HTML), XML is a tag-based markup language. Many other technologies, such as browsers, JavaScript, VBScript, Dynamic HTML (DHTML), and Cascading Style Sheets (CSS), were developed to support the HTML documents. Similarly, XML cannot be singled out as a stand-alone technology. It is actually a family of a growing set of technologies and frameworks. The major members of this family are XML parsers, Extensible Stylesheet Language Transformations (XSLT), XPath, XLink, Simple API for XML (SAX), Schema Generators, and Document Object Model (DOM), just to name a few.

Please take note that ADO.NET *is not* coded in XML but that ADO.NET revolves around XML. Some readers may confuse the terms. Microsoft has integrated the XML technology in its .NET Framework rather tightly. The core foundation of the entire ADO.NET architecture is built upon XML. The ADO.NET itself is not coded in XML; however, it provides the facilities to apply various existing and emerging XML technologies to manipulate data and information. The *System.XML* namespace offers perhaps the richest collection of classes for generating, transmitting, processing, and storing information via XML. In this chapter, we will first have a brief introduction to the structural components of an XML document. Then we will look into the architecture of the XML objects in the .NET Framework. Finally, we will study several major XML.NET objects with many examples.

An Overview of XML

XML is fast becoming a standard for data exchange in the next generation's Internet applications. XML allows user-defined tags that make XML document handling more flexible than HTML, the conventional language of the Internet. Since XML is the heart and soul of ADO.NET, sound knowledge of XML is imperative for developing applications in ASP.NET. The following section touches on some of the basic concepts of XML.

What Does an XML Document Look Like?

The idea behind XML is surprisingly simple. The major objective is to organize information in such a way so that human beings can read and comprehend the data and its context; also, the document itself is technology and platform independent. Consider the following text file:

```
F10 Shimano Calcutta 47.76
F20 Bantam Lexica 49.99
```

Obviously, it is difficult to understand exactly what information the above text file contains. Now consider the XML document shown in Figure 8.1. The code is available in the Catalog1.xml file on the accompanying CD.

Figure 8.1 Example XML Document (Catalog1.xml)

```xml
<?xml version="1.0"?>
<!— Chapter8\Catalog1.xml —>
<Catalog>
    <Product>
        <ProductID>F10</ProductID>
        <ProductName>Shimano Calcutta </ProductName>
        <ListPrice>47.76</ListPrice>
    </Product>
    <Product>
        <ProductID>F20</ProductID>
        <ProductName>Bantam Lexica</ProductName>
        <ListPrice>49.99</ListPrice>
    </Product>
</Catalog>
```

The above document is the XML's way of representing data contained in a product catalog. It has many advantages. It is easily readable and comprehendible, it is self-documented, and it is technology independent. Most importantly, it is quickly becoming the universally acceptable data container and transmission format in the current information technology era. Well, welcome to the exciting world of XML!

> **Developing & Deploying…**
>
> ### XML and Its Future
>
> XML is quickly becoming the universal protocol for transferring information from site to site via HTTP. Whereas, the HTML will continue to be the language for displaying documents on the Internet, the developers will start using the power of XML to transmit, exchange, and manipulate data using XML.
>
> XML offers a very simple solution to a complex problem. It offers a standard format for structuring data or information in a self-defined document format. This way, the data are kept independent of the processes that will consume the data. Obviously, the concept behind XML is nothing new. XML happens to be a proper subset of a massive specification named SGML developed by W3C in 1986. The W3C began to develop the standard for XML in 1996 with the motivation that XML would be simpler to use than SGML but that it will have more rigid structure than HTML. Since then, many software vendors have implemented various features of XML technologies. For example, Ariba has built its entire B2B system architecture based on XML, many Web servers (such as Weblogic Server) utilize XML specifications for configuring various server related parameters, Oracle has included necessary parsers and utilities to develop business applications in its 8i/9i suites, and finally, the .NET has also embraced the XML technology.
>
> XML contains self-defined data in document format. Hence it is platform independent. It is also easy to transmit a document from a site to another site easily via HTTP. However, the applications of XML do not necessarily have to be limited to conventional Internet applications only. It can be used to communicate and exchange information in other contexts, too. For example, a VB client can call a remote function by passing the function name and parameter values using a XML document. The server may return the result via a subsequent XML document. Basically, that is the technology behind the SOAP (Simple Object Access Protocol).

Creating an XML Document

We can use Notepad to create an XML document. VS.NET offers an array of tools packaged in the XML Designer to work with XML documents. We will demonstrate the usages of the XML Designer later. Right now, go ahead and open the Catalog1.xml file from the CD that accompanies this book in IE 5.0 or higher. You will see that the IE displays the document in a very interesting fashion with drill-down features as shown in Figure 8.2.

Figure 8.2 Catalog1.xml Displayed in IE

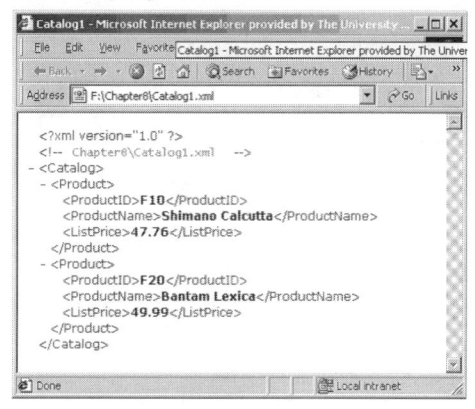

Creating an XML Document in VS.NET XML Designer

It is very easy to create an XML document in VS.NET. Use the following steps to develop an XML document:

1. From the **Project** menu, select **Add New Item**.
2. Select the **XML File** icon in the **Add New Item** dialog box.
3. Enter a name for your XML file.
4. The VS.NET will automatically load the XML Designer and display the XML document template.
5. Finally, enter the contents of your XML document.

The system will display two tabs for two views: the XML view and the Data view of your XML document. These views are shown in Figures 8.3 and 8.4. The XML Designer has many other tools to work with. We will introduce these later in this chapter.

Figure 8.3 The XML View of an XML Document in VS.NET XML Designer

Figure 8.4 The Data View of an XML Document in VS.NET XML Designer

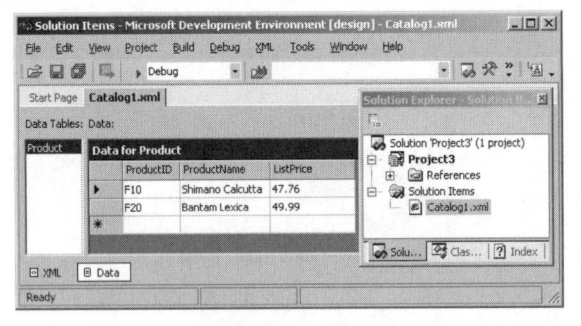

Components of an XML Document

In this section, we will introduce the major components of an XML document. An XML document contains a variety of constructs. Some of the frequently used ones are as follows:

- **Declaration** Each XML document may have the optional entry <?xml version="1.0"?>. This standard entry is used to identify the document as an XML document conforming to the W3C (World Wide Web Consortium) recommendation for version 1.0.

- **Comment** An XML document may contain html-style comments like <!--Catalog data -->.

- **Schema or Document Type Definition (DTD)** In certain situations, a schema or DTD may precede the XML document. A schema or

DTD contains the rules about the elements of the document. For example, we may specify a rule like "A product element must have a *ProductName*, but a *ListPrice* element is optional." We will discuss schemas later in the chapter.

- **Elements** An XML document is mostly composed of elements. An element has a start-tag and end-tag. In between the start-tag and end-tag, we include the content of the element. An element may contain a piece of character data, or it may contain other elements. For example, in the Catalog1.xml, the *Product* element contains three other elements: *ProductId*, *ProductName*, and *ListPrice*. On the other hand, the first *ProductName* element contains a piece of character data like Shimano Calcutta.

- **Root Element** In an XML document, one single main element must contain all other elements inside it. This specific element is often called the root element. In our example, the root element is the *Catalog* element. The XML document may contain many *Product* elements, but there must be only one instance of the *Catalog* element.

- **Attributes** Okay, we agree that we didn't tell you the whole story in our first example. So far, we have said that an element may contain other elements, or it may contain data, or both. Besides these, an element may also contain zero or more so-called attributes. An attribute is just an additional way to attach a piece of data to an element. An attribute is always placed inside the start-tag of an element, and we specify its value using the "name=value" pair protocol.

Let us revise our Catalog1.xml and include some attributes to the *Product* element. Here, we will assume that a *Product* element will have two attributes named *Type* and *SupplierId*. As shown in Figure 8.5, we will simply add the *Type="Spinning Reel"* and *SupplierId="5"* attributes in the first product element. Similarly, we will also add the attributes to the second product element. The code shown in Figure 8.5 is also available in the accompanying CD.

Figure 8.5 Catalog2.xml

```
<?xml version="1.0"?>
<!-- Chapter8/Catalog2.xml -->
<Catalog>
    <Product Type="Spinning Reel" SupplierId="5">
        <ProductID>F10</ProductID>
```

Continued

Figure 8.5 Continued

```
            <ProductName>Shimano Calcutta </ProductName>
            <ListPrice>47.76</ListPrice>
    </Product>
    <Product Type ="Baitcasting Reel" SupplierId="3">
            <ProductID>F20</ProductID>
            <ProductName>Bantam Lexica</ProductName>
            <ListPrice>49.99</ListPrice>
    </Product>
</Catalog>
```

Let us not get confused with the "attribute" label! An attribute is just an additional way to attach data to an element. Rather than using the attributes, we could have easily modeled them as elements as follows:

```
<Product>
    <ProductID>F10</ProductID>
    <ProductName>Shimano Calcutta </ProductName>
    <ListPrice>47.76</ListPrice>
    <Type>Spinning Reel</Type>
    <SupplierId>5</SupplierId>
</Product>
```

Alternatively, we could have modeled the entire product element to be composed of only attributes as follows:

```
<Product ProductID="F10" ProductName="Shimano Calcutta"
    ListPrice = "47.76" Type="Spinning Reel" SupplierId= "5" >
</Product>
```

At the initial stage, the necessity of an attribute may appear questionable. Nevertheless, they exist in the W3C recommendation, and in most situations these become handy in designing otherwise-complex XML-based systems.

- **Empty Element** We have already mentioned a couple of times that an element may contain other elements, or data, or both. However, an element does not necessarily have to have any of them. If needed, it can be kept totally empty. For example, observe the following element:

    ```
    <Input type="text" id="txtCity" runat="server" />
    ```

The *empty* element is a correct XML element. The name of the element is *Input*. It has three attributes: *type, id*, and *runat*. However, neither does it contain any sub-elements, nor does it contain any explicit data. Hence, it is an *empty* element. We may specify an empty element in one of two ways:

- Just before the ">" symbol of the start-tag, add a slash (/), as shown above, or

- Terminate the element using standard end-tag as follows:
    ```
    <Input type="text" id="txtCity" runat="server" ></Input>
    ```

Examples of some empty elements are: <br/>, <Pup Age=1 />, <Story></Story>, and <Mail/>.

Well-Formed XML Documents

At first sight, an XML document may appear to be like a standard HTML document with additional user-given tag names. However, the syntax of an XML document is much more rigorous than that of an HTML document. The HTML document enables us to spell many tags incorrectly (the browser would just ignore it), and it is a free world out there for people who are not case-sensitive. For example, we may use <BODY> and </Body> in the same HTML document without getting into trouble. On the contrary, there are certain rules that must be followed when we develop an XML document. Please, refer to the http://W3C.org Web site for the details. Some basic rules, among many others are as follows:

- The document must have exactly one root element.

- Each element must have a start-tag and end-tag.

- The elements must be properly nested.

- The first letter of an attribute's name must begin with a letter or an underscore.

- A particular attribute name may appear only once in the same start tag.

An XML document that is syntactically correct is often called a "well-formed" document. If the document is not well formed, Internet Explorer will provide an error message. For example, the following XML document will receive an error message, when opened in Internet Explorer, just because of the case sensitivity of the tag <product> and </Product>.

www.syngress.com

```
<?xml version="1.0"?>
<product>
<ProductID>F10</ProductID>
</Product>
```

Schema and Valid XML Documents

An XML document may be well formed, but it may not necessarily be a valid XML document. A valid XML document is a document that conforms to the rules specified in its Document Type Definition (DTD) or Schema. DTD and Schema are actually two different ways to specify the rules about the contents of an XML document. The DTD has several shortcomings. First, a DTD document does not have to be coded in XML. That means a DTD is itself not an XML document. Second, the data-types available to define the contents of an attribute or element are very limited in DTD. This is why, although VS.NET allows both DTD and schema, we will present only the schema specification in this chapter. The W3C has put forward the candidate proposal for the standard schema specification (www.w3.org/XML/Schema#dev). The XML Schema Definition (XSD) specification by W3C has been implemented in ADO.NET. VS.NET supports the XSD specifications.

A schema is simply a set of predefined rules that describe the data contents of an XML document. Conceptually, it is very similar to the definition of a relational database table. In an XML schema, we define the structure of an XML document, its elements, the data types of the elements and associated attributes, and most importantly, the parent-child relationships among the elements. We may develop a schema in many different ways. One way is to enter the definition manually using Notepad. We may also develop schema using visual tools, such as VS.NET or XML Authority. Many automated tools may also generate a rough-cut schema from a sample XML document (similar to reverse-engineering).

If we do not want to code a schema manually, we may generate a rough-cut schema of a sample XML document using VS.NET XML Designer. We may then polish the rough-cut schema to conform to our exact business rules. In VS.NET, it is just a matter of one click to generate a schema from a sample XML document. Use the following steps to generate a rough-cut schema for our Catalog1.xml document:

- Open the **Catalog1.xml file** in a VS.NET Project. VS.NET will display the XML document and its XML View and the Data View tabs at the bottom.
- Click on the **XML** menu pad of the Main menu.

That's all! The systems will create the schema named Catalog1.xsd. If we double-click on the **Catalog1.xsd** file in the **Solution Explorer**, we will see the screen as shown in Figure 8.6. We will see the *DataSet* view tag and the XML view tag at the bottom of the screen. We will elaborate on the *DataSet* view later in the chapter.

Figure 8.6 Truncated Version of the XSD Schema Generated by the XML Designer

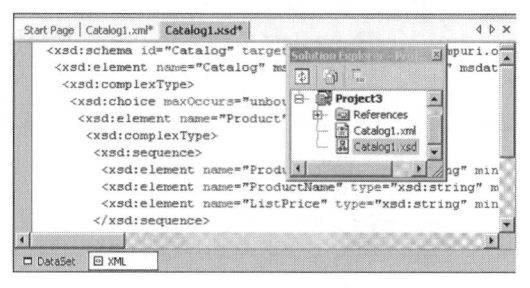

For discussion purposes, we have also listed the contents of the schema in Figure 8.7. The XSD starts with certain standard entries at the top. Although the code for an XSD may appear complex, there is no need to get overwhelmed by its syntax. Actually, the structural part of an XSD is very simple. An element is defined to contain either one or more *complexType* or *simpleType* data structures. A *complexType* data structure nests other *complexType* or *simpleType* data structures. A *simpleType* data structure contains only data.

In our XSD example (Figure 8.7), the *Catalog* element may contain one or more (unbounded) instances of the *Product* element. Thus, it is defined to contain a *complexType* structure. Besides containing the *Product* element, it may also contain other elements (for example, it could contain an element *Supplier*). In the XSD construct, we specify this rule using a *choice* structure as follows:

```
<xsd:element name="Catalog" msdata:IsDataSet="true">
    <xsd:complexType>
        <xsd:choice maxOccurs="unbounded">
            --- --- ---
            --- --- ---
```

```
            </xsd:choice>
        </xsd:complexType>
</xsd:element>
```

> **NOTE**
>
> An XSD is itself a well-formed XML document.

Because the *Product* element contains further elements, it also contains a *complexType* structure. This *complexType* structure, in turn, contains a sequence of *ProductId*, and *ListPrice*. The *ProductId* and the *ListPrice* do not contain further elements. Thus, we simply provide their data types in their definitions. The automated generator failed to identify the *ListPrice* element's text as decimal data. We converted its data type to decimal manually. The complete listing of the *Catalog.xsd* is shown in Figure 8.7. The code is also available in the accompanying CD.

Figure 8.7 Partial Contents of Catalog1.xsd

```
<xsd:schema id="Catalog"
    targetNamespace="http://tempuri.org/Catalog1.xsd"
    xmlns="http://tempuri.org/Catalog1.xsd"
    xmlns:xsd="http://www.w3.org/2001/XMLSchema"
    xmlns:msdata="urn:schemas-microsoft-com:xml-msdata"
    attributeFormDefault="qualified" elementFormDefault="qualified">
    <xsd:element name="Catalog" msdata:IsDataSet="true"
        msdata:EnforceConstraints="False">
        <xsd:complexType>
            <xsd:choice maxOccurs="unbounded">
                <xsd:element name="Product">
                    <xsd:complexType>
                        <xsd:sequence>
                            <xsd:element name="ProductID"
                                type="xsd:string" minOccurs="0" />
                            <xsd:element name="ProductName"
                                type="xsd:string" minOccurs="0" />
```

Continued

Figure 8.7 Continued

```
                        <xsd:element name="ListPrice"
                                type="xsd:string" minOccurs="0" />
                </xsd:sequence>
            </xsd:complexType>
        </xsd:element>
    </xsd:choice>
  </xsd:complexType>
 </xsd:element>
</xsd:schema>
```

Minimal knowledge about the XSD schema is required to understand the XML.NET architecture. You will find it especially useful when we discuss the *XmlDataDocument*.

> **NOTE**
>
> Readers interested in the details of DTD and Schema may explore http://msdn.microsoft.com/xml/default.asp and www.w3.org/XML.

Developing & Deploying…

XML Validation in VS.NET

VS.NET provides a number of tools to work on XML documents. One of them enables you to check if a given XML document is well formed. While on the XML view of an XML document, you may use **XML>>Validate XML Data** of the main menu to see if the document is well formed. The system displays its findings in the bottom-left corner of the status bar. Similarly, you can use the Schema Validation tool to check if your schema is well formed, too. While on the XML view of the schema, use the **Schema>>Validate Schema** of the main menu to perform this task.

However, none of the above tests guarantee that your XML data is valid according to the rules specified in the schema. To accomplish this

Continued

task, you will need to link your XML document to a particular schema first. Then you can test the validity of the XML document. To assign a schema to an XML document, perform the following steps:

1. Display the XML document in XML view (in the XML Designer).
2. Display its **Property sheet**. (It will be captioned **DOCUMENT**.)
3. Open the drop-down list box at the right-hand side of the **targetSchema**, and select the appropriate schema.
4. Now, go ahead and validate the document using the **XML>>Validate XML Data** of the main menu.

By the way, there are many other third-party software packages that can also test if an XML document is well formed, and if it is valid (against a given schema). In this context, we have found the XML Authority (by TIBCO) and XML Writer (by Wattle Software) to be very good. An excellent tool named XSV is also available from www.w3.org/2000/09/webdata/xsv.

Structure of an XML Document

In an XML document, the data are stored in a hierarchical fashion. A hierarchy is also referred to as a *tree* in data structures. Conceptually, the data stored in the Catalog1.xml can be represented as a tree diagram, as shown in Figure 8.8. Please note that certain element names and values have been abbreviated in the tree diagram, mostly to conserve real estate on the page.

In this figure, each rectangle is a node in the tree. Depending on the context, a node can be of different types. For example, each product node in the figure is an *element-type* node. Each product node happens to be a *child node* of the catalog node. The catalog node can also be termed as the *parent* of all product nodes. Each product node, in turn, is the parent of its *PId, PName,* and *Price* nodes.

In this particular tree diagram, the bottom-most nodes are **not** of element-type; rather, these are of *text-type*. There could have been nodes for each attribute and its value, too, although we have not shown those in this diagram.

The *Product* nodes are the immediate *descendants* of the *Catalog* node. Both *Product* nodes are *siblings* of each other. Similarly, the *PId, PName,* and *Price* nodes under a specific product node are also siblings of each other. In short, all children of a parent are called siblings.

At this stage, you may have been wondering why we are studying the family history rather than ASP. Well, you will find out pretty soon that all of these terminologies will play major roles in taming the beauties and the beasts of something called XML technology.

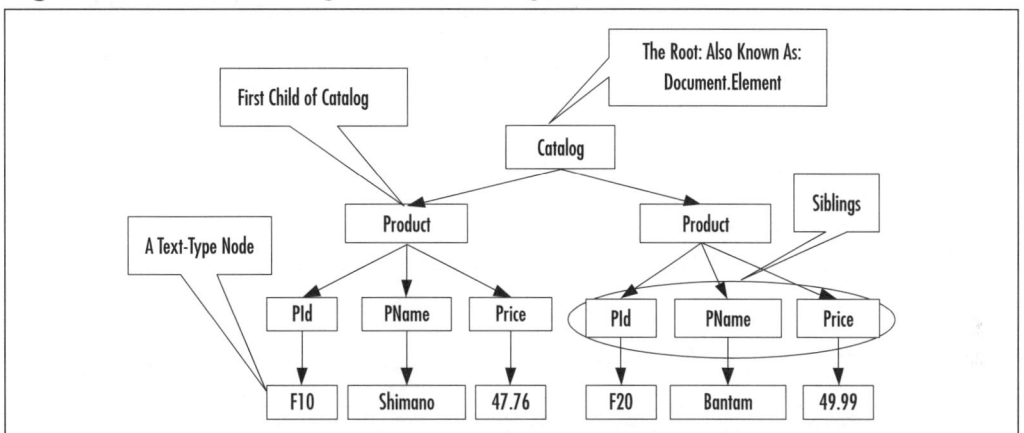

Figure 8.8 The Tree-Diagram for Catalog1.xml

Processing XML Documents Using .NET

The entire ADO.NET Framework has been designed based on XML technology. Many of the ADO.NET data-handling methodologies, including *DataTables* and *DataSets*, use XML in the background, thus keeping it transparent to us. The .NET Framework's *System.Xml* namespace provides a very rich collection of classes that can be used to store and process XML documents. These classes are also often referred to as the XML.NET.

Before we get into the details of the XML.NET objects, let us ask ourselves several questions. As ASP NET developers, what kind of support would we need from .NET for processing XML documents? Well, at the very least, we would like .NET to assist us in creating, reading, and parsing XML documents. Anything else? Okay, if we have adequate cache, we would like to load the entire document in the memory and process it directly from there. If we do not have enough cache, then we would like to read various fragments of an XML document one piece at a time. Do we want more? How about the ability for searching and querying the information contained in an XML document? How about instantly creating an XML document from a database query and sending it to our B2B partners? How about converting an XML document from one format to another format and transmitting it to other servers? Actually, XML.NET provides all of these, and much more! All of the above questions fall into two major categories:

1. How do we read, parse and write XML documents?
2. How do we store, structure, and process them in the memory?

As mentioned earlier, XML is associated with a growing family of technologies and frameworks. The major trends in this area are W3C DOM, XSLT, XPath, XPath Query, SAX, and XSLT. In XML.NET, Microsoft has incorporated almost all of these frameworks and technologies. It has also added some of its own unique ideas. There is a plethora of alternative XML.NET objects to satisfy our needs and likings. However, it's a jungle out there! In the remainder of this section, we will have a brief glance over this jungle.

> **Migrating...**
>
> **Legacy Systems and XML**
>
> Organizational data stored in legacy systems can be converted to appropriate XML documents, if needed, reasonably easily. There is third-party software like XML Authority by Tibco Extensibility and others, which can convert legacy system's data into XML format. We can also use VS.NET to convert legacy data to XML documents.

Reading and Writing XML Documents

Two primary classes in this group are *XmlReader* and *XmlWriter*. Both of these classes are abstract classes, and therefore we cannot create objects of these classes. Microsoft has provided a number of concrete implementations of both of these classes:

- **XmlTextReader** We may use an object of this class to read non-cached XML data on a forward-only basis. It checks for well-formed XML, but it does not support data validation.
- **XmlNodeReader** An object of this class can be used to access non-cached forward-only data from an XML node. It does not support data validation.

- **XmlValidationReader** This is very similar to the *XMLTextReader*, except that it accommodates XML data validation.

We may create objects of these classes and use their methods and properties. If warranted, we may also extend these classes to provide further specific functionalities. Fortunately, the *XmlWriter* class has only one concrete implementation: *XmlTextWriter*. It can be used to write XML document on a forward-only basis. These classes and their relationships are shown in Figure 8.9.

Figure 8.9 Major *XmlReader* and *XmlWriter* Classes

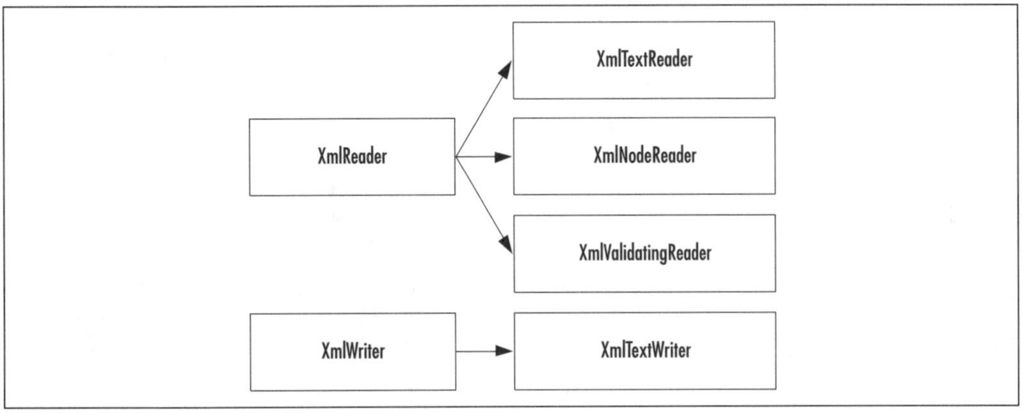

```
XmlReader ──┬──► XmlTextReader
            ├──► XmlNodeReader
            └──► XmlValidatingReader

XmlWriter ───► XmlTextWriter
```

Storing and Processing XML Documents

Once XML data are read, we need to structure these data in the computer's memory. For this purpose, the major offerings include the *XmlNode* class and the *XPathDocument* class. The *XmlNode* class is an abstract class. There are a number of concrete implementations of this class, too, such as the *XmlDocument, XmlAttribute, XmlDocumentFragment,* and so on. We will limit our attention to the *XmlDocument* class, and to one of its subsequent extensions named the *XmlDataDocument*. The characteristics of some of these classes are as follows:

- **XmlDocument** This class structures an XML document according to a DOM tree (as specified in the W3C DOM Core Level 1 and 2 specifications).

- **XmlDataDocument** This class is a major milestone in integrating XML and database processing. It allows two views of the in-cache data: the Relational Table view, and the XML Tree View.

- **XPathDocument** This class employs the XSLT and XPath technologies, and enables you to transform an XML document in to a desired format.

Above classes are essentially used for storing the XML data in the cache. Just storing data in the memory serves us no purpose unless we can process and query these data. The .NET Framework has included a number of classes to operate on the cached XML data. These classes include *XPathNavigator*, *XPathNodeIterator*, *XSLTransform*, *XmlNodeList*, etc. These classes are shown in Figure 8.10.

Figure 8.10 Major XML Classes for In-Memory Storage and Processing

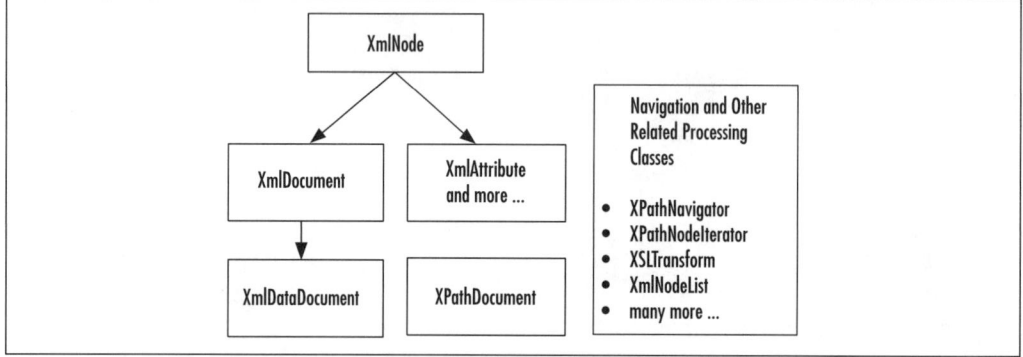

Reading and Parsing Using the XmlTextReader Class

The *XmlTextReader* class provides a fast forward-only cursor that can be used to "pull" data from an XML document. An instance of it can be created as follows:

```
Dim myRdr As New XmlTextReader(Server.MapPath("catalog2.xml"))
```

Once an instance is created, the imaginary cursor is set at the top of the document. We may use its *Read()* method to extract fragments of data sequentially. Each fragment of data is distantly similar to a node of the underlying XML tree. The *NodeType* property captures the type of the data fragment read, the *Name* property contains the name of the node, and the *Value* property contains the value of the node, if any. Thus, once a data fragment has been read, we may use the following type of statement to display the node-type, name, and value of the node.

```
Response.Write(myRdr.NodeType.ToString() + " " +
    myRdr.Name + ": " + myRdr.Value)
```

The attributes are treated slightly differently in the *XmlTextReader* object. When a node is read, we may use the *HasAttributes* property of the reader object to see if there are any attributes attached to it. If there are attributes in an element, the *MoveToAttribute(i)* method can be applied to iterate through the attribute collection. The *AttributeCount* property contains the number of attributes of the current element. Once we process all of the attributes, we need to apply the *MoveToElement* method to move the cursor back to the current element node. Therefore, the following code will display the attributes of an element:

```
If  myRdr.HasAttributes Then
   For i = 0 To myRdr.AttributeCount - 1
     myRdr.MoveToAttribute(i)
     Response.Write(myRdr.NodeType.ToString() + " : "+ myRdr.Name _
         + ": " + myRdr.Value + "</br>")
   Next i
   myRdr.MoveToElement()
End If
```

Microsoft has loaded the *XmlDocument* class with a variety of convenient class members. Some of the frequently used methods and properties are *AttributeCount*, *Depth*, *EOF*, *HasAttributes*, *HasValue*, *IsDefault*, *IsEmptyElement*, *Item*, *ReadState*, and *Value*.

Parsing an XML Document:

In this section, we will apply the *XMLTextReader* object to parse and display all data contained in our Catalog2.xml (as shown in Figure 8.5) document. The code for this example and its output are shown in Figures 8.11 and 8.12, respectively. The code shown in Figure 8.12 is available in the accompanying CD. Our objective is to start at the top of the document and then sequentially travel through its nodes using the *XMLTextReader*'s *Read()* method. When there is no more data to read, the *Read()* method returns "false." Thus, we are able to build the *While myRdr.Read()* loop to process all data. Please review the code (Figure 8.12) and its output cautiously. While displaying the data, we have separated the node-type, node-name, and values using colons. Not all elements have names or values. Hence, you will see many empty names and values after respective colons.

Chapter 8 • Using XML in the .NET Framework

Figure 8.11 Truncated Output of the *XmlTextReader1.aspx* Code

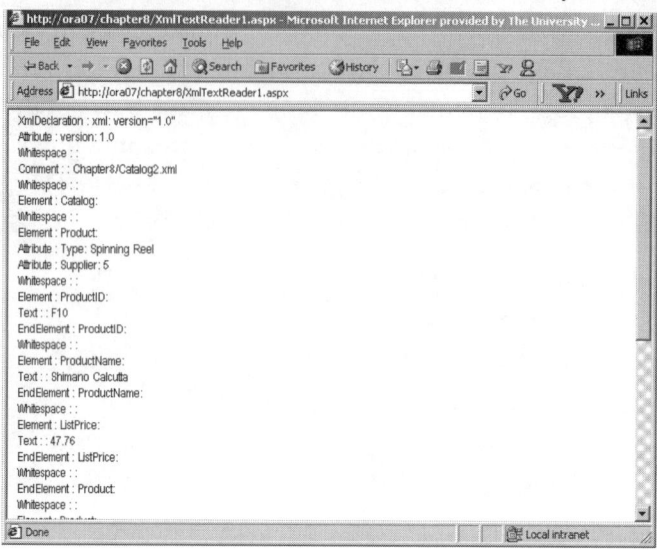

```
XmlDeclaration : xml: version="1.0"
Attribute : version: 1.0
Whitespace : :
Comment : : Chapter8/Catalog2.xml
Whitespace : :
Element : Catalog:
Whitespace : :
Element : Product:
Attribute : Type: Spinning Reel
Attribute : Supplier: 5
Whitespace : :
Element : ProductID:
Text : : F10
EndElement : ProductID:
Whitespace : :
Element : ProductName:
Text : : Shimano Calcutta
EndElement : ProductName:
Whitespace : :
Element : ListPrice:
Text : : 47.76
EndElement : ListPrice:
Whitespace : :
EndElement : Product:
Whitespace : :
```

Figure 8.12 XmlTextReader1.aspx

```
<!— Chapter8\xmlTextReader1.aspx —>
<%@ Page Language = "VB" Debug ="True" %>
<%@ Import Namespace="System.Xml" %>
<Script runat="server">
Sub Page_Load(sender As Object, e As EventArgs)
   Dim myRdr As New XmlTextReader(Server.MapPath("Catalog2.xml"))
   Dim i As Integer
   While myRdr.Read()
     Response.Write(myRdr.NodeType.ToString() + " : " + myRdr.Name _
        + ": " + myRdr.Value + "<br/>")
     If  myRdr.HasAttributes Then
        For i = 0 To myRdr.AttributeCount - 1
          myRdr.MoveToAttribute(i)
          Response.Write(myRdr.NodeType.ToString() + " : "+ myRdr.Name _
             + ": " + myRdr.Value + "</br>")
        Next i
        myRdr.MoveToElement()
```

Continued

Figure 8.12 Continued

```
    End If
  End While
  myRdr.Close()
End Sub
</Script>
```

Navigating through an XML Document to Retrieve Data

In the previous section, we extracted and displayed all data, including the "whitespaces" contained in an XML document. Now, we will illustrate an example where we will navigate through the document and pick up only those data that are necessary for an application. The output of this application is shown in Figure 8.13. In this example, we will display the names of our products in a list box. We will load the list box using the *Product Name* data from the XML file. The user will select a particular product. Subsequently, we will search the XML document to find and display the price of the product. We will travel through the XML file twice, once to load the list box, and once to find the price of a selected product. Please be aware that we could have easily developed the application by building an array or arraylist of the products during the first pass through the XML data, thus avoiding a second pass. Nevertheless, we are reading the file twice just to illustrate various methods and properties of the *XmlTextReader* object.

Figure 8.13 Output of the Navigation ASPX Example XmlTextReader2.aspx

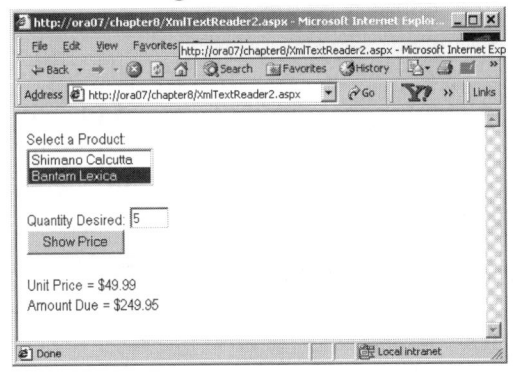

To load the List Box, we will go through the following process: We will load the list box in the *Page_Load* event. Here, we will read the nodes one at a time. If the node type is of element-type, we will check if its name is *ProductName*. If it is a *ProductName* node, we will perform a *Read()* to get to its text node and then apply the *myRdr.ReadString()* method to extract the value and load it in the list box. Finally, we will close the reader object. **Caution:** We are assuming that there is no "whitespace" between the *ProductName* and its Text node. If there is a "whitespace," we will need to put the second *Read()* in a loop until the node-type is Text.

```
While myRdr.Read()
        If   XmlNodeType.Element
              If myRdr.Name="ProductName" Then
                    myRdr.Read()
                    lstProducts.Items.Add(myRdr.ReadString)
              End If
        End If
End While
myRdr.Close()
```

To find the price of the selected product, we will go through the following process: We will include the necessary code in the "unclick" event code of the command button "Show Price." We will create a second *XmlTextReader* object based on the catalog2.xml file. Of course, we may scan all nodes sequentially to find the price. However, the *XmlTextReader* class enables you to skip undesirable nodes, such as the "whitespace" or the declaration nodes via the *MoveToContent()* method. According to Microsoft, all nonwhitespace, Element, End Element, EntityReference, and EndEntity nodes are *content nodes*. The *MoveToContent()* method checks whether the current node is a content node. If the node is not a content node, then the method skips to the next content node. You need to be careful though. If the current node happens to be a content node, the cursor does not move to the next content node automatically on a further *MoveToContent()*.

Initially, when we instantiate the *reader* object, its node type is *None*. It happens to be a noncontent node. Hence our first *MoveToContent()* statement takes us to a content node. There, we check if it is an Element-type node named "ProductName" and if its *ReadString()* is equal to the name of the selected product. If all are true, then we apply a *Read()* to go to the next node. This *Read()* may take us to a "whitespace" node, and thus we have applied a *MoveToContent()*

to get to the ListPrice node. Figure 8.14 shows an excerpt of the relevant code. The complete code is available in XmlTextReader2.aspx file in the CD.

Figure 8.14 Excerpt of XmlTextReader2.aspx

```
Sub showPrice(s As Object, e As EventArgs)
  Dim myRdr2 As New XmlTextReader(Server.MapPath("Catalog2.xml"))
  Dim unitPrice As Double
  Dim qty AS Integer
  Do While Not myRdr2.EOF()
   If (myRdr2.MoveToContent() = XmlNodeType.Element _
     And myRdr2.Name ="ProductName" _
     And myRdr2.ReadString()=lstProducts.SelectedItem.ToString())
     myRdr2.Read()
     If (myRdr2.MoveToContent() = XmlNodeType.Element _
       And myRdr2.Name ="ListPrice")
       unitPrice=Double.Parse(myRdr2.ReadString())
       lblPrice.Text= "Unit Price = " + FormatCurrency(unitPrice)
       Exit Do
     End If
   End If
   myRdr2.Read()
  Loop
  qty = Integer.Parse(txtQty.Text)
  lblAmount.Text = "Amount Due = " + FormatCurrency(qty * unitPrice)
  myRdr2.Close()
End Sub
```

By the way, we could have also used the *MoveToContent()* method to load our list box more effectively. However, we just wanted to show the alternative methodologies.

NOTE

We may also read XML files from remote servers as follows:
```
Dim myRdr As New XmlTextReader("http://ahmed2/Chapter8/
    Catalog2.xml")
```

Writing an XML Document Using the XmlTextWriter Class

The *XmlTextWriter* class is a concrete implementation of the *XmlWriter* abstract class. An *XmlTextWriter* object can be used to write data sequentially to an output stream, or to a disk file as an XML document. The data to be written may come from the user's input and/or from a variety of other sources, such as text files, databases, *XmlTextReaders*, or *XmlDocuments*. Its major methods and properties include *Close, Flush, Formatting, WriteAttribues, WriteAttributeString, WriteComment, WriteElementString, WriteElementString, WriteEndAttribute, WriteEndDocument, WriteState,* and *WriteStartDocument*.

Generating an XML Document Using *XmlTextWriter*

In this section, we will collect user-given data via an .aspx page, and write the information in an XML file. The run-time view of the application is shown in Figure 8.15. On the *click* event of the "Create XML File," the application will create the XML file (in the disk) and display it back in the browser as seen in Figure 8.16.

Figure 8.15 Output of the XmlTextReader2.aspx

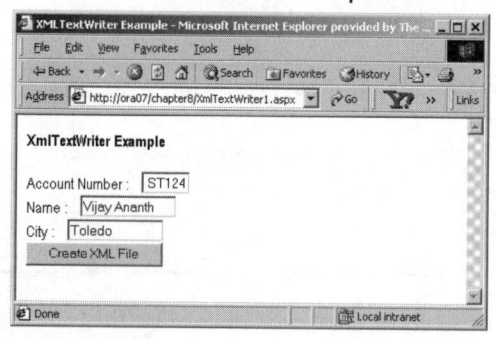

We have included the necessary code in the *click* event of the command button. Our objective is to write the data in a disk file named Customer.xml. In the code, first we have created an instance of the *XmlTextWriter* object as follows:

```
Dim myWriter As New XmlTextWriter _
    (Server.MapPath("Customer.xml"), Nothing)
```

Figure 8.16 Generated XML File

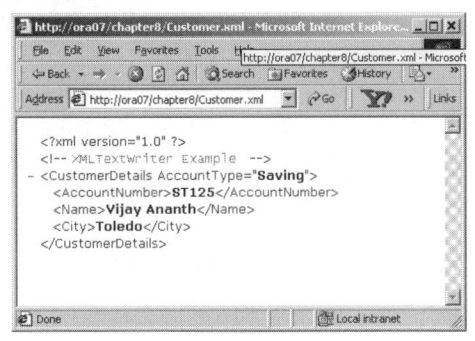

![Screenshot of browser showing Customer.xml with CustomerDetails element containing AccountNumber ST125, Name Vijay Ananth, City Toledo, AccountType Saving]

The second parameter "Nothing" is specified to map the file to a UTF-8 format. Then it is just a matter of writing the various elements, attributes, and their values judiciously. Once the file is written, we simply employed the *Response.Redirect(Server.MapPath("Customer.xml"))* to display the XML documents information in the browser. The complete code for the application is shown in Figure 8.17. Both Customer.xml and XmlTextWriter1.aspx files are available in the accompanying CD.

Figure 8.17 XmlTextWriter1.aspx

```
<!-- Chapter8\XmlTextWriter1.aspx -->
<%@ Page Language="VB" Debug="True"%>
<%@ Import Namespace="System.Xml"%>
<HTML><HEAD><title>XMLTextWriter Example</title></HEAD>
<body><form runat="server">
<b>XmlTextWriter Example</b><br/><br/>
<asp:Label id="lblAcno" Text="Account Number :"
    runat="server"/>  
<asp:TextBox id="txtAcno" runat="server" width="50" _
    text=" ST124" /><br/>
<asp:Label id="lblName" Text="Name :" runat="server" />  
<asp:TextBox id="txtName" runat="server" width="100" text="Vijay
    Ananth"/><br/>
<asp:Label id="lblCity" Text="City :" runat="server"/>  
<asp:TextBox id="txtCity" runat="server" width="100"
    text="Toledo"/><br/>
```

Continued

Figure 8.17 Continued

```
<asp:Button id="cmdWriteXML" Text="Create XML File" runat="server"
    onclick="writeXML"/>
<br></form>

<Script Language="vb" runat="server">

Sub writeXML(sender As Object,e As EventArgs)
    Dim myWriter As New XmlTextWriter _
        (Server.MapPath("Customer.xml"), Nothing)
    myWriter.Formatting = Formatting.Indented
    myWriter.WriteStartDocument()       'Start a new document
    ' Write the Comment
    myWriter.WriteComment("XMLTextWriter Example")
    ' Insert an Start element tag
    myWriter.WriteStartElement("CustomerDetails")
    ' Write an attribute
    myWriter.WriteAttributeString("AccountType", "Saving")
    ' Write the Account element and its content
    myWriter.WriteStartElement("AccountNumber","")
    myWriter.WriteString(txtAcno.Text)
    myWriter.WriteEndElement()
    ' Write the Name Element and its data
    myWriter.WriteStartElement("Name","")
    myWriter.WriteString(txtName.Text)
    myWriter.WriteEndElement()
    'Write the City element and its data
    myWriter.WriteStartElement("City","")
    myWriter.WriteString(txtCity.Text)
    myWriter.WriteEndElement()

    'End all the tags here
    myWriter.WriteEndDocument()
```

Continued

Figure 8.17 Continued

```
    myWriter.Flush()
    myWriter.Close()

    'Display the XML content on the screen
    Response.Redirect(Server.MapPath("Customer.xml"))

End Sub

</Script>
```

Exploring the XML Document Object Model

The W3C Document Object Model (DOM) is a set of specifications to represent an XML document in the computer's memory. Microsoft has implemented the W3C Document Object Model via a number of .NET objects. The *XmlDocument* is one of these objects. When an *XmlDocument* object is loaded, it organizes the contents of an XML document as a "tree" (as shown in Figure 8.18). Whereas the *XMLTextReader* object provides a forward-only cursor, the *XmlDocument* object provides fast and direct access to a node. However, a DOM tree is cache intensive, especially for large XML documents.

An *XmlDocument* object can be loaded from an *XmlTextReader*. Once it is loaded, we may navigate via the nodes of its tree using numerous methods and properties. Some of the frequently used members are the following: *DocumentElement* (root of the tree), *ChildNodes* (all children of a node), *FirstChild*, *LastChild*, *HasChildNodes*, *ChildNodes.Count* (# of children), *InnerText* (the content of the sub-tree in text format), *Name* (node name), *NodeType*, and *Value* (of a text node) among many others.

If needed, we may address a node using the parent-child hierarchy. The first child of a node is the ChildNode(0), the second child is ChildNode(1), and so on. For example, the first product can be referenced as *DocumentElement.ChildNodes(0)*. Similarly, the price of the second product can be addressed as *DocumentElement.ChildNodes(1).ChildNodes(2).InnerText*.

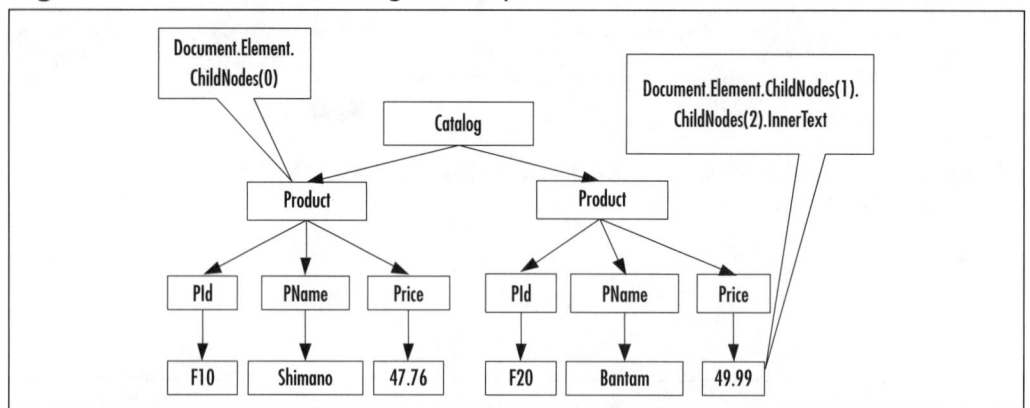

Figure 8.18 Node Addressing Techniques in an XML DOM Tree

```
Document.Element.
ChildNodes(0)                              Document.Element.ChildNodes(1).
                                           ChildNodes(2).InnerText
              Catalog

       Product              Product

   PId  PName  Price    PId   PName   Price

   F10  Shimano 47.76   F20   Bantam  49.99
```

Navigating through an *XmlDocument* Object

In this example we will implement our product selection page using the XML document object model. The output of the code is shown in Figure 8.19.

Figure 8.19 Output of the *XmlDocument* Object Example

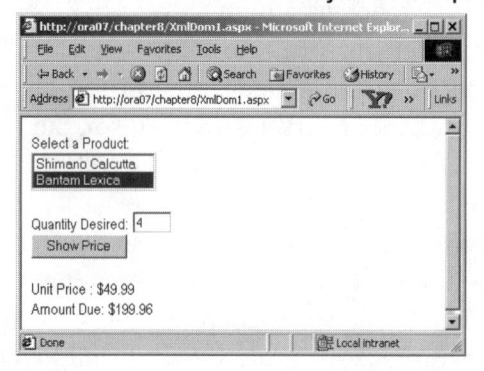

Let's go through the process of loading the *XmlDocument* (DOM tree). There are a number different ways to load an *XML Document* object. We will load it using an *XmlTextReader* object. We will ask the reader to ignore the "whitespaces" (more or less to conserve cache). As you can see from the following code, we are loading the tree in the *Page_Load* event. On "PostBack", we will not have access to this tree. That is why we are storing the "tree" in a *Session* variable. When the user makes a selection, we will retrieve the tree from the session, and search its node for the appropriate price.

```
Private Sub Page_Load(s As Object,   e As EventArgs)
   If Not Page.IsPostBack Then
      Dim myDoc As New XmlDocument()
      Dim myRdr As New XmlTextReader(Server.MapPath("Catalog2.xml"))
      myRdr.WhitespaceHandling = WhitespaceHandling.None
      myDoc.Load(myRdr)
      Session("sessionDoc") = myDoc  ' Put it in a session variable
```

Once the tree is loaded, we can load the list box with the *InnerText* property of the *ProductName* nodes.

```
For i = 0 To myDoc.DocumentElement.ChildNodes.Count - 1
              lstProducts.Items.Add _
(myDoc.DocumentElement.ChildNodes(i).ChildNodes(1).InnerText)
Next i
      myRdr.Close()
```

Next, let's investigate how to retrieve the price of a selected product. On click of the **Show Price** button, we simply retrieve the tree from the session, and get to the *Price* node directly. The *SelectedIndex* property of the list box does a favor for us, as its Selected Index value will match the corresponding child's ordinal position in the *Catalog (DocumentElement)*. Figure 8.20 shows an excerpt of the relevant code that is used to retrieve the price of a selected product. The complete code is available in the XmlDom1.aspx file in the accompanying CD.

Figure 8.20 Partial Listing of XmlDom1.aspx

```
Private Sub showPrice(s As Object,   e As EventArgs)
  Dim i As Integer
  Dim qty As Integer = 1
  Dim price As Double
  Dim myDoc As New XmlDocument()
  myDoc = Session("sessionDoc")
  i = lstProducts.SelectedIndex    ' The Row number selected
  qty = Integer.Parse(txtQty.Text)
  price = Double.Parse _
      (myDoc.DocumentElement.ChildNodes(i).ChildNodes(2).InnerText)
  lblPrice.Text = FormatCurrency(price)
```

Continued

Figure 8.20 Continued

```
    lblAmount.Text = FormatCurrency(qty * price)
End Sub
```

Parsing an XML Document Using the *XmlDocument* Object

A *tree* is composed of nodes. Essentially, a node is also a tree because it contains all other nodes below it. A node at the bottom does not have any children; hence, most likely it will be of a text-type node. We will employ this phenomenon to travel through a tree using a VB recursive procedure. The primary objective of this example is to travel through DOM tree and display the information contained in each of its nodes. The output of this exercise is shown in Figure 8.21.

Figure 8.21 Parsing an *XmlDocument* Object

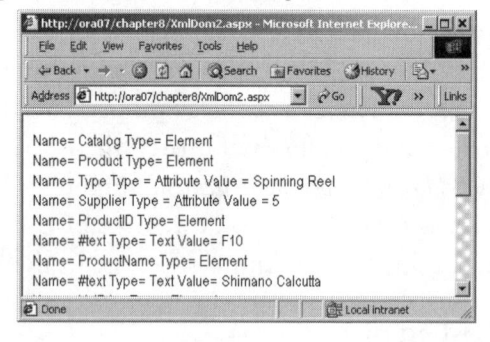

We will develop two subprocedures:

1. **DisplayNode(node As XmlNode)** It will receive a node and check if it is a terminal node. If the node is a terminal node, this subprocedure will print its contents. If the node is not a terminal node, then the subprocedure will check if the node has any attributes. If there are attributes, it will print them.

2. **TravelDownATree(tree As XmlNode)** It will receive a tree, and at first it will call the DisplayNode procedure. Then it will pass the sub-tree of the received tree to itself. This is a recursive procedure. Thus, it will actually fathom all nodes of a received tree, and we will get all nodes of the entire tree printed.

The complete listing of the code is shown in Figure 8.22. The code is also available in the file named XmlDom2.aspx in the accompanying CD. As usual, we will load the *XmlDocument* in the *Page_Load()* event using an *XmlTextReader*. After the DOM tree is loaded, we will call the *TravelDownATree* recursive procedure, which will accomplish the remainder of the job.

Figure 8.22 The Complete Code *XmlDom2.aspx*

```
<!— Chapter8\xmlDom2.aspx —>
<%@ Page Language = "VB"  Debug ="True" %>
<%@ Import Namespace="System.Xml" %>
<Script Language="vb" runat="server">
Sub Page_Load(s As Object, e As EventArgs)
  If Not Page.IsPostBack Then
    Dim myXmlDoc As New XmlDocument()
    Dim myRdr As New XmlTextReader(Server.MapPath("Catalog2.xml"))
    myRdr.WhitespaceHandling = WhitespaceHandling.None
    myXmlDoc.Load (myRdr)
    TravelDownATree(myXmlDoc.DocumentElement)
    myRdr.Close()
  End If
End Sub
Sub TravelDownATree(tree As XMLNode)
  If Not IsNothing(tree) Then
     DisplayNode(tree)
  End If
  If tree.HasChildNodes Then
    tree = tree.FirstChild
    While Not IsNothing(tree)
       TravelDownATree(tree) //Call itself and pass the subtree
       tree = tree.NextSibling
    End While
  End If
End Sub
Sub DisplayNode(node As XmlNode)
  If Not node.HasChildNodes Then
```

Continued

Figure 8.22 Continued

```
      Response.Write( "Name= " + node.Name + " Type= " _
        + node.NodeType.ToString()+" Value=   "+node.Value +"<br/>")
    Else
      Response.Write("Name= " + node.Name + " Type= " _
        + node.NodeType.ToString() + "<br/>")
      If node.NodeType = XmlNodeType.Element   Then
          Dim x As XmlAttribute
          For each x In node.Attributes
              Response.Write("Name= " + x.Name   +   " Type = " _
                + x.NodeType.ToString()+" Value = "+x.Value +"<br/>")
          Next
      End If
   End If
 End Sub
</Script>
```

Using the *XmlDataDocument* Class

The *XmlDataDocument* class is an extension of the *XmlDocument* class. It more-or-less behaves almost the same way the *XmlDocument* does. The most fascinating feature of an *XmlDataDocument* object is that it provides two alternative views of the same data, the "XML view" and the "relational view." The *XmlDataDocument* has a property named *DataSet*. It is through this property that *XmlDataDocument* exposes its data as one or more related or unrelated *DataTables*. A *DataTable* is actually an imaginary table-view of XML data. Once we load an *XmlDataDocument* object, we can treat it as a DOM tree, or we can treat its data as a *DataTable* (or a collection of *DataTables*) via its *DataSet* property. Figure 8.23 shows the two views of an *XmlDataDocument*. Because these views are drawn from the same *DataDocument* object, these are automatically synchronized. That means that any changes in any one of them will change the other. In this section, we will provide three examples.

- We will demonstrate how to load an XML document as an *XmlDataDocument* object, and process it as a Dom tree.
- We will illustrate how to retrieve the data from a *DataTable* view of the *XmlDataDocument*'s *DataSet*.

- Finally, We will demonstrate when and how the *XmlDataDocument* object provides multiple-table views.

Figure 8.23 Two Views of an *XmlDataDocument* Object

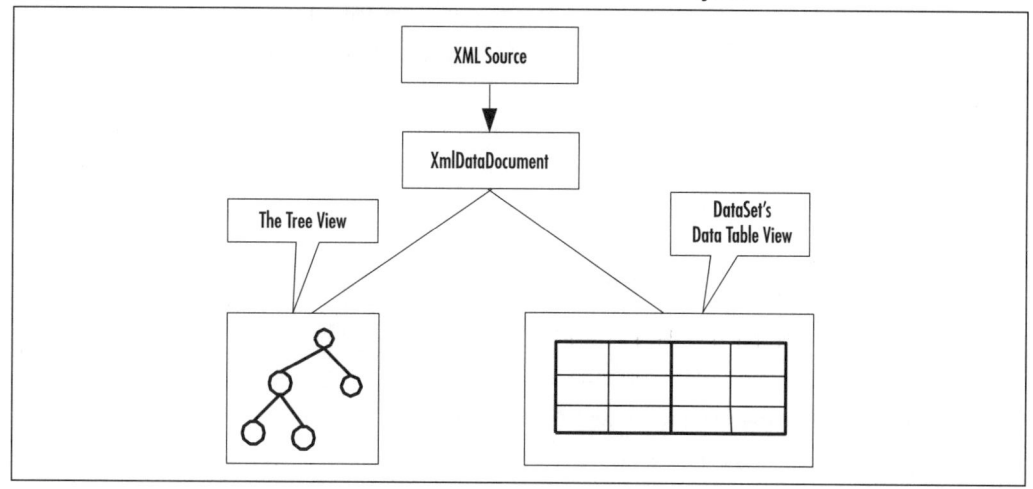

Loading an *XmlDocument* and Retrieving the Values of Certain Nodes

In this section we will load an *XmlDataDocument* using our Catalog2.xml file. After we load it, we will retrieve the product names and load them in a list box. The output of this example is shown in Figure 8.24. The code for this application is listed in Figure 8.25, and it is also available in the file named XmlDataDocument1.aspx in the accompanying CD.

Figure 8.24 Output of XmlDataDocument1.aspx

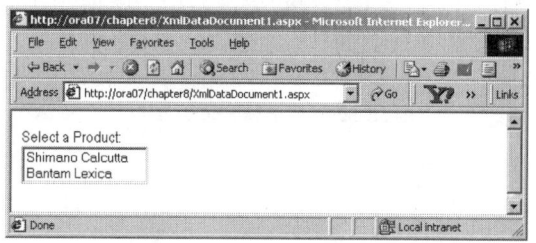

The *XmlDataDocument* is a pleasant object to work with. In this example, the code is pretty straightforward. After we have loaded the *XmlDataDocument*, we have declared an *XmlNodeList* collection named *productNames*. We have populated the collection by using the *GetElementsByTagName*("ProductName") method of the *XmlDataDocument* object. Finally, it is just a matter of iterating through the *productNames* collection and loading each of its members in the list box.

At this stage, you will probably ask why we are not finding the unit price of the selected product. Actually, therein lies the beauty of the *XmlDataDocument*. Because it has extended the *XmlDocument* class, all of the members of the *XmlDocument* class are also available to us. Thus, we could use the same technique as shown in our previous example to find the price. Nevertheless, the reason for not showing the searching technique here is that we will cover it later when we discuss the *XPathIterator* object.

Figure 8.25 XmlDataDocument1.aspx

```
<!--\Chapter8\xmlDataDocument1.aspx -->
<%@ Page Language = "VB"  Debug ="True" %>
<%@ Import Namespace="System.Xml" %>
<html><head></head><body><form runat="server">
Select a Product: <br/>
<asp:ListBox id="lstProducts" runat="server" rows = "2" /><br/><br/>
</body></form><html>
<Script Language="vb" runat="server">
Sub Page_Load(s As Object, e As EventArgs)
    If Not Page.IsPostBack Then
        Dim myDataDoc As New XmlDataDocument()
        myDataDoc.Load(Server.MapPath("Catalog2.xml"))
        Dim productNames As XmlNodeList
        productNames= myDataDoc.GetElementsByTagName("ProductName")
        Dim x As XmlNode
        For Each x In productNames
            lstProducts.Items.Add (x.FirstChild().Value)
        Next
    End If
End Sub
</Script>
```

Using the Relational View of an *XmlDataDocument* Object

In this example, we will process and display the Catalog3.xml document's data as a relational table in a *DataGrid*. The Catalog3.xml is exactly the same as Catalog2.xml except that it has more data. The Catalog3.xml file is available in the accompanying CD. The output of this example is shown in Figure 8.26.

Figure 8.26 Output of *XmlDataDocument DataSet* View Example

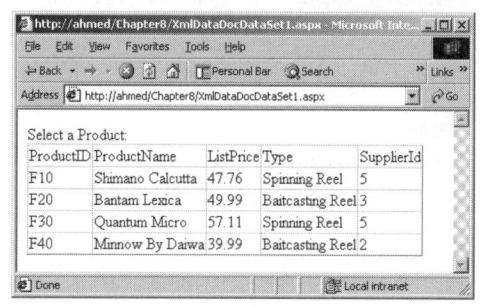

If we want to process the XML data as relational data, we need to load the schema of the XML document first. We have generated the following schema for the Catalog3.xml using VS.NET. The schema specification is shown in Figure 8.27 (also available in the accompanying CD).

Figure 8.27 Catalog3.xsd

```
<xsd:schema id="Catalog" targetNamespace="http://tempuri.org
    /Catalog3.xsd" xmlns="http://tempuri.org/Catalog3.xsd"
    xmlns:xsd="http://www.w3.org/2001/XMLSchema" xmlns:msdata
    ="urn:schemas-microsoft-com:xml-msdata" attributeFormDefault
    ="qualified" elementFormDefault="qualified">
 <xsd:element name="Catalog" msdata:IsDataSet="true"
   msdata:EnforceConstraints="False">
  <xsd:complexType>
   <xsd:choice maxOccurs="unbounded">
    <xsd:element name="Product">
     <xsd:complexType>
      <xsd:sequence>
       <xsd:element name="ProductID" type="xsd:string" minOccurs="0"
```

Continued

Figure 8.27 Continued

```
            msdata:Ordinal="0" />
        <xsd:element name="ProductName" type="xsd:string"
        minOccurs="0" msdata:Ordinal="1" />
        <xsd:element name="ListPrice" type="xsd:string" minOccurs="0"
        msdata:Ordinal="2" />
      </xsd:sequence>
      <xsd:attribute name="Type" form="unqualified" type="xsd:string"/>
      <xsd:attribute name="SupplierId" form="unqualified"
        type="xsd:string" />
    </xsd:complexType>
   </xsd:element>
  </xsd:choice>
 </xsd:complexType>
</xsd:element>
</xsd:schema>
```

> **NOTE**
>
> When we create a schema from a sample XML document, VS.NET automatically inserts an *xmlns* attribute to the root element. The value of this attribute specifies the name of the schema. Thus when we created the schema for Catalog3.xml, the schema was named Catalog3.xsd and VS.NET inserted the following attributes in the root element of Catalog3.xml:
>
> `<Catalog xmlns="http://tempuri.org/Catalog3.xsd">`

In our .aspx code, we loaded the schema using the *ReadXmlSchema* method of our *XmlDataDocument* object as:

`myDataDoc.DataSet.`**`ReadXmlSchema`**`(Server.MapPath("Catalog3.xsd")).`

Next, we have loaded the *XmlDataDocument* as:

`myDataDoc.Load(Server.MapPath("Catalog3.xml")).`

Since the *DataDocument* provides two views, we have exploited its *DataSet* *.Table(0)* property to load the *DataGrid* and display our XML file's information in the grid. The complete listing of the code is shown in Figure 8.28. The code is also available in the XmlDataDocDataSet1.aspx file in the accompanying CD.

Figure 8.28 Complete Listing XmlDataDocDataSet1.aspx

```
<!-- Chapter8\XmlDataDocDataSet1.aspx -->
<%@ Page Language = "VB"  Debug ="True" %>
<%@ Import Namespace="System.Xml" %>
<%@ Import Namespace="System.Data" %>
<html><head></head><body><form runat="server">
Select a Product: <br/>
<asp:DataGrid id="myGrid"  runat="server"/>
</body></form></html>
<Script Language="vb" runat="server">
Sub Page_Load(s As Object, e As EventArgs)
    If Not Page.IsPostBack Then
      Dim myDataDoc As New XmlDataDocument()
      ' load the schema
      myDataDoc.DataSet.ReadXmlSchema(Server.MapPath("Catalog3.xsd"))
      ' load the xml data
      myDataDoc.Load(Server.MapPath("Catalog3.xml"))
      myGrid.DataSource = myDataDoc.DataSet.Tables(0)
      myGrid.DataBind()
    End If
End Sub
</Script>
```

Viewing Multiple Tables of a *XmlDataDocument* Object

In many instances, an XML document may contain nested elements. Suppose that a bank has many customers, and a customer has many accounts. We have modeled this simple scenario in an XML document with nested elements. This

Chapter 8 • Using XML in the .NET Framework

document, named Bank1.xml, is shown in Figure 8.29. It is also available in the accompanying CD.

Figure 8.29 Bank1.xml

```xml
<?xml version="1.0" encoding="utf-8" ?>
<Bank xmlns="http://tempuri.org/Bank1.xsd">
    <Customer>
        <CustomerID>C100</CustomerID>
        <CustomerName>Alfred Smith</CustomerName>
        <City>Toledo</City>
        <Account>
            <Type>Savings</Type>
            <Balance>1500.00</Balance>
        </Account>
        <Account>
            <Type>Checking</Type>
            <Balance>111.11</Balance>
        </Account>
        <Account>
            <Type>Home Equity</Type>
            <Balance>50000</Balance>
        </Account>
    </Customer>
    <Customer>
        -- -- --
        -- -- --
    </Customer>
</Bank>
```

If we load the above XML document and its schema in an *XmlDataDocument* object, it will provide two relational tables' views: one for the customer's information, and the other for the account's information. Our objective is to display the data of these relational tables in two *DataGrid*s as shown in Figure 8.30.

To develop this application, first we had to generate the schema for our Bank1.xml file. We used the VS.NET XML designer to accomplish this task. It is interesting to observe that while creating the schema, VS.NET automatically generates the 1:Many relationship between the *Customer* and *Accounts* elements. To establish the relationship, it also creates an auto-numbered primary key column (*Customer_Id*) in the *Customer* DataTable. Simultaneously, it inserts the appropriate values of the foreign keys in the *Account* DataTable. The *DataSet* view of the generated schema is shown in Figure 8.31.

Figure 8.30 Displaying Customer and Accounts Data in Two Data Grids

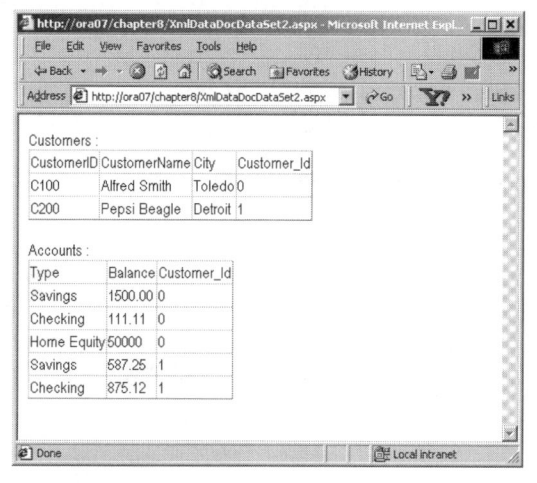

Figure 8.31 *XmlDataDocument DataSet* Representation in Visual Studio .NET

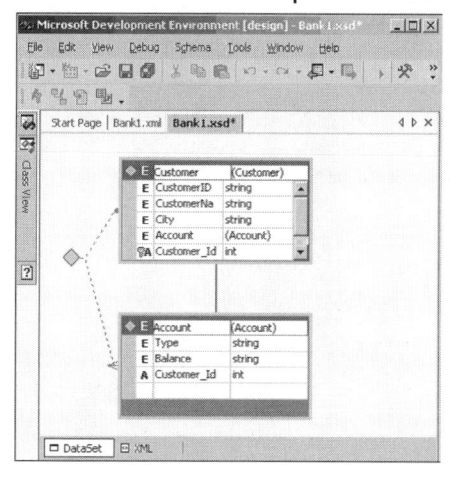

In order to provide the relational view of our XML document (Bank1.xml), VS.NET included the *Customer_Id* attributes in both *Customer* and *Account* elements in its generated schema. It also generated the necessary schema entries to

describe the implied relationship among the *Customer* and *Account* elements. Figure 8.32 shows an excerpt of the generated schema for our XML file. The complete schema is available in a file named Bank1.xsd in the accompanying CD.

Figure 8.32 Primary Key and Foreign Key Specifications in the Bank1.xsd

```
<xsd:unique name="Constraint1" msdata:PrimaryKey="true">
          <xsd:selector xpath=".//Customer" />
          <xsd:field xpath="@Customer_Id" /></xsd:unique>
<xsd:keyref name="Customer_Account"
    refer="Constraint1"msdata:IsNested="true">
          <xsd:selector xpath=".//Account" />
          <xsd:field xpath="@Customer_Id" />
</xsd:keyref>
```

In the above fragment of the generated schema, the *xsd:unique* element specifies the *Customer_Id* attribute as the primary key of the *Customer* element. Subsequently, the *xsd:keyref* element specifies the *Customer_Id* attribute as the foreign key of the *Account* element. XPath expressions have been used to achieve the afore-mentioned objectives.

The complete listing of the application is shown in Figure 8.33. It is also available in the xmlDataDocDataSet2.aspx file in the accompanying CD. The code is pretty straightforward. We have loaded two data grids from two *DataTables* of the *DataSet,* associated with the *XmlDataDocument* object.

Figure 8.33 Complete Code of XmlDataDocDataSet2.aspx

```
<!- Chapter8\XmlDataDocDataSet2.aspx -->
<%@ Page Language = "VB"  Debug ="True" %>
<%@ Import Namespace="System.Xml" %>
<%@ Import Namespace="System.Data" %>
<html><head></head><body><form runat="server">
Customers : <br/>
<asp:DataGrid id="myCustGrid"   runat="server"/><br/>
Accounts : <br/>
<asp:DataGrid id="myAcctGrid"   runat="server"/><br/>
</body></form></html>
<Script Language="vb" runat="server">
```

Continued

Figure 8.33 Continued

```
Sub Page_Load(s As Object, e As EventArgs)
    If Not Page.IsPostBack Then
      Dim myDataDoc As New XmlDataDocument()
      ' load the schema
      myDataDoc.DataSet.ReadXmlSchema(Server.MapPath("Bank1.xsd"))
      ' load the xmldata
      myDataDoc.Load(Server.MapPath("Bank1.xml"))
      myCustGrid.DataSource = myDataDoc.DataSet.Tables("Customer")
      myCustGrid.DataBind()
      'load the Account grid
      myAcctGrid.DataSource = myDataDoc.DataSet.Tables("Account")
      myAcctGrid.DataBind()
    End If
End Sub
</Script>
```

> **NOTE**
>
> In a Windows Form, the *DataGrid* control by default provides automatic drill-down facilities for two related *DataTables.* Unfortunately, it does not work in this fashion in a Web form. Additional programming is needed to simulate the drill-down functionality.

In this example, we have illustrated how an *XmlDataDocument* object maps nested XML elements into multiple *DataTable*s. Typically, an element is mapped to a table if it contains other elements. Otherwise, it is mapped to a column. Attributes are mapped to columns. For nested elements, the system creates the relationship automatically.

Querying XML Data Using XPathDocument and XPathNavigator

The *XmlDocument* and the *XmlDataDocument* have certain limitations. First of all, the entire document needs to be loaded in the cache. Often, the navigation process via the DOM tree itself gets to be clumsy. The navigation via the relational views of the data tables may not be very convenient either. To alleviate these problems, the XML.NET has provided the *XPathDocument* and *XPathNavigator* classes. These classes have been implemented using the W3C XPath 1.0 Recommendation (www.w3.org/TR/xpath).

The *XPathDocument* class enables you to process the XML data without loading the entire DOM tree. An *XPathNavigator* object can be used to operate on the data of an *XPathDocument*. It can also be used to operate on *XmlDocument* and *XmlDataDocument*. It supports navigation techniques for selecting nodes, iterating over the selected nodes, and working with these nodes in diverse ways for copying, moving, and removal purposes. It uses *XPath* expressions to accomplish these tasks.

The *W3C XPath 1.0* specification outlines the query syntax for retrieving data from an XML document. The motivation of the framework is similar to SQL; however, the syntax is significantly different. At first sight, the *XPath* query syntax may appear very complex. But with a certain amount of practice, you may find it very concise and effective in extracting XML data. The details of the *XPath* specification are beyond the scope of this chapter. However, we will illustrate several frequently used *XPath* query expressions. In our exercises, we will illustrate two alternative ways to construct the expressions. The first alternative follows the recent *XPath 1.0* syntax. The second alternative follows *XSL Patterns*, which is a precursor to *XPath 1.0*. Let us consider the following XML document named Bank2.xml. The Bank2.xml document is shown in Figure 8.34, and it is also available in the accompanying CD. It contains data about various accounts. We will use this XML document to illustrate our *XPath* queries.

Figure 8.34 Bank 2.xml

```
<!-- Chapter8\Bank2.xml -->
<Bank>
    <Account>
        <AccountNo>A1112</AccountNo>
        <Name>Pepsi Beagle</Name>
```

Continued

Figure 8.34 Continued

```
        <Balance>1200.89</Balance>
        <State>OH</State>
    </Account>
        --- --- ---
        --- --- ---
    <Account>
        <AccountNo>A7833</AccountNo>
        <Name>Frank Horton</Name>
        <Balance>8964.55</Balance>
        <State>MI</State>
    </Account>
</Bank>
```

Sample Query Expression 1: Suppose that we want the names of all account holders. The following alternative *XPath* expressions will accomplish the job equally well:

- Alternative 1: **descendant::Name**
- Alternative 2: **Bank/Account/Name**

The first expression can be read as "Give me the descendents of all Name nodes." The second expression can be read as "Give me the Name nodes of the Account nodes of the Bank node." Both of these expressions will return the same node set.

Sample Query Expression 2: We want the records for all customers from Ohio. We may specify any one of the following expressions:

- Alternative 1: **descendant::Account[child::State='OH']**
- Alternative 2: **Bank/Account[child::State='OH']**

Sample Query Expression 3: Any one of the following alternative expressions will return the Account node-sets for all accounts with a balance more than 5000.00:

- Alternative 1: **descendant::Account[child::Balance > 5000]**
- Alternative 2: **Bank/Account[child::Balance > 5000.00]**

Sample Query Expression 4: Suppose that we want the Account information for those accounts whose names start with the letter "D."

- Alternative 1: **descendant::account[starts-with(child::Name, 'D')]**
- Alternative 2: **Bank/Account[starts-with(child::Name, 'D')]**

Which of the alternative expressions would you use? That depends on your personal taste and on the structure of the XML document. The second alternative appears to be easier than the first one. However, in the case of a highly nested document, the first alternative will offer more compact expressions. Regardless of the syntax used, please be aware that each of the above queries will return a set of nodes. In our ASP code, we will have to extract the desired information from these sets using an *XPathNodeIterator*.

> **NOTE**
>
> We found the http://staff.develop.com/aarons/bits/xpath-builder/ site to be very good in learning *XPath* queries interactively.

Okay, now that we have traveled through the *XPath* waters, we are ready to venture into the usages of the *XPathDocument*. In this context, we will provide two examples. The first example will extract the names of the customers from Ohio and load a list box. The second example will illustrate how to find a specific piece of data from an *XPathDocument*.

Using *XPathDocument* and *XPathNavigator* Objects

In this section we will use the *XPathDocument* and *XPathNavigator* objects to load a list box from our Bank2.xml file (as shown in Figure 8.34). We will load a list box with the names of customers who are from Ohio. The output of this application is shown in Figure 8.35. The complete code for this application is shown in Figure 8.36. The code is also available in the XPathDoc1.aspx file in the accompanying CD.

We loaded the Bank2.xml as an *XPathDocument* object as follows:

```
Dim Doc As New XPathDocument(Server.MapPath("Bank2.xml"))
```

Figure 8.35 Using *XPathDocument* Object

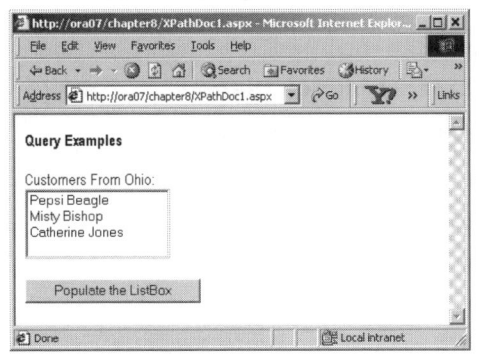

At this stage, we need two more objects: an *XPathNavigator* for retrieving the desired node-set, and an *XPathNodeIterator* for iterating through the members of the node-set. These are defined as follows:

```
Dim myNav As XPathNavigator
myNav= myDoc.CreateNavigator()
Dim myIter As XPathNodeIterator
myIter=myNav.Select("Bank/Account[child::State='OH']/Name")
```

The **Bank/Account[child::State='OH']/Name** search expression returns the Name nodes from the Account node-set whose state is "OH." To get the value inside a particular name node, we need to use the *Current.Value* property of the *Iterator* object. Thus, the following code loads our list box:

```
While (myIter.MoveNext())
        lstName.Items.Add(myIter.Current.Value)
End While
```

Figure 8.36 Complete Code XPathDoc1.aspx

```
<!– Chapter8/XPathDoc1.aspx –>
<%@ Page Language="VB" Debug="True"%>
<%@ Import Namespace="System.Xml"%>
<%@ Import Namespace="System.Xml.XPath"%>
<%@ Import Namespace="System.Xml.Xsl"%>
<html><head></head><body>
<form runat="server"><h4>
```

Continued

Figure 8.36 Continued

```
Query Examples</h4>
Customers From Ohio:<br/>
<asp:ListBox id="lstName1" runat="server"
      width="150" rows="4"/>  
<br/><br/>
<asp:Button id="cmdDetails" Text="Populate the ListBox"
     runat="server"  onClick="showNames"/><br/>
</form></body></html>
<Script Language="vb" runat="server">
 Sub showNames(s As Object, e As EventArgs)
    Dim Doc As New XPathDocument(Server.MapPath("Bank2.xml"))
    Dim myNav As XPathNavigator
    myNav=Doc.CreateNavigator()
    Dim myIter As XPathNodeIterator
    myIter=myNav.Select("Bank/Account[child::State='OH']/Name")
    While (myIter.MoveNext())
       lstName1.Items.Add(myIter.Current.Value)
    End While
  End Sub
</Script>
```

Using *XPathDocument* and *XPathNavigator* Objects for Document Navigation

This section will illustrate how to search an *XPathDocument* using a value of an attribute, and using a value of an element. We will use the Bank3.xml to illustrate these. A partial listing of the Bank3.xml is shown in Figure 8.37. The complete code is available in the accompanying CD.

Figure 8.37 Bank3.xml

```
<!-- Chapter8\Bank3.xml -->
<Bank>
    <Account AccountNo="A1112">
```

Continued

Figure 8.37 Continued

```
        <Name>Pepsi Beagle</Name>
        <Balance>1200.89</Balance>
        <State>OH</State>
    </Account>
    --- --- ---
    --- --- ---
</Bank>
```

The *Account* element of the above XML document contains an attribute named *AccountNo*, and three other elements. In this example, we will first load two combo boxes, one with the account numbers, and the other with the account holder's names. The user will select an account number and/or a name. On the click event of the command buttons, we will display the balances in the appropriate text boxes. The output of the application is shown in Figure 8.38. The application has been developed in an .aspx file named XpathDoc2.aspx. Its complete listing is shown in Figure 8.39. The code is also available in the accompanying CD.

Figure 8.38 The Output of XPathDoc2.aspx

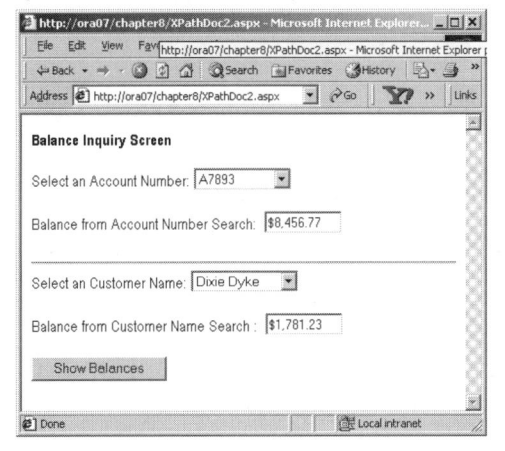

To search for a particular value of an attribute (e.g., of an account number) we have used the following expression:

```
Bank/Account[@AccountNo='"+accNo+"']/Balance
```

394 Chapter 8 • Using XML in the .NET Framework

To search for a particular value of an element (e.g., of an account holder's name), we have used the following expression:

```
descendant::Account[child::Name='"+accName+"']/Balance
```

We needed to call the *MoveNext* method of the *Iterator* object in order to get to the balance node. The following expression illustrates the construct:

```
Bank/Account[@AccountNo='"+accNo+"']/Balance
```

Figure 8.39 Complete Code XPathDoc2.aspx

```
<!— Chapter8/XPathDoc2.aspx —>
<%@ Page Language="VB" Debug="True"%>
<%@ Import Namespace="System.Xml"%>
<%@ Import Namespace="System.Xml.XPath"%>
<%@ Import Namespace="System.Xml.Xsl"%>
<html><head></head><body>
<form runat="server"><h4>
Balance Inquiry Screen</h4>
Select an Account Number:
<asp:DropdownList id="cboAcno" runat="server" width="100" />  
<br/><br/>
Balance from Account Number Search: 
<asp:Textbox id="txtBalance1" runat="server" width="80" />  
<br/><br/><hr/>
Select an Customer Name:
<asp:DropdownList id="cboName" runat="server" width="110" />  
<br/><br/>
Balance from Customer Name Search : 
<asp:Textbox id="txtBalance2" runat="server" width="80" />  
<br/><br/>

<asp:Button id="cmdDetails" Text="Show Balances" runat="server"
    onClick="showNames"/><br/>
</form></body></html>
<Script Language="vb" runat="server">
```

Continued

Figure 8.39 Continued

```
Sub Page_Load(s As Object, e As EventArgs)
  If Not Page.IsPostBack Then
    Dim myDoc As New XPathDocument(Server.MapPath("Bank3.xml"))
    Dim myNav As XPathNavigator
    myNav=myDoc.CreateNavigator()
    Dim myIter As XPathNodeIterator
    ' Populate the DropDownList with Account Number values
    myIter=myNav.Select("//@*")   ' Load all attributes
    While (myIter.MoveNext())
      cboAcno.Items.Add(myIter.Current.Value)
    End While

    ' Populate the  DropDown list with the name values
    myIter=myNav.Select("/Bank/Account/Name")
    While (myIter.MoveNext())
      cboName.Items.Add(myIter.Current.Value)
    End While
  End If
End Sub


Sub showNames(s As Object, e As EventArgs)
   'Get the value of the selected Item
   Dim accNo As String = cboAcno.SelectedItem.Text.Trim()
   Dim accName As String = cboName.SelectedItem.Text.Trim()
   Dim myDoc As New XPathDocument(Server.MapPath("Bank3.xml"))
   Dim myNav As XPathNavigator
   myNav=myDoc.CreateNavigator()
   Dim myIter As XpathNodeIterator

   '  Query to get the balance from AccountNo
   myIter=myNav.Select("Bank/Account[@AccountNo='"+accNo+"']/Balance")
   myIter.MoveNext()
   'Display the values of  Balance
```

Continued

Figure 8.39 Continued

```
    txtBalance1.Text=FormatCurrency(myIter.Current.Value)
    ' Query to get the balance from Name
    myIter = myNav.Select _
       ("descendant::Account[child::Name='"+accName+"']/Balance")
    myIter.MoveNext()
    'Display the values of  Balance
    txtBalance2.Text=FormatCurrency(myIter.Current.Value)
End Sub
</Script>
```

Transforming an XML Document Using XSLT

Extensible Stylesheet Language Transformations (XSLT) is the transformation component of the XSL specification by W3C (www.w3.org/Style/XSL). It is essentially a template-based declarative language, which can be used to transform an XML document to another XML document or to documents of other types (e.g., HTML and Text). We can develop and apply various XSLT templates to select, filter, and process various parts of an XML document. In .NET, we can use the *Transform()* method of the *XSLTransform* class to transform an XML document.

Internet Explorer (5.5 and above) has a built-in XSL transformer that automatically transforms an XML document to an HTML document. When we open an XML document in IE, it displays the data using a collapsible list view. However, the Internet Explorer cannot be used to transform an XML document to another XML document. Now, why would we need to transform an XML document to another XML document? Well, suppose that we have a very large document that contains our entire catalog's data. We want to create another XML document from it, which will contain only the *productId* and *productNames* of those products that belong to the "Fishing" category. We would also like to sort the elements in the ascending order of the unit price. Further, we may want to add a new element in each product, such as "Expensive" or "Cheap" depending on the price of the product. To solve this particular problem, we may either develop relevant codes in a programming language like C#, or we may use XSLT to accomplish the job. XSLT is a much more convenient way to develop the application, because XSLT has been developed exclusively for these kind of scenarios.

Before we can transform a document, we need to provide the Transformer with the instructions for the desired transformation of the source XML document. These instructions can be coded in XSL. We have illustrated this process in Figure 8.40.

Figure 8.40 XSL Transformation Process

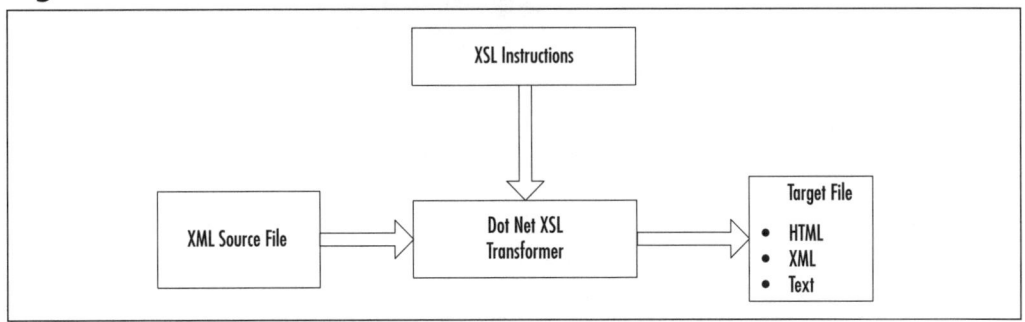

In this section, we will demonstrate certain selected features of XSLT through some examples. The first example will apply XSLT to transform an XML document to an HTML document. We know that the IE can automatically transform an XML document to a HTML document and can display it on the screen in collapsible list view. However, in this particular example, we do not want to display all of our data in that fashion. We want to display the filtered data in tabular fashion. Thus, we will transform the XML document to a HTML document to our choice (and not to IE's choice). The transformation process will select and filter some XML data to form an HTML table. The second example will transform an XML document to another XML document and subsequently write the resulting document in a disk file, as well as display it in the browser.

Transforming an XML Document to an HTML Document

In this example, we will apply XSLT to extract the account's information for Ohio customers from the Bank3.xml (as shown in Figure 8.37) document. The extracted data will be finally displayed in an HTML table. The output of the application is shown in Figure 8.41.

If we need to use XSLT, we must at first develop the XSLT style sheet (e.g., XSLT instructions). We have saved our style sheet in a file named XSLT1.xsl. In this style sheet, we have defined a template as <xsl:template match="/"> … </xsl:template>. The match="/" will result in the selection of nodes at the root of the XML document. Inside the body of this template, we have first included the necessary HTML elements for the desired output.

Figure 8.41 Transforming an XML Document to an HTML Document

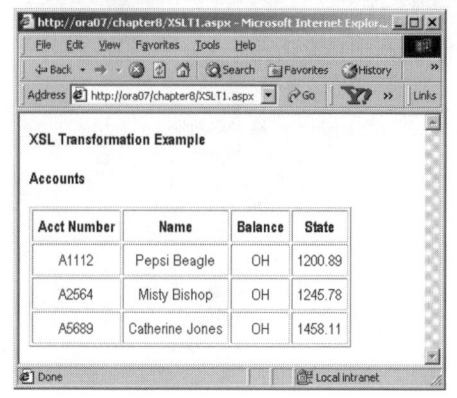

The "<xsl:for-each select="Bank/Account[State='OH']" >" tag is used to select all *Account* nodes for those customers who are from "OH." The value of a node can be shown using a <xsl:value-of select=*attribute* or *element name*>. In case of an attribute, its name must be prefixed with an @ symbol. For example, we are displaying the value of the State node as <xsl:value-of select="State"/>. The complete listing of the XSLT1.xsl file is shown in Figure 8.42. The code is also available in the accompanying CD. In the .aspx file, we have included the following asp:xml control.

```
<asp:xml id="ourXSLTransform" runat="server"
      DocumentSource="Bank3.xml" TransformSource="XSLT1.xsl"/>
```

While defining this control, we have set its *DocumentSource* attribute to "Bank3.xml", and its *TransformSource* attribute to XSLT1.xsl. The complete code for the .aspx file, named XSLT1.aspx, is shown in Figure 8.43. It is also available in the accompanying CD.

Figure 8.42 Complete Code for XSLT1.xsl

```
<?xml version="1.0" ?>
<!— Chapter 8\XSLT1.xsl —>
<xsl:stylesheet version="1.0"
      xmlns:xsl="http://www.w3.org/1999/XSL/Transform">
<xsl:template match="/">
```

Continued

Figure 8.42 Continued

```
  <h4>Accounts</h4>
  <table border="1" cellpadding="5">
    <thead><th>Acct Number</th><th>Name</th>
    <th>Balance</th><th>State</th></thead>

    <xsl:for-each select="Bank/Account[State='OH']" >
      <tr align="center">
      <td><xsl:value-of select="@AccountNo"/></td>
      <td><xsl:value-of select="Name"/></td>
      <td><xsl:value-of select="State"/></td>
      <td><xsl:value-of select="Balance"/></td>
      </tr>
    </xsl:for-each>
  </table>
 </xsl:template>
</xsl:stylesheet>
```

Figure 8.43 XSLT1.aspx

```
<!-- Chapter8\XSLT1.aspx -->
<%@ Page Language="VB" Debug="True"%>
<%@ Import Namespace="System.Xml"%>
<%@ Import Namespace="System.Xml.Xsl"%>
<html><head></head><body><form runat="server">
<b>XSL Transformation Example </b><br/>
<asp:Xml id="ourXSLTransform" runat="server"
     DocumentSource="Bank3.xml" TransformSource="XSLT1.xsl"/>
</form></body></html>
```

Transforming an XML Document into Another XML Document

Suppose that our company has received an order from a customer in XML format. The XML file, named OrderA.xml, is shown in Figure 8.44. The file is also available in the accompanying CD.

Figure 8.44 An Order Received from a Customer in XML Format (OrderA.xml)

```
<?xml version="1.0" ?>
<!— Chapter 8\OrderA.XML —>
<Order>
      <Agent>Alfred Bishop</Agent>
      <Item>50 GPM Pump</Item>
      <Quantity>10</Quantity>
      <Date>
           <Month>8</Month>
           <Day>24</Day>
           <Year>2001</Year>
      </Date>
      <Customer>Pepsi Beagle</Customer>
</Order>
```

Now we want to transmit a purchase order to our supplier to fulfill the previous order. Suppose that the XML format of our purchase order is different from that of our client as shown in Figure 8.45. The OrderB.xml file is also available in the accompanying CD.

Figure 8.45 The Purchase Order to Be Sent to the Supplier in XML Format (OrderB.xml)

```
<?xml version="1.0" encoding="utf-8"?>
<Order>
  <Date>2001/8/24</Date>
  <Customer>Company A</Customer>
  <Item>
    <Sku>P 25-16:3</Sku>
```

Continued

Figure 8.45 Continued

```
      <Description>50 GPM Pump</Description>
      <Quantity>10</Quantity>
   </Item>
</Order>
```

The objective of this example is to automatically transform OrderA.xml (Figure 8.44) to OrderB.xml (Figure 8.45). The outputs of this application are shown in Figures 8.46 and 8.47.

Figure 8.46 Transformation of an XML Document to Another XML Document

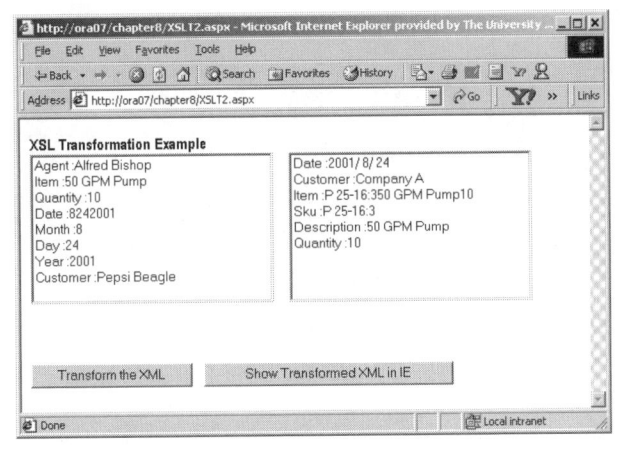

Figure 8.47 The Target XML File as Displayed in Internet Explorer

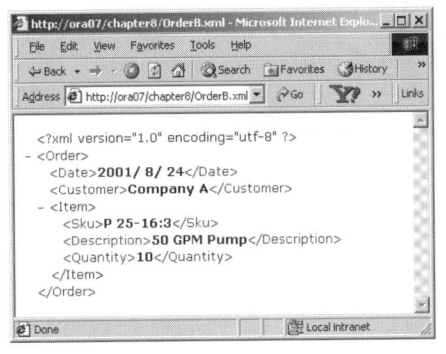

We have developed an XSLT file (shown in Figure 8.48) to achieve the necessary transformation. In the XSLT code, we have used multiple templates. The

complete listing of the XSLT code is shown in Figure 8.48. The code is also available in the order.xsl file in the accompanying CD.

Figure 8.48 Complete Listing of order.xsl

```xml
<?xml version="1.0" ?>
<!— Chapter 8\order.xsl —>
<xsl:stylesheet version="1.0"
xmlns:xsl="http://www.w3.org/1999/XSL/Transform">
<xsl:output method="xml" indent="yes" />
<xsl:template match="/">
  <Order>
    <Date>
      <xsl:value-of select="/Order/Date/Year" />/
      <xsl:value-of select="/Order/Date/Month" />/
      <xsl:value-of select="/Order/Date/Day" />
    </Date>
    <Customer>Company A</Customer>
    <Item>
      <xsl:apply-templates select="/Order/Item" />
      <Quantity><xsl:value-of select="/Order/Quantity"/></Quantity>
    </Item>
  </Order>
</xsl:template>
<xsl:template match="Item">
  <Sku>
    <xsl:choose>
      <xsl:when test=". ='50 GPM Pump'">P 25-16:3</xsl:when>
      <xsl:when test=". ='100 GPM Pump'">P 35-12:5</xsl:when>
      <!—other Sku would go here—>
      <xsl:otherwise>00</xsl:otherwise>
    </xsl:choose>
  </Sku>
  <Description>
    <xsl:value-of select="." />
  </Description>
```

Continued

Figure 8.48 Continued

```
</xsl:template>
</xsl:stylesheet>
```

Subsequently, we have developed the XSLT2.aspx file to employ the XSLT code in the order.xsl file to transform the OrderA.xml to OrderB.xml. The complete listing of the .aspx file is shown in Figure 8.49. This code is also available in the accompanying CD. The transformation is performed in the *ShowTransformed()* subprocedure of our .aspx file. In this code, the *Transform* method of an *XSLTransform* object is used to transform and generate the target XML file.

Figure 8.49 Complete Listing for XSLT2.aspx

```
<!--Chapter8/XSLT2.aspx-->
<%@ Page Language="VB" Debug="True"%>
<%@ Import Namespace="System.Xml"%>
<%@ Import Namespace="System.Xml.XPath"%>
<%@ Import Namespace="System.Xml.Xsl"%>
<%@Import Namespace="System.IO"%>
<html><head></head><body><form runat="server">
<b>XSL Transformation Example </b><br/>
<asp:ListBox id="lstInitial" runat="server" rows="9"
    width=250/>   
<asp:ListBox id="lstFinal" runat="server" rows="9" width=250/><br/><br/>
<br/><br/>
<asp:Button id="cmdTransform" Text="Transform the XML" runat="server"
      onClick="showTransformed" />  
<asp:Button id="cmdDisplayTgt" Text="Show Transformed XML in IE"
    runat="server" onClick="showTarget" />
</form></body></html>

<Script Language="vb" runat="server">

 Sub Page_Load(sender As Object, e As EventArgs)
    If Not Page.IsPostBack Then
      Dim myDoc As New XPathDocument(Server.MapPath("OrderA.xml"))
```

Continued

Figure 8.49 Continued

```
    Dim myNav As XPath.XPathNavigator
    Dim myIterator As XPath.XPathNodeIterator
    ' Set nav object
    myNav = myDoc.CreateNavigator()
    ' Iterate through all the attributes of the descendants
    myIterator =myNav.Select("/Order")
    myIterator=myNav.SelectDescendants(XPathNodeType.Element,false)
    myIterator.MoveNext()
    While myIterator.MoveNext()
      ' Add the Items to the DropdownList
      lstInitial.Items.Add _
        (myIterator.Current.Name+" :"+myIterator.Current.Value)
    End While
  End If
End Sub


Sub showTransformed(sender As Object,e As EventArgs)
  ' Load the XML Document
  Dim myDoc As New XPathDocument(Server.MapPath("OrderA.xml"))
  ' Declare the XSLTransform Object
  Dim myXsltDoc As New XSLTransform
  ' Create the filestream to write a XML file
  Dim myfileStream As New FileStream _
    (Server.MapPath ("OrderB.xml"),FileMode.Create,FileShare.ReadWrite)
  ' Load the XSL file
  myXsltDoc.Load(Server.MapPath("order.xsl"))
  ' Tranform the XML file according to XSL Document
  myXsltDoc.Transform(myDoc,Nothing,myfileStream)
  myfileStream.Close()
  lstFinal.Items.Clear
  Dim myDoc2 As New XPathDocument(Server.MapPath("OrderB.xml"))
  Dim myNav As XPath.XPathNavigator
  Dim myIterator As XPath.XPathNodeIterator
  ' Set nav object
```

Continued

Figure 8.49 Continued

```
    myNav = myDoc2.CreateNavigator()
    ' Iterate through all the attributes of the descendants
    myIterator =myNav.Select("/Order")
    myIterator=myNav.SelectDescendants(XPathNodeType.Element,false)
    myIterator.MoveNext()
    While myIterator.MoveNext()
      ' Add the Items to the DropdownList
      lstFinal.Items.Add _
         (myIterator.Current.Name+" :"+myIterator.Current.Value)
    End While
End Sub
Sub showTarget(sender As Object,e As EventArgs)
    Response.Redirect(Server.MapPath("OrderB.xml"))
End Sub
</Script>
```

Working with XML and Databases

Databases are used to store and manage organization's data. However, it is not a simple task to transfer data from the database to a remote client or to a business partner, especially when we do not clearly know how the client will use the sent data. Well, we may send the required data using XML documents. That way, the data container is independent of the client's platform. The databases and other related data stores are here to stay, and XML will not replace these data stores. However, XML will undoubtedly provide a common medium for exchanging data among sources and destinations. It will also allow various software to exchange data among themselves. In this context, the XML forms a bridge between ADO.NET and other applications. Since XML is integrated in the .NET Framework, the data transfer using XML is lot easier than it is in other software development environments. Data can be exchanged from one source to another via XML. The ADO.NET Framework is essentially based on *Datasets*, which, in turn, relies heavily on XML architecture. The *DataSet* class has a rich collection of methods that are related to processing XML. Some of the widely used ones are *ReadXml, WriteXml, GetXml, GetXmlSchema, InferXmlSchema, ReadXmlSchema,* and *WriteXmlSchema.*

In this context, we will provide two simple examples. In the first example, we will create a *DataSet* from a SQL query, and write its contents as an XML document. In the second example, we will read back the XML document generated in the first example and load a *DataSet*. What are the prospective uses of these examples? Well, suppose that we need to send the products data of our fishing products to a client. In earlier days, we would have sent the data as a text file. But in the .NET environment, we can instead develop a XML document very fast by running a query, and subsequently send the XML document to our client. What is the advantage? It is fast, easy, self-defined, and technology independent. The client may use any technology (like VB, Java, Oracle, etc.) to parse the XML document and subsequently develop applications. On the other hand, if we receive an XML document from our partners, we may as well apply XML.NET to develop our own applications.

Creating an XML Document from a Database Query

In this section, we will populate a *DataSet* with the results of a query to the *Products* table of SQL Server 7.0 Northwind database. On the click event of a command button, we will write the XML file and its schema. (The output of the example is shown in Figure 8.50). We have developed the application in an .aspx file named DataSet1.aspx. The complete listing of the .aspx file is shown in Figure 8.51. The file is also available in the accompanying CD.

Figure 8.50 Output of DataSet1.aspx Application

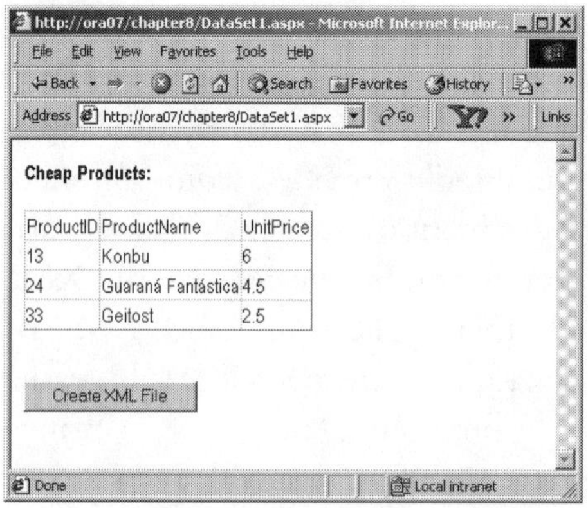

The XML file created by the application is as follows:

```
<myXMLProduct>
```

```
    <dtProducts>
        <ProductID>13</ProductID>
        <ProductName>Konbu</ProductName>
        <UnitPrice>6</UnitPrice>
    </dtProducts>
    --- --- ---
    --- --- ---
</myXMLProduct>
```

The code for the illustration is straightforward. The *DataSet*'s *WriteXml* and *WriteXmlSchema* methods were used to accomplish the desired task.

Figure 8.51 Complete Listing DataSet1.aspx

```
<!— Chapter8\DataSet1.aspx —>
<%@ Page Language = "VB"  Debug ="True" %>
<%@ Import Namespace="System.Xml" %>
<%@ Import Namespace="System.Data" %>
<%@ Import Namespace="System.IO" %>
<%@ Import Namespace="System.Data.SqlClient" %>
<html><head></head><body><form runat="server">
<b>Cheap Products:</b> <br/><br/>
<asp:DataGrid id="myGrid"  runat="server"/><br/><br/>
<asp:Button id="cmdWriteXML" Text="Create XML File" runat="server"
    onclick="writeXML"/>
</body></form></html>
<Script Language="vb" runat="server">
Sub Page_Load(s As Object, e As EventArgs)
 If Not Page.IsPostBack Then
    Dim myDataSet As New DataSet("myXMLProduct")
    Dim myConn As New _
    SqlConnection("server=ora07;uid=sa;pwd=ahmed;database=Northwind")
    Dim mydataAdapter As New SqlDataAdapter _
      ("SELECT ProductID,ProductName,UnitPrice FROM Products WHERE
          UnitPrice <7.00",myConn)
    mydataAdapter.Fill(myDataSet,"dtProducts")
    myGrid.DataSource=myDataSet.Tables(0)
```

Continued

Figure 8.51 Continued

```
    myGrid.DataBind
    Session("sessDs")=myDataSet
 End If
End Sub

Sub writeXML(s As Object, e As EventArgs)
Dim myFs1 As New FileStream _
    (Server.MapPath _
       ("myXMLData.xml"),FileMode.Create,FileShare.ReadWrite)
Dim myFs2 As New FileStream(Server.MapPath _
   ("myXMLData.xsd"),FileMode.Create,FileShare.ReadWrite)
Dim myDataSet As New DataSet _
    myDataSet=Session("sessDs")
' Use the WriteXml method of DataSet object to write an XML file
' from  the DataSet
myDataSet.WriteXml(myFs1)
myFs1.Close()
myDataSet.WriteXmlSchema(myFs2)
myFs2.Close()

End Sub
</Script>
```

Reading an XML Document into a *DataSet*

Here, we will read back the XML file created in the previous example (as shown in Figure 8.50) and populate a *DataSet* in the *Page_Load* event of our .aspx file. We will use the *ReadXml* method of the *DataSet* object to accomplish this objective. The output of the application is shown in Figure 8.52. The application has been developed in an .aspx file named DataSet2.aspx. The complete code for this application is shown in Figure 8.53. The code is also available in the accompanying CD. The code is self-explanatory.

Figure 8.52 Output of DataSet2.aspx Application

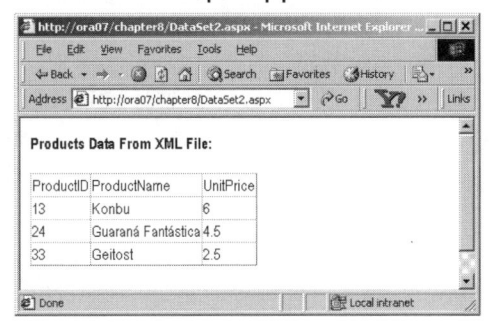

Figure 8.53 Complete Listing of DataSet2.aspx

```
<!-- Chapter8\DataSet2.aspx -->
<%@ Page Language = "VB"  Debug ="True" %>
<%@ Import Namespace="System.Xml" %>
<%@ Import Namespace="System.Data" %>
<%@ Import Namespace="System.IO" %>
<%@ Import Namespace="System.Data.SqlClient" %>
<html><head></head><body><form runat="server">
<b>Products Data  From XML File:</b>  <br/><br/>
<asp:DataGrid id="myGrid"  runat="server"/><br/><br/>
</body></form></html>

<Script Language="vb" runat="server">
Sub Page_Load(s As Object, e As EventArgs)
 If Not Page.IsPostBack Then
   Dim myDataSet As New DataSet("myXMLProduct")
   Dim myFs As New FileStream _
      (Server.MapPath("myXMLData.xml"),FileMode.Open,FileShare.ReadWrite)
   myDataSet.ReadXml(myFs)
   myGrid.DataSource=myDataSet.Tables(0)
   myGrid.DataBind
   myFs.Close
 End If
End Sub
</Script>
```

Summary

In this chapter, we have introduced the basic concepts of XML, and we have provided a concise overview of the .NET classes available to read, store, and manipulate XML documents. The examples presented in this chapter also serve as good models for developing business applications using XML and ASP.NET.

The *.NET's System.Xml* namespace contains probably the richest collection of XML-related classes available thus far in any other software development platform. The *System.Xml* namespace has been further enriched by the recent addition of *XPathDocument* and *XPathNavigator* classes. We have tried to highlight these new features in our examples. Since XML can be enhanced using a family of technologies, there are innumerable techniques a reader should judiciously learn from other sources to design, develop, and implement complex real-world applications.

Solutions Fast Track

An Overview of XML

- ☑ XML stands for eXtensible Markup Language. It is a subset of a larger framework named SGML. The W3C developed the specifications for SGML and XML.

- ☑ XML provides a universal way for exchanging information between organizations.

- ☑ XML cannot be singled out as a stand-alone technology. It is actually a framework for exchanging data. It is supported by a family of growing technologies such as XML parsers, XSLT transformers, XPath, XLink, and Schema Generators.

- ☑ An XML document may contain Declaration, Comment, Elements, and Attributes.

- ☑ An XML element has a start-tag and an end-tag. An element may contain other elements, or character data, or both.

- ☑ An attribute provides an additional way to attach a piece of data to an element. An attribute must always be enclosed within start-tag of an element, and its value is specified using double quotes.

- ☑ An XML document is said to be well formed when it satisfies a set of syntax-related rules. These rules include the following:
  - The document must have exactly one root element.
  - Each element must have a start-tag and end-tag.
  - The elements must be properly nested.
- ☑ An XML document is case sensitive.
- ☑ DTD and schema are essentially two different ways two specify the rules about the contents of an XML document.
- ☑ An XML schema contains the structure of an XML document, its elements, the data types of the elements and associated attributes including the parent-child relationships among the elements.
- ☑ VS.NET supports the W3C specification for XML Schema Definition (also known as XSD).
- ☑ XML documents stores data in hierarchical fashion, also known as a node tree.
- ☑ The top-most node in the node tree is referred to as the root.
- ☑ A particular node in a node tree can be of *element-type,* or of *text-type.* An element-type node contains other element-type nodes or text-type node. A text-type node contains only data.

Processing XML Documents Using .NET

- ☑ The *Sytem.Xml* namespace contains *XmlTextReader, XmlValidatingReader,* and *XmlNodeReader* classes for reading XML Documents. The *XmlTextWriter* class enables you to write data as XML documents.
- ☑ *XmlDocument, XmlDataDocument*, and *XPathDocument* classes can be used to structure XML data in the memory and to process them.
- ☑ *XPathNavigator* and *XPathNodeIterator* classes enable you to query and retrieve selected data using *XPath* expressions.

Reading and Parsing Using the *XmlTextReader* Class

- ☑ The *XmlTextReader* class provides a fast forward-only cursor to pull data from an XML document.

- ☑ Some of the frequently used methods and properties of the *XmlTextReader* class include *AttributeCount, Depth, EOF, HasAttributes, HasValue, IsDefault, IsEmptyElement, Item, ReadState,* and *Value*.

- ☑ The *Read()* of an *XmlTextReader* object enables you to read data sequentially. The *MoveToAttribute()* method can be used to iterate through the attribute collection of an element.

Writing an XML Document Using the *XmlTextWriter* Class

- ☑ An *XmlTextWriter* class can be used to write data sequentially to an output stream, or to a disk file as an XML document.

- ☑ Its major methods and properties include *Close, Flush, Formatting, WriteAttribues, WriteAttributeString, WriteComment, WriteElementString, WriteElementString, WriteEndAttribute, WriteEndDocument, WriteState,* and *WriteStartDocument*.

- ☑ Its constructor contains a parameter that can be used to specify the output format of the XML document. If this parameter is set to "Nothing," then the document is written using UTF-8 format.

Exploring the XML Document Object Model

- ☑ The W3C Document Object Model (DOM) is a set of the specifications to represent an XML document in the computer's memory.

- ☑ *XmlDocument* class implements both the W3C specifications (Core level 1 and 2) of DOM.

- ☑ *XmlDocument* object also allows navigating through XML node tree using *XPath* expressions.

- ☑ *XmlDataDocument* is an extension of *XmlDocument* class.

- ☑ It can be used to generate both the XML view as well as the relational view of the same XML data.
- ☑ *XmlDataDocument* contains a *DataSet* property that exposes its data as relational table(s).

Querying XML Data Using *XPathDocument* and *XPathNavigator*

- ☑ *XPathDocument* class allows loading XML data in fragments rather than loading the entire DOM tree.
- ☑ *XPathNavigator* object can be used in conjunction with *XPathDocument* for effective navigation through XML data.
- ☑ *XPath* expressions are used in these classes for selecting nodes, iterating over the selected nodes, and working with these nodes for copying, moving, and removal purposes.

Transforming an XML Document Using XSLT

- ☑ You can use XSLT (XML Style Sheet Language Transformations) to transform an XML document to another XML document or to documents of other types (e.g., HTML and Text).
- ☑ XSLT is a template-based declarative language. We can develop and apply various XSLT templates to select, filter, and process various parts of an XML document.
- ☑ In .NET, you can use the *Transform()* method of *XSLTransform* class to transform an XML document.

Working with XML and Databases

- ☑ A *DataSet*'s *ReadXml()* can read XML data as *DataTable*(s).
- ☑ You can create an XML document and its schema from a database query using *DataSet*'s *WriteXml()* and *WriteXmlSchema()*.
- ☑ Some of the widely used ones include *ReadXml, WriteXml, GetXml, GetXmlSchema, InferXmlSchema, ReadXmlSchema,* and *WriteXmlSchema*.

Frequently Asked Questions

The following Frequently Asked Questions, answered by the authors of this book, are designed to both measure your understanding of the concepts presented in this chapter and to assist you with real-life implementation of these concepts. To have your questions about this chapter answered by the author, browse to **www.syngress.com/solutions** and click on the **"Ask the Author"** form.

Q: What is the difference between DOM Core 1 API and Core 2 API?

A: DOM Level 2 became an official World Wide Web Consortium (W3C) recommendation in late November 2000. Although there is not much of difference in the specifications, one of the major features was the namespaces in XML being added, which was unavailable in prior version. DOM Level 1 did not support namespaces. Thus, it was the responsibility of the application programmer to determine the significance of special prefixed tag names. DOM Level 2 supports namespaces by providing new namespace-aware versions of Level 1 methods.

Q: What are the major features of System.XML in the Beta 2 edition?

A: The most significant change in the Beta 2 edition was the restructuring the *XmlNavigator* Class. *XmlNavigator* initially was designed as an alternative to the general implementation of DOM. Since Microsoft felt that there was a mismatch in the *XPath* data model and DOM-based data model, *XmlNavigator* was redesigned to *XpathNavigator*, employing a read-only mechanism. It was conceived of using with *XPathNodeIterator* that acts as an iterator over a node set and can be created many times per *XPathNavigator*.

Alternatively, one can have the DOM implementation as *XmlNode*, and methods such as *SelectNodes()* and *SelectSingleNodes()* can be used to iterate through a node set. A typical code fragment would look like this:

```
Dim nodeList as XmlNodeList
Dim root as XmlElement = Doc.DocumentElement
nodeList =
root.SelectNodes("descendant::account[child::State='OH']")
Dim entry as XmlNode
    For Each entry in nodeList
        'Do the requisite operations
    Next
```

Although *XPathNavigator* is implemented as a read-only mechanism to manipulate the XML documents, it can be noted that certain other classes like *XmlTextWriter* can be implemented over *XPathNavigator* to write to the document.

Q: How is *XPath* different from XSL Patterns?

A: XSL Patterns are predecessors of *XPath 1.0* that have been recognized as a universal specification. Although similar in syntax, there are some differences between them. XSL pattern language does not support the notion of axis types. On the other hand, the *XPath* supports axis types. Axis types are general syntax used in *Xpath*, such as descendant, parent, child, and so on. Assume that we have an XML document with the root node named Bank. Further, assume that the *Bank* element contains many *Account* elements, which in turn contains *account number, name, balance,* and *state* elements. Now, suppose that our objective is to retrieve the *Account* data for those customers who are from Ohio. We can accomplish the search by using any one of the following alternatives:

- XSL Pattern Alternative: Bank/Account[child::State='OH']
- XSL Path 1.0 Alternative: descendant::Account[child::State='OH']

Which of the above alternatives would you use? That depends on your personal taste and on the structure of the XML document. In case of a very highly nested XML document, the XSL Path offers more compact search string.

Chapter 9

Debugging ASP.NET

Solutions in this chapter:

- Handling Errors
- Page Tracing
- Application Tracing
- Using Visual Studio .NET Debugging Tools

☑ Summary
☑ Solutions Fast Track
☑ Frequently Asked Questions

Introduction

Before ASP 3.0, error handling was never a strong suit of ASP. Despite taking great efforts to handle possible error conditions, it is not uncommon to see ASP applications crash and display cryptic error messages. For applications critical to a company's success, this is a huge embarrassment. You may have seen something like this quite often:

```
Microsoft VBScript runtime error '800a0006'
Overflow
/wad/vote.asp, line 25
```

Besides handling errors, how many times have you forgotten to remove debugging statements in your application? Often, due to the unrealistic and tight deadlines imposed by management, you end up rushing to deploy your application. In the midst of doing that, a few debugging statements occasionally get left out.

In this chapter, we will look at the new error handling mechanisms available in .NET. We will discuss how to anticipate various kinds of errors and their possible remedies. We will also look at how the new *Trace* class in ASP.NET allows programmers to trace the flow of ASP.NET applications as well as explore the various capabilities available in the *Trace* class. Finally, we will show you how to use the Object browser and Class Viewer to look for specific libraries.

Handling Errors

While it is the hope of every programmer to write bug-free programs, it can prove a tasking goal. Bugs in programs can be incredibly frustrating, usually disrupting the programs they infect. Such errors can be classified into these four categories, which we'll discuss in the following sections:

- **Syntax Errors** Errors caused by writing codes that do not follow the rules of the language. An example would be a misspelled keyword.

- **Compilation Errors** Errors that can be detected during the compilation stage. An example would be assigning a big number to an integer variable, causing it to overflow.

- **Runtime Errors** Errors that happen after the codes are compiled and executed. An example would be a division-by-zero error.

- **Logic Errors** Errors due to incorrect implementations of algorithms. This is the kind of error that programmers dread most since they are the most difficult to debug.

Syntax Errors

A syntax error is one of the most common errors in programming. This is especially true if you are new to a particular language. Fortunately, syntax errors can be resolved quite easily. In Visual Studio .NET, syntax errors are underlined as shown in Figure 9.1.

Figure 9.1 Syntax Errors Are Underlined

```
Dim sum As Interger
              Type is not defined: 'Interger'
```

To know the cause of the error, simply position the mouse over the underlined word and the tool tip box will appear. The cause of the error in Figure 9.1 is the misspelled word "Integer." To correct the error, simply change the word "Interger" to "Integer."

Compilation Errors

Compilation errors occur when the compiler tries to compile the program and realizes that the program contains codes that may potentially trip up a program. As an illustration, consider the following example, which declares two variables of different data types:

```
Dim shortNum As Int16
Dim intNum As Int32
...
shortNum = intNum
```

The last line of the code tries to assign the value of an *Int32* variable to another variable of type *Int16*. The risk here is that during runtime, *intNum* might contain a value that is larger than the range represented by the *Short* data type. Hence this assignment is not safe (although it will compile and may run without error). This form of assignment where the value of a "wider" data type is assigned to a variable of a "narrower" data type is known as *narrowing*. The reverse is known as *widening*. Narrowing is dangerous and could possibly result in runtime errors.

VB.NET supports the *Option Strict* statement to ensure that only widening conversions are allowed, otherwise it will generate an error message. Modifying our codes, we get:

```
Option Strict On
...
...
        Dim shortNum As Int16
        Dim intNum As Int32
        ...
        shortNum = intNum
```

In this case, our compiler will generate an error message to indicate that such a conversion is not allowed.

The *Option Strict On* statement must be placed at the first line of your program. Using the *Option Strict On* also implies *Option Explicit On* (the *Option Explicit* statement ensures that variables are declared prior to usage). Thus undeclared variables would also generate error messages.

> **NOTE**
>
> In VB6, the array index can be changed using the *Option Base* statement. In VB.NET, the *Option Base* statement is not supported.

Runtime Errors

Runtime errors occur during the time when the application is running and something unexpected occurs. It happens regularly in projects that have very tight deadlines. Programmers stretched to their limits are often satisfied that their program runs. They do not have the time to carefully consider all the different possible scenarios in which their programs may be used, hence the result is often a buggy program. To ensure that an application is as robust and bug-free as possible, it is important to place emphasis on anticipating all the errors that can occur in your program.

Error handling got a new lease on life in the .NET Framework, particularly within the .NET languages. In VB6, error handling was unstructured, done using the primitive *On Error* statement. In the .NET languages, specifically in VB.NET, error handling can both be structured and unstructured. We will examine the two modes of handling errors in the next section.

Unstructured Error Handling

Using our previous example on narrowing conversions (assuming we use the *Option Strict off* statement), the following codes will trigger a runtime error:

```
Dim shortNum As Int16
Dim intNum As Int32

intNum = 999999
shortNum = intNum   ' narrowing will fail!
```

You should see the error as shown in Figure 9.2.

Figure 9.2 Runtime Error

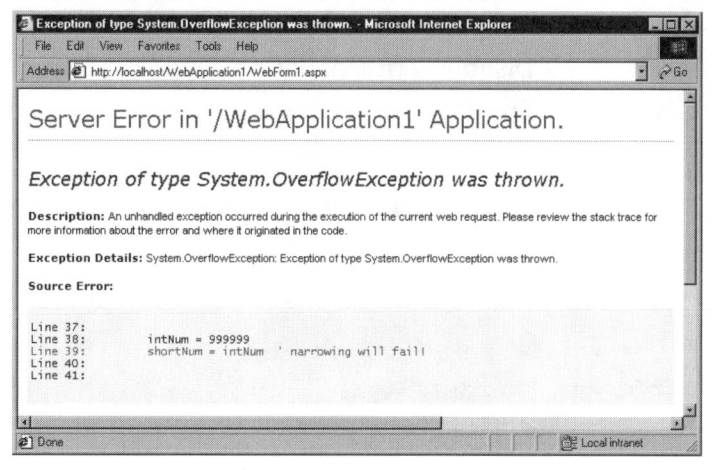

To prevent the error from happening, VB.NET supports the unstructured *On Error* statement:

```
        Dim shortNum As Int16
        Dim intNum As Int32

On Error Resume Next
```

```
        intNum = 999999
        shortNum = intNum   ' narrowing will fail!
        If Err.Number <> 0 Then
            Response.Write(Err.Description)
        End If
```

The *On Error Resume Next* statement ignores any error that happens and continues as though no error has occurred. The error information is contained within the *Err* object. If an error has occurred, the property *Number* of the *Err* object would contain a nonzero value. The *Description* property will contain the description of the error. Some common errors and their descriptions are shown in Table 9.1.

Table 9.1 Common *On Error* Statements and Descriptions

On Error Statement	Description
On Error Resume Next	Specifies that in the event an error occurs, resume execution.
On Error Goto −1	Disables enabled exception in the current subroutine and resets it to Nothing.
On Error Goto 0	Disables error handling.
On Error Goto *label*	Specifies the location to jump to when an error occurs.

The following codes show an extended example outlining use of the *On Error* statement:

```
Private Sub Page_Load(ByVal sender As System.Object, ByVal e As
    System.EventArgs) Handles MyBase.Load
        On Error Goto ErrorHandling
        Dim shortNum As Int16
        Dim intNum As Int32

        intNum = 999999
        shortNum = intNum   ' error #1 will be trapped

        On Error Resume Next
        shortNum = intNum   ' error #2 will be ignored
```

```
        On Error Goto 0
    shortNum = intNum   ' error #3 will cause program to fail

    Exit Sub ' exits the subroutine
ErrorHandling:
    If Err.Number <> 0 Then
        Response.Write(Err.Description)
    End If
    Resume Next
End Sub
```

In the preceding example, we examine three errors. The first error will cause the execution to jump to the *ErrorHandling* block and after the error description has been printed, it resumes execution at the point it was interrupted. The second error will be ignored while the third error will cause the program to fail.

As you can see, unstructured error handling makes your code messy and difficult to debug, and also affects future maintenance. Hence, the recommended way to handle errors is to use structured error handling, which is covered in the next section.

Structured Error Handling

Using unstructured error handling usually results in messy and difficult-to-maintain codes. Rather than placing an *On Error* statement at the beginning of a block to handle potential errors, .NET supports structured error handling using the *Try-Catch-Finally* construct. Structured error handling uses the *Try-Catch-Finally* construct to handle exceptions. The *Try-Catch-Finally* construct allows developers to actively "catch" different forms of errors and respond to them appropriately. It has the following syntax:

```
Try
    ' Executable statements that may cause
    ' an exception.
Catch [optional filters]
    ' Catches the error and responds to it
Catch [optional filters]
    ' Catches the error and responds to it
[Additional Catch blocks]
```

```
Finally
    ' Always executed, with or without error
End Try
```

Rewriting our codes using structured error handling, we get:

```
Dim shortNum As Int16
Dim intNum As Int32

intNum = 999999
Try
    shortNum = intNum    ' narrowing will fail!
Catch anyException As Exception
    Response.Write(anyException)
End Try
```

When executed, the error message printed is:

`System.OverflowException: Exception of type System.OverflowException was thrown. at WebApplication1.WebForm1.Page_Load(Object sender, EventArgs e) in C:\Documents and Settings\lwm\VSWebCache\LWM\WebApplication1\WebForm1.aspx.vb:line 31`

When the line in the *Try* block is executed, it generates an exception, which is then caught by the *Catch* block. The statement in the *Catch* block prints out the reason for causing that exception.

The previous example doesn't really do justice to the structured error-handling construct in VB.NET. Consider the following revised example:

```
Dim shortNum As Int16
Dim intNum As Int32

intNum = 999999
Try
    shortNum = intNum    ' narrowing will fail!
Catch outofMemoryException As System.OutOfMemoryException
    Response.Write("Out of memory!")
Catch overflowException As System.OverflowException
```

```
        Response.Write("Overflow!")
Catch anyException As Exception
        Response.Write("Some exception!")
End Try
```

Here we have multiple *Catch* statements. Each *Catch* statement tries to catch the different kinds of exceptions. If discovered, the exception is evaluated from top to bottom. Once a match is found, the codes within the *Catch* block are executed. If no match is found, an error message is displayed.

The three exceptions in the preceding list include:

- **OutOfMemoryException** Thrown when there is not enough memory to continue the execution of a program.
- **OverflowException** Thrown when an operation results in an overflow condition.
- **Exception** The base class for exception. This means all unmatched exceptions would be matched here.

When the statement within the *Try* block generates an exception, the few *Catch* statements are evaluated in order. First, it compares with the initial *Catch* block and checks to see if it matches the kind of exception specified in the *Catch* statement. If it doesn't, it will compare it with the next, and so on. It only stops when a match is found. In our case, the exception is an overflow exception and hence the second *Catch* block is matched. If no match is found, an error message will be generated.

Lastly, the *Finally* block allows you to perform whatever cleaning up operation codes need doing, regardless of whether the exception occurs.

```
    ...
    Catch anyException As Exception
        'Response.Write(anyException)
        Response.Write("Some exception!")
    Finally
        '---codes here are always executed
        '---regardless of the exception
    End Try
```

> **NOTE**
>
> You cannot use both structured and unstructured error handling in the same subroutine.

Logic Errors

Logic errors are the most difficult problem to solve! While the previous errors can be taken care of with the help of special language constructs and the compilers, logic errors cannot be resolved so easily. Logic errors result when a piece of code does not work as intended. As an example, consider the following code snippets:

```
Dim i, factorial As Integer
For i = 1 To 5
    factorial *= i
Next
Response.Write(factorial)
```

The code is trying to calculate the factorial of a number. Though there are no syntax errors, the code is not producing the expected answer (120). In fact, no result is printed. Only through some tracing and checking is it found that the culprit is actually forgetting to initialize the value of the *factorial*. To facilitate the debugging of logic errors, ASP.NET provides tracing ability. We will elaborate on the tracing feature available in ASP.NET in the next section.

Page Tracing

During the development stage, you may often need to monitor the value of some variables or functions, especially if they are not giving the correct results. Tracing through the codes is another important debugging method to make sure your codes flow in the intended manner.

ASP.NET provides tracing ability to easily map the flow of an application. In ASP, debugging is a painful process. You must often use the *Response.Write()* method to output the values of variables:

```
Dim i As Integer
Dim factorial As Integer
```

```
factorial = 1
For i = 1 To 5
    factorial *= i
    Response.Write("value of i is " & i & "<br>")
    Response.Write("value of factorial is" & factorial &
        "<br>")
Next
Response.Write(factorial)
```

How often have you forgotten to remove the debugging statements after you have tracked the error and deployed your application?

Using the *Trace* Class

ASP.NET includes the *Trace* class to help trace the flow of an application. Instead of using the *Response* object for debugging, we now get:

```
factorial = 1
For i = 1 To 5
    factorial *= i
    Trace.Write("value of i is " & i)
    Trace.Write("value of factorial is" & factorial)
Next
Trace.Write(factorial)
Response.Write("The factorial of 5 is " & factorial)
```

To activate the trace, the page directive needs to have a *Trace* attribute with its value set to "true," as shown in Figure 9.3. By just changing the value of the *Trace* attribute, we can turn tracing on or off. When the application is ready for deployment, simply set the *Trace* attribute to the value "false." There is no need to remove the *Trace* statements in your application.

When the ASP.NET application is run, the following output is shown (Figure 9.4). Table 9.2 contains the following sections of the *Trace* page (not all are shown in Figure 9.4).

Figure 9.3 Enabling Tracing

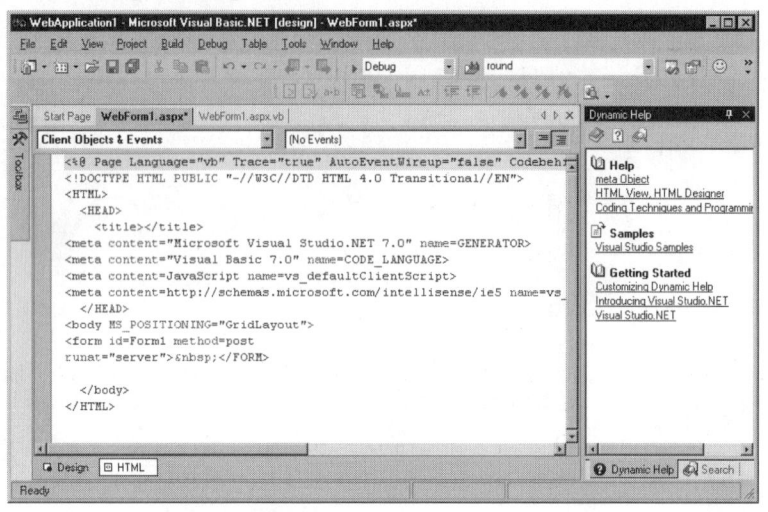

Figure 9.4 Displaying the *Trace* Information

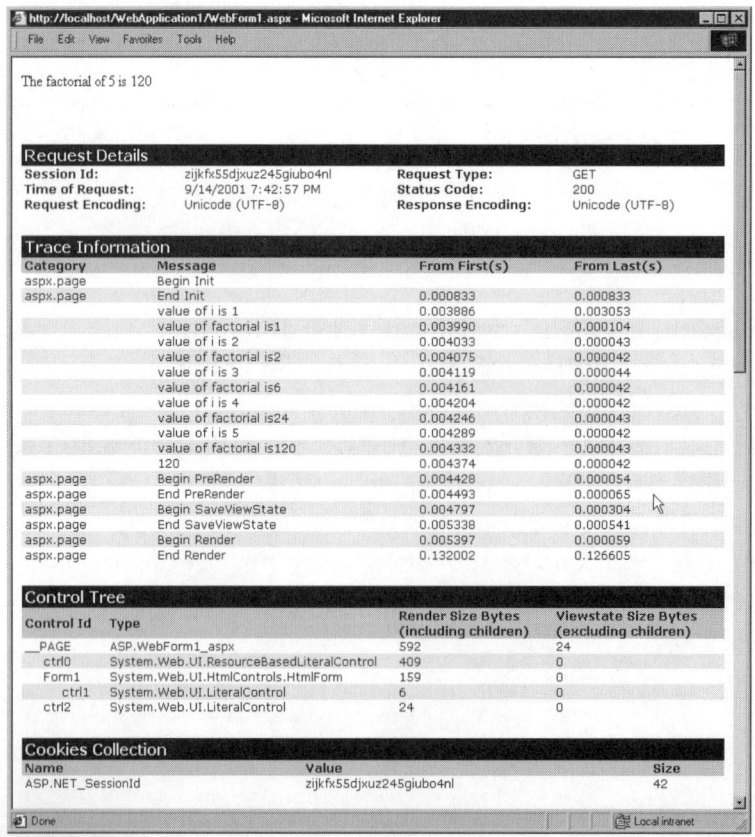

Table 9.2 Sections in a *Trace* Page

Sections	Description
Request Details	Describes information pertaining to the request (e.g., SessionID, Encoding, and time of request).
Trace Information	Contains detailed information about the application currently running. Trace information is displayed in this section.
Control Tree	Displays information about controls used in a page and the size of the Viewstate hidden field.
Cookies Collection	Displays the cookie set by the page and its value.
Headers Collection	Displays HTTP header information like content length and user agent.
Forms Collection	Displays the name of controls in a page and its value.
Server Variables	Displays the environment variables on the server side.

Notice that our *Trace* message is written under the "*Trace* Information" section. The *Trace* class contains the following members (Table 9.3 and Table 9.4).

Table 9.3 Properties in the *Trace* Class

Property	Description
IsEnabled	Indicates whether tracing is enabled for the current request.
TraceMode	Sets the trace mode: sortByCategory or sortByTime.

Table 9.4 Methods in the *Trace* Class

Methods()	Description
Warn	Writes the trace information in red.
Write	Writes the trace information.

For example, the *Warn()* method of the *Trace* class causes the *Trace* information to be printed in red as shown in Figure 9.5 (all the nonshaded lines you see are displayed in red).

```
For i = 1 To 5
    factorial *= i
    Trace.Warn("value of i is " & i)
```

```
            Trace.Write("value of factorial is" & factorial)
Next
```

Figure 9.5 Using the *Warn()* Method to Display *Trace* Information

value of i is 1	0.004144	0.003268
value of factorial is1	0.004250	0.000106
value of i is 2	0.004295	0.000045
value of factorial is2	0.004337	0.000042
value of i is 3	0.004380	0.000043
value of factorial is6	0.004422	0.000042
value of i is 4	0.004465	0.000042
value of factorial is24	0.004507	0.000042
value of i is 5	0.004549	0.000042
value of factorial is120	0.004592	0.000042

NOTE

Turning tracing on and off is just a matter of modifying the value of the *Trace* attribute in the page directive.

Sorting the *Trace* Information

Inserting multiple *Trace* statements in an application can sometimes be messy. It is useful if the *Trace* information is classified into different categories to make tracing easier. The *Trace* class allows us to create different debugging categories and sort the *Trace* information based on these categories. The following example shows how to group the different categories of *Trace* information:

```
factorial = 1
Trace.TraceMode = TraceMode.SortByCategory
For i = 1 To 5
    factorial *= i
    Trace.Warn("counter", "value of i is " & i)
    Trace.Write("Factorial", "value of factorial is" & factorial)
Next
Trace.Write(factorial)
Response.Write("The factorial of 5 is " & factorial)
```

The output of the preceding code is shown in Figure 9.6.
Let's dissect the preceding codes:

```
Trace.TraceMode = TraceMode.SortByCategory
```

Figure 9.6 Sorting by Category (All Lines in the "Counter" Category Are Displayed in Red)

Category	Message	From First(s)	From Last(s)
	120	0.009814	0.000049
aspx.page	Begin Init		
aspx.page	End Init	0.001325	0.001325
aspx.page	Begin PreRender	0.009876	0.000063
aspx.page	End PreRender	0.009930	0.000054
aspx.page	Begin SaveViewState	0.010268	0.000338
aspx.page	End SaveViewState	0.011253	0.000984
aspx.page	Begin Render	0.011329	0.000077
aspx.page	End Render	0.146525	0.135196
counter	value of i is 1	0.004630	0.003305
counter	value of i is 2	0.004778	0.000051
counter	value of i is 3	0.004882	0.000056
counter	value of i is 4	0.004977	0.000047
counter	value of i is 5	0.009663	0.004638
Factorial	value of factorial is1	0.004727	0.000097
Factorial	value of factorial is2	0.004827	0.000049
Factorial	value of factorial is6	0.004930	0.000048
Factorial	value of factorial is24	0.005025	0.000047
Factorial	value of factorial is120	0.009765	0.000102

The *TraceMode* property sets the modes supported by the trace:

- **SortByCategory** *Trace* information is sorted by category.
- **SortByTime** *Trace* information is displayed in the sequence of execution.

Since we are sorting the *Trace* mode by category, notice that Figure 9.6 shows the messages are sorted by category.

```
Trace.Warn("counter", "value of i is " & i)
```

The *Warn* method displays the message in red and notes that this method is overloaded. In this case, we pass in two arguments. The first goes into the *Category* and the second is for the *Message*.

```
Trace.Write("Factorial", "value of factorial is" & factorial)
```

The *Write()* method of the *Trace* object is also overloaded, just like the *Warn()* method. This time around, we write the message into the "Factorial" category.

Besides using the *Trace* class to set the *Trace* mode, you can also use the Page directive to set the *Trace* mode:

```
<%@ Page Language="vb" Trace="true" TraceMode="SortByCategory"
        AutoEventWireup="false" Codebehind="WebForm1.aspx.vb"
        Inherits="WebApplication1.WebForm1" %>
```

Writing the *Trace* Information to the Application Log

Although displaying the *Trace* information within the page is useful, sometimes you need to trace the page while users are utilizing your application. In such cases, the user should not see the *Trace* information. ASP.NET provides a mean for the *Trace* information to be written to a log file. The following example shows how the *Trace* information is written to the application log:

```
...
Response.Write("The factorial of 5 is " & factorial)
Dim appLog As New System.Diagnostics.EventLog()
appLog.WriteEntry("Factorial ASP.NET application", "The factorial of 5
    is " & factorial)
```

The *System.Diagnostics* namespace provides the class to debug our application. In particular, we used the EventLog component to help us write messages to the application log. To view the message, use the Event Viewer. Our message is shown in Figure 9.7.

Figure 9.7 Writing to the Application Log

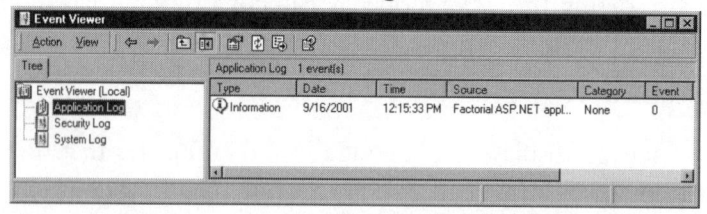

To see the message details, double-click the event item. The detailed message is shown in Figure 9.8.

Application Tracing

This last section discusses page tracing which maps the flow within a page. ASP.NET also supports tracing at the application level. Application-level tracing is set in the web.config file, under the trace section:

```
<trace enabled="false"
       requestLimit="10"
       pageOutput="false"
       traceMode="SortByTime"
```

```
            localOnly="true"
    />
```

Figure 9.8 Details of the Message

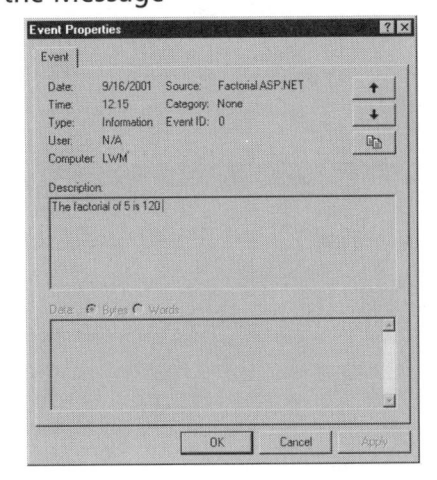

To enable an application-level trace, set the following values shown in Table 9.5.

Table 9.5 Attributes of the *Trace* Element

Attribute	Value	Description
enabled	true	Enables or disables application-level tracing.
requestLimit	10	Sets the maximum number of requests to trace.
pageOutput	false	Displays the trace at the end of the page.
traceMode	SortByTime	Trace information sort order.
localOnly	true	Sets the ability to see trace viewer on a nonlocal machine.

When the application is loaded, the *Trace* information does not appear on the page. To view the *Trace* information, we need to use the *Trace* viewer (trace.axd) shown in Figure 9.9.

Figure 9.9 shows the *Trace* information of the last ten requests to the application. To view the detailed information of each request, click the **View Details** link of each row.

Figure 9.9 Application Level Tracing

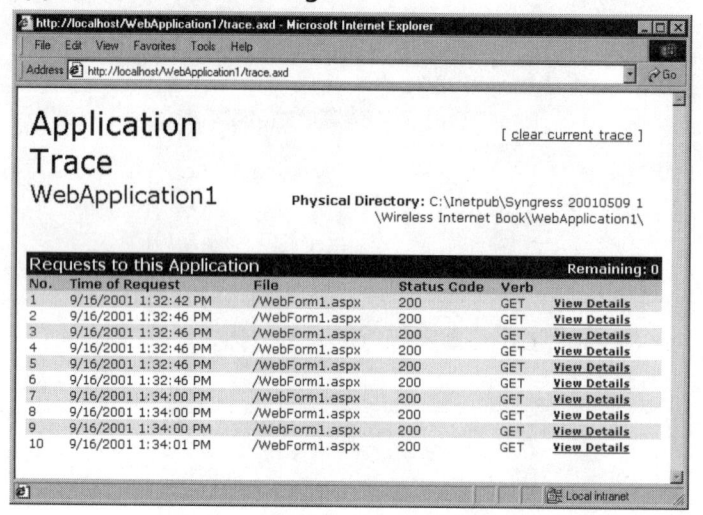

> **NOTE**
>
> If the trace is set to "true" in the web.config file and set to "false" in the page directive, tracing is disabled.

Using Visual Studio .NET Debugging Tools

Visual Studio .NET contains a rich set of debugging tools to help developers debug their applications. In this section, we look at some of the tools available.

Setting Breakpoints

Besides using the *Trace* class to trace the value of variables in your application, another method is to set breakpoints in your application. Visual Studio .NET allows you to do this so you can examine and trace the flow of your application during runtime. Figure 9.10 shows a breakpoint (indicated by a dot, which shows up as red on the screen).

Figure 9.10 Setting a Breakpoint (Designated by Red Dot)

```
Private Sub Page_Load(ByVal sender As System.Object, ByVal e As S
    'Put user code to initialize the page here
    Response.Write("The factorial of 5 is " & Factorial(5))
End Sub
Private Function Factorial(ByVal i As Integer) As Integer
    Factorial = 1
    For i = 1 To 5
        Factorial *= i
    Next
End Function
```

> **NOTE**
>
> Visual Studio 6 developers should be familiar with setting breakpoints in the IDE.

When the application is run, the execution would stop at the breakpoint. Three options are available:

- **Step Into** The execution would then move into the function named Factorial. Each step would execute a line (by pressing **F11**).

- **Step Over** The execution would execute the function (without stepping through the codes within the function) and treat the function as a single line. This is achieved by pressing **F10**.

- **Step Out** This option is available if the current execution point is in the function and you want to execute the rest of the codes in the function without stepping through them. It then returns to the calling function.

Besides tracing the flow, you can also examine the values of variables during a breakpoint. There are two ways to examine the values of variables:

- **Tool tip help** Position the cursor over the variable you want to examine. The value will be displayed in a tool tip dialog box.

- **Watch window** Examine the value of variables by using the Watch window (activated by choosing **Debug | Windows | Watch**).

Enabling and Disabling Debug Mode

By default, your ASP.NET application is in debug mode. The *<compilation>* element in the web.config file controls this:

```
<compilation defaultLanguage="vb" debug="true" />
```

During compilation, debugging symbols (.pdb information) are inserted into the compiled page. As a result, the application will run slower than without the debugging symbols. As such, remember to set the *debug* attribute to *false* when you deploy your application.

Viewing Definitions Using the Object Browser

One of the key aspects of successful .NET programming is the ability to use the appropriate class libraries provided by the framework. While the MSDN documentation is a good place to find out about the class libraries, a better option would be to use the Object Browser provided by the .NET SDK. To launch the Object Browser in Visual Studio .NET, press **Ctrl+Alt+J**.

Figure 9.11 shows the Object Browser with the *System* assembly and its associated namespaces exposed. Members of the class *UriFormationException* are shown on the right window, while the bottom window shows the description of the selected member.

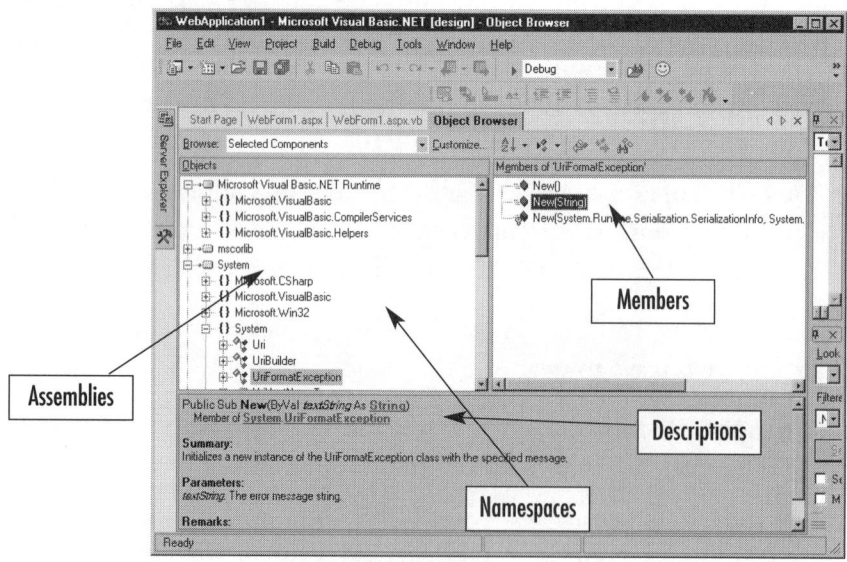

Figure 9.11 Using the Object Browser

Using the Class Viewer

Besides employing the Object Browser to view the various class libraries available, you can also use the Class Viewer. To launch the Class Viewer, type **WinCV** at the command prompt. Figure 9.12 shows the Class Viewer.

Figure 9.12 Using the Class Viewer

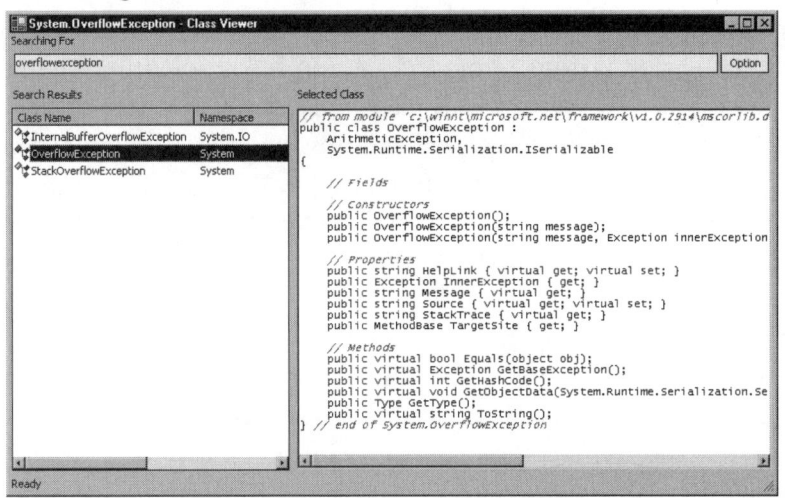

The Class Viewer allows you to type in the keyword to search and display all matching instances of the search word. For example, Figure 9.12 shows the search result for "overflowexception." It also displays the corresponding namespace and the members of the selected class.

Summary

Error handling is an important aspect of software development. Good robust applications anticipate various errors and take an active role in resolving them without crashing the program. In this chapter, we have seen two distinctive methods of error handling—structured and unstructured. While the unstructured error handling mechanism continues to be supported in .NET, it is recommended that programmers make the switch to the structured error handling mechanism using the *Try-Catch-Finally* statement. Besides handling errors, the new tracing capability found in .NET makes the life of a programmer much easier. No longer do you have to insert *Response.Write* statements into your application, you can now trace your application using the *Trace* class. Removing the *Trace* statements during deployment is simply a matter of setting an attribute. Finally, Visual Studio .NET allows you to set breakpoints in your application so that the flow of variables and codes can be examined during runtime.

Solutions Fast Track

Handling Errors

- ☑ There are four main categories of programming errors: syntax, compilation, runtime, and logic errors.
- ☑ Visual Studio .NET IDE provides help for detecting syntax errors.
- ☑ Runtime errors can be handled using structured and unstructured error handling mechanisms.
- ☑ Structured handling using the *Try-Catch-Finally* statement is the recommended mode for handling runtime errors in .NET.

Page Tracing

- ☑ The *Trace* class provides tracing capability.
- ☑ Turning tracing on and off is easy.
- ☑ *Trace* information can be grouped into multiple categories for easier viewing and it can be written into log files, viewable using the Event Viewer.
- ☑ Tracing can be done at the page level or at the application level.

Using Visual Studio .NET Debugging Tools

- ☑ Programmers can use the Visual Studio .NET IDE to set breakpoints in their application.

- ☑ Breakpoints allow you to examine variables and trace the execution flow of your application.

- ☑ The Object Browser and Class Viewer provide quick reference to the various class libraries.

Frequently Asked Questions

The following Frequently Asked Questions, answered by the authors of this book, are designed to both measure your understanding of the concepts presented in this chapter and to assist you with real-life implementation of these concepts. To have your questions about this chapter answered by the author, browse to **www.syngress.com/solutions** and click on the **"Ask the Author"** form.

Q: Is the *Try-Catch-Finally* block available in C# as well?

A: Yes, the *Try-Catch-Finally* block is available in both VB.NET and C#.

Q: Can I use both structured and unstructured error handling within a function/subroutine?

A: No, you cannot use both error handling mechanisms at the same time. It is recommended you use structured error handling in .NET.

Q: When I try to run my ASP.NET application in VS.NET, I encounter this error message "Error while trying to run project: Unable to start debugging on the Web server. The project is not configured to be debugged." Why does this occur?

A: This is caused by the setting of the *debug* attribute within the *<compilation>* element. During development stage, set the value of the *debug* attribute to "true." Remember, however, to set this attribute to "false" when you are ready to deploy your application.

Q: I noticed during tracing that the Session ID for my application changes when I refresh my page or when I do a postback. Why is this happening?

A: For performance reasons, the .NET Framework does not maintain state between the Web server and the Web browser automatically, hence the Session ID is always different between submissions. However, when the *Session* object is used or when the *Session_OnStart()* event is added to the global.asax file, the Session ID would be maintained between postbacks.

Chapter 10

Web Services

Solutions in this chapter:

- **Understanding Web Services**
- **Using XML in Web Services**
- **An Overview of the System.Web.Services Namespace**
- **Type Marshalling**
- **Using DataSets**

☑ **Summary**

☑ **Solutions Fast Track**

☑ **Frequently Asked Questions**

Introduction

Web Services provide a new level of interaction to ASP.NET applications. The ability to access and use a remote Web service to perform a function within an ASP.NET Web application enables programmers to quickly deliver a more sophisticated app in less time. The programmer no longer has to create and maintain all functions of the application. Reusability is also greatly enhanced by creating multiple Web services that perform functions in multiple applications, thus freeing up time and resources to work on other aspects of specific projects. See Figure 10.1, which shows a graphical representation of this process.

Figure 10.1 Where Do Web Services Fit In?

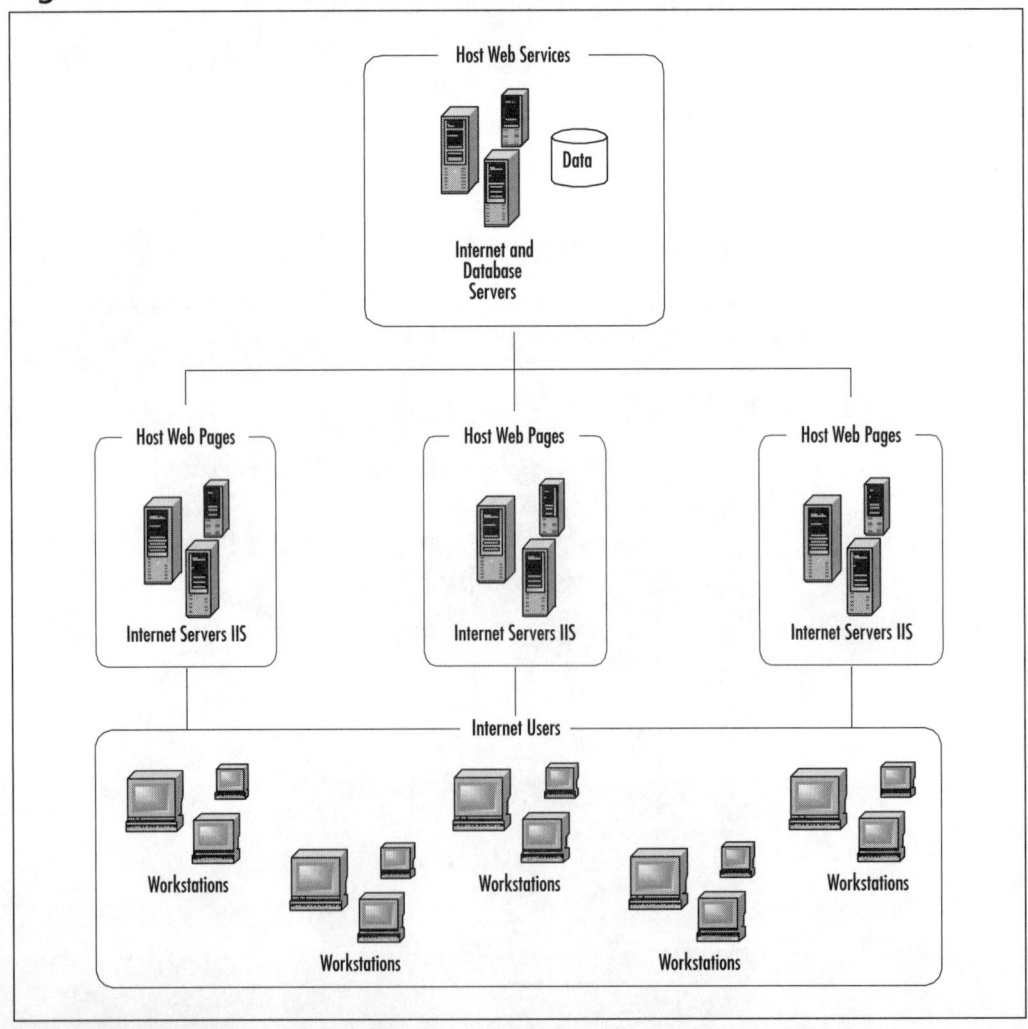

Web Services function primarily through XML in order to pass information back and forth through the Hypertext Transfer Protocol (HTTP). Web Services are a vital part of what the .NET Framework offers to programmers. XML-based data transfer is realized, enabling primitive types, enumerations, and even classes to be passed through Web Services to the application performing the request. This brings a whole new level of reusability to an application. XML is the backbone from which the whole Framework is built. The user interface (UI) can be created by applying Extensible Stylesheet Language Transformations (XSLTs) or by loading the data into *DataSets* and binding to Web Controls. Having XML as the intermediary enables new avenues of client design.

Understanding Web Services

Web Services are objects and methods that can be invoked from any client over HTTP. Web Services are built on the Simple Object Access Protocol (SOAP). Unlike the Distributed Component Object Model (DCOM) and Common Object Request Broker Architecture (CORBA), SOAP enables messaging over HTTP on port 80 (for most Web servers) and uses a standard means of describing data. SOAP makes it possible to send data and structure easily over the Web. Web Services capitalizes on this protocol to implement object and method messaging. Web Services are easy to create in VS.NET. Here is an ASP.NET *Hello World* class in C#:

```
public class hello
    {
        public string HelloWorld()
        {
            return "Hello World";
        }
    }
}
```

This class describes a *hello* object that has one method, *HelloWorld*. When called, this method will return data of type *string*. To convert this to a Web Service method, we simply have to add one line of code:

```
public class hello
    {
        [WebMethod]
        public string HelloWorld()
```

```
        {
                return "Hello World";
        }
    }
}
```

A little bit more code is involved to make this a method of a Web Service. This is the code that VS.NET auto-generates when we create a new .asmx page, along with our *Hello World* method:

```
using System;
using System.Collections;
using System.ComponentModel;
using System.Data;
using System.Diagnostics;
using System.Web;
using System.Web.Services;

namespace Hello
{
    public class Hello : System.Web.Services.WebService
    {
    public Hello()
        {
                InitializeComponent();
        }
        private void InitializeComponent()
        {
        }
        protected override void Dispose( bool disposing )
        {
        }
        [WebMethod]
        public string HelloWorld()
        {
                return "Hello World";
```

```
        }
    }
}
```

You can quickly create this class in VS.NET by creating and opening a C# Web Application project or Web Service project and adding a new WebService page.

If you prefer, similar code could be written to create a VB.NET Service:

```
Imports System.Web.Services

Public Class Service1
    Inherits System.Web.Services.WebService
<WebMethod()> Public Function HelloWorld() As String
        HelloWorld = "Hello World"
    End Function

End Class
```

Configuring & Implementing...

Setting the Start Page

When testing a Web service in a project that contains other .aspx or .asmx files, be sure to set the file you are debugging/testing to be the Start page, before running. To do this, right-click the filename in the **Solution Explorer** and select **Set as start page**.

To run this sample in VS.NET, simply press **F5**. It will take a few moments to build and compile. When that phase is complete, you should see the Hello service screen shown in Figure 10.2.

The top line on the screen states that the operations listed below it are supported. This is followed by a bulleted list of links to each of the Web methods that belong to the Web service. In our case, we created only one Web method, *HelloWorld*. If you click the link **HelloWorld**, you will be taken to that service's description page (see Figure 10.3).

Figure 10.2 Hello Service

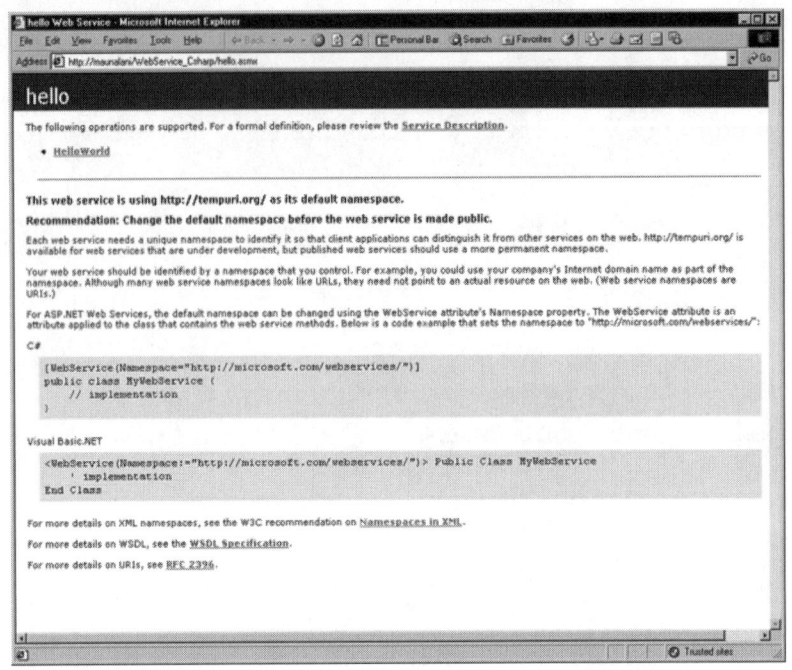

Figure 10.3 *HelloWorld* Service Description Page

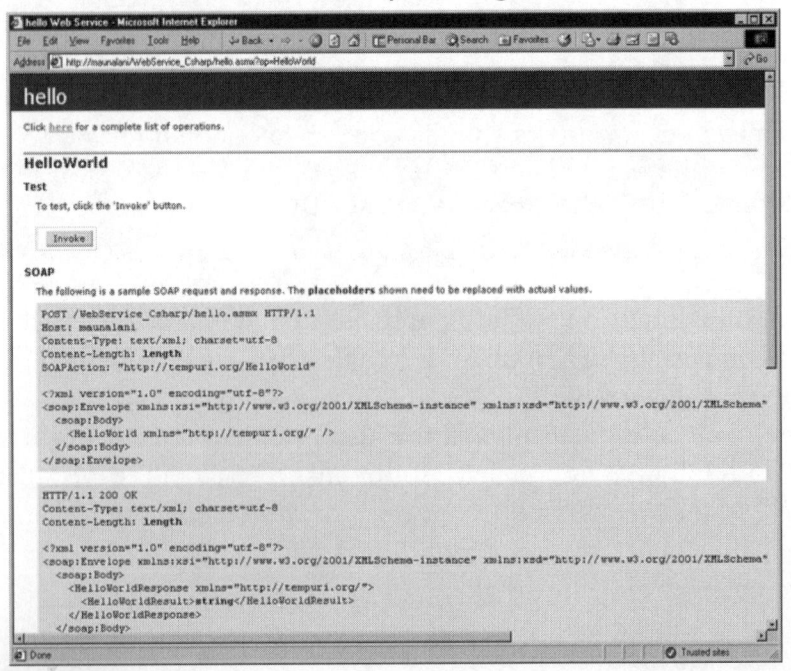

To test our Hello Web Services *HelloWorld* Web method, simply click the **Invoke** button and our method will be called. Recalling our method returns the string "hello world"; the result is returned in an XML wrapper (see Figure 10.4).

Figure 10.4 Results from Invoking the *HelloWorld* Web Method

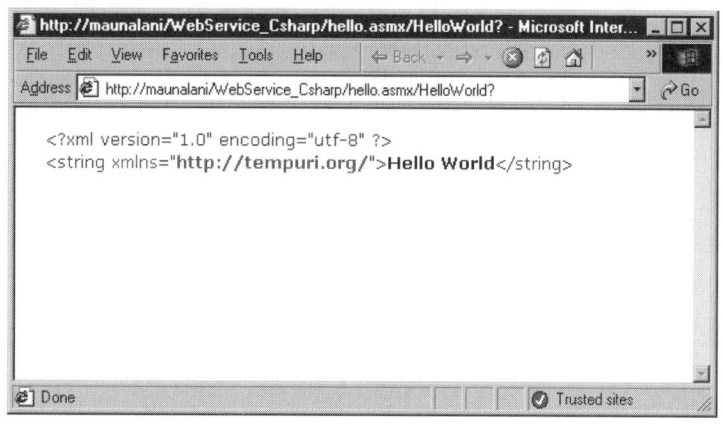

```
<?xml version="1.0" encoding="utf-8" ?>
<string xmlns="http://tempuri.org/">Hello World</string>
```

Note that the XML node reflects the datatype of the method's return value, *string*. This XML message is received and converted to the string "Hello World". This means that any variable (of type *string*) in our code can be assigned to the result of our Web method.

Configuring & Implementing...

Building and Compiling

If you have experience programming in C/C++ or Java, you will be familiar with the building and compiling steps. If you are a Web Developer who hasn't really played with a compiled language before, these steps will be new to you. Think of it as the phase in which the compiler gets all your code together and checks it for unassigned variables, variable type mismatches, and other syntactic errors. In this phase, it also converts your code into the Common Language Runtimes (CLR) Intermediate Language (IL), and then into machine language. This will allow the code to run faster and more efficiently than uncompiled script. After this phase completes, the code is run in the Browser. So, testing Web page output may seem to take longer in the .NET environment.

Communication between Servers

The concept of sending messages between servers or remotely calling functions is not new. Technologies such as DCOM and CORBA are well-known proprietary protocols that have been in use for years. What is new is the use of a standard protocol to transfer messages over HTTP, that protocol is SOAP. SOAP makes it possible for applications written in different languages running on different platforms to make remote procedure calls (RPC) effectively, even through firewalls. DCOM doesn't use port 80, which is reserved for HTTP traffic; this causes DCOM calls to be blocked by firewalls. SOAP calls use port 80, which makes it possible to call procedures that exist behind firewalls. Figure 10.5 shows a high level overview of how Web Services can be used, both for customer interactions with a company from multiple client types as well as for internal company data gathering and reporting between all company servers, including legacy systems.

Figure 10.5 Overview: Where Do Web Services Fit In?

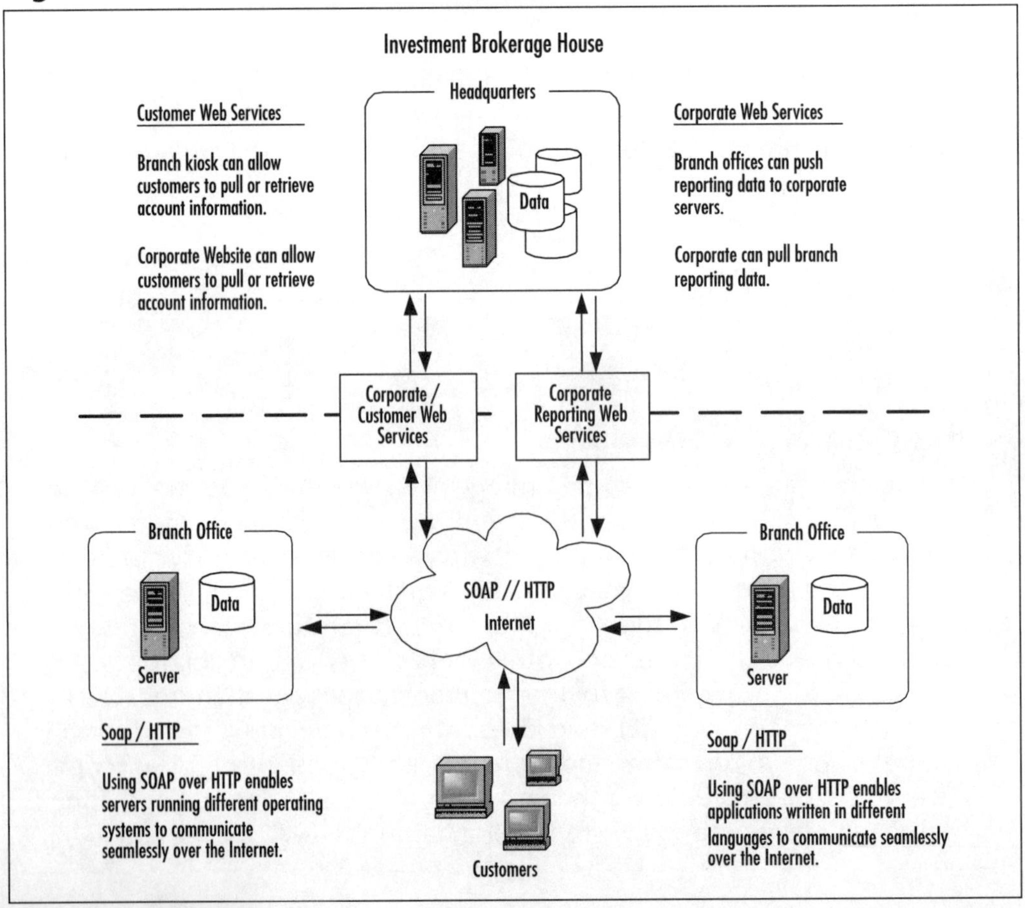

In ASP.NET, Web Services and their methods are defined in pages with the .asmx extension. When we create Web Services, the .NET Framework generates a Web Services Description Language (WSDL) file on the server hosting the Service; this WSDL file describes the Web Service interface. On the Web server that hosts our .aspx pages, VS.NET generates a WSDL proxy when we click **Add Web reference** in the **Solutions Explorer** and select the server and Service (see Figure 10.6).

Figure 10.6 Overview: Where WSDL and WSDL Proxies Fit into the Internet User Page Request Process

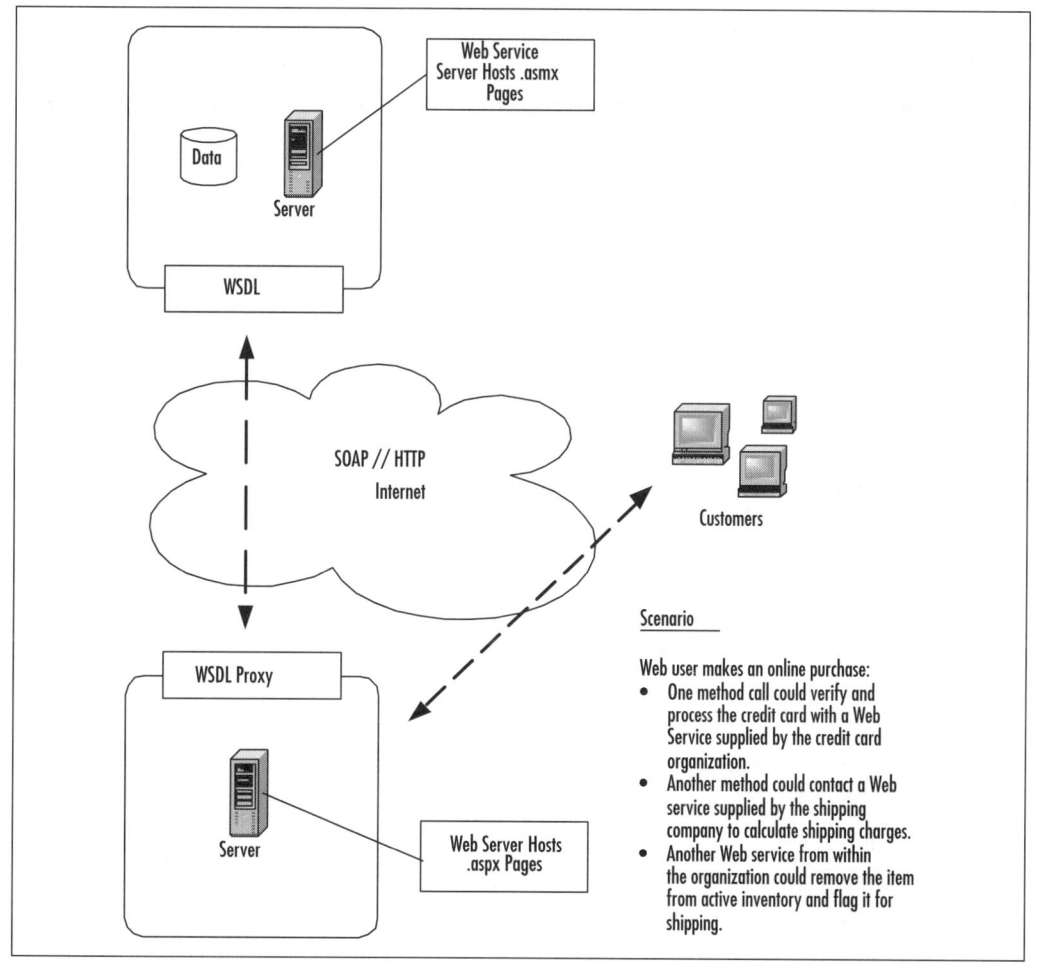

Figure 10.7 shows a Web reference for "localhost" and the WSDL proxies for each Web Service that exists on that server.

Figure 10.7 Web References in VS.NET's Solution Explorer Window

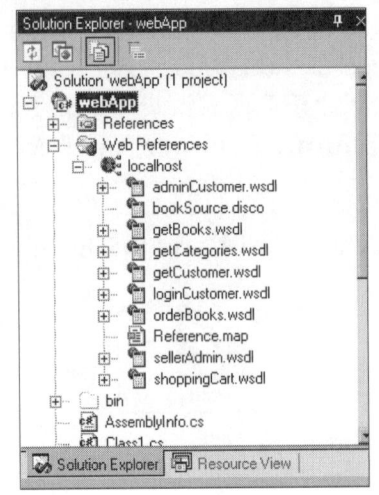

> **NOTE**
>
> A single application hosted on the Web server may access several Web Services residing on different servers. Likewise, many Web servers may access one Web Service.

.asmx Files

ASP.NET uses the .asmx file extension for defining ASP.NET Web Services. The code-behind pages are .asmx.cs and .asmx.vb for C# and VB.NET, respectively.

Migrating...

What Is the Difference between .asmx and .aspx?

In ASP, we have the .asp extension to denote an Active Server Page. When IIS sees this extension, it knows it has some extra processing to do. This is the same with ASP.NET, except that we have two new extensions, .aspx and .asmx.

Continued

> Lets do a quick comparison:
> - Both file types have a template, which includes references to the primary namespaces.
> - .aspx pages have references to *System.Drawing* since their purpose is to generate a user interface.
> - .asmx pages have references to *System.Web.Services* since their purpose is to generate an interface for external programs.
> - You can add UI components and Data Connections to an .aspx page.
> - You can add Server and Data Connections to an .asmx page.
> - .aspx pages usually begin with an @Page directive to designate: this is a Web Form.
> - .asmx pages usually begin with an @WebService directive to designate: this is a Web Service.
> - Using the wrong @ directive with the wrong type of file extension will generate an error.

While the client for an .aspx page is the Web browser, the client for an .asmx file is the Web server. Since they are used as programming interfaces and not directly utilized by the Web user, .asmx files should not contain any UI. To get a better understanding of how this all works, lets create an .aspx page that calls our "Hello" service.

1. In the **Solutions Explorer**, right-click the project name.
2. Select **Add | New Item**.
3. Select **Web Form**. Name the file **helloPage.aspx**.
4. While in design view, open the toolbox and drag onto the page a label and a button control from the selection of Web Forms (see Figure 10.8).
   While still in design mode double-click the new button. This will generate event code in the code behind page (see Figure 10.9).
5. Right-click **References** in the **Solution Explorer** and select **Add Web Reference**. This is basically a graphical user interface (GUI) for the WSDL.exe command line utility.
6. When the **Add Web Reference** dialog opens (see Figure 10.10) click the link **Web References on local server**.

Figure 10.8 Adding a Web Form Control to an .aspx Page

Figure 10.9 Auto-Generated Button Event Code

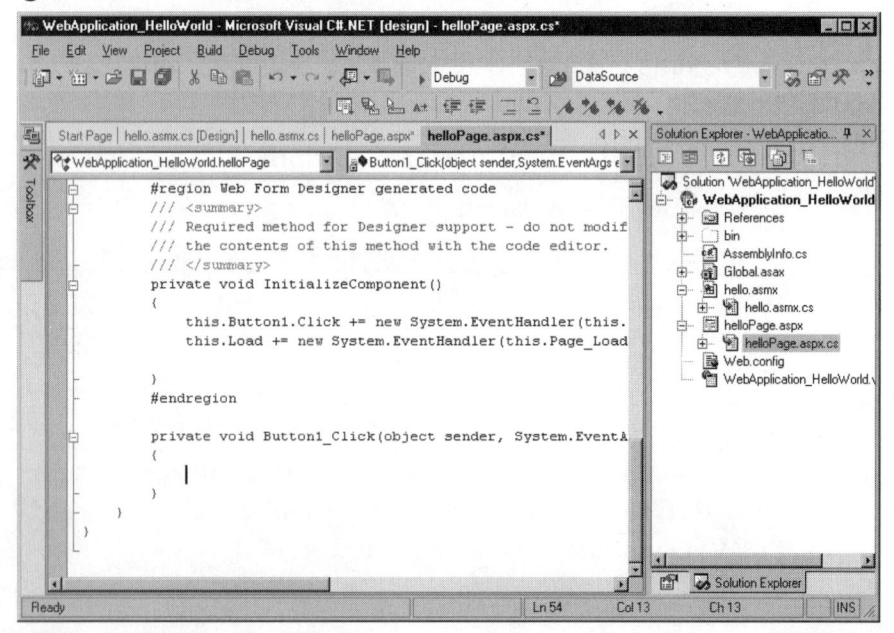

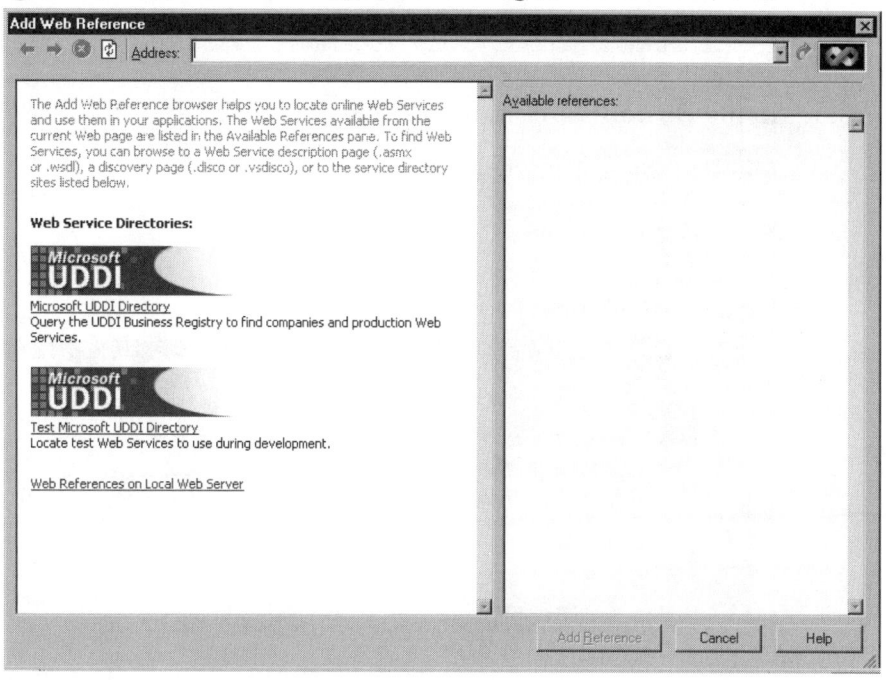

Figure 10.10 Add Web Reference Dialog Box

The dialog will pause while it searches your local machine for a list of services available.

7. When the list appears, click the name of the service that matches the name of your project, **WebApplication_HelloWorld**.
8. When the service loads, click the **Add Reference** button. This will create several new entries in your Solutions Explorer.
9. Now take a look at helloPage.aspx in HTML view. You should see code similar to the following:

```
<body MS_POSITIONING="GridLayout">
  <form id="helloPage" method="post" runat="server">
    <asp:Button id=Button1 Text="Button" runat="server" >
      </asp:Button>
    <asp:Label id=Label1 runat="server">Label</asp:Label>
  </form>
</body>
```

10. Note the name of the label control is Label1. Now open **helloPage.aspx.cs** and add the following code below the label and button code.

    ```
    localhost.hello test = new localhost.hello();
    ```

11. In the **Button Click handler**, add the following:

    ```
    Label1.Text = test.HelloWorld();
    ```

12. Your code should now look like Figure 10.11.

    Figure 10.11 helloPage.aspx.cs

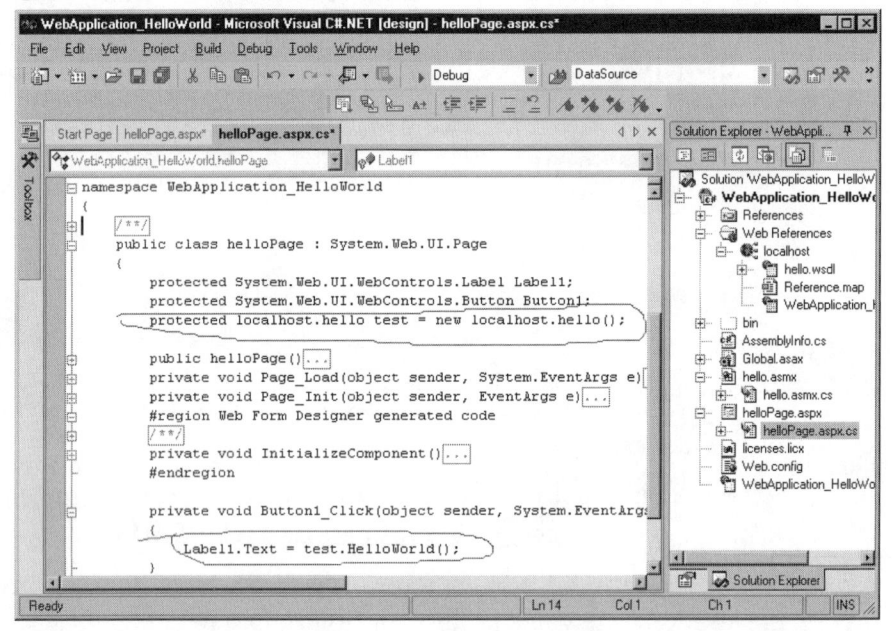

    ![Figure 10.11 screenshot showing helloPage.aspx.cs code in Visual C#.NET]

13. Right-click **helloPage.aspx** and click **Set as start page**.
14. Press **F5** to run the application.
15. When the browser loads, click the button, this will invoke our *helloWorld* method and assign its value to the label text. After clicking the button, your page should look like Figure 10.12.

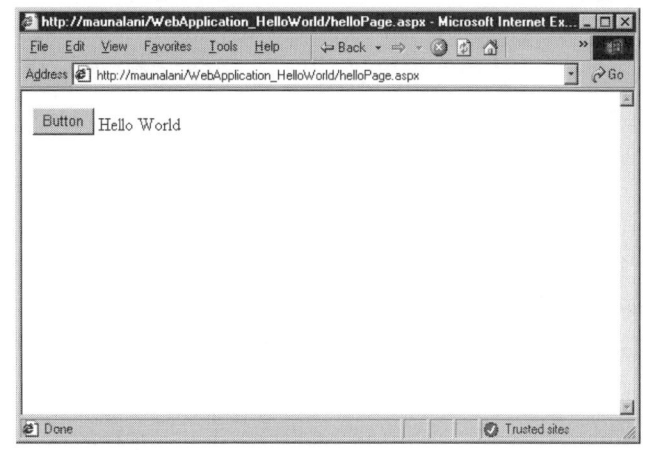

Figure 10.12 HelloPage.aspx in the Browser after Clicking the Button

Developing & Deploying…

VS.NET Beta 2: Generated Template Code

When using VS.NET to develop ASP.NET pages it's actually easier to develop using code behind than to code in the same document. When we create a new Web Form or Web Service VS.NET automatically generates a corresponding code-behind page with template code. While the template code generated may seem like more than is necessary for simple applications, the generated code makes it easy to quickly create larger event driven Web applications.

WSDL

WSDL is an XML-based language that describes Web Services. It is the composite of work done by Ariba, IBM, and Microsoft. Currently, it only supports SOAP as a messaging protocol.

The thought behind WSDL is that in future applications it will be a collection of networked-Web Services. WSDL describes what a service can do, where it lives, and how to invoke it. WSDL describes the Web Service method interfaces thoroughly enough for it to be used to create proxy methods that enable other classes to invoke its members as if they were local methods. IBM and Microsoft both have WSDL command line utilities available that do just that. IBM does it for Java, and Microsoft does it for Visual Studio. VS.NET has this ability built into the GUI. In VS.NET, we simply right-click **add Web Reference** and select the service we want to generate a proxy class for. Here is an example of a WSDL file for a Web Service used in Chapter 12: getCategories.wsdl. This file is auto-generated by the .NET Framework.

While the auto-generated file will cover the basic functionality, it may do more or less than you intended. The auto-generated code can be simplified by removing support for asynchronous operations if you do not need to support this type of operation. Also, you could add custom SOAP headers and customize other parts of the SOAP envelope by creating your own class.

```xml
<?xml version="1.0" encoding="utf-8"?>
<definitions xmlns:s="http://www.w3.org/2001/XMLSchema"
    xmlns:http="http://schemas.xmlsoap.org/wsdl/http/"
    xmlns:mime="http://schemas.xmlsoap.org/wsdl/mime/"
    xmlns:tm="http://microsoft.com/wsdl/mime/textMatching/"
    xmlns:soap="http://schemas.xmlsoap.org/wsdl/soap/"
    xmlns:soapenc="http://schemas.xmlsoap.org/soap/encoding/"
    xmlns:s0="http://tempuri.org/"
targetNamespace="http://tempuri.org/"
    xmlns="http://schemas.xmlsoap.org/wsdl/">
  <types>
    <s:schema attributeFormDefault="qualified"
elementFormDefault="qualified" targetNamespace="http://tempuri.org/">
      <s:import namespace="http://www.w3.org/2001/XMLSchema" />
      <s:element name="AllCat">
        <s:complexType />
      </s:element>
      <s:element name="AllCatResponse">
        <s:complexType>
          <s:sequence>
            <s:element minOccurs="1" maxOccurs="1" name="AllCatResult"
              nillable="true">
              <s:complexType>
                <s:sequence>
                  <s:element ref="s:schema" />
```

```xml
            <s:any />
          </s:sequence>
        </s:complexType>
      </s:element>
    </s:sequence>
  </s:complexType>
</s:element>
<s:element name="DataSet" nillable="true">
  <s:complexType>
    <s:sequence>
      <s:element ref="s:schema" />
      <s:any />
    </s:sequence>
  </s:complexType>
</s:element>
</s:schema>
</types>
<message name="AllCatSoapIn">
  <part name="parameters" element="s0:AllCat" />
</message>
<message name="AllCatSoapOut">
  <part name="parameters" element="s0:AllCatResponse" />
</message>
<message name="AllCatHttpGetIn" />
<message name="AllCatHttpGetOut">
  <part name="Body" element="s0:DataSet" />
</message>
<message name="AllCatHttpPostIn" />
<message name="AllCatHttpPostOut">
  <part name="Body" element="s0:DataSet" />
</message>
<portType name="getCategoriesSoap">
  <operation name="AllCat">
    <documentation>
```

```xml
        This will return all categories in an XML String
      </documentation>
      <input message="s0:AllCatSoapIn" />
      <output message="s0:AllCatSoapOut" />
    </operation>
  </portType>
  <portType name="getCategoriesHttpGet">
    <operation name="AllCat">
      <documentation>
        This will return all categories in an XML String
      </documentation>
      <input message="s0:AllCatHttpGetIn" />
      <output message="s0:AllCatHttpGetOut" />
    </operation>
  </portType>
  <portType name="getCategoriesHttpPost">
    <operation name="AllCat">
      <documentation>
        This will return all categories in an XML String
      </documentation>
      <input message="s0:AllCatHttpPostIn" />
      <output message="s0:AllCatHttpPostOut" />
    </operation>
  </portType>
  <binding name="getCategoriesSoap" type="s0:getCategoriesSoap">
    <soap:binding style="document"
      transport="http://schemas.xmlsoap.org/soap/http" />
    <operation name="AllCat">
    <soap:binding style="document"
      soapAction="http://tempuri.org/AllCat" />

      <input>
        <soap:body use="literal" />
      </input>
```

```xml
        <output>
           <soap:body use="literal" />
        </output>
     </operation>
  </binding>
  <binding name="getCategoriesHttpGet" type="s0:getCategoriesHttpGet">
     <http:binding verb="GET" />
     <operation name="AllCat">
        <http:operation location="/AllCat" />
        <input>
           <http:urlEncoded />
        </input>
        <output>
           <mime:mimeXml part="Body" />
        </output>
     </operation>
  </binding>
  <binding name="getCategoriesHttpPost" type="s0:getCategoriesHttpPost">
     <http:binding verb="POST" />
     <operation name="AllCat">
        <http:operation location="/AllCat" />
        <input>
           <mime:content type="application/x-www-form-urlencoded" />
        </input>
        <output>
           <mime:mimeXml part="Body" />
        </output>
     </operation>
  </binding>
  <service name="getCategories">
     <port name="getCategoriesSoap" binding="s0:getCategoriesSoap">
        <soap:address
          location="http://ubid/bookSource/getCategories.asmx" />
     </port>
```

```
      <port name="getCategoriesHttpGet"
binding="s0:getCategoriesHttpGet">
        <http:address
          location="http://ubid/bookSource/getCategories.asmx" />
      </port>
      <port name="getCategoriesHttpPost"
binding="s0:getCategoriesHttpPost">
        <http:address
          location="http://ubid/bookSource/getCategories.asmx" />
      </port>
   </service>
</definitions>
```

Developing & Deploying…

When Moving a VS.NET Web Service to Another Server

When transferring a project to another server, make sure the page namespaces match the project name and be sure to update Web references.

Using XML in Web Services

Web Services use SOAP as a messaging protocol. SOAP is a relatively simple XML language that describes the data to be transmitted. Why use XML? XML is a standard language designed to be understandable by humans, and structured so it can be interpreted programmatically. XML does not only describe data, it can also describe structure, as we will see when we take a closer look at the ADO.NET *DataSet*.

Consider the case of replicating a database into cache. We might want to do this to reduce the load on the database server, to speed client processing, or to provide an offline data handling scenario. We could transport an XML document that contains the new W3C XML Schema Definition Standard (XSD) schema describing the database tables, relations, and constraints, along with the actual data (see the section "Using DataSets" later in this chapter). Because XSD can describe relational data and can be embedded within an XML document, any database can be converted to a ubiquitous data source. That is, a data source that can be accessed on any platform by any application. This is possible because the transfer protocol, SOAP, uses XML over HTTP and because XML, XSD, SOAP, and HTTP are all nonproprietary industry standards.

It is the use of non proprietary industry standards that makes Web Services so powerful. By using XML to describe structure and content, Web Services can provide an interface to data on legacy systems, or between incompatible platforms from acquisitions or between vendors over intranets, extranets, or the Internet.

An Overview of the System.Web.Services Namespace

System.Web.Services is the namespace from which all Web service classes are derived. It consists of all the classes needed to create Web Services in the .NET Framework. When using VS.NET most of the *System.Web.Services* classes and subclasses are transparent to the developer, so we won't go into much depth here. The three primary child classes of *System.Web.Services* are: Description, Discovery, and Protocols.

The *System.Web.Services.Description* Namespace

The *System.Web.Services.Description* namespace contains the classes needed to describe a Web Service using the Microsoft SDL (Service Definition Language), a Microsoft implementation of the WSDL standard. VS.NET uses these classes to create the .disco or .vsdisco file. Many of the subclasses of this class are related to binding: *MessageBinding*, *OperationBinding*, *OutputBinding*, and so on. One of the more interesting subclasses is the *ServiceDescription* class. It takes as a parameter an XML file and enables the creation of a valid WSDL file.

```
ServiceDescription MyDescription = new ServiceDescription();
ServiceDescription MyDescription =
    ServiceDescription.Read("MyTestFile.xml");
```

The *System.Web.Services.Discovery* Namespace

The *System.Web.Services.Discovery* namespace consists of the classes that enable Web Service consumers to locate available Web Services. In VS.NET when we create a Web Reference, these classes find the .vsdisco files that describe Web Services.

Disco file from our Hello World example:

```
<?xml version="1.0" encoding="utf-8"?>
<discovery xmlns:xsi="http://www.w3.org/2001/XMLSchema-instance"
           xmlns:xsd="http://www.w3.org/2001/XMLSchema"
           xmlns="http://schemas.xmlsoap.org/disco/">
   <contractRef
       ref="http://localhost/WebApplication_HelloWorld/hello.asmx?wsdl"
       docRef="http://localhost/WebApplication_HelloWorld/hello.asmx"
       xmlns="http://schemas.xmlsoap.org/disco/scl/" />
</discovery>
```

The *System.Web.Services.Protocols* Namespace

The *System.Web.Services.Protocols* namespace consists of the classes used to define the protocols that enable message transmission over HTTP between ASP.NET Web Services and ASP.NET Web Service clients. These classes are used in our WSDL proxy classes. They are mostly involved with the formatting, bindings, and settings of the SOAP message.

WSDL proxy from our Hello World example:

```
namespace WebApplication_HelloWorld.localhost {
    using System.Diagnostics;
    using System.Xml.Serialization;
    using System;
    using System.Web.Services.Protocols;
    using System.Web.Services;


    [System.Web.Services.WebServiceBindingAttribute(Name="helloSoap",
                        Namespace="http://tempuri.org/")]
    public class hello :
        System.Web.Services.Protocols.SoapHttpClientProtocol {

        [System.Diagnostics.DebuggerStepThroughAttribute()]
        public hello() {
```

```
            this.Url =
"http://localhost/WebApplication_HelloWorld/hello.asmx";
        }

        [System.Diagnostics.DebuggerStepThroughAttribute()]
        [System.Web.Services.Protocols.SoapDocumentMethodAttribute(
         "http://tempuri.org/HelloWorld",
        Use=System.Web.Services.Description.SoapBindingUse.Literal,
        ParameterStyle=
System.Web.Services.Protocols.SoapParameterStyle.Wrapped)]
        public string HelloWorld() {
            object[] results = this.Invoke("HelloWorld", new object[0]);
            return ((string)(results[0]));
        }

        [System.Diagnostics.DebuggerStepThroughAttribute()]
        public System.IAsyncResult BeginHelloWorld(
          System.AsyncCallback callback, object asyncState)
        {
            return this.BeginInvoke(
              "HelloWorld", new object[0], callback, asyncState);
        }

        [System.Diagnostics.DebuggerStepThroughAttribute()]
        public string EndHelloWorld(System.IAsyncResult asyncResult) {
            object[] results = this.EndInvoke(asyncResult);
            return ((string)(results[0]));
        }
    }
}
```

Type Marshalling

Type marshalling refers to the translation of datatypes from an application or database as it is mapped to a SOAP datatype. When any datatype, object, method, or string (xml, or a simple string) is passed as a SOAP request or response, it is automatically converted into an XML representation of itself. Since any programming language can use SOAP, SOAP has defined its own set of datatypes. When data is passed in a SOAP envelope its datatypes are translated or converted to a SOAP equivalent. This enables different languages with different names for similar datatypes to communicate effectively. The datatypes supported when using Web Services include:

- **Standard primitive types** String, char, Boolean, byte, single, double, DateTime, int16, int32, int 64, Uint16, and so on.

    ```
    string "hello World" is represented as:
    <string>hello World</string>
    ```

- **Enum Types** Enumerations like enum weekday {sun=0, mon=1, tue=2, wed=3, thu=4, fri=5, sat =6}

- **Arrays of Primitives or Enums**

    ```
    MyArray[ 5,7 ] is represented as:
    <ArrayOfInt>
       <int>5</int>
       <int>7</int>
    </ArrayOfInt>
    ```

- **Classes and Structs**

    ```
    struct Order( OrderID, Price ) is represented as:
    <Order>
       <OrderID>12345</OrderID>
       <Price>49.99</Price>
    </Order>
    ```

- **Arrays of Classes (Structs)**

    ```
    MyArray Orders( order1, order2 ) may be represented as:
    <ArrayOfOrder>
    ```

```xml
<Order>
    <OrderID>int</OrderID>
    <Price>double</Price>
</Order>
<Order>
    <OrderID>int</OrderID>
    <Price>double</Price>
</Order>
</ArrayOfOrder>
```

- **DataSets** The representation of a DataSet is rather lengthy; it includes an inline XSD schema defining the structure followed by the XML data. For an example of a DataSet, see the next section, "Using *DataSets*."

- **Arrays of DataSets**

- **XmlNodes**

    ```xml
    <book id=1><title>book1</title><price>25.00</price></book>
    ```

- **Arrays of XmlNodes**

    ```xml
    <ArrayOfBook>
        <book id="1">
            <title>book1</title>
            <price>25.00</price>
        </book>
        <book id="2">
            <title>book2</title>
            <price>49.99</price>
        </book>
    </ArrayOfBook>
    ```

It is important to note that when we create and use Web Services in VS.NET, the marshalling of data is transparent to the developer. This is also true when using the WSDL.exe command line utility. While it is important to have some understanding of how data is transported between the Web Service and the Service proxy or client, this layer is and should be transparent to the developer, just as packet structures for transmitting data over HTTP is transparent to the Web developer.

Using DataSets

A *DataSet* can be used to cache an entire database within an ASP application variable. This would reduce the Database Server Load and speed data access over the life of the application object. The following is a code snippet that calls a Web Service that returns a *DataSet*. The *DataSet* in turn stores the data in an application object.

```
myServer.getBooks DataSource = new myServer.getBooks();
Application["AllBooks"]  = DataSource.AllBooks();
```

This makes the *DataSet* available to all instances of the Web application, which is very efficient. Operations can be performed on the *DataSet* and, on *Application_End* the Database can be updated.

DataSets store database structure information and contain *DataTable*, *DataColumn*, *DataRow*, and *DataView* children. *DataSet RowFilter* operations are very much like SQL Queries. The *DataSet* can easily be databinded to ASP.NET UI controls. It also has an XML output format that makes it easily translated to XML for XML processing.

Here is an example of the Books *DataSet* returned by the getBooks.allBook service:

```xml
<?xml version="1.0" encoding="utf-8"?>
<DataSet xmlns="http://tempuri.org/">
  <xsd:schema id="NewDataSet" targetNamespace="" xmlns=""
    xmlns:xsd=http://www.w3.org/2001/XMLSchema
    xmlns:msdata="urn:schemas-microsoft-com:xml-msdata">
    <xsd:element name="NewDataSet" msdata:IsDataSet="true">
      <xsd:complexType>
        <xsd:choice maxOccurs="unbounded">
          <xsd:element name="Books">
            <xsd:complexType>
              <xsd:sequence>
                <xsd:element name="isbn" type="xsd:string"
                  minOccurs="0" />
                <xsd:element name="name" type="xsd:string"
                  minOccurs="0" />
                <xsd:element name="id" type="xsd:int" minOccurs="0" />
```

```xml
            <xsd:element name="imgSrc" type="xsd:string"
             minOccurs="0" />
            <xsd:element name="author" type="xsd:string"
             minOccurs="0" />
            <xsd:element name="price" type="xsd:decimal"
             minOccurs="0" />
            <xsd:element name="title" type="xsd:string"
             minOccurs="0" />
            <xsd:element name="description" type="xsd:string"
             minOccurs="0" />
          </xsd:sequence>
        </xsd:complexType>
      </xsd:element>
    </xsd:choice>
  </xsd:complexType>
</xsd:element>
</xsd:schema>
<diffgr:diffgram xmlns:msdata="urn:schemas-microsoft-com:xml-msdata"
  xmlns:diffgr="urn:schemas-microsoft-com:xml-diffgram-v1">
  <NewDataSet xmlns="">
    <Books diffgr:id="Books1" msdata:rowOrder="0">
      <isbn>0072121599      </isbn>
      <name>cisco</name>
      <id>2</id>
      <imgSrc>ccda.gif</imgSrc>
      <author>Syngress Media Inc</author>
      <price>49.99</price>
      <title>Ccda Cisco Certified Design Associate Study Guide</title>
      <description>
        Written for professionals intending on taking the CCDA test,
        this special guide covers all the basics of the test and
        includes hundreds of test questions on the enclosed CD.
      </description>
    </Books>
```

```
        <Books diffgr:id="Books2" msdata:rowOrder="1">
          <isbn>0072126671       </isbn>
          <name>cisco</name>
          <id>2</id>
          <imgSrc>ccna.gif</imgSrc>
          <author>Cisco Certified Internetwork Expert Prog</author>
          <price>49.99</price>
          <title>CCNA Cisco Certified Network Associate Study
Guide</title>
          <description>
             Cisco certification courses are among the fastest-growing
             courses in the training industry, and our guides are
designed
             to help readers thoroughly prepare for the exams.
          </description>
        </Books>
</NewDataSet>
        </diffgr:diffgram>
</DataSet>
```

Summary

In this chapter, we discussed Web Services, along with their related technologies, protocols, and standards, such as Simple Object Access Protocol (SOAP), Web Services Description Language (WSDL), Extensible Markup Language (XML), and the XML Schema Definition (XSD) standard. We examined the role of Web Services and how messages are passed between servers and data sources.

We created simple Web Services (producers) as well as Web Services (consumers) using the .NET Framework and VS.NET Beta 2 to show how the Web Service messaging infrastructure works and how it can be used transparently to the developer.

The power of Web Services is due to its foundation in nonproprietary protocols and standards. Web Services would not be as useful if it were not built on XML for defining data and structure, XSD for defining structure, SOAP for defining a messaging transport mechanism over the well-established HTTP, WSDL for defining method interfaces in XML, Universal Description, Discovery, and Integration (UDDI, a Web Service discovery mechanism), and DISCO, the Web Service discovery description document.

We've covered a lot of ground here. For in-depth examples, see Chapter 12, where we develop several Web Services as wrappers around our data source, for use by an ADO application.

Solutions Fast Track

Web Services

- ☑ Web Services provide an XML interface that can be accessed by any SOAP-enabled client, which means a Web Service developed with .NET can be accessed by a Java application, a Web page, or any SOAP-enabled desktop application.
- ☑ Web Services can be accessed over HTTP through port 80, which means remote procedure calls can be made to objects behind firewalls.

Using XML in Web Services

- ☑ XML is the enabling standard upon which SOAP and Web Services are built.

- ☑ The SOAP envelope is an XML document. The SOAP message, meanwhile, describes the data being passed as an XML representation of the original datatype or object.

An Overview of the *System.Web.Services* Namespace

- ☑ *System.Web.Services* is .NET Framework's namespace of classes that enable .NET Web Services. The three primary subclasses or subnamespaces are:

    1. **System.Web.Services.Description** Classes that support WSDL, used to define the methods, parameters, and datatypes of Web Services.

    2. **System.Web.Services.Discovery** Classes that support UDDI and the generation of WSDL proxies for Web Service clients.

    3. **System.Web.Services.Protocols** Classes that support the generation and customization of Web service protocols, and can be used for things such as creating custom SOAP headers.

Type Marshalling

- ☑ Type marshalling is the mapping of types from Web Service method calls to SOAP datatypes.
- ☑ When remote calls are made using Web Services and the SOAP protocol; datatypes and objects that are passed are represented as XML descriptions of themselves. (Datatypes are marshalled as one of many SOAP standard datatypes.)

Using *DataSets*

- ☑ *DataSets* are ADO.NET objects that provide database type operations.
- ☑ *DataSets* enable the transfer of database structure and content to and from Web Services.

Frequently Asked Questions

The following Frequently Asked Questions, answered by the authors of this book, are designed to both measure your understanding of the concepts presented in this chapter and to assist you with real-life implementation of these concepts. To have your questions about this chapter answered by the author, browse to **www.syngress.com/solutions** and click on the **"Ask the Author"** form.

Q: Why replace COM objects with Web Services?

A: Web Services have a platform neutral interface. This enables Web Services to be easily utilized by multiple clients on different platforms developed with different programming languages. Note that existing COM components can be wrapped by Web Services.

Q: Can I create access to Web Services from a standard ASP page?

A: Yes, you can; however, you might want to look into Microsoft's SOAP toolkit.

Q: How do I know I need Web Services?

A: If you have data that is needed by various customers (different departments, different levels of management, vendors, industry partners, consumers and so on) and getting to that data is hindered or prevented by issues involving platform, programming language, legacy hardware or other types of incompatibility, developing Web Services can help.

Q: What area of development are Web Services best for?

A: I believe that Web Services development like COM development will remain in the hands of the middle tier programmer. Traditionally this was accomplished with C++ and VB programmers, however simple data access type components may be developed by intermediate and advanced ASP developers. While this might still be the case, ASP.NET developers need a firmer grasp of programming with a strongly typed compiled language then their ASP predecessors. This makes the ASP.NET developer more of a middle tier programmer and less of a front-end Web developer. Since building and deploying Web classes and Web Services are relatively easy with VS.NET as compared to traditional COM development. I think the proportion of components built by the ASP developer (using ASP.NET) will be larger than it has been in the past.

Q: Is it possible to try out Web Services using only my local computer?

A: Yes, it is. Using the WSDL.exe command line tool, you can point to any Web server. This is even easier with the VS.NET UI. Simply right-click **Web references**, then select any Web service from the UDDI directory or your local machine, or simply type the URL of a disco file on any server. You can easily generate a WSDL proxy and use it as long as you are connected to the Internet.

Q: I'm currently in the process of migrating. What considerations should I take with my existing COM components?

A: Here are a few things to consider:

- *Who is the customer?* If the customer is only within the intranet and there are no external customers in the foreseeable future, an existing DCOM infrastructure needn't be changed.

- *What type of clients do I have?* If the client is a desktop application, switching to Web Services would require updating the client, which may include updating the OS, and possibly the hardware so that the client has enough memory to host the .NET Framework.

- *Will I need to support Mobile devices in the near future?* Using the .NET Mobile Framework to access Web Services is as simple as it is with .NET. Updating the existing clients to .NET will make adding future clients simple and cost-effective.

Chapter 11

Creating an XML.NET Guestbook

Solutions in this chapter:

- **Functional Design Requirements of the XML.NET Guestbook**
- **Adding Records to the Guestbook**
- **Viewing the Guestbook**
- **Advanced Options for the Guestbook Interface**

☑ Summary
☑ Solutions Fast Track
☑ Frequently Asked Questions

Introduction

Your first case study is a simple online guestbook application, completely coded in ASP.NET. You are going to need to provide the basic functions through this guestbook, namely the ability to do the following:

1. Enable guests to enter messages.
2. Display all messages on one page.
3. Show author, e-mail address of author, and comment from the author of the message.

The flowchart in Figure 11.1 shows the user interaction process that you want to achieve.

Figure 11.1 Basic Functionality Layout

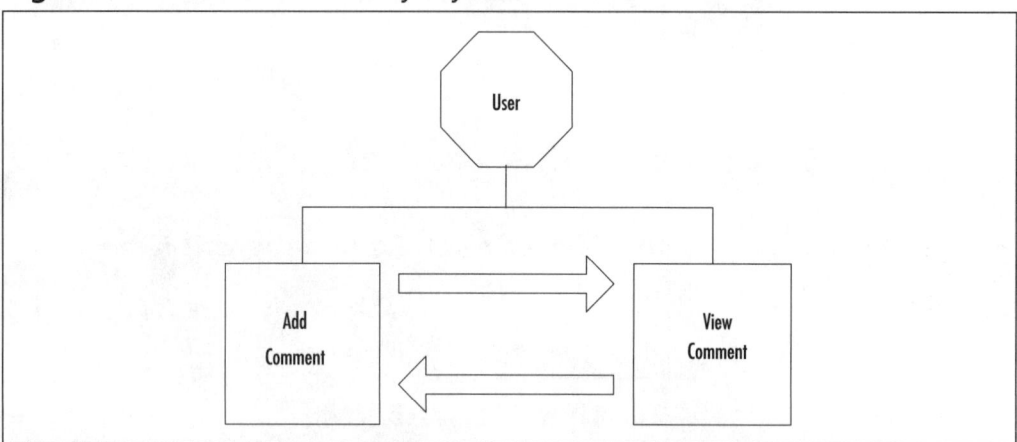

In essence, the user will come to the site and decide if he or she wants to view previous messages or add new messages. The user will be redirected to the view comments page after filling out a new message, or the user viewing the messages has the option to fill out a message.

> **NOTE**
>
> In the CD there are two folders for this chapter, representing two ways of going about this guestbook: one is labeled "basic" and the other is labeled "advanced." We are going to explore both of these.

All of these functions need to be kept as compact as possible. Our backend needs to store the following information for every message that is left on the guestbook:

- Name
- E-mail
- Subject Line
- Actual Comment

The Name, E-mail, Subject Line, and Actual Comment need to be required fields and you need to provide validation for the e-mail field. Also, you need to provide the user with an easy-to-use interface. A basic interface would consist of the user being able to do the following:

1. Choose between adding a new entry and viewing previous entries.
2. Properly locate the corresponding text areas for the entry points.
3. Have real-time validation take place where needed.
4. Reply to a comment left by a user via e-mail.

Functional Design Requirements of the XML Guestbook

Several guestbooks are already available online for download, but most require either a Microsoft Access database or an SQL Server database for storing the guestbook entries and other information pertinent to that guestbook. While both of these tools provide their own strengths and weaknesses, you want to provide an application that is small, quick, and able to stand alone without requiring a separate application to make it work. This type of thought also implies that the application will be small and easy to transfer, if needed. You also need to keep an eye on the code and keep it as small as possible. You need to be able to write directly to the database and read from the database with as little code as possible. Just because you are trying to make the code portable doesn't mean you need to make the code bloat!

So, if you are not going to use a traditional database (such as Microsoft Access or SQL Server), then what can you use that won't kill the application requirements? Back in Chapter 8 we talked about a technology that is turning into a strong database alternative, called XML. XML will enable you to use a text-based approach to your database that does not rely on any ODBC connections or even any server (although your code will pretty much lock you into a server that uses ASP.NET). Also, through an XML schema you can define how our XML "row" will look and what each value must contain.

With your backend solution set at XML you need to determine how you are going to work with the XML file. The logical choice is the *System.XML* namespace, but you can actually find a faster method by using the XML tools that accompany the *System.Data* namespace. Even though *System.XML* is more powerful than *System.Data* when it comes to XML, you simply don't need to rely on so much coding to see your results.

> **NOTE**
>
> The choice of *System.Data* over *System.XML* does *not* mean that *System.XML* is in any way inefficient. It simply means that, as programmers, we sometimes have to choose between a solution that requires more time but is more flexible, and a solution that is quicker but more rigid. *System.XML* is more flexible with XML than *System.Data* will ever be, but all you need for this case study is just to be able to read and write to an XML file. In other words, you are following an age-old adage of programming—K.I.S.—"Keep It Simple!"

Constructing the XML

Even though *System.Data* is viewed more or less as a method of working with traditional database connections, such as a SQL database or an Access database, it can also work with XML data, provided the XML has an inline schema that it can match the data against; almost like looking at the table structure first and then the data within it.

The file gbook.xml (shown in Figure 11.2, and in the Basic directory on the CD that accompanies this book) displays the XML code that we will be working with.

Figure 11.2 gbook.xml (Basic Version)

```
01: <gbook>
02: <xsd:schema id="gbook"
03:             targetNamespace=""
```

Continued

Figure 11.2 Continued

```
04:                xmlns=""
05:                xmlns:xsd="http://www.w3.org/2001/XMLSchema"
06:                xmlns:msdata="urn:schemas-microsoft-com:xml-msdata">
07:
08: <xsd:element name="gbook"
09:              msdata:IsDataSet="true">
10:     <xsd:complexType>
11:     <xsd:choice maxOccurs="unbounded">
12:     <xsd:element name="gbooky">
13:     <xsd:complexType>
14:     <xsd:sequence>
15:         <xsd:element name="Name" type="xsd:string" minOccurs="0" />
16:     <xsd:element name="Chrono" type="xsd:string" minOccurs="0" />
17:     <xsd:element name="Email" type="xsd:string" minOccurs="0" />
18:     <xsd:element name="Comments" type="xsd:string" minOccurs="0" />
19:     </xsd:sequence>
20:     </xsd:complexType>
21:     </xsd:element>
22:     </xsd:choice>
23:     </xsd:complexType>
24: </xsd:element>
25:
26: </xsd:schema>
27: </gbook>
```

Lines 1 and 26 have the root tags for the XML file. In this example, we are using "gbook" but you can use anything. Lines 2 through 6 are one line that we used whitespace to organize the attributes in order for the tag to be more readable. The *targetNamespace* and *xmlns* attributes in the <xsd:schema> tag are left blank since both the *targetNamespace* and *xmlns* are inline. The *xsd* attribute is pointing to the current schema, and the special Microsoft attribute *msdata* points to a Microsoft data compatibility namespace.

> **NOTE**
>
> If you want more information on the XSD and MSDATA attributes, you can find documentation for XML schemas online through http://msdn.microsoft.com/library and www.w3.org/XML/Schema.html.

Lines 8 through 24 construct the element that will store the data. When the data is entered into the corresponding .aspx file, it will format the data within the XML per the data outline within the schema. In this case, a sample entry in our guestbook will appear as the following:

```
<gbooky>
    <Name>Jon Ortiz</Name>
    <Chrono>Time Posted</Chrono>
    <Email>somewhere@overthereainbow.com</Email>
    <Comments>Hola!</Comments>
</gbooky>
```

This information will be created by your application through the *System.Data* namespace. In order to be able to do it, *System.Data* matches the information input to the inline schema and creates the appropriate record. Now that you have set up the "template," you can get started with the code that adds records. Refer to Figure 11.3 for the logic behind the XML file.

Adding Records to the Guestbook

Any veteran ASP developers are going to notice in this section a distinct change. Remember in desktop applications that you formed your GUIs using a Form? Well, in ASP.NET, the Form has been brought to Web development and is referred to as a *Panel*. You are going to work with your code inline for just this chapter so that you can get a good grasp of what a *Panel* looks like and how it works within ASP.NET.

There are no real differences between using a Form for desktop applications and a *Panel* for online applications. Many of the same subs are intact, such as *OnLoad*, and *Panel* can reference any item within the *Panel*, just like in desktops. A great place to view the *Panel* in ASP.NET is within the UI for adding guestbook records. Your file will be called add.aspx, and is the code is displayed in Figure 11.4 (note that some lines wrap), and in the Basic directory on the CD that accompanies this book.

Figure 11.3 Creating a Record Using the XML Schema

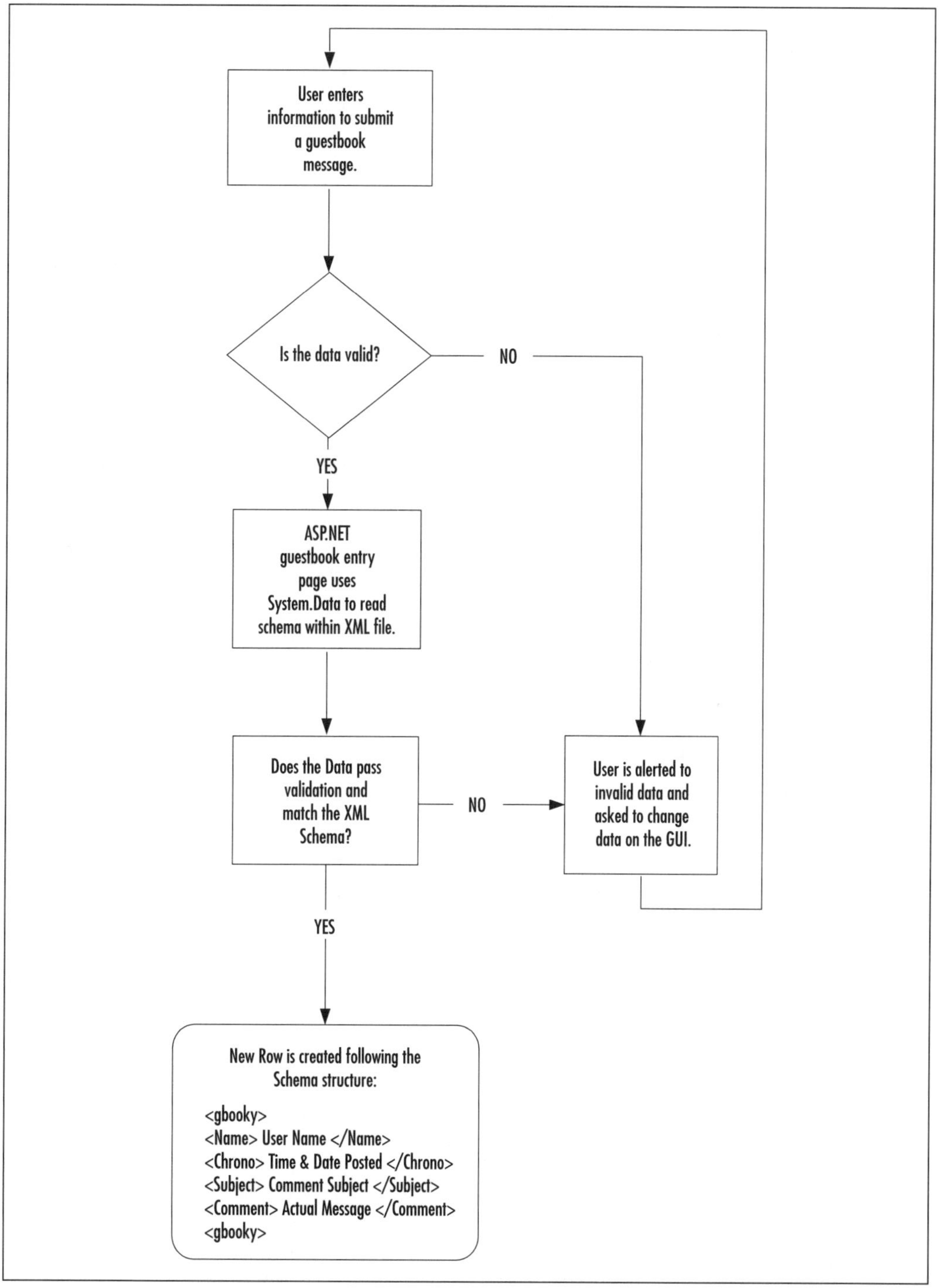

Figure 11.4 Sample ASPX Code add.aspx (Basic Version)

```
01: <%@ Page Language="VB" EnableSessionState="False"%>
02:
03: <%@ Import Namespace="System.IO" %>
04: <%@ Import Namespace="System.Data" %>
05: <html>
06: <head>
07: <title>Add Entry</title>
08: </head>
09: <script language="VB" runat="server" >
10: <!— event handling code here—>
11: </script>
12: </head>
13: <body topmargin="0" leftmargin="0" rightmargin="0" marginwidth="0"
    marginheight="0">
14: <br>
15: <br>
16: <h3 align="center">Guestbook Post Page.</h3>
17: <br>
18: <asp:label id="err" text="" style="color:#FF0000" runat="server" />
19: <asp:Panel id=pnlAdd runat=server>
20: <form action="add.aspx" runat=server>
21:     <table border="0"  width="80%" align="Center">
22:     <tr>
23:     <td><b>Sign-in My GuestBook</b></td>
24:     <td> </td>
25:     </tr>
26:     <tr>
27:     <td>Name :</td>
28:     <td><asp:textbox text="" id="Name" runat="server" />
    <asp:RequiredFieldValidator ControlToValidate=Name display=static
    runat=server>*</asp:RequiredFieldValidator></td>
29:     </tr>
30:     <tr>
```

Continued

Figure 11.4 Continued

```
31:      <td>E-Mail :</td>
32:      <td><asp:textbox text="" id="Email" runat="server"/>
    <asp:RequiredFieldValidator ControlToValidate=Email display=static
    runat=server> *</asp:RequiredFieldValidator>
    <asp:RegularExpressionValidator runat="server"
            ControlToValidate="Email"
            ValidationExpression="[\w-]+@([\w-]+\.)+[\w-]+"
            Display="Static"
            Font-Name="verdana" Font-Size="10pt">Please enter a valid
            e-mail address</asp:RegularExpressionValidator>
33:      </td>
34:      </tr>
35:      <tr>
36:      <td>Comments :</td>
37:      <td><asp:Textbox textmode=multiline id="Comments" columns="25"
         rows="4" runat="server" />
38:      </td>
39:      </tr>
40:      <tr>
41:      <td colspan="2" >
42:      <asp:Button Text="Submit Post" onClick="AddClick"
         runat="server" /></td>
43:      </tr>
44: </table>
45: </form>
46: </asp:Panel>
47:
48: <asp:Panel id=pnlThank visible=false runat=server>
49: <p align=center><b>Thank you for posting in my Guestbook!</b><br>
50: <a href="viewbook.aspx">Click here </a> to view GuestBook.
51: </p>
```

Continued

Figure 11.4 Continued

```
52:     </asp:Panel>
53:   </body>
54: </html>
```

It may look daunting at first, but it really is quite simple. Remember that in ASP.NET you first should declare the language the page is going to be using. While it is redundant, since the language declaration on the <script> tag determines the actual language use, it is still a good coding practice to get into. Lines 2 through 4 declare the namespaces that you are going to use—*System*, *System.IO*, and *System.Data*. Lines 5 through 8 just display the HTML code that needs to be in every single HTML page.

You then hit the script tag that controls the **Submit** button event (lines 9 through 10). For now it's just a placeholder for the code you'll be adding in later. Notice that the code is placed at the head of the html file, which means that it will be processed before anything else. You'll look at the Submit button event after you dissect this portion of the ASP.NET page.

Understanding the *pnlAdd* Panel

On line 19 of Figure 11.4, *pnlAdd* is declared; it is the name of the panel that contains the programming code displaying the messages and text boxes that the user will be viewing on the page, in order to enter the guestbook entry data; e.g., the name area, the name entry textbox, the e-mail area, the e-mail entry textbox, the comment area, the comment entry textbox, and the Submit button. In other words, it is your run-of-the-mill HTML form but with ASPX. In reality there are only two "normal" form objects; the name textbox is your standard text object, and the comment area is your standard multilane textbox.

The e-mail area, however, is another story. Take a look at the behemoth of a line that you'll find in line 32:

```
<asp:textbox text="" id="Email" runat="server"/
    ><asp:RequiredFieldValidator ControlToValidate=Email display=static
    runat=server> *</asp:RequiredFieldValidator>
    <asp:RegularExpressionValidator runat="server"
            ControlToValidate="Email"
            ValidationExpression="[\w-]+@([\w-]+\.)+[\w-]+"
            Display="Static"
```

```
            Font-Name="verdana" Font-Size="10pt">Please enter a valid
    e-mail address</asp:RegularExpressionValidator>
```

Starting from the top, you find your standard *ASPcontrol* declaration as a textbox with its default text set to empty and an ID of "E-mail." Right after it comes the ASP control declaration for *RequiredFieldValidator* set to validate the control labeled "E-mail" and with a static display. You then implement two types of validation to the field. The first validation is through the *RegularFieldValidator* control:

```
<asp:RequiredFieldValidator ControlToValidate=Email display=static
    runat=server>This is required.</asp:RequiredFieldValidator>
```

All you are doing here is a quick check to see if the field is empty or not. If the user skips the field and leaves it empty, then a little message in red shows up saying that "This is required." You don't have to use that text but it works for this example. Our second round of validation begins right after that line with the more intense *RegularExpressionValidator* object:

```
<asp:RegularExpressionValidator runat="server"
            ControlToValidate="Email"
            ValidationExpression="[\w-]+@([\w-]+\.)+[\w-]+"
            Display="Static"
            Font-Name="verdana" Font-Size="10pt">Please enter a valid
            e-mail address</asp:RegularExpressionValidator>
```

Developing & Deploying…

Stricter E-Mail Validation

The method of e-mail validation demonstrated in this chapter is not the only option available to you. There is a stricter method for e-mail validation that would only enable the user to input a .com, .org, .edu, .mil, .gov, or .net:

```
ValidationExpression = "^[\w-]+@[\w-]+\.(com|net|org|edu|mil|gov)$"
```

You first set the object to bind itself to the E-mail control. It will be analyzing the contents within the E-mail object to see if it falls under the Validation Expression that it has been given; in this case, it checks to see that an "@" symbol as well as a "." is present within the string. You may want to read up on *RegEx* to fully understand what variables can be used with Regular Expressions.

Adding a Thank-You Panel with *PnlThank*

All you are doing here is declaring a panel that will show up after a successful guestbook entry has been added to the XML file. The link in order to view the guestbook is declared and set. Very simple and very quick, to the point, starting on line 48 (Figure 11.4):

```
<asp:Panel id=pnlThank visible=false runat=server>
<p align=center><b>Thank you for posting in my Guestbook!</b><br>
<a href="viewbook.aspx">Click here </a> to view GuestBook.
</p>
</asp:Panel>
```

Exploring the Submit Button Handler Code

Now that you have established your design and layout, you can take a look at the code that actually handles the addition of new entries into the guestbook. The basic functionality of this code is to react to the Submit button when pressed, and write the necessary items to the XML file. Figure 11.5 walks you through an overview of the Submit button code.

Figure 11.5 Submit Button Handler Code for add.aspx (Basic Version)

```
01:     Sub AddClick(Sender As Object, E As EventArgs)
02:
03:         Try
04:         Dim dataFile as String = "gb/gbook.xml"
05:
06:         'the next line wraps
07:         Dim fin as New FileStream (Server.MapPath(dataFile),
    FileMode.Open,FileAccess.Read,FileShare.ReadWrite)
08:
09:         'this line also wraps
```

Continued

Figure 11.5 Continued

```
10:            Dim fout as New FileStream (Server.MapPath(dataFile),
     FileMode.Open,FileAccess.Write,FileShare.ReadWrite)
11:
12:            Dim guestData as New DataSet()
13:            Dim newRow as DataRow
14:            err.Text = ""
15:            guestData.ReadXml(fin)
16:            fin.Close()
17:            newRow = guestData.Tables(0).NewRow()
18:            newRow("Name")=Name.Text
19:            newRow("Chrono")=DateTime.Now.ToString()
20:            newRow("Email")=Email.Text
21:            newRow("Comments")=Comments.Text
22:            guestData.Tables(0).Rows.Add(newRow)
23:            guestData.WriteXml(fout, XmlWriteMode.WriteSchema)
24:            fout.Close()
25:            pnlAdd.Visible=false
26:            pnlThank.Visible=true
27:
28:            Catch edd As Exception
29:            err.Text="Error writing file at: " & edd.ToString()
30:
31:            End Try
32:
33: End Sub
34: </script>
```

Line 1 starts you off with your VB code, declaring itself a code segment that is run on the server-side and written using VB. Line 1 uses an ASP.NET form subnamed "AddClick"; this code segment will be providing all of the functionality of the Submit button.

On line 3, you start taking advantage of one of VB's newest and very useful feature, error trapping. Your try/catch segment starts out by declaring a variable to store the location of your XML file, which can be any directory. You can just assume that for this example it's in the *gb* directory on the root folder of the site. With the location of the file stored, you can open up a *FileStream* object to open and process the XML file for you. *FileStream* needs to know the actual location of the file (not the virtual location) of the file, so you use *Server.MapPath()* to return the actual location of the file to your *FileStream* object, which you can then open (*FileMode.Open*) and start reading (*FileAccess.Read*). You can also tell *FileStream* how to handle other events, such as sharing; by telling *FileStream* to allow read/write sharing of the file (*FileShare.ReadWrite*), you don't have to worry about your XML file suffering from any file locking, which would prevent any other user from editing the file and getting them a nasty error.

> **Migrating ...**
>
> **Online Forms**
>
> As you have noticed and learned throughout this book, ASP.NET enables programmers to use Web forms, which can be described as the VB6.0 desktop form. In this particular example, your "AddClick" sub would be placed within the *OnClick()* event for whatever button you wanted to use as your trigger for this action. One other little trick is to view each "panel" as a small form within an mdi, namely the browser window, with their own "hide" and "show" features.

With your XML file stored within the *fout* object (line 10 in Figure 10.5) you can start to create the object that will handle parsing the data, *DataType*, and properly formatting it and writing to the XML file, *DataRow*. Specifically, *DataType* will handle reading the information and transforming it to a table format. *DataRow* will then use the information stored within your *DataType* object to create a new row with the columns that it finds within the *DataType* object. In other words, when *DataType* reads your XML file, it will see the root element "gbook" as your table, "gbooky" as your rows, and all the information within "gbooky" as columns. It will write the information out accordingly to the XML file. It will know what it's writing since it's using the inline schema (Figure 10.2) to write to the file per the schema, using the *WriteXML* class of the *DataType* object and having it write the stream matching the XMLSchema (XMLWriteMode.WriteSchema). You then hide the panel that contains the text boxes and Submit button, and make the panel that contains the "Thank You" message. Figures 10.6 and 10.7 show the basic add.aspx file before and after filling out a new entry.

Figure 11.6 Before Adding a New Entry

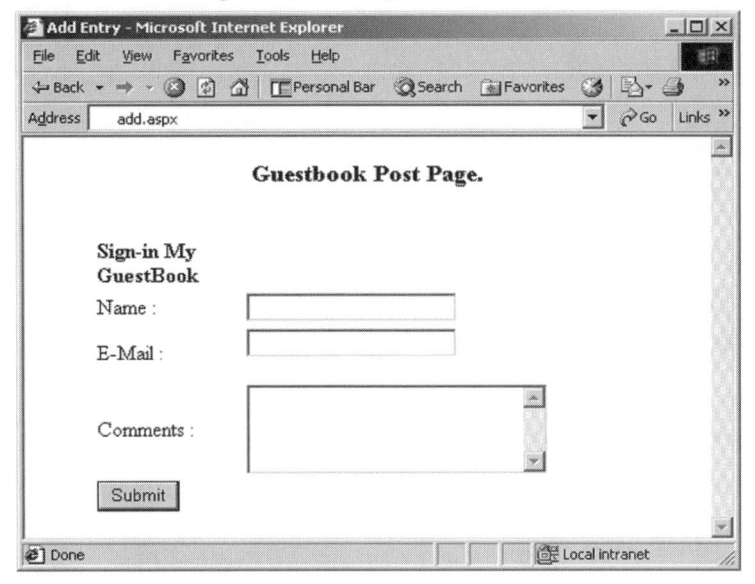

Figure 11.7 After Adding a New Entry

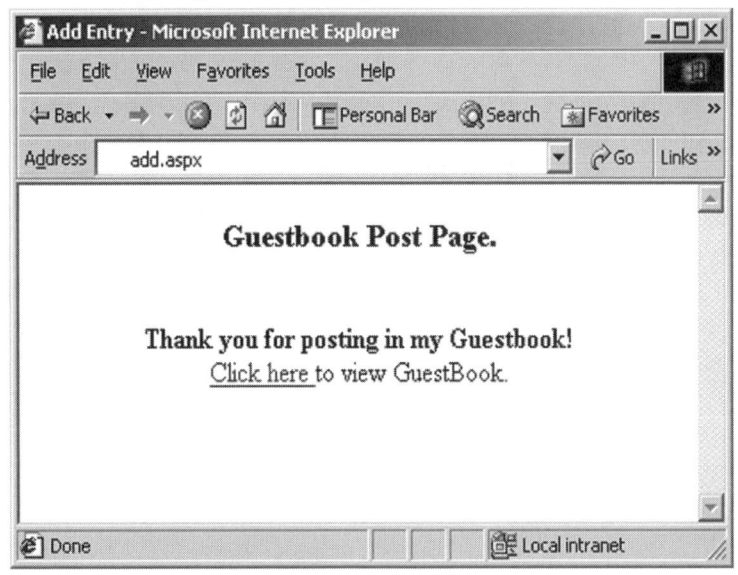

> **Developing & Deploying…**
>
> **File Locking**
>
> File Locking is a basic response to multiple users trying to read and modify the same file at around the same time. I say at "around" the same time because File Locking will take place if the file is accessed at the same time, or if access is attempted after someone already has access to it. By preventing multiple users from reading and writing the file, you avoid file corruption and constant backup restorations. File Locking allows a temporary "lock" to be placed to the file that allows for changes to be made one after the other without damaging the integrity of the file.

Viewing the Guestbook

One line of actual ASPX code—that's about as simple as it gets, and done just by using the built-in XML server control. You may remember in Chapter 3 that ASP.NET has several controls built in to facilitate many different HTML functions, such as displaying radio buttons and handling forms, which allows ASP.NET to generate items fairly on-the-fly. XML is no exception to this rule.

Displaying Messages

Here is our one-line masterpiece, as shown in Figure 11.8. In essence, all we did to get the sample output shown in Figure 11.8 was just to tell the ASP.NET XML control to read the data in gbook.xml, and to transform it according to the XSL information in gbook.xsl. It is displayed in Figure 11.9 and can be found in the gb folder in the Basic directory on the CD that accompanies this book. Figure 11.10 shows us the output.

Figure 11.8 viewplain.aspx (Basic Directory)

```
01: <html>
02: <head>
03: <title>XML Control Test</title>
04: </head>
05: <body bgcolor="#000000">
```

Continued

Figure 11.8 Continued

```
06: <!-- line 7 wraps -->
07: <asp:xml id="gbook" DocumentSource="gb/gbook.xml"
    TransformSource="gb/gbook.xsl" runat="server"/>
08: </body>
09: </html>
```

Figure 11.9 gbook.xsl

```
01: <?xml version="1.0"?>
02:
03: <!-- this line wraps -->
04: <xsl:stylesheet xmlns:xsl="http://www.w3.org/1999/XSL/Transform"
    version="1.0">
05:
06: <xsl:template match="/">
07:
08: <xsl:for-each select="gbook/gbooky">
09: <table width = "400">
10: <!-- this line wraps -->
11: <tr><font color="#FFFFFF" face="Arial Black"><xsl:value-of
    select="Name"/></font></tr>
12:
13: <!-- this line wraps -->
14: <tr><font color="#FFFFFF" face="Arial Black"><br /><xsl:value-of
    select="Chrono"/></font></tr>
15:
16: <!-- this line wraps -->
17: <tr><font color="#FFFFFF" face="Arial Black"><br /><xsl:value-of
    select="Email"/></font></tr>
18:
19: <!-- this line wraps -->
20: <tr><font face="Arial, Helvetica, sans-serif" size="2"
    color="#C7B29A"><p><xsl:value-of
```

Continued

Figure 11.9 Continued

```
         select="Comments"/></p><p></p></font></tr>
21:
22: </xsl:for-each>
23: </table>
24: </xsl:template>
25: </xsl:stylesheet>
```

Figure 11.10 Viewing Basic Guestbook Entries

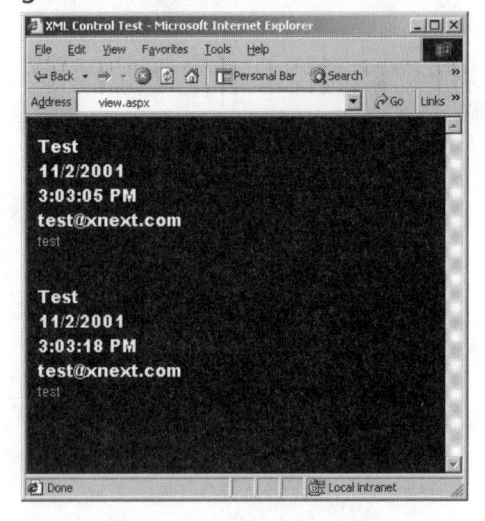

> **NOTE**
>
> If you have no other recourse but to use XSL to also generate your hyperlinks, the fastest work around to this is will be to simply add the <a> element with an attribute of *href* and nesting the *e-mail* element.

Advanced Options for the Guestbook Interface

Now that you have a good understanding of a guestbook and how it works, you can try to do something you haven't done yet—actually make it look cool! Just because you are working with ASP.NET does not mean that you cannot use its new tricks to come up with some really jazzy items and tweak your XML a bit. Let's start by looking at your guestbook entry page.

Manipulating Colors and Images

Clearly this is a design point and not a very strong showing of ASP.NET. However, how you design your page is just as vital as how you design a graphical user interface. In this example, I made the design pleasing to the eye, and I try to use a couple of design techniques to lure the user's eye to the proper areas on the add screen. While these are basic points, it's a good idea to keep the following in mind:

1. Is the area visible on most monitors? (Start off at 800x600 resolution.)
2. Will the user be able to understand what to do?
3. If the user cannot easily figure out what to do, should an easy-to-find help link be visible, or should you perhaps change the design?

One of the nice things about ASP.NET controls is that you can still use tags with them. In fact, this second version of my add entry page looks so nice because I'm using a Cascading Style Sheet (CSS) script with it (in the CD that accompanies this book as gbook.css in the Advanced directory). Another part of this new design that you haven't seen before are the emoticons. Emoticons add a little bit of interactivity to the guestbook by enabling users to pick an image that reflects their "feelings" at the time of posting. You will have to add a couple of changes to the XML file and to the add.aspx file as well as to the view.aspx file in order to display the images. Figure 11.11 will show you how the new add.aspx page will look before and Figure 11.12 after entering a message.

Line 16 in Figure 11.13 reflects the change from the previous XML code; all that happened was just to create a new element of "img" to under complex type "gbook." Your code will read this value and assign the correct image for it. For right now all you are doing is just preparing the inline schema to support the value so that when you store the data it will know where to put it.

Figure 11.11 add.aspx Before Entering a Comment (Advanced Version)

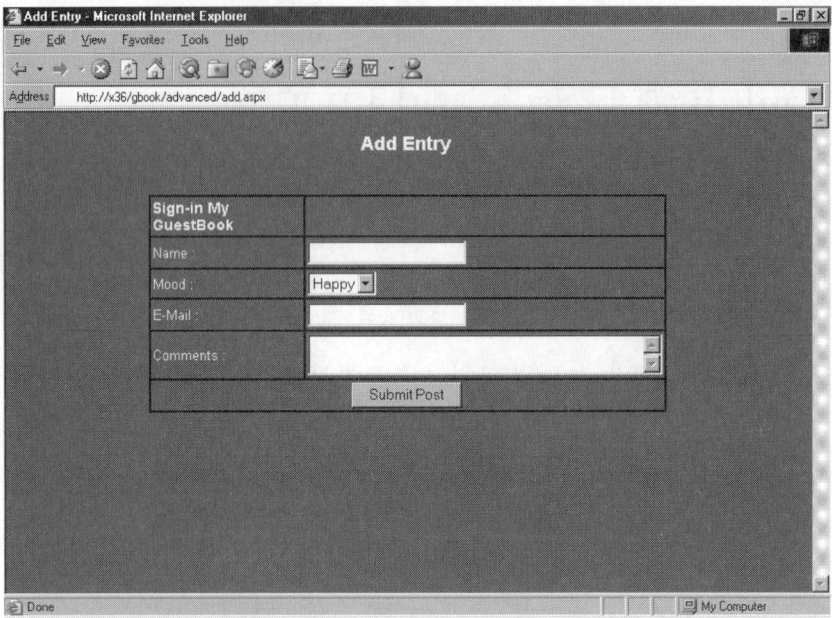

Figure 11.12 add.aspx After Entering a Comment (Advanced Version)

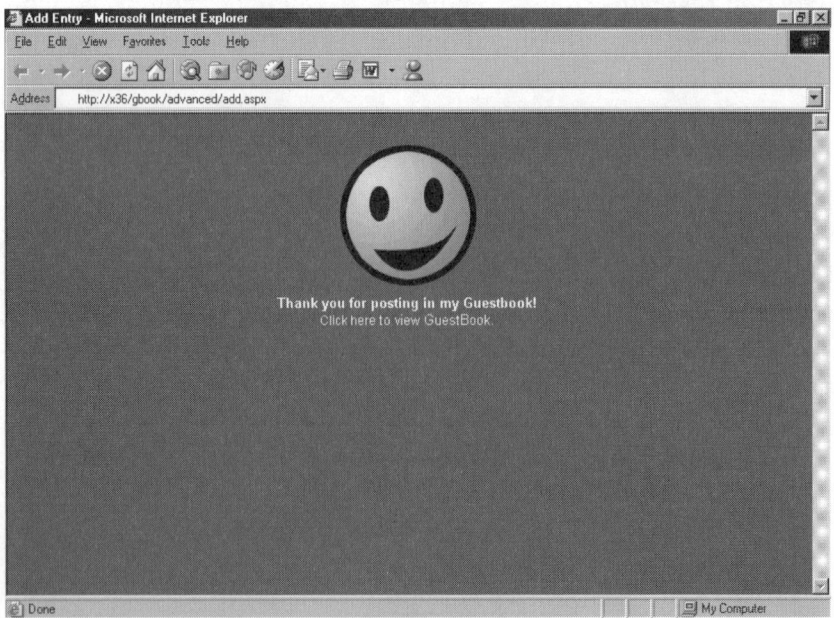

Figure 11.13 gbook.xml (Advanced Version)

```
01:    <gbook>
. . .
14:        <xsd:sequence>
15:            <xsd:element name="Name" type="xsd:string" minOccurs="0" />
16:         <xsd:element name="Emoticon" type="xsd:string" minOccurs="0" />
17:            <xsd:element name="Email" type="xsd:string" minOccurs="0" />
18:            <xsd:element name="Comments" type="xsd:string" minOccurs="0" />
19:            <xsd:element name="DateTime" type="xsd:string" minOccurs="0" />
20:        </xsd:sequence>
```

Now for your code; first, you have to add the new row to your Submit button handler at the top in order to include the new *Emoticon* element within the XML (Figure 11.14).

Figure 11.14 Your Changed add.aspx Submit Handler Code (Advanced Version)

```
10:        Sub AddClick(Sender As Object, E As EventArgs)
11:
12:            Try
13:                Dim dataFile as String = "gb/gbook.xml"
14:
15:                'the next line wraps pretty badly
16:                Dim fin as New FileStream (Server.MapPath(dataFile),
        FileMode.Open,FileAccess.Read,FileShare.ReadWrite)
17:
18:                'this line also wraps pretty badly
19:                Dim fout as New FileStream (Server.MapPath(dataFile),
        FileMode.Open,FileAccess.Write,FileShare.ReadWrite)
20:
21:                Dim guestData as New DataSet()
```

Continued

Figure 11.14 Continued

```
22:             Dim newRow as DataRow
23:             err.Text = ""

24:             guestData.ReadXml(fin)
25:             fin.Close()
26:             newRow = guestData.Tables(0).NewRow()
27:             newRow("Name")=Name.Text
28:             newRow("Emoticon")=Emoticon.Value
29:             newRow("Chrono")=DateTime.Now.ToString()
30:             newRow("Email")=Email.Text
31:             newRow("Comments")=Comments.Text
32:             guestData.Tables(0).Rows.Add(newRow)
33:             guestData.WriteXml(fout, XmlWriteMode.WriteSchema)
34:             fout.Close()
35:             formPanel.Visible=false
36:             thankPanel.Visible=true
37:
38:         Catch edd As Exception
39:             err.Text="Error writing file at: " & edd.ToString()
40:
41:         End Try
42:
43: End Sub
44: </script>
```

The final change to your add entry is an option button for the image selection; you can add this code anywhere in the add.aspx within the display area. We set ours right after the name.

```
<tr>
<td>Mood :</td>
<td><select id="Emoticon" runat="server">
<option Value="01.gif">Happy</option>
<option Value="02.gif">Sad</option>
<option Value="03.gif">Cute</option>
```

```
<option Value="04.gif">Ugly</option>
</select>
</td>
</tr>
```

Modifying the Page Output

You don't really want to display the same boring, old structured output, so try using some tables to break things up a bit. You are going to take a look at this code a bit differently by starting with the page load code (Figure 11.15).

Figure 11.15 view.aspx (Advanced Version)

```
Sub Page_Load(Src As Object, E As EventArgs)
 Dim ds As New DataSet
 Dim fs As New FileStream(Server.MapPath("gb\gbook.xml"),
FileMode.Open)
 ds.ReadXml(fs)
 gbook.DataSource = ds.Tables(0).DefaultView
 gbook.DataBind()
 fs.close()
End Sub
```

You are telling the server that when the page loads (before ANYTHING else is processed, including HTML) create a dataset (ds) and a filestream (fs) to the XML file. Then you tell the dataset (ds) to read the XML file and bind the information to the *"gbook"* object with the information contained in the dataset. You close the *filestream* and finish your initialization code. Your display code has undergone some major changes as well (see Figure 11.16, note that some lines wrap).

Figure 11.16 Your Changed Display Code add.aspx (Advanced Version)

```
01: <%@ Page Language = "VB" Debug="true" %>
02: <%@ Import Namespace="System.IO" %>
03: <%@ Import Namespace="System.Data" %>
04: <html>
05: <script language="VB" runat="server">
        . . .
```

Continued

Figure 11.16 Continued

```
06: </script>
07:
08: <body>
09: <h3>Advanced Guestbook</h3>
10: <ASP:Repeater id="gbook" runat="server">
11: <headertemplate>
12: <table width="350" style="font: 12pt Arial">
13: </headertemplate>
14:
15: <itemtemplate>
15:    <tr>
16:       <%# DataBinder.Eval(Container.DataItem, "Name") %>
17:       <img src="<%# DataBinder.Eval(Container.DataItem, "Emoticon")
          %>" >
18:       <%# DataBinder.Eval(Container.DataItem, "Chrono") %>
19:    </tr>
20:    <tr>
21:       <a href="mailto: <%# DataBinder.Eval(Container.DataItem,
          "Email") %>"><%# DataBinder.Eval(Container.DataItem, "Email")
          %></a>
22:    </tr>
23:    <tr>
24:       <%# DataBinder.Eval(Container.DataItem, "Comments") %>
25: </tr>
26: </itemtemplate>
27:
28: <footertemplate>
29: </table>
30: </footertemplate>
31:
32: </ASP:Repeater>
33: </body>
34: </html>
```

> **NOTE**
>
> This code has had all of the graphical changes stripped; if you want to see the code as the screenshots display it, please check the code on the accompanying CD.

Instead of using the asp:xml server control, you are using the Repeater control and a *DataSource*. Lines 2 and 3 have the two namespaces that you are going to need for your script tag. *System.IO* handles the *Filestream* object and *System.Data* handles the *DataSource* object. The information acquired from the *Page_Load* sub will generate the information that is bound to the *Repeater* object. The *Repeater* object (id="gbook") will read the information bound to it, write the header, and then repeat the sequence within the item template until it finishes; then the footer will be written and the *asp:repeater* object will close. Line 17 shows your only change to the *Repeater* by adding the link to the image stored by the image tag. The code above plus the graphical add-ons gives you the happy result as seen in Figure 11.17.

Figure 11.17 view.aspx + graphics (Advanced Version)

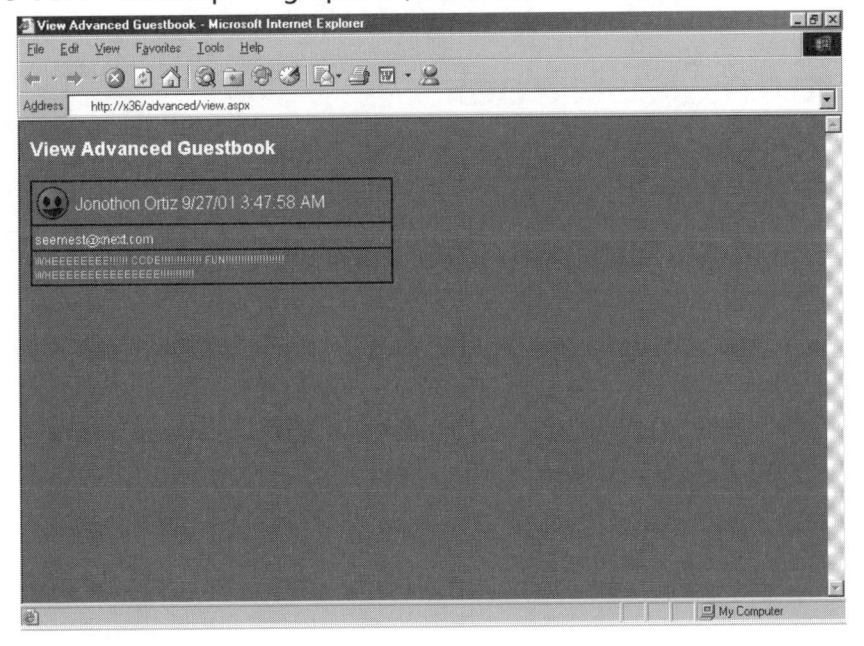

Summary

Well, we started off with basically nothing and finished up with something that is not only useful but can be pleasing to the eye as well. Hopefully this chapter has introduced some concepts that are useful, not only to your hobby programming but also in your work.

XML and ASP.NET can work well together in a variety of ways: from simple reading and writing to proper design and look. Using a combination of either the *System.Data* namespace and the ASP server objects, you can create a single-line parsing .aspx page or a more robust page with tables, rows, columns, and different colors and graphics. In order to achieve the best performance available, the *System.Data* namespace requires an inline schema within the XML file, which the *System.Data* namespace can reference against when reading or writing XML.

ASP server objects themselves are very flexible in that they can be stand-alone and provide an area to insert inline ASPX code. In the Advanced guestbook, you made heavy use of the inline functions, wrapping table rows and columns around them to provide a view that was readable. Also, by using an inline function you were able to receive the correct image file associated for an emoticon, by placing it within the image html tag. Combined with Cascading Style Sheets (CSS), this method proved capable and provided ample room to grow with.

Solutions Fast Track

Functional Design Requirements of the XML.NET Guestbook

- ☑ XML enables you to use an interface that is both universally read and universally accessed. You do not have to use bulky components such as SQL or Access databases for simple—and even some complicated—database solutions.

- ☑ XML provides a schema to use with XML in order to provide validation for data.

Adding Records to the Guestbook

- ☑ When working with the *System.Data* namespace and planning to write XML, you need to make sure that you have a properly validated inline XML schema, or else the code will not work.

- ☑ Even though you can use the XML schema to help determine certain validation points, it is better to have the ASP.NET provide the validation of certain entries, such as e-mail, due to the powerful use of Regular Expressions.

Viewing the Guestbook

- ☑ Using *System.Data* can provide a fast, efficient forward-only read and write solution that is perfect for reading and writing to XML files that are not dependant on heavy node interaction, and that just need information added to them.

- ☑ Cascading Style Sheets provide a way to create a more pleasing guestbook without having to change any code structure.

Advanced Options for the Guestbook Interface

- ☑ The ASP.NET controls are very versatile and efficient. Keep in mind that by combining them with Cascading Style Sheets, their obvious lack of visual aids are easily bypassed for a true eye-candy feel.

- ☑ The *asp:repeater* object needs to have a <headertemplate>, an <itemtemplate>, and a <footertemplate> within it to function.

- ☑ The only part of the *asp:repeater* object that actually repeats is the <itemtemplate> section.

www.syngress.com

Frequently Asked Questions

The following Frequently Asked Questions, answered by the authors of this book, are designed to both measure your understanding of the concepts presented in this chapter and to assist you with real-life implementation of these concepts. To have your questions about this chapter answered by the author, browse to **www.syngress.com/solutions** and click on the **"Ask the Author"** form.

Q: Why does the add.aspx code need the inline XML schema?

A: Add.aspx uses the schema to retrieve the way it needs to write the data to the XML file in the proper order. Say that instead of name before e-mail, you had e-mail before name; add.aspx would write the row with the e-mail field first instead of the name field.

Q: Why won't the simple guestbook show?

A: .NET expects www.w3.org/1999/XSL/Transform as the XSLT namespace. This does limit you a bit, since the Working Draft version is extremely better than the 1999 version.

Q: I get an error that says, "compilation error, (*addClick* or *Page_Load*) is not part of asp:(add.aspx or viewbook.aspx)". What does that mean?

A: Unfortunately, some of the error handling for ASP.NET still needs tweaking; this is a perfect example. When running the aspx page, it will spit out errors when it finds them within the asp objects, but is not very good at reporting errors within the subs located within the <head> tag. When you see these errors, check the code and try again.

Chapter 12

Creating an ADO.NET Shopping Cart

Solutions in this chapter:

- **Setting Up the Database**
- **Creating the Web Services**
- **Using WSDL Web References**
- **Building the Site**
- **Site Administration**
- **Customer Administration**
- **Creating an ADOCatalog**
- **Building an XMLCart**
- **Creating the User Interface**
- ☑ Summary
- ☑ Solutions Fast Track
- ☑ Frequently Asked Questions

Introduction

Now that we've gotten XML under our belt, let's start working with ADO.NET. A good way to really see what ADO can do is within the frame of a shopping cart application. In this chapter, we will create a shopping cart application for a fictitious online bookseller called "Book Shop."

To enable online shoppers to purchase books from our site, our shopping cart application must be able to: authenticate users, show current contents of the cart, and enable add, update, and checkout operations.

We will also need to create a catalog that our shoppers can browse through to add items to their cart. Users should also be able to query books by category and view a range of books at a time. In order to achieve these goals, we will create the following:

- A database to store all book details
- Stored procedures (MS SQL 2000) or parameterized queries (MS Access 2000) for all add, update, delete, and retrieve operations
- Web Services that will handle all database interactions
- Web Services Description Language (WSDL) Web references to our Web Services
- Server-side classes that will connect the Web Services with our user interface (UI)
- Web interface for displaying both our catalog and cart

We will also need to create admin interfaces to handle add, update, delete, and retrieve operations for our customers (site users) and site administrators. The interface that will be created in our example can be seen in Figure 12.1.

Setting Up the Database

First, we will design the database for our shopping cart. We will start out by designing an MS Access 2000 database which we will then upsize to a SQL Server 2000 database.

We are creating what is called a *relational database*. A relational database is a series of tables that represent entities related to one another. Let's look at a simple example to help illustrate this point: our database. See Figure 12.2.

Figure 12.1 The "Book Shop" User Interface

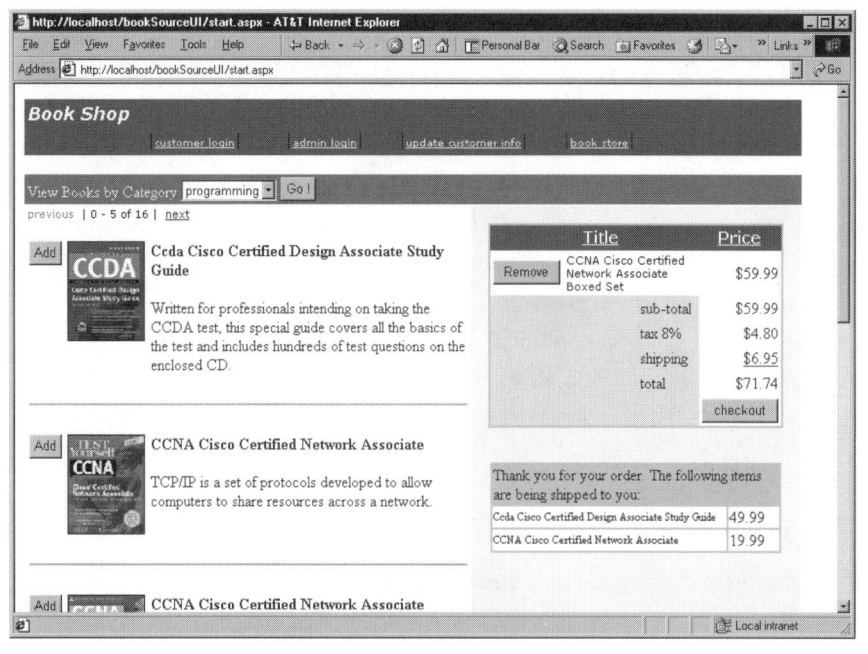

Figure 12.2 Table Relationship

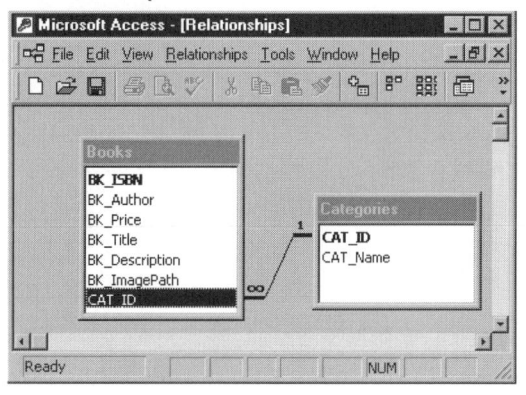

> **NOTE**
>
> To set up the database in this example, you will need to know some basic fundamentals of database design. A good source is Syngress Publishing's *Designing SQL Server 2000 Databases for .NET Enterprise Servers*.

Table "Books" is an entity that represents all the attributes of a book. Table "Categories" is an entity that represents all the attributes for a specific category. A relationship between the two tables is created by the use of *primary* and *foreign keys*. Table "Categories" has an attribute named *CAT_ID*, which is the primary key for the table. This means simply that *CAT_ID* uniquely identifies every row in the table. This will ensure we won't get duplicate rows of data. The same concept is true for the table "Books." We can create the relationship between the two tables by putting the attribute *CAT_ID* into the table "Books." By doing so, we have created a foreign key in the table "Books" which references the table "Categories." We have now created a *one-to-many* relationship between the table "Books" and the table "Categories."

There are three different types of table relationships:

- **One-to-one** Exactly one row corresponds with a matching row of the related table.

- **One-to-many** One row corresponds to many rows of the related table.

- **Many-to-many** Many rows correspond to many rows of the related table.

> **WARNING**
>
> A many-to-many relationship between tables is not a recommended practice. When this type of relationship is created in the design of your database, use a splitter table in-between the two tables that have the affected relationship. This will create two one-to-many relationships and ensure data integrity for your database.

We will now create the *entities* for our shopping cart application. Entities enable us to map the real world. Since we are making a shopping cart, we need some basic objects to start off with. First of all, we need product. We have chosen to use "Books" as the product for the shopping cart but this could be anything. Next, we need an object that will be using the shopping cart, "Customers." As in the previous paragraph, we have more than one category of product, or in our case "Books," so we have another object to map which is "Categories." The last piece to finish off the whole design is a way to track what is bought, "BookOrders." Now we need to go over each entity to explain why we have selected the attributes included in each.

Setting Up the Table "Books"

The Books table will contain the following attributes:

- **BK_ISBN** This will also be our Primary key for the table since an ISBN is already a global unique identifier.
- **BK_Author** This contains the author's full name.
- **BK_Price** The price of the book.
- **BK_Title** The book title.
- **BK_Description** A brief description of the book.
- **BK_ImagePath** The path to where we will store the image.
- **CAT_ID** Our foreign key attribute to table "Categories."

Setting Up the Table "Categories"

The Categories table will contain the following attributes:

- **CAT_ID** The primary key for the table which will be an auto generated number; I will cover this in the next two sections.
- **CAT_Name** The name of the category.

Setting Up the Table "Customer"

The Customer table will contain the following attributes:

- **CT_ID** The primary key for the table, an auto generated number.
- **CT_FirstName** Customer first name.
- **CT_LastName** Customer last name.
- **CT_Email** Customer e-mail.
- **CT_Password** Customer password.

Setting Up the Table "Orders"

The Orders table will contain the following attributes:

- **OR_ID** The primary key for the table, an auto generated number.
- **CT_ID** This is our foreign key attribute to table "Customers."

- **OR_Date** The date of the order.
- **OR_ShippedDate** The date the order ships.

Setting Up the Table "BookOrders"

The BookOrders table is the split table for the handling of our relationship between the tables "Books" and "Orders." This table includes the following attributes:

- **OR_ID** This is our foreign key attribute to table "Orders." This is also part of the composite Primary key for the table.
- **BK_ISBN** This is our foreign key attribute to table "Books." This is the other part of the composite primary key.
- **BKOR_Quantity** The total of number of books.
- **BKOR_Price** The total amount of the order.

Now, lets implement this database in Microsoft Access.

> **NOTE**
>
> It is good practice to come up with a naming convention for your database. The naming convention can be anything of your choosing, just make sure you're consistent throughout your database. A naming convention is a uniformed way to document your code. In our example, *OR_denotes* the table "Orders."

Creating an Access Database

To create a database in Microsoft Access, simply navigate to your program files and select the Access icon. The main window will pull up, prompting you to either pick a database from the list of current databases, create a blank database, or use the wizard. See Figure 12.3.

We want to select the **Blank Database** option and not the wizard. Select **OK**, then give the database the name **shopDb**. Next, select the **Tables** object. From here, we choose the option **Create table in design view**. We can now transfer the attributes for the tables into the interface (see Figure 12.4).

Figure 12.3 Setting Up the Access Database

Figure 12.4 Creating Tables in Design View

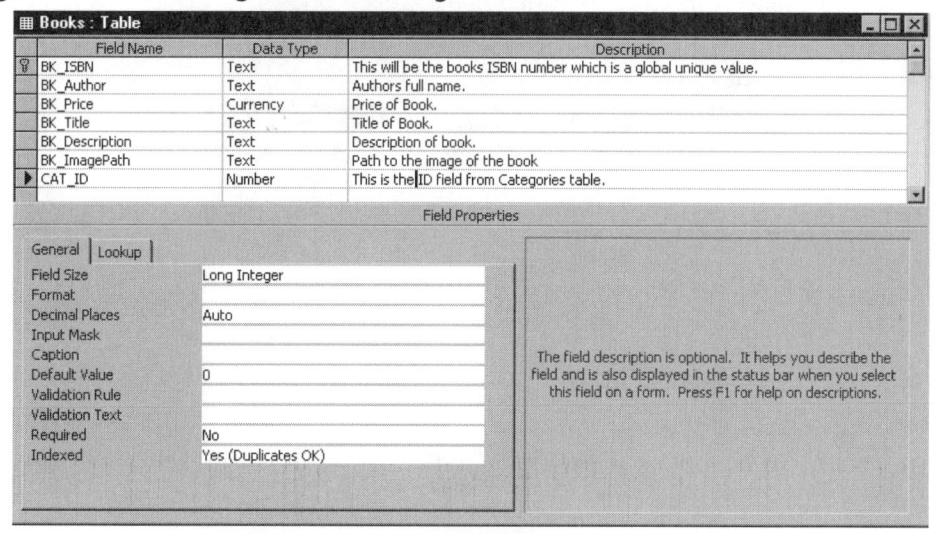

Now we can transfer almost everything that's been done into the interface. One thing we have not discussed is *datatypes*.

The following is a list of datatypes we will implement in the database:

- **Text** Text or combinations of text and numbers: maximum size 255 characters.

- **Currency** Used for monetary functions, prevents rounding off of total: size 8 bytes.

- **AutoNumber** Unique number automatically inserted when a record is added: size 4 bytes.
- **Number** Numeric data to be used for mathematical calculations: size 1, 2, 4, or 8 bytes.
- **Date/Time** Stores date/time: size 8 bytes.
- **Yes/No** Boolean value, 0 or 1: size 1bit.
- **Memo** Used for storing large amounts of text: maximum size 64,000 characters.
- **OLE Object** Can store Word docs, Excel files, and so on: maximum size 1 gigabyte.

Continue this process for the rest of the tables. If you want, you can load the shopDb.mdb from the CD that accompanies this book, then view the complete database. Let's look at the complete diagram generated by Access after we finish filling in our tables (shown in Figure 12.5).

Figure 12.5 A Database Diagram

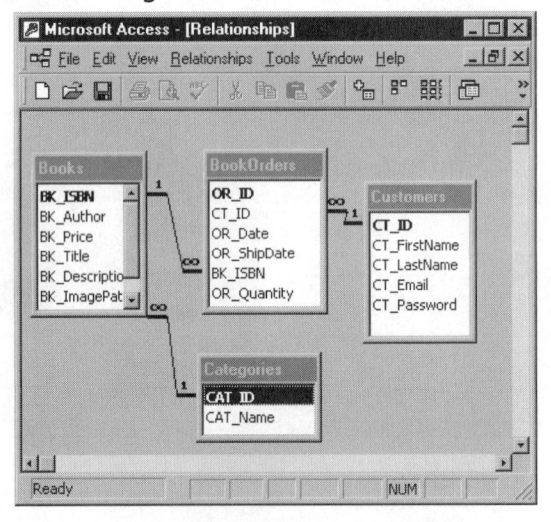

To generate the preceding diagram, go to the **Tools** menu and select the **Relationships option**. You will be prompted for what tables to add. Select the tables you have created and hit **OK**. To create the relationships between the tables, left-click the attribute you want to make a relationship with and drag it over to the table that has the matching attribute, release the mouse and you will be prompted with a set of options for the relationship. See Figure 12.6.

Figure 12.6 Defining Relationships in Access

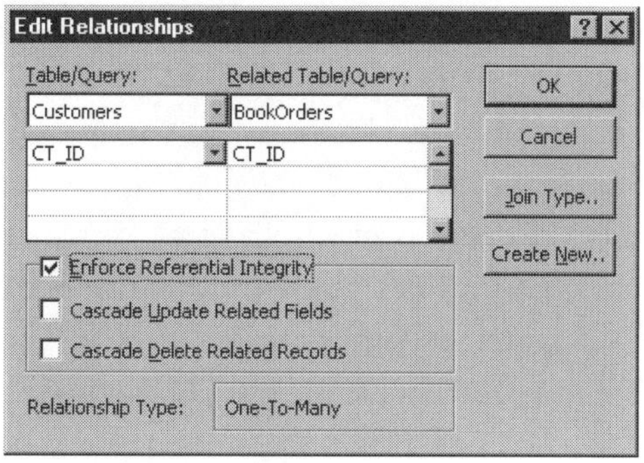

The default is to have the Enforce Referential Integrity option selected. This is good enough for our example; the other two options will enable cascading deletes and updates.

> **WARNING**
>
> When defining relationships, make sure the column is of the same datatype as the one you are trying to make a relationship with, otherwise Access will throw an error.

We will do what is called *de-normalize* the database for the Access version to make things flow between the Data tier of our application and the two different databases. Since our shopping cart uses all OleDb connections to the database regardless of source, the stored procedures created in the SQL Db are the same for the Access version, but we have some limitations when it comes to Access. We cannot easily return the submitted record ID from the table like we can in SQL using the global variable *@@identity*, so we must solve this by eliminating the Orders table in the schema for Access and adding those rows to the BookOrders table. This will result in customers having multiple order entries, but keeps all data handling code the same for both databases. If you were to program this application, you would select one or the other and optimize accordingly—we are going to straddle the fence here and show both in the same logic.

Now that we have our database schema done, we can upsize the database using the Access Upsizing Wizard and make a SQL server version. Go to **Tools**, select **Database Utilities**, then select **Upsizing Wizard**. Follow the wizard and choose all the defaults.

SQL Server Database

Now that we have our schema upsized into SQL, we can easily create the rest of our database components. We primarily need a set of stored procedures that will run all of our operations against the database. This will enable us not to have to use ad hoc queries in our code for our Data Tier interaction.

One thing we need to do first is ensure that all our primary keys were transcribed into the upsized version. Let's open up the **Enterprise Manager of MSSQL 2000** (EM). Navigate to your program files and select the **SQL Server** group, then select **EM**. From EM, we can quickly navigate to our database (shopDB). See Figure 12.7.

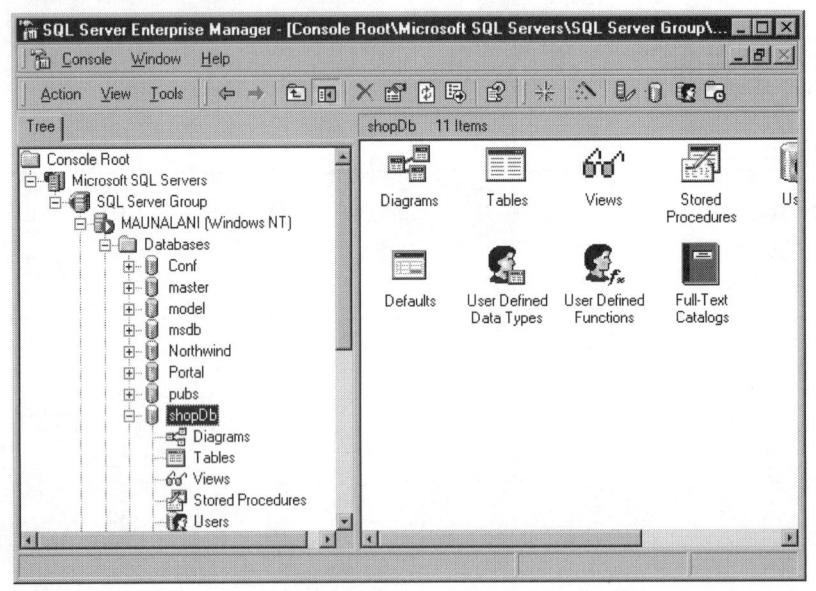

Figure 12.7 The SQL EM Interface

Select **Tables** and you'll notice our tables from Access are now here. Right-click a table and select **Design Table**. From here, we can check to see if our tables made the move without ill effects. If everything looks correct, check the rest of the tables—you'll see the Access datatype "autonumber" does not come over to SQL Server as an "int" identity column datatype, which it needs to be. So, for the tables that have autonumber, you will have to change it to the "int" datatype with identity, and give them a seed and increment value. See Figure 12.8.

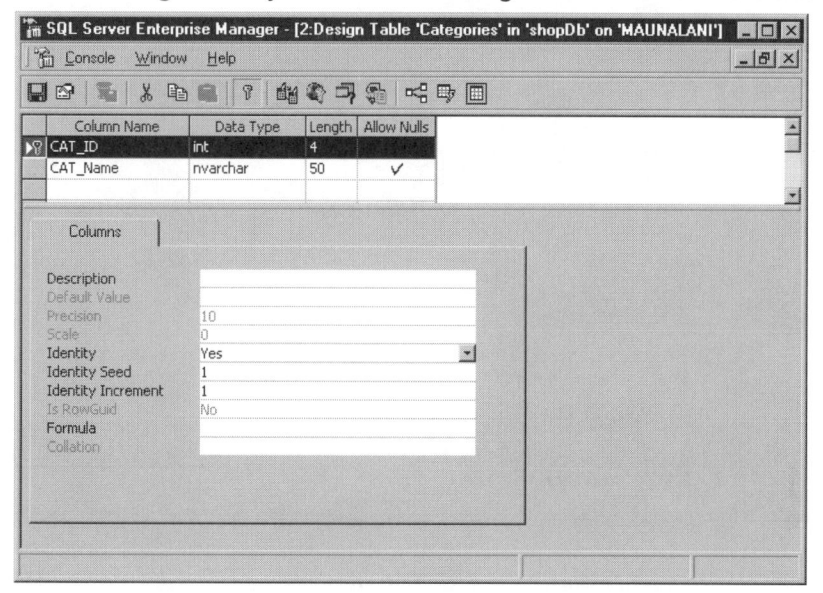

Figure 12.8 Setting Identity to Yes and Giving Seed and Increment Value

You must also uncheck **Allow Nulls**. This is because the field we are working with is a primary key and we cannot have a null value for a primary key field. Also, we are using the option identity in this instance, which requires that null not be allowed.

We will also separate the table "BookOrders" into its original design since SQL Server can easily give us a value for the identity field returned. After we have done all of this, we can create a new diagram in SQL and apply our new relationships. In the EM view, right-click diagrams and select **New Diagram**. The wizard will prompt you for the tables you want to select for the database diagram. Add only the tables we have created, leave out all the system tables. We will now view our new diagram generated by SQL Server (see Figure 12.9).

We can create relationships in the same manner as before. Click the column you want to make a relationship with and drag and drop it into to the appropriate column and table. We will go with the selected defaults. We have a normalized database now completed in SQL Server. We will now create the stored procedures (procs) we'll need for the rest of the application.

Figure 12.9 A SQL Server Diagram

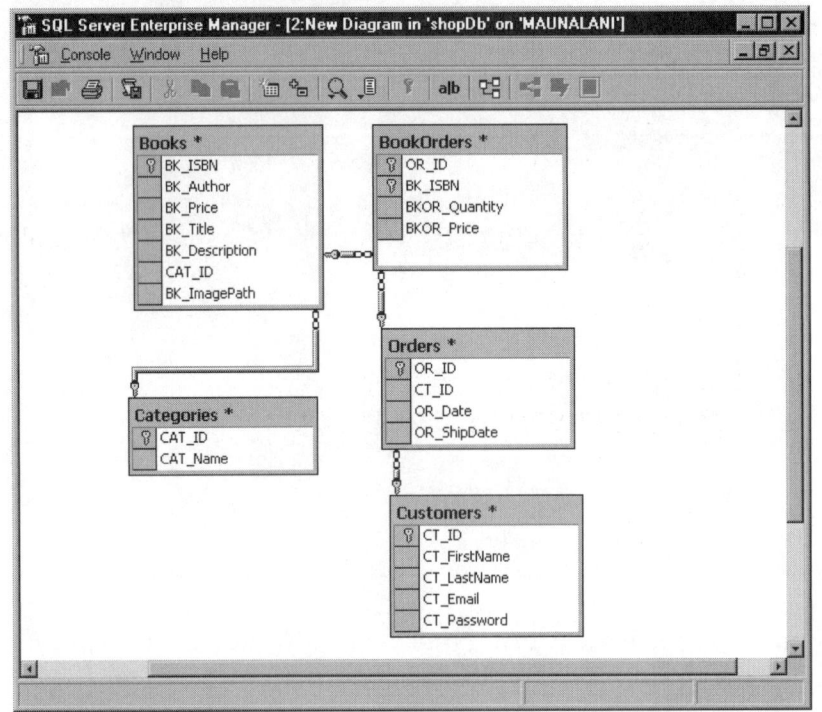

Creating the Stored Procedures

We'll now create the following list of stored procedures:

- AdminAddBook
- AdminAddCustomer
- AdminAddCat
- AdminDeleteCat
- AdminDeleteCustomer
- AdminDeleteBook
- AdminUpdateBook
- AdminUpdateCat
- AdminUpdateCustomer
- AllCustById

- GetAllBooks
- GetAllCat
- LoginCustomers
- OrderBook

Don't be intimidated. We'll use the SQL Server Wizard to create most of these procedures. Now we need to begin creating all our stored procedures. Go to the **Tools** menu and select **Wizards**. From there, a new window will pop up with a listing of items. Double-click the first item, **Database**, then select **Create Stored Procedure Wizard**. You should see the screen shown in Figure 12.10.

Figure 12.10 The Create Stored Procedure Wizard

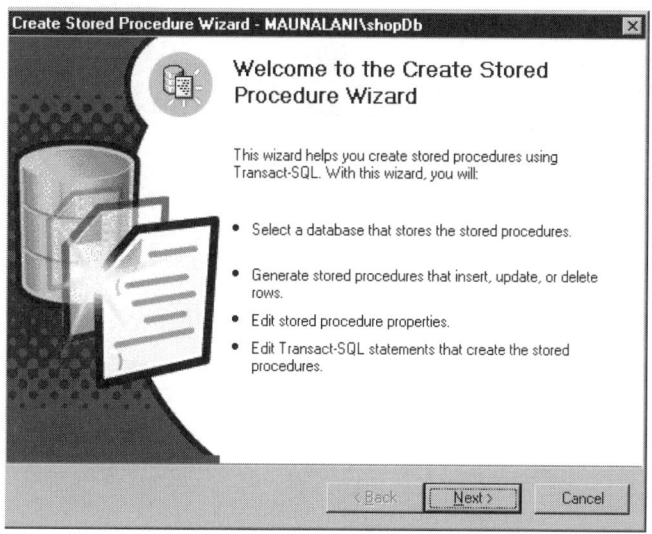

Click **Next** and select the database, which is **shopDb**. The next window will show all the tables on the left and the subsequent procedures that can be created on the right. Mark the check box labeled **insert** in the row of options listed for the **Customers** table. Click **Next**. The window that appears will give you the choice to edit the SQL syntax—select this option. We need to give the procedure a name, which in this case will be AdminAddCustomer. See Figure 12.11.

In Figure 12.11, we see that all columns are selected for insert; however, we do not need one for *CT_ID* because the identity field generates that. Uncheck that option and rename the proc **AdminAddCustomer**. Select **Edit SQL**. Let's look at the code generated by this; it's shown in Figure 12.12 and found on the CD as ShopDB.sql.

Figure 12.11 The Stored Procedure Wizard's Properties Dialog Box

Figure 12.12 ShopDB.sql

```
USE [shopDb]
GO
CREATE PROCEDURE [AdminAddCustomer]
       (@CT_FirstName      [nvarchar](20),
       @CT_LastName        [nvarchar](50),
       @CT_Email           [nvarchar](75),
       @CT_Password        [nvarchar](6))

AS INSERT INTO [shopDb].[dbo].[Customers]
       ([CT_FirstName],
       [CT_LastName],
       [CT_Email],
       [CT_Password])

VALUES
       (@CT_FirstName,
       @CT_LastName,
       @CT_Email,
       @CT_Password)
```

Here we have the SQL syntax to insert a row of new data. In the code view window, SQL Server likes to put numbers on all the variables. You can delete this so the code looks cleaner and will be easy to use when we write the Web service that will hit this proc and execute it. Create the rest of the Admin procs in this same manner.

Now that we have completed a majority of the stored procedures needed for our database through the use of the wizards, we have to create more complex stored procedures using the Query Analyzer. Open up **Query Analyzer** from the **Tools** menu of **EM**. Connect the server you are running. In the drop-down menu, select the database **shopDb**. The next proc we need to build is AllCustById. We will write a simple select statement with one parameter.

Let's look at some code which can be executed in Query Analyzer:

```
CREATE   PROC AllCustById
@CT_ID int
AS
SELECT *
FROM customers
WHERE CT_ID = @CT_ID
GO
```

The next procedure in the list after AllCustById is GetAllBooks. No need for parameters—just give up the data.

```
CREATE    PROCEDURE GetAllBooks

AS

SELECT BK_ISBN isbn,
    category.CAT_Name "name",
    category.CAT_ID "id",
    BK_ImagePath imgSrc,
    BK_author author,
    BK_Price price,
    BK_Title title,
    BK_Description "description"
FROM Books book inner Join Categories category
on book.CAT_ID = category.CAT_ID
```

```
ORDER BY "name"
```

> **NOTE**
>
> In the code in this section, we are using aliasing so the column headers returned will have easy-to-use names. The *DataSet* will use the column names as XML element names when the data is converted to XML.

Now we need to get a selection of categories from the database for our drop-down menus:

```
CREATE   PROC GetAllCat
AS
SELECT * FROM Categories
```

This will populate with all category names and associated IDs.

Now we need to create a proc that will query the database and return a Customer's ID. This is our Login proc:

```
CREATE   proc LoginCustomers
    @CT_Email nvarchar(75),
    @CT_Password nvarchar(6)


as


SELECT [CT_ID]
FROM Customers
WHERE CT_Email = @CT_Email And CT_Password = @CT_Password
```

This will return a value of either the Customers ID or −1, which we can check for on the page load.

Now we need to handle the ordering of a book. We can load and run the OrderBook procedure to do that:

```
CREATE    Procedure OrderBook
(
    @CT_ID int,
```

```sql
    @BK_ISBN int,
    @BKOR_Quantity int,
    @BKOR_Price money
)
AS

declare @OR_Date datetime
declare @OR_ShipDate datetime
declare @OR_ID int

select @OR_Date = getdate()
select @OR_ShipDate = getdate()

begin tran NewBook

INSERT INTO Orders
(
    CT_ID,
    OR_Date,
    OR_ShipDate
)
VALUES
(
    @CT_ID,
    @OR_Date,
    @OR_ShipDate
)

SELECT @OR_ID = @@Identity

INSERT INTO BookOrders
(
    OR_ID,
    BK_ISBN,
```

```
        BKOR_Quantity,
        BKOR_Price
)
VALUES
(
        @OR_ID,
        @BK_ISBN,
        @BKOR_Quantity,
        @BKOR_Price
)
commit tran NewBook
```

We are using *begin tran* and *end tran*. This simply means that if there is an error during any part of the previous query the transaction will be aborted and rolled back. That's it for the stored procedures. Now to make these all work in the Access DB, we need to trim out some stuff from the preceding code.

As a rule of thumb, we can grab all the code after the key word *AS*. This is then pasted into Access query SQL mode and saved as the same file name. Open up the shopDB.mdb file and see the differences in the code.

Creating the Web Services

This section will provide an overview of the Web Services needed for our site, and describe the processes of creating the data connection, creating a Web Service, and, finally, testing the Web Service.

Overview of the Book Shop Web Services

We will be using Web Service methods to wrap our database logic (stored procedures for SQL, or parameterized queries for Access). This will provide separation of the data tier from the UI. This will also enable our data to be accessed from multiple clients including Java-servlets, JSP, PHP, desktop application with Hypertext Transfer Protocol (HTTP) connections, and, of course, ASP.NET applications.

We will be creating the following Web Services (see Figure 12.13):

- sellerAdmin
- adminCustomer
- getCustomer

- loginCustomer
- getBooks
- getCategories
- orderBooks

Figure 12.13 An Overview of Web Services and Their Methods

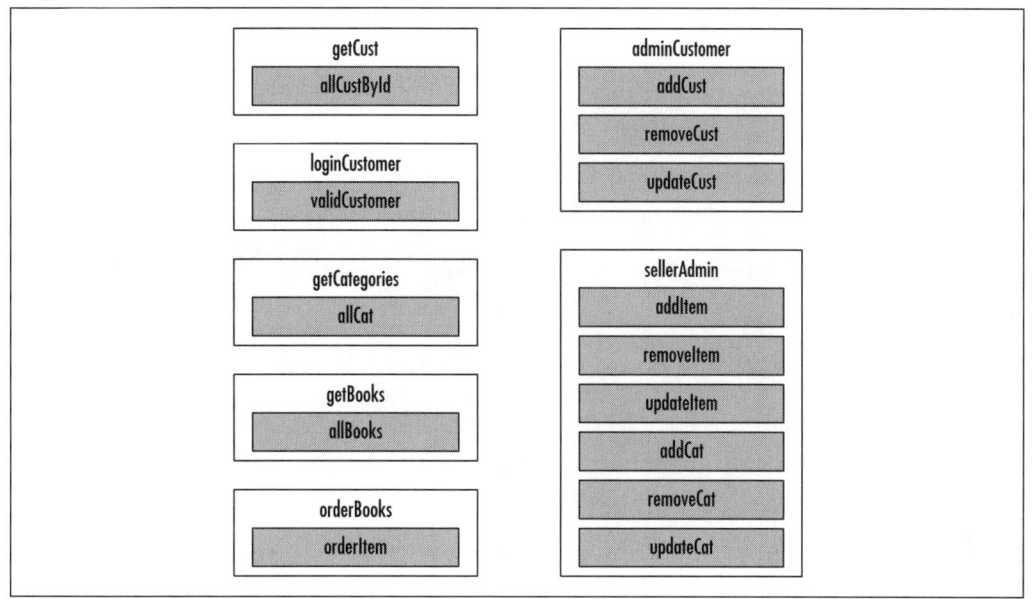

getCust	adminCustomer
allCustById	addCust
	removeCust
loginCustomer	updateCust
validCustomer	
	sellerAdmin
getCategories	addItem
allCat	removeItem
	updateItem
getBooks	addCat
allBooks	removeCat
	updateCat
orderBooks	
orderItem	

Earlier in this chapter (see the section "Setting Up the Database"), we created stored procedures for use with an SQL database, as well as the equivalent parameterized queries for use with an Access database, to make the interface to the data source consistent; this allows us to write ADO.NET code that can be used against both SQL and Access.

We will also use the OleDb data connection object since most databases have an OleDb provider. This will enable our code not only to work with SQL and Access but with any database that has an OleDb interface. So, our application will work with an SQL database and our application will work with an Access database. And the only code that will need to be changed with this approach is the connection string.

Let's create a new project to host all our Web Services. Open **Visual Studio .NET Beta 2** (VS.NET), and select **New Project**. We want to create a C# ASP.NET Web Service application named "booksource" (see Figure 12.14); next, we will create the data connection.

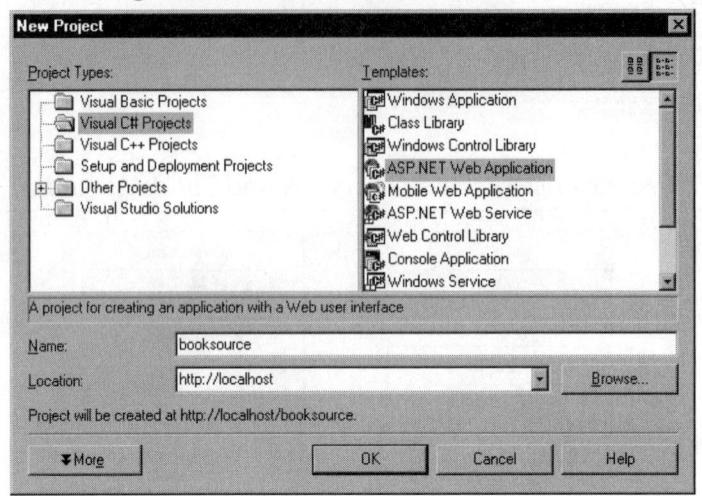

Figure 12.14 Creating the Booksource Web Service

Creating the Data Connection

Data Connections can be created in several ways. Let's look at how the VS.NET Wizard does this. For this example, we'll create a connection to an Access database. The steps for MS SQL will be slightly different.

1. Open the **Server Explorer**, and select **View | Server Explorer** from the menu.
2. Right-click **Data Connection,** then select **Add connection.**
3. Select the **Provider** tab.
4. Select the appropriate provider. For access, select **Jet 4.0 OLEDB Provider**.
5. Click **Next**.
6. Select the database name by clicking the **Browse…** button and navigating to your database.
7. Click **Test Connection**. You should get a pop-up window that says **Connection succeeded**.
8. Click **OK**.
9. Click **OK**. You now have a data connection.

While in design mode, you can drag and drop this connection onto your .asmx page. This will add the following to our code-behind page as the first line in the *service* public class:

```
private System.Data.OleDb.OleDbConnection oleDbConnection1;
```

Connection string information will also be added to the *InitializeComponent()* method. Alternatively, we can still create a connection string by creating a .udl file on the desktop, double-clicking it and following the dialogs. With this method, we will have to insert the code ourselves, as follows:

1. In C#, add **Using System.Data.OleDb** to the top "using" section.
2. Then add the following inside the *service* class:

    ```
    private OleDbConnection myConnection = new OleDbConnection();
    ```

3. Add the following to a method (*Page_onload*, or a method of your own creation):

    ```
    myConnection.ConnectionString =
    [the string obtained from the udl file]
    ```

We will take a closer look at adding a connection when we create the "sellerAdmin" service in the next section.

Creating a Web Service

All of the code for the Web Services in this chapter can be found on the CD. (See adminCustomer.asmx.cs, sellerAdmin.asmx.cs, getBooks.asmx.cs, getCategories.asmx.cs, getCustomer.asmx.cs, loginCustomer.asmx.cs, orderBooks.asmx.cs, and sellerAdmin.asmx.cs.)

Let's take a closer look at adding a connection by creating the "sellerAdmin" Service. To create this service follow these steps:

1. Create the connection object.
2. Set the connection string.
3. Create the Command object.
4. Create the Parameter objects and assign their values.
5. Execute the procedure. We will be using the AdminAddBook proc. It takes the following parameters: *BK_ISBN, BK_Author, BK_Price, BK_Title, BK_Description, CAT_ID, BK_ImagePath*.
6. Return string indicating success or failure of the operation.

Now let's get started. To accomplish Step 1 (creating the connection object), first create a new C# Web Service and name it **sellerAdmin.asmx**. Add this directive to the top "using" section:

```
Using System.Data.OleDb;
```

Scroll down to below the method named *Dispose(bool disposing)*. Add the following:

```
protected OleDbConnection sellerAdminConn = new OleDbConnection();
```

This accomplishes the creation of the connection object. Now, for Step 2 (setting the connection string), add the following:

```
protected void init()
{
this.sellerAdminConn.ConnectionString =
@"Provider=SQLOLEDB.1;
Persist Security Info=False;
User ID=[user id]; password=[password]; Initial Catalog=[Database Name];
Data Source=[Server Name]"
}
```

Note that the use of the "@" before the connection string is required. This accomplishes Step 2.

For Step 3, (creating the Command object), first create a new method called *addItem*. It should have parameters corresponding to the stored procedures parameters, and should return a string indicating success or failure of the operation:

```
public string addItem(string ISBN,string author,double price, string
    title,string description,string imagePath, int CAT_ID)
```

Now create a Command object that references the AdminAddBook proc:

```
OleDbCommand addItem =
new OleDbCommand("AdminAddBook",this.sellerAdminConn);
addItem.CommandType = CommandType.StoredProcedure;
```

This accomplishes Step 3.

For Step 4 (creating the Parameter objects and assigning their value), we will create Parameter objects for ISBN, author, price, title, description, imagePath, and CAT_ID, then set their values. Here is the code for "isbn":

```
OleDbParameter addISBN =
addItem.Parameters.Add("@BK_ISBN",OleDbType.Char,15);
addISBN.Value = ISBN;
```

Note that "@BK_ISBN" is the name of the parameter we are assigning a value to; "OleDbType.Char" is its datatype (it should be compatible with the field in the database); and "15" refers to the character size as defined for the field in the database.

The code to create Parameter objects for each of the method parameters is nearly identical, and can be found on the CD (see: sellerAdmin.asmx.cs). This accomplishes Step 4.

Now, for Step 5 (executing the procedure), we will open the connection and execute the query. Since the stored procedure performs an insert operation it will return an "int" containing the number of rows affected. Therefore, we will use the command *ExecuteNonQuery*.

```
this.sellerAdminConn.Open();
int queryResult = QueryObject.ExecuteNonQuery();
```

This accomplishes Step 5. Now close the connection and return the result of executing the proc (this is Step 6). Note that our method returns the following string: "success" or the generated error message.

```
        this.sellerAdminConn.Close();
        if ( queryResult != 0)
        {
            return "Success";
        }
        else
        {
            return "error: QueryResult= " + queryResult;
        }
```

This accomplishes Step 6. Since all of the Web methods have similar logic, we can combine some of this code into a method that each Web method calls:

```
protected string ExecuteQuery( OleDbCommand QueryObject)
{
        this.sellerAdminConn.Open();
        int queryResult = QueryObject.ExecuteNonQuery();
```

524 Chapter 12 • Creating an ADO.NET Shopping Cart

```
        if ( queryResult != 0)
        {
            this.sellerAdminConn.Close();
            return "Success";
        }
        else
        {
            return "error: QueryResult= " + queryResult;
        }
}
```

We need to add one more thing to our method to make it accessible as a Web method:

```
[ WebMethod(Description="Adds a new book to the books table",
        EnableSession=false)]
```

Putting it all together, we get the following:

```
using System;
using System.Collections;
using System.ComponentModel;
using System.Data;
using System.Diagnostics;
using System.Web;
using System.Web.Services;
using System.Data.OleDb;

namespace bookSource
{
    public class sellerAdmin : System.Web.Services.WebService
    {
        public sellerAdmin()
        {
            InitializeComponent();
        }

        protected override void Dispose( bool disposing )
```

```csharp
    {
    protected OleDbConnection sellerAdminConn =
            new OleDbConnection();
    }

    protected void init()
    {
        this.sellerAdminConn.ConnectionString =
                    @"Provider=SQLOLEDB.1;
                    Persist Security Info=False;
                    User ID=[user id];
                    password=[password];
                    Initial Catalog=[Database Name];
                    Data Source=[Server Name]";
    }

    protected string ExecuteQuery( OleDbCommand QueryObject)
    {
        this.sellerAdminConn.Open();
        int queryResult = QueryObject.ExecuteNonQuery();
        if ( queryResult != 0)
        {
            this.sellerAdminConn.Close();
            return "Success";
        }
        else
        {
            return "error: QueryResult= " + queryResult;
        }
    }


[ WebMethod(Description="Adds a new book to the books
                table", EnableSession=false)]
 public string addItem(string ISBN,string author,
            double price, string title,string description,
```

```csharp
                        string imagePath, int CAT_ID)
        {
            try
            {
                this.init();
                OleDbCommand addItem =
                        new OleDbCommand(
                                    "AdminAddBook",
                                        this.sellerAdminConn);
                addItem.CommandType =
                            CommandType.StoredProcedure;

                OleDbParameter addISBN =
                            addItem.Parameters.Add(
"@BK_ISBN",OleDbType.Char,15);
                addISBN.Value = ISBN;

                OleDbParameter addAuthor = addItem.Parameters.Add(
                            "@BK_Author",OleDbType.Char,80);
                addAuthor.Value = author;

                OleDbParameter addPrice =
addItem.Parameters.Add(
                            "@BK_Price",OleDbType.Currency,8);
                addPrice.Value = price;

                OleDbParameter addTitle =
addItem.Parameters.Add(
                            "@BK_Title",OleDbType.Char,75);
                addTitle.Value = title;


                OleDbParameter addDescription
=addItem.Parameters.Add(
```

```
"@BK_Description",OleDbType.Char,255);
                addDescription.Value = description;


                OleDbParameter addImage = 
addItem.Parameters.Add(
                        "@BK_ImagePath",OleDbType.Char,50);
                addImage.Value = imagePath;



                OleDbParameter addCatId = 
addItem.Parameters.Add(
                        "@CAT_ID",OleDbType.Integer,4);
                addCatId.Value = CAT_ID;

                return this.ExecuteQuery( addItem );
            }
            catch(Exception e)
            {
                return e.ToString();
            }
        }
```

.
.
.

In this section, we created the *sellerAdmin* Web Service and the *additem* Web Service method. In the next section, we will look at how to test the Web Service and its methods.

Testing a Web Service

We can test our service by performing the following steps:

1. In VS.NET right-click the .asmx file (sellerAdmin.asmx), and select **Set as start page**.
2. Press **F5** to run it. This will take a few seconds to compile and run.
3. When the browser loads, you should see something like Figure 12.15.

Figure 12.15 Web Service Listing

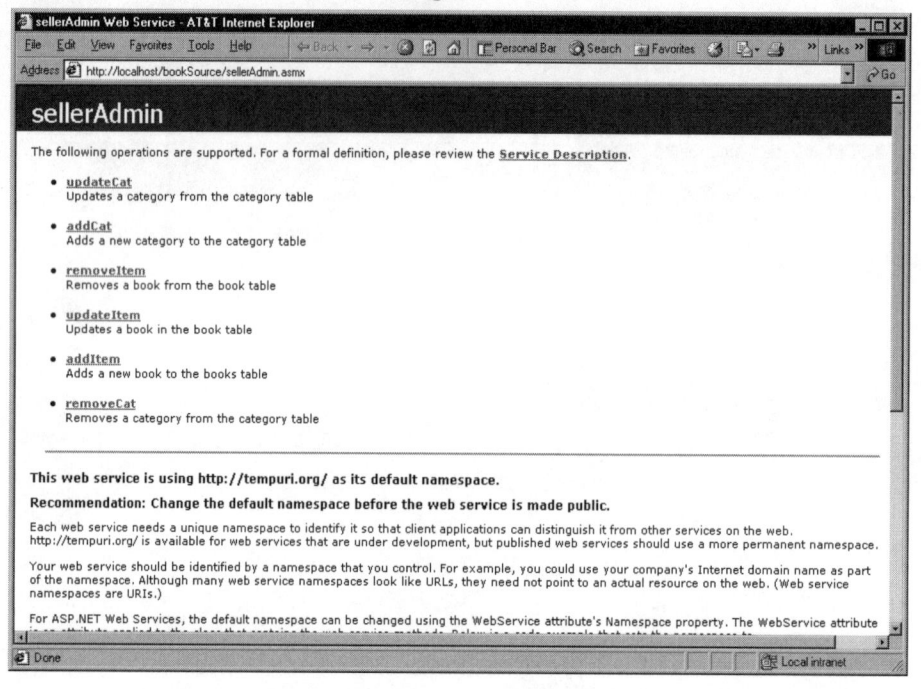

[Screenshot: sellerAdmin Web Service page in Internet Explorer listing supported operations: updateCat, addCat, removeItem, updateItem, addItem, removeCat, with descriptions and namespace recommendation notes.]

4. To test the service *addItem*, click its link. An input form will be displayed, prompting you for values for its parameters. See Figure 12.16.

5. Fill in the appropriate textboxes and click **Invoke**.

6. Since this service returns a datatype *string*, we should see something like Figure 12.17.

This shows that the method has completed successfully and returned the corresponding output. These steps can be repeated for each of the remaining methods: *removeItem*, *updateItem*, *addCat*, *removeCat*, and *updateCat*. Each of these methods is coupled with a corresponding stored procedure (MSSQL) or parameterized query (MS Access).

The following is a function prototype overview of the process-flow or steps involved in creating each of these Web methods. See if you can create and test these Web methods on your own, then compare them to the source on the CD. The *sellerAdmin* Web service and all of its methods can be found on the CD (see sellerAdmin.asmx.cs).

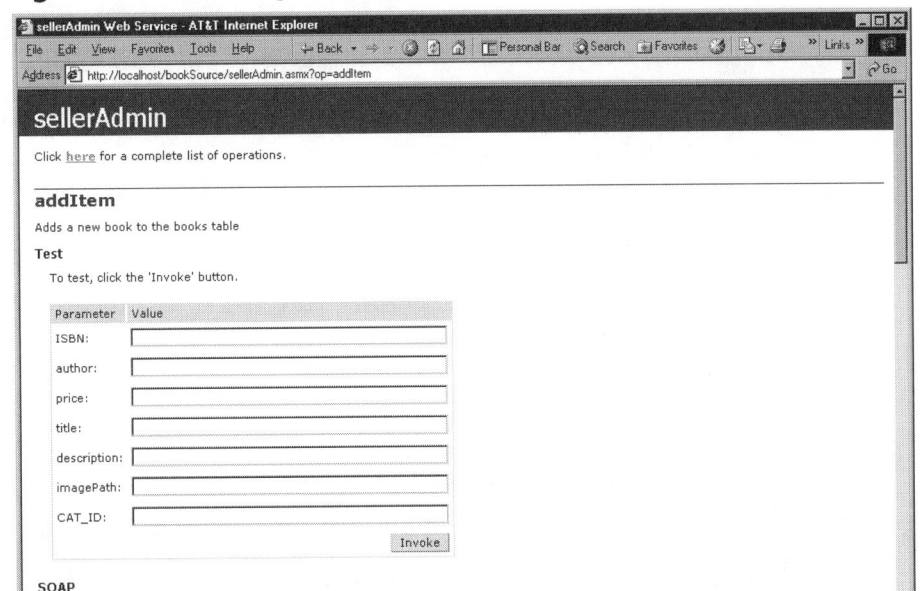

Figure 12.16 Testing a Web Service

Figure 12.17 Results of invoking the *addItem* Web Service

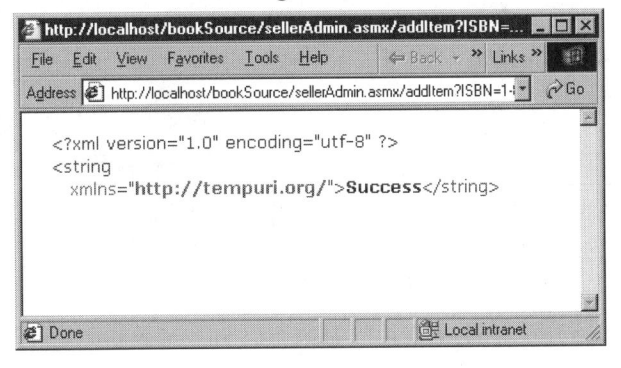

- **removeItem (int isbn)** Removes a book item from the database.
    1. Call **init()**.
    2. Create Command object accessing the AdminRemoveBook proc.
    3. Create the Parameter object and assign its value.
    4. Execute the procedure. Call **ExecuteQuery(commandObj)**.

5. Return string indicating success or failure of the operation.

- **updateItem (string ISBN, string author, double price, string title, string description, string imagePath, int CAT_ID)** Updates a book item's information.
    1. Call **init()**.
    2. Create Command object accessing the AdminUpdateBook proc.
    3. Create the Parameter objects and assign their values.
    4. Execute the procedure. Call **ExecuteQuery(commandObj)**.
    5. Return string indicating success or failure of the operation.

- **addCat (string CAT_Name)** Adds a category name to the database.
    1. Call **init()**.
    2. Create Command object accessing the AdminAddCat proc.
    3. Create the Parameter object and assign its value.
    4. Execute the procedure. Call **ExecuteQuery(commandObj)**.
    5. Return string indicating success or failure of the operation.

- **updateCat (int CAT_ID, string CAT_Name)** Updates category details.
    1. Call **init()**.
    2. Create Command object accessing the AdminUpdateCat proc.
    3. Create the Parameter objects and assign their values.
    4. Execute the procedure. Call **ExecuteQuery(commandObj)**.
    5. Return string indicating success or failure of the operation.

- **removeCat (int CAT_ID)** Removes a category from the database.
    1. Call **init()**.
    2. Create Command object accessing the AdminUpdateCat proc.
    3. Create the Parameter object and assign its value.
    4. Execute the procedure. Call **ExecuteQuery(commandObj)**.
    5. Return string indicating success or failure of the operation.

> **NOTE**
>
> This application contains several different Web Services. The code for these Web Services can be found on the CD. (See adminCustomer.asmx.cs, sellerAdmin.asmx.cs, getBooks.asmx.cs, getCategories.asmx.cs, getCustomer.asmx.cs, loginCustomer.asmx.cs, orderBooks.asmx.cs, and sellerAdmin.asmx.cs.)

Now that we know the Web Service and its methods are working correctly, the next step will be to create our UI for the Web application and generate proxy classes for it to retrieve data from our Web Services. In the next section, we will see how VS.NET works with WSDL and Universal Description, Discovery, and Integration (UDDI) to enable our ASP.NET Web Application to connect to and retrieve data from our booksource Web Service project.

Using WSDL Web References

We will use WSDL and disco in our Web application project to connect to and add a reference to our Web Services Application (bookSource) and its individual Web Services and their Web methods. To learn more about WSDL, disco, and Web Services, please see the discussion of this topic in Chapter 10.

Let's create a new C# Web application, named "bookSourceUI." The first thing we want to do is create a reference to our Web Services so that we can easily access the methods in our code.

1. In the **Solution Explorer** pane, right-click **Web References**.

2. Select **Add Web Reference**. A new dialog will appear.

3. Select the last UDDI option, which is your local machine. VS.NET will check your server for all Web Services. It will then present you with a list of services you can view or select to add a reference to. See Figure 12.18.

4. Select the service group you would like to add a reference to. Look for your Web Service project name (http://localhost/bookSource.vsdisco).

5. The Services available will be displayed. See Figure 12.19.

Figure 12.18 UDDI Server Discovery Dialog

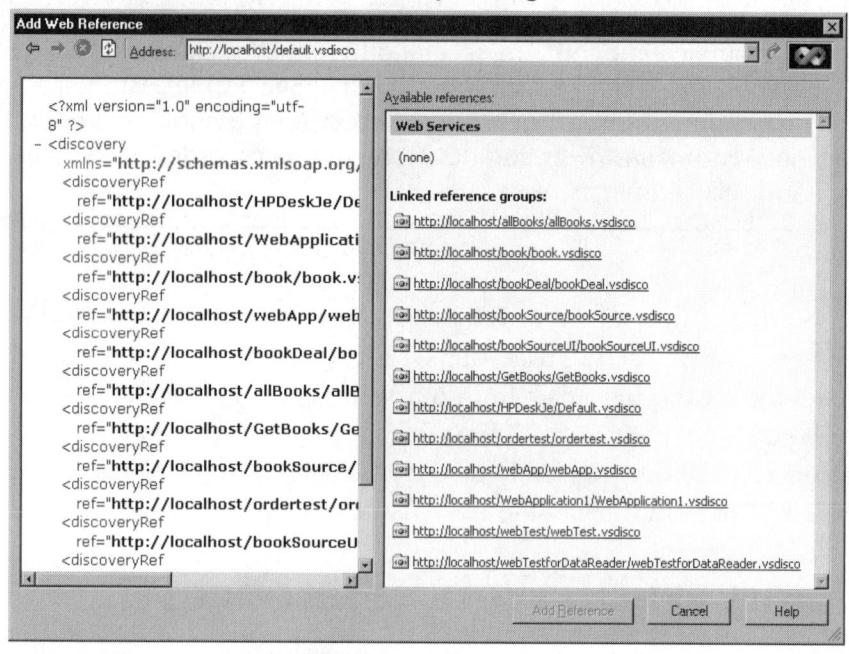

Figure 12.19 Services Available

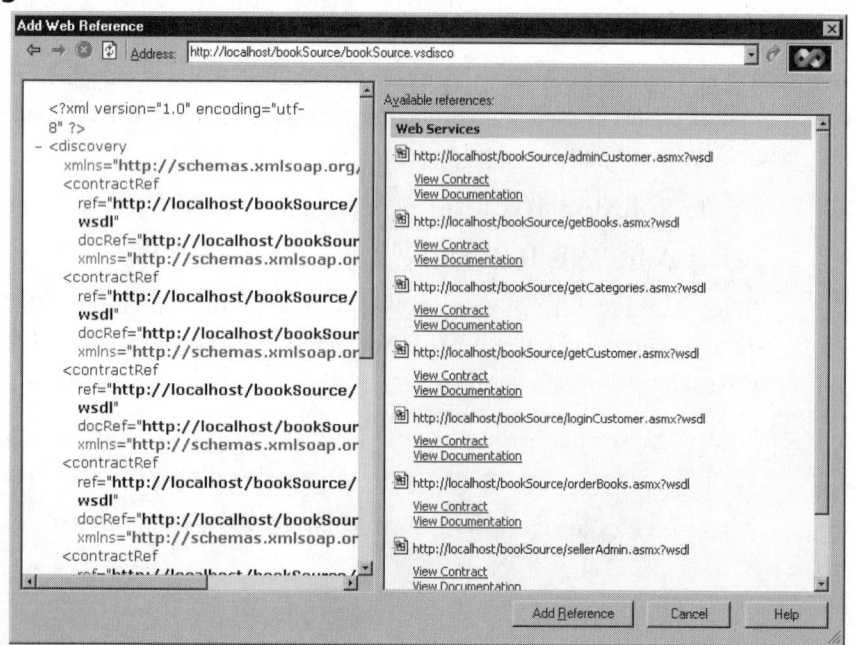

6. You can view the Simple Object Access Protocol (SOAP) contracts and documentation for each Service method by clicking on the link. Be sure to add the reference from this level in the menu. To add this Web Service and all its methods, click **Add Reference**. VS.NET will create proxy classes for each Service method so that the method can be accessed just like a local class method. See Figure 12.20.

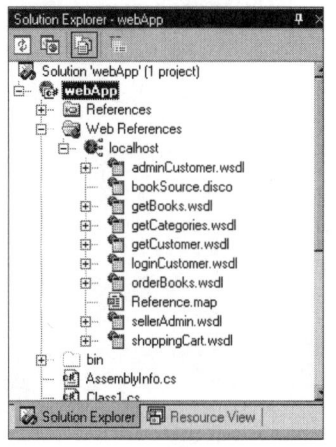

Figure 12.20 Proxy Classes Added to Solution Explorer in VSNET UI

Building the Site

Now that the backend database interfaces and Web Services have been completed, we will turn our focus to the middle tier data classes and controls that act as a bridge between the backend and the Web UI. Our site structure will look something like that depicted in Figure 12.21.

Site Administration

In this section, we will develop the code that allows us to tie our site administration interface to our Web Services (see Figure 12.22). While creating the pages needed, we will cover creating the Administration login, creating the Administration page, and an *addBook* page for the administrator.

534 Chapter 12 • Creating an ADO.NET Shopping Cart

Figure 12.21 BookShop Site Overview

Figure 12.22 Site Administration Page Group Overview

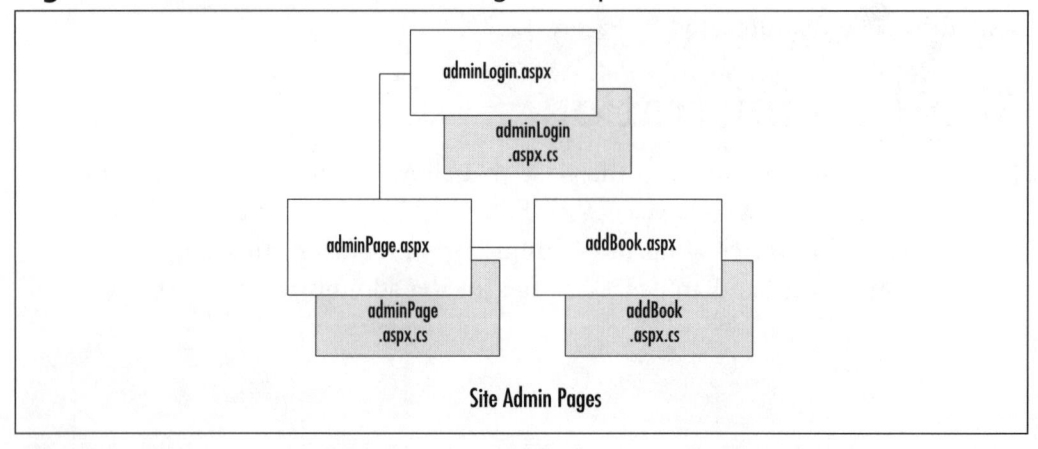

Creating the Administration Login (adminLogin.aspx)

This is a fairly simple page that uses the asp:*RequiredFieldValidator* server control. There are several server controls that enable HTML form validation:

- RequiredFieldValidator
- CompareValidator
- RangeValidator
- RegularExpressionValidator
- CustomValidator
- ValidationSummary

All of these controls work in a similar fashion. In this example page, we use *RequiredFieldValidator* in a code behind page to show how to use a server control to validate user data in HTML forms.

1. In the Web application **bookSourceUI**, create a new aspx page, and name it **adminLogin.aspx**.
2. In **Design view**, drag and drop a **RequiredFieldValidator**.
3. Be sure not to position this element in Design view; in the **aspx page**, remove the style attribute from the element and use HTML layout techniques to position it. (See the sidebar in this section on ASP.NET and Netscape.)

Let's look at the code from the .aspx page:

```
<tr>
  <td><FONT face="Verdana" size="2">User:</FONT> </td>
  <td style="WIDTH: 127px">
    <asp:textbox id="txtUser" runat="server"
        Width="106px" Height="24px">
    </asp:textbox>
  </td><td>
    <asp:requiredfieldvalidator id="passUser" runat="server"
        ErrorMessage="You must supply a user name"
        ControlToValidate="txtUser" Width="121px" Height="57px">
```

```
        </asp:requiredfieldvalidator>
      </td>
  </tr>
```

Lets look at a code snippet from the code-behind file (the aspx.cs page). When we drag the RequiredFieldValidator onto the page, VS.NET will add the following:

```
protected System.Web.UI.WebControls.RequiredFieldValidator passUValid;
```

And that's all there is to it. When the page is run, a reference is made to a client-side JavaScript file that includes crossbrowser code to ensure that this field contains a value before allowing a "submit." If the user tries to submit without filling in the text box, the error message "You must supply a user name" will appear in the table cell to the right of the text box (it actually appears wherever the **asp:requiredfieldvalidator** tag is placed in the HTML, in this case an adjacent table cell). Next, we will look at the admin page itself.

Debugging…

ASP.NET Server Controls Do Not Display Correctly in Netscape 4.x

A lot has happened over the last few years with Netscape and the open source Mozilla project. While the newer versions of Mozilla version .094 and later should handle this fine, there is still a significant Netscape 4.x user base. When we develop Web front-ends for our clients, we strive to ensure at least Netscape 4.72 will display and function correctly.

What's the issue? It seems that most of the examples showing you how to use server controls have you drag and drop the control to where you want it on the screen. In HTML, this creates span tags with inline style attributes containing "absolute positioning." Those of us that have dealt with cross-browser Dynamic HTML (DHTML) issues know that this can cause problems in Netscape. The solution: Use "FlowLayout" and good old-fashioned HTML elements and tricks for positioning. To do this, simply right-click a page in either "Design" or "HTML" view and switch the *pageLayout* property to FlowLayout.

Creating the Administrator Page (adminPage.aspx)

The purpose of this page is to allow the site administrator the ability to remove and update book item information. In the following sections, we'll look specifically at retrieving the data, displaying the data, adding new books to the database, deleting books, and updating book details.

Retrieving the Data: Creating the *getBooks.AllBooks* Web Method

To retrieve the list of books stored in the database, we will need to access the "GetAllBooks" stored procedure (MSSQL) or parameterized query (MS Access). We will do this by creating the *allBooks* method of the *getBooks* Web Service. This method will take no parameters, and will return a *DataSet* containing all Book data as well as the table structure of the Database table that the data originated from. The Web method *getBooks.AllBooks* can be found on the CD that accompanies this book (see getBooks.asmx.cs).

1. To create this method, we must first create a new Web Service named "getBooks". (See the section on Web Services earlier in this chapter.)
2. Inside the code-behind page of getBooks (getbooks.asmx.cs), we need to create the method *allBooks*. AllBooks should return a *DataSet*:

```
public DataSet AllBooks()
```

3. Set the connection string:

```
string source = "Provider=SQLOLEDB.1;Persist Security Info=False …
```

4. Create the Connection object:

```
OleDbConnection conn = new OleDbConnection ( source ) ;
```

5. Create the Command object accessing the "GetAllBooks" proc:

```
OleDbCommand  cmd = new OleDbCommand ( "GetAllBooks" , conn ) ;
cmd.CommandType = CommandType.StoredProcedure;
```

6. Create a *DataAdapter* object for the Command object:

```
OleDbDataAdapter da = new OleDbDataAdapter (cmd) ;
```

7. Create a new *DataSet* and use the *DataAdapter* to fill it from the results of executing the stored procedure:

```
DataSet ds = new DataSet ( ) ;
da.Fill ( ds , "Books" ) ;
```

8. Close the connection and return the *DataSet*:

```
conn.Close();
return ds;
```

Here is the method in its entirety:

```
[WebMethod(Description="This will return all books in an XML String",
    EnableSession=false)]
public DataSet AllBooks()
{
  string source = "Provider=SQLOLEDB.1;Persist Security
     Info=False;User ID=[userID];password = [password];
     Initial Catalog=[database name];
     Data Source=[server name];Use Procedure for Prepare=1;
     Auto Translate=True;Packet Size=4096;
  OleDbConnection conn = new OleDbConnection( source );
  conn.Open ( ) ;
  OleDbCommand cmd = new OleDbCommand ("GetAllBooks" , conn);
  cmd.CommandType = CommandType.StoredProcedure;
  OleDbDataAdapter da = new OleDbDataAdapter (cmd) ;
  DataSet ds = new DataSet ( ) ;
  da.Fill ( ds , "Books" ) ;
  conn.Close();
  return ds;
}
```

The data returned contains an embedded xsd schema describing the Database table "Books".

```
<?xml version="1.0" encoding="utf-8"?>
<DataSet xmlns="http://tempuri.org/">
<xsd:schema id="NewDataSet" targetNamespace=""
xmlns="" xmlns:xsd="http://www.w3.org/2001/XMLSchema" xmlns:msdata=
```

```xml
         "urn:schemas-microsoft-com:xml-msdata">
  <xsd:element name="NewDataSet" msdata:IsDataSet="true">
   <xsd:complexType>
     <xsd:choice maxOccurs="unbounded">
       <xsd:element name="Books">
         <xsd:complexType>
           <xsd:sequence>
             <xsd:element name="isbn" type="xsd:string" minOccurs="0" />
             <xsd:element name="name" type="xsd:string" minOccurs="0" />
             <xsd:element name="id" type="xsd:int" minOccurs="0" />
             <xsd:element name="imgSrc" type="xsd:string" minOccurs="0" />
             <xsd:element name="author" type="xsd:string" minOccurs="0" />
             <xsd:element name="price" type="xsd:decimal" minOccurs="0" />
             <xsd:element name="title" type="xsd:string" minOccurs="0" />
             <xsd:element name="description" type="xsd:string"
                 minOccurs="0" />
           </xsd:sequence>
         </xsd:complexType>
       </xsd:element>
     </xsd:choice>
   </xsd:complexType>
  </xsd:element>
</xsd:schema>
```

The next section is the diffgram node, which contains all the table records:

```xml
<diffgr:diffgram xmlns:msdata="urn:schemas-microsoft-com:xml-msdata"
xmlns:diffgr="urn:schemas-microsoft-com:xml-diffgram-v1">
  <NewDataSet xmlns="">
   <Books diffgr:id="Books1" msdata:rowOrder="0">
     <isbn>0072121599</isbn>
     <name>cisco</name>
     <id>2</id>
     <imgSrc>ccda.gif</imgSrc>
     <author>Syngress Media Inc</author>
     <price>49.99</price>
```

```xml
    <title>Ccda Cisco Certified Design Associate Study Guide</title>
    <description>Written for professionals intending on taking the CCDA
      test, this special guide covers all the basics of the test and
      includes hundreds of test questions on the enclosed CD.
    </description>
  </Books>
  <Books diffgr:id="Books2" msdata:rowOrder="1">
    <isbn>0072126671</isbn>
    <name>cisco</name>
    <id>2</id>
    <imgSrc>ccna.gif</imgSrc>
    <author>Cisco Certified Internetwork Expert Prog</author>
    <price>49.99</price>
    <title>CCNA Cisco Certified Network Associate Study Guide</title>
    <description>Cisco certification courses are among the fastest-
      growing courses in the training industry, and our guides are
      designed to help readers thoroughly prepare for the exams.
    </description>
  </Books>.
```

This XML file is interpreted by ASP.NET as a *DataSet* object and can be easily loaded into any variable of type *DataSet*. The *DataGrid* control is designed to be *DataBinded* to a *DataSet* object. This makes it easy to "data bind" to a Web Service method that returns a *DataSet*. Data Binding a *DataSet* to the *DataGrid* is almost the same as loading the *DataSet* into the *DataGrid*. The *DataGrid* is then able to iterate through and perform operations on the *DataSet* as if it were an Access Form connected to an Access database. The *DataSet* in actuality is an in-memory XML representation of the database including the Books table.

Displaying the Data: Binding a *DataGrid* to the *DataSet*

The *DataGrid* is actually bound to the *DataTable* Books which is a table within the *DataSet* returned by *getBooks.AllBooks*. We create a *DataView* of the Books table so that we can sort the data. This *DataView* is then bound to the *DataGrid*.

In the following code, *changeBooks* is the name of our *DataGrid* object:

```
Dt = Books.AllBooks().Tables["Books"];
myView = new DataView(Dt);
myView.Sort = "isbn";
    changeBooks.DataSource = myView;
    changeBooks.DataBind();
```

Adding New Books to the Database: Creating the *allBooks.addItem* Web Method

The creation of this method was shown as an example earlier in the chapter, under the section "Web Services."

Deleting Books: Deleting from the *DataGrid* and the Database

Using the *DataGrid* event *changeBooks_DeleteCommand*, fired when a user clicks the **Delete** button in the *DataGrid UI*, we will select the row in the *DataGrid* to remove by using the *RowFilter* property. The following code selects the individual book by performing a filter on ISBN. It is analogous to the SQL statement:

```
Select * from Books where isbn = "@isbn"
```

The equivalent code for the *DataView* is:

```
myView.RowFilter = "isbn='"+upISBN+"'";
```

This will return an array or collection of items. Since ISBN is our primary key in the Books table, we know that this filter will return only one item. We delete this row from the *DataView* by simply calling the *Delete* method:

```
myView.Delete(0);
```

Next, we reset the filter so we can re-access the entire Books table:

```
myView.RowFilter = "";
```

Now we need to resync the *DataGrid* with the in-memory Books Table View so that the *DataGrid UI* reflects the change:

```
changeBooks.DataSource = myView;
changeBooks.DataBind();
```

Next, we need to update the database to sync it with the *DataGrid*. This is accomplished by calling the Web method and passing it the ISBN of the book to delete:

```
removeBook.removeItem(upISBN);
```

Updating Book Details: Updating the *DataGrid* and the Database

Using the *DataGrid* event *changeBooks_UpdateCommand*, fired when a user clicks the **Update** button in the *DataGrid UI*, we will select the row in the *DataGrid* to update by using the *RowFilter* property.

1. Select the row to update by using the *RowFilter* property of the *DataView* (see the example in the preceding section).

2. Create a new *DataRow* Item and populate it with the changes (new Data). Store updated column values in local variables:

    ```
    string upISBN = e.Item.Cells[2].Text;
    string upAuthor = ((TextBox)e.Item.Cells[3].Controls[0]).Text;
    double upPrice =
    double.Parse(((TextBox)e.Item.Cells[4].Controls[0]).Text);
    string upTitle = ((TextBox)e.Item.Cells[5].Controls[0]).Text;
    string upDescription =
    ((TextBox)e.Item.Cells[6].Controls[0]).Text;
    int upCatId = int.Parse(e.Item.Cells[7].Text);
    string upImage = ((TextBox)e.Item.Cells[8].Controls[0]).Text;
    ```

3. Delete the row that is being updated (see the example in the preceding section).

4. Create a new *DataRow* and populate it with the new data.

    ```
    DataRow dr = Dt.NewRow();
    dr["isbn"] = upISBN;
    dr["author"] = upAuthor;
    dr["price"] = upPrice;
    dr["title"] = upTitle;
    dr["description"] = upDescription;
    dr["id"] = upCatId;
    ```

```
dr["imgSrc"] = upImage;
```

Insert the new *DataRow*:

```
Dt.Rows.Add(dr);
```

5. Resync the *DataGrid* with the *DataView* (see the example in the preceding section).

To update the database, simply call the Web method *sellerAdmin.updateItem*, passing it the new data.

```
localhost.sellerAdmin newData = new localhost.sellerAdmin();
    newData.updateItem(upISBN,upAuthor,upPrice,upTitle,upDescription,
                            upImage,upCatId);
```

One limitation of the *DataGrid* is that it doesn't provide a UI for adding new records. We will handle this case by creating another page: addBook.aspx.

Creating the *addBook* Page (addBook.aspx)

The *addBook* is another fairly straightforward page. It provides a UI where the site administrator can fill out a simple HTML form and submits. This data is handled by the code-behind page addBook.asmx.cs. This page simply passes the data to the database via the Web method *sellerAdmin.addBook*:

```
addNewBook = new localhost.sellerAdmin();

resultAdd =
addNewBook.addItem(addISBN,addAuthor,addPrice,addTitle,addDescription,
addPath,addCatId);
```

Customer Administration

In this section, we will develop the code that allows us to tie our customer administration interface to our Web Services (see Figure 12.23).

Creating the Customer Admin Section

This section of the site deals with user authentication, including creating a customer account and login. We use this to simulate order processing.

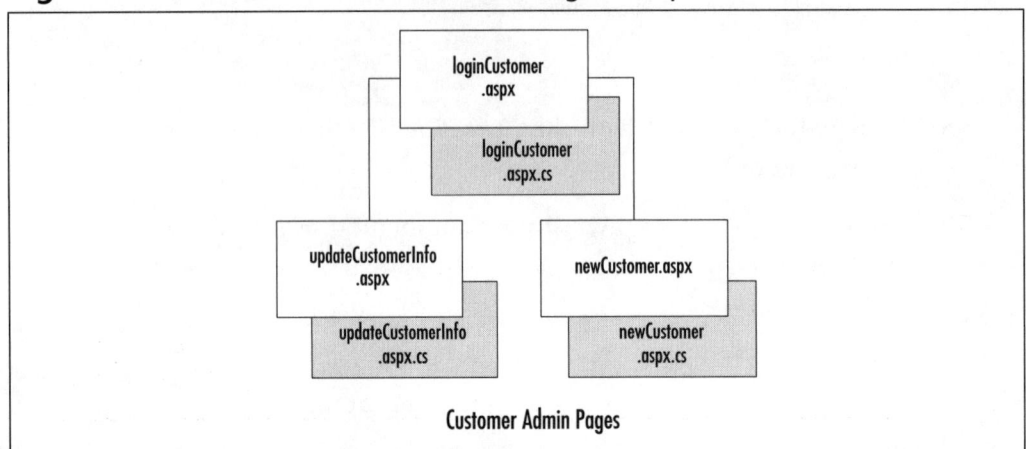

Figure 12.23 Customer Administration Page Group Overview

Customer Admin Pages (loginCustomer.aspx, loginCustomer.aspx.cs, updateCustomerInfo.aspx, updateCustomerInfo.aspx.cs, newCustomer.aspx, newCustomer.aspx.cs)

Creating the *loginCustomer* Page

We will use the same form layout as we did for the admin login described in the preceding section. One change we'll implement is that we'll call a Web Service to verify the login of the customer.

1. Make a call to the Web Service *loginCustomer*. This should be routine by now, but let's look at the code to call the Web Service:

    ```
    loggedCust = new WebReference1.loginCustomer();
    ```

2. Access the Web method *validCustomer*. Now we have access to all the methods contained in the class.

    ```
    string resultId =
    loggedCust.validCustomer(validEmail,validPassword);
    ```

3. Return a value. We can now check the value of the variable *resultId* and either grant the customer access or return an error message.

    ```
    if(resultId == "-1")
    {
    loginLabel.Text = "Invalid Login please re-enter your password
        and email!";
    ```

```
          }
          else
          {
          loginLabel.Text ="Welcome";
          Session["userId"] = int.Parse(resultId);
          Server.Transfer((string)Session["return2Page"]);
          }
```

Now we have the customer logged in to the site and they can go to any page without having to sign in again.

> **NOTE**
>
> We are using a session variable to track where the user is coming from when they are prompted to login. This will enable us to redirect them back to the page where they came from rather then sending them to some nonspecific page and having them navigate through the site from scratch.

Creating the *updateCustomerInfo* Page

We can now add a page that will let the customer update his or her information. This will be done identically to the example from site admin where we brought in all books and then enabled the site administrator to go through the books listed and delete, update, or add books at will. In this case, we will enable the customer to update only.

1. Select the row to update by using the *RowFilter* property of the *DataView*.
2. Create a new *DataRow* Item and populate it with the changes (new Data).
3. Delete the row that is being updated.
4. Insert the new *DataRow*.
5. Resync the *DataGrid* with the *DataView*.

All five steps are the same as covered in earlier examples. Let's look at the code one more time:

```
Dt = Customers.AllCustById((int)Session["userId"]).Tables["Customers"];
        myView = new DataView(Dt);
        myView.Sort = "CT_ID";
```

Set the *DataTable* value into the *DataView*:

```
custGrid.DataSource = myView;
custGrid.DataBind();
```

Set the data source of *DataGrid*:

```
myView.RowFilter = "CT_ID='"+upId+"'";
    if (myView.Count > 0)
    {
    myView.Delete(0);
    }
    myView.RowFilter = "";

    DataRow dr = Dt.NewRow();
    dr[0] = upId;
    dr[1] = upFName;
    dr[2] = upLName;
    dr[3] = upEmail;
    dr[4] = upPassword;
    Dt.Rows.Add(dr);
```

Delete the bad data row and the new one:

```
    WebReference1.adminCustomer newData = new
        WebReference1.adminCustomer();


    newData.updateCust(upId,upFName,upLName,upEmail,upPassword);
```

Lastly, update the database by calling the Web service.

In the previous examples we have made extensive use of the *DataGrid* control for *DataBinding DataSet* information to the UI. We must admit we were a bit reluctant to use the *DataGrid* since it seemed reminiscent to the *DataGrid* Design Time Controls (DTCs). DTCs were included with many versions of FrontPage, Visual InterDev, and Office. They made it easy for novice developers to quickly create data driven Web sites. Lets just say DTCs had some drawbacks, to put it politely! In the next two sections, *ADOCatalog* and *XMLCart*, we will use XSL/Transforms against XML data to produce our UI. This is accomplished by using the asp:xml server control as well as client side script and hidden asp:text controls. The *ADOCatalog*'s primary interfaces will return *DataSet* objects so it could be easily tied to a *DataGrid* control. We will leave that as an exercise for you. The *XMLCart* is primarily a wrapper class around the *XmlDocument* object. Its primary interfaces will return *XmlDocument* objects. Let's get started!

Creating an ADOCatalog

In this section, we will develop the code that allows us to tie our catalog interface to our Web Services. We will store a *DataSet* in an *Application* variable to reduce the load on the database, perform copy, clone, import, create, and filter operations on ADO.NET *DataSet* objects, and use XML and Extensible Stylesheet Language Transformations (XSLT) to render data stored in a *DataSet* as HTML via the asp:xml server control.

In our *ADOCart* application, all database interaction is handled via Web Services. Since our "Books" data is fairly static, we can retrieve the data in a *DataSet* once and store that *DataSet* in an application-level variable. This reduces the database traffic, while still providing quick access to the data. Here is an overview of the process we will be following:

- Load all Books data to an *application* variable:

    ```
    Application["AllBooks"];
    ```

- Create an instance of *ADOCatalog* (a.k.a., *BookCatalog*).

    ```
    In Page_onload
    ```

- Initialize the instance by passing it.

    ```
    (DataSet)Application["AllBooks"];
    ```

- Call **BookCatalog.CatalogRange(0,5)** to return the first five books.
- Convert return data to XML.
- Load XSLT.
- Set *Document* and *Transform* properties of the asp:xml control.

Now, lets create the code. To store our data in an application object, open the Global.asax file. Add this to the *Application_onstart* method:

```
localhost.getBooks DataSource = new localhost.getBooks();
Application["AllBooks"]  = DataSource.AllBooks();//DataSet
```

This will create an instance of the *getBooks* object called *DataSource*. Using this instance, we call the *AllBooks* method, which returns a *DataSet*. We then save the *DataSet* in an application-level variable, *allbooks*.

> **NOTE**
>
> localhost is a reference to the name of the Web Reference containing the *getBooks* Web Service proxy (getBooks.wsdl).

Now add a new page to the Web Application project (bookSourceUI). Name it **start.aspx**. Below the *#endregion* section in the *WebForm1* class, we will create a new class called *bookCatalog*.

Creating the *BookCatalog* Class

The *BookCatalog* class will contain the following public methods: *InitCatalog*, *Catalog*, *CatalogItemDetails*, *CatalogRange*, *CatalogByCategory*, and the private methods *CatalogRangeByCategory*, and *CreateSummaryTable*. The following is a rough prototype of the *ADOCatalog* class that we'll be building in this section:

```
public class bookCatalog
{
    protected WebReference1.getBooks DataSource;
    protected DataSet dsAllBooks;
    protected DataTable dtSummary;

    protected DataTable createSummaryTable(
       int startPos, int range, int RecordCount)
    public DataSet catalog()
    public void initCatalog(DataSet ds )
    public DataSet catalogItemDetails( string book_isbn )
    public DataSet catalogRange(int startPos, int range)
```

```
    public DataSet catalogByCategory( int catId)
    protected DataSet catalogRangeByCategory(
       int startPos, int range, int catId, string book_isbn)
}
```

Creating the *CreateSummaryTable* Method

The *CreateSummaryTable* method creates a *DataTable* that contains summary information about the *DataSet* being returned. This data is used by the XSLT to display Metadata (i.e., viewing records 6 through 12 of 25). It is also useful when making a fetch next range of records call.

Based on the prototype, this method will take the parameters *int startPos*, *int range*, and int *RecordCount* and will return a *DataTable*. Let's get started.

1. Create a new empty DataTable named "summary".

   ```
   DataTable dtSummary = new DataTable("Summary");
   ```

   In the XSD schema this makes the DataTables parent

   ```
   element a summary tag (i.e. <summary> )
   ```

2. Now add the Columns RecordCount, FirstItemIndex, and LastItemIndex to the Summary DataTable.

   ```
   dtSummary.Columns.Add(
   new DataColumn("RecordCount", typeof(int)));
     dtSummary.Columns.Add(
   new DataColumn("FirstItemIndex", typeof(int)));
     dtSummary.Columns.Add(
   new DataColumn("LastItemIndex", typeof(int)));
   ```

3. Create a new *DataRow* object and assign it to a new *DataTable* row.

   ```
   DataRow drSummary;
   drSummary = dtSummary.NewRow();
   ```

4. Populate the *DataRow* object and add it to the *DataTable*.

   ```
   drSummary["RecordCount"]    = RecordCount;
   drSummary["FirstItemIndex"] = startPos;
   drSummary["LastItemIndex"]  = startPos + range;
   dtSummary.Rows.Add( drSummary );
   ```

5. Return the new DataTable.

   ```
   return dtSummary;
   ```

Creating the *InitCatalog* Method

The *InitCatalog* method loads a *DataSet* into the *BookCatalog* object, then adds a default summary table to the private *DataSet dsAllBooks*. Based on the prototype, this method will take the only parameter, a *DataSet*, and will return nothing.

```
public void initCatalog(DataSet ds )
{
    dsAllBooks = ds;
    int recordCount = dsAllBooks.Tables[0].Rows.Count;
    dsAllBooks.Tables.Add(
            createSummaryTable(0, recordCount-1, recordCount) );
}
```

Creating the *Catalog* Method

The *Catalog* method returns the entire *DataSet* stored in the private variable *dsAllBooks*:

```
public DataSet catalog()
{
   return dsAllBooks;
}
```

Creating the *catalogItemDetails*, *catalogRange*, and *catalogByCategory* Methods

The three methods, *catalogItemDetails*, *catalogRange*, and *catalogByCategory*, are specialized cases of *catalogRangeByCategory* and are really only logical interfaces to obtain desired result sets.

The method *catalogItemDetails* will return all data corresponding with the given ID (*Book_isbn*):

```
public DataSet catalogItemDetails( string book_isbn )
{       // returns a DataSet containing a single book
        return catalogRangeByCategory( -1, -1, -1, book_isbn);
```

}

The method *catalogRange* will return all data for items in a given range:

```
public DataSet catalogRange(int startPos, int range)
{     //returns a given range of books
    return catalogRangeByCategory( startPos, range, -1, null);
}
```

The method *catalogByCategory* will return all data for items in a given category:

```
public DataSet catalogByCategory( int catId)
{     //returns all books with the given categoryId
    return catalogRangeByCategory( -1, -1, catId, null);
}
```

Creating the *catalogRangeByCategory* Method

The *catalogRangeByCategory* method creates a new *DataSet* containing a new Books Table, appends the appropriate Summary Table, and returns this new *DataSet*. It is used by the preceding methods to return a single item's node (to add to the shopping cart), to return a range of books (to handle browsing the catalog), and to return all books in a given category (to handle viewing by category). A method could easily be added that enables browsing by category.

In order to return a subset of the *DataSet allBooks*, we need to create a new DataTable object that has the same table structure as Books. We can then import rows that meet our criteria into this new table. When the table is filled, we create a new *DataSet* object and add the new DataTable as well as a Summary Table. The resulting *DataSet* will contain the request subset of data and some Meta-information (supplied by the Summary table).

Now, let's examine the code. Create a temporary DataTable that holds *allBooks* data:

```
DataTable dtTemp = dsAllBooks.Tables["Books"];
```

Clone the structure of this table in a new DataTable:

```
DataTable dtBooks = dtTemp.Clone();//create Empty Books Table
```

Set the filter expression property based on input parameters:

```
if( catId == -1)
{ //no filter is applied strExpr = "";
```

```
}
else
{ //select only one category
    strExpr = "id='" + catId + "'";
}
if( book_isbn != null)
{ //return a single item
    strExpr = "isbn='" + book_isbn + "'";
}
```

Set our Data filter to affect all current rows, sort by title, and apply the filter expression:

```
strSort ="title";
recState = DataViewRowState.CurrentRows;
foundRows = dtTemp.Select(strExpr, strSort, recState);
RecordCount = foundRows.Length;
```

Add *foundRows* to the *DataTable dtBooks*:

```
for(int i = startPos; i < endPos; i ++)
{
    dtBooks.ImportRow( (DataRow)foundRows[i] );
}
```

Add the *DataTable dtBooks* to the new *DataSet* along with *DataTable Summary*, then return this new *DataSet*:

```
dsBookRange = new DataSet();
dsBookRange.Tables.Add(  dtBooks );
dsBookRange.Tables.Add(
    createSummaryTable( startPos, range, RecordCount) );
return dsBookRange;
```

On page load, we will instantiate the object, retrieve Application["AllBooks"], return the requested subset *DataSet* object, convert it to XML using the *GetXml()* method of the *DataSet* object, and apply an XSL/Transform to render the Catalog in the UI.

In order to enable browsing, we will store the FirstRecord, LastRecord, recordCount, and user action (**previous | next | by CategoryID**) into hidden

Text fields on the client, so this data can be read to determine which *bookCatalog* method to call and with which parameters to return the desired subset of *AllBooks*.

You can see the code on the CD for a closer look at how to implement this class (see start.aspx and start.aspx.cs). The CD also contains the *XSLT used* to render the UI (Catalog.xslt).

Building an XMLCart

In this section, we will develop the code that allows us to tie our catalog to the shopping cart. We will use XML node operations to update our cart's contents, XSLT/XPath operations to calculate cart totals and taxes, XML and XSLT to render cart data as HTML, and the asp:XML server control to process transforms. The code for this class can be found on the CD (see start.aspx and start.aspx.cs).

The *XMLCart* is really a wrapper class around common XML functions. It performs the following basic operations: load data, add new item, remove item, and empty cart.

Looking at the class, you'll see there really isn't much to it.

```
public class xmlShoppingCart
{
    protected XmlDocument myCart;
    public void initCart( string dataSource )
{
myCart = new XmlDocument();
if( dataSource != null )
{
    myCart.LoadXml(dataSource);
}
else
{
    myCart.LoadXml( "<shopcart-items></shopcart-items>" );
}
}

public string addItem2Cart( XmlDocument book )
{
```

```csharp
        try
        {
          //Import the last book node from doc2 into the original document.
          XmlNode newBook =
          myCart.ImportNode(book.DocumentElement.FirstChild, true);
          myCart.DocumentElement.AppendChild(newBook);
          return "Success";
        }
        catch(Exception e)    {
        return e.ToString();
        }}

public string removeItemFromCart( string isbn )
{
    XmlNode curnode =
    myCart.SelectSingleNode("//Books[isbn='" + isbn + "']");
    try
    {
      myCart.DocumentElement.RemoveChild( curnode );
      return "Success";
    }
    catch(Exception e)
    {
      return e.ToString();
    }
}
public void clearCart()
{
    XmlElement root = myCart.DocumentElement;
    root.RemoveAll();
}
public XmlDocument getCartDescription()
{
    return myCart;
}
```

```
public string getCartDescriptionString()
{
   return myCart.OuterXml;
}
}
```

When the page loads, the cart must be initialized. This is handled with the *init* method. If there is no data to load into the cart, the root node (<shopcart-items>) is added so that child nodes can be imported from the catalog.

```
public void initCart( string dataSource )
{
   myCart = new XmlDocument();
   if( dataSource != null )
   {
      myCart.LoadXml(dataSource);
   }
   else
   {
      myCart.LoadXml( "<shopcart-items></shopcart-items>" );
   }
}
```

When a user chooses to add an item to the shopping cart, the *onclick* event will call *bookCatalog.catalogItemDetails* and supply an ISBN. The resulting data will be an XML node for that item. The node will then be imported to the *XmlCart* document via the method *addItem2Cart*. The string representation will then be stored in Session["myShoppingCart"].

```
public string addItem2Cart( XmlDocument book )
{
    //Import the last book node from doc2 into the
    //original document.
    XmlNode newBook =
    myCart.ImportNode(book.DocumentElement.FirstChild, true);
    myCart.DocumentElement.AppendChild(newBook);
    return "Success";
}
```

When a user selects to remove an item from the shopping cart, the *onclick* event will remove the node specified by the supplied ISBN via the *removeItemFromCart* method, and update Session["myShoppingCart"].

```
public string removeItemFromCart( string isbn )
{
    XmlNode curnode = myCart.SelectSingleNode(
            "//Books[isbn='" + isbn + "']");
    myCart.DocumentElement.RemoveChild( curnode );
}
```

When a user selects Checkout from the shopping cart, the *onclick* event will call the Web Service *orderBooks.OrderItem* to update the orders table in the Database, clear the cart via the *clearCart* method, and display confirmation information to the UI.

```
public void clearCart()
{
    XmlElement root = myCart.DocumentElement;
    root.RemoveAll();
}
```

When the page is reloaded and the UI needs the latest version of cart, the XML representation is passed via the *getCartDescription* method:

```
public string getCartDescriptionString()
{
    return myCart.OuterXml;
}
```

Creating the User Interface

ADOCatalog and *XMLCart* alone do not provide that much functionality; the real functionality is handled by the *showCatalog* and the *showCart* page methods. Before we take a closer look at that, let's see how the start.aspx page is laid out.

Creating the start.aspx Page

The start.aspx page is the Web form that hosts the controls to generate the UI for our catalog and cart. Here's the HTML:

```
<body onload="initializePagevariables()">
```

The preceding code makes a call to a JavaScript function that initializes the values of our hidden field variables.

This next line adds the HTML necessary to draw the navbar. You can also find this file on the CD (see header.htm).

```
<!— #Include file="header.htm" —>
<form id="formstart" method="post" runat="server">
<div style="PADDING-RIGHT: 3px; PADDING-LEFT: 3px; PADDING-BOTTOM: 3px;
WIDTH: 800px; COLOR: white; PADDING-TOP: 3px; BACKGROUND-COLOR:
dimgray" align="left">
View Books by Category
```

The following asp:dropdown control reads the list of categories from the database and generates a drop-down select box:

```
<asp:dropdownlist id="CategoryList" runat="server"
    DataValueField="CAT_ID"
DataTextField="CAT_Name"></asp:dropdownlist>
<input type="button" id="btnGo" value="Go !" onclick=
    "formstart.categoryState.value='Go';formstart.submit();">
</div>
<table width="800">
<tr>
<td>
```

The following asp:xml server control transforms the supplied XML data with catalog.xslt (see catalog.xslt on the CD):

```
<asp:xml id="catalog" runat="server"></asp:xml>
</td>
<td valign="top" align="middle" bgcolor="cornsilk">
```

The following asp:xml server control transforms the supplied XML data with cart.xslt (see cart.xslt on the CD):

```
<asp:xml id="cart" runat="server"></asp:xml>
<br>
```

The following asp:Label server control is used to insert HTML that is dynamically generated when the user clicks checkout:

```
<asp:Label id="lblFeedBack" runat="server"></asp:Label>
</td>
</tr>
</table>
```

The following div is used to hide a group of text box server controls—so why use a div to hide asp:textbox controls? First, while the asp:textbox control does have a visibility attribute, setting this attribute to hidden prevents the HTML from being written to the client, so when we view page source, the HTML for the text box isn't even there. Second, while using the HTML control **<input type="hidden" runat="server">** is also an option, this control lacks postback ability.

Each time a user clicks Add, Remove, Checkout, Previous, Next, or makes a change to the drop-down menu for category, we set these hidden variables accordingly and submit the page. Program control is then passed to our code-behind page "start.aspx.cs" (this file can also be found on the CD).

```
<div style="VISIBILITY: hidden">
    <asp:textbox id="addItem" runat="server" AutoPostBack="True" />
    <asp:TextBox id="removeItem" runat="server" AutoPostBack="True" />
    <asp:textbox id="firstRecord" runat="server" AutoPostBack="True"/>
    <asp:textbox id="lastRecord" runat="server" AutoPostBack="True"/>
    <asp:textbox id="direction" runat="server" AutoPostBack="True"/>
    <asp:textbox id="recordCount" runat="server" AutoPostBack="True"/>
    <asp:TextBox id="categoryState" runat="server" AutoPostBack="True"/>
    <asp:TextBox id="Ready4Checkout" runat="server" AutoPostBack="True"/>
</div>
</form>
</body>
```

In the following sections, we will see how the user-generated events are handled in our code-behind page: start.aspx.cs.

Rendering the Catalog

On *Page_load*, we retrieve Application["AllBooks"] and apply an XSL/Transform to render the Catalog in the UI. In order to enable browsing, we store the FirstRecord, LastRecord, recordCount, and user action (**previous | next | by CategoryID**) into hidden Text fields on the client, so this data can be read to determine which *bookCatalog* method to call and with which parameters to return the desired subset of AllBooks.

Rendering the Cart

When a user makes a selection from the catalog ("Add item to cart," Previous, Next, or selects a category) or the cart (Remove item, or Checkout), the user's action is stored in hidden text boxes that are passed to the code-behind *onsubmit()*. In the *Page_load* method, we will test for addItem, removeItem, or Checkout and handle each accordingly.

Creating the Code

The code for this page can be found on the CD (see:start.aspx.cs). Here is an overview of the page process flow:

- **In Page_Load()**
  1. Get list of categories and bind to asp:dropdownlist control "categories."
  2. Display the default catalog UI by calling *showCatalog()*.
  3. Display the default cart UI by calling *showCart()*.
  4. Test for Add, Remove, and Checkout. Handle each appropriately.

- **In showCatalog()**
  1. Create an instance of *ADOCatalog* (a.k.a., bookCatalog).
  2. Initialize the instance by loading all book data from Application["AllBooks"].
  3. Test for data filters.
     - Did user make a change to the category drop-down? Filter "AllBooks" for only the selected category.
     - Did user click Previous or Next? Filter "AllBooks based on the contents in our hidden textboxes: direction, recordCount, firstRecord, and lastRecord.
     - If no filters, use default.
     - Set the Document property of the asp:xml control, "catalog" to the filter results.
  4. Load XSLT (see catalog.xslt on the CD).

5. Set Transform properties of the asp:xml control "cart" to catalog.xslt.

- **In showCart()**
    1. Create an instance of *XMLCart* (a.k.a., xmlShoppingCart).
    2. Initialize the instance by loading any previous cart information from Session["myShoppingCart"].
    3. Load XSLT (see cart.xslt on the CD).
    4. Set Document and Transform properties of the asp:xml control, "cart" to cart.xslt.

Note that cart and catalog will have already been initialized and rendered before the next three cases can occur.

- **In AddItem**
    1. Retrieve from "AllBooks" the node corresponding to the ISBN value stored in the hidden text box "addItem".
    2. Add this node to our shopping cart.
    3. Store updated cart information in Session["myshoppingCart"].
    4. Rewrite the cart to update the UI.

- **In RemoveItem**
    1. Using the ISBN stored in the hidden text box "removeItem," remove the corresponding XML node from cart.
    2. Store updated cart information in Session["myshoppingCart"].
    3. Rewrite the cart to update the UI.

- **In Checkout**
    1. Login user to simulate order processing.
    2. Loop through the Nodes in cart and update the orders table, then remove ordered item from cart, while generating the HTML necessary to display the items ordered in an HTML table.
    3. Store updated cart information in Session["myshoppingCart"]; the cart is empty at this point.
    4. Rewrite the cart to update the UI.

There are many ways to display data held in a *DataSet* in XML, or for that matter in ASP.NET. In fact, there are a multitude of controls, including the popular *DataGrid* control that make this relatively simple. We have opted to use XML and XSLT to show other approaches to the same problem. Also, if your current ASP application uses XML and XSLT, the migration to ASP.NET is fairly easy. In fact, your existing XSLT stylesheets and XML content can still be used. For more information on XSLT, visit www.w3c.org/TR/xslt, www.w3c.org/Style/XSL/#Learn, and www.w3schools.com/XSL.

It is important to note that the *Application* and *Session* objects still have issues with regards to server farms and scalability. We used *Session* in this example for simplicity and to show that it can still be useful. Relatively simple changes can be made to the Start page to convert Session variables into hidden fields stored on the page, or state can be stored in a database.

Summary

We have developed an application that enables customers to browse a catalog of books by category or range, add selections to a virtual shopping cart, remove items from the cart and simulate processing an order by logging in and submitting updates to the order table in the database. We have leveraged the power of XML and its ability to represent data and structure, explored Web Services and their methods, designed databases and stored procedures, developed custom code-behind classes in C# and covered a multitude of uses for ADO.NET.

We also explored database design and implementation, creating two databases for the application, one for Access and one for SQL. We then covered entities and their attributes and how both work with each other to create a normalized database. Lastly, we developed a set of stored procedures that will handle all data interaction with the database, preventing the use of "ad hoc" queries against the database. To see the *ADOCart* application on the Web (it is available on the CD accompanying this book), visit www.DotThatCom.com.

Solutions Fast Track

Setting Up the Database

- ☑ A relationship between the two tables is created by the use of *primary* and *foreign keys*.

- ☑ The different types of relationships between tables are one-to-one, one-to-many, and many-to-many. In a one-to-one relationship, exactly one row corresponds with a matching row of the related table. In a one-to-many relationship, one row corresponds to many rows of the related table. In a many-to-many relationship, many rows correspond to many rows of the related table.

- ☑ Using parameterized queries in MS Access and stored providers in MS SQL results in performance gain. In addition, you no longer have to run ad hoc queries against the database. Pre-complied queries perform better.

Creating the Web Services

- ☑ Web Services provide separation of the data tier from the user interface (UI). This also makes it possible to access our data from any platform.

- ☑ Web Services help separate our data tier from our application logic. This creates a more robust and portable application.
- ☑ Web Services leverage the power of XML and its interoperability. All pages can communicate with the common language and exist in the same context.

Using WSDL Web References

- ☑ Disco, or vsdisco, written in WSDL, enables access to all Web Services and methods for that site. This provides a one-stop shop, if you will, into the server's cupboards.
- ☑ Proxy classes can easily be generated using WSDL, which enables code to access remote services as if they were local classes.

Building the Site

- ☑ Create an overview of the site structure: what pieces need to be built and how the pages relate to one another. In our example, we focus on the middle tier data classes and controls that act as a bridge between the backend and the Web UI.

Site Administration

- ☑ Tie the site administration to the Web Services, enabling the administration functions for the site to be done without accessing the code or database. The adminPage.aspx page in our example allows the site administrator to retrieve and display data, and to add, delete, and update product.
- ☑ To retrieve the list of books stored in the database, we need to access the "GetAllBooks" stored procedure (MSSQL) or parameterized query (MS Access) by creating the *allBooks* method of the *getBooks* Web Service. This method will take no parameters, and will return a *DataSet* containing all Book data as well as the table structure of the Database table that the data originated from.
- ☑ The *DataSet* is an in-memory XML representation of the database, including the Books table.

- Display the data by binding a *DataGrid* to the *DataSet*. The *DataGrid* is actually bound to the DataTable Books which is a table within the *DataSet* returned by *getBooks.AllBooks*. We create a *DataView* of the Books table so we can sort the data. This *DataView* is then bound to the *DataGrid*.

- Using the *DataGrid* event *changeBooks_DeleteCommand*, fired when a user clicks the **Delete** button in the *DataGrid UI*, we can select a row in the *DataGrid* to delete by using the *RowFilter* property.

- Using the *DataGrid* event *changeBooks_UpdateCommand*, fired when a user clicks the **Update** button in the *DataGrid UI*, we can select the row in the *DataGrid* to update by using the *RowFilter* property.

Customer Administration

- The Customer Administration pages tie our customer administration interface to our Web Services, enabling the customer to update their personal information. This is an added benefit to the user of the site.

- Customer administration will be identical to the example of the site administrator, except we will enable the customer to update only.

Creating an *ADOCatalog*

- Creating an ADOCart application allows us to tie our catalog interface to our Web Services. In our ADOCart application, all database interaction is handled via Web Services.

- Create a new class to explore ADO.NET *DataSet* operations in order to: copy, clone, import, create, and filter.

- Since our "Books" data is fairly static, we can retrieve the data in a *DataSet* once and store that *DataSet* in an application-level variable. This reduces the database traffic, while still providing quick access to the data.

- Use XML and XSLT to render data stored in a *DataSet* as HTML via the asp:Xml server control.

Building an *XMLCart*

- ☑ Building an XMLCart allows us to tie our catalog to the shopping cart.
- ☑ We will use XML node operations to update our cart's contents, XSLT/XPath operations to calculate cart totals and taxes, XML and XSLT to render cart data as HTML, and the asp:XML server control to process transforms.
- ☑ An *XmlDocument* wrapper class provides add, remove, clear, and checkout operations.

Creating the User Interface

- ☑ *ADOCatalog* and *XMLCart* alone do not provide that much functionality; the real functionality is handled by the *showCatalog* and the *showCart* page methods.
- ☑ The start.aspx page is the Web Form that hosts the controls to generate the UI for our catalog and cart.
- ☑ Use of XML and XSLT generates portions of the UI via the asp:xml server controls.

Frequently Asked Questions

The following Frequently Asked Questions, answered by the authors of this book, are designed to both measure your understanding of the concepts presented in this chapter and to assist you with real-life implementation of these concepts. To have your questions about this chapter answered by the author, browse to **www.syngress.com/solutions** and click on the **"Ask the Author"** form.

Q: My project has a few different pages in it. Unfortunately, the last page I created is the one that is loaded when I run the project. How do I set the first page to open when I run the project?

A: In your **Project Explorer**, right-click the file you want and set it to **Start Page**.

Q: I am working with the *XmlDocument* object in my code-behind page, and I am not getting any IntelliSense. What am I doing wrong?

A: Make sure you have included "Using System.Xml" in the top section of the page.

Q: I just started using VS.NET Beta 2 and I am trying to create a WSDL proxy to my Web Service. Is there an easy way to do this in VS.NET?

A: Right-click your Project Explorer and select **Add Web reference**.

Q: I renamed a file in my Solutions Explorer, but the corresponding ".aspx.cs" and ".aspx.resx" names did not change. Because of this, the project will not compile correctly. How can I fix this?

A: In your Solutions Explorer, make sure all child files are collapsed in the parent when renaming and this will change all the associated files. If you have already changed one file, change it back to the name prefix of the other files, then collapse the children and rename it to the new name. Also, check the first line in the .aspx page and ensure that the Inherits attribute lists the correct filename.

Chapter 13

Creating a Message Board with ADO and XML

Solutions in this chapter:

- **Setting Up the Database**
- **Designing Your Application**
- **Designing the User Interface**
- **Setting Up General Functions**
- **Building the Log-In Interface**
- **Designing the Browsing Interface**
- **Creating the User Functions**
- **Building the Administrative Interface**

- ☑ Summary
- ☑ Solutions Fast Track
- ☑ Frequently Asked Questions

Introduction

In the case study presented in this chapter, we take both of our previous case studies and use what we've learned together to form a big project. We'll be calling this our dotBoard! This case study will detail the process necessary to design and implement your own message board using ADO.NET and a bit of XML. First, we will go through the process necessary to create the data structures in MS Access and SQL Server. We will analyze our application and break down the data into small pieces in order to represent them in a database. Next, we will determine the best way to design our application and go through the design of all the classes we will use to power the message board, and determine what methods and properties each class should contain.

Once the data analysis is done, we are going to develop our classes that will represent the core "business objects" in our application. These objects will be the guts of dotBoard and are what we will use in our User Interface to allow our users to interact indirectly with the data in our database. The last step we will perform is creating the User Interface itself and allow users to interact with our message board.

One major point we should realize, however, is that no matter how large a project this message board seems, it is in fact incredibly simple once broken down into its smaller pieces. In fact, as you delve deeper and deeper into .NET, you will notice how much simpler it is to build most applications. With the right programming practices and .NET as your technology of choice, you can build complex applications in a much more efficient manner than some of the older technologies in existence.

Setting Up the Database

Setting up the database is one of the most important parts of any application. How do you represent your ideas in a structured, well-formed way? The first and most important step is to break down what you know you want your application to do, analyze those tasks, and then extract the important parts.

A message board has several distinguishable elements once you start to analyze it. The first and most obvious is you need to store information on subjects and threads. If you've ever looked at a message board before, you'll notice that it's broken down into three levels. The first level is a general heading, describing what it is going to contain. We'll call this level *Board*. Board can contain any number of *Threads*. Finally, a Thread contains any number of *Messages*. The last area of data involved is data representative of a message board user. Users do not fit into this three level hierarchy, but instead are a distinct part of each level. This very distinct hierarchy is a great place to start when defining your data.

The first thing to do is break down the type of information that describes a Board. This can be done many different ways: brainstorm, use your vast knowledge of all things data, or actually go to some bulletin boards on the Web and take a look at the kind of information they capture and display. This last option is probably the easiest, as there are numerous examples on the Web to look at.

That said, let's go through a Board and determine what type of information a Board uses. Our board will have the following information displayed on the user interface: name, description, list of threads, thread count, post count, the moderator, and some sort of unique identifier. Not all of those fields need their values to be saved in the database. For instance, the thread count and post count can be easily retrieved at runtime by just calculating them. That leaves Name, Description, Moderator, and a Unique Identifier.

Threads are less complex than Boards. A Thread contains the following fields: board ID, subject, post count, creator, and some sort of unique identifier. The board ID should be created by a relationship between the two tables, and post count can be retrieved at runtime. That leaves subject and creator.

A Post is composed of the following fields: subject, body, creator, thread ID, and some sort of unique identifier. All of these must be captured in order to successfully represent a Post.

Finally, the last item we must capture is the user data. Most bulletin boards you visit do not allow anonymous posting. That is, in order to post, you must have your own user data. Our message board will function the same way. This makes it much easier to write your SQL statements and preserve database integrity. User information will contain the following fields: a unique identifier, username, password, first name, last name, e-mail address, whether or not this user is an administrator, and whether or not this user has been banned from posting.

MSAccess Database

Setting up your Access database is a pretty quick process. You can use the dotBoard.mdb file located on your CD, or follow the steps provided next. If you want to create your own database, open up Microsoft Access (either 97 or 2000), and create a new database called dotBoard.mdb.

The Microsoft Access database is rather straightforward. As was described previously, the Board table (see Figure 13.1) will contains four fields: BoardID, BoardName, BoardDescription, and ModeratorID. BoardID should be an **AutoNumber**, with Indexed set to **Yes (No Duplicates)**, and should also be the primary key. BoardName is a **Text** field, with **Required** set to **Yes**, and with a **Field Size** of 100. BoardDescription is a **Text** field, with **Field Size** set to the maximum access allows, which is 255.

Figure 13.1 The Boards Table

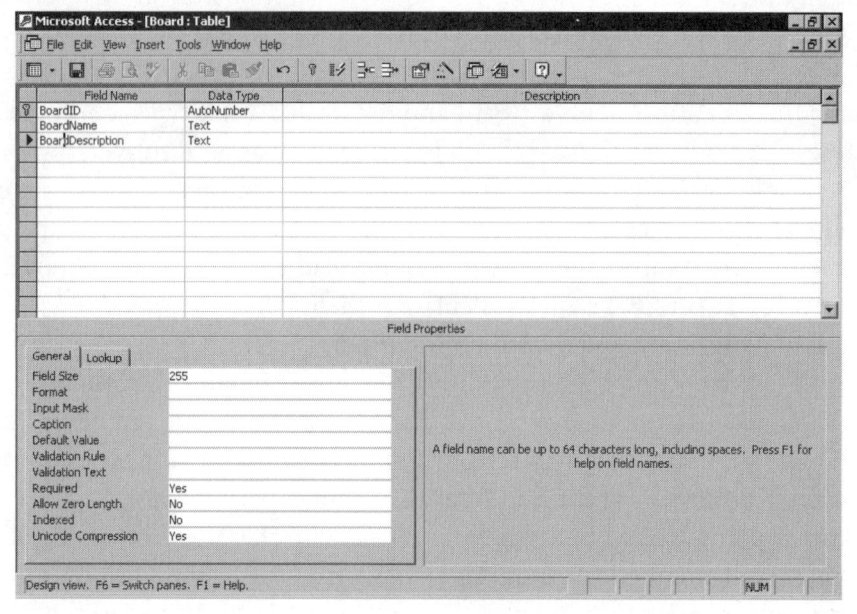

The Threads table will also contain four fields: ThreadID, ThreadSubject, CreatorID, and BoardID. ThreadID should be an **AutoNumber**, with **Indexed** set to **Yes (No Duplicates)**, and should also be the primary key. ThreadSubject is a **Text** field, with **Field Size** set to the maximum access allows, which is 255. CreatorID is a **Number**, with **Field Size** set to **Long Integer**, and **Required** set to **Yes**. BoardID is a **Number**, with **Field Size** set to **Long Integer**, and **Required** set to **Yes** (see Figure 13.2).

The Posts table will contain six fields: PostID, PostSubject, PostBody, CreatorID, ThreadID, and PostDate. PostID should be an **AutoNumber**, with **Indexed** set to **Yes (No Duplicates)**, and should also be the primary key. PostSubject is a **Text** field, with **Field Size** set to the maximum access allows, which is 255. PostBody is a **Memo** field with **Required** set to **Yes**. CreatorID is a **Number**, with **Field Size** set to **Long Integer**, and **Required** set to **Yes**. ThreadID is a **Number**, with **Field Size** set to **Long Integer**, and **Required** set to **Yes**. PostDate will be a Date/Time field with a **Default Value** of **Now()** and **Required** set to **Yes**. See Figure 13.3 for the Posts table.

Figure 13.2 The Threads Table

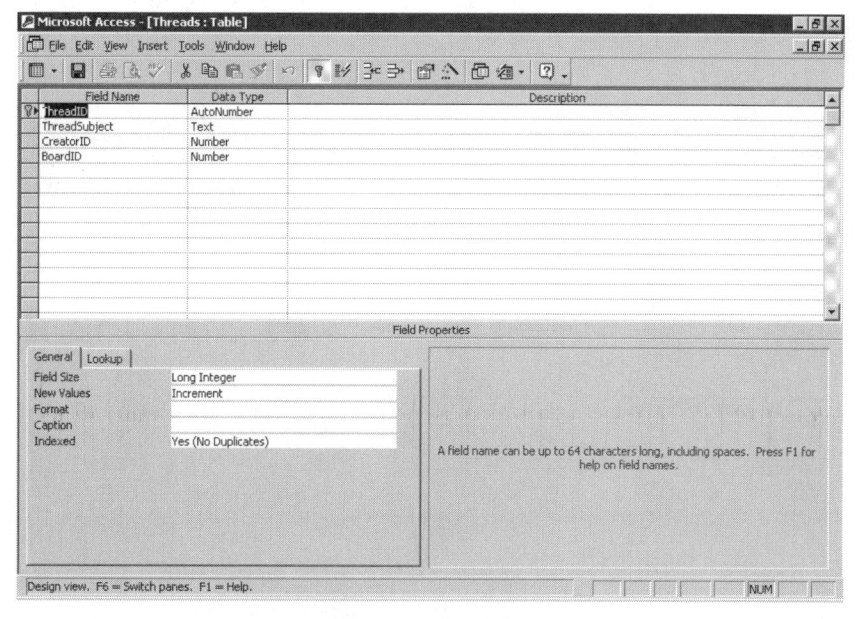

Figure 13.3 The Posts Table

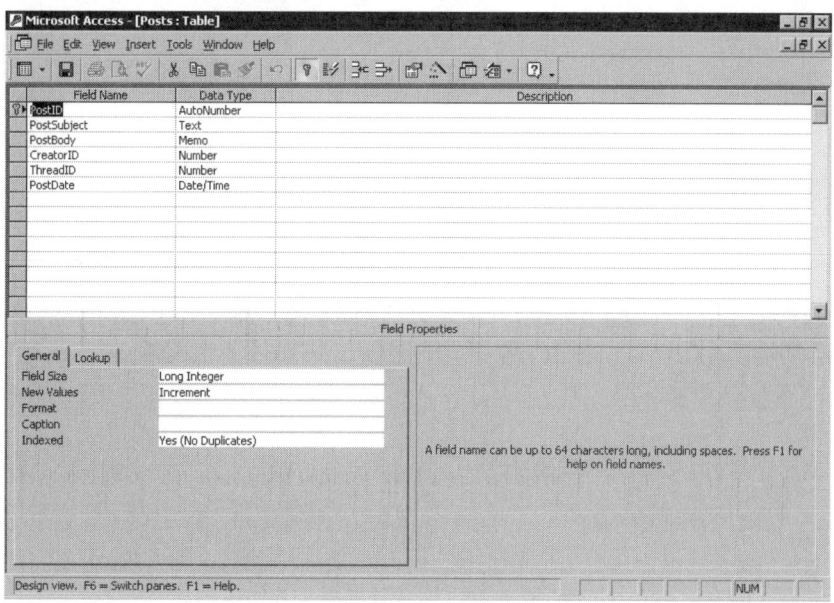

The Users table will contain eight fields: UserID, Username, Password, FirstName, LastName, Email, IsAdmin, IsBanned. UserID should be an

AutoNumber, with **Indexed** set to **Yes (No Duplicates)**, and should also be the primary key. Username is a **Text** field, with its **Field Size** set to **50** and **Required** set to **Yes**. Password is a **Text** field, with its **Field Size** set to **50** and **Required** set to **Yes**. FirstName is a **Text** field, with its **Field Size** set to **100** and **Required** set to **Yes**. LastName is a **Text** field, with its **Field Size** set to **200** and **Required** set to **Yes**. Email is a **Text** field, with its **Field Size** set to **255** and **Required** set to **Yes**. IsAdmin and IsBanned are **Yes/No** fields, with **Format** set to **True/False** and **Required** set to **Yes**. See Figure 13.4 for the Users table.

Figure 13.4 The Users Table

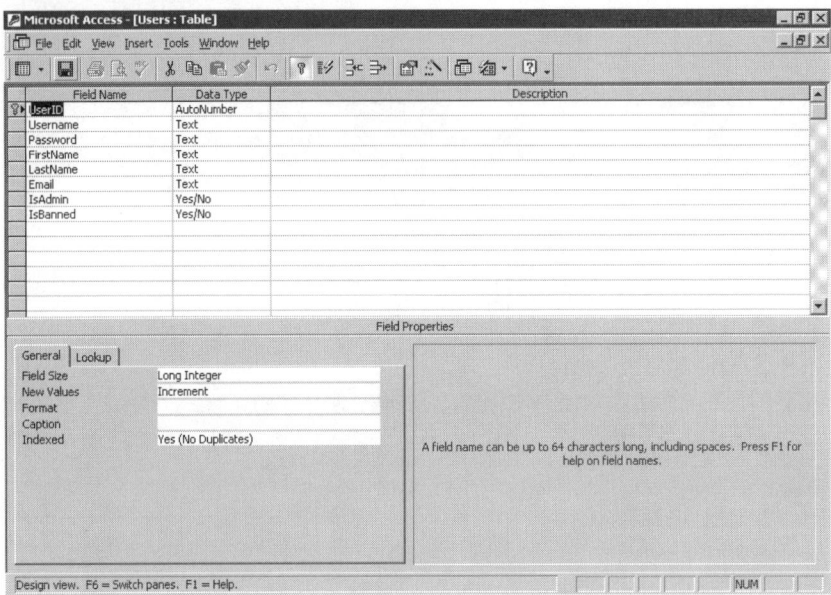

The last step is to define the relationships between the tables. Posts relates to Threads on ThreadID. Threads relates to Board on BoardID. Users relates to Posts on CreatorID, to Threads on CreatorID, and Board on ModeratorID (see Figure 13.5).

SQL Server Database

Setting up a SQL Server database is rather effortless, especially since you can let the database do everything for you by executing a SQL script. The only thing you need to do is open up your **SQL Enterprise Manager**, navigate to the server you want to create your database on, and open up the **Databases** node. Right-click the **Databases** node and select **New Database**. Name your database **dotBoard** and select **OK**.

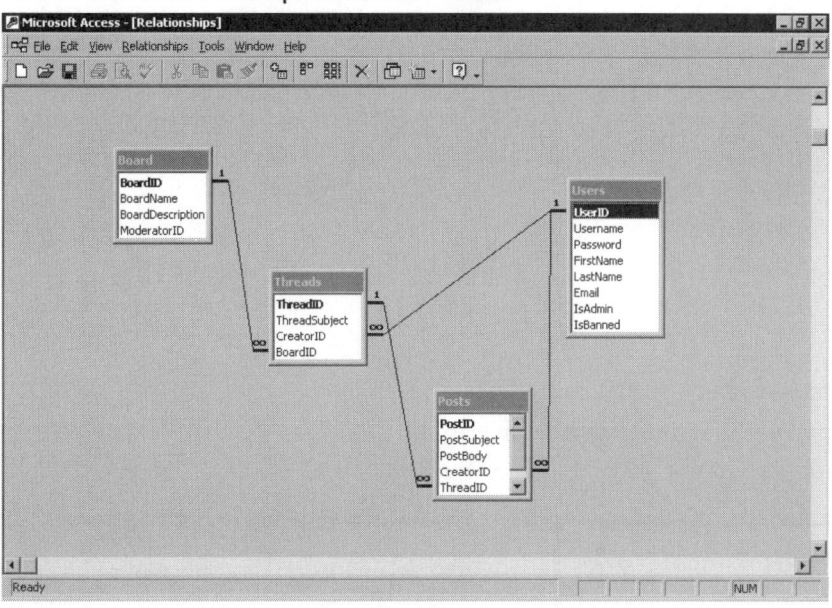

Figure 13.5 The Relationships between Tables

The only other action you need to take is open up **SQL Query Analyzer**, and execute the SQL Script shown in Figure 13.6 (which can also be found on your CD, called dotBoard Setup.sql).

Figure 13.6 SQL Server Database Creation Script (dotBoard Setup.sql)

```
CREATE TABLE [dbo].[Board] (
    [BoardID] [int] IDENTITY (1, 1) NOT NULL ,
    [BoardName] [varchar] (100) COLLATE SQL_Latin1_General_CP1_CI_AS
        NOT NULL ,
    [BoardDescription] [varchar] (255) COLLATE SQL_Latin1_General_
        CP1_CI_AS NOT NULL
) ON [PRIMARY]
GO
CREATE TABLE [dbo].[Posts] (
    [PostID] [int] IDENTITY (1, 1) NOT NULL ,
    [PostSubject] [varchar] (255) COLLATE SQL_Latin1_General_CP1_CI_AS
        NOT NULL ,
    [PostBody] [text] COLLATE SQL_Latin1_General_CP1_CI_AS NOT NULL ,
```

Continued

Figure 13.6 Continued

```
        [CreatorID] [int] NOT NULL ,
        [ThreadID] [int] NOT NULL ,
        [PostDate] [datetime] NOT NULL DEFAULT getDate()
) ON [PRIMARY] TEXTIMAGE_ON [PRIMARY]
GO
CREATE TABLE [dbo].[Threads] (
        [ThreadID] [int] IDENTITY (1, 1) NOT NULL ,
        [ThreadSubject] [varchar] (255) COLLATE SQL_Latin1_General_
            CP1_CI_AS NOT NULL ,
        [CreatorID] [int] NOT NULL ,
        [BoardID] [int] NOT NULL
) ON [PRIMARY]
GO
CREATE TABLE [dbo].[Users] (
        [UserID] [int] IDENTITY (1, 1) NOT NULL ,
        [Username] [varchar] (50) COLLATE SQL_Latin1_General_CP1_CI_AS NOT
            NULL ,
        [FirstName] [varchar] (100) COLLATE SQL_Latin1_General_CP1_CI_AS
            NOT NULL ,
        [LastName] [varchar] (200) COLLATE SQL_Latin1_General_CP1_CI_AS
NOT
            NULL ,
        [Email] [varchar] (255) COLLATE SQL_Latin1_General_CP1_CI_AS NOT
            NULL ,
        [IsAdmin] [bit] NOT NULL ,
        [IsBanned] [bit] NOT NULL
) ON [PRIMARY]
GO
ALTER TABLE [dbo].[Board] WITH NOCHECK ADD
        CONSTRAINT [PK_Board] PRIMARY KEY  CLUSTERED
        (
                [BoardID]
        )  ON [PRIMARY]
```

Continued

Figure 13.6 Continued

```
GO
ALTER TABLE [dbo].[Posts] WITH NOCHECK ADD
     CONSTRAINT [PK_Posts] PRIMARY KEY  CLUSTERED
     (
          [PostID]
     )  ON [PRIMARY]
GO
ALTER TABLE [dbo].[Threads] WITH NOCHECK ADD
     CONSTRAINT [PK_Threads] PRIMARY KEY  CLUSTERED
     (
          [ThreadID]
      )  ON [PRIMARY]
GO
ALTER TABLE [dbo].[Users] WITH NOCHECK ADD
     CONSTRAINT [PK_Users] PRIMARY KEY  CLUSTERED
     (
          [UserID]
     )  ON [PRIMARY]
GO
ALTER TABLE [dbo].[Users] WITH NOCHECK ADD
     CONSTRAINT [DF_Users_IsAdmin] DEFAULT (0) FOR [IsAdmin],
     CONSTRAINT [DF_Users_IsBanned] DEFAULT (0) FOR [IsBanned]
GO
ALTER TABLE [dbo].[Posts] ADD
     CONSTRAINT [FK_Posts_Threads] FOREIGN KEY
     (
          [ThreadID]
     ) REFERENCES [dbo].[Threads] (
          [ThreadID]
      ) ON DELETE CASCADE  ON UPDATE CASCADE ,
     CONSTRAINT [FK_Posts_Users] FOREIGN KEY
     (
          [CreatorID]
```

Continued

Figure 13.6 Continued

```
        ) REFERENCES [dbo].[Users] (
            [UserID]
        )
GO
ALTER TABLE [dbo].[Threads] ADD
    CONSTRAINT [FK_Threads_Board] FOREIGN KEY
    (
        [BoardID]
    ) REFERENCES [dbo].[Board] (
        [BoardID]
    ) ON DELETE CASCADE  ON UPDATE CASCADE ,
    CONSTRAINT [FK_Threads_Users] FOREIGN KEY
    (
        [CreatorID]
    ) REFERENCES [dbo].[Users] (
        [UserID]
    )
GO
```

Lastly, go back to your SQL Enterprise Manager, navigate to your database, and select the **Diagrams** node. Right-click and select **New Database Diagram**. Click **Next**, then select our four database tables and hit **Next**. The diagram should be created automatically for us and should look a lot nicer than the MS Access version. (see Figure 13.7).

Designing Your Application

When designing an application, there are two possible main routes. The first is the procedural approach (anyone familiar with ASP 3.0 and earlier who did not use COM objects to handle logic knows exactly what I mean): the simple "Page1" does this, "Page2" does this, and so on. You have a set of "top-down" ASP scripts (that is, your code starts at the top and executes until it hits the bottom), with functions including files, which make up your application. There is technically nothing wrong with this approach, as there are many large-scale applications that are written exactly this way.

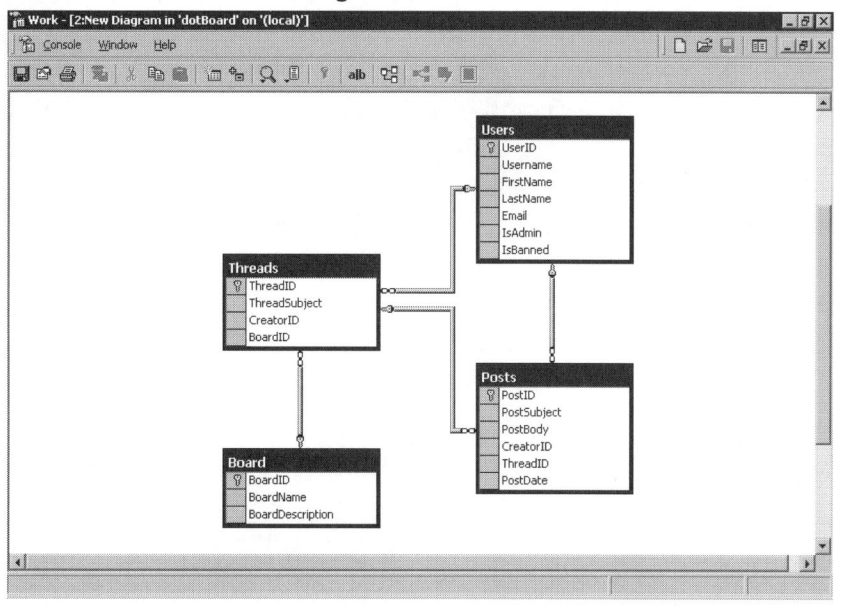

Figure 13.7 The SQL Server Diagram

Your other choice is to take a more Object-Oriented (OO) approach. In an OO world, you create a set of classes and interfaces that make up the core of your application. Using these classes, you create a user interface that will define what an average user would consider your "application." This approach allows the designer of the classes to encapsulate a good majority of all the code and logic behind the application, without exposing it to whomever might be building the user interface (and likely, the same person will be building both). An OO approach also allows your application to be used in a variety of ways, and would allow someone to build multiple user interfaces on top of the exact same set of classes.

Both approaches have their merits and flaws. With the procedural approach, you will be stuck in ASP.NET for your user interface, and if you want to "copy" logic from one place to another, you either have to create globally scoped functions, or copy and paste code. The procedural approach does tend to be a bit easier to create, though, because you do not have the additional overhead of having to create classes to handle your logic and data. The Object-Oriented approach effectively encapsulates your entire application into a small set of classes, grouped into an assembly .dll file, which can be created from another application and used. This allows you to hand another developer your assembly file, and let him or her go about building the actual user interface without you ever needing to know what the user interface was. The drawback to building an application in an OO-manner is whomever is developing the classes needs to take a lot of care to get it done properly, and be able to build it in such a manner as to not tie it exclusively to one type of user interface.

When deciding whether or not dotBoard should be procedural or Object-Oriented, take into account these things. First and foremost, you need to be able to maintain your code. If your code is modularized into multiple functions and organized very well, then the procedural approach doesn't seem too bad. However, if your code is placed haphazardly throughout your application, finding your bugs and improving code at a later date might be harder. If your code is organized into a set of classes and public interfaces (the methods and procedures that an application can "see"), it is typically easier to maintain your code, as each piece of each class is a very small piece of the application as a whole, and making changes won't likely take a large amount of code.

The other thing you should think about is that dotBoard is being written in VB.NET. For anyone who has built an application in straight ASP, you would probably be more comfortable with the procedural approach. For anyone who has built an application in ASP and created VB COM objects, you would most likely be more comfortable with the Object-Oriented approach, but feel some trepidation about speed and performance issues. For the master gurus out there who are building C++ ATL COM objects and using them in ASP, you might scoff at VB.NET and think you would rather stick with C++ ATL COM. Well, all of you have very valid points. A straight procedural approach is generally looked down upon in a professional environment, VB COM objects in ASP are typically regarded as slow and frequently memory- and processor-intensive, and well, nobody can read the C++ ATL code anyway, so it doesn't count!

Seriously, though, every point made is very valid about every technology discussed. That's where VB.NET comes in. The .NET runtime is remarkably fast. The Just-In-Time (JIT) compilation of your code only happens the first time it is executed; so, after that initial execution, your code runs incredibly fast until you change it (at which point the JIT compilation happens again). VB.NET is also a fully Object-Oriented language. It provides developers with every good OO technique available, and it is actually quite easy to write OO applications with it.

All that said, it's pretty obvious dotBoard should be an Object-Oriented application. Don't worry if you've never written any OO code before. Object-Oriented techniques are relatively easy to implement, and even if you don't think you've ever used any objects before, you probably have (especially if you've done any development in ASP).

Designing Your Objects

Now that we've decided on object orientation, we need to analyze our application and determine what our objects will "look like." At this point, you might say, "we've already done that while analyzing and building our database," and you'd be right. We have already done that. Half of our design work is now already done! The only other part we have to do is map the data we've already analyzed to VB.NET types and group them accordingly. We're going to do that with the wonder of UML (Unified Modeling Language). If you don't know what UML is, don't worry; all we're using it for here is to show you some pretty pictures of what our classes are going to look like. Please note that all of these objects and all files will be found on the CD that accompanies this book.

Creating Your Data Access Object

To make it easier for each of your objects to have access to the database, we're going to create a singular data access object that does everything for you. We're going to call this class *DataControl*, and it is going to be comprised of solely shared methods. A shared method means you do not need to create an instance of a *User* object to call it. *DataControl* will contain two Shared methods, *GetDataSet* and *ExecuteNonQuery*. *GetDataSet* returns a *DataSet*, and *ExecuteNonQuery* executes a SQL statement and returns nothing. This class is pretty straightforward, and is shown in Figure 13.8 (likewise, it can also be found on your CD as DataControl.vb).

Figure 13.8 DataControl.vb

```vb
Imports System.Data
Imports System.Data.OleDb
Imports System.Web
Imports System.Configuration
Imports System.Collections.Specialized

Public Class DataControl
    Public Shared Function GetDataSet(ByVal SQL As String) As DataSet
        Dim connectionString As String
        Dim settings As ConfigurationSettings
        Dim appSettings As NameValueCollection
```

Continued

Figure 13.8 Continued

```vb
        appSettings = settings.AppSettings()
        connectionString = appSettings.Item("ConnectionString")

        Dim connection As New OleDbConnection(connectionString)
        connection.Open()

        Dim adapter As New OleDbDataAdapter(SQL, connection)
        Dim myData As New DataSet()

        adapter.Fill(myData)
        adapter.Dispose()
        connection.Close()

        Return myData
    End Function

    Friend Shared Sub ExecuteNonQuery(ByVal SQL As String)
        Dim connectionString As String
        Dim settings As ConfigurationSettings
        Dim appSettings As NameValueCollection

        appSettings = settings.AppSettings()
        connectionString = appSettings.Item("ConnectionString")

        Dim connection As New OleDbConnection(connectionString)
        connection.Open()

        Dim myCommand As New OleDbCommand()
        myCommand.Connection = connection
        myCommand.CommandText = SQL
        myCommand.CommandType = CommandType.Text
        myCommand.ExecuteNonQuery()
        'clean up
```

Continued

Figure 13.8 Continued

```
            connection.Close()
            myCommand.Dispose()
            connection.Dispose()
        End Sub
End Class
```

You see that the two methods in *DataControl* are in fact, rather simple. As was discussed earlier in this book, these functions connect to the database and do a specific function (execute SQL scripts and one returns a *DataSet*). The one thing to note is that the connection string is being retrieved from the ConfigurationSettings.AppSettings. These are dynamic settings that the .NET runtime gives you access to. When you're running an ASP.NET application, they are located in the *web.config* file. In another type of application, they are located in *ProjectName.exe.config*. That's it for our Data object. The next step is to take a look at our *User* object.

Designing the *User* Class

When we looked at the user information when thinking about the database, we discovered a number of fields that needed to reside in the User table. Luckily all our classes will be structured in a way to nearly match the database; the *User* class is no exception. The only difference is that this *User* is a VB.NET class and not a database table.

There are four basic types of users: Guests, Registered users, Administrators, and Moderators. All of these should be represented when we build our User class. Again, you might say something like "but this is an object-oriented application, and if we have multiple types of one object, shouldn't they be separate?" Again, you would be right. There are three types of users. All have similar properties; the only difference is that some do certain things that others can't. For instance, a registered user in a bulletin board would have the ability to post threads and messages, whereas a guest user would not. A registered user would also have the ability to edit his or her profile and edit his or her messages, whereas a guest user would not be able to. An administrator would have the ability to do everything a registered user could, except globally. A moderator can modify posts and threads in boards he or she has moderator privileges to.

Now that we've identified the multiple types of users, we need to determine if we should have multiple types of users in our application. A Guest can only browse a bulletin board, as no security is necessary for browsing. A Registered User can create and edit posts, and modify his or her profile. An Administrator can do anything he or she wants to the bulletin board. A Moderator can do what a Registered User can, and can act like an Administrator on the board he or she is given moderation rights to.

You may want to build some neat OO objects here, but all these things can be accomplished through a single *User* class. Take a look at Figure 13.9.

Figure 13.9 The *User* Object Diagram

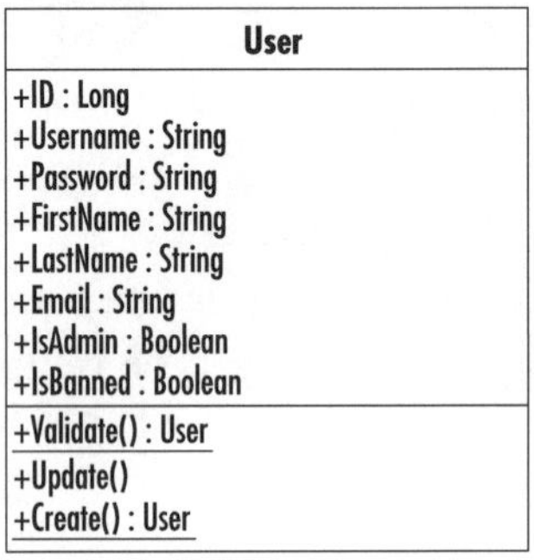

```
User
+ID : Long
+Username : String
+Password : String
+FirstName : String
+LastName : String
+Email : String
+IsAdmin : Boolean
+IsBanned : Boolean
+Validate() : User
+Update()
+Create() : User
```

You see that our *User* object will have the exact same fields as our database table, which is named exactly the same. This makes it a bit easier to remember which field in the object matches up to which field in the database. The other thing you should notice is the three items down at the bottom of the diagram: *Create*, *Validate*, and *Update*. All are methods the *User* object will have. *Update()* will update the user's details and save them to the database. *Validate* is a shared method of the *User* class, and can be used to perform all user validation. Create is also a shared method, and can be used to create a brand new user in the database.

That's it. That's the whole *User* object. Not much to it is there? It has a Boolean field to signify whether or not it is an administrator, and each Board object will store the ID of the administrator of that Board, so the *User* object doesn't have to. The only other thing to mention is guest users—a guest user will just be a User that is Nothing. That is, if you are currently a guest in the application, you won't have a *User* object created for you. Let's take a look at the code involved to create this *User* object in Figure 13.10 (which can also be found on your CD called User.vb).

Figure 13.10 The Basics (User.vb)

```
Public Class User
    Private mUsername As String
    Private mPassword As String
    Private mFirstName As String
    Private mLastName As String
    Private mUserID As Long
    Private mIsAdmin As Boolean
    Private mEmail As String
    Private mUserID As Long
End Class
```

That part is clear enough. We declare the *User* class, and the private variables necessary to represent each user. Next, declare the public properties for each of these private variables as shown in Figure 13.11.

Figure 13.11 Public Properties (User.vb)

```
    Public WriteOnly Property Password() As String
        Set(ByVal Value As String)
            MPassword = Value
        End Set
    End Property

    Public ReadOnly Property ID() As Long
        Get
            Return mUserID
        End Get
    End Property

    Public Property LastName() As String
        Get
            Return mLastName
        End Get
        Set(ByVal Value As String)
```

Continued

Figure 13.11 Continued

```
            mLastName = Value
        End Set
    End Property

    Public Property FirstName() As String
        Get
            Return mFirstName
        End Get
        Set(ByVal Value As String)
            mFirstName = Value
        End Set
    End Property

    Public Property Username() As String
        Get
            Return mUsername
        End Get
        Set(ByVal Value As String)
            mUsername = Value
        End Set
    End Property

    Public Property IsAdmin() As Boolean
        Get
            Return mIsAdmin
        End Get
        Set(ByVal Value As Boolean)
            mIsAdmin = Value
        End Set
    End Property

    Public Property IsBanned() As Boolean
        Get
```

Continued

Figure 13.11 Continued

```
            Return mIsBanned
        End Get
        Set(ByVal Value As Boolean)
            mIsBanned = Value
        End Set
    End Property

    Public Property Email() As String
        Get
            Return mEmail
        End Get
        Set(ByVal Value As String)
            mEmail = Value
        End Set
    End Property
```

With that out of the way, let's look at the methods the *User* object will have. As we saw earlier, there will be three methods: *Validate*, *CreateUser*, and *Update*. *Validate* is a shared method which will give a developer the ability to validate and return a valid *User* object, or throw an exception. *CreateUser* is also a shared method that gives the developer the ability to create a new *User* object. Finally, *Update* will allow a developer to update the private fields in the *User* object and commit them to the database. This will be for tasks like saving passwords and updating e-mail addresses. Let's take a look at the first method, *Validate*, in Figure 13.12.

Figure 13.12 The *Validate* Method (User.vb)

```
Public Shared Function Validate(ByVal username As String, _
    ByVal password As String) As User
    If password.Equals("") Then
        Throw New ArgumentException("You must enter a password.")
    Else
        Dim myData As DataSet = DataControl.GetDataSet("SELECT * " & _
            "FROM [Users] WHERE [UserName] = '" & username & "'")
        If myData.Tables(0).Rows.Count <= 0 Then
```

Continued

Figure 13.12 Continued

```
                Throw New ArgumentException("Username does not exist.")
        Else
            If CBool(myData.Tables(0).Rows(0)("IsBanned")) = True Then
                Throw New Exception("User is banned")
            Else
                If password <> _
                    CStr(myData.Tables(0).Rows(0)("Password")) Then
                        Throw New ArgumentException("Invalid password")
                Else
                    Return New User(myData.Tables(0).Rows(0))
                End If
            End If
        End If
    End If
End Function
```

The *Validate* method accepts a username and a password as parameters, and attempts to verify that those parameters are a valid combination for a registered user. If the password is empty, it throws an ArgumentException. If, while looking up the username, it finds that the username is not present in the database, it again throws an *ArgumentException*. If the username exists, but the user is banned, then it throws an Exception. If the username exists, the user is not banned, and the password passed in was incorrect, once again it throws an ArgumentException. Finally, if the username is valid and the password is correct, it returns a new *User* object, passing in the first *DataRow* to the *User* constructor.

At this point, you're probably wondering why we haven't discussed the constructor of the *User* object. Well, wait no longer! Here's the code for the *User* object constructor in Figure 13.13.

Figure 13.13 Constructors (User.vb)

```
    Public Sub New(ByVal userId As Long)
        Dim myData As DataSet
        myData = DataControl.GetDataSet("SELECT * FROM Users " & _
            "WHERE UserID = " & Me.mUserID)
```

Continued

Figure 13.13 Continued

```
        If myData.Tables(0).Rows.Count <= 0 Then
            Throw New ArgumentException("The requested user " & _
                does not exist.")
        Else
            inflate(myData.Tables(0).Rows(0))
        End If

        myData.Dispose()
    End Sub

    Public Sub New(ByVal row As DataRow)
        inflate(row)
    End Sub
```

There are two constructors here. The second constructor is what the *Validate* method called. That constructor forwards the *DataRow* on to another method called *inflate*, which will be discussed in a moment. The first constructor accepts a user ID as a parameter. This user ID is synonymous with the UserID field in the User table. The constructor looks up the user based on the user ID. If that user ID is not found, it throws an ArgumentException. If the user ID *is* found, it forwards the first *DataRow* in the *DataSet* to the *fillData* method in Figure 13.14.

Figure 13.14 The *fillData* Method (User.vb)

```
Private Sub inflate(ByVal row As DataRow)
    Me.mUsername = CStr(row("Username"))
    Me.mFirstName = CStr(row("FirstName"))
    Me.mLastName = CStr(row("LastName"))
    Me.mIsAdmin = CBool(row("IsAdmin"))
    Me.mEmail = CStr(row("Email"))
    Me.mUserID = CLng(row("UserID"))
    Me.mPassword = CStr(row("Password"))
End Sub
```

As you can see, the *inflate* method accepts a *DataRow* as a parameter, and populates all the private fields with values from the database. This is frequently called "inflating" your objects, hence the appropriately named subroutine. The other thing to notice is that inflate is a private subroutine. This is because you don't want any objects outside of the current *User* object to have access to this method. It does "utility" work on the object, and is unnecessary for any other object to call this method.

Now that we've discussed how to Validate and return a valid *User* object, let's move on to creating users. Any user can have any username. The only restriction is that no two users can have the same username. This is because if you had two users with the same username, the only way to identify which one you wanted is to have some other sort of unique identifier. Unfortunately, people can typically remember names and usernames much better than they could some (relatively) random number. So, in order to keep this username unique, you have to manually check. If you were a database administrator, you would probably insist on creating a unique index on the username field in the database, which is completely reasonable. If you feel you need the extra "security" in place to make sure the same username isn't taken twice, go ahead and put it in there, but it's in the *CreateUser* method as well, which we will now take a look at in Figure 13.15.

Figure 13.15 The *CreateUser* Method (User.vb)

```
Public Shared Function CreateUser(ByVal userName As String, _
    ByVal password As String, _
    ByVal firstName As String, _
    ByVal lastName As String, ByVal email As String) As User

    Dim sql As String
    Dim myData As DataSet

    sql = "SELECT userName FROM Users WHERE userName = '" & _
        userName & "'"
    myData = DataControl.GetDataSet(sql)
    If myData.Tables(0).Rows.Count <= 0 Then
        'this username has not been taken
        sql = "INSERT INTO [Users] ([Username], [Password], " & _
            "[FirstName], [LastName], " & _
```

Continued

Figure 13.15 Continued

```
                "[Email], [IsAdmin], [IsBanned]) VALUES ('" & userName & _
            "','" & password & "','" & firstName & "','" & lastName & _
            "','" & email & "',0,0)"
        DataControl.ExecuteNonQuery(sql)
        Return User.Validate(userName, password)
    Else
        'this username has already been taken
        Throw New ArgumentException("The username is already taken")
    End If
End Function
```

First, the *CreateUser* function scans the database to see if the request username already exists. If it does, it throws an ArgumentException. If the username doesn't exist, it builds a SQL statement to insert a new row into the user table and executes it. Finally it calls the *Validate* method and returns the result.

The last method to discuss is the *Update* method. This method updates the database with the current state of the object. See Figure 13.16 for the *Update* method.

Figure 13.16 The *Update* Method (User.vb)

```
Public Sub Update()
    Dim sql As String
    sql = "UPDATE [Users] SET [Password] = '" & mPassword & _
        "', [FirstName] = '" & mFirstName & _
        "', [LastName] = '" & mLastName & _
        "', [Email] = '" & mEmail & "'"
    If Me.IsAdmin = True Then
        sql = sql & ", [IsAdmin] = 1"
    Else
        sql = sql & ", [IsAdmin] = 0"
    End If
    If Me.IsBanned = True Then
        sql = sql & ", [IsBanned] = 1"
    Else
```

Continued

Figure 13.16 Continued

```
        sql = sql & ", [IsBanned] = 0"
    End If
    sql = sql & " WHERE [UserID] = " & mUserID.ToString()
    DataControl.ExecuteNonQuery(sql)
End Sub
```

Again, this method is rather simple. It generates a SQL statement to update the database. The If statements are there to insert the correct Boolean value into the database instead of "True" or "False." Finally, after building the SQL statement, it executes it and exits the method.

Debugging…

Creating Console Applications to Test Your Progress

Visual Studio .NET gives us an easy way to test and debug our applications, without actually needing to have a decent User Interface to look at. They call it a Console Application. Sure, Console Applications are useful by themselves when you don't need a UI, but when you are building a relatively large application and you don't want to get yourself confused trying to build the UI and the classes at the same time, consider using a Console Application to debug your project.

Go ahead and try it.

1. Add a new Console Application to your project.
2. Add a reference to your **dotBoardObjects** project to the Console Application.
3. Set your new Console Application as the start-up project.
4. Start putting in some code to test the classes you've written. Maybe something like this:

```
Dim myUser As User
myUser = User.CreateUser("myuser", "mypassword", "joe", _
    "blow", "joe.blow@email.com")
```

Continued

```
Console.WriteLine(myUser.FirstName)
Console.WriteLine("Press enter to finish")
Console.ReadLine()
```

>   Before you run this, put a break point on the line that creates a user.
>
> 5. Step through the code using F8 (if you set up your Visual Studio to use the Visual Basic Profile) and watch as the execution moves into the *User* class you created. You can step through your application and watch as every line of code gets executed. If an error pops up, stop your application, fix the error, and run the application again.
>
> You should use and abuse this technique as much as possible. Not only does it allow you to test and debug your classes, but it also does it without your needing to build a UI at the same time you build the objects.

Designing the *Board* Class

Now that we've designed the *User* class, let's take a look at the *Board* class. A lot of the concepts in the *User* class will be taken from the *Board* class. That is, the *Board* class will mimic the Board table in the database, and will have a couple of similarly named methods as in the *User* class. Let's take a look at a UML diagram of the *Board* class in Figure 13.17.

Figure 13.17 The *Board* Class

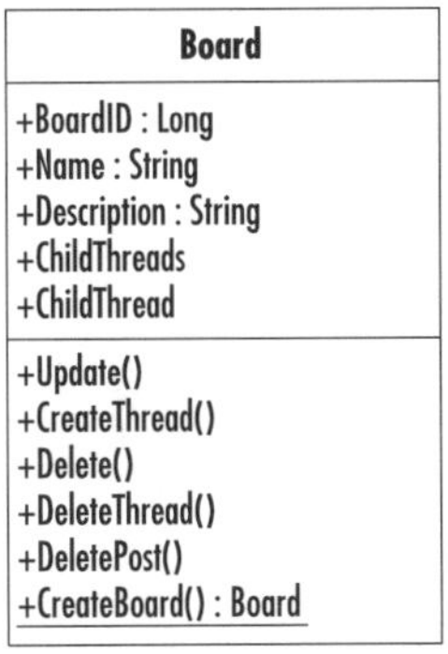

Board
+BoardID : Long
+Name : String
+Description : String
+ChildThreads
+ChildThread
+Update()
+CreateThread()
+Delete()
+DeleteThread()
+DeletePost()
+CreateBoard() : Board

Just by looking at this diagram, you can see that the *Board* class has a lot more functionality than the *User* class. Notice the four fields from the Board table: BoardID, Name, and Description. Just like the *User* class, these are directly representative of what exists in the database. The other two fields you shouldn't recognize. ChildThreads returns a list of the Threads that exist in this Board. ChildThread is a property that accepts a ThreadID to return a specific Thread that is directly located in a specific Board.

The methods available to a *Board* object should be somewhat self-explanatory. The *Update* method does exactly what the *User* class *Update* method did: updates the database with the private fields in the database. The *Delete* method deletes the Board from the database. DeleteThread deletes a specific Thread from the database. DeletePost deletes a specific Post that is located somewhere in this Board. CreateThread creates a new Thread and adds it to the private list of Threads in this Board. Like the *User* class, the *Board* class has a way to create new Boards, called *CreateBoard*. Let's start off by showing the basics of the *Board* class in Figure 13.18 (which can also be found on your CD under the name Board.vb).

Figure 13.18 Private Fields and Public Properties (Board.vb)

```
Public Class Board
    Private mBoardID As Long
    Private mName As String
    Private mDescription As String
    Private myThreads As ThreadList

    Public ReadOnly Property ChildThread(ByVal threadId As Long) As _
        Thread
        Get
            'lookup the correct thread
            Dim i As Integer
            For i = 0 To Me.ChildThreads.Count - 1
                Dim myThread As Thread = Me.ChildThreads.Item(i)
                If myThread.ID = threadId Then
                    Return myThread
                End If
            Next i
            'if we've gotten to this point, there is no thread
```

Continued

Figure 13.18 Continued

```
            'with that ID in this board. throw an exception
            Throw New ArgumentException("Thread does not exist")
        End Get
    End Property


    Public ReadOnly Property ChildThreads() As ThreadList
        Get
            Return myThreads
        End Get
    End Property


    Public ReadOnly Property ID() As Long
        Get
            Return mBoardID
        End Get
    End Property


    Public Property Name() As String
        Get
            Return mName
        End Get
        Set(ByVal Value As String)
            mName = Value
        End Set
    End Property


    Public Property Description() As String
        Get
            Return mDescription
        End Get
        Set(ByVal Value As String)
            mDescription = Value
        End Set
    End Property
```

The public properties in this class are a little more complex than the properties in the *User* class. The public properties for the private fields are easy to understand, but ChildThread and ChildThreads are a bit more complex, as is the private *myThread* variable. Let's start with myThread, which is defined as being of type *ThreadList*. If you're familiar with the *System.Collections* namespace, you'll definitely notice that this is not one of the built-in .NET collections. ThreadList is actually a custom list that wraps an ArrayList, which will be discussed a bit later. For now, just accept the fact that this list collects all the Threads in a given Board.

The *ChildThreads* property returns the private *myThreads* variable. The *ChildThread* property accepts a ThreadID as a parameter, and looks up that ThreadID in the myThreads list. It loops through the list, and compares the ID of the Thread in the list with the ThreadID passed in. If it finds a match, it returns that Thread, otherwise it throws an ArgumentException. Again, ThreadList will be discussed later, but for now, let's move on to the shared *CreateBoard* method, as shown in Figure 13.19.

Figure 13.19 The *CreateBoard* Method (Board.vb)

```
Public Shared Function CreateBoard(ByVal name As String, _
    ByVal description As String, _
    ByVal creator As User) As Board

    Dim sql As String
    Dim myData As DataSet

    If creator.IsAdmin = True Then
        sql = "SELECT BoardName FROM [Board] WHERE [BoardName] = '" & _
            name & "'"
        myData = DataControl.GetDataSet(sql)
        If myData.Tables(0).Rows.Count <= 0 Then
            'this board name does not already exist.
            sql = "INSERT INTO [Board] ([BoardName], " & _
                "[BoardDescription], " & _
                ") VALUES ("
            sql &= "'" & name & "','" & description & _
                "')"
```

Continued

Figure 13.19 Continued

```
            'create the board
            DataControl.ExecuteNonQuery(sql)
            'return the board
            Return New Board(name)
        Else
            'board name already exists
            Throw New Exception("This board name already exists")
        End If
    Else
        Throw New Exception("Only admins may create boards")
    End If
End Function
```

The first step in this method is to check to see if the user that is requesting a new Board be created is an admin. If the user is not an admin, it throws an exception. If the user is an admin, it then checks to see if a Board with that name has already been created. Like the username field in the *User* class, the name field in the *Board* class should be unique. This makes it easier to manage your Boards and to make sure they're named appropriately. If the Board name already exists, it throws an exception, otherwise it generates the SQL statement necessary to create a Board. It then executes the SQL statement and returns a new *Board* object based on the Board name. Let's take a look at the Board constructor, shown in Figure 13.20, to see what it does.

Figure 13.20 Constructor (Board.vb)

```
Public Sub New(ByVal name As String)
    Dim sql As String
    Dim myData As DataSet
    sql = "SELECT * FROM [Board] WHERE [BoardName] = '" & _
        name & "'"
    myData = DataControl.GetDataSet(sql)

    If myData.Tables(0).Rows.Count > 0 Then
        Me.inflate(myData.Tables(0).Rows(0))
```

Continued

Figure 13.20 Continued

```
        Else
            Throw New Exception("Board does not exist")
        End If
    End Sub

    Private Sub inflate(ByVal myRow As DataRow)
        mName = CStr(myRow("BoardName"))
        mDescription = CStr(myRow("BoardDescription"))
        mBoardID = CLng(myRow("BoardID"))

        myThreads = New ThreadList(mBoardID)
    End Sub
```

The Board constructor takes the Board name as a parameter, and looks in the database for that Board name. If it cannot find the Board, it throws an Exception, otherwise it passes the first DataRow in the *DataSet* to the inflate method. The inflate method functions exactly as it did in the *User* class: it fills up the private fields with values. The only difference here is that the *myThreads* variable is initialized and the BoardID is passed to it. Again, the ThreadList will be discussed a bit later, but trust that the ThreadList takes the BoardID passed in and creates a collection of the Threads in this Board. Next, let's take a look at the *Update* method in Figure 13.21.

Figure 13.21 The *Update* Method (Board.vb)

```
Public Sub Update(ByVal requestor As User)
    If requestor.IsAdmin Then
        'update the database with this board's details
        Dim sql As String
        sql = "UPDATE [Board] SET [BoardName] = '" & mName & _
            "', BoardDescription = '" & mDescription & _
            " WHERE [BoardID] = " & mBoardID.ToString()
        DataControl.ExecuteNonQuery(sql)
    End If
End Sub
```

The *Update* method in the *Board* class does exactly what the *User* class's *Update* method did. The only real difference here is that it checks to make sure the user requesting the update is really an admin. If the user is not an admin, then it throws an exception. Next, take a look at Figure 13.22 for the *CreateThread* method.

Figure 13.22 The *CreateThread* Method (Board.vb)

```
Public Sub CreateThread(ByVal subject As String, _
    ByVal creator As User)

    Dim sql As String
    sql = "INSERT INTO [Threads] ([ThreadSubject], " & _
        "[CreatorID], [BoardID]) VALUES ('" & subject & _
        "'," & creator.ID.ToString() & "," & _
        mBoardID.ToString() & ")"
    DataControl.ExecuteNonQuery(sql)

    'reinitialize the thread list
    myThreads.InitializeThreads()
End Sub
```

The *CreateThread* method builds the SQL statement necessary to insert a new Thread into the database, and then reinitializes the private *ThreadList* variable by calling its *InitializeThreads* method. You may be wondering why the *Board* class has the *Create* method for its child objects, whereas both the *User* class and *Board* class have their *Create* method located in their class definitions. This is because both the *User* class and *Board* class do not have any parent-child relationships with any other classes. When you have a parent object and multiple child objects, the typical place to put the creation of the child objects is in the parent object. This is a matter of semantics— if you prefer to have your child objects create themselves, feel free to do it that way.

Let's explore how to delete objects. The *Board* class contains the *Delete*, *DeleteThread*, and *DeletePost* methods. The *Board* class can obviously delete itself, but why would it also contain the ability to delete both threads and posts? It has these two methods because the *Board* class is where the ModeratorID lives, and Moderators can delete both threads and posts, so it just seems natural to put these two delete methods in the *Board* class. Look at Figure 13.23 for the code.

Figure 13.23 The *Delete* Method (Board.vb)

```
Public Sub Delete(ByVal requestor As User)
    'only admins can delete boards
    If requestor.IsAdmin Then
        Dim sql As String
        sql = "DELETE FROM Boards WHERE BoardID = " & _
            mBoardID.ToString()
        DataControl.ExecuteNonQuery(sql)
    Else
        Throw New ArgumentException("User not permitted to delete")
    End If
End Sub
```

The first step in the *Delete* method is to check to make sure the requesting user has the appropriate access rights to delete this board. If the user is not an admin, then an ArgumentException is thrown. If the user does have access rights to delete a Board, then the SQL statement is built to delete the Board from the database. The SQL statement is executed, and the Board is officially deleted. You can see the *DeleteThread* method in Figure 13.24.

Figure 13.24 The *DeleteThread* Method (Board.vb)

```
Public Sub DeleteThread(ByVal thread As Thread, ByVal requestor As User)
    If requestor.IsAdmin Then
        Dim sql As String
        sql = "DELETE FROM Threads WHERE ThreadID = " & _
            thread.ID.ToString()
        DataControl.ExecuteNonQuery(sql)
        'reinitialize the threads
        myThreads.InitializeThreads()
    Else
        Throw New ArgumentException("User not permitted to delete")
    End If
End Sub
```

The first step in the *DeleteThread* method is to make sure the requesting user has the appropriate access to delete this thread. If the user is neither an admin nor a moderator of this Board, then an ArgumentException is thrown. If the user does have access to delete a thread, then the SQL statement is built to delete the thread from the database. The SQL statement is executed, and the ThreadList is reinitialized by calling its *InitializeThreads* method.

The next method we need is the *DeletePost* method. Take a look at Figure 13.25 for its implementation.

Figure 13.25 The *DeletePost* Method (Board.vb)

```
Public Sub DeletePost(ByVal thread As Thread, ByVal post As Post, _
    ByVal requestor As User)

    If requestor.IsAdmin Then
        Dim sql As String
        sql = "DELETE FROM Posts WHERE PostID = " & _
            post.ID.ToString()
        DataControl.ExecuteNonQuery(sql)
        'reinitialize the posts in the thread
        thread.ChildPosts.InitializePosts()
    Else
        Throw New ArgumentException("User not permitted to delete")
    End If
End Sub
```

Just as in the *DeleteThread* method, the first step in the *DeletePost* method is to make sure the requesting user has the appropriate access rights to delete this post. If the user is neither an admin nor a moderator of this Board, then an ArgumentException is thrown. If the user does have access to delete a post, then the SQL statement is built to delete the post from the database. The SQL statement is executed, and the Threads *ChildPosts* property is reinitialized by calling its *InitializePosts* method.

Designing the *ThreadList* Class

We promised you that we would discuss the *ThreadList*, and here it is. As was mentioned earlier, the *ThreadList* class is a class that wraps an ArrayList. By wraps, we mean it contains a private ArrayList thereby holding its list of Threads, and exposes certain custom functionalities not necessarily pre-built into the *ArrayList* class. Let's take a look at a UML diagram for the *ThreadList* class in Figure 13.26.

Figure 13.26 The *ThreadList* Class

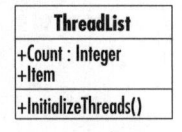

ThreadList
+Count : Integer
+Item
+InitializeThreads()

As you can see from this diagram, there isn't much to the *ThreadList*. It contains a count of the number of Threads in the list, contains an *Item* property to allow you to access the Threads in the list, and gives you the ability to manually force the reinitialization of the list through the *InitializeThreads* method. Again, let's start at the basics and build up from there in Figure 13.27 (which can also be found on your CD under the name ThreadList.vb).

Figure 13.27 The Basics (ThreadList.vb)

```
Public Class ThreadList
    Private list As ArrayList
    Private mBoardID As Long

    Public Sub New(ByVal BoardID As Long)
        mBoardID = BoardID
        Me.InitializeThreads()
    End Sub

    Public ReadOnly Property Count() As Integer
        Get
            Return list.Count
        End Get
    End Property
End Class
```

The *ThreadList* class contains only two private fields: list and mBoardID. The list variable is used to hold all your Threads, and mBoardID is used to look up the Threads in a given Board. The constructor accepts a BoardID, and calls the *InitializeThreads* method, as shown in Figure 13.28.

Figure 13.28 The *InitializeThreads* Method (ThreadList.vb)

```
Public Sub InitializeThreads()
    Dim myData As DataSet
    Dim sql As String
    sql = "SELECT [Threads].*, [Users].* FROM [Threads] " & _
        "INNER JOIN [Users] " & _
        "ON [Users].[UserID] = [Threads].[CreatorID] " & _
        "WHERE " & _
        "[BoardID] = " & mBoardID.ToString() & _
        " ORDER BY [Threads].[ThreadID] DESC"
    myData = DataControl.GetDataSet(sql)
    list = New ArrayList()

    Dim myRow As DataRow
    For Each myRow In myData.Tables(0).Rows
        list.Add(myRow)
    Next
End Sub
```

The *InitializeThreads* method is rather straightforward, but there is one major concept that needs to be mentioned. First, a SQL statement is built to select the Threads located in the appropriate Board (this is where the mBoardID variable comes into play). The SQL statement also joins on the Users table, to allow for the *Thread* object to know about the User who created the Thread. Next, the list is initialized, and each *DataRow* in the resultant *DataSet* is added to the list. This is where the important concept is. The private list currently contains a set of *DataRow* objects. Obviously, you do not want to expose a bunch of *DataRow* objects as your list of Threads, so this is where the *Item* property comes into effect. See Figure 13.29 regarding the *Item* property.

Figure 13.29 The *Item* Property (ThreadList.vb)

```
    Public Function Item(ByVal index As Integer) As Thread
1       Dim myObject As Object = list.Item(index)
2       If myObject.GetType() Is GetType(Thread) Then
3           'it is already a thread, so nothing further is needed
4       Else
5           Dim myThread As Thread
6           myThread = New Thread(CType(list.Item(index), DataRow))
7           'replace the item in the list with
8           'an actual thread object
9           list.Item(index) = myThread
10      End If
11
12      Return CType(list.Item(index), Thread)
    End Function
```

The *Item* property is a little more complex than the average property. Let's review it, line by line. Line 1 creates a variable called *myObject* of type *Object* and sets it equal to the object that is at the specified index of the ArrayList. Line 2 compares the type of the object to the type of the *Thread* class. If they are the same, it does nothing; if not, it enters the Else part of the If statement (lines 5 – 9). Next, a *Thread* variable called *myThread* is declared and set to a new Thread on line 6, passing in the object that is in the specified index in the ArrayList. That object is cast to a *DataRow* using CType. Line 9 sets the object at the specified index in the ArrayList to the *myThread* variable. Finally, on line 12 it returns the Thread that is in the specified index of the ArrayList (and again, is cast to be a *Thread* object).

You may be wondering to yourself exactly what all of this accomplishes. Well, if you remember from the *InitializeThreads* method, the ArrayList is filled with *DataRow* objects. We do not want to directly expose anyone using our objects to *DataRow* objects, so we need to instead give them *Thread* objects. So, behind the scenes, every time a new index is requested from the ArrayList, we quietly "switch" the variable in that index from a *DataRow* to the appropriate *Thread* object. You may also ask why this class doesn't just put the Threads into the ArrayList from the start instead of doing it this way. The answer is simple: there is no need for the overhead of having multiple Thread objects (each with other objects inside them) in the list when you can save memory and time instantiating objects by just keeping the data for each *Thread* object until it is actually requested. When developing large-scale applications with many parent-child hierarchical relationships, a technique like this will save you and your application a lot of time.

Designing the *Thread* class

The *Thread* class is the "middle child" in our hierarchy of objects. Luckily for us, a lot of its functionality and concepts are borrowed directly from the *Board* class, so this should be pretty quick. Let's take a look at another UML diagram in Figure 13.30.

Figure 13.30 The *Thread* Class

```
┌─────────────────┐
│     Thread      │
├─────────────────┤
│ +ID : Long      │
│ +Subject : String│
│ +Creator : User │
│ +ChildPost      │
│ +ChildPosts     │
├─────────────────┤
│ +CreatePost()   │
└─────────────────┘
```

Like every class we've examined so far, the *Thread* class shares the same private fields as the Thread table in the database. Like the *Board* class, the *Thread* class contains two properties to access its children: *ChildPost* and *ChildPosts*. *ChildPost* retrieves an individual *Post* object from its list, and *ChildPosts* returns the entire PostList. PostList will be discussed a bit later. Thread also contains the method to create child Posts. Let's start with the basics in Figure 13.31.

Figure 13.31 The Basics (Thread.vb)

```vb
Public Class Thread
    Private mThreadID As Long
    Private mSubject As String
    Private mCreator As User
    Private myPosts As PostList

    Public Sub New(ByVal myRow As DataRow)
        inflate(myRow)
    End Sub
```

Continued

Figure 13.31 Continued

```vb
    Private Sub inflate(ByVal myRow As DataRow)
        mSubject = CStr(myRow("ThreadSubject"))
        mThreadID = CLng(myRow("ThreadID"))
        mCreator = New User(myRow)
        myPosts = New PostList(mThreadID)
    End Sub

    Public ReadOnly Property ChildPost(ByVal postId As Long) _
        As Post
        Get
            'lookup the correct Post
            Dim i As Integer
            For i = 0 To Me.ChildPosts.Count - 1
                Dim myPost As Post = Me.ChildPosts.Item(i)
                If myPost.ID = postId Then
                    Return myPost
                End If
            Next i
            'if we've gotten to this point, there is no Post
            'with that ID in this board. throw an exception
            Throw New ArgumentException("Post does not exist")
        End Get
    End Property

    Public ReadOnly Property ChildPosts() As PostList
        Get
            Return myPosts
        End Get
    End Property

    Public ReadOnly Property ID() As Long
        Get
```

Continued

Figure 13.31 Continued

```
            Return mThreadID
        End Get
    End Property

    Public Property Subject() As String
        Get
            Return mSubject
        End Get
        Set(ByVal Value As String)
            mSubject = Value
        End Set
    End Property

    Public ReadOnly Property Creator() As User
        Get
            Return mCreator
        End Get
    End Property
End Class
```

First, you'll notice the private fields that are the same as the fields in the database. You'll also notice that a Thread has a Creator field and property that are *User* objects representing the user that created this Thread. Like the *Board* class, this class has a constructor that accepts a *DataRow* as a parameter and then calls inflate to fill up the private fields using that *DataRow*. Also like Board, you have two child object properties, *ChildPost* and *ChildPosts*. *ChildPost* is used to return a single Post, and *ChildPosts* is used to return the entire PostList. Let's take a look at the next method in the Thread class, *CreatePost*, in Figure 13.32.

Figure 13.32 The *CreatePost* Method (Thread.vb)

```
Public Sub CreatePost(ByVal subject As String, _
    ByVal body As String, _
    ByVal creator As User)
```

Continued

Figure 13.32 Continued

```
    Dim sql As String
    sql = "INSERT INTO [Posts] ([PostSubject], " & _
        "[PostBody], " & _
        "[CreatorID], [ThreadID]) VALUES ('" & subject & _
        "','" & body & "'," & creator.ID.ToString() & "," & _
        mThreadID.ToString() & ")"
    DataControl.ExecuteNonQuery(sql)

    'reinitialize the thread list
    myPosts.InitializePosts()
End Sub
```

Taking a look at the *CreatePost* method, you'll notice that it does almost exactly what *CreateThread* did in the Board class. It builds a SQL statement to create a new Post, then executes that statement and reinitializes the private *PostList* object.

Designing the *PostList* Class

Being that we're almost finished creating our classes, it's time to look at the *PostList* class. You may be thinking to yourself "I wonder if the *PostList* class is similar to the *ThreadList* class". Such thinking should be rewarded. *PostList* and *ThreadList* are nearly identical, except for in regards to what type of object they collect. Again, let's take a look at the UML diagram for the class first in Figure 13.33, then in Figure 13.34 we'll review the basics of this class (something which can also be found on your CD as PostList.vb).

Figure 13.33 The *PostList* Class

PostList
+Count : Integer
+Item
+InitializePosts()

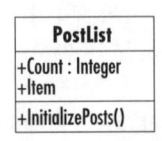

Figure 13.34 The Basics (PostList.vb)

```
Public Class PostList
    Private list As ArrayList
    Private mThreadID As Long
```

Figure 13.34 Continued

```vb
    Public Sub New(ByVal ThreadID As Long)
        mThreadID = ThreadID
        Me.InitializePosts()
    End Sub


    Public Sub InitializePosts()
        Dim myData As DataSet
        Dim sql As String
        sql = "SELECT [Users].*, [Posts].* FROM " & _
            "[Posts] INNER JOIN [Users] " & _
            "ON [Users].[UserID] = [Posts].[CreatorID] " & _
            "WHERE " & _
            "[ThreadID] = " & mThreadID.ToString() & _
            " ORDER BY PostDate DESC"
        myData = DataControl.GetDataSet(sql)

        list = New ArrayList()

        Dim myRow As DataRow
        For Each myRow In myData.Tables(0).Rows
            list.Add(myRow)
        Next
    End Sub


    Public ReadOnly Property Count() As Integer
        Get
            Return list.Count
        End Get
    End Property
End Class
```

Just like *ThreadList*, *PostList* contains a Count property, a method to initialize posts in a thread, and a constructor that accepts the ID of the parent object. The only real difference here is that this class gets values from the User table instead of the Thread table. Next, let's examine the *Item* function in Figure 13.35.

Figure 13.35 The *Item* Function (PostList.vb)

```
Public Function Item(ByVal index As Integer) As Post
    Dim myObject As Object = list.Item(index)
    If myObject.GetType() Is GetType(Post) Then
        'it is already a post, so nothing further is needed
    Else
        Dim myPost As Post
        myPost = New Post(CType(list.Item(index), DataRow))
        'replace the item in the list with
        'an actual post object
        list.Item(index) = myPost
    End If

    Return CType(list.Item(index), Post)
End Function
```

In reviewing this *Item* function, note that it looks remarkably similar to the *Item* function in the *ThreadList* class. In fact, it is exactly the same except that it uses Post instead of Thread. Other than that difference, *PostList* is exactly the same as *ThreadList*.

Designing the *Post* Class

So far, you should have noticed most of the classes in our code share a lot of the same ideas: add, update, lists, mimicking the database tables. Well, the *Post* class is no different. In fact, it is rather similar to both the *Board* and *Thread* classes. Let's take a look at the UML diagram for this class in Figure 13.36.

Just like the other classes, this one is remarkably similar to its brothers—especially the *Thread* class. The only real difference between this class and the *Thread* class is that *Post* has a Body field, pulls its values from the Post table, and doesn't have any child objects. Let's take a look at the whole class in Figure 13.37 (which can be found on your CD as Post.vb), as there really isn't much to it.

Figure 13.36 The *Post* Class

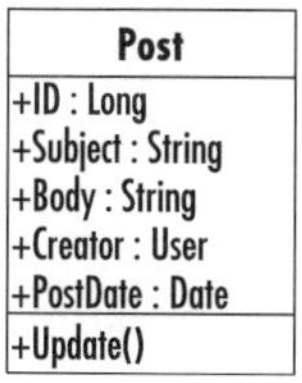

```
Post
+ID : Long
+Subject : String
+Body : String
+Creator : User
+PostDate : Date
+Update()
```

Figure 13.37 Post.vb

```
Public Class Post
    Private mPostID As Long
    Private mPostSubject As String
    Private mPostBody As String
    Private mCreator As User
    Private mPostDate As Date

    Public Sub New(ByVal myRow As DataRow)
        inflate(myRow)
    End Sub

    Public Sub Update(ByVal requestor As User)
        If requestor.ID = mCreator.ID Then
            Dim sql As String
            sql = "UPDATE [Posts] SET [PostSubject] = '" & _
                mPostSubject & "', [PostBody] = '" & mPostBody & _
                "' WHERE [PostID] = " & mPostID.ToString()
            DataControl.ExecuteNonQuery(sql)
        Else
            Throw New ArgumentException _
                ("Only the creator of a post can update it")
        End If
    End Sub

    Private Sub inflate(ByVal myRow As DataRow)
        mPostID = CLng(myRow("PostID"))
```

Continued

Figure 13.37 Continued

```
            mPostSubject = CStr(myRow("PostSubject"))
            mPostBody = CStr(myRow("PostBody"))
            mCreator = New User(myRow)
            mPostDate = CDate(myRow("PostDate"))
    End Sub

    Public ReadOnly Property ID() As Long
        Get
            Return mPostID
        End Get
    End Property

    Public Property Subject() As String
        Get
            Return mPostSubject
        End Get
        Set(ByVal Value As String)
            mPostSubject = Value
        End Set
    End Property

    Public Property Body() As String
        Get
            Return mPostBody
        End Get
        Set(ByVal Value As String)
            mPostBody = Value
        End Set
    End Property

    Public ReadOnly Property Creator() As User
        Get
            Return mCreator
```

Continued

Figure 13.37 Continued

```
        End Get
    End Property

    Public ReadOnly Property PostDate() As Date
        Get
            Return mPostDate
        End Get
    End Property
End Class
```

As you can see, this class has five private fields with the corresponding five public properties. In addition, it has a constructor that accepts a *DataRow* parameter which passes the *DataRow* to the *inflate* method. Finally, it has an *update* method, with the rule that only the creator of the Post can actually edit the Post. Doesn't seem too hard, does it?, Especially after all the other classes we've dealt with. It almost seems passé.

Designing the *MessageBoard* Class

We've finally gotten every class in our message board object library finished; now all we need is a way to get a list of every *Board* object from our database. This is accomplished using the *MessageBoard* class. We won't bother to show you a UML diagram of the *MessageBoard* class, as there is only one method in it: *GetBoards*. Let's take a look at the code in Figure 13.38 (which can be found on your CD under the name MessageBoard.vb).

Figure 13.38 MessageBoard.vb

```
Public Class MessageBoard
    Public Shared Function GetBoards() As ArrayList
        Dim list As New ArrayList()
        Dim sql As String
        Dim myData As DataSet
        Dim myRow As DataRow

        sql = "SELECT [BoardName] FROM [Board] ORDER BY [BoardName] Asc"
```

Continued

Figure 13.38 Continued

```
        myData = DataControl.GetDataSet(sql)

        For Each myRow In myData.Tables(0).Rows
            Dim myBoard As Board
            myBoard = New Board(CStr(myRow("BoardName")))
            list.Add(myBoard)
        Next myRow

        Return list
    End Function
End Class
```

This class is fairly easy to understand. What it does is look up each BoardName from the database, and create a new *Board* object based on that name. It then adds each Board to its list, and finally returns the list.

That's it. Every single one of our objects to be used in dotBoard is completely finished. You may wonder why we did all this work ahead of time instead of just jumping into the application itself. That is a very good question, and as such, has a very good answer. We did all this work designing and setting things up so that when we actually build our application, it will go smoothly, quickly, and won't require a lot of coding in the User Interface. Any good application splits the User Interface from the actual implementation of the application, which is exactly what we did. We are about to move on to the user interface of our message board application. You will see that using the work we've already done, the rest of this application is going to be very straightforward and easy.

Designing the User Interface

Finally, we've gotten to our User Interface. Our database is constructed. All of our message board classes are created; the final thing to do is to put a UI on top of it all. Just like when we created the classes our applications are going to use, we need to sit and think for a few minutes to determine exactly what it is our message board will do. The obvious requirements are that a user must be able to register, log in, and modify his or her profile. Anyone must be able to browse the Boards, Threads, and Posts. Registered users must be able to create threads and posts, and administrators must have the ability to administer users and create and delete boards.

Sound like a lot? Well, since we have a good majority of this work already built into our numerous classes, most of our work now is to create the UI and tie events to methods our objects will handle. The only other thing our message board should be able to do is be "changed" at will. That is, colors, fonts, and any other sort of styling element should be able to be changed without needing to actually modify every single control we place on our form. This will be discussed in a moment, but for now, rest assured, it will be very exciting, and most of the work will be done for us! Let's start by figuring out how to register and log in.

Developing & Deploying…

Copying ASP.NET Applications to Multiple Computers

If you are using the examples on your CD, please perform the following steps to get your ASP.NET message board up and running on your computer.

- Copy the files from your CD to a folder underneath your WWWRoot folder, typically located at C:\Inetpub\WWRoot. Name this folder **dotBoardUI**.
- Open up the **Internet Services Manager** from **Administrative Tools** in the **Control Panel**.
- Expand the **Internet Information Services** node, then your computer's node, and finally the **Default Web Site** node.
- Find your **dotBoardUI** folder. Right-click and select **Properties** to bring up the **Properties** pane.
- Look at the **Application Settings** panel, and click the **Create** button next to the grayed out Application Name label and text box.
- Hit **OK**.

Setting Up General Functions

The first step in designing our application is to create the ASP.NET application. You can either get the solution from the CD, or create your own. If you get the files from the CD, they are in a folder called "dotBoardUI" in the Chapter 13 folder. The dotBoard.sln file is the main solution file, and everything else in that folder is a part of the project. Either way, your application should be named **dotBoardUI**, to go with your *dotBoardObjects* class library. After you have created your application, add your **dotBoardObjects** project to your solution, and add a reference to the newly added project to your ASP.NET application. Next, rename **Web Form1.aspx** to **default.aspx**. This will make it easier when it comes time to deploy your application, as default.aspx is typically one of the default documents IIS serves when the browser doesn't request a specific file in your application.

Now that you have your project created and the appropriate references made, let's get started on the groundwork for our application. If you think about it, every page you make will likely need access to the currently logged in user. There are many reasons for this as you'll see later, so for now just assume that every page will need that information. There are many ways to do this. For instance, you can copy and paste the code necessary to get this information on every page. Anyone familiar with programming techniques should sense a red flag go up at that statement. Copying and pasting the code is a terrible idea, for so many reasons that we don't have space to state them here. Another solution available is to create a public module with the common functions your pages would need. This is a good solution, but let's do it a little differently. We are going to have one Web Form that all our Web Forms will inherit from. Why would we do this? So every Web Form you create will have direct access to the common methods, and every user control you put on these Web Forms will be able to get the information easily.

Add a new class to your project and name it *FormBase.vb*. We're not adding a Web Form in this case because we don't need any sort of UI for our FormBase; we just need access to a common set of methods. Take a look at the basic code in Figure 13.39 (which can also be found on your CD called FormBase.vb).

Figure 13.39 The Basics (FormBase.vb)

```
Public Class FormBase
    Inherits System.Web.UI.Page
End Class
```

Pretty easy, right? What we have here is a class that inherits from System.Web.UI.Page. This allows all our Web Forms to inherit directly from this class, instead of inheriting from System.Web.UI.Page. The next thing we need is for our FormBase to be able to have a reference to the currently logged in user (if there is one). Here is the code to do just that in Figure 13.40.

Figure 13.40 Maintaining the Current User (FormBase.vb)

```vb
Private mCurrentUser As dotBoardObjects.User

Public Property CurrentUser() As dotBoardObjects.User
    Get
        Return mCurrentUser
    End Get
    Set(ByVal Value As dotBoardObjects.User)
        mCurrentUser = Value
        'add the user's ID to the session
        Session.Add("userid", Value.ID.ToString())
    End Set
End Property

Public ReadOnly Property IsLoggedIn() As Boolean
    Get
        Return Not mCurrentUser Is Nothing
    End Get
End Property
```

All we have here is a private *dotBoardObjects.User* object, and a public property to retrieve it. The *Set* property sets the private field with the value passed in, and adds the user ID of the passed in *User* object to the session. We do this so a user does not have to log in multiple times while perusing your message board. You'll see where this comes into play later. The other property we have is one that returns a Boolean value of whether or not there is a currently logged in user. This property makes it easier for someone to determine if there is a logged in user. Basically, instead of having to test for **Nothing** over and over, you use this *Boolean* property.

That is all the state maintaining we'll need in our base class. The only other thing our *FormBase* class needs to do is fulfill that last requirement we talked about. That is, the ability to modify every control on every form without needing to actually rename the class names on elements. This is probably one of the most interesting techniques dotBoard will use. Basically, what we will do is create the code necessary to automate the process of restyling every control in every Web Form. This might sound like a daunting task, but actually once you take a look at it, it is rather simple. The first step we need to take is to open up our web.config file and add the following lines of XML directly beneath the <configuration> tag as shown in Figure 13.41 (which can also be found on your CD called web.config).

Figure 13.41 The web.config File

```
<appSettings>
    <add key="ConnectionString"
value="Provider=Microsoft.Jet.OLEDB.4.0;
        DataSource="C:\Location\To\Your\database\dotBoard.mdb;
        User ID=Admin;Password=;" />
    <add key="XmlConfigFile"
        value="C:\Inetpub\WWWRoot\dotBoardUI\styles.xml" />
</appSettings>
```

Okay, now what exactly does that mean? Your <appSettings> are custom settings you create and have access to in your application. We are creating two custom settings, which are added using the <add> tag. The *key* attribute is the name of the settings, and the *value* attribute is obviously the value. Here we are adding two keys, *ConnectionString* and *XmlConfigFile*. *ConnectionString* is what you use to connect to your database with. Remember the *DataControl* class and how it accessed *System.Configuration.ConfigurationSettings*? The *ConnectionString* key is exactly what that class will use. The other key is *XmlConfigFile*, which is used to hold the location to your XML file that will hold the style information we discussed earlier. Please change the values of each to represent where you actually have the files on your computer located.

We now have the *ConnectionString* and *XmlConfigFile* keys added to our appsettings. Let's start discussing how we will accomplish the "sweeping" change of styles, without needing to manually apply any styles on your controls. First take a look at the following Cascading Style Sheet (CSS) file you should add to your project, as shown in Figure 13.42.

Figure 13.42 Styles.css

```css
body
{
      font-family:Tahoma, Arial, Sans-Serif;
      font-size:10pt;
      color:#000000;
}
.errors
{
      font-family:Tahoma, Arial, Sans-Serif;
      font-size:10pt;
      color:#993300;
}
.link
{
      text-decoration:underline;
      font-family:Tahoma, Arial, Sans-Serif;
      color:#FF9933;
}
.header
{
      color:#003399;
      font-size:16pt;
      font-weight:bold;
      font-family:Arial, Sans-Serif;
}
.panel
{
      border: 1px solid #000000;
      padding: 10px;
}
```

Continued

Figure 13.42 Continued

```
.inputBox
{
    border: 1px solid #000000;
    background-color:#e5e5e5;
}
.label
{
    font-family:Tahoma;
    font-size:8pt;
    color:#000000;
}
.button
{
    border: 1px solid #000000;
    background-color: #FF9933;
    color: #000000;
    font-family: Arial, Sans-Serif;
    font-size: 10pt;
}
```

You can see here that we have a number of styles we will want to apply to many different elements throughout our application. Manually setting these styles is hardly desirable, and maintaining these settings if any of your class names change would be a nightmare. So, what can be done to prevent us from having to maintain this? Enter the styles.xml file in Figure 13.43 (which can also be found on your CD under the name Styles.xml).

Figure 13.43 Styles.xml

```
<?xml version="1.0" encoding="utf8"?>
<styles>
    <control type="System.Web.UI.WebControls.Label">label</control>
    <control type="System.Web.UI.WebControls.TextBox">inputBox</control>
    <control type="System.Web.UI.WebControls.Button">button</control>
```

Continued

Figure 13.43 Continued

```
    <control type="System.Web.UI.WebControls.Panel">panel</control>
    <control type="System.Web.UI.WebControls.LinkButton">link</control>
    <control
        type="System.Web.UI.WebControls.ValidationSummary">
        errors</control>
</styles>
```

You should now notice that the values of these XML tags correspond to an appropriate class name in the preceding stylesheet declaration. Now all we need to do is find a way to associate these XML tags with the appropriate controls on every single page. We can accomplish this through two methods, as shown in Figure 13.44.

Figure 13.44 Two Methods to Dynamically Apply Styles to Controls (Board.vb)

```vb
Public Sub ApplyStyles(ByRef objControls As ControlCollection)
    If objXml Is Nothing Then
        Dim xmlLoc As String
        xmlLoc = ConfigurationSettings.AppSettings()("XmlConfigFile")
        objXml = New XmlDocument()
        Try
            objXml.Load(xmlLoc)
        Catch E As Exception
            Throw New Exception("XML Style Config file not found")
        End Try
    End If

    Dim objControl As Control
    For Each objControl In objControls
        Dim style As String
        style = GetStyleName(objControl.GetType.ToString())

        If style <> "" Then
            Dim objWebControl As WebControl
            objWebControl = CType(objControl, WebControl)
```

Continued

Figure 13.44 Continued

```
                'we only want to apply these styles if we
                'haven't already explicitly set them
                If objWebControl.CssClass.Trim() = "" Then
                    objWebControl.CssClass = style
                End If
            End If
            If objControl.HasControls() Then
                ApplyStyles(objControl.Controls)
            End If
        Next objControl
    End Sub

    Public Function GetStyleName(ByVal controlType As String) As String
        Dim objNode As XmlNode
        objNode = objXml.SelectSingleNode("styles/control[@type='" & _
            controlType & "']")
        If objNode Is Nothing Then
            'do nothing
            Return ""
        Else
            'get the css class specified by this node
            Return objNode.InnerText
        End If
    End Function
```

That's a lot to digest all at once, so let's break it down. The first thing you'll see is that ApplyStyles accepts a *ControlCollection* as a parameter. This collection can be obtained from Page.Controls or Control.Controls. Next, the subroutine checks to see if the XML document has been loaded yet. If it hasn't, it retrieves the location of the styles.xml file from the AppSettings and loads it. If there was an error in the loading of the document, it throws an exception. If there are no problems with the XML document, it loops through every Control in the ControlCollection that was passed in. For every control, it sets a variable "style" to the value of what the *GetStyleName* function returns. *GetStyleName* takes your control's fully qualified type name (represented in the code by *objControl.GetType().ToString()*), and looks for that in the XML document. It does this by calling the *SelectSingleNode* function of the *XMLDocument* object. It builds an XPath query string and looks for the appropriate node with the type attribute that is the same as the type string passed into the *GetStyleName* function. If it finds that node, it returns the InnerText of the appropriate node; otherwise it returns an empty string.

Control is returned to the *ApplyStyles* method, and the style that was returned is tested to make sure it is not an empty string; there is no point in setting the value if it is empty. Next, the Control is cast to be a variable of type WebControl. Since the only Control that can have its style attribute programmatically manipulated is the WebControl, and since every control in *System.Web.UI.WebControls* inherits directly from WebControl, it is safe to perform this cast. Just make sure you do not add anything other than WebControls to your styles.xml file and this will work without error. Next, the *CssClass* property of your WebControl is tested to make sure it is currently an empty string. It does this because if you specifically set a style on one of your controls, you most likely do not want that style overridden by this method. If it is empty, it sets the *CssClass* property to the style String that was returned by the *GetStyleName* function. Finally, if the Control has child controls, it recursively calls ApplyStyles, but instead with the *Control.ChildControls ControlCollection* as the parameter.

With these two functions, every type of Control you add to your styles.xml file will automatically get CSS styles applied to them, without any maintenance on your part other than a small XML file. Wondering how this will actually get used? All you need to do is in your classes that inherit from FormBase, call the *ApplyStyles* method passing the ChildControls of the page you are currently on. Feel free to try this. Modify the stylesheet and styles.xml file all you want. Just rest assured that every control type you add to your XML file will automatically have the CSS classes applied to them that you want.

Building the Log-In Interface

Since we don't have any users created in the database yet, let's take a look at how to register with dotBoard. How to create the User Controls and Forms won't be discussed, but the source code is available on your CD, as well as multiple screen shots for each Web Form and User Control. Take a look at the register.aspx page on Figure 13.45.

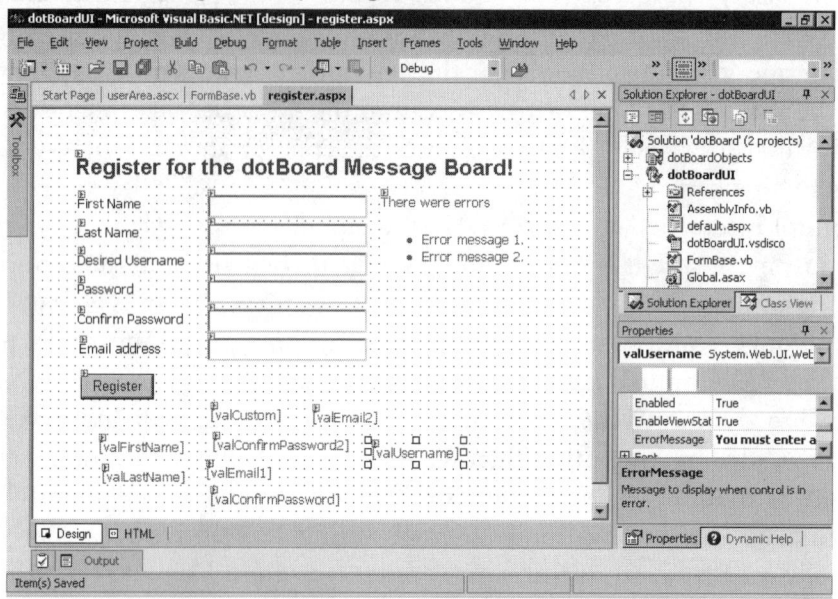

Chapter 13 • Creating a Message Board with ADO and XML

Figure 13.45 The Register.aspx Page

Let's examine the controls on this page. First, there are a number of labels and text boxes used to capture the user's information. There is also a button that will submit the form when pressed. The red-colored controls are validation controls. Validation controls allow you to place "rules" on input without needing to actually code it yourself. The display property of these controls is set to *None*, so they will never show up, but that is where the ValidationSummary comes in. The control in the top right of this page is a ValidationSummary control, which will aggregate all the errors into one area, so you do not need to place your validation controls in a custom place. The other thing on this form is a CustomValidator control. A CustomValidator is typically used to handle client-side JavaScript, but it is also quite useful to handle exceptions thrown and display them to the user. Let's take a look at the code behind this form in Figure 13.46.

Figure 13.46 The Code-Behind File (Register.aspx.vb)

```
Private Sub Page_Load(ByVal sender As System.Object, _
    ByVal e As System.EventArgs) Handles MyBase.Load
    'Put user code to initialize the page here
    Me.ApplyStyles(Me.Controls)
End Sub
```

Continued

Figure 13.46 Continued

```
Private Sub btnRegister_Click(ByVal sender As System.Object, _
    ByVal e As System.EventArgs) Handles btnRegister.Click
    'attempt to register the user
    If Me.Page.IsValid Then
        Try
            Dim myUser As dotBoardObjects.User
            myUser = dotBoardObjects.User.CreateUser( _
                txtUsername.Text, txtPassword.Text, _
                txtFirstName.Text, txtLastName.Text, _
            txtEmailAddress.Text)
            'if we've made it this far, the create worked
            Dim objPage As FormBase
            objPage = CType(Me.Page, FormBase)
            objPage.CurrentUser = myUser
            'redirect to the default page
            Response.Redirect("default.aspx")
        Catch Ex As Exception
            valCustom.ErrorMessage = Ex.Message
            valCustom.IsValid = False
        End Try
    End If
End Sub
```

First, we have the *Page_Load* subroutine, which handles the *Page.Load* event. All this event does is call the *ApplyStyles* method of the *FormBase* class. Next, we have the *btnRegister_Click* subroutine that handles the Register button's *click* event. The first thing that subroutine does is make sure the page is currently in a valid state. This validity is determined whether or not all of the validation controls you added to your form return a valid result. Only once every validation control becomes valid does Page.IsValid ever return true. Next, a *User* object is declared and the *CreateUser* method is called. If the *CreateUser* method throws an exception, then the custom validator on our form is set to invalid and its *ErrorMessage* property is set to the *Message* property of the Exception thrown. If the *CreateUser* succeeded, then a reference to the parent Page, casted to the *FormBase* type, is created and the *CurrentUser* property is set to the User that was just created. Once all this is done, the user is redirected to default.aspx.

As we discussed when we went over FormBase, every page will need to know about the currently logged in user. Likely, every page will also need a login form so the user can log in from anywhere. The best way to do this is to create a Web User Control. Take a look at our *userArea.ascx* control in Figure 13.47.

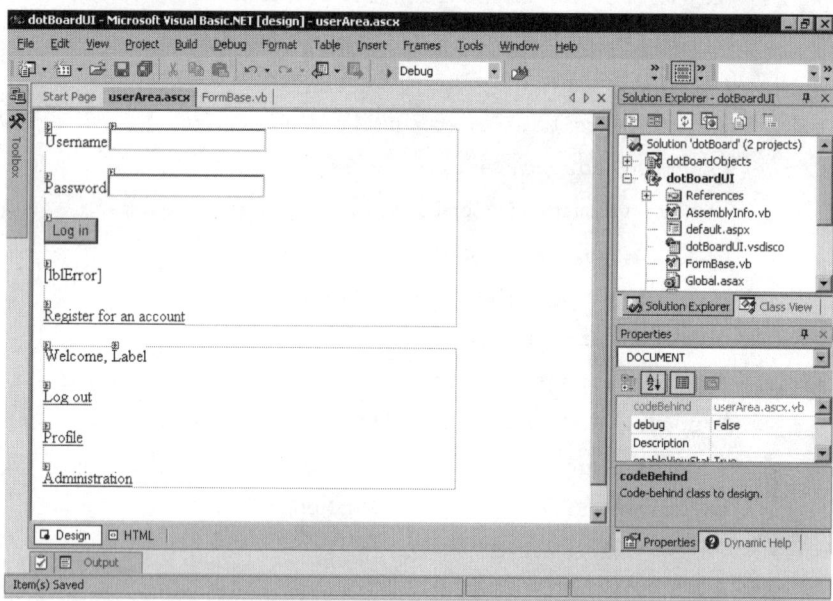

Figure 13.47 UserArea.ascx

Boy that's ugly, isn't it? Don't worry, that's why we created the style code in FormBase. Anyway, what we have here are two panels. The top panel contains the controls necessary to log a user in, while the bottom panel contains the welcome message and any specific actions the user can take. Let's take a look at the code-behind for this page in Figure 13.48.

Figure 13.48 The Code-Behind (UserArea.ascx.vb)

```
Private Sub Page_Init(ByVal sender As System.Object, _
    ByVal e As System.EventArgs) Handles MyBase.Init
    'CODEGEN: This method call is required by the Web Form Designer
    'Do not modify it using the code editor.
    InitializeComponent()
```

Continued

Figure 13.48 Continued

```
        pnlNotLoggedIn.Visible = True
        pnlLoggedIn.Visible = False
        lnkAdmin.Visible = False

        'attempt to log the user in
        If Not Session.Contents().Item("userid") Is Nothing Then
            Dim userId As Long
            userId = CLng(Session.Contents.Item("userid"))
            Dim myUser As User
            Try
                myUser = New User(userId)
                Dim objPage As FormBase
                objPage = CType(Me.Page, FormBase)
                objPage.CurrentUser = myUser
                pnlNotLoggedIn.Visible = False
                pnlLoggedIn.Visible = True

                lblWelcome.Text = myUser.FirstName & " " & myUser.LastName

                If myUser.IsAdmin Then
                    lnkAdmin.Visible = True
                End If
            Catch Ex As Exception
                lblError.Text = Ex.Message
            End Try
        End If
    End Sub

    Private Sub btnLogIn_Click(ByVal sender As System.Object, _
        ByVal e As System.EventArgs) Handles btnLogIn.Click
        'attempt to log in the user
        If txtUsername.Text.Trim() <> "" And _
```

Continued

Figure 13.48 Continued

```vb
                txtPassword.Text.Trim() <> "" Then
            Try
                Dim myUser As User = User.Validate(txtUsername.Text, _
                    txtPassword.Text)
                Dim objPage As FormBase
                objPage = CType(Me.Page, FormBase)
                objPage.CurrentUser = myUser
                'if it got this far it succeeded
                'redirect, to allow the whole page to refresh
                Response.Redirect(Request.RawUrl)
            Catch Ex As Exception
                lblError.Text = Ex.Message
            End Try
        End If
End Sub


Private Sub LinkButton1_Click(ByVal sender As System.Object, _
    ByVal e As System.EventArgs) Handles LinkButton1.Click
    'redirect to the register page
    Response.Redirect("register.aspx")
End Sub


Private Sub lnkLogOut_Click(ByVal sender As System.Object, _
    ByVal e As System.EventArgs) Handles lnkLogOut.Click
    Session.Remove("userid")
    Response.Redirect("default.aspx")
End Sub


Private Sub lnkProfile_Click(ByVal sender As System.Object, _
    ByVal e As System.EventArgs) Handles lnkProfile.Click
    Response.Redirect("profile.aspx")
End Sub
```

Continued

Figure 13.48 Continued

```
Private Sub lnkAdmin_Click(ByVal sender As System.Object, _
    ByVal e As System.EventArgs) Handles lnkAdmin.Click
    Response.Redirect("admin.aspx")
End Sub
```

Okay, there's a lot here, so let's break it down. The *Page_Init* subroutine handles the *Page.Init* event. When this subroutine gets called, it attempts to log in the user based on the Session *userId* value. If that value exists, it uses it and initializes the *CurrentUser* object; otherwise, it exits. Finally, the subroutine hides or shows the correct panel and admin link depending on whether the user was successfully logged in or not and if the use is an admin or not, and then changes the text of the welcome label to the logged in users first and last name.

BtnLogin_Click handles the event when the user clicks the Login button. The first thing it does is check to make sure values have been entered into the username and password fields. If so, it attempts to validate the user with the username and password the user entered. If an exception is thrown, the error label text is set to the message of the exception thrown. If not, it sets the *CurrentUser* property of the FormBase to the currently logged in user, and then redirects the user back to the page they are currently on. It does this to make sure all controls on the page have gotten a chance to know that the user has logged in.

Finally, we have four link buttons, the first one redirects the user to the register page we've already seen, while the other clears the user ID out of Session and redirects them back to default.aspx. The third redirects the user to profile.aspx, the user profile page. The fourth one redirects the user to admin.aspx, the admin page.

Finally, open up your default.aspx page, and drag your userArea.ascx user control onto the page. You now have a fully functioning login/register area to your message board, where anyone can register and log in and receive customized links depending on what type of user they are. See Figure 13.49 to see what the page looks like.

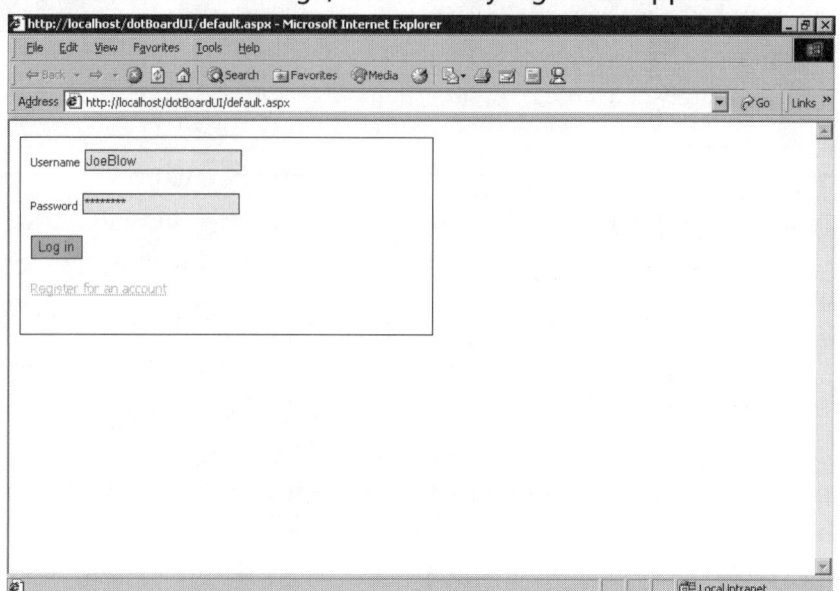

Figure 13.49 The Default Page, with the Styling Code Applied

Designing the Browsing Interface

The next step in building dotBoard is to determine how to browse through the Boards, Threads, and Posts. When a user first enters the site and views the default page, they should be shown a list of Boards and descriptions they can choose to view. This code is located in default.aspx and default.aspx.vb.

Board Browsing

Browsing through our boards isn't very difficult. All we need to do is use a *Repeater* control, and create a custom *DataSet* out of our list of Board objects. Unfortunately, the only control we can drag and drop onto a Web Form is a *Repeater* control, and you can't drag controls into the *Repeater*, so we are going to have to look at the actual quasi-HTML that ASP.NET uses and write the repeated content by hand, as shown in Figure 13.50.

Figure 13.50 The *Repeater* Control (Default.aspx)

```
<asp:Panel runat="server">
    <asp:Repeater id="Repeater1" runat="server">
        <HeaderTemplate>
```

Continued

Figure 13.50 Continued

```
            <div class="header">Available boards</div>
        </HeaderTemplate>
        <SeparatorTemplate>
            <br><br>
        </SeparatorTemplate>
        <ItemTemplate>
            <a href='board.aspx?boardid=
                <%#DataBinder.Eval(Container, "DataItem.BoardName")%>'>
                <%#DataBinder.Eval(Container, "DataItem.BoardName")%>
            </a>
            <br>
            <%#DataBinder.Eval(Container, "DataItem.BoardDescription")%>
        </ItemTemplate>
    </asp:Repeater>
</asp:Panel>
```

The repeater code creates a header template, separator template, and the actual item template. The only thing we haven't discussed thus far is what data source the *Repeater* should use. Since the *Repeater* control requires a real data source (i.e., *DataSet* or something similar), what needs to be done is our list of Boards needs to be "translated" into a *DataSet*. Take a look at the updated code-behind for the default page in Figure 13.51.

Figure 13.51 The Updated Code-Behind (Default.aspx.vb)

```
Private Sub Page_Load(ByVal sender As System.Object, _
    ByVal e As System.EventArgs) Handles MyBase.Load
    'Put user code to initialize the page here
    Me.ApplyStyles(Me.Controls)
    Me.DisplayBoards()
End Sub

Private Sub DisplayBoards()
    Dim myBoards As DataSet = New DataSet()
    Dim list As ArrayList
```

Continued

Figure 13.51 Continued

```vb
        list = dotBoardObjects.MessageBoard.GetBoards()

        myBoards.Tables.Add("boards")
        Dim myTable As DataTable = myBoards.Tables(0)
        myTable.Columns.Add("BoardName", GetType(String))
        myTable.Columns.Add("BoardDescription", GetType(String))

        Dim i As Integer
        For i = 0 To list.Count - 1
            Dim myBoard As dotBoardObjects.Board
            myBoard = CType(list(i), dotBoardObjects.Board)
            Dim fields(1) As Object
            fields(0) = myBoard.Name
            fields(1) = myBoard.Description

            myTable.Rows.Add(fields)
            myTable.AcceptChanges()
        Next i

        myBoards.AcceptChanges()

        Repeater1.DataMember = "boards"
        Repeater1.DataSource = myBoards
        Repeater1.DataBind()
End Sub
```

Notice the addition to the *Page_Load* method in this file. This subroutine now calls the *DisplayBoards* subroutine. *DisplayBoards* restructures the list of Boards into an appropriate form for a *Repeater* control to use. First, it creates a *DataSet* and gets the list of Boards from the *MessageBoard* class. Next, it creates a new table in the *DataSet* and adds three columns to it. Next, it loops through the list of Boards and builds an object array of the fields to add to the *DataSet*. It then adds a new row by passing in the object array to the *Add* method of the

Rows collection. Finally, it accepts the changes, and forces the *Repeater* control to *DataBind* to the *DataSet*. Look at Figure 13.52 to see what this page looks like.

Figure 13.52 The Default Page with Boards Displayed

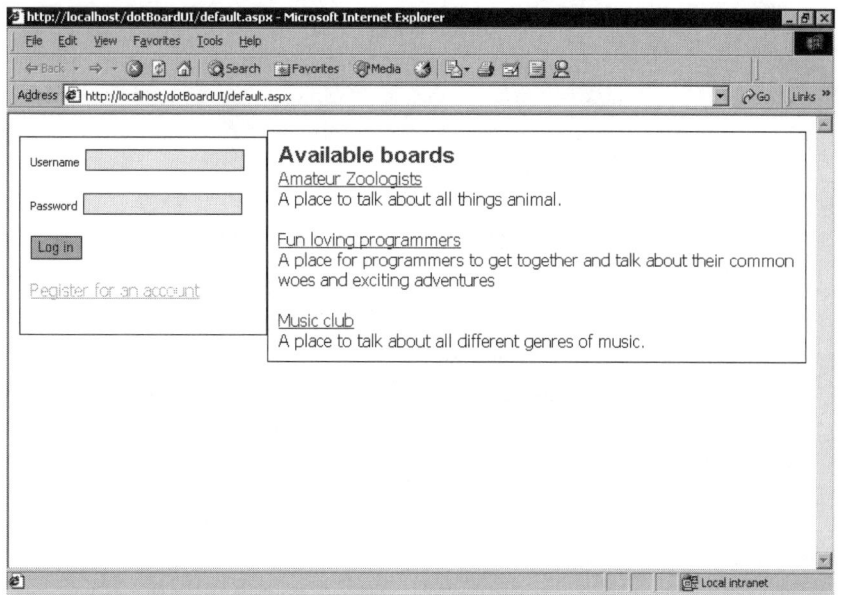

Thread Browsing

Once the user has clicked one of the board links from default.aspx, they are taken to board.aspx. This page will be responsible for determining which board was selected and for displaying the appropriate threads. Displaying the Threads in a Board will function nearly identically to how displaying Boards functioned. Let's take a look at the important quasi-HTML that this page uses in Figure 13.53.

Figure 13.53 The ASPX Code for Board.aspx

```
<table cellpadding="0" cellspacing="0" border="0">
    <asp:Repeater runat="server" id="Repeater1">
        <SeparatorTemplate>
            <tr> <td colspan="2">   </td> </tr>
        </SeparatorTemplate>
        <ItemTemplate>
            <tr>
                <td>
```

Continued

Figure 13.53 Continued

```
                started by
                <%#DataBinder.Eval(Container, "DataItem.creatorName")%>
                </td>
                <td>
                <%#DataBinder.Eval(Container, "DataItem.postCount")%>
                total posts
                </td>
            </tr>
            <tr>
                <td colspan="2">
                <a href='thread.aspx?
                <%#DataBinder.Eval(Container, "DataItem.threadLink")%>
                '>
                <%#DataBinder.Eval(Container, "DataItem.threadSubject")%>
                </a>
                </td>
            </tr>
        </ItemTemplate>
    </asp:Repeater>
</table>
```

The repeater code creates a separator template and the actual item template. It *DataBinds* the appropriate fields in the data source to items in the template. Let's take a look at how we get the data into the data source in Figure 13.54.

Figure 13.54 Board.aspx.vb

```
Private Sub Page_Load(ByVal sender As System.Object, _
    ByVal e As System.EventArgs) Handles MyBase.Load
    Dim mBoard As dotBoardObjects.board
    Dim boardId As String
    boardId = Request.QueryString.Item("boardid")

    Dim myLabel As Label
    myLabel = CType(Me.FindControl("lblHeader"), Label)
```

Continued

Figure 13.54 Continued

```vb
        myLabel.Text = boardId

        mBoard = New dotBoardObjects.board(boardId)

        Dim myThreads As DataSet
        myThreads = New DataSet()
        myThreads.Tables.Add("threads")

        Dim myTable As DataTable
        myTable = myThreads.Tables(0)

        myTable.Columns.Add("threadLink", GetType(String))
        myTable.Columns.Add("threadSubject", GetType(String))
        myTable.Columns.Add("postCount", GetType(Integer))
        myTable.Columns.Add("creatorName", GetType(String))

        Dim i As Integer
        For i = 0 To mBoard.ChildThreads.Count - 1
            Dim myThread As dotBoardObjects.Thread
            myThread = mBoard.ChildThreads.Item(i)

            Dim fields(3) As Object
            fields(0) = "BoardId=" & boardId & _
                "&ThreadId=" & myThread.ID.ToString()
            fields(1) = myThread.Subject
            fields(2) = myThread.ChildPosts.Count
            fields(3) = myThread.Creator.Username

            myTable.Rows.Add(fields)
            myTable.AcceptChanges()
        Next i

        myThreads.AcceptChanges()
```

Continued

Figure 13.54 Continued

```
    Repeater1.DataMember = "threads"
    Repeater1.DataSource = myThreads
    Repeater1.DataBind()

    Me.ApplyStyles(Me.Controls)
End Sub
```

Just like default.aspx, the data binding is relatively straightforward. First, we need to get a reference to the current Board. We do this by requesting the board name from the query string and initializing the board using it. Next, we set a label's text property to the name of the board, so the user knows what board he's in. Then we create a *DataSet*, add a table to it, and add all the required columns. Afterward, we iterate through the Board's child threads and create an object array to hold the necessary fields to add to the *DataSet*. Finally, we add all the rows to the *DataSet* and force the *Repeater* control to *DataBind*. Take a look at Figure 13.55 to see what the completed page looks like.

Figure 13.55 The Board Page with Threads Displayed

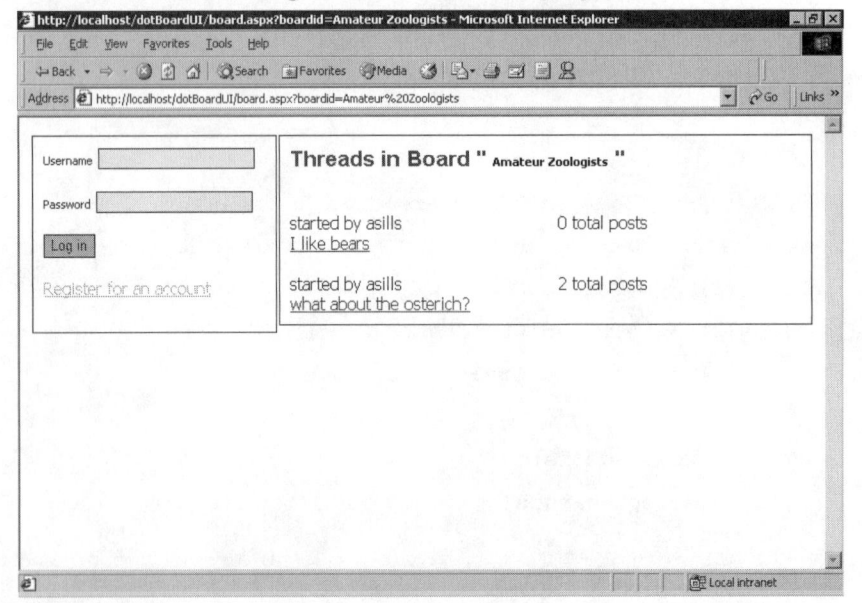

Message Browsing

The last piece to browsing the message board is to see individual Posts themselves. Just like Boards and Threads, displaying this data is accomplished by using a *Repeater* control and a *DataSet*. Let's take a look at the important quasi-HTML and the code-behind in Figures 13.56 and 13.57.

Figure 13.56 Thread.aspx

```
<asp:Repeater runat="server" id="Repeater1">
    <ItemTemplate>
        <tr>
            <td>posted by
            <%#DataBinder.Eval(Container, "DataItem.postCreatorName")%>
            <%#DataBinder.Eval(Container, "DataItem.postCreatorEmail")%>
            </td>
            <td>
                posted at
                <%#DataBinder.Eval(Container, "DataItem.postDate")%>
            </td>
        </tr>
        <tr>
            <td colspan="2">
            <b>
            <%#DataBinder.Eval(Container, "DataItem.postSubject")%>

            </b>
            </td>
        </tr>
        <tr>
            <td colspan="2">
              <%#DataBinder.Eval(Container, "DataItem.postBody")%>
            </td>
        </tr>
    </ItemTemplate>
</asp:Repeater>
```

Figure 13.57 Thread.aspx.vb

```vb
Private Sub Page_Load(ByVal sender As System.Object, _
    ByVal e As System.EventArgs) Handles MyBase.Load
    Dim boardId As String
    Dim threadId As Long

    boardId = Request.QueryString.Item("boardId")
    threadId = CLng(Request.QueryString.Item("threadId"))

    Dim myBoard As dotBoardObjects.board
    myBoard = New dotBoardObjects.board(boardId)

    Dim myThread As dotBoardObjects.thread
    myThread = myBoard.ChildThread(threadId)

    lblHeaderBoard.Text = myBoard.Name
    lblHeaderThread.Text = myThread.Subject

    Dim myPosts As DataSet
    myPosts = New DataSet()
    myPosts.Tables.Add("posts")

    Dim myTable As DataTable
    myTable = myPosts.Tables(0)

    myTable.Columns.Add("postId", GetType(Long))
    myTable.Columns.Add("postSubject", GetType(String))
    myTable.Columns.Add("postBody", GetType(String))
    myTable.Columns.Add("postDate", GetType(Date))
    myTable.Columns.Add("postCreatorName", GetType(String))
    myTable.Columns.Add("postCreatorEmail", GetType(String))

    Dim i As Integer
    For i = 0 To myThread.ChildPosts.Count - 1
```

Continued

Figure 13.57 Continued

```
    Dim myPost As dotBoardObjects.Post
        myPost = myThread.ChildPosts.Item(i)

        Dim fields(5) As Object
        fields(0) = myPost.ID
        fields(1) = myPost.Subject
        fields(2) = myPost.Body
        fields(3) = myPost.PostDate
        fields(4) = myPost.Creator.Username
        If Me.IsLoggedIn = True Then
            fields(5) = "<a href='mailto:" & myPost.Creator.Email & _
                "'>email</a>"
        Else
            fields(5) = ""
        End If

        myTable.Rows.Add(fields)
        myTable.AcceptChanges()
    Next i

    myPosts.AcceptChanges()

    Repeater1.DataMember = "posts"
    Repeater1.DataSource = myPosts
    Repeater1.DataBind()

    Me.ApplyStyles(Me.Controls)
End Sub
```

Again, this code is nearly identical to that of the last two pages we've dealt with. The only real difference is that one of the fields is actually building a short HTML string. This is because the repeater can't handle *if* statements. So, in order to hide or show users' e-mail addresses depending on whether the viewer is logged in or not, we need to build a string instead of directly inserting the value. If the user is logged in, then the anchor tag for the poster's e-mail address is built; otherwise, an empty string is used.

Creating the User Functions

Registered users (Members) get a special set of functions they can access, like creating threads and posts, editing their profile, and editing the messages they've posted. A guest (that is, an unregistered user) is limited to a very small set of functionalities—specifically, viewing the threads and messages (see Figure 13.58).

Figure 13.58 The Thread Page

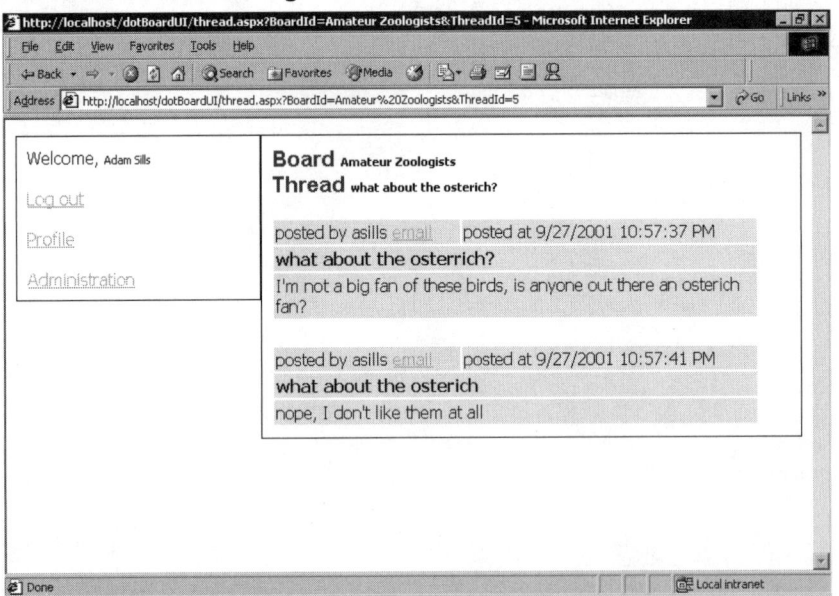

Editing the Member Profile

The next step in building our application's User Interface is to allow a registered user to modify his or her member profile. This includes first name, last name, password, and e-mail address. Let's take a look at the profile.aspx page in Figure 13.59.

The profile page contains text boxes for every field in the *User* object, except for the user ID and username. These two fields are read only, and should never be changed. Like the register page, this page contains a number of Validation controls with their display value set to none, and a ValidationSummary control added to the page to aggregate all the errors a user might receive while inputting information. When this page first loads, it should default all fields (except for passwords) with their existing values, so a user does not have to type everything over, just change the fields he or she wants to change. Upon clicking the Update Profile button, the user's details should be updated and the user given a message explaining that their profile was updated. Let's take a look at the implementation of these features in Figure 13.60.

Figure 13.59 The Profile Page

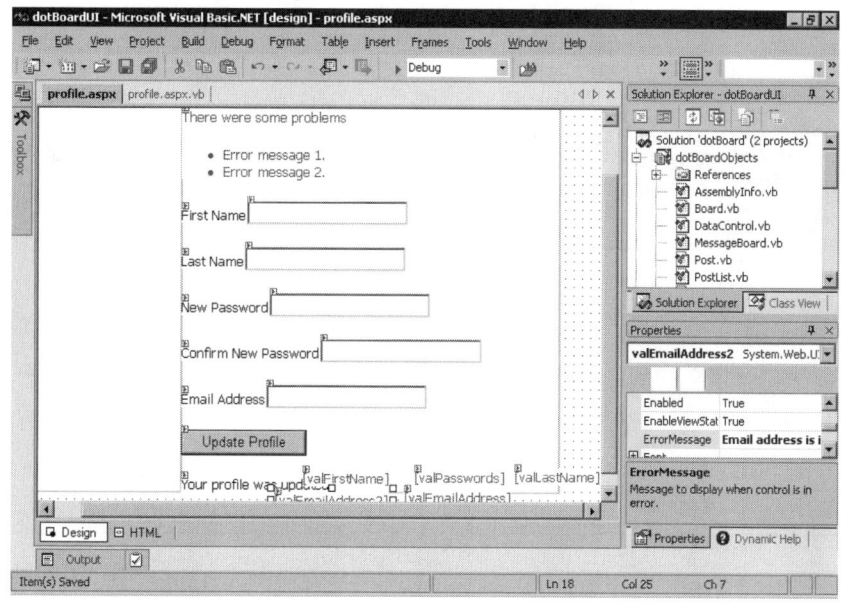

Figure 13.60 The Code-Behind (Profile.aspx.vb)

```
Private Sub Page_Load(ByVal sender As System.Object, _
    ByVal e As System.EventArgs) Handles MyBase.Load
    If Me.IsLoggedIn = False Then
        'only logged in users can access this site
        Response.Redirect("default.aspx")
    End If

    If Page.IsPostBack = False Then
        txtFirstName.Text = Me.CurrentUser.FirstName
        txtLastname.Text = Me.CurrentUser.LastName
```

Continued

Figure 13.60 Continued

```
            txtEmailAddress.Text = Me.CurrentUser.Email
        End If


        Me.ApplyStyles(Me.Controls)
    End Sub


    Private Sub btnUpdate_Click(ByVal sender As System.Object, _
        ByVal e As System.EventArgs) Handles btnUpdate.Click
        If Page.IsValid Then
            If txtNewPassword.Text.Trim() <> "" Then
                Me.CurrentUser.Password = txtNewPassword.Text
            End If
            Me.CurrentUser.FirstName = txtFirstName.Text
            Me.CurrentUser.LastName = txtLastname.Text
            Me.CurrentUser.Email = txtEmailAddress.Text
            Me.CurrentUser.Update()
            lblMessage.Visible = True
        End If
    End Sub
```

Updating the user profile is rather easy. First, the *Page_Load* method checks to make sure there is a valid, logged in user. If not, it redirects the user back to default.aspx. If the user is logged in and the page has not posted back to itself yet, then it sets the values of the text boxes to the existing values of the current user object. Afterward, it applies the styles to the page and exits.

When the Update button is clicked, the *btnUpdate_Click* method is called. The subroutine first checks to make sure all the validation controls have returned valid results. If not, it exits the subroutine. If they have returned valid results, it first checks to see if the user entered a new password, and if so, sets the current user object's password to what the user entered. Next, each of the *User* objects' fields are set to what the user entered, then the *User* object is updated to the database. Finally, the message label indicating that the profile was updated successfully is displayed.

Creating Threads and Posts

The last thing to do for registered users is generate a page for them to create new threads and posts. In order to get to this page, let's take a look at board.aspx and thread.aspx again. We need to add a LinkButton to each one. When clicked, that link button needs to redirect the user to createpost.aspx. See Figures 13.61 and 13.62.

Figure 13.61 *LinkButton1_Click* Event (Board.aspx)

```
Private Sub LinkButton1_Click(ByVal sender As System.Object, _
    ByVal e As System.EventArgs) Handles LinkButton1.Click
    Dim boardId As String
    boardId = Request.QueryString.Item("boardid")
    Response.Redirect("createPost.aspx?boardName=" & boardId)
End Sub
```

Figure 13.62 *LinkButton1_Click* Event (Thread.aspx)

```
Private Sub LinkButton1_Click(ByVal sender As System.Object, _
    ByVal e As System.EventArgs) Handles LinkButton1.Click
    Dim boardId As String
    Dim threadId As Long

    boardId = Request.QueryString.Item("boardId")
    threadId = CLng(Request.QueryString.Item("threadId"))

    Response.Redirect("createPost.aspx?boardName=" & boardId & _
        "&threadId=" & threadId.ToString())
End Sub
```

The function of these buttons is almost the same. The first one redirects the user to createpost.aspx?boardName=[*The selected Board*], and the second redirects the user to createpost.aspx?boardName=[*The selected Board*]&threadId=[*The selected Thread*]. The same page handles the creation of new Threads and Posts, so if you are creating a new Post, you just pass in the ThreadID along with the board name. If you are creating a brand new Thread, you just pass in the board name. Let's take a look at createpost.aspx to see what controls are on that page. See Figure 13.63.

Figure 13.63 The Create Post Page

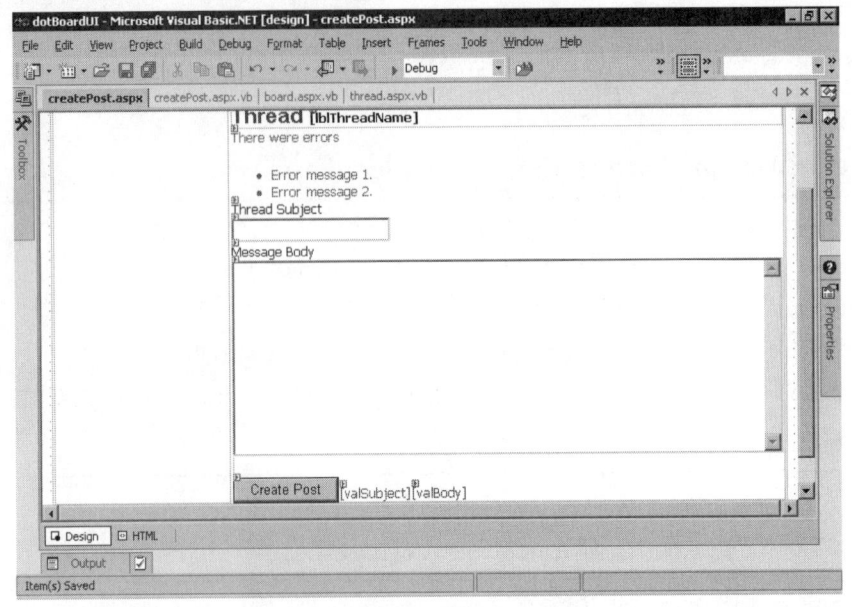

The create post page contains the necessary controls to accept user input and create a new thread and/or post. The other controls on the page are a *ValidationSummary*, two *RequiredFieldValidators*, and a *Panel* that contains the current Thread information. Obviously, if the user is creating a new Thread and Post, the Thread panel will not be visible, whereas, if the user is creating a new Post inside a Thread, the Thread panel will be visible and display the appropriate Thread subject. Let's take a look at the code necessary to initialize this form in Figure 13.64.

Figure 13.64 The Code-Behind Initialization (Createpost.aspx.vb)

```
Private Sub Page_Load(ByVal sender As System.Object, _
    ByVal e As System.EventArgs) Handles MyBase.Load
    'only logged in users are allowed in this page
    If Me.IsLoggedIn = False Then
        Response.Redirect("default.aspx")
    End If
```

Continued

Figure 13.64 Continued

```
    mBoardName = Request.Item("boardName")
    If Request.Item("threadId") Is Nothing Then
        mThreadID = 0
    Else
        mThreadID = CLng(Request.Item("threadId"))
    End If

    mBoard = New dotBoardObjects.board(mBoardName)
    lblBoardName.Text = mBoard.Name

    If mThreadID = 0 Then
        pnlShowThread.Visible = False
    Else
        pnlShowThread.Visible = True
        mThread = mBoard.ChildThread(mThreadID)
    End If

    If Not Me.IsPostBack Then
        'put the default values in the thread and board text boxes
        If mThreadID <> 0 Then
            txtThreadSubject.Text = mThread.Subject
            lblThreadName.Text = mThread.Subject
        End If
    End If

    Me.ApplyStyles(Me.Controls)
End Sub
```

First, what we do is verify that there is a logged in user. If there isn't, we redirect the user back to the default page. If the user is valid, we get a reference to the current board and if the ThreadID was passed in, we get a reference to the appropriate Thread as well. Finally, if the page hasn't posted back to itself and we have a current Thread, we default the text box and label values with the Thread's subject. All that's left is to take a look at the code that actually creates Posts and Threads, as shown in Figure 13.65.

Figure 13.65 *btnCreatePost_Click* Code (Createboard.aspx.vb)

```
Private Sub btnCreatePost_Click(ByVal sender As System.Object, _
    ByVal e As System.EventArgs) Handles btnCreatePost.Click
    If Me.IsValid = True Then
        If mThreadID <> 0 Then
            'we're adding a post to a thread. do nothing here
        Else
            'we're creating a new thread and adding a post
            mBoard.CreateThread(txtThreadSubject.Text, Me.CurrentUser)
            'let's find that thread. it will be the first one
            'in the list
            mThread = mBoard.ChildThreads.Item(0)
        End If

        mThread.CreatePost(txtThreadSubject.Text, _
            TextBox1.Text, Me.CurrentUser)
        'redirect the user to the current thread
        Response.Redirect("thread.aspx?boardId=" & mBoardName & _
            "&threadId=" & mThread.ID.ToString())
    End If
End Sub
```

What happens in this bit of code is that we first check to make sure the page is valid. If not, we do nothing; otherwise, we attempt to create the Thread and/or Post. If the ThreadID is currently "0" (that is, no ThreadID was given to the page), then we create a new Thread and set the private *mThread* variable to the new Thread (remember that when adding a new Thread, since Threads are ordered by their ThreadID field, new Threads appear at the top of the ThreadList). Lastly, we create a new Post from the current *Thread* object and redirect the user to the thread.aspx page to view the new and/or updated Thread.

Building the Administrative Interface

Administrators need to do a few things that other people can't. First, they need the ability to delete anything—boards, threads, and posts. They also need the ability to edit any post, and modify any user's admin or banned status. Let's take a look at the useradmin.aspx screen in Figure 13.66.

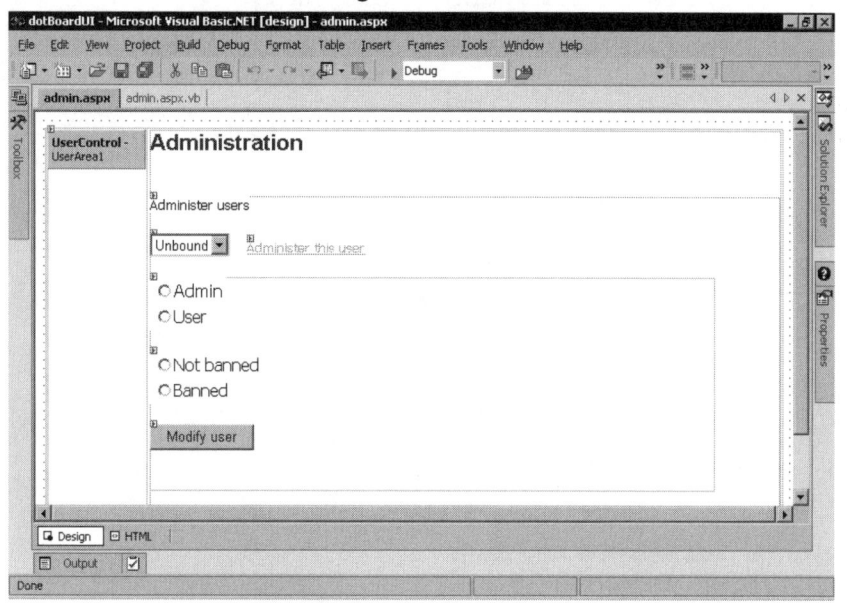

Figure 13.66 The User Admin Page

This page allows administrators to promote other users to administrator status, and ban problematic users from logging into the site. First, we have a *DropDownList* control that we will *DataBind* to a *DataSet*. There is also a *LinkButton* that will show the admin panel at the bottom once we've selected a user to administer. The two radio button lists will be used to display and set the current admin/banned status of the selected user. Finally, when the user clicks the Modify User button, the current user will be updated with the new banned and admin values the administrator entered. Let's first take a look at the code necessary to set up the form in Figure 13.67.

Figure 13.67 The *Page_Load* Method (Admin.aspx.vb)

```vb
Private Sub Page_Load(ByVal sender As System.Object, _
    ByVal e As System.EventArgs) Handles MyBase.Load
    'only logged-in admins can enter this page
    If Me.IsLoggedIn = False Then
        Response.Redirect("default.aspx")
    ElseIf Me.CurrentUser.IsAdmin = False Then
        Response.Redirect("default.aspx")
    End If
    'get the users bound to the drop down list
    If Not Me.IsPostBack Then
        Dim myUsers As DataSet
        Dim sql As String
        sql = "SELECT UserID, UserName FROM Users"
        myUsers = dotBoardObjects.DataControl.GetDataSet(sql)
        dlUsers.DataTextField = "Username"
        dlUsers.DataValueField = "UserID"
        dlUsers.DataMember = "data"
        dlUsers.DataSource = myUsers
        dlUsers.DataBind()
    End If
    Me.ApplyStyles(Me.Controls)
End Sub
```

The first thing this method does is guarantee that there is a logged in user, and that the currently logged in user is an administrator. If either of these is not true, it sends the user back to default.aspx. Next, it makes sure the page has not posted back to itself; since there's no need to *DataBind* a drop-down list every time the page is executed, as ASP.NET will handle that for us. If the page has not posted back to itself, it builds a SQL statement to retrieve the UserIDs and Usernames from the Users table in the database. It then gets a *DataSet* from the *dotBoardObjects.DataControl* class, and dynamically binds the *DropDownList* to the *DataSet*. Finally, it applies the styles to this page and exits.

The next thing we need to do is get the ability to select a user from the drop-down list, and have the page load that user's information. The click event handler for the Choose User link handles this. Let's take a look at the code for it in Figure 13.68.

Figure 13.68 The *lnkChooseUser_Click* Method (Admin.aspx.vb)

```
Private Sub lnkChooseUser_Click(ByVal sender As System.Object, _
    ByVal e As System.EventArgs) Handles lnkChooseUser.Click
    Dim userID As Long
    userID = CLng(dlUsers.SelectedItem.Value)
    Dim myUser As dotBoardObjects.User
    myUser = New dotBoardObjects.User(userID)

    If myUser.IsBanned = True Then
        rblBanned.Items(1).Selected = True
    Else
        rblBanned.Items(0).Selected = True
    End If

    If myUser.IsAdmin = True Then
        rblAdmin.Items(0).Selected = True
    Else
        rblAdmin.Items(1).Selected = True
    End If

    rblBanned.Visible = True
    rblAdmin.Visible = True

    Panel1.Visible = True
End Sub
```

This gets the user ID from the DropDownList's *SelectedItem.Value* property, and creates a new user object from it. Next, the appropriate radio buttons are selected depending on whether or not the user is banned or is an admin. Finally, the admin panel and the two radio button lists are set to visible so they will appear when the page refreshes. Next, we need to handle when the administrator clicks the Modify User button and update the selected user based on what the administrator entered in. See Figure 13.69 for the code involved.

Figure 13.69 The *btnModify_Click* Method (Admin.aspx.vb)

```vb
Private Sub btnModify_Click(ByVal sender As System.Object, _
    ByVal e As System.EventArgs) Handles btnModify.Click
    Dim userID As Long
    userID = CLng(dlUsers.SelectedItem.Value)
    Dim myUser As dotBoardObjects.User
    myUser = New dotBoardObjects.User(userID)

    'we now have the user, so let's set his admin/banned properties
    If rblBanned.Items(0).Selected = True Then
        'the user is not banned
        myUser.IsBanned = False
    Else
        myUser.IsBanned = True
    End If

    If rblAdmin.Items(0).Selected = True Then
        'the user is an admin
        myUser.IsAdmin = True
    Else
        myUser.IsAdmin = False
    End If

    myUser.Update()
End Sub
```

Just like before, the first thing we do is get a reference to the selected *User* object. The next step is to determine which radio buttons were selected, and set the *IsAdmin* and *IsBanned* properties accordingly. The last step is to update the selected user by calling its *Update* method. Now you can promote other users to be administrators or ban them from entering your site again. If a banned user attempts to log on, they will receive an error explaining to that their account was banned. You may be wondering why we don't just delete the banned user. We don't do this because the Thread and Post tables are dependent on the User table, and deleting a User from the User table would not be allowed due to the relationships involved.

The other thing that administrators can do is create and delete boards, delete threads, and delete posts. Let's start with creating a board. The first step involved in this is adding a new LinkButton to the user area user control. This button will be named "lnkCreateBoard" and will have its text property set to Create New Board. Once clicked, it should redirect the user to createboard.aspx. Let's take a look at that code in Figure 13.70.

Figure 13.70 The *lnkCreateBoard_Click* Code (Userarea.ascx.vb)

```
Private Sub lnkCreateBoard_Click(ByVal sender As System.Object, _
    ByVal e As System.EventArgs) Handles lnkCreateBoard.Click
    Response.Redirect("createboard.aspx")
End Sub
```

Now that we have the administrator going to the create board page, let's take a look at that page. See Figure 13.71.

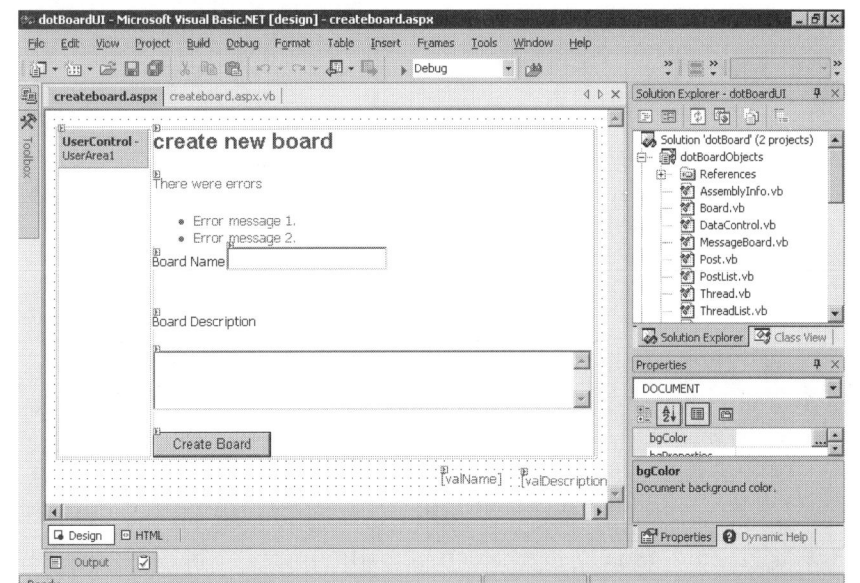

Figure 13.71 The Create Board Form

Like all our other pages that accept user input, this page has controls on it for every piece of information we need to perform the task at hand. Also, like the other pages, there is a validation control for every text box to make sure the user enters the required information. Let's take a look at the code-behind for this form in Figure 13.72.

Figure 13.72 The Code-Behind (Createboard.aspx.vb)

```vb
Private Sub Page_Load(ByVal sender As System.Object, _
    ByVal e As System.EventArgs) Handles MyBase.Load
    'only logged-in admins can enter this page
    If Me.IsLoggedIn = False Then
        Response.Redirect("default.aspx")
    ElseIf Me.CurrentUser.IsAdmin = False Then
        Response.Redirect("default.aspx")
    End If
End Sub


Private Sub btnCreate_Click(ByVal sender As System.Object, _
    ByVal e As System.EventArgs) Handles btnCreate.Click
    If Me.IsValid = True Then
        'create the new board
        dotBoardObjects.Board.CreateBoard(txtBoardName.Text, _
            txtBoardDescription.Text, _
            Me.CurrentUser)
        Response.Redirect("default.aspx")
    End If
End Sub
```

Like every other admin page so far, this page guarantees that the current user is a logged-in administrator, and if not, redirects to the default page. After the user has entered the required information to create a board and clicks the Create Board button, the *btnCreate_Click* method is called. First, the method checks to make sure the page is valid, then it creates the board based on the values the administrator entered. Finally, it redirects the administrator back to the default page so he can see his newly created board.

The last things an administrator should be able to do are delete Boards, Threads, and Posts. This functionality can be placed on the appropriate pages

Creating a Message Board with ADO and XML • Chapter 13

where this information is actually displayed. What we will do is next to every Board, Thread, and Post we will place an *HtmlAnchor* control next to each item that will point to an .aspx page named delete[*type of object to delete*].aspx. For instance, deleting Boards will link to deleteBoard.aspx. Let's go over the three places in our code that need to change because of this new feature in Figures 13.73, 13.74, and 13.75.

Figure 13.73 The *DisplayBoard* Method Changes (Default.aspx.vb)

```
Dim fields(1) As Object
fields(0) = myBoard.Name
fields(1) = myBoard.Description
If Me.IsLoggedIn = True Then
    If Me.CurrentUser.IsAdmin = True Then
        fields(1) &= "<br><br><a href='deleteBoard.aspx?boardName=" & _
            myBoard.Name & "'>&gt;&gt;delete</a>"
    End If
End If
```

Figure 13.74 The *Page_Load* Method Changes (Board.aspx.vb)

```
Dim fields(3) As Object
fields(0) = "BoardId=" & boardId & _
    "&ThreadId=" & myThread.ID.ToString()
fields(1) = myThread.Subject
If Me.IsLoggedIn = True Then
    If Me.CurrentUser.IsAdmin = True Then
        fields(1) &= "<br><br><a href='deleteThread.aspx?" & _
            "boardName=" & mBoard.Name & _
            "&threadId=" & myThread.ID.ToString() & _
            "'>&gt;&gt;delete</a>"
    End If
End If
```

Figure 13.75 The *Page_Load* Method Changes (Thread.aspx.vb)

```
Dim fields(5) As Object
fields(0) = myPost.ID
fields(1) = myPost.Subject
fields(2) = myPost.Body
If Me.IsLoggedIn = True Then
    If Me.IsLoggedIn = True Then
        fields(2) &= "<br><br><a href='deletePost.aspx?" & _
            "boardName=" & myBoard.Name & _
            "&threadId=" & myThread.ID.ToString() & _
            "&postId=" & myPost.ID.ToString() & _
            "'>&gt;&gt;delete</a>"
    End If
End If
```

You can see that all of these changes is very similar. Each gets slightly more complicated as you get further down the object hierarchy; you need to pass more information to get a reference to the correct objects. Now all we need to do is create the three pages that will handle deleting our objects. All three are very similar, and are shown in the following figures, Figures 13.76, 13.77, and 13.78.

Figure 13.76 DeleteBoard.aspx.vb

```
Private Sub Page_Load(ByVal sender As System.Object, _
    ByVal e As System.EventArgs) Handles MyBase.Load
    If Me.IsLoggedIn = True Then
        If Me.CurrentUser.IsAdmin = True Then
            Dim boardName As String
            boardName = Request.QueryString.Item("boardName")
            Dim myBoard As dotBoardObjects.board
            myBoard = New dotBoardObjects.board(boardName)
            myBoard.Delete(Me.CurrentUser)
        End If
    End If
```

Continued

Figure 13.76 Continued

```vb
        Response.Redirect("default.aspx")
End Sub
```

Figure 13.77 DeleteThread.aspx.vb

```vb
Private Sub Page_Load(ByVal sender As System.Object, _
    ByVal e As System.EventArgs) Handles MyBase.Load
    If Me.IsLoggedIn = True Then
        If Me.CurrentUser.IsAdmin = True Then
            Dim boardName As String
            Dim threadId As Long
            boardName = Request.QueryString.Item("boardName")
            threadId = CLng(Request.QueryString.Item("threadId"))

            Dim myBoard As dotBoardObjects.board
            myBoard = New dotBoardObjects.board(boardName)
            Dim myThread As dotBoardObjects.thread
            myThread = myBoard.ChildThread(threadId)

            myBoard.DeleteThread(myThread, Me.CurrentUser)
        End If
    End If

    Response.Redirect("default.aspx")
End Sub
```

Figure 13.78 DeletePost.aspx.vb

```vb
Private Sub Page_Load(ByVal sender As System.Object, _
    ByVal e As System.EventArgs) Handles MyBase.Load
    If Me.IsLoggedIn = True Then
        If Me.CurrentUser.IsAdmin = True Then
            Dim boardName As String
```

Continued

Figure 13.78 Continued

```
            Dim threadId As Long
            Dim postId As Long

            boardName = Request.QueryString.Item("boardName")
            threadId = CLng(Request.QueryString.Item("threadId"))
            postId = CLng(Request.QueryString.Item("postId"))

            Dim myBoard As dotBoardObjects.board
            myBoard = New dotBoardObjects.board(boardName)
            Dim myThread As dotBoardObjects.thread
            myThread = myBoard.ChildThread(threadId)
            Dim myPost As dotBoardObjects.Post
            myPost = myThread.ChildPost(postId)

            myBoard.DeletePost(myThread, myPost, Me.CurrentUser)
        End If
    End If

    Response.Redirect("default.aspx")
End Sub
```

A lot of code, for sure, but it should all be relatively easy to follow. Each page retrieves the objects necessary to delete whatever it is trying to delete, then calls the appropriate delete method on the board object. When it finishes, each one redirects the user back to the default page. If the person accessing this page is neither logged in nor an admin, it does nothing but the final redirect. You don't want anyone who is not an admin deleting your boards, so even on pages in which the user never sees the UI, it's still a good idea to perform every security check necessary.

The final administrative interface we need to create is to give the Administrators the ability to edit posts, in the case of offensive or undesired language that doesn't necessarily need to be deleted. First, we'll need to add another button to the view thread page right next to the Delete button. See Figure 13.79 for the changes.

Figure 13.79 Page_Load Changes (Thread.aspx.vb)

```
If Me.IsLoggedIn = True Then
    If Me.IsLoggedIn = True Then
        fields(2) &= "<br><br><a href='deletePost.aspx?" & _
            "boardName=" & myBoard.Name & _
            "&threadId=" & myThread.ID.ToString() & _
            "&postId=" & myPost.ID.ToString() & _
            "'>&gt;&gt;delete</a>"
        fields(2) &= "   " & _
            "<a href='editPost.aspx?" & _
            "boardName=" & myBoard.Name & _
            "&threadId=" & myThread.ID.ToString() & _
            "&postId=" & myPost.ID.ToString() & _
            "'>&gt;&gt;edit</a>"
    End If
End If
```

All that has changed is a new HTML anchor tag is added that points to a new page called editPost.aspx. Let's take a look at this page and examine what controls are on it (see Figure 13.80).

Figure 13.80 editPost.aspx

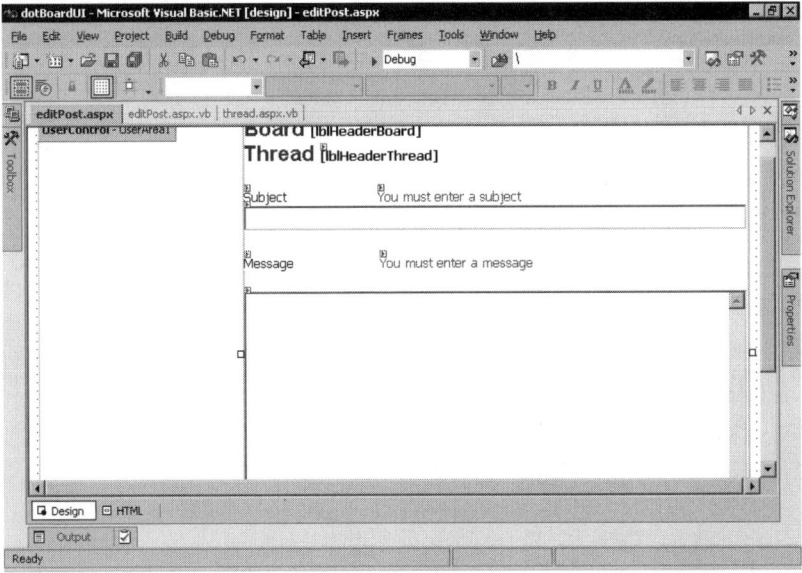

You should notice that this page looks very similar to the create post page. In fact, it is nearly identical — so identical that we could have reused the same page instead of creating the new one. The only reason we aren't using the create post page is for the sake of simplicity; there's no need to complicate pages we have already finished for new functionality. All we need to do now is take a look at the code-behind page in Figure 13.81.

Figure 13.81 The Code-Behind (editPost.aspx)

```
Public Class editPost
    Inherits FormBase

    Private mBoard As dotBoardObjects.Board
    Private mThread As dotBoardObjects.Thread
    Private mBoardName As String
    Private mThreadID As Long
    Private mPostID As Long
    Private mPost As dotBoardObjects.Post

    Private Sub Page_Load(ByVal sender As System.Object, _
        ByVal e As System.EventArgs) Handles MyBase.Load
        'only logged in users are allow in this page
        If Me.IsLoggedIn = False Then
            Response.Redirect("default.aspx")
        ElseIf Me.CurrentUser.IsAdmin = False Then
            Response.Redirect("default.aspx")
        End If

        mBoardName = Request.Item("boardName")
        mThreadID = CLng(Request.Item("threadId"))
        mPostID = CLng(Request.Item("postId"))

        mBoard = New dotBoardObjects.board(mBoardName)
        mThread = mBoard.ChildThread(mThreadID)
        mPost = mThread.ChildPost(mPostID)
```

Continued

Figure 13.81 Continued

```
            lblHeaderBoard.Text = mBoard.Name
            lblHeaderThread.Text = mThread.Subject

            If Not Me.IsPostBack Then
                txtSubject.Text = mPost.Subject
                txtMessage.Text = mPost.Body
            End If

            Me.ApplyStyles(Me.Controls)
        End Sub

        Private Sub btnEditPost_Click(ByVal sender As System.Object, _
            ByVal e As System.EventArgs) Handles btnEditPost.Click
            If Me.IsValid Then
                mPost.Subject = txtSubject.Text
                mPost.Body = txtMessage.Text
                mPost.Update(Me.CurrentUser)
                Response.Redirect("thread.aspx?boardID=" & _
                    mBoard.Name & "&threadId=" & _
                    mThread.ID.ToString())
            End If
        End Sub
End Class
```

You should immediately notice how similar the code-behind of the edit post page is to create post page. Again, we could have used the same page, but to keep things simple we're using two separate pages. The *Page_Load* method first checks to make sure there is a logged in user, and that the user is an administrator. Next, it gets a reference to the appropriate Board, Thread, and Post objects, and fills the label and text box controls on the page with values. The *btnEditPost_Click* method makes sure the page is valid, then sets the values on the *Post* object, commits it to the database, and redirects to the thread view page so the user can see the changes.

Summary

Our message board is 100 percent complete and ready for use. We have analyzed our message board and created a solution to fit with all our requirements. Our message board is an Object-Oriented application that is scalable, maintainable, and well-defined. We have created all the necessary classes to maintain our data and the relationships between our data through the use of custom list objects and classes. We also have a built-in security model where every action that requires administrative access is checked before the requestor is allowed to perform the operation.

Our User Interface is somewhat extensible in that it dynamically applies styles to multiple types of WebControls that we defined using CSS and an XML document. Each Web Form we created inherits the *FormBase* class, which allows all our Web Forms to have access to a few common methods and properties, in addition to the *System.Web.UI.Page* methods and properties. Our User Interface contains all the necessary interfaces to browse through Boards, Threads, and Messages, as well as interfaces to administer users, and those that contain interfaces to create and delete Boards, Threads, and Messages.

All in all we have a functioning message board that could be placed anywhere and run on top of SQL Server or MS Access. It was accomplished in an Object-Oriented manner and hopefully by now you understand the use for designing OO applications. We have also separated the UI and UI logic from the actual "business rules" applied to our objects. If we wanted, we could take our *dotBoardObject* class library and put a Windows Form front end on it, a Web Service front end on it, or even attach a Console Application front end. All because we kept our UI completely separate from our implementation.

Solutions Fast Track

Setting Up the Database

☑ Analyze your data and create the tables necessary to represent the solution to our problem. Make sure you have broken down each piece of data into the smallest possible representation of that data. For instance, you wouldn't want to have a field in your database for the user's full name; instead, you would want first and last name fields.

- ☑ Analyze your data and create the relationships necessary between the different sets of data.

Designing Your Application

- ☑ Analyze your data and find a way to fit it into an Object-Oriented environment. Many times you can use the analysis you performed while building your database in this step.
- ☑ Map the fields in the database to appropriate fields in each object.
- ☑ Analyze our solution and determine the types of methods each of our objects will contain. You need to provide interfaces to modify, add, and delete every relationship and field in each of your objects.

Designing the User Interface

- ☑ Analyze what type of actions our users will need to perform, then create the necessary Web Forms.
- ☑ Analyze what type of actions our administrators will need to perform and create the necessary Web Forms.

Setting Up General Functions

- ☑ Create the *FormBase* class that contains all the necessary properties and methods our Web Forms will need to hold. Determine what functionality you need shared throughout every Web Form and build it into this class.

Building the Log-In Interface

- ☑ Create the user area user control. Place this control on every Web Form so each form can have a reference to the currently logged in user.
- ☑ Create the registration page, which allows users to register for your message board.

Designing the Browsing Interface

- ☑ Create the Board browsing. Create the Web Form and use the *Repeater* control and *DataBind* it to a *DataSet*.
- ☑ Create the Thread browsing. Create the Web Form and use the *Repeater* control and *DataBind* it to a *DataSet*.
- ☑ Create the Post browsing. Create the Web Form and use the *Repeater* control and *DataBind* it to a *DataSet*.

Creating the User Functions

- ☑ Generate the Thread creation. Create the Web Form and use *Validation* controls and text boxes to get the necessary information.
- ☑ Generate the Post creation. Create the Web Form and use *Validation* controls and text boxes to get the necessary information.

Building the Administrative Interface

- ☑ Create the interface to ban and promote users. Make sure only administrators can access this functionality using the properties built into the *FormBase* class.
- ☑ Create the interfaces necessary to delete Board, Thread, and Post pages. Modify the existing View Board, Thread, and Post pages to create the links to the delete pages.
- ☑ Create the interfaces necessary to edit Posts. Modify the existing view Post page to create the links to edit Posts.

Frequently Asked Questions

The following Frequently Asked Questions, answered by the authors of this book, are designed to both measure your understanding of the concepts presented in this chapter and to assist you with real-life implementation of these concepts. To have your questions about this chapter answered by the author, browse to **www.syngress.com/solutions** and click on the **"Ask the Author"** form.

Q: When designing applications, do I need to design them in an Object-Oriented manner?

A: Absolutely not, although when applications are designed in an OO manner, they are typically more scalable and maintainable, and allow for the use of multiple User Interfaces. You are not forced to create applications in an OO manner, but good programming practices typically stress Object Orientation.

Q: Are there any performance issues when using an OO approach versus a more procedural approach?

A: Yes, typically the OO approach adds a bit of overhead to everything you do. For instance, the creation of the custom *DataSet* in order to view Boards, Threads, and Posts spends extra time that wouldn't have been lost if you had gone directly to the database instead of accessing the data through objects. The price of scalability and maintainability is a possible performance loss. Luckily, with .NET, execution is very fast after the initial compile, so it's also very likely that you would never notice the speed loss.

Q: How important is it to use Validation controls?

A: Very important. In ASP 3.0 and 2.0 (heck, even ASP 1.0), all validation had to be done by hand. Empty fields needed to be validated as well as e-mail addresses and URIs. With Validation controls, ASP.NET does all of this for us, allowing us to focus more on the logic and business rules in our application.

Q: How can I ban a list of IP addresses in the future?

A: First, you would need to create a table in your database to store the list of IP addresses, and provide a way for an administrator to enter an IP address into it. Then, at every page you want to disallow this list of IP addresses from viewing, compare the IP address of the requesting user and compare it to the list of IP addresses you have banned. If it exists in your list of banned addresses, redirect them to another page or do whatever else you feel is appropriate.

Index

@ OutputCache directive, usage, 269–277, 279

A

absoluteExpiration, 258
Accept-Language
  header values, 274
  parameter, 274
Access control, authorization tag (usage), 208–209
Access database, creation, 506–509
Access datatype, 510
Access object, creation. *See* Data
Access times, 267
Account element, 393
Accounts element, 385, 386
Action events, 77
Active Server Pages (ASP). *See* Classic ASP
  applications, 87
    ASP.NET applications, contrast, 231
  ASP 1.x, development, 5–6
  ASP 2.x
    changes, 6–7
    development, 6–7
    weaknesses, 7
  ASP 3.0
    development, 7–9
    weaknesses, 8–9
  code, 12
  control declaration, 483
  controversy, 4–5
  developers, 78, 130
  editing environment, 5
  Engine, 62, 76
  file execution, Web server usage, 15–27
  history, 2–11
  model
    ASP.NET improvements, comparison, 14–15
    need, 9
    need, 3–4
  original model, changes, 8
  origins, 2–5
  pages, 86, 161
  scripts, 576
  skills, obsolescence, 86
  timeline, 10–11
  upgrading. *See* Classic ASP
  version 4, 11
ActiveX controls, 164, 167
ActiveX Data Objects (ADO), 6, 8
  ADO-related codes, 86
  update, 19
  usage. *See* Message board creation
  version 2.5, 10
Actual comment, 475
add attribute, 203
add (processing directive), 189
Add stored procedure, 335
add subtag, 190, 192–193, 202, 207
add tag, 616
addBook page, 533
  addBook.aspx, creation, 543
addBook.aspx, creation. *See* addBook page
addCat, 528, 530
Address book application, creation, 314–341
Address.aspx, 314
AdminAddBook, 512
AdminAddCat, 512
AdminAddCustomer, 512
adminCustomer, 518

663

AdminDeleteBook, 512
AdminDeleteCat, 512
AdminDeleteCustomer, 512
Administration login (adminLogin.aspx), creation, 535–536
Administrative interface, construction. *See* Message board creation
Administrator page (adminPage.aspx), creation, 537–543
Administrators, 581. *See also* Logged-in administrator
adminLogin.aspx, creation. *See* Administration login
adminPage.aspx, creation. *See* Administrator Page
AdminUpdateBook, 512
AdminUpdateCat, 512
AdminUpdateCustomer, 512
ADO. *See* ActiveX Data Objects
ADOCatalog, creation, 547–553
ADO.NET, 12
  ADO contrast, 53
  changes, understanding, 300–310
  FAQs, 345–346
  introduction, 299, 300
  solutions, 343–344
  supported connectivity, 305
ADO.NET shopping cart
  creation, 501
  database, setup, 502–518
  FAQs, 566
  introduction, 502
  site
    administration, 533–547
    construction, 533
  solutions, 562–565
AdRotator controls, 62
ADSI, 13

allBooks.addItem Web method, creation, 541
AllCustById, 512
Allow Paging property, 144
allowOverride attribute, 174, 176, 177, 214
AllowPaging, 152
AllowSorting property, 144, 150
AlternatingItemStyle property, 147
AlternatingItemTemplate, 132
Anchor tag. *See* HyperText Markup Language
Application. *See* ASP.NET application
  cache object, 233–234
  class, 250
  configuration, 179–184
  creation. *See* ASP.NET application
  design. *See* Message board creation
  events
    support, 236–237
    usage, 236–239
  identity configuration, identity tag (usage), 181
  locking, 239
  log, Trace information (writing), 432
  testing/error-checking. *See* ASP.NET application
  tracing, 432–434
  variables, 229, 234
Application state, 63
  session states, comparison, 246–258
  understanding, 232–236
  usage, 232–234
Application-level trace, 433
Application-level variable, 547
Application_onstart method, 548
Application-specific configuration section handlers, 212
Application-wide issues, 246

Index

ApplyStyles, 620
AppSettings, 620
appSettings
  node, 312
  tag, usage, 220. *See also* Static variables
ArgumentException, 586, 587, 599
Ariba, 350, 455
Array class, 44
Array-like addressing, usage, 96
ArrayList, 95, 602
  ListControl, binding, 111–113
.ascx file, 163
.asmx
  .aspx, contrast, 450–451
  file, 445
    extension, 450
  page, 444
ASP. *See* Active Server Pages
asp:Button, 62, 135
ASPError object, removal, 27
asp:Label, 62, 102
  control, 162
ASP.NET
  browser capability function, 21
  controls, 68
  delivery, 18
  developers, 46
  Engine, 66
  FAQs, 32–33
  flexibility, utilization, 12–14
  framework, 69
  improvements, comparison. *See* Active Server Pages
  introduction, 2
  object, 47
  pages, 51. *See also* Data-enabled ASP.NET pages
    compilation, 18, 37

  platform basics, review, 11–15
  scripts, 15
  server controls, display. *See* Netscape 4.x
  server-side processing, 65
  solutions, 29–31
  techniques, 95
ASP.NET application, 37, 227
  contrast. *See* Active Server Pages
  copying, 613
  creation, 20–26, 229
  debugging, 27
  deployment, 13
  FAQs, 262–263
  introduction, 228
  solutions, 259–262
  testing/error-checking, 235–236
  understanding, 228–229
ASP.NET configuration, 173
  FAQs, 224–225
  introduction, 174
  overview, 174–177
  solutions, 223–224
ASP.NET debugging, 417
  FAQs, 439–440
  introduction, 418
  solutions, 438–439
ASP.NET Web
  application, 86
  controls, 66
  form, structure, 75–76
  pages, running, 19–26
asp:RequiredFieldValidator server control, 535
asp:requiredfieldvalidator tag, 536
asp:TextBox, 62
.aspx
  contrast. *See* .asmx

extension, 65
file, 77, 314, 478
   scripts, inclusion, 69–72
page, 451
ASPX code, 488
ASPX page, 65, 162
asp:XML server control, 553
asp:xml server control, 547
ATG, 7
Attribute name, 355
AttributeCount property, 365
Attributes, 353
Authentication, 204. See also Biometric authentication; Windows authentication
  cookie data, encryption/decryption. See Forms
  modules, removal, 207
authentication tag, 205, 206
  usage. See User authentication
authenticationModules tag, usage. See Security
authorization tag, usage. See Access control
AutoGenerate, usage, 209
AutoGenerateColumn property, 144, 147
Automatic drill-down facilities, 387
AutoNumber, datatype, 508
AutoPostBack
  attributes. See Server controls
  property, 85, 106

B

B2B partners, 361
BackColor, 101
Backend database failure, 208
Back-end databases, 3
Back-end Web programming, 5
bin subdirectory, 78, 81, 106
Binary code, 18. See also Machine-specific binary code
bindDataGrid
  procedure, 152
  routine, 150
Binding, usage. See Data
bindListControl sub-procedure, 131
Biometric authentication, 207
BK_Author, 505
BK_Description, 505
BK_ImagePath, 505
BK_ISBN, 505, 506
BKOR_Price, 506
BKOR_Quantity, 506
BK_Price, 505
BK_Title, 505
Board
  browsing, 628–638
  class, design, 591–612
  object, 592, 657
BoardDescription, 569
BoardID, 569, 570, 596
BoardName, 569, 570, 612
/body, 130–161
Body field, 608
Book Shop Web services, overview, 518–520
BookCatalog class, creation, 548–553
bookCatalog method, 553
bookCatalog.catalogItemDetails, 555
Books
  addition. See Database
  deletion, 541–542
  details, updating, 542–543
bookSourceUI, 548
Booleans, 38, 40

BorderColor, 101
bordercolor property, 122
BorderStyle, 101
BorderWidth, 101
Borland, 14
Bottom-most nodes, 360
BoundColumn, 147
Breakpoints, setting, 434–435
Broadvision, 7
Browser. *See* Down-level browsers; Up-level browsers
  communication. *See* Client/browser communication
  type, 16
Browser-based state solution, 230
browserCaps tag, usage. *See* Client capabilities determination
Browser-compliant HTML, 75
Browsing interface, design, 628–638
btnEditPost_Click method, 657
btnRegister_Click subroutine, 623
btnUpdate_Click method, 640
Bug fixes, 300
Built-in applications, 25
Built-in features, 62
BulletList, 123
Business objects, 568
Byte data types, 39

C

C, 3, 447
  programmers, 24
C#, 9, 11–13, 26, 247, 450
  class file, 78
  source file, 79, 81
  syntax, 24, 248
  usage, 20, 79, 82
  Web Service, 522
C++, 3, 8, 14, 25, 447. *See also* Visual C++
  ATL
    code, 578
    COM, 578
  bolted-on approach, 11
C# .NET, 306
Cache
  duration, 280
  expiration, 258
  method, usage, 282–284
  object. *See* Application
  optimization, 268–269
  values, 234
Cache Insert method, 258
cache.add method, usage, 282, 285–292
Cached configuration, 220
Cache-filling statements, 258
cache.insert method, usage, 282, 285–292
CacheItemPriority setting, 289
CacheItemPriorityDecay setting, 289
CacheItemRemoved option, 290
CacheItemRemovedCallback delegate, usage, 289–292
Cache.Remove method, usage. *See* /HTML
Caching, 273. *See also* Data; Fragment caching; Output caching
  data, 282
  facility, 252
  implementation, 293
  overview, 266–269
  uses, 293–294
Caching methods, optimization, 265
  FAQs, 297–298
  introduction, 266

668   Index

solutions, 296–297
Calendar controls, 62
Camel-cased attributes, 211
Carriage return, 24
Cascading Style Sheet (CSS), 348
  code, 62
  file, 617
  script, 491
  styles, 622
Case sensitivity, 355
Catalog
  element, 353
  method, creation, 550
  node, 360
  rendering, 558–559
catalogByCategory method, creation, 550–551
catalogItemDetails method, creation, 550
catalogRange method, creation, 550–551
catalogRangeByCategory method, creation, 551–553
Catalog.xsd, 358
Catch statements, 425
CAT_ID, 504–505, 522
CAT_Name, 505
C-compiled languages, 5
CDalAddress class, 319
CGI. *See* Common Gateway Interface
Change events, 77
Char data type, 40
CheckBoxes, usage, 103–106
CheckBoxList, 108
  control, 101, 106
Child node, 360
Child objects, 597
ChildControls, 621
ChildNodes, 373

ChildNodes.Count, 373
ChildPost property, 599, 603, 605
ChildPosts property, 599, 603, 605
ChildThread, 594
Class file, compiling, 78
Class viewer, usage, 436–437
Classes, 464
  arrays, 464–465
Classic ASP, 14, 17, 22
  pages, 37
  projects, 24
  upgrading, 26–27
ClassViewer, 437
clear attribute, 203
clear (processing directive), 189
clear subtag, 190, 192–193, 202, 207
Clear (value), 206
click() event, 70
Client capabilities determination, browserCaps tag, usage, 184–186
Client/browser communication (enabling), System.Web namespace (usage), 45–52
  supplied functionality, 45–52
Client-server interaction, 16–17
Client-side JavaScript validation, 120
Client-side scripts, 75
Client-side validation, 120, 121
  function. *See* CustomValidator
ClientValidationFuncation property, 121
C-like shorthand, 250
CLR. *See* Common Language Runtime
cmdCompute, 164
cntApplication, 250
COBOL.NET, 13
Code
  conversion. *See* Multiple languages

Index 669

creation. *See* eXtensible Markup Language Cart
  development activities, 78
  listing, 328
Code-Behind, 63, 78
  attribute, 82
  class file, development, 83
  file, 312
Code-behind, 106, 635, 650, 657
  classes, 66, 181
  in-page coding, contrast, 77–87
  onsubmit(), 559
  pages, 15, 450, 455, 543
  usage
    compilation, inclusion, 81–84
    compilation, non-inclusion, 79–81
CodeBehind.aspx file, 80
ColdFusion, 7
Collection objects, 111
Colors, manipulation, 491–495
Column mapping, usage. *See* DataGrid control
COM. *See* Component Object Model
COM+ components, 27
Command object, 325, 328, 332, 335
  usage, 337
Command-line tools, 12
CommandSource, 136
Comment, 352. *See also* Actual comment
Common Gateway Interface (CGI), 4
  programs, 3
Common Language Runtime (CLR), 11–13, 27, 37, 63
  CLR-supported language, 75
  Intermediate Language (IL), 447
  languages, 300
  usage, 45, 75, 313

Common Object Request Broker Architecture (CORBA), 443, 448
CompareValidator, 113, 127–128, 535
  control, 117–118
Compilation
  command, 81
  errors, 418–420
  inclusion/non-inclusion. *See* Code-behind
  options (setting), compilation tag (usage), 187–190
compilation subtags, 189
compilation tag, usage. *See* Compilation
compiler subtag, 188
Compiling. *See* World Wide Web services
complexType data structures, 357–358
Component Object Model (COM), 6
  components, 24, 27
  foundations, 9
  objects, 8, 231, 576
Comprehensive Perl Archive Network (CPAN), 5
comptePay procedure, 166
configSections tag, 212
Configuration. *See* Application; ASP.NET configuration; Encryption; HyperText Transfer Protocol; Request; Security; Session state; Sessions; System; World Wide Web
  file, 174
    anatomy, 211–222
    creation, 215–219
    overriding, 175
    uses, 177–211
  hierarchy, 176
  inheritance, 176
  section handlers, 212

670 Index

settings, retrieval, 220–222
trace tag, usage. *See* Tracing
configuration tag, opening, 215
ConfigurationSettings.appSettings method, 220
ConfigurationSettings.GetConfig method, 220
Connection strings
  creation, 310–313
  placement, 312–313
  security, 313
connectionManagement tag, usage. *See* Connections control
Connections control, connectionManagement tag (usage), 190–191
ConnectionString, 616
Connectivity. *See* ADO.NET
Console applications, creation, 590–591
Constraints, 127–128
Control.ChildControls Control Collection, 621
ControlCollection, 620
Controls. *See* Custom controls; Server controls; Validation; World Wide Web
  usage. *See* DataGrid control; DataList control
ControlToCompare property, 128
Cookies, 230, 241
  data, encryption/decryption. *See* Forms
Copy methods, 44
CORBA. *See* Common Object Request Broker Architecture
Corel, 14
CPAN. *See* Comprehensive Perl Archive Network (CPAN)
CreatePost method, 606

CreateSummaryTable method, creation, 549–550
CreateThread method, 606
CreateUser, 585, 624
  function, 589
CreateUser method, 623
Creator field, 605
CreatorID, 570
credentials subtag, 206
Cross-discipline teams, 4
CSS. *See* Cascading Style Sheet
CT_Email, 505
CT_FirstName, 505
CT_ID, 505, 513
CT_LastName, 505
CT_Password, 505
CType, usage, 602
Currency, datatype, 507
CurrentUser
  object, 627
  property, 624
Current.Value property, 391
Custom controls, 63
Custom errors definition, customErrors tag (usage), 191–192
Custom server user controls, creation, 161–167
Customer
  Admin section, creation, 543–547
  administration, 543–547
  element, 385, 386
Customer_Id attributes, 385
customErrors tag, usage. *See* Custom errors definition
CustomValidator, 113, 535, 622
  client-side validation function, 120–122
  control, 118–120

Index 671

D

DAL, 319, 332
  example, 337
Data
  access code, 335
  access layer, value retrieval, 312
  access object, creation, 579–581
  binding, usage, 95–97
  caching, 252–257, 266, 281–294
    usage, advantages, 292–293
  collection, HTML forms (usage), 63–65
  connection, creation, 520–521
  display, 540–541. *See also* Formatted data; Repeater control
    default column mapping, usage. *See* DataGrid control
    editing capability, providing. *See* DataGrid control
  filters, testing, 559
  non-updateable stream, 303
  provider, 300, 341
  retrieval, 367–369, 537–540
  table, 154
  types (grouping), System.Collections namespace (usage), 43–44
    supplied functionality, 43–44
  updating. *See* Database
Data source, 302, 319
  System.Data namespace, usage, 52–53
    supplied functionality, 52
data source agnostic namespace, 306
DataAdapter, 302, 303
  usage, 538
Database. *See* MSAccess database; SQL Server database; SQLServer database
  access, 51
  addition, 330–335
  books, addition, 541
  browsing, 323–330
  connection, 319–323, 476
    information, 236
  connectivity issues, 130
  creation. *See* Access database
  data, updating, 335–339
  deleting, 339–341, 541–542
  level, 330
  query, usage. *See* eXtensible Markup Language document
  replication, 460
  setup. *See* ADO.NET shopping cart; Message board creation
  updating, 542–543
  usage, 405–409
Database-driven interactivity, 4
DataBind, 101
  Repeater control, interaction, 634
DataBind() method, 111
DataBinded, 540
DataBinds, 632
Databound ListControls, 100
  family, 130–161
DataColumn, 306
  children, 466
DataColumns, 301
DataControl, 579
Data-enabled ASP.NET pages, 52
DataException, 306
DataGrid, 49
  binding, 323. *See* DataSet
  contents, 146
  control, 387, 540, 561
  deleting, 541–542
  event, 542
  loading, 383

672 Index

paging, providing, 152–154
relational table, 381
resync, 543
sorting, 149–152
tag, 158
UI, 541
updating, 542–543
DataGrid control
  data display, default column mapping (usage), 145–146
  data editing capability, providing, 157–161
  usage, 144–152
DataGridPageChangedEventArgs
  parameter, 152, 157
  usage, 158
DataItem fields, 132
DataKeyField property, 158
DataList, 314. *See also* Page-level DataList
  binding, 316, 323
  control, 157
  definition, 142
  RepeatColumn property, usage, 139–141
  RepeatDirection property, usage, 139–141
DataList control
  items, capturing, 141–144
  usage, 139–144
DataReader, 303, 305, 325
  object, 301
  usage, 314
DataReaders, 52
DataRepeater, binding, 323
DataRow, 486, 586, 596, 601
  children, 466
  creation, 542

CType, usage, 602
passing, 611
DataRows, 301
DataSet, 303, 306, 319, 465, 516. *See also* XmlDataDocument
  allBooks, 551
  arrays, 465
  creation, 538, 634
  DataGrid, binding, 540–541
  dsAllBooks, 550
  object, 408, 540, 547, 552
  property, 378
  requirement, 302
  returning, 537
  RowFilter operations, 466
  storage, 547
  type, 540
  usage, 301, 314, 466–468, 601
  view tag, 357
  XML document, reading, 408–409
DataSets, 52–53, 361
DataSource object, 497
DataTable, 306, 361, 386
  children, 466
  filling, 323
  returning, 549
  value, 546
  view, 378
DataType, 486
Datatypes, 507. *See also* AutoNumber; Currency; Date/Time; Memo; Number; OLE Object; Text; Yes/No
DataView, 306, 541
  children, 466
  object, 151
  usage, 543
DataViews collection, 301

Dates, 40
  structures, 38
  validating, 126–129
Date/Time, datatype, 508
datetime.maxvalue option, usage, 287
DB2, 327
DCOM. *See* Distributed Component Object Model
Debug mode, enabling/disabling, 435–436
Debugging. *See* ASP.NET debugging tools, usage. *See* Visual Studio .NET
Declaration, 352
decryptionKey attribute, 209
Default column mapping, usage. *See* DataGrid control
defaultRedirect attribute, 191
Definitions (viewing), object browser (usage), 436
Delete method, 592, 598
DELETE records, 303
Delete Stored procedure, 341
Delete syntax, usage, 339, 340
deleteBoard.aspx, 651
DeletePost method, 597, 599
DeleteThread method, 597
Delphi, 3
Dependency option, usage, 285–287
Depth, 365
Description property, 422
Design Time Control (DTC), 546
Desktop application, 229
DHTML. *See* Dynamic HTML
Dictionary-style interface, 282
Display, 114
Display= "dynamic," 114
Display= "none," 114
Display= "static," 114

DisplayBoards subroutine, 630
displayMode, 123
DisplayNode, 376
Dispose, 101
Distributed Component Object Model (DCOM), 443, 448
Distributed Internet Applications (DNA), 5, 9
DLL. *See* Dynamically linked library
DNA. *See* Distributed Internet Applications
DNS. *See* Domain Name System
Document Object Model (DOM), 348, 373
  exploration. *See* eXtensible Markup Language
  tree, 374, 376–378, 388
Document Type Definition (DTD), 352–353, 356
DocumentElement, 373
DocumentElement.ChildNodes(0), 373
Documents. *See* eXtensible Markup Language; Valid XML documents; Well-formed XML documents
  components. *See* eXtensible Markup Language document
  creation. *See* Visual Studio .NET
  navigation
    XPathDocument objects, usage, 392–396
    XPathNavigator objects, usage, 392–396
  structure. *See* eXtensible Markup Language
DocumentSource attribute, 398
DOM. *See* Document Object Model
Domain Name System (DNS), 13, 15
doPaging sub-procedure, 152
dotBoard

674 Index

construction, 628
Setup.sql, 573
dotBoardObjects, 590, 614
dotBoardObjects.DataControl class, 646
dotBoardObjects.User object, 615
dotBoardUI, 613, 614
Down-level browsers, 100
Drill-down facilities. *See* Automatic drill-down facilities
Drop-down list, 303, 646
  boxes, 233
DropDownList, 646, 647
  control, 645
DropDownLists, usage, 103–106
DSN sources, 176
DTC. *See* Design Time Control
DTD. *See* Document Type Definition
dtProducts, 132, 135
Dynamic compilation, 75
Dynamic HTML (DHTML), 348, 536
Dynamic SQL, 327
Dynamically Linked Library (DLL), 36, 192
  file, 78, 81, 83, 577

E

editItemIndex, 314
EditItemIndex, setting, 316
EditItemTemplate, 139
editPost.aspx, 655
Electronic business (E-business), 12
Electronic commerce (E-commerce), 12
Electronic mail (E-mail), 475
  address, 474, 569, 638
  object, 484
  validation, 483

Elements, 353. *See also* Empty element; Root element
  nesting, 355
  termination, 355
Element-type node, 368
element-type node, 360
EM. *See* Enterprise Manager
Email, 571
Embedded SQL, 327
  statements, 327
Emoticon element, 493
Empty element, 354–355
Enabled, 101
Encryption, 204, 206
  keys configuration, machineKey tag (usage), 209–210
End-tag, 353, 355
English-language systems, 180
Enterprise JavaBeans, 9
Enterprise Manager (EM), 510–511, 515, 572, 576
Enum types, 464
Enums, arrays, 464
EOF, 365
ErrorHandling block, 423
ErrorMessage, 114
Errors. *See* Compilation; Logic errors; Runtime; Syntax errors
  definition. *See* Custom errors definition
  handling, 418–426. *See also* Structured error handling; Unstructured error handling
  message, 114, 420, 424
    display, 122
Events, 237–239
  bubbling, 132
    usage, 135–138
  capturing. *See* Repeater control

Index

execution, order, 77
item, 432
usage. *See* Application; Sessions
Exception, 425. *See also* OutOfMemoryException; OverflowException
EXEC usp_tblAddress_sel, 326
ExecuteNonQuery method, 335, 339, 341, 579
ExecuteQuery, 530
ExecuteReader, 325
Execution environment, 75
executionTimeout attribute, 194
Expiration policy, 285
  option, usage, 287
eXtensible Markup Language Cart (XMLCart)
  construction, 553–556
  rendering, 559
eXtensible Markup Language Schema Definition (XSD), 356–357, 460
  attributes, 478
  schema, 359
eXtensible Markup Language (XML), 51
  Authority, 362
  construction, 476–478
  data, 13, 52, 465, 557
    representation, 53
  data, querying
    XPathDocument, usage, 388–396
    XPathNavigator, usage, 388–396
  Designer, XML document creation. *See* Visual Studio .NET
  DOM, exploration, 373–387
  element, 355
  files, 15, 52, 285, 484
    change, 286
  files (processing), System.XML namespace (usage), 53–54
    supplied functionality, 53–54
  format text files, 13
  formatting, 174
  functions, 553
  future, 350
  interactions. *See* Legacy systems
  node, 362, 560
  overview, 348–361
  parser, 174, 348
  specifications, 350
  tags, 619
  tree, 364
  usage, 405–409. *See also* Message board creation; .NET framework; World Wide Web services
  validation. *See* Visual Studio .NET
  XML-based systems, 354
  XML-based text files, 8
  XML-RPC, 9
eXtensible Markup Language (XML) document, 70, 312. *See also* Valid XML documents; Well-formed XML documents
  appearance, 349
  components, 352–355
  creation, 350–352. *See also* Visual Studio .NET
    database query, usage, 406–408
  generation, XmlTextWriter (usage), 370–373
  loading, 378
  navigation, 367–369
  parsing, 365–367
    XmlDocument object, usage, 376–378
    XmlTextReader class, usage, 364–369
  processing, .NET (usage), 361–364

reading, 362–363. *See also* DataSet
   XmlTextReader class (usage),
   364–369
  storing/processing, 363–364
  structure, 360–361
  transformation, 400–405. *See also*
   HyperText Markup Language
   XSLT, usage, 396–405
  writing, 362–363
   XmlTextWriter class, usage, 370–373
eXtensible Markup Language (XML)
   XML.NET guestbook
  creation, 473
  FAQs, 500
  functional design requirements,
   475–478
  interface, advanced options, 490–497
  introduction, 474–475
  records, addition, 478–488
  solutions, 498–499
  viewing, 488–490
eXtensible Stylesheet Language
   Transformations (XSLT), 348, 362,
   396, 549
  code, 401–403
  file, 401
  style sheet, 397
  usage. *See* eXtensible Markup
   Language document

F

Factorial, value, 426
Failure point, 27
File locking, 488
File Transfer Protocol (FTP), 5, 16, 231
fileControl.PostedFiled.SaveAs, 93
Filestream, 495

Finally block, 425
firehose Recordset, 303
Firewalls, 448
FirstChild, 373
FirstName, 571
FirstRecord, 558
Floating point numbers, 38
Floating-point numbers, 39–40
Font, 101
Footer template, 132, 133
FooterTemplate, 132
ForeColor, 101
forecolor property, 122
/form, 130–161
Formatted data, display, 146–149
Formatting, 370
Formatting-related HTML elements,
   139
FormBase.vb, 614
Forms. *See* Online forms
  authentication cookie data,
   encryption/decryption, 209
  controls. *See* World Wide Web
  objects, 482
  usage. *See* Data collection
forms subtag, 205, 206
Form-type server controls, 62
Forward-only basis, 362–363
Foundation class libraries, 12
Fragment caching, 266, 267, 277–281,
   294
  usage, advantages, 281
fragment_cache.aspx, 279
FrontPage, 5
FTP. *See* File Transfer Protocol
Functionality. *See* Supplied functionality

G

Generated template code, 455
GET, 16, 192
  query string parameter, 270
  requests, 17
GetAllBooks, 513
GetAllCat, 513
GetBoards, 611
getBooks, 519, 540
getBooks.AllBooks Web method,
    creation, 537–540
getByID function, 316
getCartDescription method, 556
getCategories, 519
getCustomer, 518
GetDataSet, 579
GetElementsByTagName, 380
GetStyleName, 620–621
  function, 621
GetValueList method, 97
GetXml, 405
GetXml() method, 552
GetXmlSchema, 405
Global Assembly Cache, 27
Global files, 24
Global support (providing), globalization tag (usage), 180–181
Global unique identifier, 505
Global variables, 233
Global.asa, 313
Global.asax, 228, 234, 250
  analysis, 231–232
  creation, 245
  files, 238
globalization tag, usage. *See* Global support
grossWage property, 164

Guestbook. *See* eXtensible Markup Language XML.NET guestbook
Guests, 581
GUIs, 478

H

HasAttributes property, 365
HasChildNodes, 373
HashTable, 95
HasValue, 365
Header
  information, 17
  template, 133
HeaderStyle property, 147
HeaderTemplate, 132
headerText, 123
Height, 101
Hidden fields, 69
HTML. *See* HyperText Markup Language
/html, 130–161
/HTML tag, cache remove method (usage), 292
HTMLAnchor, 47
  object, 36
HtmlAnchor control, 651
  usage, 88, 89
HtmlButton control, usage, 91–93
HtmlCheckBox control, usage, 98–99
HtmlImage control, usage, 91–93
HtmlInputButton, 91
HtmlInputFile control, usage, 93–95
HtmlInputRadioButton control, usage, 98–99
HtmlInputText control, usage, 90–91
HTMLInputTextBox object, 36
HtmlSelect control
  binding, 111

usage, 95–97
HtmlTable
  construction, 89
  control, usage, 88–90
HtmlTextArea control, usage, 90–91
HTTP. *See* HyperText Transfer Protocol
HttpApplication class, 46
HttpCachePolicy class, 46
  methods, 269
  usage, 275–277
httpHandlers, 192
  tag, usage. *See* Requests mapping
httpModules tag, usage. *See* HyperText Transfer Protocol modules configuration
HttpRequest object variables, 45
HttpResponse object variables, 45
HttpResponse.Cache property, 269
httpRuntime tag, 194
  usage. *See* Runtime options
HttpServerUtility object, 45
HTTP_USER_AGENT variable, 184
HyperLink controls, usage, 110–111
Hyperlinks, display, 88
HyperText Markup Language (HTML), 4, 53, 212, 557. *See also* Dynamic HTML
  anchor tag, 655
  code, 482
  controls, 47, 75, 558
    usage, 66–67
  counterparts, 48
  display, 26
  document, 64, 348
    XML document transformation, 397–399
  elements, 62, 87, 93, 95. *See also* Formatting-related HTML elements

form
  element, 64
  usage. *See* Data
  validation, 535
functions, 488
head/body information, 257
HTML-user interface controls, 36
layout techniques, 535
markup, 20
metatag, 232
page, 47
rendering, 303
server controls, 62, 102
  usage, 87–100
  Web controls, contrast, 100
string, 637
table, 133, 397
tables/lists, 48
version 3.2, 100
version 4.0, 100
view, 453
HyperText Transfer Protocol (HTTP), 350, 443
  connections, 518
  data transmission, 462, 465
  header, 230
    value, 273
  HTTP-header client-side implementation, 8
  message, 63, 65
  methods, 16
  modules, 200
    configuration, httpModules tag (usage), 193–194
  processing, 194
  protocol, 67
  reponse information, 45
  request, 18, 267, 281

Index

header, 17
traffic, 448
usage, 461

I

IBM, 7
IconfigurationSectionHandler interface, 212
IDC. *See* Internet Database Connector
  technology, 10
@@IDENTITY
  function, 330
  selection, 332
@@identity, 509
identity tag, usage. *See* Application
If statements, 27, 637
IHttpHandler, 192
IhttpHandlerFactory, 192
IIS. *See* Internet Information Server
IL. *See* Common Language Runtime
Image selection, 494
ImagePath, 130
Images
  folder, 92
  manipulation, 491–495
img (element), 92
Imports keyword, 306
In AddItem, 560
In Checkout, 560
In Page_Load(), 559
In RemoveItem, 560
In showCart(), 560
In showCatalog(), 559–560
InferXmlSchema, 405
inflate method, 588, 611
Inheritance, 75. *See also* Configuration
.ini files, 174

Init, 101
init(), 529, 530
InitCatalog method, creation, 550
Initialization code, 495
InitializeComponent() method, 521
InitializeThreads method, 599–601
InkCreateBoard, 649
Inline coding, 77
In-memory relational database, 301
InnerText, 373
In-Page Code, 63
In-page coding, contrast, 77. *See also* Code-behind
Input/Output, 335
INSERT records, 303
Insurance-related data, 103
Int16 variable, 419
Int32 variable, 419
Integers, 38
  data types, 39
  number, 250
Integral numbers, 38, 39
Intermediate Language (IL). *See* Common Language Runtime
Internet Database Connector (IDC), 3
Internet Information Server (IIS), 2–3, 10, 18
  application parameters, 228
  environment, 63
  infancy, 5
  usage, 266, 450
  version 5, 8, 10
Internet Server Application Programming Interface (ISAPI), 3–5, 10
Internet Service Provider (ISP), 19
Intrinsic state methods, 220
IsAdmin, 571, 648

680   Index

ISAPI. *See* Internet Server Application Programming Interface
IsBanned, 571, 648
ISBN, 522, 541, 556
  supplying, 555
  usage, 560
IsDefault, 365
IsEmptyElement, 365
ISP. *See* Internet Service Provider
IsPostBack property, usage. *See* Pages
Item, 365
  capturing. *See* DataList control
  Command event, 132
  function, 608
  property, 602
  Template, 132
ItemIndex, 314
ItemTemplate, 135, 137
Iterator object, 394

J

J++, 14
J2EE. *See* Java 2 Enterprise Edition
Java, 11, 24, 447, 456
  support, 7
Java 2 Enterprise Edition (J2EE), 9
Java Server Pages (JSP), 7
JavaScript, 3, 24, 62, 120, 348
  validation, 121. *See also* Client-side JavaScript validation
Java-servlets, 518
Jet, 326
JIT. *See* Just-In-Time
JScript
  developers. *See* .NET.Experience JScript developers
  programmers, 26
JScript.NET, 13

JSP, 518. *See* Java Server Pages
Just-In-Time (JIT) compilation, 578

K

Key attribute, 179
Key-field, 97

L

Labels, usage, 103–106
Large-scale applications, 603
LastChild, 373
LastName, 571
LastRecord, 558
Legacy systems, XML interactions, 362
Length properties, 44
Let assignments, 27
level attribute, 211
Link buttons, usage, 141
LinkButton, 641, 645
List, 123
List box loading, script usage, 70–72
ListBox control, 85, 106
ListControl, 108, 141–142. *See also* Databound ListControls
  abstract class, usage, 106–109
  binding. *See* ArrayList
  examples, 132
ListPrice
  element, 353, 358
  node, 369
Load, 101
Local files, usage, 51
location (tag), 177, 214, 216
Logged-in administrator, 650
Logic errors, 419, 426
Log-in interface, construction, 621–628
loginCustomer, 519

Index

page, creation, 544–545
LoginCustomers, 513
Long data types, 39
Lower-level configuration file, 177
Lower-level file, 175

M

machine.config, 174, 183
  file, 176, 184, 212
machineKey tag, usage. *See* Encryption
Machine-specific binary code, 14
Macromedia. *See* Ultradev
.majorversion properties, 22
Many-to-many table relationship, 504
Mark-up codes, 63
mBoardID variable, 601
MD5 hash algorithm, usage, 206
MD5 (value), 206
Member profile, editing, 638–640
Memo, datatype, 508
Memory
  implications, 233
  resources, 269, 293
Message
  board, 568
  browsing, 635–638
  display, 488–490
  transmission, 462
Message board creation, ADO/XML
    usage, 567
  administrative interface, construction,
    645–657
  application design, 576–612
  database, setup, 568–576
  FAQs, 661–662
  general functions, setup, 614–621
  introduction, 568
  solutions, 658–660

user functions, creation, 638–644
MessageBinding, 461
MessageBoard class, 630
  design, 611–612
Metatag. *See* HyperText Markup
    Language
Microsoft Data Engine (MSDE), 19, 28
Microsoft Intermediate Language
    (MSIL), 14, 18, 37
Microsoft Management Console
    (MMC), 10, 13, 229
  usage, 231, 239
Microsoft Message Queue, 7
Microsoft Office, 51
Microsoft Transaction Server (MTS),
    7, 10
Middle child, 603
.minorversion properties, 22
MMC. *See* Microsoft Management
    Console
mode attribute, 191, 205
ModeratorID, 569
Moderators, 581
Modern Relational Database
    technology, 323
Modified URL, 241
Modules configuration,
    webRequestModule tag (usage).
    See Request
Mono, 14
MoveNext method, 394
MoveToAttribute(i) method, 365
MoveToContent()
  method, 369
  statement, 368
MoveToElement method, 365
MSAccess database, 569–572
MSDATA attributes, 478
MSDE. *See* Microsoft Data Engine

MSDN documentation, 436
MSIL. *See* Microsoft Intermediate Language
MSSQL, 537
mThread variable, 644
MTS. *See* Microsoft Transaction Server
Multi-line comments, 24
Multi-line text, 90
Multi-page bank account sign-up form, 228
Multiple languages, code conversion, 13–14
Multiple tables, viewing. *See* XmlDataDocument
Multiple-table views, 379
Multi-process environment, 233

N

Name, 475
  property, 364
name attribute, 210, 212
  acceptance, 213
name parameter, 270
name value, 203
namespace subtag, 189
Namespaces. *See* System
  FAQs, 58–59
  function, review, 36–37
  introduction, 36
  set. *See* System.Web.Services namespace set; System.Web.UI namespace
  solutions, 56–57
  understanding. *See* Root namespace
  usage, 37. *See also* Client/browser communication; Data; eXtensible Markup Language files; Objects; .VisualBasic namespace
NavigateUrl property, 110

Nested controls, 100
Nested elements, 387
.NET, 11
  class, 234
  environment, 406
  language code, 14
  namespaces, 232
  objects, 12
  obtaining/installation, 19
  technology, 13
  usage. *See* eXtensible Markup Language document
.NET DLLs, 36
.NET Framework, 12, 13, 26, 421, 449
  FAQs, 414–415
  introduction, 348
  solutions, 410–413
  XML usage, 347
Net SDK Collection Class, 95
.NET-based modules, 26
Net.Commerce, 7
.NET.Experience JScript developers, 14
Netscape 4.72, 536
Netscape 4.x, ASP.NET server controls display, 536
Netscape Netsite server, 10
Network communication, 233
Network-handling functions, 12
newPageIndex property, 152
Nodes, values retrieval, 379–380
NodeType, 373
  property, 364
Non-indexed default properties, 27
Non-windows platforms, 14
Normal default value, 288
Notepad, 4, 174
  usage, 350, 356
nothing object, 287

Null, 246
Number, datatype, 508

O

objControl.GetType().ToString(), 621
Object Browser, usage, 436
Object-oriented (OO)
  application, 581
  approach, 577–578
  objects, 582
Objects, 40–43. *See also* Application; Request; Response objects
  browser, usage. *See* Definitions
  creation. *See* Data
  design, 579
  grouping, System.Collections namespace (usage), 43–44
    supplied functionality, 43–44
  hierarchy, 652
  orientation, 14
ODBC. *See* Open DataBase Connectivity
OLE Object, datatype, 508
OleDb
  connection string, 305
  data connection object, 519
  provider, 519
OleDbCommand, 307
  object, 326, 332
OleDbConnection, 307
  connection string, 310
OleDbDataAdapter, 307
OleDbDataReader, 307
  object, 319
OLTP. *See* Online Transaction Processing
On Error Resume Next statement, 422
On Error statement, 421–423

OnCancelCommand, 157
onclick event, 556
OnClick() event, 486
OnDataBinding, 101
OnDeleteCommand, 157
OnEditCommand, 157, 314
OnEditCommandEvent, 157
One-to-many table relationship, 504
One-to-one table relationship, 504
OnInit, 101
Online forms, 486
Online Transaction Processing (OLTP), 323
OnLoad, 101
OnPageIndexChanged, 152
OnRemove, 289
onSelectedIndexChanged attribute/event, 73
onserverchange attribute, 90
OnServerValidate property, 120
onServerValidate property, 119
OnSortCommand, 150
onsubmit(), 559
OnUpdateCommand, 157
OO. *See* Object-oriented
Open DataBase Connectivity (ODBC), 3
  connections, 476
Open Source projects, 22
Opera browser, 275
OperationBinding, 461
Option Explicit, 27
Option Strict On statement, 420
Oracle, 7, 327
OR_Date, 506
OrderBook, 513
orderBooks, 519
orderBooks.OrderItem, 556

OR_ID, 505, 506
originUrl attribute, 211
OR_ShippedDate, 506
OutOfMemoryException, 425
Output Cache directive, usage.
  See @ OutputCache directive
Output caching, 266–267, 269–277, 294
  advantages, 276–277
OutputBinding, 461
output_cache.aspx, 271
OverflowException, 425

P

Page, 101
  Declarative statement, 79
@Page directive, 451
Page_Init, 77
Page.InitOutputCache method, 269
Page.IsPostBack, 72
Page-level DataList, 319
Page_Load, 77
  event, 71–72, 77, 97, 108, 162, 281
    usage, 368, 374, 408
  method, 630, 640, 657
  sub, 497
  subroutine, 623
Page.Load event, 623
Page_Load() event, 377
Page_OnLoad event, 316
Page_PreRender event, 281
PagerStyle-HorizontalAlign, 152
Pages. See Active Server Pages
  class file, 65
  compilation. See ASP.NET
  directive, 434
  directives, 76–77
  events, 75
    option, 181

IsPostBack property (usage), 72–73
  navigation, 154–156
  output, modification, 495–497
  running. See ASP.NET
  tracing, 426–434
pages tag, usage. See Page-specific
    attributes
PageSize, 152
Page-specific attributes (setting), pages
    tag (usage), 181–182
Page_Unload, 77
Paging, providing. See DataGrid
Parallel processing, 24
Parameterized stored procedure, 154
Parent, 101
Parent-child relationships, 356
Parentheses, usage, 27
passport subtags, 205, 206
Passwords, 176, 236, 569, 571
  validating, 126–129
Password-type textbox, 90
path attribute, 214
Patterned strings, validating, 126–129
Payroll user control
  consuming, 166–167
  development, 164–166
Perl, 3–5, 117. See also Comprehensive
    Perl Archive Network
  5, 7
Perl.NET, 13
Permissions, 208
Per-server basis, 174
Personal identification number
    (PIN), 230
PHP, 7, 518
PIN. See Personal identification number
pnlAdd panel, understanding, 482–484
PnlThank, Thank-You panel
    (addition), 484

policyFile attribute, 210
Portable.NET, 14
POST, 16, 192
  method, 17
  parameters, 270
Post
  class, design, 608–611
  creation, 641–644
  object, 603, 657
PostBack, role, 63
Postbacks, 166
PostList class, design, 606–608
Price, 146
Primitive types. *See* Standard primitive types
Primitives, arrays, 464
Priority option, usage, 288–289
Process model options (setting), processModel tag (usage), 195–200
processModel tag, usage. *See* Process model options
Product element, 353, 357–358
Product Name, 353, 367
Product nodes, 360
ProductId, 135–137, 146, 353
  field, 158
  usage, 358
ProductName, 130, 146
  node, 368
Provider
  attribute, 304, 310
  property, 305
Proxy
  classes. *See* Web Services Description Language
PUT, 192
Python, 13

Q

Quasi-HTML, 628, 631, 635
Query
  expressions, samples, 389–390
  plan, optimization, 327
  running, 276
  usage. *See* eXtensible Markup Language document
Query Analyzer, 515
Querystring parameter values, 17

R

RAD. *See* Rapid Application Development
RadioButtonList control, 101, 106
RadioButtons, usage, 103–106
RangeValidator, 113–114, 128, 535
  control, 118
Rank properties, 44
Rapid Application Development (RAD), 63
  features, 11
Read() method, 364, 365, 368
Read-only forward-only cursor, 323
ReadOnly property, 158, 164
ReadState, 365
ReadString(), 368
ReadXml method, 408
ReadXmlSchema, 405
Real-time value verification, 62
RealXml, 405
recordCount, 558
Recordset. *See* firehose Recordset
  object, 53
  usage, 301
Recursive procedure, 376
redirectUrl attribute, 206

Register
  directive, 162
Registered users, 581
Regular Expressions, 4
  support, 6
RegularExpression property, 115
RegularExpressionValidator, 113, 535
  control, 115–117
Relational database, 502
Relational view, 378, 384
  usage. *See* XmlDataDocument
Remote database, access, 181
Remote procedure call (RPC), 448
remove attribute, 203
remove (processing directive), 189
remove subtag, 190, 192–193, 202, 207
removeCat, 528, 530
removeItem, 528–530
removeItemFromCart method, 556
RepeatColumn property, usage. *See* DataList
RepeatDirection
  attribute, 107
  property, usage. *See* DataList
Repeater code, 632
Repeater control, 52, 145, 628–631
  data display, 132–135
  events, capturing, 135–138
  interaction. *See* DataBind
  usage, 635
Repeater server control, usage, 132–138
RepeaterCommandEventArgs, 136
Request
  modules configuration, webRequestModule tag (usage), 202–203
  objects, 21, 45–46
Request.Browser.Browser, 22

Request.Browser.Type property, 275
requestEncoding, default, 180
Requests mapping, httpHandlers tag (usage), 192–193
RequiredFieldValidator, 113, 535
  control, 114–115
RequiredFieldValidators, 642
Resource buffering, 216
Response
  buffering options, 181
  messages, 63
  objects, 45–46, 63, 427
responseEncoding, default, 180
Response.Write() method, 426–427
ReturnValue, 335
Reverse engineering, 356
Rexx, 3
Root element, 353, 355, 382
Root namespace, understanding, 38–43
  supplied functionality, 38–43
Root node, 555
RowFilter property, 542, 545
RPC. *See* eXtensible Markup Language; Remote procedure call
Runtime
  errors, 418, 420–426
  options (setting), httpRuntime tag (usage), 194
Run-time display, 119
Run-time view, 114, 155

S

SAX. *See* Simple API for XML
Schema, 352–353
  documents, 356–360
Schema Generators, 348
Screen scrape, 12

Index

Scripts
  execution changes, 8
  inclusion. *See* .aspx file
  tags, entering, 239
  usage. *See* List box loading
SDK. *See* Service Definition Language; Software Development Kit
section tag, 212
sectionGroup, usage, 213
Security. *See* Connection strings
  configuration, 179, 204–211
  modules configuration, authenticationModules tag (usage), 207–208
  policies mapping, securityPolicy tag (usage), 210–211
  precautions, 28
securityPolicy tag, usage. *See* Security
Select statement, 326
SelectedIndex property, 375
SelectedIndexChange events, 106
SelectedItem property, 72
SelectedItemTemplate, 139
SelectedItem.Value property, 647
SelectSingleNode function, 621
sellerAdmin, 518
Semi-static page, 292
SeparatorTemplate, 132
Server controls, 72. *See also* Form-type server controls; HyperText Markup Language; World Wide Web
  AutoPostBack attributes, 73–77
  FAQs, 171
  features, 62–65
  introduction, 62
  mapping, 69
  solutions, 168–171
  states, preservation, 69
  usage, 68–69. *See also* HyperText Markup Language; Repeater server control
Server resources
  utilization, 268
Server resources, optimization, 268–269
Server Side Include (SSI), 4
Server user controls, creation. *See* Custom server user controls
ServerControl3.aspx, 73
Server.HTMLEncode, 45
Server.MapPath, 45
Server.MapPath(), usage, 486
Servers, communication, 448–460
Server-side code, 65, 90, 92
  development, 118
Server-side controls, 113
Server-side processing, 17–18, 65–77. *See also* ASP.NET
Server-side programmability, 98
Server-side redirects, 8
Server-side scripting, 65
Server-side scripts, 75
  tag, 120
Server-side validation, 120, 121
Server-side Web form components, 257
Server-side-only custom validator, 120
ServerValidateEventArgs class, 120
Service Definition Language (SDL), 461
ServiceDescription class, 461
Servlets technology, 7
Session
  configuration, 241–243
  events, usage, 243–245
  information, 232
  object, 97
  userId value, 627
  variable, 240

688 Index

usage, 545
Session ID, 15, 240
Session state, 63, 242
  comparison. *See* Application state
  configuration, sessionState tag (usage), 200–202
  information, 26
  understanding, 240–241
Session_OnStart event, 245
sessionState tag, usage. *See* Session state
Set assignments, 27
setEditMode procedure, 157
SetSlidingExpiration method, 276
Settings, retrieval. *See* Configuration
SGML, 350
SHA1 algorithm, usage, 206
SHA1 (value), 206
Short data types, 39
Show Price button, 375
showCart page methods, 556
showCatalog(), 559
showCatalog page methods, 556
showSelection
  function, 142
  procedure, 97, 142
ShowSummary, 123
Simple API for XML (SAX), 348
Simple Mail Transfer Protocol (SMTP), 6, 10
Simple Object Access Protocol (SOAP), 9, 12, 51, 350, 443
  contracts, 533
  datatype, 464
  headers, 456
  message, 462
  usage, 448, 460–461
SimpleType data structures, 357
Singleparagraph, 123
Site, 101

Site, construction/administration. *See* ADO.NET shopping cart
Sliding expiration, 287
slidingExpiration, 258
Smart cards, usage, 207
SMTP. *See* Simple Mail Transfer Protocol
SOAP. *See* Simple Object Access Protocol
Socket, 211
Software Development Kit (SDK), 19
Sort methods, 44
SortByCategory, 431
SortByTime, 431
SortedList
  creation/loading, 97
  structure, 95–97
sortGrid sub-procedure, 150
Source data, 283
Splitter table, 504
SQL. *See* Structured Query Language
SQL 2000, 317, 502
SQL database, 476
SQL mode, 518
SQL ORDER BY clause, 149
SQL Query, 406
  Analyzer, 28, 573
SQL scripts, 581
SQL Server, 19, 52, 307–308, 330, 511
  7.0 Northwind database, 406
  2000 database, 502, 503
  database, 475, 572–576
  installation, 28
  stored procedures, 327
  usage, 313
  Wizard, 513
SQL Server 2000, 300
SQL Statement, 324, 326, 541, 579
  construction, 597–598, 646

usage, 589–590, 595, 599–601
SQL string, 132, 158
SqlClient
  connection string, 305
  namespace, 307
SqlCommand, 308
  object, 332
SqlConnection, 308, 312
  connection string, 310
  object, 319
  type, 322
SqlDataAdapter, 308
SqlDataReader, 308
SqlDbType enumeration, usage, 339
SqlDbTypes enumeration, 309
SQLServer database, 510–518
SSI. *See* Server Side Include
Standard primitive types, 464
Start page, setting, 445
start.aspx page, creation, 556–558
Start-tag, 353, 355
State. *See* Application state; Session state
  example, 234–236
  management, 229–231
State Bags, 16
State-full ASP Net controls, 63
State-full phenomenon, 68
State-full values, 97
State-less ASP controls, 63
Static texts, 75
Static values, 249–258
Static variables, 234, 249
  counter, 252
  setting, appSettings tag (usage), 179–180
Step Into, 435
Step Out, 435
Step Over, 435

Stored procedures
  creation, 512–518
  name, 324
strConnection property, 322
strConStr, 322
Strings, 38, 40
  data type, 40
  values, 38
  variable, 22
Structs, 464
  arrays, 464–465
Structured error handling, 423–426
Structured Query Language (SQL). *See* Dynamic SQL; Embedded SQL
  server, 327
Sub-application, 176
Subject line, 475
Submit button, 64, 67, 230
  event, 482
  removal, 73
Submit Button Handler code, exploration, 484–488
Sun, 7, 9, 11
Supported connectivity. *See* ADO.NET
Syntax errors, 418, 419
System
  configuration, 179, 184–204
  namespace, 38–43
System.Collections, 41, 43
  namespace, usage, 594. *See also* Data; Objects
System.Configuration.NameValueFileActionHandler class, 212
System.Data, 478
  namespace, 37, 305–308, 476
    usage. *See* Data
  object, 52

System.Data.Common namespace, 307–310
System.Data.OleDb namespace, 304, 305, 307
System.Data.SqlClient namespace, 304, 305, 308
System.Data.SqlTypes namespace, 308–310
System.Int, 39
System.Int16, 39
System.Int32, 39
System.IO, 497
System-level capabilities, 184
System.Net.FileWebRequestCreator module, 202
System.Web namespace, usage. *See* Client/browser communication
system.web node, 312
System.Web.HttpForbiddenHandler handler, 192
System.Web.HttpResponse
  class, 45
  object, 45
System.Web.Services namespace
  overview, 461–463
  set, 51–52
System.Web.Services.Description namespace, 461
System.Web.Services.Discovery namespace, 461–462
System.Web.Services.Protocols namespace, 462–463
System.Web.UI
  namespace set, 46–51
  sub-namespace, 46
system.WebUI.Control object, 46
System.Web.UI.HtmlControls subnamespaces, 47
System.Web.UI.HtmlControls .HTMLControl, 87

System.Web.UI.Page, 615
System.Web.UI.WebControls
  namespace, 62, 80
  sub-namespaces, 47
System.Web.UI.webControls, 621
System.XML, 36
  namespace, 348
    usage. *See* eXtensible Markup Language files
System.Xml namespace, 361
System.Xml.Schema sub-namespaces, 54
System.Xml.Serialization subnamespaces, 54
System.Xml.XPath subnamespaces, 54
System.Xml.Xsl subnamespaces, 54

T

TabIndex, 101
Table
  BookOrders, setup, 506
  books, setup, 505
  categories, setup, 505
  customer, setup, 505
  orders, setup, 505–506
Tag-based markup language, 348
tagname attribute, 163
tagprefix attribute, 162–163
Tags, system, 53
targetNamespace attribute, 477
TCP/IP. *See* Transmission Control Protocol/Internet Protocol
Template code. *See* Generated template code
Template-based declarative language, 396
Templated Web Controls, 100
Terminal node, 376
Text
  boxes, 638

databases, 53
datatype, 507
files. *See* eXtensible Markup Language
Text CommandType, 328
TextBoxes, usage, 103–106
Text-type node, 376
Thank-You panel, addition. *See* PnlThank
Third-party support, 5
Third-party tool vendors, 6
Thread
  browsing, 631–634
  class, design, 603–606
  creation, 641–644
  ID, 569
  object, 657
ThreadID, 570, 572, 594, 643–644
Threading
  model. *See* Visual Basic
  usage, 239
ThreadList, 600, 608
  class, 606
    design, 599–603
ThreadSubject, 570
TIBCO, 360
Tibco Extensibility, 362
Time delay, 257
Time structures, 38
timespan.zero option, usage, 287
Timestamp, 233
TimeUserControl.ascx, 162
Title property, 166
Tool tip help, 435
ToolTip, 101
tooltip property, 122
ToString, 101
Trace. *See* Application-level trace
  attribute, 427

class, 418
  usage, 427–430
information
  sorting, 430–431
  writing. *See* Application
message, 429
mode, 431
page, 427
statements, 430
trace tag, usage. *See* Tracing service
Tracing. *See* Application; Pages
  service configuration, trace tag (usage), 183–184
Transact SQL (T-SQL), 323, 327
  asterisk, usage, 340
  command, 326
Transaction sites, 6
Transfer protocol, 461
Transform() method, usage, 396
TransformSource attribute, 398
Transmission Control Protocol/Internet Protocol (TCP/IP), 12, 15
TravelDownATree, 376
True-or-false values, 40
Trust levels application, trust tag (usage), 211
trust tag, usage. *See* Trust levels application
Try block, 425
Try Catch block, 325
Try-Catch-Finally construct, 423
T-SQL. *See* Transact SQL
Two-way communication, 164
txtConfirmPassword, 128
txtDateOfBirth, 127
type attribute, 212
Type marshalling, 464–465
Type safety, 75

U

UI. *See* User interface
Ultradev (Macromedia), 6
UML. *See* Unified Modeling Language
Unicode, 40
Unified Modeling Language (UML), 579
  diagram, 591, 600, 603, 606, 611
Unique Identifier, 569
UNIX, 3
Unload, 101
Unstructured error handling, 421–423
UPDATE
  query, 158
  records, 303
Update, 585
  method, 589, 592, 597, 648
  profile, 639
Update(), 582
updateCat, 528, 530
updateCustomerInfo page, creation, 545–547
updateItem, 528, 530
Up-level browsers, 100
useFullyQualifiedRedirectUrl attribute, 194
User action, 558
User authentication, authentication tag (usage), 205–207
User class, 583, 592
  design, 581–591
User constructor, 586
User controls
  consuming. *See* Payroll user control
  creation. *See* Custom server user controls; World Wide Web
  development. *See* Payroll user control
  properties, exposure, 163–167

User functions, creation. *See* Message board creation
User IDs, 176, 587, 647
User information, 569
User interface (UI), 46–49, 478, 638, 654. *See also* World Wide Web
  components, 451
  creation, 556–561
  design, 612–613
  producing, 547
  usage, 51, 518, 612
User lists, usage, 51
User object, 585, 588, 615
User page request, 252
User table, 649
userArea.ascx control, 624
UserControlPayrollText.aspx, 166
userCtrlPayroll, 166
User-defined tags, 348
UserID, 571, 646
userId value. *See* Session
Usernames, 236, 571, 588

V

Valid XML documents, 356–360
Validate, 582, 585
  method, 586
validateDeptNum, 119
Validation
  controls, 63, 100, 113–129
  function. *See* CustomValidator
validationKey attribute, 209
ValidationSummary, 113, 535, 622, 642
  control, 123–126
ValidatorControls, 123
validCustomer, 544
Value, 365
  attribute, 179, 616

Variables
  setting. *See* Static variables
  values, 435
VaryByControl attribute, 280, 281
VaryByCustom, 270
  attribute, 275, 280
VaryByHeader, 270
  attribute, 273, 274, 280
VaryByParam, 270
  attribute, 269, 271, 280
VB. *See* Visual Basic
vbCb.dll file, 79, 81
VBCodeProvider, 38
View states, 181
Virtual directory, 83, 229
  structure, 176
Visible, 101
Visual Basic (VB), 2–4, 8, 25
  ASP.NET project, 84
  class file, 80
  objects, 232
  Profile, 591
  Rapid Development, 15
  Scripting, 4
  source file, 79, 81
  threading model, 239
  VB.NET, 27
    language, 20
    statement, 40
  VBScript, 14, 37, 348
    programmers, 10
Visual C++, 9
Visual Source Safe, 6
Visual Studio .NET (VS.NET), 11, 13, 75–78, 246
  Beta 2, 455
  debugging tools, usage, 434–437
  usage, 318. *See also* World Wide Web
  Web service, movement, 460
  XML Designer, XML document creation, 351–352
  XML validation, 359–360
Visual Studio (VS) project, 232
.VisualBasic namespace, usage, 38
VS.NET. *See* Visual Studio .NET

W

W3C. *See* World Wide Web Consortium
Wall, Larry, 5
Warn property, 431
Watch window, 435
Wattle Software, 360
Web Custom Controls, 161
Web Services Description Language (WSDL), 455–460, 502, 531
  file, 449, 461
  proxy classes, 463
  web references, usage, 531–533
Web User Controls, 161
web.config setting, 242
web.config.files, 174, 217, 243
WebControls namespace, 47
WebRequest, 211
webRequestModule tag, usage. *See* Request
@WebService directive, 451
webServices tag, usage. *See* World Wide Web
Websphere, 7
Well-defined documents, 301
Well-formed XML documents, 355–356
Whitespace, 368
Wildcards, 202, 207
Win32 API, 9
Windows authentication, 217
Wireless Markup Language (WML), 18

Wizard-style developer toolkits, 6
WML. *See* Wireless Markup Language
WMLScript, 18
World Wide Web Consortium (W3C), 396, 460
  DOM, 362
  recommendation, 354, 356
World Wide Web (WWW / Web)
  application, 174, 228, 267
    development, VS.NET (usage), 84–87
    folder, creation, 239
  browser, 235
  configuration files, 236
  controls, 62, 75, 87, 101–113
    contrast. *See* HyperText Markup Language
    usage, 100–161
  developers, 3
  farm, 240
  form, 319, 455
    components. *See* Server-side Web form components
    controls, 62
    structure. *See* ASP.NET
  interface, 502
  method, creation. *See* allBooks.addItem Web method; getBooks.AllBooks Web method
  pages, 63
    running. *See* ASP.NET
  programming. *See* Back-end Web programming
  references, usage. *See* Web Services Description Language
  root folder, 229
  server
    controls, 62
    usage. *See* Active Server Pages

services configuration, webServices tag (usage), 203–204
UI, 533
user control, creation, 161–163
World Wide Web (WWW / Web)
  services, 51, 441
  building/compiling, steps, 447
  creation, 518, 521–527
  FAQs, 471–472
  introduction, 442–443
  method interfaces, 455
  overview. *See* Book Shop Web services
  solutions, 469–470
  testing, 527–531
  understanding, 443–460
  XML, usage, 460–461
Write() method, 431
WriteAttributes, 370
WriteAttributeString, 370
WriteComment, 370
WriteElementString, 370
WriteEndAttribute, 370
WriteEndDocument, 370
WriteStartDocument, 370
WriteXml, 405
  method, 407
WriteXML class, 486
WriteXmlSchema, 405
  method, 407
WSDL. *See* Web Services Description Language
WYSIWYG editing tools, 75

X

XML. *See* eXtensible Markup Language
XmlAttribute, 363
XMLCart, 547

XmlCart document, 555
XmlConfigFile, 616
XmlDataDocument, 363
  class, usage, 378–387
  DataSet, 378
  object, 379, 382
    multiple tables, viewing, 383–387
    relational view, usage, 381–383
XmlDocument, 363
  loading, 379–380
  object
    navigation, 374–376
    usage. *See* eXtensible Markup Language document
XmlDocumentFragment, 363
XmlDocuments, 370
XmlElement, 54
XmlNode, 54, 376, 465
  arrays, 465
  class, 363
XmlNodeList, 364
XmlNodeList collection, 379
XmlNodeReader, 362
xmlns attribute, 382, 476
XmlReader, 362
XMLTextReader, 363
  object, 373
XmlTextReader, 362, 368
  class, usage. *See* eXtensible Markup Language document
  object, 367, 374
  usage, 377
XmlTextReader object, 365
XmlTextReaders, 370
XmlTextWriter, 363
  class, usage. *See* eXtensible Markup Language document
  object, 370

  usage. *See* eXtensible Markup Language document
XmlTextWriter1.aspx, 371
XmlValidationReader, 363
XmlWriter, 362
XPath expressions, 389
XPath query syntax, 388
XPathDocument, 364
  objects, usage, 390–392. *See also* Documents
  searching, 392
  usage. *See* eXtensible Markup Language
XPathNavigator
  objects, 388
    usage, 390–392
  usage. *See* eXtensible Markup Language
XPathNodeIterator, 364, 390–391
XSD. *See* eXtensible Markup Language Schema Definition
XSL, 490
XSLT. *See* eXtensible Stylesheet Language Transformations
XSLTransform, 364
  class, 396
XSV, 360

Y

Yes/No, datatype, 508

Z

Zero-based odd indexed items, 132
.ZIP extension, 192

Global Knowledge™

Train with Global Knowledge

The right content, the right method, delivered anywhere in the world, to any number of people from one to a thousand. Blended Learning Solutions™ from Global Knowledge.

Train in these areas:

Network Fundamentals
Internetworking
A+ PC Technician
WAN Networking and Telephony
Management Skills
Web Development
XML and Java Programming
Network Security
UNIX, Linux, Solaris, Perl
Cisco
Enterasys
Entrust
Legato
Lotus
Microsoft
Nortel
Oracle

www.globalknowledge.com

Global Knowledge™

*Every hour, every business day all across the globe Someone just **like you** is being trained by Global Knowledge.*

Only Global Knowledge offers so much content in so many formats—Classroom, Virtual Classroom, and e-Learning. This flexibility means Global Knowledge has the IT learning solution you need.

Being the leader in classroom IT training has paved the way for our leadership in technology-based education. From CD-ROMs to learning over the Web to e-Learning live over the Internet, we have transformed our traditional classroom-based content into new and exciting forms of education.

Most training companies deliver only one kind of learning experience, as if one method fits everyone. Global Knowledge delivers education that is an exact reflection of you. No other technology education provider integrates as many different kinds of content and delivery.

www.globalknowledge.com

Blended Learning Solutions™ from Global Knowledge

The Power of Choice is Yours.

Get the IT Training you need— how and when you need it.

Mix and match our Classroom, Virtual Classroom, and e-Learning to create the exact blend of the IT training you need. You get the same great content in every method we offer.

Self-Paced e-Learning
Self-paced training via CD or over the Web, plus mentoring and Virtual Labs.

Virtual Classroom Learning
Live training with real instructors delivered over the Web.

Classroom Learning
Train in the classroom with our expert instructors.

1-800-COURSES   www.globalknowledge.com

Global Knowledge

9000 Regency Parkway, Suite 500
Cary, NC 27512
1-800-COURSES
www.globalknowledge.com

At Global Knowledge, we strive to support the multiplicity of learning styles required by our students to achieve success as technical professionals. We do this because we know our students need different training approaches to achieve success as technical professionals. That's why Global Knowledge has worked with Syngress Publishing in reviewing and recommending this book as a valuable tool for successful mastery of this subject.

As the world's largest independent corporate IT training company, Global Knowledge is uniquely positioned to recommend these books. The first hand expertise we have gained over the past several years from providing instructor-led training to well over a million students worldwide has been captured in book form to enhance your learning experience. We hope the quality of these books demonstrates our commitment to your life-long learning success. Whether you choose to learn through the written word, e-Learning, or instructor-led training, Global Knowledge is committed to providing you the choice of when, where and how you want your IT knowledge and skills to be delivered. For those of you who know Global Knowledge, or those of you who have just found us for the first time, our goal is to be your lifelong partner and help you achieve your professional goals.

Thank you for the opportunity to serve you. We look forward to serving your needs again in the future.

Warmest regards,

Duncan M. Anderson
President and Chief Executive Officer, Global Knowledge

P.S.   Please visit us at our Web site www.globalknowledge.com.

SYNGRESS SOLUTIONS...

AVAILABLE NOW
ORDER at
www.syngress.com

VB.NET Developer's Guide
The introduction of VB.NET has sent many Visual Basic gurus back to the drawing board! VB.NET introduces a new set of standards, protocols, and syntax that previous users of Visual Basic will need to learn to regain their guru status and be positioned to create enterprise-critical applications. *VB.NET Developer's Guide* will help you master VB.NET!
ISBN: 1-928994-48-2
Price: $49.95 USA, $77.95 CAN

AVAILABLE JANUARY 2002
ORDER at
www.syngress.com

BizTalk Server 2000 Developer's Guide for .NET
Written for developers responsible for installing, configuring, and deploying BizTalk Server. This book discusses B2B application integration, BizTalk enhancements, XML, and the tools incoporated into BizTalk.
ISBN: 1-928994-40-7
Price: $49.95 US, $77.95 CAN

AVAILABLE JANUARY 2002
ORDER at
www.syngress.com

C#.NET Web Developer's Guide
Teaches Web developers to build solutions for the Microsoft .NET platform. Web developers will learn to use C# (C Sharp) components to build services and applications available across the Internet.
ISBN: 1-928994-50-4
Price: $49.95 US, $77.95 CAN

solutions@syngress.com

SYNGRESS®